Terminal Illness

A Guide to Nursing Care

SECOND EDITION

Charles Kemp, MSN, RN, CRNH
Baylor University School of Nursing
Dallas, Texas

Lippincott
Philadelphia • New York • Baltimore

Acquisitions Editor: Lisa Marshall
Sponsoring Editor: Sandra Kasko
Project Editor: Nicole Walz
Senior Production Manager: Helen Ewan
Production Coordinator: Pat McCloskey
Design Coordinator: Brett MacNaughton
Indexer: Ellen Murray

2nd Edition

9 8 7 6 5 4 3 2 1

Library of Congress Cataloging-in-Publications Data
Kemp, Charles, 1944-
   Terminal illness : a guide to nursing care / Charles Kemp—2nd ed.
      p.   cm.
   Includes bibliographical references and index.
   ISBN 0-7817-1772-8 (alk. paper)
   1. Terminal care.   2. Nursing.   I. Title.
   [DNLM: 1. Terminal Care—methods. 2. Nursing Care—methods.
   3. Palliative Care—methods.   WY 152 K32t 1999]
   RT87.T45K45   1999
   610.73´61—dc21
   DNLM/DLC
   for Library of congress   98-43501
                                                CIP

Care has been taken to confirm the accuracy of the information presented and to describe generally
accepted practices. However, the authors, editors, and publisher are not responsible for errors or omissions
or for any consequences from application of the information in this book and make no warranty, express or
implied, with respect to the contents of the publication.

The authors, editors, and publisher have exerted every effort to ensure that drug selection and dosage set
forth in this text are in accordance with current recommendations and practice at the time of publication.
However, in view of ongoing research, changes in government regulations, and the constant flow of information relating to drug therapy and drug reactions, the reader is urged to check the package insert for each
drug for any change in indications and dosage and for added warnings and precautions. This is particularly
important when the recommended agent is a new or infrequently employed drug.

Some drugs and medical devices presented in this publication have Food and Drug Administration
(FDA) clearance for limited use in restricted research settings. It is the responsibility of the health care
provider to ascertain the FDA status of each drug or device planned for use in his or her clinical practice.

I lay dreaming that I was near an outdoor marketplace, watching a group of musicians set up to play. One by one, they began to tune, softly. Then in a soft clear voice, a woman sang the words, "Who knows . . . where the time goes . . ." and at that moment I awoke and said, "to Leslie." A true vision.
This book is dedicated with love to
my wife, Leslie.

When my son, David, was about five years old, I dreamed one night that the end of the world had come. Everything was just slowing, slowing, slowing and I was drifting in space. I knew when it all stopped, that would be the end. David drifted into my arms as a voice said, "Into the loving arms of his father." It was a calm encompassing peace.
This book is also dedicated with love to
my son, David

and to
my Mother and Father

Acknowledgments

Writing a book is a formidable task and there is much gratitude to express. First and always, I could not have done this without unending help from my wonderful and beloved wife, Leslie—who is immensely patient and supportive. My wonderful and deeply loved son, David, has also been patient, understanding, and a sanity-saver where the computer is concerned.

To the ever-growing Roster of Gratitude carried over from the first edition, I need to add (with only a little repetition) these people, on whom so much depends:

The work in community must go on and would not have done so without my comrades-in-arms and brothers in the hood—Lance Rasbridge and Martin Hironaga; and my colleagues out there in the East Dallas streets—Luisa Rondon, Jim Walton, Chindavanh (Thoy) Vongsavath, Daniel Au, J. R. Newton, Leslie Kemp, David Kemp, Viengxay Lounnarath, Sandy Pol, MyTrang Nguyen, Paul Thai, Lek Keovilay, and Han Chung.

Life is better because of our friends at the East Dallas police Storefront—Rick (Move on) Janich, Tri Ngo, Lynne y Lynn, Benito Hernandez, Eric Conde, Tony (Vato) Medrano, Jim Little, and Wes Stout.

Life is more complete because of Wednesday morning Bible study. For the wisdom and other support, thank you to Jim Carvell, Mike Haney, Chris Harper, Al (Standing Tall) Hobrecht, Chuck Hudson, Bryce Weigand, and Hu Warden. Dan Foster is always with me and I am far richer because of him.

Thanks to my colleagues at Baylor—Becky Robbins, Stephanie Allen, Leonard Brown, Anita Comley, Melanie McEwen, Phyllis Karns, Melinda Mitchell, Alice Pappas, Rosie Taylor, Cheryl Vandiver, Barbara Worth, and especially the Baylor LRC guys—Sally Spafford, Kathryn Leonard, and Jody Guenther. Thank you to all my students, especially those in the streets with me.

This is an opportunity to thank two of the finest educators I know—St. Mark's Headmaster Arnold Holtberg and St. Mark's Head of Middle School Warren Foxworth—and to thank Mitta Angell, Louise Rossi, and Sachiko Mori for all the beauty they give.

My thanks to Dr. Aziz Sheikh for reviewing the Islam section in Chapter 5. Most of his suggestions are incorporated.

Thank you to Lisa Marshall, Sandy Kasko, Nicole Walz, and others at Lippincott Williams & Wilkins.

Jeff, I'm filled with joy that you finally came home from Khe Sanh. Life is richer with you here. Jerry, we miss you. This broke–down palace just isn't the same.

The Photographs

The photographs in this book were taken by Debora Hunter, associate professor of art at Southern Methodist University. After being with her father as he died, Debora developed an interest in hospice care. Through her volunteer work with hospice patients, she worked to promote understanding of the human process of dying. These pictures are part of an extended documentary project entitled "Waiting: Portraits of the Terminally Ill." We are all deeply grateful for Debora's gift.

Preface

In the years since the first edition of this book was published in 1995, I have been pleased and honored to hear from many nurses and others who found it useful in their practice. Many of the changes in this edition are based on their comments and suggestions.

Great advances were made in the first several decades of the contemporary care of patients with terminal illness. Brompton's cocktail, the stages of dying, and the hospice concept once were revolutionary. Now, Brompton's is obsolete, stages passé, and hospice programs abound. Yet, the care of patients with terminal illness still has a long way to go. Despite advances in terminal and palliative care, pain and symptoms of terminal illness remain poorly managed in too many patients. Because of inadequately managed symptoms and for other reasons, many patients never have an opportunity to live as well as they might during their terminal illness. Too many patients enter hospice or palliative care programs in the last weeks or even days of life. Other patients may never receive care from a person or program skilled and knowledgeable in providing terminal care. Denied peace and dignity in dying, some patients are unable to work toward the reconciliations—with God, others, and self—that humans seek.

The second edition of *Terminal Illness: A Guide to Nursing Care* has been completely updated to reflect advances in knowledge and clinical practice. New material has been added and some material deleted. While the focus remains on clinical care, the new material should make the book more relevant to educators. As a practical tool, it is about patient and family needs in all domains of being and how to facilitate meeting those needs. This book is based on experience, research, and field-tested theory. It is patient- and family-centered and is oriented toward prevention. The rest of the book is a tool for *doing* the care of the dying.

Conceptual Framework

There are three major organizing concepts to *Terminal Illness: A Guide to Nursing Care*. First, effective care of persons who are terminally ill includes competent action in all areas of human needs: physiological, psychosocial, and spiritual. The book presents fundamental concepts, issues, problems, and interventions in each of these areas. Second, while there is always individual variation, some terminal illnesses such as cancer are relatively predictable in their natural history. Knowing the natural history and attendant problems allows practitioners to anticipate what physiological problems may occur and act first to prevent them; or failing prevention, to recognize and treat problems early and minimize their effects. Third, superior care proceeds concurrently along two parallel tracks:

● competent action in all areas of human needs, and
● watching or being with the person who is dying (and/or family).

Thus in the first track caring means aggressive action on the part of the nurse to manage problems and facilitate the patient and family's ability to manage problems. It may appear to be paradoxical but caring in the second track means accepting suffering and frailty, and despite being unable to manage all problems and suffering, staying or watching with the patient and family. It is here, when it *seems* like there is nothing more than can be done that terminal care reaches its highest and deepest level. It is here, facing and staying with overwhelming suffering and fear that we reach an ancient and essential human function: the priestly function of accompanying another through suffering and to the awesome finality of death.

Organization

The book is divided into four units: Psychosocial Care, Pain and Symptom Management, Advanced Cancer: Metastatic Spread, and Terminal Illnesses (other than cancer). Problems and interventions are detailed in all chapters.

Unit I, *Psychosocial Care* presents terminal illness from the perspective of patient and family, and covers psychological and social issues, spiritual issues, major faiths, grief and bereavement care, and socio-cultural issues. Chapters directed to the nurse are on hospice and palliative care, ethical issues, and stress and health care providers.

Unit II, *Pain and Symptom Management* is divided into twelve chapters. The first chapter discusses principles of pain management; the second chapter covers classification and assessment of pain; and the final chapter is a comprehensive and detailed discussion of exactly how to manage the various pain syndromes. The remaining chapters address the major problems, other than pain, of terminal illness. Problems are divided into chapters as follows: Neurological; respiratory and cardiac, skin, oral, gastrointestinal, genitourinary, dehydration, fatigue, and sleep, oncology emergencies and paraneoplastic syndromes, and imminent death.

Unit III, *Advanced Cancer: Metastatic Spread, Common Symptoms, and Assessment* presents a summary of the natural history and attendant problems of the 18 most common tumor sites that each cause more than 5,000 deaths annually in the U.S. This section allows the practitioner to anticipate and thus prevent or minimize at least some of the problems and complications of advanced disease. The section is divided into chapters on cancers of major organs, female reproductive, gastrointestinal, urinary tract, and blood/lymph and skin.

Unit IV, *Management of Other Terminal Illnesses* covers diseases other than cancer that lend themselves to palliative care. These include HIV infection, degenerative neurological disorders. Alzheimer's and related disorders, and cardiovascular and chronic obstructive pulmonary diseases.

Contents

UNIT II
Pain and Symptom Management

UNIT III
Advanced Cancer: Metastatic Spread, Common Symptoms, and Assessment

Psychosocial Care

DEBORA HUNTER

INTRODUCTION

THIS section addresses an array of psychosocial issues typical of the situations of people who are dying and of their families. The section begins with a chapter on hospice and palliative care. Although hospice and palliative care encompass physical and psychosocial issues, the growth and development of hospice and palliative care have been major social trends in health care in the western world. Along with chapters on individual and family psychosocial needs and problems, there are also chapters on spiritual care, the major faiths, sociocultural issues, and grief and bereavement. The section ends with chapters on ethical issues and on stress in health care providers.

Although specific direction is provided on various situations and problems, no general information is given on counseling or teaching theories and strategies. Theories and strategies are beyond the scope of this book, and one may accurately view the entire book as a compilation of teaching points. However, several key issues on psychosocial care are helpful to keep in mind when working with people who are dying:

● The first step in addressing psychosocial needs and problems of people who are dying is to manage distressing physical symptoms. Few people caught up in suffering from severe physical problems can muster the emotional strength to deal with psychosocial problems. At the same time, however, it is important to understand that physical suffering may be affected or even caused by emotional, spiritual, or other psychosocial problems.

● The essence of helping, caring, or effective intervention in the nurse–patient relationship "is the engagement, the identification of the nurse with the patient" (Morse, Bottorff, Anderson, O'Brien, & Solberg, 1992, p. 819). This "connected" engagement helps the nurse focus on the patient's response to illness, whether physical or emotional, and thus increases the likelihood of providing the needed care. Staying completely focused on a person who is suffering and dying is terribly difficult. "The hardest state to be in is one in which you keep your heart open to the suffering . . . and simultaneously keep your discriminative wisdom. . . . It takes a good while to get the balance" (Ram Dass, 1978, p. 1).

● Trust is an essential component in all communications. The patient must trust the nurse always (1) to tell the truth and (2) to be competent. Trusting and being honest with oneself and the patient are central in the process of engagement.

The nurse's fundamental beliefs about humankind and caring have a profound influence on the quality of care provided and the response of the patient to the practitioner and the situation. While basic beliefs are infinite in number and variation, several have a positive effect on all concerned, including belief in the intrinsic worth of humans, belief that it is worthwhile to relieve suffering, and belief that there is hope.

As noted in the preface of the book, health care workers sometimes fall short of the goals for self and for the patients. Usually, though, competent loving work in all dimensions of care helps patients and families move toward healing and reconciliation.

There are also times when, with or without care, a patient or family will reach astonishing levels of human potential. The art of dying is really about the art of living, and many lives show how much richness is possible within the fierce context of terminal illness. Like war, dying can bring to light previously unknown strength and beauty, especially in courage and relationships.

Practitioners who choose this work are fortunate to be in the presence of such people and to be in the presence of those who seemingly do not reach higher levels of human existence. Health care workers need to pay attention to all patients because through them they will learn about their own strengths and weaknesses. Each patient does have something to teach, and it is a blessing for that teaching to occur.

The teaching and learning are not always apparent. Sometimes it is because there is so much suffering or unpleasantness, because the teaching and learning are so subtle, or because of the fears or agendas of the health care workers.

Mrs. C was a 58-year-old Cambodian woman who had undetected cervical cancer when she was found in door-to-door outreach in one of Dallas' refugee communities. She had an 11-year-old son with Down syndrome, a 13-year-old daughter who provided most of Mrs. C's care, and a 15-year-old son who was sent to prison midway through the course of care. My students and I cared for her for 2 years. We were with her through many clinic visits and two courses of treatment (surgery and radiation). Until 2 months before she died, we provided all her home care following crises related to complications of disease, treatment, and alcoholism, including septicemia, stroke, seizures, bowel obstruction, malnutrition, and dehydration. For 2 years, Mrs. C received at least three home visits each week. For 2 years she misled caregivers, was noncompliant with care and treatment, and treated family and others in an unkind manner. She seemed to find no peace in our presence and work, and she seemed to be unaffected by Christianity, Buddhism, or the Morman missioners who came to visit. Hospice was helpful, but little changed. She died at home with her family and me in attendance.

This woman taught us how tough a person can be, and her daughter taught us how strong a child can be. She taught us all that we could persevere longer than we thought. It took a while before any of us figured out what we had learned.

This section of the book presents a number of problems and issues followed by actions (interventions) practitioners can take to address the problems and issues. These are not "the" answers, nor are they intended as "cookbook" answers. Rather, they are starting places given with the respectful knowledge that each person and each family is unique and not necessarily amenable to "cookbook" answers. Nevertheless, one must start somewhere beyond simply appreciating the uniqueness of an individual and family.

REFERENCES

Ram Dass. (1978, December). Introduction. *Hanuman Foundation Dying Project Newsletter,* 1.
Morse, J. M., Bottorff, J., Anderson, G., O'Brien, B., & Solberg, S. (1992). Beyond empathy: Expanding expressions of caring. *Journal of Advanced Nursing, 17,* 809–821.

CHAPTER 1

Hospice and Palliative Care

KEY POINTS

- The growth of modern hospice and palliative care is due to several factors, especially the basic human need for dignity and meaning in life.

- Although there are some programmatic differences between hospice and palliative care, both are based on core principles, such as relieving suffering, the intrinsic worth of all human beings, and cooperation among team members.

- The standards and services of hospice programs address the core principles of hospice and palliative care.

- The standards of hospice nursing practice are based on the needs of patients and the core principles of hospice and palliative care.

Improvements in end-of-life care for patients with terminal illness have been a major advance in modern health care. The enormous medical/technological advances made in the 1940s to 1960s were accompanied by a decline in the incidence of dying as a family and community affair. Often, the patient and family were seen as irrelevant to the purposes of modern curative medicine. Because of exalting cure at all costs, immense suffering frequently resulted—often with no attendant extension of life quality or even life span.

However, some essential human quality moves people toward attaining dignity and meaning in life. In terminal care, this quality was manifested primarily through the efforts of the hospice movement; through the work of Edwin Shneidman, Avery Weisman, Elisabeth Kübler-Ross, and other well-known clinicians; and through the work of many unnamed and unknown nurses, physicians, and others.

General Principles and Philosophy of Hospice and Palliative Care

Hospice care is broader in scope than palliative care and has certain programmatic components, but both hospice and palliative care are based on the same or similar concerns and concepts. General principles and philosophy of hospice and palliative care (or terminal care) include the following:

● The purpose of hospice and palliative care is to relieve suffering and thus promote healing. This may seem obvious, but it bears explication that the practitioner intentionally and specifically seeks to prevent or relieve the physical, emotional, and spiritual suffering that often accompanies the process of dying.

● Preventing or relieving suffering requires a high level of competence and is an active, even aggressive endeavor. In pain and other symptom management, it is essential that medications or treatments be given before the problem occurs rather than in response to the problem.

● There is always hope, always something that can be done. An effective practitioner always has and always gives hope. The hope is not necessarily that the patient will not die (although many patients hold that hope to the very end), but rather that suffering will lessen, reconciliation will be achieved, a goal will be met, meaning will be found, or any number of other possibilities.

● Human beings have intrinsic worth. It is not necessary to believe that all humans are "good" or noble. There is reason to believe that many are not. However, if the practitioner operates from the perspective that people have at least the potential for worth (which may not always be apparent), then the relationship is more likely to be productive, and the patient is more likely to achieve the dignity and meaning that are basic human needs.

● It is worthwhile to help uncover, or help actualize, the worth, beauty, empowerment, or whatever one calls the positive potential of people. The time of dying is the last chance many people have to become who they really are rather than who they pretend to be. Dying can be a time of reconciliation with God, self, and others. Practitioners must also accept that some patients will never achieve reconciliation.

● Patient, family, and practitioner share dynamic responsibility for what happens in the process of dying. The practitioner gives the patient and family the benefit of her or his knowledge and expertise so that patient and family are able to achieve autonomy and make informed decisions about what is happening and what will happen.

● Working cooperatively with others is necessary. A host of providers can and should be involved in the care of a human being in the final days of life. These include the obvious (eg, family, nurses, doctors, chaplains, volunteers, aides) and the perhaps not so obvious (neighbors, relatives, family clergy, work colleagues, and others in the social sphere of the patient).

● Terminal care is not always a successful endeavor. No matter what is done, most patients will suffer to some extent, and some will suffer terribly. Suffering may be physical, mental, and/or spiritual. It is imperative that the practitioner be able to stay gracefully in the presence of people who are suffering. There is always something that can be done. Waller and Caroline (1996) note that practitioners must "learn to enjoy small accomplishments" (p. xiv).

● Living or working with uncertainty is acceptable. For the practitioner, the human need for understanding, order, and predictability must sometimes be set aside in terminal situations, even as the practitioner provides or creates as much understanding, order, and predictability for others as is possible in the situation.

● For most practitioners, it is necessary to go beyond self-limitations—not with respect to responsible care, but in terms of working to become more competent, more skilled, and better able to confront the fears and inadequacies about death and suffering.

The Development of Hospice and Palliative Care

The word hospice is derived from the Latin, *hospes*, the root word for *hospitium*, a place of hospitality. Originally places of hospitality and welcome for travelers, especially pilgrims, *hospitia* evolved in the Middle Ages into hospitals for the sick and hospices for the poor and dying. As the Crusades and widespread pilgrimages ended, most hospices disappeared from Europe until the 19th century. Two of the early hospices that still serve are the Hospices of the Great Saint Bernard and the Little Saint Bernard. In the late 19th and early 20th centuries, several hospices designed specifically for the dying were established in Europe, most notably Our Lady's Hospice and St. Joseph's Hospice, both operated by the Irish Sisters of Charity.

Most of the credit for modern hospice care is due to Dame Cicely Saunders. Saunders began her work with terminally ill patients as a volunteer nurse at St. Luke's Hospital. After completing her medical degree in 1957, Saunders worked first at St. Joseph's Hospice and then in 1967 founded St. Christopher's Hospice where the modern concepts of hospice and symptom management were realized (Sheehan & Foreman, 1996). The critical concept of giving oral opioids around the clock was established as a basic hospice protocol by Saunders and her colleagues.

The development of hospice care was supported at least philosophically by the work of Elisabeth Kübler-Ross and others. Kübler-Ross, a Swiss psychiatrist working at the University of Chicago, wrote the enormously influential book, *On Death and Dying*, first published in 1969. *On Death and Dying* was the first widely read and accessible book on the experience of terminal illness and provided early direction in how to provide quality care for patients and families facing death.

A growing sense of empowerment among consumers and questions about the *human* quality of health care for the terminally ill and others also helped in the development of hospice care. Other factors contributing to the growth of hospice care were the "natural death consumer movement," increased interest and research in grief and bereavement, development and acceptance of the holistic nursing practice model, discussion about the cost of care versus the quality of life, increased concern about decisions at the end of life, and more recently, questions about physician-assisted suicide and the continuing problem of a high prevalence of uncontrolled symptoms at the end of life (Hospice and Palliative Nurses Association, 1997).

The first hospice in the United States was the Connecticut Hospice, a home hospice program founded in 1974 by Florence Wald, the dean of the graduate nursing program at Yale University. Following the New Haven lead, most hospice programs in the United States were at least initially focused on home care. In Canada, Balfour Mount founded the Palliative Care Service at the Royal Victoria Hospital in Montreal in 1975. In the press of developing programs incorporating the hospice concept, the early and often lonely work done at such institutions as Calvary Hospital in New York should never be forgotten.

Initially, almost all hospice patients had a primary diagnosis of cancer. Gradually, people with other diagnoses, such as advanced neuromuscular disease, pulmonary disease, heart failure, renal failure, liver disease, acquired immunodeficiency syndrome (AIDS), and other conditions were admitted to hospice. People with dementias or Alzheimer's disease are admitted to some, but not all, hospices. The Jacob Perlow Hospice is one of a very few hospices specializing in Alzheimer's disease care. In the mid-1990s, there were many patients with AIDS in hospices. This number decreased significantly with the advent of improved antiretroviral therapy (Palella et al., 1998). Currently, most patients in most hospices have a primary diagnosis of cancer.

By the late 1990s in the United States, many hospice programs shifted the focus of care from exclusively the home setting to home and inpatient settings. Basic models for hospice include:

● Home hospice, either freestanding or a part of a home health care agency. Most have agreements with inpatient facilities to provide beds, either in a dedicated unit or served by a palliative care or hospice team.
● Hospice facility, either freestanding or a unit within a larger inpatient facility. Most also have a home care team or an arrangement with a home hospice.

In most cases, short- or long-term inpatient care is best provided in acute care hospitals or skilled nursing facilities associated with acute care hospitals so that sophisticated testing or treatments are available *if appropriate*. In the early years, hospices were nonprofit, community-based organizations. Although many hospices remain nonprofit, there has been a steady growth in for-profit hospices.

Definitions, Principles, and Standards

Following is a current and widely accepted definition of hospice (National Hospice Organization [NHO], 1993):

> *Hospice provides support and care for persons in the last phases of incurable disease so that they may live as fully and comfortably as possible. Hospice recognizes dying as part of the normal process of living and focuses on maintaining the quality of remaining life. Hospice affirms life and neither hastens nor postpones death. Hospice exists in the hope and belief that through appropriate care, and the promotion of a caring community sensitive to their needs, patients and families may be free to attain a degree of mental and spiritual preparation that is satisfactory to them. (p.2)*

The philosophy of hospice may be summarized as a dedication to comfort, dignity, autonomy, quality of life, and empowerment for the client and family (National Board for Certification of Hospice Nurses [NBCHN], 1997). The NHO "Standards of a Hospice Program of Care" (1994) include the following principles of hospice:

Access to Care
"Hospice offers palliative care to all terminally ill people and their families regardless of age, gender, nationality, race, creed, sexual orientation, disability, diagnosis, availability of a primary caregiver, or ability to pay" (p. 2). Standards of implementing this principle include conducting community assessments (especially of underserved populations), providing services sensitive to culturally diverse communities, conducting diversity training for staff, and providing care for medically indigent patients.

Patient/Family as the Unit of Care
"The unit of care in hospice is the patient/family" (p. 7). Standards of implementing this principle include encouraging the patient/family to participate in developing the plan of care, being respectful of patient/family values and beliefs, and teaching primary caregivers how to provide care.

Hospice Interdisciplinary Team
"A highly qualified, specially trained team of hospice professionals and volunteers work together to meet the physiological, psychological, social, spiritual, and economic needs of hospice patients/families facing terminal illness and bereavement" (p. 12). Standards of implementing this principle include identification and maintenance of an interdisciplinary team of professionals and volunteers, coordination of the hospice team by a qualified health professional, supervision and support for volunteers, provision of appropriate and quality care, and maintenance of appropriate fiduciary and professional boundaries and relationships with patients and families.

Interdisciplinary Team Plan of Care
"The hospice interdisciplinary team collaborates continuously with the patient's attending physician to develop and maintain a patient-directed, individualized plan of care" (p. 24). Standards of implementing this principle include a written plan of comprehensive care developed for each patient/family by the attending physician, the hospice physician, and the interdisciplinary team.

Scope of Hospice Services
"Hospice provides a safe, coordinated program of palliative and supportive care, in a variety of appropriate settings, from the time of admission through bereavement, with the focus on keeping terminally ill patients in their own

homes as long as possible" (p. 29). Standards of implementing this principle include the presence of a knowledgeable hospice medical director, inclusion of the attending physician, registered nursing (RN) services based on nursing assessments, nursing assistant services based on the RN's assessments and supervision, social work services based on the social worker's assessments, counseling services, spiritual care services consistent with patient/family beliefs, volunteer services, nutritional counseling, services to meet the pharmaceutical needs of patients (including provision of medications), pathology and laboratory services, radiology services, access to emergency medical services, and bereavement services.

Coordination and Continuity of Care

"Hospice care is available 24 hours a day, seven days a week, and services continue without interruption if the patient care setting changes" (p. 69). Standards of implementing this principle include assessing the patient/family's needs and coordinating continuity of care, and ensuring that care is available 24 hours a day, 7 days a week.

Utilization Review

"Hospice is accountable for the appropriate allocation and utilization of its resources in order to provide optimal care consistent with patient/family needs" (p. 78). The standard of implementing this principle is focused on regular monitoring and evaluation of services.

Hospice Services Record

"Hospice maintains a comprehensive and accurate record of services provided in all care settings for each patient/family" (p. 81). The standard of implementing this principle is focused on complete and accurate recordkeeping.

Governing Body

"Hospice has an organized governing body that has complete and ultimate responsibility for the organization" (p. 84). Standards of imple-

menting this principle include the governing body determining the mission and other program issues, monitoring the program and services, ensuring effective planning and management, taking fiscal and fiduciary responsibility, ensuring compliance with legal and regulatory requirements, and assessing its own performance.

Management and Administration

"The hospice governing body entrusts the hospice administrator with overall management responsibility for operating the hospice including planning, organizing, staffing, and evaluating the organization and its services" (p. 95). Standards of implementing this principle include the administrator taking responsibility for day-to-day operations, making policies that define management and administration, ensuring that personnel policies are comprehensive, ensuring that the program reflects community diversity, overseeing financial data, creating policies to guide the team in making ethical decisions, involving clients and families in hospice activities, and representing the program objectively to the public.

Quality Assessment and Improvement

"Hospice is committed to continuous assessment and improvement of the quality and efficiency of its services" (p. 108). The standard of implementing this principle is focused on assessment and improvement of all aspects of the program.

In her chapter on The Philosophy of Terminal Care, Saunders (1981) lists the essential elements in terminal and hospice care:

● Concern for the patient and family as the unit of care
● Management by an experienced clinical team
● Expert control of the common symptoms of terminal cancer, especially pain in all its aspects
● Skilled and experienced nursing
● An interprofessional (ie, interdisciplinary) team

● A home care program
● Bereavement follow-up
● Methodical recording and analysis
● Teaching in all aspects of terminal care
● Imaginative use of the architecture available
● A mixed (with respect to prognosis) group of patients
● An approachable central administration (and in this day of for-profit hospices, ownership and administration that understands the spirit and philosophy of hospice)
● The search for meaning

Except for the exclusive focus on cancer, Saunders' work remains fresh today, almost 20 years after publication.

The Hospice Team and Services

Hospice care is provided by a core interdisciplinary team. An interdisciplinary team is one in which each team member is responsible for decision making in his or her own field of expertise. This is in contrast with the multidisciplinary team structure in which leadership and decision making rest with the highest ranking member of the team (eg, the physician). Core team members as defined in the Medicare hospice regulations include physician, RN, social worker, and pastoral or other counselor. Essential team members as defined in the Medicare hospice regulations include home health aide, pharmacist, physical or occupational therapist, and volunteer. Hospice philosophy mandates inclusion of the patient and family as members of the team. Some hospice program teams have a music or art therapist, nutritionist, respiratory therapist, and other personnel. Team member roles and qualities include the following:

Attending Physician
The patient's primary physician is usually considered a member of the team. The attending may or may not contribute to the work of the team and in some cases withdraws from the care of the patient. However, inclusion of the attending is usually helpful to the patient and family's sense of continuity and stability.

Hospice Physician
Medicare-eligible hospices must have a physician who functions as the medical director. Clinically, the hospice physician's role may include consultation and collaboration with the attending and the hospice nurse and ongoing assessment of the patient's status. The hospice medical director determines and certifies (and recertifies) patient eligibility for hospice, reviews policies, and participates in quality assurance. The hospice physician also may provide professional and community education, liaison with other professionals, and program planning and support. The hospice physician should have expanded knowledge in the pathophysiology, progression, and terminal stages of the diseases common to the program in which she or he works; and expertise in hospice and palliative care, especially symptom management. Hospice physicians are expected to make home visits when indicated.

Registered Nurse
Hospice nurse roles commonly include physical, psychosocial, and spiritual assessment; analysis; planning; implementation of plans (interventions); and evaluation of interventions directed to the problems and needs of patients and families. The nursing care plan is generally focused first on symptom management and takes into account the unique psychological and emotional characteristics of the individual patient, family or social support system dynamics, socioeconomic factors, spirituality, grief and loss issues, and environmental and safety factors (NBCHN, 1997). Coordination of care or case management, supervision (eg, of home health aides), consultation, education, advocacy, and discharge planning also are common activities (Nyman, 1997).

Definition of hospice nursing: "Hospice nursing practice is the provision of palliative nursing care for the terminally ill and their families, with the emphasis on their physical, psycho-social, emotional, and spiritual needs. This is accomplished in collaboration with an interdisciplinary team in a setting which provides 24 hour nursing availability, pain and symptom management, bereavement support, and volunteer services" (NBCHN, 1997).

The hospice nurse should have abilities related to those noted in the discussion of the hospice physician, including expanded knowledge in the pathophysiology, progression, and terminal stages of the diseases common to the program in which she or he works; expertise in hospice and palliative care, especially symptom management; and the ability to work effectively and coordinate care with patients, families, and the interdisciplinary team.

Social Worker
The hospice social worker is responsible for assessing psychosocial problems and needs and developing a psychosocial plan of care to address these. The hospice social worker provides emotional support to patients and families and helps to develop the patient–family support system. In addition to the unique issues of particular situations, hospice social workers commonly provide counseling or assistance related to financial problems, advance directives, funerals, grief, and community resources.

Pastoral (Chaplain) or Other Counselor
The hospice chaplain provides spiritual care and related counseling to patients, families, and the interdisciplinary team. When patients do not have a source of spiritual care, the chaplain serves as the source of care, including providing the funeral service. The chaplain also works and consults with the patient's clergy and provides community education for religious and other institutions. The hospice chaplain should have specialized knowledge in spiritual and psychosocial processes in dying, death, and grief; an understanding of family dynamics; an ability to work with clergy from diverse belief systems; and an ability to provide spiritual care across different belief systems.

Home Health Aide
The hospice home health aide (or nursing assistant or homemaker) provides personal care for the patient, such as bathing, grooming, feeding, assisting with medications, carrying out certain procedures, ensuring safety, and providing light housekeeping; respite (relief) for the family; and although not always included in job descriptions, emotional support to the patient and family. The home health aide also monitors and reports changes in the patient's and family's physical and mental status. The home health aide is supervised by the primary nurse who is responsible for developing the aide's plan of care, including which procedures the aide will undertake. Home health aides should have training in the physical and psychosocial aspects of terminal illness and be skilled in providing physical and emotional care.

Pharmacist
The hospice pharmacist usually works at a pharmacy under contract to the hospice in a managed care plan or other agreement. The hospice pharmacist should have current knowledge of the pharmacologic management of pain and other symptoms and must maintain adequate stock of the necessary medications, such as various formulations of opioids.

Therapist (Physical, Occupational, Speech)
In most hospices, the various therapies are available on an as-needed basis through contract agreements.

Volunteer
Part of the foundation of hospice care is affirmation of the connections among patient, family, community, and the hospice itself. Community volunteers have thus been an integral part of hospice from the earliest days. Volunteers are not just part of the team, they are vital to the purpose and meaning of hos-

pice. The role of the hospice volunteer is as varied as the needs and problems of patients and families. Under direction from the volunteer coordinator and in collaboration with various team members, volunteers may provide emotional or spiritual support, physical care, transportation or errands, housekeeping or lawn care, and a host of other services. Volunteers also provide specialized services, such as bereavement care or pastoral (assistant) care. Hospice volunteers should have training in physical and psychosocial aspects of terminal illness and be skilled in providing care or in other roles as needed.

Patient and Family

The patient and family are considered the hospice "unit of care." Moreover, hospice philosophy includes patient and family as partners in care so that the relationship between hospice and patient and family is collaborative rather that just provider–recipient of care.

Team Operations

The plan of care is developed out of the interdisciplinary team assessment and takes into account problems, needs, and strengths in all spheres of being. Coordination of care or case management is the responsibility of the nurse in most programs. In both home and inpatient hospice settings, the team conference is an important means of coordination and communication.

Although team conferences vary from hospice to hospice, they have some characteristics in common (Martinez, 1996):

● Formal team conferences are regularly scheduled. Medicare regulations require that each patient be conferenced at least every 2 weeks.
● Evaluation of client status, outcomes of care, and need for changes in care plan are central to the conference.
● All team members document patient status, outcomes of care, changes in plans, and other material pertinent to the plan.

● Learning is an integral part of team conferences.

Team conferences may or may not function (along with addressing patient issues) to provide staff support and include members sharing personal feelings or responses to clients, families, or stresses. The degree to which emotional, spiritual, or other personal issues emerge depends on the policies, procedures, and milieu of the hospice or on circumstances within the hospice, team, or one or more patients or families.

As Kübler-Ross (1969) and Saunders (1981) noted in the early days of hospice and palliative care, education is a vital component of this work. The importance of educating patients and families seems almost self-evident. Without education on symptom management, personal care, disease process, and a host of other issues, problems or even disasters are inevitable. However, Kübler-Ross, Saunders, and others had more in mind than teaching only patients and families.

Individuals involved in terminal care, hospice, and palliative care programs have traditionally sought opportunities to educate other health care professionals, health professions students, and the community. Readers may recall that the seminal *On Death and Dying* grew out of interviews of terminally ill patients with students in attendance. The tradition and importance of education in terminal care come from the realization that work with people who are dying is important work and puts its practitioners face to face with the most fundamental issues of human existence: life, death, meaning, hope, and suffering. Whether for health professionals, students, or community, education on terminal care thus touches on clinical and philosophic areas.

Working in hospice and palliative care, we also seek to educate ourselves—in part about the art and science of palliative care and in part about *ars moriendi*, the art of dying. In learning the art of dying, one also learns much of the art of living.

For more specific information on patient and family teaching, please see the chapter on family caregivers and teaching points through-out the book.

Legal and Ethical Issues

Although there is an in-depth discussion of ethical (and some legal) issues in terminal care in a later chapter, several legal and ethical issues specific to hospice are discussed here.

Informed Consent

Informed consent includes the following "essential elements of a hospice admission consent" (HNSG, 1997, p. 27):

● Definition and explanation of palliative services
● Explanation of all service settings
● Bereavement services
● Services that are covered and those that are not
● Explanation of recordkeeping
● Financial responsibilities
● Withdrawal or discharge criteria
● Signatures—including the patient's, if competent

Patient Bill of Rights and Responsibilities

Patient rights and responsibilities are based on Medicare and state licensing regulations and in some cases on the ethical stance of the hospice program. Below are summarized points covered in the NHO guide to developing hospice client rights and responsibilities (1994). The patient (and family) has the right to:

● Receive quality care from a qualified team
● Have clear understanding of availability and access to services
● Receive appropriate and compassionate care regardless of diagnosis, race, ability to pay, or other characteristics
● Be fully informed of health status and thus be able to participate in planning care

● Be fully informed of all potential risks and benefits of treatment and to be free to accept or refuse treatments or services
● Be treated with dignity and respect
● Have family and other caregivers trained to provide care when self-care is not possible
● Expect privacy and confidentiality in all aspects of care and condition
● Voice grievances through confidential procedures without fear of retribution
● Be informed of fees or charges before services are provided

The patient may be responsible for the following:

● Participating in developing and updating the plan of care
● Providing hospice with accurate and complete health information
● Remaining under a doctor's care while receiving hospice services
● Assisting staff in developing and maintaining a safe environment for care to be provided

Resuscitation and Advance Directives

Contrary to popular belief, resuscitation of hospice patients is required in the absence of a do-not-resuscitate (DNR) physician's order (HNSG, 1997). Moreover, NHO standards do not require DNR orders for admission to hospice, although resuscitation is not covered under hospice benefits. As a practical matter, advance directives (living will) and Durable Power of Attorney for Health Care are usually completed before or during the admission process. Depending on the state and county or parish, the hospice nurse may pronounce death with agreement from the patient's physician (who does not need to be present).

Federal and State Regulations

Medicare Hospice Regulations, Part 418, cover most patients in most hospice programs. To be certified under Medicare Hospice Regulations, a hospice must provide core services in a manner consistent with that described under NHO guidelines. Core Medicare hospice services that must be available 24 hours, 7 days per week for all patients are nursing, physician, and drugs and biologicals. The core team consists of physician, RN, social worker, and pastoral or other counselor. Other services are available 24 hours, 7 days per week according to the individual needs of patients. These services include (but are not limited to) physical therapy, occupational therapy, speech pathology, medical social services, home health aide and homemaker, counseling, short-term inpatient care, medical appliances and supplies, and bereavement care. Some of these services may be contracted. Levels of care include:

● Routine home care, usually regularly scheduled visits from at least the core team members. The frequency and duration of visits increase when patient/family problems increase.
● Continuous home care is 24-hour home care provided during a period of crisis but is not reimbursable for longer than 5 days.
● Inpatient care for respite is short-term inpatient care for the purpose of relieving family or other caregivers. Respite care is not reimbursable for more than 5 consecutive days.
● General inpatient care is provided for the purpose of carrying out symptom management measures that cannot be provided in another setting. Inpatient care is not provided on an indefinite basis—there must be a problem to be managed. Inpatient care days (respite and general) reimbursed by Medicare may not exceed 20% of the total number of days for which a patient had elected hospice care (the 80/20 rule).

Patient eligibility for Medicare Hospice Benefits includes entitlement to Part A of Medicare and certification as terminally ill with a life expectancy of less than 6 months. Benefit periods consist of an initial and subsequent 90-day period, a subsequent 30-day period, followed by a subsequent indefinite extension period for as long as the patient is appropriate for hospice care.

State requirements for licensure and Medicaid reimbursement vary, and some states do not have hospice licensure. Most state requirements are similar to Medicare requirements.

Standards of Hospice Nursing Practice and Professional Performance

The standards of hospice nursing practice and professional performance are described in detail in Standards of Hospice Nursing Practice and Professional Performance (Hospice Nurses Association [HNA], 1995). The HNA is now the Hospice and Palliative Nurses Association (HPNA). HNA/HPNA standards are summarized:

I. Assessment: The hospice nurse collects patient and family data.
II. Diagnosis: The hospice nurse analyzes the assessment data in determining outcomes.
III. Outcome Identification: The hospice nurse identifies expected outcomes individualized to the client and family.
IV. Planning: The hospice nurse develops a nursing plan of care that prescribes interventions to attain expected outcomes.
V. Implementation: The hospice nurse implements the interventions identified in the plan of care.
VI. Evaluation: The hospice nurse evaluates the patient's and family's progress toward attainment of outcomes.

Standards of Professional Performance follow:

I. Quality of Care: The hospice nurse systematically evaluates the quality and effectiveness of nursing practice.

II. Performance Appraisal: The hospice nurse evaluates his or her own nursing practice in relation to professional practice standards and relevant standards and regulations.

III. Education: The hospice nurse acquires and maintains current knowledge in hospice nursing practice.

IV. Collegiality: The hospice nurse contributes to the professional development of peers, colleagues, and others.

V. Ethics: The hospice nurse's decisions and actions on behalf of patient and family are determined in an ethical manner.

VI. Collaboration: The hospice nurse collaborates with the patient and family, other members of the interdisciplinary team, and other health care providers in providing patient and family care.

VII. Research: The hospice nurse uses research findings in practice.

VIII. Resource Utilization: The hospice nurse considers factors related to safety, effectiveness, and cost when planning and delivering patient and family care.

Palliative Care

Palliative care "is a direct outgrowth of the hospice movement" (Waller & Caroline, 1996, p. xvii) and, like hospice, has as its aim the relief of suffering in all spheres of being. Palliative care is defined in several ways, including "management of patients with active, progressive far advanced disease for whom the prognosis is limited and the focus of care is quality of life" (Doyle, 1993, p. 253). The World Health Organization defines palliative care as "the active total care of patients whose disease is not responsive to curative treatment" (1990, p. 11). The NHO (1994) defines palliative care as "treatment which enhances comfort and improves the quality of a patient's life. The goals of intervention are pain control, symptom management, quality of life enhancement, and spiritual-emotional comfort for patients and their primary care support. Each patient's needs are continually assessed and all treatment options are explored and evaluated in the context of the patient's values and symptoms" (p. 29). Note that all treatment options, including curative and resuscitation, are available. There are several primary differences between hospice and palliative care:

● Although there is a point at which hospice care begins, there often is overlap with palliative and curative care. Indeed, palliation of symptoms is "important in the practice of cancer medicine in *all* patients" (Cleary & Carbone, 1997, p. 1335). Palliative care, then, may begin before a patient is or is known to be terminally ill and takes on increasing importance as the disease progresses (Tamburini, Brunelli, Rosso, & Ventifridda, 1996).

● Hospice programs have certain specified services or elements of care (see above) that may or may not exist in a particular palliative care program or service.

Curative care (Time/effort →)

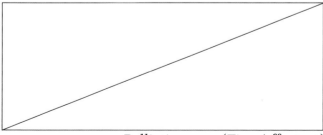

Palliative care (Time/effort →)   **FIGURE 1-1.** Curative and Palliative Care

Otherwise, there is no essential difference in philosophy or focus of care.

Although modern hospices and palliative care programs embody a relatively young concept, their effects have been enormous, both in the lives of patients and families served and less directly in their influence on society as a whole and in humanizing modern health care. However, much remains undone. Pain and other symptoms of terminal illness are often poorly managed in medical and oncology centers (Ahmedzai, 1997; Cleary & Carbone, 1997; Stolberg, 1997; Zhukovsky, Gorowski, Hausdorff, Napolitano, & Lesser, 1995) and even in hospices (McMillan, 1996). In many settings, there still remains a focus on medical answers to problems that may be psychological, social, or spiritual. Hospice is not a magic bullet for suffering, but it has been a huge step forward.

REFERENCES

Ahmedzai, S. (1997). Current strategies for pain control. *Annals of Oncology*, 8(Suppl. 3), s21–s24.

Chaisson, R. E., & Moore, R. D. (1997). Prevention of opportunistic infections in the era of improved retroviral therapy. *Journal of Acquired Immune Deficiency Syndromes and Human Retrovirology*, 16(Suppl. 1), s14–s22.

Cleary, J. F., & Carbone, P. P. (1997). Palliative medicine in the elderly. *Cancer*, 80(7), 1335–1347.

Doyle, D. (1993). Palliative medicine: A time for definition? *Palliative Medicine*, 7, 253–255.

Hospice and Palliative Nurses Association (1997). *The hospice nurses study guide: A preparation for the CRNH candidate* (2nd ed.). Pittsburgh: Author.

Hospice Nurses Association (1995). *Standards of hospice nursing practice and professional performance*. Pittsburgh: Author.

Kübler-Ross, E. (1969). *On death and dying*. MacMillan: New York.

Martinez, J. M. (1996). The interdisciplinary team. In D. C. Sheehan & W. B. Forman (Eds.), *Hospice and palliative care*. Sudbury, MA: Jones and Bartlett.

McMillan, S. C. (1996). Pain and pain relief experienced by hospice patients with cancer. *Cancer Nursing*, 19(4), 298–307.

National Board for Certification of Hospice Nurses (1997). *Certification examination for hospice nurses: Handbook for candidates*. Pittsburgh: Author.

National Hospice Organization (1993). *Standards of a hospice program of care*. Arlington, VA: Author.

National Hospice Organization (1994). *Standards of a hospice program of care: Self assessment tool*. Arlington, VA: Author.

Nyman, S. (1997). *Guidelines for nursing in hospice*. Unpublished manuscript.

Palella, F. J., Delaney, K. M., Moorman, A. C., Loveless, M. O., Fuhrer, J., Satte, G. A., Aschman, D. J., Holmberg, S. D., & the HIV Outpatient Study Investigators (1998). Declining morbidity and mortality among patients with advanced human immunodeficiency virus infection. *New England Journal of Medicine*, 338(13), 853–860.

Saunders, C. M. (Ed.). (1981). *The management of terminal disease*. London: Edward Arnold.

Sheehan, D. C., & Foreman, W. B. (1996). *Hospice and palliative care*. Boston: Jones and Bartlett.

Stolberg, S. G. (1997, June 30). Cries of the dying awaken doctors to a new approach. *New York Times*, A1.

Tamburini, M., Brunelli, C., Rosso, S., & Ventifridda, V. (1996). Prognostic value of quality of life scores in terminal cancer patients. *Journal of Pain and Symptom Management*, 11(1), 32–41.

Waller, A., & Caroline, N. L. (1996). *Palliative care in cancer*. Boston: Butterworth-Heinemann.

The World Health Organization Expert Committee (1990). *Cancer pain relief and palliative care*. Geneva: Author.

Zhukovsky, D. S., Gorowski, E., Hausdorff, J., Napolitano, B., & Lesser, M. (1995). Unmet analgesic needs in cancer patients. *Journal of Pain and Symptom Management*, 10(2), 113–119.

CHAPTER 2

Psychosocial Needs, Problems, and Interventions: The Individual

The process of dying creates unfamiliar psychosocial problems and brings old ones into focus. The complexity of these problems—large and small, individual and family, new and old, new influencing old, old influencing new—is overwhelming and confusing at times. This section presents common problems, processes, and interventions in terminal ill-ness—all of which do not necessarily apply to every person and circumstance. In some cases, the presentation of problems and solutions appears almost recipe-like. However, the purpose is not to present recipes, but to offer a means of *beginning* to understand and help in complex and confusing situations. What these concepts do is to break into manageable parts something (a human dying) that is too much to comprehend as a whole. Having some understanding of the parts allows a better understanding of the whole.

Profile of the Dying

Caring for people who are dying is based, as much as possible, on appreciation and understanding of the experience of living with terminal illness. While each person goes through terminal illness in a different way, there are often many similarities in the experience or responses to it.

An important point of departure in viewing the experience of and response to terminal illness is the recognition that each person is different. At the same time, it is important to be aware of and responsive to cultural differences, gender and sexual orientation issues, problems common to various diagnoses—in short, any related circumstances or means through which sense can be made of confusing situations. Therefore, while approaching each individual without preconceptions, the nurse is prepared for predictable patient/family responses.

One way to begin appreciating the person who is dying and his or her experience is to work toward understanding the whole person. All people come to their time of dying with unique life experiences, with strengths and weaknesses, and with some psychosocial and spiritual issues resolved and some unresolved. Seeing and accepting all that a person brings to his or her last days honors the wholeness of the person. If each patient is seen and appreciated—both in his or her fullness and in his or her incompleteness—then the care given is based on the reality of that patient and is thus more likely to succeed.

Appreciating the person also means appreciating who he or she is in the present moment. For many people, facing death is the greatest challenge of life. Some meet that challenge with great courage and dignity; others meet it with less courage or less dignity. Nearly all people meet it in the best way possible.

The Process of Terminal Illness

Understanding and appreciating the person who is dying also implies understanding and appreciating his or her experience with illness.

Typically, the process of a terminal illness begins with an ominous symptom. That symptom—a persistent cough, bleeding, lump, or pain—brings fear and often denial. Eventually, the symptom cannot be ignored, and help is sought. In the process of assessment, testing, and waiting for results, there is hope, fear, anxiety, and denial. Receiving the diagnosis and discussing treatment and prognosis are overwhelming and confusing situations. Waves of hope and fear wash over the person, and for many people, the common illusion of living indefinitely is shattered. At a time like this, few people are capable of processing all that they are hearing, and later they often ask: "What exactly is wrong with me, and what does it mean to me?" (The practitioner should follow-up at this point in the process, including clarifying what the patient understands and providing correct information about what was misunderstood.)

Among the components of various treatments for terminal illnesses are many that, unfortunately, bring with them a host of side effects and other problems. The physical side effects and difficulties caused by some cancer treatments, for example, are generally well documented. One relatively unrecognized problem, however, is that of negative expectations in relation to pain—the most feared aspect of cancer other than death. How do so many people with cancer come to believe that their pain will be uncontrollable?

One explanation may be that postoperative pain (a common aspect of diagnosis and treatment for a variety of tumor types) is often undertreated. When undertreatment is preceded by the usual preoperative promise—"We'll control your pain after surgery"—then a negative expectation, or response, to similar words later in the disease process is created.

Side effects and other treatment problems also give the patient and his or her family intimations of suffering and mortality. People unfamiliar with cancer, AIDS, and other catastrophic illnesses often are surprised at how sick patients can become. The prospect of advanced disease becomes overwhelming.

Treatment decisions are complicated and often do not offer clear-cut benefits and liabilities. The amount of information is overwhelming and is complicated by a number of factors, including uncertainty of disease, competency (sometimes) of the patient, unfamiliar or stressful setting for the decision making, economic considerations, and (sometimes) conflict within the health care team (Davison & Degner, 1998). Lack of clarity, misunderstanding, and anxiety are hallmarks of life and death medical decision making.

Treatment often results in remission of disease or diminished disease-related problems. Hope rises, but the specter of mortality and more intense suffering lurks in the background. When symptoms recur, hope falls. With the vast array of both legitimate and spurious treatments available, the patient and family may find themselves on a veritable roller-coaster ride of responses. At some point, however, people tire, hope wanes, and the prospect of suffering and mortality becomes reality. Everyone involved is emotionally and physically exhausted, tired of hoping and failing, tired of sickness, tired of worry, and tired of feeling tired. It is a deep weariness that surpasses all previous experience.

Terminal Illness as a Developmental Stage of Life

Having advanced disease is an important developmental stage in the life of a person and in the lives of that person's family. Within the disease's overall developmental stage are a series of smaller stages, sometimes referred to as "the process of cancer." This process is adaptable to other diseases discussed in this book.

Colin Murray Parkes, one of the pioneers in the care of people with terminal illness, wrote that cancer is a process that forces everyone involved gradually to give up assumptions about life. There is a series of setbacks, each causing a negative reaction, followed (hopefully) by acceptance of the loss. These setbacks are characterized as "crisis points," or "partial deaths," the responses to which have positive or negative effects on subsequent crises (Parkes, 1978, p. 52). Sullivan gave profound insight into the opportunities presented by these crisis points when he wrote, "It is at the developmental thresholds that the chance for notable favorable change" is the greatest (1953a, p. 247).

Every crisis point, or stage, in the process of cancer is a developmental threshold and an obvious intervention point, offering an opportunity for responses that are growth producing or not. Even positive changes, remission, for example, are stressful and provide opportunities for positive or negative responses.

Terminal illness is a developmental stage in the life of the family/social system and in the life of the person who is dying. In some cases, except for the patient's physical needs, the family is the focus of care (see Chapter 3).

Erikson's developmental stages and psychosocial crises, shown in Table 2-1, help in understanding patients and families (Holland, 1997). Although ages and psychosocial crises suggest general directions in the care of clients

TABLE 2-1	Developmental Stages/Psychosocial Crises	
Stage and Typical Age	**Psychosocial Crisis**
Infant (birth–2 y)	Trust versus mistrust
Toddler (2–4 y)	Autonomy versus shame and doubt
Early school age (5–7 y)	Initiative versus guilt
Midschool age (8–12 y)	Industry versus inferiority
Early adolescence (13–17 y)	Group identity versus alienation
Late adolescence (18–22 y)	Individual identity versus role diffusion
Young adult (23–30 y)	Intimacy versus isolation
Middle adult (31–50 y)	Generativity versus stagnation
Later adult (50–death)	Integrity versus despair

and families, Erikson's last stage (integrity versus despair) is broadly applicable to terminal situations, regardless of patient or family age or developmental stage. In many respects, terminal illness is a struggle to maintain or achieve integrity rather than despair.

When looking at a person's life, the nurse may see unresolved psychosocial crises emerge as major conflicts in dying. Conversely, earlier crises resolved in an effective manner can serve as points of strength around which the patient may rally. A fundamental technique in crisis intervention is to help the person in crisis use past coping skills to adapt to the current situation. Helping a person recall how he or she handled receiving the original diagnosis (if it was well handled) or how he or she might have handled it (if it was not well handled), for example, may bring to mind strengths and coping skills that were forgotten in the current crisis.

Psychosocial and Related/Interrelated Problems

Loss and Grief

Much is lost in the process of dying, including some or even most of the following:

- Physical health
- The belief in remaining healthy indefinitely—of living indefinitely
- Confidence in the certainty, order, predictability, and security of life
- Family
- Roles, identity
- Job, employment
- Being productive, feeling competent
- Independence
- Control (of bowels, of life—everything)
- People thought to be friends
- Things (ie, possessions)
- The future
- Superficial relationship with God
- Hope
- Meaning

Not everyone experiences all these losses, but everyone experiences at least some of them. Valued, comfortable aspects of life, beliefs, illusions, and much more all inevitably fall away. Nothing can be done to prevent some of these losses. What can be done is to modify the responses to the losses.

The natural response to loss is grief. A number of contemporary theoretical constructs of the stages of grief have been proposed since Lindemann's pioneering work (1944). To the extent that they delineate and normalize certain expressions or experiences of grief and mourning, they are helpful. In terms of predicting behavior, they are less helpful (Lev & McCorkle, 1998). Most can be summarized as a series of phases or responses that merge with one another and include an initial (visceral) alarm phase followed by emotional distress (sadness, depression, anger, anxiety, guilt, yearning, and other such feelings), which gradually diminishes until the final stage of recovery (Lev & McCorkle, 1998). Full recovery may never be achieved.

The power of grief should not be underestimated. Not only does grief have profound effects on individuals and families, but it also has profound effects on the human race as a whole. "Grief appears prominently in all great systems of thought (religious and philosophical), although it does not always go by that name" (Carse, 1980, p. 8).

Basic interventions and responses to people experiencing the overwhelming losses in dying include the following:

- Acknowledge the losses and their magnitude. Saying simply (words to the effect), "You're really losing a lot," can bring relief to the person who is grieving for the losses that dying and death bring. It tells the person that you understand not necessarily *what* the person feels, but *that the person feels*. In other words, connection is made.
- Help the patient explore losses and their meaning. Whether losses are physical beauty, a loving relationship, meaning in life, or whatev-

er, the opportunity to talk about and understand them promotes growth in the process of dying. It is not necessary for all these losses to be accepted, resolved, and forgotten. Some are resolved and forgotten, others remain painful, and still others serve as a means of growth and change. Losses such as a (perhaps comfortable) superficial relationship with God or dependence on physical beauty can result in significant personal growth.

● Help the patient resolve conflicts and complete unfinished relationships. As noted under the list of losses, dying means losing the future (ie, the common illusion of living indefinitely).

● Help the patient explore what is possible for the future. The person who is able to grieve about loss of beauty, relationships, and old meanings in life may find that physical beauty passes and the loss is not great; loving relationships thought to be gone live on in the heart; and meaning in life may change and deepen as growth occurs.

Loneliness and Isolation

Dying can be hard, lonely work. Often, friends fall away or are not available in the most difficult times. Many people go through the dying process emotionally, spiritually, or physically alone.

No matter who or what is there, in flesh or faith, virtually everyone, sometime during the process of dying, conceives of him- or herself as utterly alone. This age-old, universal conception of isolation in the face of death is reflected, for example, in psalms and in Christ's cry as he died, "My God, my God, why hast thou forsaken me?" (Psalm 22:1; Mark 15:34)

The loneliness inherent in the process of living and dying is obviously affected by the presence of others. The quality of the presence is what is important, and not everyone who is present must be alive. A loving memory may often bring more comfort than a living person. To a widow, a nurse might say, for example, "Tell me what you valued most about your husband. What would he say to you if he were here now? What would you say to him?"

The following are two superficially contradictory forms of valued presence in the process of dying:

● The presence of one who works consistently and skillfully to manage symptoms and problems.

● The presence of one who "can be silent with us in a moment of despair or confusion, who can stay with us in an hour of grief and bereavement, who can tolerate not knowing, not curing, not healing, and face with us the reality of our helplessness . . ." (Nouwen, 1974, p. 34).

One of these presences does everything; one does nothing. In reality, both are doing what the patient needs, and both exhibit the vital quality of consistency.

Feelings of Uselessness

Feelings of uselessness can arise from the physical and emotional or social limitations that come with terminal illness. These feelings of uselessness are probably greatest in cultures or social systems that value people primarily for what they accomplish and achieve. In western cultures, this "being-by-doing" ethic is so powerful that even elderly people, sick unto death, are troubled by being unable to "do." The drive to do may also function as a means of avoiding dealing with "being." Feelings of uselessness can be approached in several ways:

● When possible, help the person be—not just feel—useful. This is accomplished by getting the patient involved in his or her own care, by helping him or her participate in decisions, and in general, by including the patient as much as possible in normal life activities.

● One of the most helpful things to do for a person who is dying is to help that person help others, rather than remaining simply the object of others' care and protection. Terminal illness often brings great insights into the meaning of life. Reciprocal sharing of feelings and knowledge can turn passive patients into vital partners in possession of an important gift they can leave behind.

● Explore losses, and whenever possible, help the patient achieve resolution or acceptance.

Anger

Anger is a response to anxiety or threat and may be expressed directly or indirectly. Although often ascribed to the patient's response to illness, anger in terminal illness may arise in reaction to other issues. This displacement of anger to illness is actually less threatening than when the anger is directed to its underlying target of self or others.

Regardless of how it is expressed, anger is an important theme in many lives. Expressed directly and excessively, anger may result in a chronically hostile life. Excessive anger that is repressed or suppressed may result in a life characterized by depression, superficiality, or passive aggressive behavior. A pattern of internalizing anger may also predispose some to certain physical diseases. The stress of terminal illness often brings anger sharply into focus. Old, unresolved anger emerges and becomes a central issue in the process of dying.

Common targets for anger include individual family members, the entire family, health care personnel, the disease, institutions, self, fate, or God. Some anger is reasonable and should be expressed. Enmeshment in anger, however, is destructive. If expressing anger is a lifestyle, or if there is a pattern of repressing or suppressing anger, change is difficult.

Chronically angry people drive others away with anger and blaming. Anger then has a cyclic nature, in which anger promotes isolation, isolation promotes anxiety, and anxiety promotes more anger.

A process for understanding and addressing anger as a problem includes these steps:

● Understand one's own response to anger. Being with a person who is angry can be extremely difficult. It is difficult not to have a negative emotional response to the angry person, especially when the anger is directed at the practitioner.

● Accept that anger or irritability is present in many people who are dying and is considered a natural part of the process of dying by some (eg, Kübler-Ross, 1969).

● Help the person verbally express the anger and name the object of the anger.

● When anger is reasonable, or justifiable, and the object or precipitating factor can be changed, then facilitate the change—injustice in the health care system, for example.

● Help identify the precursors to angry feelings: the situations, words, behaviors, and feelings that trigger anger.

● Help identify the underlying feeling, for example, betrayal, frustration, or anxiety. This can be done by discussing with the patient what was occurring and what he or she was feeling just before getting angry. This is best done when the person is not angry.

● Help identify alternatives to anger as ways of expressing feelings of frustration and anxiety. The patient or family member can discuss or practice with the nurse more productive ways of expressing the feelings.

● Help identify consequences of angry behavior.

● Because anxiety underlies much anger and because anxiety and poor self-concept are related, assisting the patient or family member to examine and improve self-concept may also be helpful.

Anxiety and Fear

Anxiety is "apprehension or uneasiness that results from the anticipation of danger, usually of intrapsychic origin and therefore unconscious." Fear, on the other hand, is "apprehension resulting from a consciously recognized, usually external, threat or danger" (Nicholi, 1978, p. 34). Along with sadness, some degree of fear and anxiety can be expected in most people who are dying. Although anxiety and fear are often indistinguishable in the patient's experience and expression, they are considered here, at least theoretically, as separate concepts.

Anxiety is the "most common form of psychological distress in patients with cancer" (Holland, 1997, p. 1333). It may be experienced as diffuse dread and attributed to fear of the disease, of dying, of nonbeing, or of being dead; or it may result from tension associated with not having fundamental interpersonal needs met. In some cases, anxiety may also be a result of disease process (eg, abnormal metabolic states, hormone-secreting tumors, paraneoplastic syndromes, pain) or other disease-related factors, including medication side effects, medication withdrawal, or painful procedures (Holland, 1997). The great problem of anxiety in general and the terrible anxiety felt by many who are dying is that *its source is often outside the awareness of the individual* (Sullivan, 1953b) and thus less amenable to problem-solving interventions. In general, anxiety must be addressed in the context of the illness and interpersonally. Interventions can help address the problem of anxiety:

● Manage pain and other problems.
● Decrease the unknowns in the disease process and in the care given. The patient and family should be given as much information as they are able to absorb about their situations. There is no better judge of how much a particular person can tolerate than that person. Overprotection often is a misdirected kindness. Understanding helps promote a sense of control or order.
● Involve the patient and family in the patient's care. Skills to help build a sense of purpose and competence can help replace anxiety.
● Help the patient talk about his or her anxious feelings (without insisting that it be called anxiety). This intervention alone is helpful for many because expressing and discussing the feeling brings it more into awareness, making it less mysterious and threatening.
● As anxiety is recognized, assist the patient to identify associated feelings or threats. Associated feelings point to the threat underlying the anxiety. Fear of abandonment is a very common threat. Some threats may be realistic, and some are not. Both should be acknowledged as valid for that client at that time.
● Understanding the feelings or threat underlying the anxiety allows the nurse and patient to explore together the meaning of the threat or feeling.
● While not usually prescribed as a counseling technique, frequent and realistic reassurance is often helpful for a patient who is dying. The reassurance is not that the patient will not die, but that he or she can go through the process and will not be alone.
● For some patients, it is necessary to set limits on talking about anxiety. Scrutiny of interactions in which anxiety is endlessly discussed may show that the nurse is not helping the patient move beyond talking about the anxiety.
● Antianxiety medications should be considered early in the process. Counseling is not sufficient for severe anxiety in people with limited life expectancy.
  ● Benzodiazepines are commonly used, especially the short- to intermediate-acting agents, such as alprazolam, 0.25 to 0.5 mg orally (PO) every 4 to 8 hours; midazolam, 2 to 5 mg intramuscular (IM) or subcutaneous orally (SC) every 1 to 2 hours or continuous SC infusion; or lorazepam, which is also recommended for insomnia, 1 to 2 mg PO or sublingual (SL) every 6 to 8 hours, (Waller & Caroline, 1996; Woodruff, 1997).
  ● Other medications (Holland, 1997; Waller & Caroline, 1996) include haloperidol (Haldol), 0.5 to 1.5 mg PO or IM every 4 to 6 hours for more severe anxiety and chlorpromazine (Thorazine), 12.5 to 25 mg PO every 6 to 8 hours for anxiety and to increase sedation. When anxiety and depression are present, antidepressants are used. When the patient is agitated or has insomnia, sedating antidepressants, such as doxepin (Sinequan) 25 to 50 mg PO at night or amitriptyline (Elavil), 25 to 50 mg PO at night helps with sleep, depression, and anxiety. When sedation is not desired or anticholinergic effects should be avoided (eg,

the patient has stomatitis or prostatism), desipramine (Norpramin) 25 mg increased every 3 days up to more than 100 mg at night is the drug of choice. Tricyclic antidepressants are also helpful in managing pain, especially neuropathic pain. Note that some doses are smaller than those given for psychiatric disorders.

Anxiety is a complex problem that is too often confused with fear and too often attributed to external and identifiable events. Some anxiety is normal in any patient who is dying. Fear, on the other hand, results from a consciously recognized, usually external, threat or danger. The following is a list of common fears related to death and the potential responses to them.

● Fear of death itself, perhaps as annihilation or as not being: Many people, regardless of their religious faith, at some time in the process of dying experience this fear. The fear of death itself is one of the great existential challenges of life, something everyone must face, and there are no quick or easy answers to this challenge. We should be especially wary of assuming that a patient's religious faith can supply the answers to these questions or to the crisis of death itself. Even individuals of strong faith can feel abandoned by their God at some point during the process of dying. To respond arbitrarily to such a crisis with prayer or with words from holy scriptures may be to deny the dying person the fullness of his or her own doubt and experience. The nurse remains with the person who is dying in the time of his or her darkness and in the light. Sometimes only going through the darkness with a person can help them find the light.
● Fear of punishment for sins: Death, from the point of view of religions, brings with it judgment. In psychological terms, death forces people to come to terms with a final self-judgment: What have they made of their lives? The tendency to look for quick and easy answers to the doubts and confusion posed by this final

reckoning of an individual with his or her life should be avoided. Exploring mistakes and regrets can be productive when feelings of guilt and fear of punishment are present in the individual. Guilt imposed by parents or by others is another common, but often unrecognized, factor. Terrible and lifelong guilt often occurs when people have been abused as children. The process of helping a patient deal with fear of judgment and guilt includes helping the person in the following ways:
  ● Express guilty feelings
  ● Identify the source of guilt
  ● Accept responsibility for that for which he or she is responsible and reject responsibility for that for which he or she is not responsible
  ● Accept the forgiveness of others and understand blame from others
  ● Identify and accept positive aspects of self
  ● Forgive herself or himself—something many people have great difficulty in doing. Those who are able to accept fully their own mistakes and failings and fully accept forgiveness can experience a powerful healing.
● Fear of dying: Fantasized events are almost invariably worse than the reality. Determining what expectations the person has about her or his death and judiciously furnishing factual information on the manner in which people actually die generally decreases this fear.
● Fear of the symptoms of terminal illness, especially unrelieved pain and suffocation. Fear of symptoms often is based on unfortunate experiences in the earlier stages of illness or experience with other people's dying. While assurances that symptoms will be controlled helps, prompt attention to symptom relief is the most effective intervention.

Depression
The sadness common in terminal illness is often described as depression. Sadness is a normal response to many situations, and although it includes some aspects of depression, it is distinguished from depression by generally responding to supportive interventions, lack-

ing deep self-blame or worthlessness, and encompassing less impairment in cognitive functioning. Depression, on the other hand, is a pathologic state that does not respond to supportive interventions, includes feelings of deep self-blame and worthlessness, and includes cognitive impairment. Hopelessness is basic in depression. (Also see the discussion of suicide following this section.)

American Psychiatric Association (APA) diagnostic criteria (APA, 1994) for a "major depressive episode" include at least five of the following being present nearly every day during the same 2-week period and not due to medication or illness or better accounted for by bereavement, unless the symptoms persist for more than 2 months:

1. Depressed mood (an essential feature)
2. Markedly decreased interest or pleasure in daily activities (an essential feature)
3. Significant weight loss or gain
4. Sleep changes, especially insomnia
5. Psychomotor agitation or retardation
6. Fatigue or loss of energy
7. Feelings of worthlessness or excessive guilt
8. Diminished cognitive ability
9. Recurrent thoughts of death or suicide

Clearly, the determination of depression is a major challenge in the context of the complex psychological and physical matrix of terminal disease. Among the factors confounding diagnosis are similar symptomatology (fatigue, weight loss, thoughts of death); the presence of acute, and often chronic, grief; and the frequent presence of pain or other symptoms. In practical terms, however, an accurate diagnosis is not necessary, and many patients who do not meet the criteria for a major depressive episode are appropriately treated with antidepressants.

Tricyclic antidepressants are the mainstay in the pharmacologic treatment of depression or depression-like distress in terminal illness (Woodruff, 1997) and in treating insomnia and the neuropathic pain that may occur in AIDS, multiple sclerosis, cancer, and other diseases.

Further indication for using this class of medication is the mutually reinforcing relationship of pain, physical deterioration, and depression common in clients with advanced disease (Coyle, Adelhardt, Foley, & Portenoy, 1990).

● When the patient is agitated or has insomnia, sedating antidepressants, such as doxepin, 25 to 50 mg PO at night, or amitriptyline, 25 to 50 mg PO at night, helps with sleep, depression, and anxiety.

● When sedation is not desired or anticholinergic effects should be avoided (eg, the patient has stomatitis or urinary retention), desipramine, 25 mg increased every 3 days up to more than 100 mg at night, is the drug of choice. Psychostimulants are occasionally used for withdrawn or apathetic clients (Waller & Caroline, 1996).

Independent or nonpharmacologic interventions with patients with depression or depression-like distress include the following:

● Evaluate for external causes, including uncontrolled symptoms, medications, and syndromes known to cause depression. Medications that can cause depression include methyldopa, reserpine, barbiturates, diazepam, propranolol, prednisone, dexamethasone, and some chemotherapeutic agents. Some metabolic, nutritional, endocrine, and neurologic disorders can cause depressive symptoms, notably abnormalities in potassium, sodium, or calcium; hyperthyroidism; and adrenal insufficiency (Massie, et al, 1995).

● Maintain or improve physical status. The patient may be apathetic about medications, hygiene, diet, and other aspects of physical care and thus may require direct intervention.

● Be aware of one's own response to unrelieved depression. Working with a person who is depressed can be frustrating, especially when, as is frequently the case, the depression is refractory to supportive care and other interventions.

● Throughout the course of care, help the patient set achievable (usually small) goals.

These may be related to self-care, expression of feelings, or anything else relevant to the client's concerns. While not curative, achieving these goals gives objective proof of success and can build self-esteem in a person who generally sees himself or herself as a hopeless case.

● Help the patient directly express and accept feelings of sadness, worthlessness, guilt, and other feelings common with depression. A major challenge in such expression is the tendency for some patients to ruminate endlessly about sadness, poor self-image, guilt, and hopelessness. When expression of feelings becomes repetitive or consistently results in greater depression, the nurse should help the patient:

  ● Identify attitudes or other factors that contribute to the feeling(s)
  ● Identify origins of those attitudes or factors
  ● Identify realistic and unrealistic aspects of such attitudes or factors
  ● Explore the possibility that irrational beliefs or attitudes can be reexamined and perhaps rejected

● Anger often underlies depression. Expressing and accepting anger may be central to overcoming depression. See the preceding discussion of anger.

● Help the patient do something for another person. This may help decrease the low self-esteem and self-absorption of depression.

The process of expressing, accepting, and exploring feelings; achieving success in small goals; and helping another person contributes to a sense of control over self and the situation. Ultimately, the patient may experience alternatives to her or his depressed mood.

Suicide

Physician-assisted suicide, euthanasia, and "self-deliverance" are discussed in the chapter on ethics. This discussion is concerned about patients with advanced disease and the potential for suicide.

Although the exact rate of suicide among cancer patients is unknown, the incidence is somewhat higher among patients with cancer than among the general population and is likely to be underreported (Holland, 1997). Among patients with AIDS, suicide risk likely exceeds that of patients with cancer (D. Overton, personal communication, May 1998).

General thoughts of suicide and suicidal ideation (more specific thoughts) among patients with advanced disease are both a risk factor and an attempt to exert control over a terribly difficult situation (Lesko, 1997). Risk factors given for depression apply also to suicide: personal or family history of depressive episode(s), substance abuse, suicide (attempts), isolation, and unresolved grief. Having a terminal illness is itself a risk factor, as are inadequate social support, recent knowledge of terminal prognosis, mild dementia, and poorly managed symptoms. A history of suicide attempt(s) indicates very high risk. The risk is increased by the presence of guns or large amounts of medications easily used for suicide.

Suicidal ideation may not be apparent in the context of terminal illness. With death a central issue and feelings of despair not uncommon, nurses may not take particular note of behaviors that might otherwise indicate suicide risk. Clues that alert the nurse to the possibility of suicide in people who are not terminally ill are functional behaviors in terminal illness (eg, giving away possessions, sudden desire to make a will, and talking about death). Nevertheless, clues often exist. Despair, for example, is not a state of mind to accept without concern in patients.

The primary indication of suicide risk is the patient talking indirectly or directly about suicide. Examples of possible hints about suicide include statements such as: "I wish it was over with. Anything would be better than this." "I wish there was a way to finish this." People with persistent despair, hopelessness, or depression should also be evaluated for risk.

● Evaluation is direct and begins with asking, "Are you thinking about killing yourself?" Questions about suicide are difficult to ask, but there is no substitute for direct questions. If the answer is "yes," the degree of risk is determined by the interrelation of the following factors: feelings of hopelessness; specific plan; talk of method, time, and other details; and lethal, available method. A firearm is the most lethal, but other means are also lethal. Extremely high lethality (the client feels hopeless, has lethal means, intends to use the means in a specific way at a specific time) is often an indication for hospitalization and in some cases, a 911 call for emergency personnel. Such a patient should never be left alone—including in the bathroom. A few very determined individuals commit suicide after giving only the slightest hint to those around them that they intend to take their lives.

● Remove the most lethal means of suicide. It is not possible, however, to remove all means from a home. It is important for the nurse to get help at this point. Suicide intervention should not be an individual effort.

● As with intervening in other manifestations of psychological distress, an engaged relationship is most effective. Interventions suggested under the previous headings for "loneliness" and "depression" are appropriate for a person who is suicidal.

● Suicidal ideation in a person who is not historically suicidal may be relatively transitory. The risk of suicide decreases if such a person is able to exert some control over the situation and is supported through the crisis of despair that leads to the thoughts of suicide.

● A "no-suicide contract" is an effective intervention. In this written contract, the patient agrees that she or he will not hurt or kill herself or himself during a specific time period; that if such thoughts or feelings arise, she or he will contact the nurse or other involved person; and that if the nurse is difficult to contact, the patient will keep trying.

Loss of Sexual Intimacy

Sex and intimacy are central issues in human behavior. The varieties of their meaning and expression are infinite. It is impossible to pre-dict what sex and intimacy might mean to a particular individual who is dying or to his or her partner, but it is likely to mean *something* to them. While terminal illness is not usually a time of great libido, sexual or physical intimacy may be sorely missed. Most practitioners, however, are ill-prepared to discuss sex, and even when the need is obvious (Schover, Montague, & Lakin, 1997). The nurse's purpose is not to provide sex therapy, but rather to identify problems of the whole person and to at least try to support the person in coping with the problems.

Many nurses (and other professionals) are reluctant to bring up sex in patient or family assessments. The best way for most practitioners is simply to ask in a direct manner. The nurse might ask, "What has this illness meant to your sex life or your special times together?" (There is an assumption that the illness has had an effect.)

Common etiologies of sexual dysfunction in terminal illness include emotional problems, physical aspects of the disease itself, physical aspects of treatment, and medications. Physical barriers to sexuality are discussed in the section about genitourinary problems.

● Psychological difficulties are a frequent cause of sexual dysfunction and include alteration in body image, decreased self-esteem, role changes, attitudes, beliefs and misconceptions, anxiety or depression, and lack of availability of a partner.

● Physical aspects of cancer related to sexual dysfunction include genital tumors, fistulas, pain, dyspnea, nausea, fatigue, and similar problems. Hodgkin's disease and tumors adjacent to genitalia, related nerve plexi, or the spinal cord often cause sexual problems (Schover et al., 1997). Other diseases associated with sexual dysfunction are AIDS, multiple sclerosis, Parkinson's disease, epilepsy, diabetes mellitus, arteriosclerosis, chronic renal disease, hepatic disease, chronic lung disease, heart disease, and endocrine disorders (Sawczuk, 1989).

● Physical aspects of treatment that are most troublesome are surgery for prostate cancer, pelvic exenteration, abdominal (especially colon) surgery, and mastectomy. Whether from disease, treatment, or both, fatigue is a problem for many patients. Both radiation and chemotherapy also may create problems.

● Medications that commonly cause sexual dysfunction include antihypertensives, antidepressants, antipsychotics, and opioids. Alcohol also causes sexual dysfunction.

As noted previously, most nurses (or physicians, social workers, psychologists, and so forth) are not prepared to provide sex therapy. Realistically, though, it is highly unlikely that anyone is available who is better able to deal with sexual problems (especially in home care) than the nurse. Interventions include the following:

● Bring the problem into the open. This alone is farther than many people ever go in dealing with changes in sexuality.

● When the problem is one that can be readily addressed, for example, patient or partner feeling that sexual desire is wrong "at a time like this," poorly maintained colostomy or wound dressing, or pain, take appropriate action. This action could include giving information to correct misconceptions, teaching wound or colostomy care, or managing symptoms.

● Many problems are less readily addressed. Severe depression, for example, results in loss of virtually all pleasure (anhedonia), including pleasure from sex or intimacy. Whether the etiology of the sexual difficulty is resolved or not, it is generally helpful to teach the partner of the affected person about the etiology of the sexual problem.

● Some problems are insurmountable. People with invasive vulvar disease or penectomy are unable to have sex as before. In situations in which the etiology cannot be changed, it is still possible at times to help the patient and partner explore alternatives. One alternative is to change the focus from sexual dysfunction to intimacy. The process of changing the focus includes the following:

● Help the patient and partner openly admit and face the losses and resultant grief.

● Explore with one or both people the meaning of sex to them. Alternatives to intercourse—for example, oral sex—may emerge in such discussions.

● Give permission or encourage the patient and partner to try alternative(s). Too often, people quit sleeping in the same bed or even in the same room because of the illness. At times, lying down together is all a couple can do. However, the comfort each can give the other by the simplest touch, or just close physical proximity, can be beyond measure.

Manipulation

When all aspects of life spiral out of control, it is small wonder that many patients resort to manipulation as a means of control. Not all manipulation is problematic. One of the challenges that manipulation provides for practitioners is that it often works effectively as a means of meeting dependency needs. The patient may then be reluctant to stop. In terminal situations, manipulation may take the form of frequent calls for attention. These calls may not be direct requests for help, but instead may manifest as a series of problems: running out of medication on the weekend; delayed reporting of problems; family conflict in which the patient refuses care or a family member refuses to give care; splitting staff or family; overdependence; and so on. The key to recognizing dysfunctional manipulation is seeing a pattern of direct and indirect demands that have negative consequences.

Once staff members realize they are being manipulated, the response too often is to label such patients manipulative and respond with avoidance, rigidity, or their own passive-aggressive retaliation: "She's not going to manipulate me!"

Patients with a history of chemical dependency, antisocial personality disorder, or borderline personality disorder present major challenges with respect to manipulation. A psychiatrist, clinical nurse specialist, or related consultant should be used.

When working with patients who overuse manipulation, it is important to involve all other staff on the case. Otherwise, the patient is likely to redirect the manipulative behavior to whomever will best respond as the patient desires. Following are some interventions:

● Staff members must remain aware of personal feelings engendered by the manipulative behavior. Resentment, anger, and pity are common. These feelings should not be denied, but they also should not be shared with the patient. Sharing responses to or feelings about manipulation with the team is important in understanding that one is not alone!

● Care, especially schedules, should be carefully organized. The patient and family should have full understanding of who will do what and when it will be done. A written plan should be given to the patient and family.

● Limits on behavior should be set and consistently followed; however, too many limits or requirements should be avoided. In other words, battles should be chosen carefully, while ensuring that no harm is done to the patient.

● Patients' attention should be focused on their own behavior rather than on the staff's. Some people are incredibly skilled at diverting attention from the initiating behavior to others' responses.

● Socially acceptable expressions of anger should be allowed. Patients should then be helped to relate the anger to their underlying feelings; often, the feeling present will be one of being out of control or inadequate.

● The patient should explore the feelings leading to manipulation. Understanding those feelings helps lead to their acceptance. Once underlying feelings are exposed and accepted, they may no longer need to be acted out through manipulation.

● As the patient works toward accepting underlying feelings, the nurse plans and implements the care in such a way that there is maximum patient involvement in both planning and implementation.

Dependence

Dependence and manipulation are related, hence interventions are similar in some respects. Some aspects differ, and they are discussed separately. As with patients who are manipulative, a lifelong pattern of dependence is unlikely to change in the last stages of life. To intervene with patients who are overly dependent, the nurse should consider the following:

● Stay aware of personal feelings engendered by the behavior. It is beneficial to the nurse to take note of the extent—over time—to which patients becomes dependent on him or her. A pattern of dependent clients offers insight into the nurse's needs and behavior.

● Carefully organize the care. Activities that the patient can perform should be specified. These are determined by physical and psychological potential. Hopefully there will be progression toward increased independence.

● Set and consistently follow expectations. For extremely dependent individuals, expectations should not be too high. If, for example, the patient is expected to perform certain hygiene measures and does not, what options exist other than performing them for him or her? Again, the team members should all be involved in setting and following through on this and other aspects of the plan.

● Help the patient identify consequences of dependency, and explore what can be done to become more independent.

● Help the patient explore feelings associated with dependency. Some of the most passively dependent patients are filled with the greatest repressed or suppressed anger.

● Throughout the course of care, help the patient gradually increase independence. Almost any increase addresses several of the needs that are fundamental to human existence.

Other Perspectives on Dying and Death

Works by several authors on concepts dealing with the care of the dying have contributed significantly to efforts to understand human perspectives on dying and death. With a better understanding of these perspectives, the awe and the trivialities inherent in dying and death can be easier to handle. These concepts break into manageable parts something (a human dying) that is too much to comprehend as a whole. Having some understanding of the parts, creates a better understanding of the whole.

No one concept, as expressed in these works, is better or worse, more or less useful, than another. However, some concepts may be more suitable for a particular nurse to use or may be used to greater advantage in understanding a particular patient. These concepts can be seen as sets of different tools, for different workers, for different jobs. They help give direction to care.

Avery Weisman has spent many years studying people who are dying. His book, *On Dying and Denying* (1972), is a significant contribution to the field of thanatology. Weisman developed the concept of "appropriate death," a death in which the following qualities characterize the person who is dying:

● Remain relatively pain free; suffering reduced; emotional and social impoverishments kept to a minimum
● Within limits of disability, operate on as high and effective a level as possible (even though only token forms of fulfillment can be offered)
● Recognize and resolve residual conflicts and satisfy whatever remaining wishes that are consistent with present situation and ego ideal
● Be able to yield control to others in whom one has confidence, with the option of seeking or relinquishing significant key people

These characteristics serve well as basic or generic goals in caring for people who are dying.

James Birren is less known in thanatology.

His "tasks" of the person who is dying (1964) apply very well to patients and families and give direction to care:

● Manage reaction to pathophysiology. Implicit in this task is that the nurse manages the symptoms of the pathophysiology.
● Prepare for separation. The nurse might ask from what, both good and bad, is a particular patient separating?
● Manage the prospect of transition to unknown state.
● Deal with the question of how life was lived in relation to what might have been. This is a potent question that includes at least two major issues: mistakes made and, simply, the way life worked out. We all understand making mistakes in life. There may also be issues beyond the control of the person who is dying. Clients can be helped to address this task if the nurse says words to the effect that "In looking at your life, what do you wish had been different?" As noted elsewhere, a curiosity of humans is that it is common to be unable to see the positives in life until the negatives are faced. Unfortunately, some have great difficulty facing negatives and regrets without assistance. It must also be noted that facing negatives does not guarantee that positives will then emerge without assistance. The nurse who builds a working relationship with patients and then helps them to face negative aspects of self may be rewarded by seeing significant growth in the patient.

Any discussion of dying and death should include Elisabeth Kübler-Ross' stages of dying. Her book, *On Death and Dying* (1969), blew wide open the secretive and misunderstood way in which people were dying (and continue to die) in the United States. Kübler-Ross' concept of stages, and some of her other ideas, received considerable criticism. We would do better to thank her for the work she has done and the price she paid. The stages of dying identified by Kübler-Ross are denial, anger, bargaining, depression, and acceptance. These

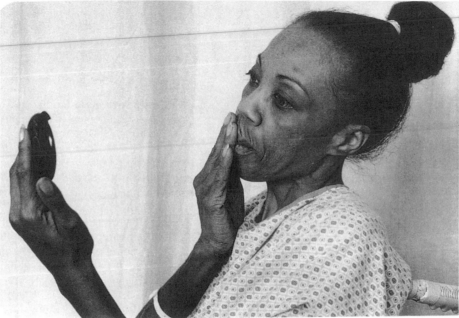

DEBORA HUNTER

are most useful if examined as states of mind common to people who are dying rather than as sequential stages. It is also helpful to remember that Kübler-Ross considers these stages, or states of mind, as "helpful" guidelines, rather than as absolutes (p. 82). Her stages are as follows:

● Denial is a defense mechanism that can be healthy or unhealthy. In psychiatric terms, denial is unconscious. As popularly used in relation to people who are dying, denial may also be a conscious effort not to think about what is happening, or a mix of belief and disbelief.

● Anger replaces "not me" with "why me?" Anger about being terminally ill, or about the fact that one's spouse or child is terminally ill, is common. This anger is often an expression of feeling overwhelmed or frightened or part of a lifelong pattern of responding to stress with anger. Finally, although we operate in a world that constantly looks at and judges psychosocial processes and needs in terms of psychopathology, anger may sometimes be appropriate and justified. The fact is that health care staff and institutions sometimes treat people with insensitivity and even, at times, with gratuitous cruelty.

● Bargaining is an old tradition; throughout literature, and even in the Scriptures, humans have sought to bargain for life with both God and the Devil. However, no matter what the bargain offered, death comes. Bargains can sometimes be made to fulfill some wish; indeed, lack of fulfillment of a wish or need may slow death, even when it seems physiologically overdue and desired by all concerned.

● Depression comes when the preceding defenses have run their course and are no longer functional; when the person realizes, "Yes, I too will die." Operatively, this depression might best be thought of as grief. The person experiences a deep sadness about the many losses already experienced and the prospect of separation from "life's web of connectedness" (Carse, 1980, p. 5).

● Acceptance, as Kübler-Ross sees it, is more than a state of mind in which the person says,

"Okay, I accept that I will die." Acceptance is closer to Merton's "freedom and transcendence . . . that nobody can touch" (Merton, 1968, p. 342). It is enlightenment, or a sense of grace. The patient is looking squarely at infinity, and does not fear.

Edwin Shneidman is a pioneer in the study of suicide. He has also contributed significantly to the understanding of people who are dying from terminal illness.

Shneidman says that "one dies as one has lived in the terrible moments of one's life" (1980, p. 112). Thus, responses to previous difficulties presage responses to terminal illness.

Shneidman offers the following "principles, goals, and beliefs" in psychotherapeutic work with people who are dying:

● Increased psychological comfort. Shneidman emphasizes the need for comfort in "a grim situation."
● Autonomy of the individual. This includes the individual having control of treatment, maintaining a sense of dignity, and being "as free as possible of unnecessary pain."
● The importance of transference. Transference, positive, negative, or ambivalent, is operative in any therapeutic relationship.
● Limited goals. Few people die "right on psychological target" with everything worked through completely. This is supremely important to understand. Expecting or desiring all or many patients to reach a state of complete acceptance dooms the nurse to disappointment in his or her abilities and in the abilities of patients.

Final Note

Humans are remarkable in their strength and adaptability. The adversity of dying enables some to resolve past and present relationships and thus bring their lives to completion.

Entering healing beyond ideas of life and death, we become who we have always been, that which preceded birth and survives death. (Levine, 1987, p. 290)

REFERENCES

American Psychiatric Association. (1994). *Diagnostic and statistical manual of mental disorders* (4th ed.). Washington, DC: Author.

Birren, J. E. (1964). *Relations of development and aging.* Salem, NH: Ayer Press.

Carse, J .P. (1980). *Death and existence: A conceptual history of human mortality.* New York: John Wiley & Sons.

Coyle, N., Adelhardt, J., Foley, K. M., & Portenoy, R. K. (1990). Character of terminal illness in the advanced cancer patient: Pain and other symptoms in the last four weeks of life. *Journal of Pain and Symptom Management, 5*(2), 83–93.

Davison, B. J., & Degner, L. F. (1998). Promoting patient decision making in life-and-death situations. *Seminars in Oncology Nursing, 14*(2), 129–136.

Holland, J. C. (1997). Principles of psycho-oncology. In J. F. Holland, R. C. Bast, D. L. Morton, E. Frei, D. W. Kufe, & R. W. Weischselbaum (Eds.), *Cancer medicine* (4th ed.) (pp. 1327–1343). Baltimore: Williams & Wilkins.

Kübler-Ross, E. (1969). *On death and dying.* New York: MacMillan.

Lesko, L. M. (1997). Psychologic issues (in cancer). In V. T. DeVita, S. Hellman, & S. A. Rosenberg (Eds.) *Cancer: Principles and practice of oncology* (5th ed.) (pp. 2879–2891). Philadelphia: Lippincott-Raven.

Lev, E. L., & McCorkle, R. (1998). Loss, grief, and bereavement in family members of cancer patients. *Seminars in Oncology Nursing, 14*(2), 145–151.

Levine, S. (1987). *Healing into life and death.* Garden City, NY: Anchor Press.

Lindemann, E. (1944). Symptomatology and management of acute grief. *American Journal of Psychiatry, 101,* 141–148.

Massie, M. J., Speigel, E., Lederberg, M. S., & Holland, J. C. (1991). Psychiatric complications in cancer patients. In G.P. Murphy, W. Lawrence, & R.E. Lenhard (Eds.), *Clinical oncology* (pp. 685-698). Atlanta: American Cancer Society.

Merton, T. (1968). *The Asian journal of Thomas Merton.* New York: New Directions Books.

Nicholi, A. M. (1978). History and mental status. In A. M. Nicholi (Ed.), *The Harvard guide to modern psychiatry* (pp. 25–40). Cambridge, MA: The Belknap Press of Harvard University.

Nouwen, H. J. M. (1974). *Out of solitude.* Notre Dame: Ave Maria Press.

Parkes, C. M. (1978). Psychological aspects. In C. M. Saunders (Ed.), *The management of terminal disease* (pp. 44–64). London: Edward Arnold.

Sawczuk, I. (1989). Impotence. In T. D. Walsh (Ed.), *Symptom control* (pp. 265–270). Oxford: Blackwell Scientific Publications.

Schover, L. R., Montague, D. K., & Lakin (1997). Sexual problems. In V. T. DeVita, S. Hellman, & S. A. Rosenberg (Eds.), *Cancer: Principles and practice of oncology* (5th ed.) (pp. 2879–2891). Philadelphia: Lippincott-Raven.

Shneidman, E. (1980). *Voices of death.* New York: Harper and Row.

Sullivan, H. S. (1953a). *The interpersonal theory of psychiatry.* New York: Norton.

Sullivan, H. S. (1953b). *Conceptions of modern psychiatry.* New York: Norton.

Waller, A., & Caroline, N. L. (1996). *Handbook of palliative care in cancer.* Boston: Butterworth-Heinemann.

Weisman, A. D. (1972). *On dying and denying.* New York: Behavior Publications.

Woodruff, R. (1997). *Symptom control in advanced cancer.* Melbourne: Asperula.

CHAPTER 3

Psychosocial Needs, Problems, and Interventions: The Family

Although this chapter refers throughout to "family," readers should keep in mind that the word family may encompass a traditional extended or nuclear family, or it may refer to less traditional configurations, such as extended kinship systems, nonrelated dyads or groups, people in long-term relationships, or other people in relationships that function to support and care for each other.

The first step in addressing psychosocial needs and problems of the patient and family is to manage the patient's physical symptoms. At times, psychosocial problems are part of the etiology of physical problems, hence addressing psychosocial issues is also part of managing physical problems.

Review of Family Concepts

A review of several concepts of family dynamics is helpful in understanding families in terminal situations:

● Family systems theory: Taken together, the members of a family make up the family system. A change in one part of the system changes the rest of the system. There are often subsystems of two or more people within the family system. The ability to adapt to change is essential to maintaining optimal function in the family system. In all hospice and most palliative care programs, the family is considered the unit of care.

● Communications: Accurate and direct communications within the context of (a generally) positive emotional climate are essential to effective functioning. One of the most damaging mistakes in terminal care is telling secrets to one family member and excluding the others (eg, telling the family that the patient is dying but not telling the patient).

It is important to understand that communication patterns in families are built over time and are structured to meet the needs, expectations, and in some cases pathology of the family. Experience in hospice and with families in a variety of settings shows that in crisis, most families do not change communication patterns, so communication continues as before—whether open or closed, deep or superficial, or sometimes open and sometimes closed. Some families increase communications so that deeper feelings are shared and the family grows.

● Rules, roles, and themes: Every family has overt and covert rules, roles, and themes that may or may not be recognized by any or all family members or by others outside the family. Rules affect the various roles and boundaries of each family member. Roles should be age appropriate and boundaries clear. Rules may range from positive to negative in content and function. Universal or rigid rules, roles, and themes, such as the role of the person who is *always* bad or *always* good, or the theme that a particular family *never* has conflict or *always* has conflict, are often problematic because they do not allow for the fullness of human expression.

● Defining a family: Although there is disagreement about the definition of family, there is one constant: Each family is different. Families may consist of relatives (blood, marriage, adoption, other) living together or apart, of heterosexual or homosexual couples, of unrelated people who depend on one another, and even of people who are living and people who are dead (the memory of a loved one is a powerful presence in some families). Probably the best approach is to let a family define itself.

The Process of Terminal Illness: Appreciation and Understanding

Caring for families of people who are dying is based, like the care for the patient, on appreciation and understanding of the experience of going through a terminal illness with a loved one. Although each person goes through this process differently, there often are similarities in the experience or response to it.

Just as it was suggested that the practitioner work to understand the fullness of the person who is dying, so should he or she work to understand and appreciate the fullness of the family of the person who is dying. To see and appreciate the family and individuals within it in the fullness and incompleteness that each family and person brings to dying is an enormous step in providing care.

Many families find that facing death is the greatest challenge of their lives together. Death brings irrevocable change to the family. The effects of terminal illness on the family as a whole and on individuals within the family are profound. Grief is, of course, central to the experience. Common behavioral responses include anxiety, depression, anger, and guilt. Different families and different individuals within the family meet the challenge (or do not) in different ways.

Like the person who is dying, families go through the up-and-down experiences of illness and treatment. Hope springs up and is dashed. There are bad times and, hopefully, good times. Ultimately, there is the realization that a loved one will die. The crisis points discussed under psychosocial needs and problems of the individual apply also to the family. The family that goes through these crisis points with the patient is most likely to help the patient through the process of dying and, in turn, be helped by the patient (Holland, 1997). The developmental stage for the family in a terminal illness case is usually integrity versus despair or mutual aid versus uselessness (Cullen, 1987).

At times, the family is the focus of care. The basic concept in caring for a family when a loved one is dying is much like the basic premise of family therapy and the "identified patient." When the family gets better, the patient also gets better. The family is most often the focus of care when the patient is a child.

Coping with Terminal Illness

Although this chapter focuses on family problems in caring for people who are terminally ill, it important to have some understanding of how families cope with the problems of giving care. By looking first at the needs of family caregivers (Harrington, Lackey, & Gates, 1996; Steele & Fitch, 1996), there is direction in preventing and addressing problems. The most important needs of family caregivers (and related interventions) tend to be the following:

● Information about the illness, symptoms, and needs of the patient: The need for teaching is clear. The family is likely to want to know what is happening physically, why it is happening, and what to expect as the illness progresses.

● Hope: Families hope for many things, not the least of which is hope that the patient will not die. Hope is discussed in greater detail in the chapter on spiritual care.

● Relief: Physical, psychological, and spiritual relief are vital to the family's ability to cope. This is discussed in detail later in this chapter, especially in the section entitled Caregiver Relief and Coping.

Psychosocial and Related Family Problems

Loss and Grief

Everyone loses something in the process of dying (also see Chapter 7). Family and survivor losses are similar to the patient's. Family losses may include the following:

● Physical health: As a result of the physical and emotional demands of providing care, some caregivers take as much as 1 year to recover their strength. Some never recover.

● The idea of living forever, of health forever: The dying and death of a loved one generally destroys this illusion, if it exists.

● Confidence in the certainty, order, predictability, and security of life in general, as a family and as individuals.

● Family structure: At a minimum, the family structure changes and often a permanent void results from the death.

● Roles, identity: Some loss of role and identity of survivors is a given with any death of a loved one. A person who takes his or her identity from the person who is dying or who has a symbiotic relationship with that person obviously losses far more than one who has his or her own identity separate from the other. For the frail, elderly, and isolated survivor, the death of a spouse or other loved one may literally be the death of self.

● Feelings of competence, usefulness: If beating death is the goal, then loss and defeat are certain. If doing the best job possible to relieve suffering is the goal, even then everyone involved may sometimes feel beaten down but at least not useless.

● Independence: This loss is sometimes unrecognized by practitioners and sometimes unexpressed by a particular family member. Independence, or a semblance of it, is lost when the person who dies was the survivor's primary link to the outside world. This is a problem especially for elderly, isolated people.

● People thought to be friends: Much is learned about who can be depended on and who cannot.

● Financial security: Terminal illness is a financial disaster for some families. When this is the case, there may be resentment toward the patient by the family, and the patient may also resent himself or herself. On the other hand, a person's death may represent a financial windfall for some in a family, and there may be conflict around this issue.

● Superficial relationship with God or faith: On the surface, losing a superficial relationship with God or faith might seem like a positive event. However, such a relationship may be very comfortable; it may also serve as a precursor to, or foundation for, a deeper relationship with faith.

● Hope: The (common illusory) hope that life will go on unchanged forever is lost. Other hopes, such as that life may go on a little longer, that relationships will deepen, or that strength will be found, can replace the hope of living forever.

Not every family or survivor experiences all these losses, but some experience many or most of them. The fundamental issues are response to the loss and what, if anything, will replace the loss.

Grief is the normal reaction to loss and "any interference with it (is) useless or even harmful" (Freud, 1917, p. 239). Grief is the long, sad, road to recovery. "The deep capacity to weep for the loss of a loved one and to continue to treasure the memory of that loss is one of our noblest human traits" (Shneidman, 1980, p. 179).

Families and patients often grieve for different losses, present and anticipated, at different speeds during the process of dying. Sometimes the grief work seems done while the patient lives. When this occurs, there may be emotional distancing between family and patient, with the patient treated unconsciously as if she or he is no longer completely within the family. In other cases, anticipatory grief is associated with an ability to face great adversity with equanimity (Lev & McCorkle, 1998).

An obvious difference in family and patient grief is that the patient's grief dies with him or her, while the family's lives on and may intensify. Like any other human behavior or experience, grief and mourning may be carried to extremes in behavior or length (eg, complicated grief disorder). Grief is discussed in depth in Chapter 7.

Decisions

The widespread use of advance directives has been helpful but not completely successful in reducing misunderstandings among patients, families, and staff regarding end-of-life decisions. Even when end-of-life wishes are known, in many cases they are not honored (Conners & SUPPORT Investigators, 1995). Moreover, in one study, fewer than half of terminally ill patients had discussed their wishes with a nurse, physician, or legal surrogate (Sulmasy et al., 1998). Promoting the fulfillment of a patient's wishes about end-of-life care includes the following:

● The patient and family should receive an accurate and clear description of treatment options, expected outcomes, and potential complications. Far too often, a crisis develops, and an ill-prepared family member is confronted with making life-or-death decisions with little understanding of all the ramifications.

● Staff should promote the resolution of interpersonal issues that if unresolved, may have an impact on a family member's judgment in the incredible tension that often accompanies the last days.

● Staff should seek to understand individual and cultural issues that may impact end-of-life decisions.

Decisions at the end of life can have immense import—life or death, suffering or peace, and more. Decisions may reverberate for many years in the lives of survivors. The nurse, physician, social worker, chaplain, and other staff must all understand that they all should be advocates for the patient's right to self-determination and for the family's mental and spiritual health.

Loneliness and Isolation

It is not only the person who is dying who finds himself or herself lonely and isolated. Isolation for the family occurs when friends and other family members do not respond with their physical or emotional presence; when the enormous demands of care result in some family members—who are usually carrying on with their normal work schedule—being completely deprived of free time; and when others have no understanding of the magnitude of the pain or process of caring for a loved one who is dying. Thus, isolation can be the physical, psychological, or spiritual absence of others. One of the most isolating situations is when others seek to comfort through inappropriate cheer or through "transform(ing) bad into good or pain into privilege" (Kushner, 1981, p. 23).

Key factors contributing to isolation are that many people do not know how to ask for or accept help, and many do not know how to offer or give help. Too often, needs for help are expressed amorphously: "I wish someone would just help me in some way." Offers to help are frequently expressed in a vague manner: "Let me know if there is anything I can do to help." While these offers are often sincere, the usual outcome is that no help is requested, and no help is given.

When a family's life is characterized by isolation, there is little the practitioner can do to change the situation other than to decrease isolation through her or his own presence or through enlisting the help of volunteer or other types of programs. When the family is, to some extent, engaged with others, isolation can be decreased in several ways:

● Teach how to ask for very specific help at specific times (eg, grocery shopping twice a week, fixing a meal every Saturday, taking out the trash four times each week, organizing medical bills on a weekly basis).

● Teach that except for the one or two most dependable people, "on-call" requests should be avoided. As previously noted, two forms of presence (of others) are especially valuable: (1) those who competently perform certain tasks and (2) those able to be with one who is suffering. Most people can do one or the other, but few can do both.

● Teach that asking for help is not only okay, but that it will probably need to be done a number of times. If, for example, the family's church or clergy is unhelpful, the family can learn to confront the church in a positive and effective manner.

People in western cultures tend not to be very skilled at helping family and friends through the process of dying. Quality hospice or palliative care must sometimes include teaching in a very direct manner how to engage family, friends, church, synagogue, and so forth in this process. In the same manner in which friends sometimes are "discovered," rising to meet the needs of a person who is dying, so may friends be discovered who can help meet the needs of a dying person's family.

Uselessness

Family members' feelings of uselessness often emerge from the physical and emotional or social limitations that are a part of terminal illness. No matter how hard the family works, no matter how much they care, no matter how much money is spent, despite the prayers, despite everything, the object of the efforts continues dying. It is helpful, however, to remember that the patient's survival is not the only object of the effort. The well-being of the family members is also at stake. They are also trying to help themselves by maintaining the family system. Feelings of uselessness can be approached in several ways (also see the discussion below on helplessness):

● Help family members be—not feel, but be— useful. In general, the family should be involved in as many aspects of care as possible. This includes children. A young child's contribution may consist only of bringing the patient a glass of water. Any contribution helps children (and adults), both during the dying family member's illness and later, when the family confronts the grief.
● Help family members understand and feel as though they are making an investment in the goals of palliative care.
● Explore feelings about the situation in general, and about regrets in particular.

Helplessness (of Patient and Family)
Helplessness is related to feelings of uselessness. There is, however, a dimension of helplessness that is best examined alone: Terminal illnesses seem to have, and in some respects really do have, an inexorable quality, rolling mercilessly along to their inevitable end as patient, family, and everyone concerned stand helplessly by. This "standing by" is perceived by many as the most difficult part of caregiving (Lev & McCorkle, 1998).

An underlying dynamic in helplessness is feeling incompetent. Caring for a person who is dying is no small feat under any circumstances. In modern western culture, the difficulties inherent in caring for a person who is dying are compounded by smaller families, urban isolation, work schedules, complex technologies of patient care, and inexperience in providing care. Feeling helpless and incompetent means that some people never try to

help. They are then left with the unescapable knowledge that, whatever the reasons, they did not help. Feelings of helplessness can be addressed in two ways:

● Move the focus of care consciously from cure to care. The goal of care then shifts from the patient not dying to the client living as well as possible.
● Involve the patient and family in care. Even when the family is financially able to pay for total patient care, competently providing at least some care is beneficial both during the process and afterward.

Anxiety and Fear
The discussion on anxiety and fear covered in Chapter 2, in the section, Individual Psychosocial Needs, also applies to the family. It is not only the body that dies, but "irreversible damage (is done) to the web of connectedness between persons," and it is within that connectedness that we experience life, or meaning in life (Carse, 1980, p. 4). As is true in other psychosocial issues, the frail elderly or isolated family members are at tremendous risk. For many, beyond the (in itself terrible) horizon of a life partner dying and the attendant grief may lie the prospect of continuing life alone.

Anger/Conflict
The discussion of anger covered in Chapter 2 in the section, Individual Psychosocial Needs, also applies to the family. Grief, anxiety, fatigue, and other dynamics place enormous stress on the family. Old, unresolved conflicts, hurts, and resentments surface, and in some families, the dying process becomes a battlefield. There are times when the atmosphere in a patient's room resembles that of a psychological war zone. In many families, at some point in the illness, it seems that some sort of conflict is bound to emerge.

When the family has a history of conflict and current interactions are characterized by dysfunctional conflict, it may be wise to recall the principle of limited goals (Shneidman, 1980). In some situations, the goal may be practitioner oriented and limited to not responding negatively to conflict so as to be able to maintain contact with the patient.

In many families, anger and conflict *can* be resolved. The process for understanding and addressing family anger and conflict is similar to that used in individual situations:

● Understand one's own response to anger. This is especially important when the practitioner comes from a family in which conflict was a theme or where conflict was repressed.
● Accept that anger and conflict are normal responses to the stress of terminal illness and of providing care.
● Help family members verbally express the anger rather than act it out in a destructive or indirect manner.
● Help identify the precursors to angry feelings and the underlying feeling (eg, betrayal, frustration, anxiety). Helping family members identify underlying feelings is promoted by discussing what was occurring and what individuals were feeling before the conflict began. This is best done when the conflict is not active.
● Help identify alternatives in expressing feelings of frustration, anxiety, and so forth.
● Help identify consequences of angry behavior.
● Because anxiety underlies much anger and because anxiety and poor self-concept are related, assisting the patient or family member to address self-concept may also help.

Depression

Sadness, guilt, and other aspects of depression are common in families in which someone is dying, but clinical depression is less usual. The absence of sadness may be more problematic than sadness. Extreme or incapacitating sadness or depression also indicates problems perhaps beyond the immediate one of the dying family member. In reality, who and what is dying is not just a person,

but also dreams unfulfilled, hope lost—the essence of life itself.

As with the individual person who is dying, clear identification of depression in a family member may be difficult. Interventions discussed in Chapter 2 for the dying individual hold true for that individual's family members as well. Although depression is not classically seen as a family problem (in the same way as, for example, eating disorders are), having a family member with depression is certainly a family issue. The possibility of family members deteriorating psychologically or attempting suicide should also be considered, especially after the patient dies.

Loss of Sexual Intimacy

The dimensions of sexuality that are more specific to the spouse or partner of the dying person than to the patient are most often related to the issues of (1) sexual feelings that, due to illness or other reasons, the patient does not share and (2) confronting the loss of intimacy or sexual activity after the patient dies. These issues are most likely to develop into problems in need of understanding and guidance when the patient and spouse or partner are young, when the patient's illness is lengthy, or when the illness is one whose effects include decreased libido (eg, multiple sclerosis).

Interventions to help a spouse or partner deal with sexual feelings or impulses might include listening *without making judgments* and assisting with finding sources to help guide spouses or partners when they are in doubt. Sexuality is a private matter for most people; a consequence of that privacy is that there is scant opportunity to develop objective perspectives. Thus, most people who struggle with issues of sexuality are left alone with their thoughts, feelings, desires, and impulses. The practitioner not only can be available to listen objectively to others' sexual problems, but also help locate pertinent information among the range of self-help and other books available on the subject of sexuality.

In any case, people who struggle with sexual feelings nearly always respond positively to

DEBORA HUNTER

the opportunity to talk about their struggles. In some cases, the issue is intimacy more than sex and thus discussing ways to share intimate feelings and contact (as opposed to sexual fulfillment) is the best course of action. On the whole, it is wise to remain aware of the fact that the stress of frustrated sexual feelings and impulses during the time of illness and after the death of a spouse or partner is a little-explored area in which there is much pain and great ignorance. Specific means of dealing with physical sexual problems are addressed in the chapter on genitourinary problems and symptoms.

Caregiver Relief and Coping

The fatigue experienced both by those who are dying and by those who are watching a loved one die is all-encompassing.

Working in hospice and in other similar settings where human life is constantly ebbing away means experiencing people as they really are: often contradictory, contrary, manipulative, worrying, working, loving, steadfast, and oftentimes, in the final analysis, capable of moving beyond themselves in outpourings of love and hard work. Many are lifted up; some are not.

As with other aspects of terminal care, fatigue in the caregiver often has a cyclical nature. First, there is physical labor, coupled with sleep loss. Because of grief, anxiety, and other psychological issues, the labor seems harder to do and sleep more difficult to accomplish and less restful. Isolation, both in terms of the decreased presence of others and the unfulfilled expectations of help from others, adds to the stress. Watching helplessly as a loved one suffers and life slips away is a terrible thing to do and often the hardest part of all the work. To put it in another way, for many, this is the hardest work they have ever tried to accomplish, with the least confidence and support they have ever experienced and with the least knowledge about how to accomplish it. They are often doing this when they are old and when they have fewer physical and, in some cases, emotional resources.

Like grief, exhaustion may be considered a given when caring for a terminally ill loved one. While exhaustion obviously is a problem for many, it may also be viewed as a sort of coping mechanism, as a confirmation of the experience. Caring for a loved one who is dying is a duty prescribed by the most ancient traditions and customs of humankind. The word "role," as in "your role as the caregiver," does not adequately describe the situation: carrying out the duty of caring for a dying loved one is part of being fully human. Those who fulfill this duty come away from it exhausted but fully aware that, on the very deepest levels of human existence, they did the right thing. Caregiver exhaustion and fatigue can be addressed and to some extent prevented as follows:

● Try to understand the extent of the work and sacrifices made by the caregiver. Directly acknowledge the sacrifices made in providing care. Many people will deny that they are tired or that they are sacrificing to provide care. This does not mean they do not benefit from the acknowledgement. Both during the ordeal and when it is over, words of understanding and acknowledgement are remembered.
● The caregiver's health status is directly related to the ability to care for the patient and should be regularly assessed and action taken based on the assessment.
● Hospice and other similar services provide immense help to families and patients. Scheduling services to fit with the caregiver's schedule is extremely important. Helping families organize themselves, their friends, or their church can have a profound impact on the situation. This is discussed in the following section.

Teaching the Family

In the United States and other technological societies, most people do not know what to do when a family member is dying. Scattered families, the technological nature of dying, and other factors play roles in this phenomenon.

In the absence of extended families or experience in caring for people who are dying, a central question is what do families and others need to be taught to provide care for a family member who is dying? Some of the answers are obvious: methods of catheter care, medication administration, pump usages, and so forth. However, caring for a loved one goes far beyond technical care. Families and others also need to understand the organization of physical care, the process of dying, and what to do emotionally and spiritually.

When people know what to expect, the process of dying is not a terrible mystery. When people feel competent to care for a family member, they are far more likely to participate in the care. When people understand and participate, the situation is still extremely difficult, but it tends to go better.

Goals in Teaching the Family

The first step in teaching is to determine family/patient goals and how these and practitioner goals can fit together. Discussing goals of care gives the practitioner the opportunity to assess the family further, and family members have the opportunity to begin assessing themselves. A standard of openness is set when the family is involved directly and early in the process of providing care. Not surprisingly, the question of goals often results in family members learning that they expect and want different things.

Teaching/Learning Needs
Teaching and learning needs vary according to patient problems, family strengths, and other factors. Typical areas of need include the following:

• While not usually considered a teaching/learning need, family members must be taught who the practitioners are, what they will do to help, and how to locate them in an emergency. It is immensely helpful for the family and the patient to learn what will happen in the course of care and how to get help in difficult times.

• Medications should be understood, including what, how much, and when to give them; adverse effects; when to discontinue or ask for help; how to keep track of medications; and when to obtain refills. (For example, Saturday night is a bad time to run out of Dilaudid!)

• Technology, even the simplest kind, is often mysterious and intimidating to families and patients. If power equipment is used, the family needs to know how to turn it on and off, how to regulate flow, how to handle minor malfunctions, and who to call if problems cannot be corrected. If equipment is basic (eg, catheter, nasogastric tube), caregivers should know how to recognize and resolve problems and who to call if problems cannot be resolved.

• How to provide physical care, again including basics, is often completely new information to many people.

• Disease progression is a sensitive and complex matter, and the practitioner must find a way to resolve conflicting demands, such as anticipating to family members the likelihood of specific problems occurring and teaching about those problems and at the same time, ensuring that family and patient are not burdened with unnecessary information. Areas to consider teaching about include (1) early recognition of and action to take for likely problems, medication side effects, and so forth and (2) what to expect and do as the disease progresses. What to do when the patient dies is almost always an issue.

Clearly, the preceding five areas of teaching and learning are not inclusive, are not in the correct order for every patient/family, and cannot all be taught in one encounter.

In some families, more than one person provides care. *Clear division of responsibilities*

is extremely important in preventing conflict and gaps in care. One person may be in charge of the catheter and the medications; another person may pay bills and call around for sitters. The procedure for dealing with more than one caregiver is discussed in the following section.

Organization

Whether there is one caregiver or five, the care must be organized. Failure to organize care increases fatigue and conflict and often results in a breakdown of care. Organizing care does not just happen, nor is it something that many families can do on their own. The practitioner assists in organizing care as follows:

• Explain to the caregiver(s) and the patient that organization is necessary to meet their goals.

• Have the family make lists of (1) what help they need now and will need later and (2) everyone who has offered to help or who might help. Different people have different skills and should be used accordingly. Some will be most helpful with shopping and errands, others with cooking and cleaning, others with reading or companionship, others with organizing bills, and so on. There are ongoing jobs that must be done, even in the midst of dying. Every family presents with a unique constellation of social support. Probably the best way to pull together a support system is for the family to go through its address book, name by name, and then consult its church directories, civic clubs, places of employment, and any other such listings. The list of names resulting from such a search may be smaller than anticipated. The list will grow smaller as contact is made and help is requested.

• Help the caregiver fit tasks and helpers together. It is nearly always a mistake to ask friends for help "in general." Be specific and people will be more helpful. Where there is not a fit between tasks and helpers, a social work or volunteer service agency may be able to help.

A common problem when working on involving others is that one or several family members may want to do everything. Sometimes, when people have enough time and energy, this is possible. Other times, the desire to do everything may function as a way of dealing with guilt or conflict.

It may be obvious to an outsider that the person who wants to do it all cannot handle the workload. Often, however, the person who wants to do it all will be unable to see that he or she is virtually ensuring failure of the care effort. When this is the case, the practitioner can help the caregiver explore her or his perceptions of self as caregiver and of others who might help.

Teaching Emotional Care (and How to Meet Needs)

In part, teaching emotional care means teaching concepts discussed under psychosocial needs and problems. Family and patient benefit from learning about and helping one another. Some families and patients require no teaching about needs or emotional care, some teach the practitioner, and others need the help.

Teaching emotional care may also include teaching innovative ways of meeting needs. The people involved have basically the same needs they did before. This may seem like a simple concept, but the practice of it is more involved. A major problem in meeting these needs is that people are limited by thinking of meeting them exactly as they were met before the illness. If, for example, the need for belonging was met in some part through church activities, the common perception is that the only way to meet the need through church is to go to church for the whole service. Why not make a one-time increase in analgesic and go just long enough for communion and a hymn? Why not make a video or audio recording of the church service? Why not have a small Sunday school class in the patient's home? People are in the habit of doing things in a particular way and few people think of doing it in any other way.

Children

The fundamental purposes of any family or parent with children are to protect the children and provide means of growth. Thus, when someone in a family is dying, there is often an almost primitive urge to shield the children from the situation, and some shielding is appropriate. Just as young children do not benefit from knowing all the details of adult sexuality, they also do not benefit from knowing all the details of dying. However, as difficult as it may be, children should be told the truth about dying and death.

There are numerous articles on children and death; many use the works of Piaget, Erickson, or other developmental psychologists as a basis for understanding how children view dying and death (Backer, Hannon, & Russell, 1994). Other factors also play important and sometimes dominant roles in how children view and react to dying and death.

A child's psychosocial life experiences or circumstances, for example, are very important in how that child views and reacts to dying and death. A child who has grown up in a neighborhood in which drugs and violence are a part of life may have more experience with death than do many adults who live in other circumstances. Refugee children may have seen mass death. Such children may be numbed or dissociated from pain and death; they may also have very strong reactions.

The extent, or lack of, family social networks and support also plays a part in a child's view of and responses to dying and death (Silverman & Worden, 1992).

Gender is yet another factor that can affect the expression of feelings about dying and death. Children and their parents (especially older parents) may often reflect gender stereotypes. Girls may express and confide more, while boys may be less expressive (Silverman & Worden, 1992).

Overall, three variables deeply affect a child's view of and response to dying and death: who dies, how the death occurs, and who survives. The death of a close family member is obviously more troubling than that of a neighbor, and the nature of the child's relationship with the surviving parent or other family members also plays a part.

How the death occurs is the variable in which family and caregivers can exert some influence, because it not only encompasses the degree to which the death was a surprise or expected and the degree of suffering and related issues (eg, appearance, smell), but also the extent and nature of the child's involvement in the dying process (Gibbons, 1992). Attempting to separate or protect a child from the process may only make the process more frightening and mysterious. On the other hand, just as it is generally a mistake to attempt to hide the situation from children, so is it also generally a mistake to force inappropriate situations on them. There is no formula for calculating how much is too much or too little. A general rule is to make decisions based on sensitivity to a child's response. It is also important to keep in mind that children do not deal with life (and death) in the same way that adults do. In grief, many children, for example, "do not wish to talk about feelings or events as much as they want to reminisce" (Silverman & Worden, 1992, p. 103).

Erikson's developmental stages and psychosocial crises (see Chapter 2) give practitioners great insight into where to *begin* working with children in families in which someone is dying. Assessments and interventions directed to the child can, at least initially, be structured around these developmental stages. Work with the parents should include teaching or reminding them that the child's natural development goes on, to some extent, regardless of other events and helping the parents understand how to deal with development-related issues. For example, primary issues for a 6-year-old center around initiative versus guilt. Left to her or his own devices, a 6-year-old child is likely to figure out something to do (on her or his own initiative) to help the person who is dying. Support of this initiative, no matter how impractical the idea is, tips the bal-

ance toward reinforcing initiative. Rejecting the idea, especially in an irritable or ridiculing manner, tips the balance toward guilt. Note that Erickson's childhood stages usually center around action on the part of the child and, further, that they all imply parental support for the action.

In the case of young adolescents, responses to someone in the family who is dying can be complicated by issues of peer-group identity, which may result in the adolescent feeling pressure to choose between family and peers and may appear more problematic. Many girls and boys in early adolescence are capable of providing superb care for family members. Sometimes group identity issues can be deferred to some extent, or they can be handled effectively with the help of school teachers and staff. Some adolescents may attempt to play the role of savior for a parent who is dying or for the bereaved parent who is left behind. This can sometimes be an attempt to avoid dealing with their own pain; it can also sometimes be an expression of maturity. In either case, the young person will need help with her or his own feelings, both during and after the experience.

Piaget's work in cognitive-affective development also provides insight into how children view and experience dying and death (Backer et al., 1994). In general, children tend to progress from the egocentric and magical thinking of the preoperational period (2–7 years), to an increasing intellectual realization of the finality of death in the concrete operations period (7–11 years), and onward to an understanding of the implications of dying and death in the formal operations period (Phillips, 1975).

It is clear that many factors affect how children and adults view and experience dying and death. Using developmental concepts helps in understanding children, but this is not a substitute for understanding individuals. It is important, both before and after the death, that the child maintain connection with the parent, sibling, or other loved one. Before the death, connection is maintained through helping with care. After the death, connection is maintained through participation in mourning rituals, openly grieving, treasured keepsakes, and reminiscing.

REFERENCES

Backer, B. A., Hannon, N., & Russell, N. A. (1994). *Death and dying: Understanding and care* (2nd ed.). Albany, NY: Delmar.

Carse, J. P. (1980). *Death and existence.* New York: John Wiley & Sons.

Conners, A. F. & the other SUPPORT principle Investigators. (1995). A controlled trial to improve care for seriously ill hospitalized patients. *Journal of the American Medical Association, 274*(20), 1591–1598.

Cullen, S. I. (1987). Family dynamics. In J. Norris, M. Kunes-Connell, S. Stockard, P. M. Ehrhart, & G. N. Newton (Eds.), *Mental health-psychiatric nursing: A continuum of care* (pp. 199–222). New York: Delmar.

Freud, S. (1917). Mourning and melancholia. In J. Strachey (Ed.), *The standard edition of the complete psychological works of Sigmund Freud (Vol. 14).* London: Hogarth Press.

Gibbons, M. B. (1992). A child dies, a child survives: The impact of sibling loss. *Journal of Pediatric Health Care, 6*(2), 65–72.

Harrington, V., Lackey, N. R., & Gates, M. F. (1996). Needs of caregivers of clinic and hospice cancer patients. *Cancer Nursing, 19*(2), 118–125.

Holland, J. C. (1997). Principles of psycho-oncology. In J. F. Holland, R. C. Bast, D. L. Morton, E. Frei, D. W. Kufe, & R. W. Weischselbaum (Eds.), *Cancer medicine* (4th ed.) (pp. 1327–1343). Baltimore: Williams & Wilkins.

Kushner, H. S. (1981). *When bad things happen to good people.* New York: Avon.

Lev, E. L., & McCorkle, R. (1998). Loss, grief, and bereavement in family members of cancer patients. *Seminars in Oncology Nursing, 14*(2), 145–151.

McNulty, B. J. (1978). Out-patient and domiciliary management from a hospice. In C. M. Saunders (Ed.), *The management of terminal disease* (pp. 154–165). London: Edward Arnold.

Phillips, J. L. (1975). *The origins of intellect: Piaget's theory.* San Francisco: W.H. Freeman Company.

Shneidman, E. (1980). *Voices of death.* New York: Harper and Row.

Silverman, P. R., & Worden, J. W. (1992). Children's reactions in the early months after the death of a parent. *American Journal of Orthopsychiatry, 62*(1), 93–104.

Steele, R. G., & Fitch, M. I. (1996). Coping strategies of family caregivers of home hospice patients with cancer. *Oncology Nursing Forum, 23*(6), 955–960.

Sulmasy, D. P., Terry, P. B., Weisman, C. S., Miller, D. J., Stallings, R. Y., Vettese, M. A., & Haller, K. B. (1998). The accuracy of substituted judgments in patients with terminal diagnoses. *Annals of Internal Medicine, 128*(8), 621–629.

CHAPTER 4

Spiritual Care: Needs, Problems, and Interventions

KEY POINTS

● There is a fundamental human need for connection with the transcendent, and that need often is greatest when confronted with death.

● Basic spiritual needs are relatively consistent among humans and across different faiths.

● The ability to provide spiritual care is enhanced by personal spiritual exploration and by understanding the basic spiritual needs.

● While variations exist in each individual's spiritual needs and problems, there are strategies helpful to the practitioner in beginning to address patients' spiritual needs and problems.

When death is near, many people turn instinctively to faith, to God. Spiritually and philosophically, death—the enemy, the end—becomes "an invitation to new life" (Carse, 1980, p. 9). However, an invitation is not a map nor a companion for the journey. The invitation may be only the explication of the need for a new life, without the understanding that a new life is possible or how it can be found. Spiritual care helps in exploring that possibility and achieving it.

Spiritual care in terminal illness may be thought of as going with a person on a journey through a sometimes fearsome personal landscape. Going with (or watching with) means being there to help with, but not guide, the exploration through the fears, doubts, failures, mistakes, regrets, and feelings of abandonment that are part of many lives. Spiritual care is about compassion, failures, facing fears, and

the hope and faith that there is something far more than this.

Definitions

There are many definitions of spirituality, religion, and faith. For this book, these terms are defined as follows:

● Spirituality: The incorporation of a transcendent dimension in life.
● Religion: An organized effort, usually involving ritual and devotion, to manifest spirituality.
● Faith: The acceptance without objective proof, of some thing (eg, God).

Many nurses feel uncomfortable or ill-prepared in providing spiritual care and thus avoid addressing spiritual issues, even when the need is great (Burton, 1998). Reasons for avoiding providing spiritual care include the following:

● Some nurses lack the spiritual preparation to provide spiritual care: Personal doubts and uncertainties may result in their feeling inadequate to help patients in these matters.
● Many nurses lack basic educational preparation related to spiritual care, especially in how to provide the care.

These two factors and other barriers stand in the way of nurses and others providing beneficial spiritual care. This chapter examines what methods exist—despite the difficulties presented by personal uncertainties and lack of formal preparation—to allow practitioners to offer spiritual care to patients, families, and others. The issue of personal spiritual preparation is a good starting point.

Providing Spiritual Care: Spiritual Preparation

It is neither necessary, nor perhaps desirable, to be a person of absolute convictions, in short, to have all the answers to spiritual questions related to life and death. Spiritual care is not a matter of providing the "right" answers or explanations, nor is it a matter for argument. The essence of spiritual care is being present in the face of suffering, helplessness, fear, and despair. Being present (ie, right there, consistently, day after day, with a person who is dying) is *primary spiritual care*. Being present, or "watching" meets a fundamental spiritual need. The simple words below from the Bible recount the turmoil of Jesus Christ before his own death.

> My soul is very sorrowful, even to death; remain here, and watch with me.
> (Matthew 26:38)

This presence, or watching, requires the will to face one's own and others' suffering,

helplessness, fear, and despair. It does not require conquering, understanding, coming to terms with, or even accepting, these difficult psychological states of being. At least initially, simply being present and watching with another requires only the will to be there consistently, to come back again and again. Zerwekh (1991, p. 879) writes, "If the nurse can remain present beside a dying person, that compassionate presence converts the experience into a triumph of love and human community." Of course, the experience does not always feel like a triumph. Often it feels like unbearably hard work for the patient, family, nurse, and others involved. The outcome of this triumph is that the patient and others are supported by the presence of another to the extent that they are able to confront the doubts, fears, and questions that may accompany suffering and dying.

The first part of spiritual preparation, then, is the vital first step of doing the job, achieving the perseverance necessary to remain present and to watch with the dying person. The second part of spiritual preparation focuses on exploring one's own spiritual resources, in searching for and discovering a spiritual foundation for self and work, that is, a source of meaning beyond self and work. It is not that one finds all the answers—and certainly never "perfection." Simply put, participation in spiritually based activities, especially in religious activities where "universal values" are served by tradition (Frankl, 1969), increases the likelihood that one will better understand God and self and increase the capacity to provide spiritual care.

Many people who draw on faith for support are not necessarily religious. Almost everyone knows people of faith who operate effectively in the world and who do not participate in religious activities. Nevertheless, *this* work, caring for the dying and helping people and their loved ones face death, means operating in the midst of enormous suffering, continually confronted not only with others' but also with personal mortality. Both practitioners and patients can benefit if practitioners are possessed of a strong spiritual foundation.

The third aspect of providing spiritual care is to increase knowledge of spiritual needs, faiths, and other aspects of spirituality and spiritual care.

Providing Spiritual Care: Spiritual Needs, Problems, and Practices

Spiritual needs (Baylor University School of Nursing [BUSN], 1991; Kemp, 1994) include the need for the following:

● *Meaning* includes the reason for an event or events, the purpose of life, and the belief in a primary force in life (BUSN, 1991). For some people, meaning may be found in a review of external achievements. More frequently, the search is a moral or spiritual search. Meaning may also include the meaning of dying, human existence, suffering, and the remaining days of life (Speck, 1998).
● *Hope* is for the "expectation of a good that is yet to be" (Nuland, 1994). Hope may be to not die or to live and die in a way perceived to be good. The last irreducible hope of life for many is not to die alone. Hope in purely spiritual terms includes hope for afterlife, resurrection, or rebirth (Kemp, 1994).
● *Relatedness* where spiritual matters are concerned is to God or to a system of spiritual faith or belief. Relatedness may also include relatedness to a faith community.
● *Forgiveness* is often seen as a concept of western religions (Christianity, Judaism, Islam), but the Buddhist and Hindu concepts of karma and transmigration of souls also address forgiveness or at least another chance to rectify mistakes. Acceptance is indirectly related to forgiveness and for some people, meets the need to deal with mistakes or misfortune in life.
● *Transcendence* is that which takes us beyond self and suffering or attachment to self and suffering. Transcendence may occur as a result of

other spiritual needs being met or as grace or manifestation of the divine.

These needs, examined separately below, often overlap with one another and with many other needs and issues. Almost always, suffering is a part of these needs not being met. Expressions of unmet spiritual needs include direct expressions and less direct expressions, such as anxiety, sadness or depression, fear, irritation, loneliness, guilt, and anger. Any or all these could be related to the above spiritual needs. Fulfilling spiritual needs aids in alleviating these expressions of distress.

Meaning

One of the common tasks, or stages, in theoretical constructs of the human experience is that of life review, or some similar activity. Inherent in this activity is the search for meaning in the individual's life as it has been lived. Meaning includes the reason for an event or events, the purpose of life, and the belief in a primary force in life (BUSN, 1991). For some people, meaning may be found in a review of external achievements. More frequently, the search is a moral or spiritual search, often dwelling on mistakes and inadequacies. However, there is more to this question of meaning than a simple search through the past. The search for meaning also includes the meaning of dying, human existence, suffering, and the remaining days of life (Speck, 1998). The absence of meaning in one's life—meaninglessness—is expressed in many ways, often through hopelessness and despair.

Meaning: Assessment and Interventions
Questions of meaning, faith, hope, and similar issues are usually best addressed directly. The search for meaning in life as it has been lived is facilitated by asking the patient questions such as, "If you had your life to live over again, what would you like to be different and what the same?" This can be an enormously productive

question in terms of the issue at hand, of communications in general, and of the nurse–patient relationship.

The meaning of dying and suffering is difficult to understand in terms of psychological explanation. It can be addressed by questions such as, "What does it mean to you that this (dying and suffering) is happening?" This is a very serious question and often gets serious answers.

Often paramount to the question of suffering is the question, "Why me; why am *I* suffering?" This is a tough question, especially for the nurse who feels obliged to provide an answer. For some patients—those who belong to formal religious groups or who have grown up with a formal religious background—helping them to find and reread passages from the sacred books of their own faiths may provide the best kind of "answer." Every faith is rich in examples of compassionate reaction to human suffering.

Contemplating the questions mentioned above might lead to other questions: about forgiveness, acceptance, punishment, and even transcendence. They may lead also to patients questioning the meaning of the remaining days of their lives and the prospect of what might be done to make the most of that time. Meaning for the future is especially a problem for those patients in whom meaning in the past was habitually extracted from external achievement. However, there is almost always room for internal achievement, or personal growth, and most people remain very alive to the universal human hunger for personal and interpersonal growth. In the context of dying, the opportunities for that growth are numerous, and the chances for their success are high.

Psychosocial means of helping patients grow or work through problems and relationships are presented in Chapters 2 and 3. In this section, the focus is on meeting the need for meaning in whatever amount of life remains to the patient. Many people are amazed at the idea that there is hope for meaning in the weeks or months of remaining life. Simply presenting the possibility of meaning is a valuable intervention.

Of course, meaning must be found by the person who seeks it and cannot be given arbitrarily by another (Frankl, 1969). However, help in the search may be given in several ways. Some patients need help in sorting through what is realistic and what is unrealistic, given their circumstances. Few can write a book, for example, but many can write a poem. Few can achieve perfect interpersonal relations with all others, but many can improve a relationship. Few can achieve spiritual perfection, but many can pray.

Nurses and other caregivers also help give meaning to life by the act of consistently dispensing their loving care, whether or not meaning and hope can be achieved by the patient. "What our patients need is unconditional faith in unconditional meaning" (Frankl, 1969, p. 156).

Hope

Hope is an important factor in dealing with stress, in maintaining quality of life, and in some cases, in continuing life (Conrad, 1985). Dimensions of hope (Nowotny, 1989) or attributes of a hopeful person include the following:

● Confidence in the outcome
● Ability to relate to others
● Possibility of a future
● Spiritual beliefs
● Active involvement
● Strength that comes from within

These are not unlike the themes of hope developed by Post-White and her colleagues (1996). These "universal components of hope" include finding meaning through faith or spirituality, having affirming relationships, relying on inner resources, living everyday life, and anticipating survival.

A person who is dying may hope for many things: to live another day, for relief from suffering, for a good death, for a healed relationship, to see a loved one, or even not to die. No matter how sick a person is, more often than not, on some level, there is always the hope not to die. In terms of psychology, this is perfectly reasonable, but in terms of disease progression, unlikely.

Hope: Assessment and Interventions

The dimensions of hope identified above give guidance in helping patients and families find hope within terminal illness. Each dimension shows an implicit assessment: What do you hope for in this illness (or this situation)? What do you hope for from others? What do you hope for at this point in your life? Looking at the realities of this situation, what do you hope for in yourself? What hope do you find in your faith (or religion or spiritual life)? Do you feel that you are involved in your care? What are your strengths? These are by no means inclusive questions; they simply provide a place to begin.

Building or strengthening dimensions that are lacking and reinforcing those that are stronger facilitate the growth of hope. Nowotny (1992) offers suggestions for each dimension:

● *Confidence in the outcome:* This is a challenge. Realistically, the outcome is that the person will die. Recall, however, that how one goes about dying—psychologically, socially, and spiritually—is not predetermined. In terminal illness, many patients ask three important questions, though not necessarily out loud. First, there is the question of cure, then the question of symptoms and problems, and finally, the question of whether the patient can get through the process (ie, "Can I do this? Can I do this well?") (Dan Foster, personal communication, 1991). Thus, the nurse helps build hope by focusing on this question of how the patient goes through the process. The nurse's self-confidence, confidence in the patient, and ability to identify and support patient and fam-

ily strengths all influence the patient's confidence in the outcome. Christians, Jews, Muslims, Buddhists, Hindus, and others all have a definitive belief in outcome, that is, what happens after death. These beliefs can bring enormous confidence in, or acceptance of, the outcome (after death).

● *Ability to relate to others:* The absence of relationships creates hopelessness, and activities that support relationships help build hope. Relationships need not be with people in physical proximity. People already dead can even be central in some people's lives. Relationships that encourage spiritual growth can also be sought in both formal and informal religious settings and organizations. However, not a few people feel failed and abandoned by their faith community.

● *Possibility of a future:* Religions offer possibilities about the future (after death). Yet, what believer has not at some point thought, "What if there is only nothing, or there is only hell?" The more devout the doubter, the more difficult it is for them to express their doubts and the greater the conflict. The response to such doubts can be twofold: First, stay with and support the patient, whether he or she is doubting or not. Second, help the person who doubts to refer back to religion, by providing reading materials, facilitating visits by clergy, and so forth. Apart from questions about the "greater" future, there are also questions about the day-to-day future. With cancer or acquired immunodeficiency syndrome, the cliché, "one day at a time" is no longer a cliché, but a mighty truth.

● *Spiritual beliefs:* Spiritual well-being clearly has a positive effect on people with life-threatening illness (Ballard, Green, McCaa, & Logsdon, 1997; Burton, 1998). Over the course of a life, many people fall away from the faith of their early years; some never had a faith. There is the possibility that many people who long for faith are not aware of what they long for. The time of dying is a good time to have another look at faith. If a visit to a place of worship is not physically possible, a visit from clergy could be very helpful. The songs and rituals of a patient's faith may be even more comforting than counseling. Patients who had few spiritual resources in their early years may wish to be seen by a chaplain. Religious rituals that can take place at a bedside (for example, for Christians, communion) should be offered. Audio tapes of devotional music (available at many specialized religious bookstores) may work wonders.

● *Active involvement:* This principle is covered primarily in Chapters 2 and 3 and, at least superficially, usually has less to do with spiritual aspects of hope than it does with psychosocial aspects. The underlying principle of active involvement is autonomy. In the context of spiritual care, this means that the patient is free to choose and be in charge of her or his own spiritual direction, and the practitioner facilitates this by providing an atmosphere of acceptance.

● *Strength that comes from within:* It is essential to use the patient's own strengths in exploring the difficult psychological and spiritual landscape of terminal illness. Anything other than recognition and validation of the patient's own feelings, strengths, and weaknesses means that full exploration—hence full understanding—is unlikely. Practitioners should also be willing to leave the patient alone with the unanswered questions that the patient must face. This may be difficult but necessary: Each person needs to discover and personally experience his or her own doubts and fears. "In religious matters it is a well-known fact that we cannot understand a thing until we have experienced it inwardly" (Jung, 1953, p. 338).

Relatedness to God

Some secularists, and even some authors writing from a spiritual perspective, view relationships with other people as a fulfillment of spiritual needs (Karns, 1991). Although relationships with others are essential and even in some cases, exalting, in the case of caring for those who are dying, the focus is on relatedness with God or the eternal, universal, all-knowing, being itself, and ultimate.

While the concept of God differs everywhere, God is infinitely available to all people and to people of all faiths. The God of Judaism, Christianity, and Islam is clearly explicated. Hindus also believe in "One God, who can be understood and worshipped in many different forms" (Green, 1989, p. 50). Buddhists can believe in a divine "force" or "being," as expressed by the Buddha. Jung has written that the presence or acknowledgment of God among virtually all peoples of all religions is evidence of God as a universal archetype, that is, an "imprint" of God on the psyche (Jung, 1953, p. 339). In America, approximately 95% of people claim to believe in God, and more than 75% say they pray regularly to God (Burton, 1998). For many people, religion, including ritual, prayer, and worship, is the primary means of connecting with God.

While God is conceived of in many ways, the essential characteristic universally present for all is that God is infinitely more than human. This is central to the comfort to be derived from relatedness to God: There *is* more than this suffering, more than these fears, more than one's inadequacies.

Relatedness to God: Assessment and Interventions

Assessment begins with looking at whether the person's life is characterized by hope, meaning, open relationships, and acceptance of self or by hopelessness, meaninglessness, isolation, and guilt. Specific assessment questions might inquire about the person's belief about God or religion, the person's relationship with God, the person's spiritual and religious life when he or she was young and later in life, and missing aspects of spiritual or religious life. A particularly good question is, "What do you think God might have to say to you now?"

While God, in the many manifestations of religious belief, ancient and present, is always conceived of as greater than humans, there has also always been a corresponding conception that humans can act as instruments, or representatives, of God. Working with love, care, respect, and diligence is the right way to practice with people who are dying, no matter what one's religious or nonreligious persuasion. Working in this manner, with a "spiritual foundation," allows the concept of God that each person carries within to touch another, something Karns called "the highest form of spiritual care" (1991, p. 12).

It goes without saying that this idea of working with a spiritual foundation is not the same thing as being a particular religion's or denomination's marketing department. In providing spiritual care, the message is the care itself and not any effort to convince a patient to believe as someone else does.

Forgiveness or Acceptance

A moral or spiritual review of life on the part of someone who is dying generally uncovers the kind of defenses that help so many of us to get through painful situations in life. Suddenly, all the events, circumstances, and actions of a lifetime, including mistakes of commission and omission, are revealed. Guilt may become a central factor. Some see this process primarily as one related to sin, repentance, forgiveness, and punishment, although for everyone mistakes or sins—as defined by all major spiritual and moral belief systems—are a part of life.

It is important to remember and to remind the patient that some guilt experienced by people is related to events or circumstances completely beyond the control of the sufferer, for example, in the case of a parent whose child has died, adults who have psychologically survived the ordeals of childhood incest, or people who grew up with alcoholic parents. In all of these examples, the adults are likely to experience terrible guilt due to a distorted sense of their own sins or responsibilities in connection with the painful circumstances of their lives.

Forgiveness or Acceptance: Assessment and Interventions

The concepts of forgiveness and acceptance are central to almost all faiths or religions, though their interpretations may differ. For example, when working with Hindus and Buddhists in terminal situations, it may be more beneficial to think in terms of acceptance rather than forgiveness.

Whatever the practitioner's beliefs or the beliefs of the patients are, it is important to remember that the health care provider cannot confer forgiveness and that teaching acceptance is a major challenge. What they *can* do is manifest forgiveness and acceptance through providing consistently loving care and thereby hold out to the patient the possibility that forgiveness and acceptance can be found. No matter what the practitioner's religious or nonreligious persuasion, it is his or her duty to practice this form of mercy. Moreover, by manifesting these qualities, practitioners are allowing the concept of God that everyone carries within him or her to work through him or her and to touch others.

The idea of this form of intervention, which appears to be passive rather than active, is a difficult one for many nurses, who are accustomed to operating as problem solvers. A practitioner impatient to get at the "problem" often impedes the expression of spiritual needs. The patient's need of forgiveness and acceptance is a profound issue, very different in nature from other kinds of practical problems faced by nurses in their everyday work, and it cannot be resolved through the usual psychological or pharmacologic channels. It is best approached through our quality of care and through the example of our own mercy.

Transcendence

Transcendence is a quality of faith or spirituality that allows one to move beyond, to "transcend," what is given or presented in experience, in this case, the suffering and despair so often inherent in dying. Transcendence is the quality that can bring victory over, and carry the patient beyond, suffering and death. Transcendence redefines limited views of life (including suffering and death) and relationships (including with self, others, and with God). Transcendence is the means by which one finds meaning "retroactively . . . even in a wasted life" (Frankl, 1969, pp. 76–77).

Transcendence: Interventions

Like the need for forgiveness, the need for transcendence is a profound issue that cannot be approached as a problem in need of "solving," and interventions here also are limited to what can be accomplished through a quality of care that is persevering and patient. It is important to keep in mind, however, that transcendence can happen when a person loves as much as is possible, especially when he or she does not feel like loving and when that loving does not seem to "work." Then sometimes personal limitations may be overcome and a new or greater reality revealed.

Reflections on Providing Spiritual Care

Providing effective care in the spiritual process of dying includes the following responsibilities, eloquently expressed by Zerwekh (1991):

● Listening
● Diagnosing distress of the human spirit
● Affirming the ultimate importance of spiritual concerns at the end of life

These responsibilities may be met through the practice of watching with a person in the final time of life. The "simple and costly demand" of watching is to remain in the presence of pain, suffering, and failure (Saunders, 1978, p. 8). Watching is an active, spiritual practice that includes awareness of the pain in life and death, the hope for healing (forgiveness), awareness of the concept of God, hope

for the possibility of transcendence, and acceptance of whatever happens.

The personal qualities that are helpful in providing spiritual care include the following:

● Realism
● Hopefulness
● Truthfulness
● Conviction or faith
● Resourcefulness
● Advocacy
● Sensitivity
● Openness and expectation

Through the act of being present, or watching, even in the midst of suffering and failure of the spirit, the nurse becomes a potent symbol of the God who is within everyone and with the client.

When faith trembles (and of course it does), one stays on, even when there is no meaning, no hope, and no healing (Nouwen, 1974).

REFERENCES

Ballard, A., Green, T., McCaa, A., & Logsdon, M. C. (1997). A comparison of the level of hope in patients with newly diagnosed and recurrent cancer. *Oncology Nursing Forum, 24*(5), 899–904.

Baylor University School of Nursing. (1991). *Report of self-study.* Dallas, TX: Author.

Burton, L. A. (1998). The spiritual dimension of palliative care. *Seminars in Oncology Nursing, 14*(2), 121–128.

Carse, J. P. (1980). *Death and existence.* New York: John Wiley & Sons.

Conrad, N. L. (1985). Spiritual support for the dying. *Nursing Clinics of North America, 20*(2), 415–425.

Frankl, V. (1969). *The will to meaning.* New York: New American Library.

Green, J. (1989). Death with dignity: Hinduism. *Nursing Times, 85*(6), 50–51.

Jung, C. G. (1953). Psychology and alchemy. In J. Jacobi, R. F. C. Hull (Eds.), *C.G. Jung: Psychological reflections* (pp. 338–339). Princeton, NJ: Princeton University Press.

Karns, P. S. (1991). Building a foundation for spiritual care. *Journal of Christian Nursing, 8*(3), 10–13.

Kemp, C. E. (1994). Spiritual care in terminal illness. *American Journal of Hospice and Palliative Care, 11*(6), 31–36.

Nouwen, J. H. M. (1974). *Out of solitude.* Notre Dame: Ave Maria Press.

Nowotny, M. L. (1989). Assessment of hope in patients with cancer: Development of an instrument. *Oncology Nursing Forum, 16*(1), 57–61.

Nowotny, M. L. (1992). Strategies to facilitate hope relating to dying using the Nowotny hope scale subscales. Unpublished manuscript.

Nuland, S. (1994). *How we die.* New York: Alfred A. Knopf.

Post-White, J., Ceronsky, C., Kreitzer, M. J., Nickelson, K., Drew, D., Mackey, K. W.,

Koopmeiners, L., & Gutknecht (1996). Hope, spirituality, sense of coherence, and quality of life in patients with cancer. *Oncology Nursing Forum, 23*(10), 1571–1579.

Saunders, C. M. (1978). Appropriate treatment, appropriate death. In C. M. Saunders (Ed.), *The management of terminal disease.* London: Edward Arnold.

Speck, P. W. (1998) Spiritual issues in palliative care. In D. Doyle, G. W. C. Hanks, & N. MacDonald (Eds.), *Oxford textbook of palliative medicine* (2nd ed.) (pp. 805–818). New York: Oxford University Press.

Zerwekh, J. (1991). Supportive care of the dying patient. In S. B. Baird, R. McCorkle, & M. Grant (Eds.), *Cancer nursing* (pp. 875–884). Philadelphia: W.B. Saunders.

CHAPTER 5

Spiritual Care: Faiths

KEY POINTS

● Although there are universal aspects of spiritual needs and problems, there are differences among how those needs and problems are expressed and addressed among different religions.

● Understanding some of the basic tenets of others' religions enriches the practitioner and enhances the care provided to people of different faiths.

● It is difficult, if not impossible, to explain adequately or generalize any person's religion, but any good-faith effort to understand and explain is worthy.

This chapter focuses on particulars of major religions. The following sections summarize the basic beliefs or tenets and outline the beliefs concerning dying and death in five faiths: Judaism, Christianity, Islam, Hinduism, and Buddhism. The material is presented with a caveat: It is impossible to understand fully and communicate another person's faith. There are many denominational or sectarian variations in every major religion, many of them fiercely disputed, and there are infinite individual variations. Nevertheless, the following information provides a foundation for an initial understanding of the religious backgrounds of many different individuals.

Judaism

Jews are descended from the Patriarch Abraham and were known initially as Hebrews, or Israelites. About 1300 BC, Moses, "the Lawgiver," was, according to Jewish belief, told by God to lead the Israelites out of Egypt, (Exodus 3:10).

Judaism was born in oppression, and persecution has been a constant theme throughout its history (Carse, 1980). The Holocaust and other persecutions have at least the potential to play a conscious or unconscious role in the spiritual and psychological responses to dying, suffering, and death among those of the Jewish faith, especially the elderly.

Tenets of the Faith

Central to Judaism are belief in one God, the Ten Commandments, and the glorification of God through the practice of belief, as evidenced through individual comportment, personal work, family life, moral behavior, and so forth (Ponn, 1991). Ritual, sacred literature, the Law, sacred institutions, and "the people, Israel" are among the key "strands" of Judaism

(Steinberg, 1975, p. 3–4). The sacred literature of Judaism includes:

● The *Torah*, which is found in every synagogue: At least one copy is written in the original Hebrew, on parchment, and includes the first books of the Old Testament: Genesis, Exodus, Leviticus, Numbers, and Deuteronomy. The word *Torah* may also be taken to mean "all teachings of Judaism."
● The *Mishnah*, which is an interpretation of the Law by generations of Jewish scholars. The *Mishnah* provides direction for daily life.
● The *Talmud*, which gives further insight into the Law, and is significantly longer than the *Mishnah*.

Branches of Judaism

As with other religions, there are differences among and within the various branches of Judaism. The three main branches in the United States are Reform, Conservative, and Orthodox. Reform Judaism is a modern interpretation of the religion and is an effort to adapt to western society (Bradley, 1963). Ritual and Talmudic practices play a lesser role, while fundamental beliefs remain. Conservative Judaism hews closer to ritual and reinterprets the law for the times and society but does not seek assimilation. Orthodox Judaism holds strictly to Talmudic teachings and rules. Either through intent or as a result of religious behavior, Orthodox Jews tend to mix less than their brethren with the non-Jewish population.

The Sabbath begins before nightfall on Friday and ends when the first three stars appear on Saturday evening. For some conservative Jews and for all Orthodox Jews, writing, traveling, switching on nonessential electric appliances (lights are nonessential; suction machines are essential), elective surgical procedures, and other activities are forbidden during this time each week. Dietary law for this segment of the Jewish population explicates what foods or combinations of foods may and may not be eaten. Kosher foods are those that are

slaughtered, manufactured, or prepared under specific circumstances and conditions.

A rabbi is the ideal provider of spiritual care; however, it is appropriate for a person of another faith to read from the *Torah* section of the Old Testament or from Psalms. Tradition directs the family to support and encourage the patient, including staying at the bedside (Gordon, 1975). There is disagreement about whether or not full knowledge should be shared with the patient.

Deathbed confession and repentance and blessing and ethical instructions to the family or others present are traditional, though last rites are not. The following is the minimum confession:

> *I acknowledge (give thanks) before You, Hashem, my God and the God of my forefathers, that my recovery and death are in Your hand. May it be Your will that You heal me with total recovery, but, if I die, may my death be an atonement for all the errors, iniquities, and willful sins that I have erred, sinned, and transgressed before You. May You grant my share in the Garden of Eden, and privilege me for the World to Come that is concealed for the righteous.*
> *(Scherman, 1984, p. 795).*

Meaning has long been a major philosophical question among Jews, and Victor Frankl, who brought the question of meaning into focus for many non-Jews, developed his philosophy in a Nazi concentration camp. Hope for Jews includes the hope for "the people, Israel," for justice, for the Messiah to come, for reunification or reconciliation with God, and for the resurrection to come (Heller, 1975; Ponn, 1991). Relatedness is clearly with God, who "chose" the Jews as his people. Forgiveness is asked in the deathbed confessional, and transcendence is found in the outcome of the lifelong struggle between good and evil.

Suicide is a mortal sin, and euthanasia, like suicide, is unacceptable under any circumstances. Extraordinary or life-prolonging measures are not expected nor usually desired when a person is imminently terminally ill (Minarik, 1996).

Immediate Aftercare, Funeral, and Burial Practices

The deceased person's eyes should be closed immediately after death, preferably by one of the person's children. The body should be straightened and covered. If at all possible, a family member stays with the body until burial. Some families request that the body not be moved on the Sabbath. Autopsy is opposed but permitted; but no part of the body should be removed. Organ transplants are acceptable only after consultation with a rabbi. Burial should be within 24 hours of death, except that burial should not be on the Sabbath. Autopsy and related activities should be concluded quickly.

Most synagogues or communities have a burial society (*chevra kaddisha*) with whom certain funeral homes cooperate. This volunteer group prepares the bodies of members of the congregation according to Jewish law. "Death is death" in Jewish belief, so some of the trappings of western funerals, such as cosmetics on the body, viewing the body, satin-lined coffins, etc. are unacceptable (Gordon, 1975). The Kaddish, a formal ritual of prayer that praises God and extends through a number of days after the death, is said at the cemetery and elsewhere.

> May He give reign to His Kingship in your lifetimes and in your days, and in the lifetimes of the entire family of Israel, swiftly and soon. Now respond Amen.
> (From the Mourner's Kaddish)

There is a prescribed period of mourning, during which grief is expressed openly and in keeping with ritual. The first period of mourning is called shivah and is divided into 3 days of deep grief, followed by 7 days of mourning. During this time, personal adornment and vanities, including shaving, are forbidden, as are discussions about matters other than the issue

at hand. There are then 30 days of readjustment, followed by 11 months of remembrance and gradual healing. After a year, there is a ceremony during which the name of the deceased is inscribed in a room in the synagogue.

Christianity

Christianity began approximately 2000 years ago with the birth, teachings and miracles, crucifixion, and finally the resurrection of Jesus Christ (revealed in Christian scripture as the Son of God). This is all recounted in the New Testament, which, together with the Old Testament, constitutes the Bible. Each of the events in Christ's life is enormously significant to Christians and may be summarized in the following beliefs:

● The birth of Christ occurred according to Old Testament prophecy:

> Therefore the Lord himself will give you a sign. Behold, a young woman (a virgin) shall conceive and bear a son, and shall call his name Eman'u-el
> (Isaiah 7:14)

● The meanings of Christ's teachings, as recounted in the Bible, are sometimes hidden in parables, but some also are direct and unmistakable:

> I am the resurrection and the life; he who believes in me, though he die, yet shall he live, and whoever lives and believes in me shall never die.
> (John 11:25-26)

● Christians believe in the occurrence of miracles, like those wrought by Christ in the Bible, regarded by some as central to the faith and by others primarily as illustrations of God's power.
● The crucifixion of Jesus Christ is described in the New Testament as a religious-political torture and execution and as the fulfillment of

DEBORA HUNTER

divine prophecy. The cross on which Christ was crucified is Christianity's powerful, primary symbol, representing suffering and death and the hope of life everlasting, through the sacrifice of the Son of God.

● The resurrection of Christ is the greatest of the Christian miracles and confirms Christian belief in life everlasting. After 3 days in his tomb, Christ rose from the dead, appeared and spoke to the disciples, was taken up into heaven, and sat down at the right hand of God (Mark 16:9–19).

The ultimate meaning of the death of Jesus Christ (God's sacrifice of His son) for Christianity is that salvation is available, through grace, for all those who believe in Christ. Christianity posits the universal presence of sin and offers a way, through belief in Christ's death and resurrection, of transcendence through God's forgiveness.

The Bible is considered by Christians to be the revelation of God. There are divisions within Christianity about whether the words of the Bible are meant to be understood in a literal fashion or interpreted. There are two major groupings (Protestants and Catholics) and numerous denominations within Christianity and further divisions within these; some are involved in serious dispute with one another about who truly represents "real Christians."

The two important sacraments (or religious rituals) for Protestants are baptism and holy communion. Holy communion should be made available to consenting Christians who are dying. Participating in this rite can have a healing effect on those who feel isolated or estranged. The Catholic sacraments most relevant in dying are the anointing of the sick and the providing of holy Eucharist, the Catholic communion. These two rituals, along with confession to a priest, should be made available to consenting Catholics. Prayer and reading from the Bible are appropriate forms of spiritual care for all Christians. Comforting passages include the following:

● Psalm 23: "The Lord is my shepherd . . . " This may be preceded for a patient who is deep in a spiritual crisis of anger or estrangement by one of the lament Psalms, such as Psalm 22, "My God, my God, why hast thou forsaken me?" The lament Psalms include 13, 38, 51, and others.
● John 11:25–26: "I am the resurrection and the life . . . "
● John 14:1–4: "Let not your hearts be troubled . . . "
● I Corinthians 15:54–56: "O death, where is thy victory?"
● Matthew 6:9–13: "Our Father who art in heaven . . . "

Christian faith promises its believers that through grace, meaning can be found for any life. Hope in Christianity exists explicitly for personal salvation and for God's forgiveness through faith. Relatedness is to a personal God and savior. Christian belief urges faithful perseverance, or "constant witness" (doing what people do not want to do when they do not want to do it) as a way of living the "unfelt faith" and as an alternative to despair. Forgiveness of sin through acceptance of Christ is central to Christianity. It is through their belief in forgiveness and grace that Christians, according to the tenets of the faith, can transcend self, sin, and suffering.

Islam

Islam is based on the word of God as revealed to the Prophet Muhammad in about 610 AD, and the adherents of this faith are known as Muslims. The meaning of the word, Islam, is surrender (specifically to Allah, ie, to God),

---

Box 5-1. Notes on Faiths That Are a Part of or Related to Christianity

● Adventist (Seventh Day): Adventists interpret the Bible literally. Living in or in close relation to Adventist communities is practiced by some. There is a strong focus on maintaining health (of the body as a temple of God). Faith healing may be combined with medical care. Many Adventists are vegetarian, and alcohol is not permitted except medicinally.

● Church of Christ, Scientist: Christian Science is based on both Christianity and the writings of Mary Baker Eddy. Christian Scientists believe that sin and illness are illusions that can be overcome by prayer and faith. Although medical care is sometimes used, in general, medicine, surgery, diagnostic tests, and other such resources are not accepted. Blood and blood products are not accepted. Christian Science Practitioners provide health care.

● Church of Jesus Christ of Latter Day Saints (Mormons): This religion is based on the Bible, the Book of Mormon, and other revelatory writings of its founder, Joseph Smith. Mormons incorporate religion as an integral part of daily life. Mormons use both medical care and faith healing. Elders provide a blessing of the sick ceremony, which includes prayer and anointing the patient with consecrated oil. Sacraments (called "ordinances") may also be given by Elders to people who are ill.

● Jehovah's Witnesses: All members of the Jehovah's Witnesses are considered ministers and are charged with witnessing to others in an attempt to convert them. Although medicine, surgery, and other aspects of modern health care are accepted, blood products are rejected under all circumstances. Faith healing is prohibited, but prayer and scripture are used as a vital means of comfort in terminal and other difficult situations.

and a Muslim, then, is one who has surrendered to God. Islam repudiated the religious practices of Arabs at the time Muhammad received this revelation. It also repudiates the Christian belief in a Son of God. The scripture of Islam is the Koran, or *Al Qur'an*, which is believed to be infallible and unequivocal. The word *Qur'an* means recital, which is derived from the belief that the *Qur'an* was recited to Muhammad by (primarily) the Angel Gabriel. The *Qur'an* is divided into chapters or *surahs* that are arranged according to divine decree. There is a widespread belief that the *Qur'an* can only be read and understood with accuracy in the original Arabic. Another holy book of Islam is the multivolume *Hadith*, "The Sayings and Doings of the Prophet Muhammad." Islamic law (*Shariah*) is based on the *Qur'an* and the Hadith.

Islam has several main divisions, including those between fundamentalists (who would order all of society according to Islamic law) and secularists (who would order society on a more secular basis); significant "denominations" of Sunni and Shi`a Muslims; and various schools, or sects, within the larger divisions.

The basic belief of all Muslims is in one God, Allah:

God! There is no god but Him, the Living, the Ever-existent one.
(Qur'an The Imrans 3:2)

This belief in one God, in Allah, is central to all Muslim belief (Rahman, 1966). Muslims also believe in angels, Satan, the *jinn* (spirits), the day of reckoning, heaven and hell, and the prophets and messengers (eg, Abraham, Moses, Jesus, and Muhammad—the final Prophet and Messenger of God).

Tenets of Islam
Also central to Islam are the five pillars of faith:

1. Faith is in the one God.
2. Prayer is offered five times each day.
3. Alms-giving or *zakat* is expected.
4. Fasting or *sawm* (on holy days, from dawn through sundown) occurs principally during Ramadan, the yearly Muslim religious celebration, which lasts for 1 month. The Muslim year uses the Julian calendar, which is 10 days shorter than the solar year; therefore, Ramadan moves by 10 days each year. In the course of a lifetime, people will have the experience of fasting in all four seasons.
5. A pilgrimage, known as the *hajj*, to the Islamic holy city of Mecca (the birthplace of Muhammad, in Saudi Arabia) should be made (when possible) in one's lifetime (Cavendish, 1980).

Halal describes what is lawful and *haram* what is unlawful. Friday is the most important day of worship for Muslims. Marital and family relationships, individual behavior, prayer, and many other aspects of daily life are definitively prescribed by Islam.

Cleanliness is a major issue for Muslims, who believe in washing their mouths, hands, and feet at least five times each day, before the five required daily prayer times. Showering is preferred over bathing, and modesty is extremely important. Health care and personal hygiene care provided by people of a different gender may be distressing to Muslims. Women and men are segregated during almost all religious and social events.

Dietary restrictions include pork and any meat not slaughtered according to custom (*halal*). Kosher foods may be substituted for *halal*. During Ramadan, Muslims fast from dawn to sundown each day of the month according to a schedule issued by a local mosque. Some Muslims interpret fasting to include all medicines and fluids, while others allow medicines and fluids during the day.

Family members and friends are expected to remain with the sick person 24 hours a day, and a close relative may even sit in bed with the patient. Most patients prefer to lie down facing Mecca. Muslim patients will reaffirm their faith ("There is no god but God and Muhammad is his messenger.") on their deathbeds. The time of dying is also a time to seek forgiveness from other people. Other interventions would include making the *Qur'an* or readings from it available to consenting patients. Note that hands should be washed before handling the *Qur'an* and that there should be no marks made in or on the book. Prayers are offered by family members or friends during the dying process and afterward. The 36th surah, *Ya Sin*, is strongly associated with dying and death.

Regular five-times daily prayer should continue as long as possible. Making a prayer schedule available and staff operating around that schedule (avoiding the patient's room during prayer times) as much as possible is a great respect to the patient, family, and faith. Family and friends should also be able to pray in the patient's room or elsewhere. Offering a quiet and private room for prayer is appreciated.

Suicide is a sin, and euthanasia is not acceptable in Islam. However, death hastened by providing adequate analgesia (double-effect treatment) is not considered euthanasia or assisted suicide by Muslims (Sheikh, 1998).

Spiritual needs of Muslims can be understood, or addressed, as follows—with, of course, differences among individuals. Individualistic meaning in life, at least in the western sense, is not a major issue in Islam. Hope is available in abundance for true believers in Allah and in the words of the *Qur'an*. Relatedness to God is both clear and prescriptive and, according to Bradley (1963), the Muslim faith has more power in this sense than any other religion. Forgiveness is available but exclusively for believers and only on the basis of how life was lived in the adult years (Rahman, 1987).

> *He accepts the repentance of His servants, and pardons their sins. He has knowledge of all your actions.*
> (Qur'an, Counsel 42:25)

> *"When will the Day of Judgment be?" they ask. On that day they shall be scourged in the Fire, and a voice will say to them: "Taste this, the punishment which you have sought to hasten!"*
> (Qur'an, The Winds 51:12-14)

Islam, like Christianity, also posits the resurrection of the body, final judgment, and assignment to heaven or hell. Transcendence is readily available for all Muslims who are undoubting true believers.

Aftercare, Funeral, and Burial Practices

Non-Muslims should not touch the body. Among some Muslims, the family is responsible for washing and preparing the body, and with others, a designated person from the community performs this function. While an autopsy may be required by secular law under some circumstances, most (but not all) Muslim religious jurists agree that autopsies are not permissible (Sheikh, 1998). If an autopsy is performed, it should be carried out expeditiously so that burial can take place as soon as possible. Muslim views on organ donation are similar to those on autopsy. In the Muslim world, burial may take place within a few hours after death. Legalities and other customs in the western world are such that funerals may be delayed but in all cases, they should take place within 24 hours after death. Bodies are buried, preferably in a Muslim cemetery. Funerals are concerned only with spiritual matters, hence they are not elaborate. Some Muslims arrange for the entire *Qur'an* to be recited on the 3rd and 40th day after the death.

Hinduism

Hinduism is an ancient religion intimately intertwined with the development of life and culture in its birthplace, India. The practice of Hinduism as an organized, historic system began about 5000 years ago. The sacred literature of Hinduism includes the earlier Vedas and the more recent (beginning in about

800–300 BC) Upanishads. There are numerous other examples of Hindu literature, notably the Bhagavad-Gita, an epic of war and devotion.

Tenets of Hinduism

Hinduism has no creed or founder. It is a devotional theism (or belief in superhuman powers), taking a number of forms, with a philosophic background and a social system based on the concept of function, or karma (cause and effect in all action or inaction), and on caste observances. Hinduism depends on what a person is and does, on social conduct, rather than on any one belief. Most Hindus also believe in transmigration of the soul, or reincarnation (*samsara*), and look forward to an ultimate salvation (*nirvana*) in the form of release from the cycle of rebirth and death.

The popular practice of Hinduism incorporates numerous gods (diversity of belief is regarded as natural and inevitable), with one god singled out (usually according to sect) for most of the devotion. Practices include prayer and worship of images of gods in temples or private chapels, the making of pilgrimages, a belief in asceticism and the efficacy of yoga, and honoring and seeking the teachings of highly respected guru, or holy men. Most Hindus also adhere to dietary law (usually a strict vegetarian diet).

The rigidity of the caste system is based on the idea that people are born to be what they are and that they cannot be anything else. This and other similarly confining Vedic beliefs regarding hope for a better life helped promote the development of a large number of various sects (the most important being the *Vaishnava*, *Saiva*, and *Shakta*). Some of these sects offer increased hope of salvation through devotion (Bradley, 1963).

> Give me your whole heart,
> Love and adore me,
> Worship me always,
> Bow to me only,
> And you shall find me:
> This is my promise

Who love you dearly.
(Bhagavad-Gita [a], p. 129)

The goal of Hinduism, salvation, is release of the *atman*, or soul, from the endless cycles of suffering inherent in life. Death is viewed not as the opposite of life, but as the opposite of birth (Minarik, 1996).

Modesty is important to most Hindus, and this extends to women refusing care, examination, or to make decisions unless the husband is present. There is also a reluctance to discuss genitourinary or bowel problems, with the result that problems may be discovered late. Bathing in running water is preferred and is seen as a means of gaining both physical and spiritual cleanliness (Neuberger, 1998).

Some Hindus who have the financial resources will go back to India, especially to the sacred city, Varanasi, to die. Prayer, recitations, and hymns from Hindu scripture are appropriate in the process of dying. The presence of a Hindu priest (*pandit*) is comforting. Health care staff should expect the priest to interact with them, with the patient, or with the family in a different way than would clergy from western religions. Rituals surrounding dying and death include prayer and chanting, use of string and lustral water, and touching the patient with various objects (Green, 1989).

Hinduism can be disconcerting for westerners because it is so outside the experience of most non-Hindus. Hindus do not believe in proselytizing, and there has been little attempt to spread Hinduism among other peoples. The spiritual needs around which this chapter is partially structured might be addressed by a Hindu as follows:

● The meaning of life is devotion to God.
● Acceptance of fate is central to Hinduism. One also hopes for a better life and ultimately for release from rebirth.
● Everything is related. Relatedness to God (as manifested in devotion to one of the pantheon of gods) is very personal.

● There is no forgiveness; there is acceptance and results (of one's behavior).

● Transcendence (enlightenment) is explicit in Hinduism and may be explained in this way:

> When, however, one is enlightened with the knowledge by which nescience is destroyed, then his knowledge reveals everything, as the sun lights up everything in the daytime. (Bhagavad-Gita [b], Text 20:16)

Immediate Aftercare, Funeral, and Burial Practices

The family is responsible for washing and preparing the body, and most families prefer that others do not touch the body. If family is unavailable, the eyes should be closed, limbs straightened, and the body wrapped in a plain sheet without emblems of other religions. Autopsies are permitted, as is organ donation.

Funeral ceremonies should occur within 24 hours of death. Cremation is the means of disposing of the body, and embalming is undesirable. If possible, the oldest son should break the skull of the deceased so that the soul is easily released.

Buddhism

Buddhism began in the sixth century BC, both as a reform of Hinduism and as a response to the human condition, to the suffering epitomized by illness, aging, and death. The founder of Buddhism was Gautama Siddharta, the Buddha (which means "the awakened, the enlightened").

Tenets of Buddhism

Belief in the following Four Noble Truths is central to Buddhism:

● All sentient beings suffer. Birth, illness, death, and other separations are inescapably part of life.

● The cause of suffering is desire. Desire is manifested by attachment to life, to security, and most specifically the desire to be (Carse, 1980).

● The way to end suffering is to cease to desire.

● The way to cease to desire is to follow the eightfold path: (1) right belief, (2) right intent, (3) right speech, (4) right conduct, (5) right endeavor or livelihood, (6) right effort, (7) right mindfulness, and (8) right meditation.

Following the path leads to cessation of desire and to nirvana, or emancipation from rebirth.

Buddhism teaches tolerance of others and acceptance of life (nonattachment). The principle of karma (or *kamma*) is basic to the practice of Buddhism. Karma is popularly interpreted as a moral precept: Do right and you will be reborn into a higher state; do wrong and rebirth will be to a lower state. Karma is neither reward nor punishment but simply cause and effect. In practice, life's misfortunes are often attributed to sins in this or in a previous lifetime.

There are two primary divisions in Buddhism: Theravada Buddhism, which is practiced most often by people from Thailand, Cambodia, Laos, Burma, and Sri Lanka, and Mahayana Buddhism, or the "greater vehicle," which is practiced most often by people from Vietnam, China, Japan, and Tibet. Mahayana Buddhism includes the Zen Buddhism of Japan, the Lamaism of Tibet, and a uniquely Chinese form of Buddhism. In Theravada Buddhism, nirvana is achievable only through complete renunciation (nonattachment) and through living as a monk. The Buddha is "revered, not as a god but as one who has shown the way" (Bradley, 1963, p. 116). In practice, among the laity, the reverence is like that shown to a god. In some branches of Mahayana Buddhism, nirvana is possible for nonmonks, and among lay people, there appears to be a greater belief in (often multiple) gods, heaven, and hell. Monks are more apt to view these as states of mind.

Although Buddhist scripture has nothing to say about magic, belief in magic is common among some Buddhists, especially people from the Theravada countries of Thailand, Cambodia, and Laos, and also among Tibetans. Magico-religious practices are well integrated into Buddhism and include use of amulets, spells, and the presence and power of spirits. It is not uncommon for people from these countries to return home for the sole purpose of obtaining a talisman or blessing from a particular monk in much the same way as some Christians might journey to Lourdes or other place considered holy by some.

The Buddha did not discuss the presence or absence of God nor did he answer questions about death. On the question of immortality, the Buddha gave the fourfold denial:

> *A saint is after death,*
> *A saint is not after death,*
> *A saint is and is not after death,*
> *A saint neither is nor is not after death.*
> *(quoted by Carse, 1980)*

Buddhist scholars thus see four possibilities regarding life after death; the less scholarly, the majority of Buddhists, are likely to believe in rebirth with station, according to deeds.

A key issue in dying for many Buddhist patients and families is to maintain consciousness so that patients may "fill their minds with wholesome thoughts" (Ratanakul, 1991, p. 396). A quiet place for dying is preferred to a noisy or busy unit. A monk or lay religious leader may chant or lead chants to help promote a peaceful or insightful state of mind at death. Incense may be burned and amulets, including images of the Buddha, may be present.

Some of the spiritual needs around which this chapter is structured may seem to apply less directly to Buddhists than to others. Meaning, for example, may be seen as illusion, while emptiness, or the void, is seen as real (The Diamond Sutra, p. 29). Emptiness is not in any way the nihilistic emptiness sometimes ascribed to this belief by non-Buddhists (Suzuki, 1968), but rather the "universal causal relatedness" of existence (Carse, 1980, p. 139). Relatedness is not to God, but to the "all." Hope is leavened with acceptance and sometimes passivity, but hope for a better life now, a better next-life, and a better life for (one's) children is strong. Further, Buddhism is explicitly based on the hope of cessation of suffering. For lay people, a form of forgiveness, improved karma, is possible through merit. Practitioners of Zen Buddhism, on the another hand, live "beyond . . . the limitations of time, relativity, causality, morality, and so on" (Suzuki, 1956, p. 265).

Immediate Aftercare, Funeral, and Burial Practices

Organ transplant and autopsy are permitted. Non-Buddhists may touch the body, and there is no particular belief about how the body should be treated. In many cases, the family will wash the body and place the hands in a prayerful position.

Funeral and related practices vary according to the branch of Buddhism and to individual inclinations. Cremation is preferred by some and burial by others. Ideally, in many cases, the body should be kept at home for a day or more so that proper ceremonies may be conducted. The temple is another site for ceremonies. Most ceremonial activity is conducted at home, in a temple, or at grave or cremation site and less at funeral home chapels. Funeral ceremonies may be held a day or so after the death, and subsequent but related ceremonies held again in a week or a month or at other intervals. In some cases, ceremonies are delayed until the family saves enough money to conduct a proper ceremony.

> *Thus shall ye think of all this fleeting world:*
> *A star at dawn, a bubble in a stream;*
> *A flash of lightening in a summer cloud;*
> *A flickering lamp, a phantom, and a dream.*
> *(The Diamond Sutra [of the Buddha], p. 74)*

REFERENCES

Bhagavad-Gita (a). Translated by Swami Prabhavananda & C. Isherwood. (1951). New York: Mentor Religious Classics.

Bhagavad-Gita (b). Translated and interpreted by A. C. Bhaktivedanta Swami Prabhupada. (1972). New York: The Bhaktivedanta Book Trust.

The Bible. Revised Standard edition.

Bradley, D. G. (1963). *A guide to the world's religions*. Englewood Cliffs, NJ: Prentice-Hall.

Carse, J. P. (1980). *Death and existence*. New York: John Wiley & Sons.

Cavendish, R. (1980). *The great religions*. New York: Arco.

The Diamond sutra and sutra of Hui Neng. Translated by A.F. Price & W. Mou-Lam. (1969). Berkeley: Shambala.

Green, J. (1989). Death with dignity: Hinduism. *Nursing Times*, 85(6), 50–51.

Gordon, A. (1975). The Jewish view of death: Guidelines for mourning. In E. Kübler-Ross (Ed.), *Death: The final stage of growth* (pp. 38–43). Englewood Cliffs, NJ: Prentice-Hall.

Heller, Z. I. (1975). The Jewish view of death: Guidelines for dying. In E. Kübler-Ross (Ed.), *Death: The final stage of growth* (pp. 38–43). Englewood Cliffs, NJ: Prentice-Hall.

The Koran. Translated by N. J. Dawood (1990). New York: Penguin Books.

Minarik, P. A. (1996). Diversity among spiritual and religious beliefs. In J. G. Lipson, S. L. Dibble, & P. A. Minarik (Eds.) (pp. B1–21), *Culture and nursing care: A pocket guide*. San Francisco: UCSF Nursing Press.

Neuberger, J. (1998). Cultural issues in palliative care: Introduction. In D. Doyle, G. W. C. Hanks, & N. MacDonald (Eds.) (pp. 777–785), *Oxford textbook of palliative medicine* (2nd ed.). Oxford: Oxford University Press.

Ponn, A. L. (1991). Judaism. In C. J. Johnson & M. G. McGee (Eds.), *How different religions view death* (pp. 205–227). Philadelphia: The Charles Press.

Rahman, F. (1966). Islam. New York: Holt, Rinehart, and Winston.

Rahman, F. (1987). *Health and medicine in the Islamic tradition*. New York: Crossroad.

Ratanakul, P. (1991). Buddhism: Discussion of dying with dignity. In M. Abivan (Facilitator), *Dying with Dignity* (pp. 395–397). World Health Forum. 12(4), 375-399.

Scherman, N. (1984). *The complete art scroll Siddur*. New York: Mesorah Publications.

Sheikh, A. (1998). Death and dying—A Muslim perspective. *Journal of the Royal Society of Medicine*, 91, 138–140.

Steinberg, M. (1975). *Basic Judaism*. New York: Harcourt Brace Jovanovich Publishers.

Suzuki, D. T. (1956). *Zen Buddhism*. Garden City, NY: Doubleday Anchor Books.

Suzuki, D. T. (1968). *On Indian Mahayana Buddhism*. New York: Harper Torchbooks.

Waddell, L. A. (1972). *Tibetan Buddhism*. London: Dover Publications.

CHAPTER 6

Sociocultural Care

KEY POINTS

Cultural competency is a dynamic process that includes understanding key aspects of cultures with whom one has contact, being aware of one's own cultural and other influences on views and behavior, and application of this knowledge in caring for patients and families.

People are products of their culture and of their ethnicity, religion, experience, and other factors; nevertheless, in many cases, there are characteristics common to each culture.

Although there are enormous differences among individuals, understanding common cultural characteristics is helpful in providing effective care.

Key issues in exploring a different culture are experiences common to people of that culture: family structure, communication patterns and styles, influences on health care beliefs, and approaches to dying and death.

We have all heard the lines from Rudyard Kipling's "Ballad of East and West":

Oh, East is East and West is West, and never the twain shall meet,
Till Earth and Sky stand presently at God's great Judgement Seat.

Most take this to mean that differences between dissimilar worlds or cultures are too great for understanding or meeting—at least until judgment day. However, Kipling had more to say on the matter.

But there is neither East nor West, Border, nor Breed, nor Birth,

When two strong men stand face to face, tho' they come from the ends of the earth!
(Kipling, 1930, p. 137)

Great variations exist among all cultures in individual behavior, family structures, and community behavior. The purpose of this chapter is to give providers of care to the terminally ill a start toward a better understanding of the sociocultural differences among distinct groups in society—some things to look for and some pitfalls to avoid. The central goal in culturally competent care is not to understand completely all cultures with which one comes into contact, but rather:

● To be sensitive to and aware of the beliefs and practices of individuals, families, and populations
● To learn to fit the care with those beliefs and practices

The concept of culture includes the common values, beliefs, traditions, norms, symbols, language, and social organization of a particular group. Culture is affected by ethnicity, socialization, religion, and other forces, including common experiences. Ethnicity is a group's shared sense of identity and is based on a social and cultural heritage passed from generation to generation (Lipman, 1996; Pickett, 1993; Spector, 1996).

In seeking to understand cultural values, it is important to remember that this is a time of significant social upheaval. This may be represented, for example, by the fact that the central role of the family in many cultures is not only recognized, but also continually reaffirmed by our political and cultural institutions; however, in many instances, family systems, regardless of ethnicity or culture, are barely functional.

To understand another person and to learn to adapt oneself to his or her beliefs, it is necessary first to know oneself and to understand one's own culture. Everyone is a product of his or her own conscious and unconscious psychological makeup, and this psychological "baggage" is carried to every encounter, including patient-care encounters. People also carry conscious and unconscious cultural values that affect how they interpret what they see, hear, smell, and feel.

An overview of cultural views of health problems is helpful in assessing clients and families from diverse cultures. Many tools are available to accomplish this, but few are as functional and elegant as the work of Tripp-Reimer, Brink, and Saunders (1984). Answers to some or all of the following (slightly modified) questions, provide important insight into the different cultural (and other) perceptions of patients or family regarding health problems:

● What do you think caused your problem?
● Do you have an explanation for why it started when it did?
● What does your sickness do to you, and how does it work?
● How severe is your sickness? How long do you expect it to last?
● What problems has your sickness caused you?
● What do you fear about your sickness?
● What kind of treatment do you think you should receive?
● What are the most important results you hope to receive from this treatment?

Of course it is not possible to write accurate generalizations about any group of people, and when writing about groups, one always is open to charges of stereotyping. This chapter is not intended to serve as a blueprint for understanding or interpreting an individual's behavior. Rather, it is intended to serve as a starting point in beginning to understand and is written in a spirit of respectfully seeking to understand and to serve.

Native Americans

There are approximately 2 million Native Americans living in the United States, and the number is growing. There are more than 300 federally recognized tribes speaking a number of different languages (though most speak English), and there are significant similarities and differences among them (Cadwalader, 1997). The following are among the similarities:

● Belief in the presence of unseen powers or what is known as the Great Spirit.
● Understanding that all things are dependent on one another.
● Practice of worship as a means of reinforcing the bond between the individual, community, and the Great Spirit or God.
● Sacred traditions are imparted by people with powers received from the Great Spirit.

Native Americans are, in some ways, less assimilated into the prevailing culture of the United States than are other minority groups, and many exhibit at most a marginal interest in the mainstream culture. Reconnection with, and affirmation of, traditional culture is growing, even as more Native Americans enter mainstream American life and achieve higher levels of education.

The extended family is the primary social unit among Native Americans. The tribe to which a family belongs is very important in both individual and family life. Native Americans may view the health care system, and western culture as a whole, as separate from Native American life and thus undesirable—especially, for some, at the end of life.

Native American religions include mainstream Christianity; Mormonism; pan-Native American religions, such as Peyotism (the Native American Church); traditional religions; and in some cases, a combination of these. Many Native American religious beliefs and practices are animist, and spirits, ghosts, and other supernatural phenomena are as real to some Native Americans as are microorganisms to other people. They may sometimes view health problems as caused by spiritual forces as much or more than they are caused by other agents.

One of the unfortunate similarities among Native Americans is that, as a whole, Native Americans have poor morbidity and mortality rates and other negative health indicators (Spector, 1996). Alcoholism is a common social ill among Native Americans. This is sometimes attributed to differences in alcohol metabolism (Hanley, 1991) but may also be viewed in the context of unmet spiritual and cultural needs, such as hope, meaning, and relatedness. It may further be viewed as related to grief or chronic sorrow. Alcoholism relates to terminal illness both as a contributing factor to the leading causes of death (Spector, 1996) and as a complicating factor in providing care.

Stoicism is a deeply held value. Some Native Americans will deny pain or other problems, even in response to direct questions. History taking may be viewed as intrusive and irrelevant. Cultural values of tribal or group interdependence and their estrangement from the health care system are often such that there is significant delay in seeking care. Communication and related problems existing between the United States' health care system and Native Americans (Kramer, 1996; Spector, 1996) include the following:

● Difficulty in speech communication: Native Americans are accustomed to speaking in a quieter voice than others.
● Differences in behavioral habits: Native Americans are accustomed to expecting a degree of intuitive ability in their interlocutors; in their culture, people do not look directly into others' eyes; and they are unaccustomed to seeing others take notes on their responses during an interaction.
● Time orientation: Time is flexible among Native Americans, both in terms of appointments and the speed at which decisions are made.

Some Native Americans, especially the more traditional minded, view death as a companion and as an integral link in the chain of life. Attitudes or approaches vary among tribes; some are very accepting of death, and others view dying people and death with fear (Lewis, 1990). Some want their family members to die at home, others prefer a hospital setting, and others will stay away from places where a person has died (Kramer, 1996).

Suffering is a "major value in Indian culture" (Lewis, 1990, p. 28), and dying and grief may be met with stoicism and silence. Thus, the idea of sharing feelings is often rejected by patient and family.

Mourning may include participation in an annual memorial service for deceased relatives, such as the Sun Dance of the Plains Indians.

Asian Americans

The term Asian American illustrates how people of enormous variation often are lumped together as one homogeneous group. Asian Americans include Cambodians, Chinese from China and overseas Chinese (or those who immigrate to the United States from previous locations of emigration), Indians, Japanese, Koreans, Lao (lowland and tribal), Filipinos, Taiwanese, Thais, Vietnamese—including Amerasians, or those of mixed Vietnamese-American descent—and others.

Some Asian Americans are new refugees and some have lived in America for five or more generations. Some are Buddhist, some Shinto, some Catholic, some Protestant, some Hindu, and some Muslim. Despite the many differences, however, there are some similarities and generalizations that may apply across different Asian cultures. These last are especially relevant in the case of first-generation immigrants and refugees.

Asian Americans, in comparison to some other cultural groups in the United States, are reluctant to speak of personal or family matters in extrafamilial situations. Equanimity is a highly valued attribute. Withdrawal is far more common than complaint. In general, if you want to know if there is a problem, you must ask about that specific problem; by the same token, if you want to know the effects of a particular medication or treatment, you must ask specifically about what you want to know. Sharing deep feelings, especially those that may be negative, is uncommon.

"Yes" or "no" questions are often a source of misunderstanding and should be avoided. A "yes" answer may mean either agreement, acknowledgment that the question is heard, or simply that the person would rather say "yes" than "no."

The family unit tends to be more important operationally among Asian Americans than it is in western cultures, and whenever possible, the family should be included in decision making. Failure to do so may mean that no decision will be made. Women are sometimes unable to make a decision without consulting their husbands (though the stereotype of the submissive Asian woman is often a myth intended for public or male consumption). Mothers-in-law, despite appearances to the contrary, frequently wield tremendous power. Children are often pampered but are expected to obey instantly and without argument. The choices and freedom given to native-born American children are astonishing to most first-generation Asians. Using children to translate for adults should usually be avoided.

Asian Americans often are viewed as passive and accepting of fate. In fact, when nothing can be changed, they tend to accept the situation, but when there is hope for change, Asians and Asian Americans tend to be remarkably tenacious.

Chinese civilization and its religious-cultural concepts have influenced almost all Asian cultures (although some non-Chinese deny this) and their views of health and illness. The Chinese concept of balance (*yin-yang*, or the principle of the masculine and the feminine, the creative and the receptive, and so forth) is universal, although it may be expressed through saying a food, drink, illness, or treatment is hot or cold. Hot and cold here refer to yin or yang, respectively, and to intrinsic properties, not to temperature. Balance may also be related to the bodily "humors," such as blood, bile, and phlegm. Magico-religious amulets, strings, statues, and other items are common among some, and their power or validity should not be discounted. Spirit possession is a reality for many Cambodians, Lao, Thai, and Vietnamese. Herbal remedies, Chinese and others, are widely available in the United States and may be used along with, or in place of, western medicines. Further detail can be found at the Baylor University School of Nursing's Asian health web site: *http://www.baylor.edu/~Charles_Kemp/asian_health.html*.

Terminal illness for Asian Americans often brings overwhelming nostalgia and sadness, especially in the case of refugees. The stark reality is that they will die in a strange land that often seems uncaring and disrespectful. For many Southeast Asians, talking about the possibility of dying brings bad luck.

Some family members, especially if the family is not well educated, are likely to stay away from the terminally ill person for fear of contracting the disease or for other reasons. This can be very distressing for the staff involved with such a case. Generally, however, the family stays close by the patient at all times. Failure to do so may also be due to problems of transportation or to misunderstanding about what is permitted. Communication with western staff members may be limited by language or cultural reluctance to express personal feelings (Kemp, 1997).

African Americans

The history of our nation has been such that for a variety of reasons (by some, still bitterly debated), African Americans tend to be less educated, poorer, die sooner, and have a higher prevalence of AIDS, especially among women and children, than do most other cultural populations in the United States (Cherry & Giger, 1995). Many African Americans share feelings of resentment toward and opposition against racism, perceived as a collective and central issue of life. Interaction with others is sometimes inhibited by the effects of this perception, compounded and reinforced by the still-existing though attenuated prejudices in society; by others' lack of knowledge about African Americans, their history, and their culture; and by racial politics that seek constantly to exploit racial divisions.

Assimilation, especially in economic terms, into the dominant, mainstream culture has been a very slow process in the case of African Americans. Many native-born African Americans today are in a state of tremendous transition and redefinition. Other Africans came to the United States relatively recently, after generations spent in other diverse cultures, bringing with them traditions and cultural values that often are very different from American-born African Americans.

Since the Civil Rights Movement began almost 40 years ago, many African Americans have moved up the socioeconomic-political ladder, while others have made little or no progress. In terms of attitudes toward health care and technology, middle-class African Americans tend to be very similar to any other middle-class group.

Protestantism—often Baptist, Pentecostal, or one of a number of other smaller or fundamentalist denominations—is a common religion. Religious faith and church congregations and institutions have traditionally been extremely important in the African American community and often functioned as their only viable political force in or outside the community. While still a powerful force, Christianity now has a rival in the Muslim faith. The number of African American Muslims (both from the traditional Muslim faith and members of the Nation of Islam sect) is growing, and they provide a strong moral voice in the African American community. The pan-Africanism movement is endeavoring to build a universal African culture among African Americans through rediscovery and reaffirmation of traditional cultural practices and ideals.

Almost 50% of all African American families are headed by a woman, and though this number has been increasing for several decades (Cherry & Giger, 1995), recent data show a change in the trend. A common family scenario involves a dying parent, cared for by a daughter who is also a single parent—an extreme burden on both mother and children. Even when families are intact, socioeconomic factors sometimes prohibit working members of the family from being present during the dying process. Another common and very challenging situation is an older woman caring for her husband and several live-in grandchildren.

The family care that is given is often very good but at times is affected by finances. Personal care and good hygiene are often a high priority for African Americans caring for a sick family member. The extended kinship system is essential in providing quality care, especially if finances are an issue.

Healing practices among African American groups include faith healing (of the kind practiced by some more mainstream Americans, particularly those living in the "Bible belt" areas) and voodoo and related practices among some immigrants from the Caribbean and tropical Africa and African Americans living in the New Orleans area and in the deep (rural) south. As with any other group, folk remedies are also practiced by many African Americans. Although these vary according to several factors, they include well-known varieties, like chicken soup, oil of camphor, and so forth.

Public and communal grief are openly expressed at traditional Protestant African American funerals, which, in some areas, are termed "home-goings." As with other services, people in the congregation respond spontaneously and aloud to the sermon. The choir may sing softly in the background during the sermon and prayers. There is a gradual increase in emotion as the funeral progresses, and when the moment for the solo arrives, deep emotion is expressed by many. It is, in fact, difficult not to feel a deep communal grief at these funerals regardless of one's own ethnicity. They seem to go beyond the African American experience alone and to touch, in a real way, all of humanity's experience of suffering and grief. In the southern United States, there are usually printed programs for the funeral, and these include a photograph of the deceased. Funerals are most often held on Saturday or Sunday, so there may be a 4- or 5-day delay in burial.

Hispanic Americans

Like Asian Americans, there is a large variety of Hispanic Americans (or Latinos), and they tend to be grouped together by many non-Hispanics. Because most speak Spanish, or a dialect of Spanish, and many are Catholic, they are more similar as a group than are Asian Americans. Within the broad group, however, significant differences exist. Native-born Hispanic Americans sometimes disdain new immigrants. Mexican and Central American groups often segregate themselves from one another, although an outsider might be unaware of the dividing lines. Though commonalities exist, each Hispanic group has its own distinct culture.

Hispanics tend to be reluctant to acknowledge, report, or describe pain. At the same time, moaning, especially for women, is acceptable and may not necessarily indicate severe pain or loss of control. Carrying on with activities of daily living and stoicism are highly valued. Self-control (*controlarse*) includes the following (Calvillo & Flaskerud, 1991):

● Ability to withstand the stress of adversity (*aguantarse*)
● Acceptance of fate (*resignarse*)
● Cognitive coping, that is, working through a problem (*sobreponerse*)

This is another example of what seems to be paradox: Working through problems and acceptance of fate are both valued. If the first does not work, then there is always the second.

The widely recognized concept of *macho* also influences approaches to dying and death. Unfortunately, the concept is frequently viewed by non-Hispanics only as a foolish male arrogance. It is more functional to see *machismo* as indicative of a strong sense of honor that affects the way in which Hispanic men approach life and death.

The basis of health and illness is thought by some Hispanics to be a balance between hot and cold and wet and dry (Spector, 1996). These are intrinsic properties of various substances, and there are differences of opinion about what is hot, cold, and so forth.

Emotional or spiritual health problems, such as *susto,* a problem of the soul, may cause serious disability. As discussed previously, not all people subscribe to these beliefs, and not all subscribers can articulate them. It is not uncommon to have family members with varying beliefs, especially across generations (eg, one person invested in modern technological care and another in traditional healing). Fortunately, this does not often present a problem: Most Hispanic Americans, especially in the context of multigenerational families, are comfortable with pluralistic health care.

Traditional beliefs include preventing or treating illness through prayer, amulets, medals, candles, statues, or pilgrimages. *Curanderos,* or folk healers, practice in many communities. Healing through *Curanderos* is usually some combination of prayer, counseling, supernatural forces, herbs, and other means. *Herbalistas* are found in most communities. Many Latino homes have shrines with statues, candles, and pictures of saints.

A recent influx of new immigrants—both legal and illegal—from Caribbean countries has helped promote the growth of *Santeria,* a cult that combines spiritualism, African folk religion, and Catholicism. Santeria healers, called *Santeros,* are seldom accessible to people outside the cult.

Sickness, including dying, is usually a family affair, and many people are likely to be around the patient's bedside, although pregnant women may avoid caring for the patient or attending funerals (de Paula, Laguna, & Gonzalez-Ramirez, 1996). Religion, a part of daily life, is also part of the dying process. Catholics will want a priest to provide the rite of anointing of the sick. Pictures of saints or saint candles may be present according to the problem or the family's inclinations.

Most parishes have an active auxiliary, and members are likely to be involved in caring for the person who is dying and also in the aftercare. Autopsies and organ donations are often resisted, especially by Catholics, but also by others.

Public expression of grief is expected, especially among women (de Paula et al., 1996). Families and the social networks are materially supportive during bereavement. Among the poor, the financial disaster of death is mitigated by ongoing extended family support.

New Age Culture

One of the effects of the consciousness-raising revolution of the 1960s has been the growth of what is often referred to as "new age" beliefs or culture. These beliefs are found mainly among younger members of the mainstream culture. New age beliefs have distinct religious and philosophic aspects. Two forces were primarily instrumental in the growth of new age philosophy:

● Many members of the privileged classes in the West realized that no matter how much material wealth could be amassed and put to use, life was still empty.
● The availability of drugs like lysergic acid diethylamide (LSD) meant that anyone willing to take the risk of ingesting a psychedelic or "mind manifesting" substance was open to the unique opportunity of having a spiritual—or at least an extreme—experience.

While psychedelic drug use has declined and far fewer people are "dropping out," there are significant numbers of people who subscribe in some degree to related beliefs and practices. Nearly all the countless schools, belief systems, cults, and other manifestations of the New Age culture share at least some distrust of mainstream institutions, including religion, science, and health care. Belief tends to center around personal religious experience (seldom mainstream Protestant or Catholic) and humanistic ideals. There is usually an acceptance of alternative religious and healing practices.

While many hospice ideals are readily accepted by New Age cultural proponents, there is frequently a tendency to resist some of the technology or aggressive aspects of palliative care. Dying may be seen as an opportunity for spiritual growth and experience. Friends may be deeply involved in the process. The patient's autonomy is paramount.

Spiritual needs are directly addressed in New Age philosophy. Meaning abounds, and hope is pervasive. Relatedness often focuses on human relationships more than on God. Acceptance is more prevalent than forgiveness. Transcendence of fear, pain, and other problems of the human condition is what this is all about. "His restlessness and fear fell away with his identification with the body. His long teaching from cancer had opened him to life, to death" (Levine, 1978, p. 5).

Refugees

Refugees represent a growing sociocultural population with a number of differences and similarities. The differences include tremendous variation in countries of origin (eg, Bosnia, Cuba, Cambodia, Ethiopia, Sudan), religion, language, education, and experience.

One similarity (especially among refugees from rural areas) is a lack of awareness of choices. Most people in the world have very limited choices in food, housing, education, and health care. If a particular medication or treatment is not effective or has undesirable side effects, some people will assume that there are no other options. It is common among refugees to report neither problems nor treatment failures.

A second similarity is that more often than not, refugees present with immense psychosocial and often spiritual distress. The degree of distress is often related to degree of trauma (eg, concentration camp experience, torture, multiple deaths of relatives). However, even when there is no history of exceptional trauma, the process of displacement and efforts to adjust to new circumstances are significantly stressful. Post-traumatic stress disorder is a prototypical

model for refugee mental health, with symptoms emerging years after displacement.

Characteristics of refugees that impact their health and their response to terminal illness (Kemp, 1998) include the following:

- Displacement: Refugees leave their homeland to exist in a foreign and often hostile culture. It is difficult to die a stranger in a strange land.
- Loss/grief related to the past: Refugees lose their past. Old ways of life, people, and things are destroyed by war and, with the onset of terminal illness, will clearly never be regained.
- Loss/grief related to the present: To function in the new land, a refugee must undergo immense, wrenching, and incessant change. Whatever old ways are retained are seldom functional in the new circumstances of advanced disease.
- War/trauma experience: Terminal illness is likely to bring up suppressed memories of atrocities and of other terrible events.
- Shortage of community resources: Not only do refugees have difficulty accessing existing community resources, but there may also be a shortage of indigenous resources.

In addition to whatever beliefs, practices, or perspectives exist specific to displaced people, refugees are also almost always from cultures different from those of both mainstream and minority America. Cultural and language barriers thus compound the issues inherent in the life of a refugee. Those from rural areas are often users of folk remedies, some of which are efficacious, and some not.

Terminal illness often brings great sadness for refugees, and there are few, if any, means of sharing or dealing with the sadness and loss. Nowhere else is the concept of ministry of presence as important as when working with terminally ill refugees.

Further information on refugees is available at the Baylor University School of Nursing refugee health web site: *http://www.baylor.edu/ ~Charles_Kemp/refugee_health.htm.*

The Very Poor

The very poor, sometimes referred to as the "underclass," are people who have been poor for several generations and who seem unlikely to change in subsequent generations. The very poor are distinct from people who are poor or otherwise disadvantaged but who are able to envision for themselves a realistic potential to improve their circumstances. Defining characteristics of the very poor are hopelessness and little self-awareness of the possibility of a realistic potential for change.

The skills of people who have long been very poor are specific to their circumstances and are thus in many ways inconsistent with the skills needed to interact effectively in the health care system. Making an appointment, arriving on time, refilling a prescription before the bottle is empty, carrying identification, and many other behaviors that seem basic and logical to providers may be unfamiliar and difficult to accomplish for many of these patients.

Everything takes more time to do for people in these circumstances. Finding their way to health care facilities by private or public transportation may require enormous effort. Clinic appointments in the facilities provided for the very poor often require spending an entire day. Picking up prescriptions—paper or medicine—usually requires at least several hours' wait. Opioids are usually unavailable (legally) in the areas where this population lives, and possession of opioids in the home or apartment can draw the attention of criminals. Whatever the health care-related activity, it almost always requires more time and carries additional costs in terms of personal dignity for the very poor to accomplish than for any other group.

People who are very poor are (or should be) entitled to the same levels of competence and caring as anyone else. At times, because of socioeconomic, educational, institutional, and other limitations, the challenges to clinicians in providing quality care are greater with patients who are very poor than with other patients.

Referrals and teaching present particular challenges. Referrals to community or institutional resources are often of little use because patients or their families may have difficulty contacting and accessing resources or because resources may not respond as expected to people in this population. It may thus be necessary to provide advocacy and to help people through the system. Teaching is often a challenge because of experiential, cultural, educational, and other differences that exist between the nurse and the patient. At least in the early stages of care, limited goals are appropriate. Based on patient and family abilities to learn and use information, goals can later be expanded if possible.

Overall, an increase in frequency and duration of services may be necessary, even when the situation seems stable, and more vigilance is required. Medications and other necessary supplies and basic necessities—like rent money—may run out seemingly without warning, and this requires frequent monitoring on the part of the practitioner. In the same manner, deterioration in the patient or family status may occur without notification to the nurse.

In short, to work effectively with members of this population, it is necessary to learn patience in working around limitations, whether those limitations are the client's or those of the institutions.

Health Care Providers

Health care providers can be viewed as a significant and distinct subculture, perhaps the most homogeneous of any discussed in this chapter. The culture is generally rigid, and many roles are gender related, although as with other cultures, some of the barriers are breaking down.

Cultural values of health care providers include a strong belief in technology and "silent suffering" in response to pain. Health care providers may have goals different from those of patients, such as seeking to reduce pain rather than to relieve it (Calvillo & Flaskerud, 1991). Providers may hold the "major American cultural values" (Leininger, 1978), including the following:

- Seeking optimal health
- Belief in democracy/individualism
- Achieving and doing
- Valuing cleanliness
- Attention to timeliness
- Belief in technology

While these may seem logical and natural to some, they may not be the values of all patients and all families. On a one-to-one basis, cultural differences may be easier to deal with individually than institutionally. What may seem completely logical and natural to middle and upper-middle class health care providers may be incomprehensible to others.

The problem-solving orientation of health care professionals may come into conflict with other cultures. The psychology of the West and of middle-class, mainstream culture health care providers includes the idea that problems should be solved and that people can deal with it. This culture-specific belief is not shared by everyone!

REFERENCES

Cadwalader, S. L. (1997). Native Americans [CD-ROM]. *Encarta 98.*

Calvillo, E. R., & Flaskerud, J. H. (1991). Review of literature on culture and pain of adults with focus on Mexican-Americans. *Journal of Transcultural Nursing, 2*(2), 16–23.

Cherry, B., & Giger, J. N. (1995). African Americans. In J. N. Giger & R. E. Davidhizar (Eds.), *Transcultural nursing* (2nd ed.) (pp. 165–203). St. Louis: Mosby Year Book.

de Paula, T., Laguna, K., & Gonzalez-Ramirez, L. (1996). *Mexican Americans.*

Hanley, C. E. (1991). Navaho Indians. In J. N. Giger & R. E. Davidhizar (Eds.), *Transcultural nursing* (pp. 215–238). St. Louis: Mosby Year Book.

Kemp, C. (1997). Asian-American health site (on-line) *http://www.baylor.edu/~Charles_Kemp/asian_health.html.*

Kemp, C. (1998). Refugee mental health issues. Refugee health (On-line) *http://www.baylor.edu/~Charles_Kemp/refugee_health.htm.*

Kipling, R. (1930). The ballad of East and West. In *Barrack room ballads.* London: Standard Book Company.

Kramer, J. (1996). American Indians. In J. G. Lipson, S. L. Dibble, & P. A. Minarik (Eds.), *Culture and nursing care: A pocket guide* (pp. 7–10). San Francisco: UCSF Nursing Press.

Lang, L. T. (1990). Aspects of the Cambodian death and dying process. In J. K. Parry (Ed.), *Social work with the terminally ill: A transcultural perspective* (pp. 205–211). Springfield, IL: Charles C. Thomas.

Leininger, M. (1978). The significance of cultural concepts in nursing. In M. Leininger (Ed.), *Transcultural nursing: Concepts, theories, and practices* (pp. 121–137). New York: John Wiley & Sons.

Levine, S. (1978, December). Approaching death. *Hanuman Foundation Dying Project Newsletter, 2.*

Lewis, R. (1990). Death and dying among the American Indians. In J. K. Parry (Ed.), *Social work with the terminally ill: A transcultural perspective* (pp. 23–32). Springfield, IL: Charles C. Thomas.

Lipman, J. G. (1996). Diversity issues. In J. G. Lipson, S. L. Dibble, & P. A. Minarik (Eds.), *Culture and nursing care: A pocket guide* (pp. 7–10). San Francisco: UCSF Nursing Press.

Mollica, R. F., Caspi-Yavin, Y., Bollini, P., Truong, & T., Lavelle, J. (1992). Validating a cross-cultural instrument for measuring torture, trauma, and post-traumatic stress. *Journal of Nervous and Mental Disease, 180*(2), 111–116.

Pickett, M. (1993). Cultural awareness in the context of terminal illness. *Cancer nursing, 16*(2), 102–106.

Salcido, R. M. (1990). Mexican-Americans: Illness, death and bereavement. In J. K. Parry (Ed.), *Social work with the terminally ill: A transcultural perspective* (pp. 99–112). Springfield, IL: Charles C. Thomas.

Soto, A. R., & Villa, J. (1990). Una platica: Mexican-American approaches to death and dying. In J. K. Parry (Ed.), *Social work with the terminally ill: A transcultural perspective* (pp. 113–127). Springfield, IL: Charles C. Thomas.

Spector, R. E. (1996). *Cultural diversity in health and illness* (3rd ed.). Norwalk, CT: Appleton & Lange.

Ta, M., & Chung, C. (1990). Death and dying: A Vietnamese cultural perspective. In J. K. Parry (Ed.), *Social work with the terminally ill: A transcultural perspective* (pp. 191–203). Springfield, IL: Charles C. Thomas.

Tripp-Reimer, T., Brink, P. J., & Saunders, J. M. (1984). Cultural assessment: Content and process. *Nursing Outlook, 32*(2), 78–82.

Wilson, B., & Ryan, A. S. (1991). Working with the terminally ill Chinese-American patient. In J. K. Parry (Ed.), *Social work with the terminally ill: A transcultural perspective* (pp. 145–158). Springfield, IL: Charles C. Thomas.

CHAPTER 7

Grief and Bereavement Care

KEY POINTS

● Grief occurs as a result of loss and is thus a universal experience.

● While each person experiences grief differently, there are characteristics common to the grief process.

● Normative and complicated grief are difficult to define, but clearly, both are common phenomena.

● There are certain relatively universal tasks of bereavement, and effective interventions may be structured around these tasks.

Grief is suffering experienced "whenever the continuity of our lives has been destroyed" (Carse, 1980, p. 8). Grief may be conceptually defined as a dynamic, pervasive, highly individualized process with a normative component (Cowles & Rodgers, 1991; Horowitz et al., 1997; Parkes, 1998a). Grief is the following:

● Changing and nonlinear (dynamic or even oscillating from one state to another)
● Composed of phases requiring *work* to move through (process)
● Uniquely experienced, often with astonishing power and pain, and expressed by individuals (individualized)
● Experienced and manifested physically, psychologically, socially, and spiritually (pervasive)
● While experienced or expressed uniquely, usually composed of relatively predictable problems, extending over a relatively predictable period of time (normative)

It is important to understand that the bereaved person does not proceed in an orderly manner through sequential stages and reach a positive resolution in a prescribed period of time. Moreover, there are cultural variations in the expression but not necessarily the internal experience of grief (Cowles, 1996). When a significant other dies, grief may be related to losses in addition to that of the loss of the person, such as life role, companionship, intimacy, financial status, living arrangements, and having someone on whom to depend (Parkes, 1998a).

The terms grief, bereavement, and mourning are sometimes used interchangeably, and there is disagreement about their precise meanings. For this book, the definitions provided by Parkes (1998b) are used:

● Bereavement: The situation of anyone who has lost a person to whom he or she is attached
● Grief: The psychological and emotional reactions to bereavement
● Mourning: The social face of grief

Note that grief and mourning may be expressed through physical means, such as illness or, in the case of Cambodians and other Southeast Asians, through dermabrasion or "coining" (Kemp, 1998)

Characteristics of Grief

Grief following the death of a loved one may be expressed by denial, shock, inertia, loss of affect, intense yearning, anger, guilt, insomnia, sadness, depression, and spiritual despair and (feelings of) losing control (Parkes, 1998a; Jacob, 1996). Also, a person for whom grief is felt is usually one who has been loved in the conventional sense of warm, loving feelings. At times, however, tremendous grief or related feelings may be experienced in relation to a person for whom the bereaved felt primarily anger, rejection, or other negative emotion. Grief after death is felt not just for a person as a love object; it can also be felt for love unexpressed, anger unresolved, and so forth.

Seeking help, holding on (to the deceased), withdrawal, loneliness, inertia, and aimlessness are common themes in grief (Jacob, 1996). Avoidance of potentially painful stimuli, intrusive thoughts and feelings, hallucinations (visions), or a strong sense of the presence of the deceased are not uncommon (Horowitz et al., 1997; Parkes, 1998a). Family conflict is common, as is increased prescription and other drug use. Physiologic manifestations of grief include anorexia, gastrointestinal disturbances, menstrual irregularities, fatigue, and shortness of breath (Lindemann, 1944). Morbidity and mortality are greater among people who are bereaved than among people who are not (Sheldon, 1998). Health risks related to bereavement include myocardial infarction, hypertension, rheumatoid arthritis, depression, alcohol and other drug abuse, and malnutrition (Carman, 1997).

Several theorists have proposed stages or phases in grief. Common to several important models are the phases of numbness and blunt-ing, pining and yearning, disorganization and despair, and reorganization and recovery (Parkes, 1998b). Such phases are helpful to the extent that they may help (1) make sense of a global or overwhelming situation and (2) keep the focus on the process rather than on each separate problem. These phases do not, however, reliably predict grief-related behaviors.

Like any other human behavior or experience, grief and mourning may be carried to extremes in behavior or in length. What constitutes extreme is subject to debate and is discussed under complicated grief. Grief may also precipitate great personal or spiritual growth.

Anticipatory Grief

Anticipatory grief has long been thought to have beneficial effects on later grief (Rando, 1986). This idea is in part related to the knowledge that unexpected death may result in greater grief than the expected death of someone after an extended illness. Denial of the reality of a terminal situation or impending death is sometimes a temporarily helpful defense in patients and caregivers. However, in general, confronting or otherwise coming to grips with the realities (anticipatory grief) leads to a greater ability to cope with the situation and may improve family and patient communications (Parkes, 1998b). On the other hand, anticipatory grief may lead the family to withdraw from the patient to protect themselves from the pain of the grief (McCabe, 1997).

Complicated Grief and Assessment Parameters

Many different terms have been used to give a name to grief or mourning that exceeds normative boundaries (of time and degree of distress) and are related to poor outcomes. The term complicated grief is gaining increasing acceptance over pathologic grief, distorted grief, dysfunctional grief, and so on. It should be emphasized that identification of complicated grief is not a matter of placing a value judgment on whether sadness or similar emotions are felt for a lengthy period after a death. It is clear that for some people and some situations, grief has no end and that in some cultures, it is inappropriate for grief to come to a complete end. However, complicated grief does result in physical and mental disability and predisposes people to suicide (Prigerson, Houck, Ehrenpreis, & Reynolds, 1997; Sheldon, 1998).

Behaviors or symptoms not characteristic of normal bereavement (American Psychiatric Association, 1994) and perhaps more characteristic of depression include guilt about things other than what occurred at the time of death or illness, thoughts of death *other* than the survivor feeling she or he would be better off dead or should have died with the deceased, morbid preoccupation with worthlessness, psychomotor retardation, prolonged and marked functional impairment, and hallucinatory experiences *other* than thinking she or he hears the voice of the deceased person or transiently sees the deceased person.

Indications that complicated grief exists (Horowitz et al., 1997) may be summarized as follows:

● Bereavement began at least 14 months ago (12 months is avoided because of potential impact of the anniversary of the loss).
● Any three of the following seven symptoms exist in the last month:

INTRUSIVE SYMPTOMS

● Unbidden memories or intrusive fantasies related to the lost relationship
● Strong spells or pangs of severe emotion related to the lost relationship
● Distressingly strong yearnings or wishes that the deceased were there

SIGNS OF AVOIDANCE AND FAILURE TO ADAPT

● Feelings of being far too much alone or personally empty
● Excessively staying away from people, places, or activities that remind the subject of the deceased
● Unusual levels of sleep interference
● Loss of interest in work, social, caretaking, or recreational activities to a maladaptive degree

These are proposed diagnostic criteria for a complicated grief disorder. Although certain symptoms may be added, deleted, or restated, these summarize much of what is known about grief.

Types of complicated grief (Hospice and Palliative Nurses Association, 1997; Parkes, 1998b) include the following:

1. Grief related to traumatic loss would include the sudden unexpected death of a child, death by murder, or multiple deaths. The response to such deaths might include absent grief, characterized by no expression of grief, psychic numbing, and permanent withdrawal from social activity, or distorted grief, characterized by distortion, usually exaggeration, of one or more components of grief—with anger and guilt the most common.

2. Absent or inhibited grief is characterized by no or little expression of grief or by psychic numbing. Absent grief is sometimes related to trauma as discussed previously. Absent grief may shift to delayed grief and thus first be experienced because of another loss or event that breaks through defenses.

3. Conflicted grief may occur when the survivor had a conflicted or ambivalent relationship with the deceased and serious unfinished business remains. Feelings of anger and guilt grow over time, and the survivor is likely to feel "haunted" by the deceased person.

4. Chronic grief is unending grief that may even intensify with time. It is associated with the

deceased person being highly dependent on the survivor.

The following personal and family attributes may be seen as indicators of increased risk for poor outcomes in grief (Cooley, 1992; Kissane, Bloch, & McKenzie, 1997; Sheldon, 1998):

● Little or no time to prepare for the death, especially when the deceased was young
● Highly dependent, conflicted, or ambivalent relationship with the deceased
● Dependence on emotion-focused coping strategies alone (versus balance of emotion and cognitive or problem-solving strategies)
● Young age (eg, young adult with children at home)
● Perceived lack of social support
● Older, isolated person with no history of working outside the home
● Previous poor physical or mental health status, including history of depression or drug dependence
● Family coping styles classified as hostile (high conflict, low cohesiveness, poor expressiveness), sullen (exhibiting characteristics of hostile family but not as severe), or intermediate (intermediate cohesiveness, low control, and low achievement orientation)

While the presence of one or more of these factors does not necessarily lead to a poor outcome, they do alert the practitioner to a higher degree of risk and thus may function as assessment parameters. Additionally, bereaved people should be assessed for physical problems related to, or exacerbated by, grief (eg, cardiac and gastrointestinal problems and any other preexisting chronic illnesses).

Interventions

Intervention in grief begins with primary prevention before death. Involving the family in caring for the person who is dying is important to all involved before death and to the family after death. To know that they are or were helpful is something solid to which people can cling. Resolving or attempting to resolve conflicts is immensely beneficial. Managing symptoms, keeping the family informed of changes and their significance in the patient's condition, and providing reassurance and comfort are nursing actions that are helpful before and after the death.

Bereavement care is likely to accomplish the most during the first few months of mourning, before defense mechanisms have hardened. Many hospice programs plan the first bereavement contact for about 2 weeks after the death. This is when the usual rush of support immediately following the death decreases, and 2 to 4 weeks lies within the parameters of length of time during which to provide crisis intervention (Sheldon, 1998). Holidays, birthdays, and other significant times are when the need for support tends to be highest. The first anniversary of the death is usually very difficult for survivors. Subsequent anniversaries are also significant.

Tasks of Bereavment: A Structure for Intervention

Certain tasks of bereavement (Castiglia, 1988; Cooley, 1992; Harr & Thistlethwaite, 1990; Parkes, 1998b; Jacob, 1996) help to guide interventions. Consistent with the process and development of grief, the tasks are not subject to the mourner completing one and then moving on to the next. There is not a "next" task. Mourners typically move from one to another, address several at once, move back to a previous task, go deeper into feelings or understanding, do nothing, move on to another, and so on. The seven "tasks of bereavement" are discussed in the following section. Making progress in these tasks results in making progress in the process of grief. The long-term goals of grief work are as follows:

● Gradual reintegration into life and adjustment to life without the person who died
● Prevention of prolonged changes in psychosocial patterns, especially prevention of depression

Telling the "Death Story"

There is an almost universal need among the bereaved to describe and redescribe events and feelings around the death (Cooley, 1992). Every detail is discussed again and again—often past the time that family and friends are willing to listen. The need to tell this story more than others want to hear it may play some part in the common problem of diminished social support. The need to tell the story also conflicts with the desire to avoid the pain of grief. Interventions related to the mourner's need to tell the story include the following:

● Actively listening to the story: Among the specific directions for listening to the story are helping the mourner sequence the events in time and place, promoting acuity in perceiving the events (increasing detail), and separating what is real from what is not.
● Teaching family members and other sources of the mourner's social support system about this common need
● Suggesting to the bereaved person that he or she write the story.

Expressing and Accepting the Sadness

There are several impediments common initially to expressing and accepting the sadness of grief. Some people will be aware of their feelings but fear a psychological catastrophe if the feelings are expressed and acknowledged. "If I start to cry, I'll never stop." Another problem is a family or social norm of not expressing feelings. It is common among some to accept the practice of pseudocomfort that really only encourages people to be quiet and to repress their feelings: "There, there, it's going to be alright." Expressing feelings may also be inhibited by institutions. Most hospitals are set up for efficiency—perhaps amenable to, at the most, quiet crying but not to the deep anguish

that may be felt when a loved one dies.

For those stuck playing a role of not hurting, a simple statement of what might be felt can help: "I'm so sorry. This must hurt terribly." Too many words can get in the way and constant attempts to fill the pain with words is not helpful. Silence may ease the expression of feelings. The old "psych nurse" technique of changing the setting to change the behavior may also facilitate the emergence of feelings.

The loneliness of grief is not unexpected by most mourners. What is often surprising is the power of it overall and the unexpectedness of the small moments of intense pain that appear amidst all the things once taken for granted (Yalom & Vinogradov, 1988).

Expressing and Accepting Guilt, Anger, and Other Feelings Perceived as Negative

In the immense stress of dying, death, and grief lies an illogical and almost universal trap for survivors: regret, which is concentrated often in the illusion that after a lifetime of imperfection: "I/he/she/we/it should have been perfect!" Decisions, behavior, and words said are obsessively reviewed and found lacking. Regrets are inescapable and accepted by most people. Excessive guilt, blame, and anger are more problematic for many and are commonly associated with complicated grief (Hyrkas, Kaunonen, & Paunonen, 1997).

Guilt is an integral part of grief (Parkes, 1998a) and often has its origin in a separation fear or anxiety. Problems in expressing guilt include the shame felt about whatever real or perceived transgressions are related to the guilt and a conscious or unconscious fear of punishment.

Acknowledging and expressing guilt is the first step in resolving it. Because shame and a fear of punishment are barriers in expressing guilt, a nonjudgmental relationship is essential to this expression. While some rumination on perceived causes and feelings of guilt is productive, greater progress is made in the process of exploring the moral code associated with the guilt. Many people struggle to live under unrealistic moral codes. Changing such beliefs is difficult and is not practical under most circumstances. Many people, however, can come to see which aspects of their values are realistic and which are unrealistic.

Once guilt is expressed and to some extent understood, the process of acceptance of self or behavior can begin. Some (intellectual) acceptance may occur through expressing the guilt. People experiencing difficulties with guilt need to do additional work. Apologizing or otherwise communicating with the person who died can be done through writing a letter to him or her. It is important to understand that it is common for people who have been abused to carry at least as much, if not more, guilt than those who have hurt others. In essence, the nurse helps the survivor to accomplish the following:

● Accept feelings of guilt
● Recognize realistic and unrealistic reasons for guilt
● Find means to apologize or otherwise atone for the guilt
● Begin to forgive self

Anger may range from the bitterness of unfulfillment to the poignancy of a loving relationship lost:

After he died I was smelling his clothes and there was no smell of him anywhere and I was really mad that he . . . that . . . I mean, what if you were here trying to smell me. Because he didn't even leave any scent.
(Levine, 1988)

For some, anger is more difficult to deal with than guilt. Indeed, guilt may be felt about feelings of anger toward the deceased. More often than not, hostility is turned inward and experienced as anger, depression, or guilt, or it may be turned outward toward others, rather than toward the idealized deceased (Switzer, 1970). For many, it feels normal to feel guilty and abnormal to feel angry. Anger is nevertheless a common component of grief.

Anger is addressed in Chapter 2, under psy-

chosocial needs of the individual. While much of that discussion applies to this one as well, anger in grief can also be addressed separately. Interventions include advising and helping mourners:

● Maintain awareness of their own responses to anger, whether it is expressed directly or indirectly
● Directly express the anger about whatever object is perceived as at fault
● Identify and explore the underlying feelings (eg, separation anxiety, frustration, betrayal)
● Deal with those underlying feelings.

While separation anxiety is a broad issue encompassing multiple settings, it can be addressed here in terms of the person feeling bad about being apart from the one who died. The separation, however, is not just from the person, but also from roles (forever lost), hopes (never to be fulfilled), and other key aspects of self, not the least of which is a deep awareness of mortality.

Reviewing the Relationship with the Deceased
While this occurs in part through other tasks and extends throughout the person's life, some support specific to this task may be helpful. Reviewing the relationship with the deceased is similar to a life review but focuses on the relationship. Elements of this task, or direction, to encourage in working with the mourner include the following:

● Exploring the early days of the relationship: For spouses or life partners, this includes how they met, courtship remembrances, and similar matters, which are seldom discussed with others. For parents, siblings, children (adult or child) of a parent who died, and similar people, talking about early remembrances is vitally important. Because much conflict has its roots in early relationships, negatives should be covered along with positives.
● Exploring what might have been had the death not occurred: While painful, this is an

important issue to confront in the process of healing.

Exploring Possibilities in Life After the Death

Behind or within the pain of grief lies the forbidding question, "What now?" In the early days after the death, the answer often appears to be, sadly, this—this pain, this despair, this emptiness. Thus, the task of exploring possibilities is filled with dread. Existing for some time in grief's suffering is a necessary precursor to looking to the future with anything other than dread. How long that time might be is impossible to estimate, and there is no specific point at which that task takes precedence over others. Rather, there (usually) is a gradual awareness that the future will not necessarily be without hope.

As the person comes to understand that life can go on and perhaps be good in some respects (and for some, this understanding seems to do an injustice to the memory of the deceased), the ability to think of the future increases. Along with this growing awareness is progress in other tasks and a concomitant increase in energy. Gradual progress with periods of regression and progression is the norm.

Some people will go on to form new intimate relationships. Men tend to be quicker than women to seek intimacy (Yalom & Vinogradov, 1988). Either may fall into relationships that are emotionally damaging, especially if alcohol or drug use is involved. The nurse can help the client go on with life by using the following interventions:

● Help the mourner to identify goals and hopes that are achievable and those that are not.
● Give the mourner the opportunity to regrieve about the reality of life going on or about other issues.
● Give the mourner the opportunity to explore possibilities for the future. There is no rush to know the future. Some of the person's ideas or hopes may be nonproductive or illogical. The freedom to express such ideas to another can allow the mourner the freedom to develop more practical plans.
● Teach the mourner problem-solving techniques, if needed. It is essential that the mourner begin by solving a small problem. Few people in these situations have the psychological reserves to fail and try again. Because emotion-based coping is positively correlated with dysfunctional grief, rational problem solving may help decrease the likelihood of complications.
● Social support is a key element in resolving grief, and directive assistance can be given in locating and using appropriate resources. Bereaved people often feel less welcome than they did before the death at church or with other former sources of social support. Although the nurse helps the mourner deal with his or her responses to this perceived rejection, more direct assistance can also be given. The nurse can respond to, or prevent, withdrawal by encouraging the person to go back to church or to former sources of support, to *ask* for help, to ask *again* if help is denied, and to look elsewhere if help is again denied. Bereavement groups, while generally a temporary source of support (Yalom, 1990), can function as a kind of gateway to exploring a new life.

Understanding Common Processes and Problems in Grief

Many people have little or no understanding of the power of grief; the flood of emotions is thus a terrible surprise. The duration of grief is also a surprise for many. Providing normative information is thus extremely important in bereavement care. Having such information does not change any of the experiences of grief; it does, however, give the mourner a kind of voice in the background that says, "This is grief; it is not the beginning of breakdown." Information should be given verbally and in writing.

Working through these normative levels of grief leads to finding a way to reorganize or adjust to the environment or life without the deceased. In addressing grief, it is essential that the nurse remember that complete resolution, that is, complete acceptance and lack of pain may not be achieved. Most people get better, but many never return to their former level of functioning. Some, thankfully, achieve a higher level of functioning.

Being Understood or Accepted by Others

The depth of the emotion of grief and its intrinsic characteristics result in isolation. Indeed, there is a time to be alone, to mourn, and to refrain from embracing. Just as the person who is dying must at some time be alone, so must the bereaved. The purpose is not to get the family and others to intervene in or to change the process, but rather to promote understanding of some of what the bereaved person is feeling. Although this does not solve the problem of isolation, it does, ironically enough, render the mourner's situation less lonely than it could be.

Funerals and Other Rituals

There is a universal need for funerals or similar rituals, and every religion provides a structure for them. Rando (1984) provides a definitive discussion of the purposes and benefits of funerals. These are summarized in Box 7-1.

A variety of options exist in funerals and related rituals. Funerals, planned within the context of the various faiths and denominations of the faiths, are the most common rituals. Memorial services or gatherings are increasingly common. Whatever the choice of the person who is dying or the family, the key issue is that a choice should be made before the death whenever possible. Making choices and arrangements after the death is a difficult burden for mourners. Moreover, the process of making choices prior to death can be helpful in the psychosocial and spiritual care of the client and family. At some point in client and family discussions, it should usually be suggested that they make plans. Most will have already thought of this, but many will not

---

Box 7-1. Purposes and Benefits of Funerals

- Provide the last rite of passage for the person who died

- Confirm and reinforce the reality of the death and the separation of the living and the dead

- Assist in acknowledging and expressing feelings of loss and facilitating mourning

- Stimulate recollections of the deceased and help validate the deceased person's life

- Allow participation of the community in memorializing the person who died

- Provide the comfort or other benefits of community and ritual

- Provide means for the community to give and receive social and spiritual support

- Begin the process of helping the bereaved back into the community

- Help in the search for meaning

- Affirm the social order: the community goes on despite death

- Remind the living of their own and others' mortality

- Furnish means and method in disposing of the body

---

have known how to bring up such a sensitive subject.

Health care providers are seldom involved in funerals, except through attendance at times. They should, from time to time, attend the funerals of clients. They too benefit from participating in these ancient rituals.

REFERENCES

American Psychiatric Association. (1994). *Diagnostic and statistical manual of mental disorders* (4th ed.). Washington, DC: Author.

Carman, M. B. (1997). The psychology of normal aging. *The Psychiatric Clinics of North America, 20*(1), 15–24.

Carse, J. P. (1980). *Death and existence: A conceptual history of human mortality*. New York: John Wiley & Sons.

Castiglia, P. T. (1988). Death of a parent. *Journal of Pediatric Health Care, 2*(3), 157–159.

Cooley, M. E. (1992). Bereavement care: A role for nurses. *Cancer Nursing, 15*(2), 125–129.

Cowles, K. V., & Rodgers, B. L. (1991). The concept of grief: A foundation for nursing research and practice. *Research in Nursing and Health, 14*(2), 119–127.

Cowles, K. V. (1996). Cultural perspectives of grief: An expanded concept analysis. *Journal of Advanced Nursing, 23,* 287–294.

Harr, B. D., & Thistlethwaite, J. E. (1990). Creative intervention strategies in the management of perinatal loss. *Maternal-Child Nursing Journal, 19*(2), 135–142.

Horowitz, M. J., Siegel, B., Holen, A., Bonanno, G. A., Milbrath, C., & Stinson, C. H. (1997). Diagnostic criteria for complicated grief disorder. *American Journal of Psychiatry, 154*(7), 904–910.

Hospice and Palliative Nurses Association. (1997). *The hospice nurses study guide: A preparation for the CRNH candidate* (2nd ed.). Pittsburgh: Author.

Hyrkas, K., Kaunonen, M., & Paunonen, M. (1997). Recovering from the death of a spouse. *Journal of Advanced Nursing, 25,* 775–779.

Jacob, S. R. (1996). The grief experience of older women whose husbands had hospice care. *Journal of Advanced Nursing, 24,* 280–286.

Kemp, C. (1998). Asian-American health site (on-line): *http://www.baylor.edu/~Charles_Kemp/asian_health.html.*

Kissane, D. W., Bloch, S., & McKenzie, D. P. (1997). Family coping and bereavement outcome. *Palliative Medicine, 11*(3), 191–201.

Levine, S. (Facilitator). (1988). Conscious living/dying (Cassette Recording No. SL1-27-8811). Delray Beach, FL: Hanuman Foundation.

Lindemann, E. (1944). Symptomatology and management of acute grief. *American Journal of Psychiatr, 101,* 141–148.

McCabe, M. J. (1997). Clinical response to spiritual issues. In R. K. Portenoy & E. Bruera (Eds.), *Topics in palliative care* (Vol. 1) (pp. 279–290). New York: Oxford University Press.

Nuss, W. S., & Zubenko, G. S. (1992). Correlates of persistent depressive symptoms in widows. *American Journal of Psychiatry, 149*(3), 346–351.

Parkes, C. M. (1998a). Coping with loss: The dying adult. *British Medical Journal, 316,* 1313–1315.

Parkes, C. M. (1998b). Bereavement. In D. Doyle, G. W. C. Hanks, & N. MacDonald (Eds.), *Oxford textbook of palliative medicine* (2nd ed.) (pp. 995–1010). Oxford: Oxford University Press.

Prigerson, S. K., Houck, H., Ehrenpreis, L., & Reynolds, C. F. (1997). Suicidal ideation in elderly bereaved: The role of complicated grief. *Suicide and Life Threatening Behavior, 27*(2), 194–207.

Rando, T. A. (1984). *Grief, dying, and death.* Champaign, IL: Research Press Company.

Rando, T. A. (Ed.) (1986). *Loss and anticipatory grief.* Lexington, MA: D.C. Heath.

Sheldon, F. (1998). ABC of palliative care: Bereavement. *British Medical Journal, 316,* 456–458.

Speck, P. (1998). Spiritual issues in palliative care. In D. Doyle, G. W. C. Hanks, & N. MacDonald (Eds.), *Oxford textbook of palliative medicine* (2nd ed.) (pp. 805–814). Oxford: Oxford University Press.

Switzer, D. K. (1970). *The dynamics of grief.* New York: Abdingdon Press.

Yalom, I., & Vinogradov, S. (1988). Bereavement groups: Techniques and themes. *International Journal of Group Psychotherapy, 38*(4), 419–446.

Yalom, I. (1990). Response to discussion of bereavement groups: Techniques and themes. *International Journal of Group Psychotherapy, 40*(1), 105–107.

Ethics

All the major ethical issues or dilemmas are brought into full focus in the process of providing end-of-life care. The most fundamental moral or ethical principle is respect for people (American Nurses Association [ANA], 1985, p. i). From this principle follows more specific principles. Each of these principles is a concrete and nonacademic issue when caring for people who are dying:

- Respect for autonomy—the patient's right of self-determination
- Beneficence or benevolence—doing good or meeting needs
- Nonmaleficence—doing no harm
- Veracity—truth telling
- Confidentiality—respecting privileged information
- Fidelity—keeping promises
- Justice—treating fairly

The ANA task force to revise the Nursing Code of Ethics is currently examining the 1985 document and will make changes and clarifications in the revised code (not available as this book goes to press). It is unlikely that the basic principles will change. However, technologic and treatment advances and issues such as assisted suicide require a careful examination of the profession's stance on all issues that affect patient welfare and the dilemmas facing nurses.

Ethical principles should also be considered in a religious and cultural context because ethical and moral values are not the same in all religions and cultures. From at least some perspectives, autonomy is central to such questions as abortion and euthanasia. The latter is discussed at the end of this chapter, in the section "Decisions Near the End of Life."

For purposes of clarity, this chapter is structured around the principles given in the

Code for Nurses with Interpretive Statements (ANA, 1985).

Autonomy

Autonomy, or the individual's freedom of self-determination, is "basic to respect for persons" (ANA, 1985, p. i) and is central to ethical professional practice and especially to patient decision making. While competence—the mental capacity to make a decision—is necessary to practice autonomy, practically speaking, autonomy is affected by economic, political, legal, and other issues (Kleinman, 1997).

Decision making, especially to forgo or withdraw treatment, is a central issue in terminal care and autonomy. To reach the conclusion that one is dying and will therefore decide to forgo further curative treatment moves a person from a primarily dependent role of "patient" to a far more autonomous role of "the person who is dying" (Van Eyes, 1991). Autonomous decisions are made by competent or "normal choosers," and the following factors are inherent in these decisions: (1) intentionality, (2) understanding, and (3) voluntariness or the absence of "controlling influences" (Beauchamp & Childress, 1994, p. 123). Therefore, the central issues within the principle of respect for autonomy are competence, informed consent, and voluntariness (intentionality either does or does not exist).

Competence
The capacity to perform a task is the "single core meaning" of competence (Beauchamp & Childress, 1994, p. 134). In the context of terminal care decisions, the primary task is to understand the risks and benefits of treatment and thus make a rational decision about what treatment to forgo and when to forgo it. Competence operates along a continuum and may change, for example, with the onset and resolution of hypercalcemia, depression, and other physical or psychological problems.

Informed Consent
Fully realized, informed consent includes the following elements (Beauchamp & Childress, 1994; Butow, Maclean, Dunn, Tattersall, & Boyer, 1997; Davison & Degner, 1998):

● Competence exists.
● Disclosure includes full explication of the procedure, including risks, benefits, and alternatives such that a "reasonable person" has sufficient information to make a decision. There is general agreement that the extent of disclosure should be based on the individual's needs for information and ability to understand (Scanlon, 1998).
● Understanding often is not complete but should always be adequate to the extent that the patient has capacity for understanding the essential elements necessary to achieve understanding: diagnosis, prognosis, nature and purpose of intervention, alternatives, risks and benefits, and recommendations (including conflicting recommendations).
● Voluntariness is narrower than autonomy and includes the freedom to act without being under the coercive or manipulative control of another influence. Voluntariness may also be decreased by disease, substance dependence, and other factors.
● Consent is given.

Autonomy becomes impossible for some patients, especially as disease advances and problems and symptoms grow in number and magnitude. The presence of an advance directive increases autonomy, but in too many cases, advance directives are not followed (SUPPORT Principal Investigators, 1995).

In the absence of an advance directive or in the case of a child who is ill, a surrogate decision maker must be used and that person's substituted judgment taken in place of the patient's. Note, however, that "increasingly, the assent of a child must be obtained, in addition to the consent of the parents, before a medical procedure is performed" (Collins, 1998, p.

DEBORA HUNTER

259). The use of a surrogate decision maker is facilitated when there is a properly executed "Durable Power of Attorney for Health Care" or related document. When there is neither an advance directive nor power of attorney document, a family member (closest competent relative) is usually designated to make the substituted decisions. All the elements of informed decision making apply to surrogate decision makers precisely as they do to patients.

Beneficence

Beneficence (or benevolence) is commonly defined as doing good (ANA, 1985). More completely defined, beneficence requires providing benefit to another (positive benefi-

cence) and balancing benefits and harms (utility). The question of balancing good and harm is a central question in terminal care: What treatment is appropriate, and when should treatment be discontinued?

Beneficence is a moral obligation to practice mercy, kindness, compassion, and charity (Beauchamp & Childress, 1994) and is considered by some as the highest duty in health care and in all human endeavors. Competent terminal care is focused completely on the patient's needs.

Beneficence (and nonmaleficence) is sometimes called into question when care is or seems to be futile. Making an absolute determination that care is futile is extremely difficult or even impossible in some cases. The issue is further complicated by patient or family requests to "do anything that can be done."

Superficially, it may seem that there is not a clear distinction between beneficence and non-maleficence. However, beneficence goes well beyond the minimal admonition to do no harm and includes action to do good (Thomasina, 1997). At least one noted ethicist makes the definitive statement that "the notion that there is no morally significant difference between omission and commission is just wrong" (Callahan, 1992, p. 52).

Nonmaleficence

Nonmaleficence encompasses not inflicting physical, psychological, social, spiritual, or any other harm, including harm to the patient's dignity. An "assault of truth," for example, may be a maleficent act (Latimer, 1991, p. 330). The duty of nonmaleficence, to do no harm "on balance" (American Medical Association [AMA], 1992, p. 2230), may come into conflict with wishes or duties of patients, families, or nurses in terminal care situations. The questions of what treatment is best, when it should be provided, and when it should be discontinued are major issues in many situations.

Veracity

Veracity includes not lying and not deceiving (Beauchamp & Childress, 1994). The question of what to tell and how to tell patients and families has long troubled health professionals who care for the terminally ill (Saunders, 1978a). Truth telling affects not only the relationship between the patient and the nurse, but also significantly influences the patient's quality of life. While in the past, nurses often operated as if in primary relationship with physicians or with hospital hierarchies and in secondary relationships with patients (Bernal, 1992), the primary relationships are now indisputably with patients.

Traditionally, and appropriately, the physician first tells the patient the diagnosis and prognosis. When such information is not given in a reasonable period of time and a patient asks about diagnosis or prognosis, the nurse may experience conflict about the best course of action. In such cases, the nurse should be guided by the "universal moral principles" (ANA, 1985) cited in the nurses' Code and discussed in this section: The truth should be told. How the truth is told and its extent may vary, but given the choice between lying and telling the truth, one should opt for the truth, except in the most extraordinary circumstances, such as protecting a person from external threats (eg, political persecution). Telling the truth may be personally uncomfortable and may result in difficulties at work. Nevertheless, the principles of beneficence, autonomy, and veracity take precedence over the desire to avoid conflict.

Confidentiality

The nurse's duty is to "hold all information in confidence" except that which is "pertinent to a client's treatment and welfare." This information is shared "only to those directly concerned with the client's care" (ANA, 1985, p. 4–5). The nurses' Code also specifies that the duty of confidentiality is "not absolute when innocent parties are in direct jeopardy." (p. 5)

Evidence exists that confidentiality is often violated, both among individuals and institutionally (Roy & MacDonald, 1998). As with other ethical principles, confidentiality can present difficult dilemmas. How much "direct jeopardy" warrants overriding confidentiality, and where do legal obligations fit? If, for example, a competent patient hints at suicide, what actions might the nurse take? If the same patient presents with behavior indicating a high risk for suicide, what actions might be appropriate?

Fidelity

Fidelity can be interpreted as fundamentally "a covenant . . . of faithfulness" between human beings (Ramsey, 1970, p. xii) or "keeping promises" (ANA, 1985, p. i). In either case, fidelity means more than "doing what one says one will do." Fidelity includes the implicit or explicit contracts or covenants that exist by virtue of one person seeking health care from another (Beauchamp & Childress, 1994). Practicing fidelity means doing what one says one will do and holding true to the ethical principles of nursing. As with veracity, the principle of fidelity may bring the nurse into moral conflict. A basic dilemma or conflict is choosing actions when the patient's welfare is in conflict with institutional or other demands.

Justice

The practice of justice includes delivering care without discrimination or prejudice "in every situation" (ANA, 1985, p. 4). The principle of distributive justice often refers to the allocation of scarce resources, whether in giving care to an individual or participating in or planning a program. Major theories of justice (Beauchamp & Childress, 1994) include egalitarian (equal access), communitarian (justice that evolves through community traditions), and utilitarian (mixed criteria to maximize public utility). Utilitarian theories have commonly been practiced in western health care systems, but managed care and "the transvaluation of clinical values into economic ones" are removing traditional moral issues (Kleinman, 1997), including in the hospice "industry." The philosophy of hospice and palliative care is explicitly just in the treatment of individuals and of humanity (Saunders, 1978b). The practice of justice does not ignore injustice, and nursing acknowledges this: The nurse seeks to promote the acceptance of justice by others (ANA, 1985).

Decisions Near the End of Life

The ability of advanced knowledge and technology to maintain life and increased societal concern about quality of life and the shift from medical paternalism to patient self-determination have brought the issue of end-of-life decisions into sharp focus (Feinberg, 1997; Scanlon, 1998). Specific events have aroused intense public, legal, ethical, and other debate:

● Karen Ann Quinlan became comatose in 1976 as a result of alcohol and drug ingestion. Her parents fought successfully in court to have her taken off a respirator, and she unexpectedly lived 9 more years after being removed from life support.
● Nancy Cruzan was in a vegetative state as a result of an automobile accident in 1990. At the request of her parents and on the basis of testimony by two friends, her feeding tube was removed, and she died.
● Articles were published in the *Journal of the American Medical Association* (1988) and the *New England Journal of Medicine* (1991) in which physicians described assisting patients to commit suicide.
● A best-selling book of arguments for "self-deliverance" and suicide recipes (*Final Exit*) was published in 1991.
● The Patient Self-Determination Act was passed by the U.S. Congress in 1991, officially ending medical paternalism by promoting the use of advance directives.
● Dr. Jack Kevorkian ("Dr. Death") has been using a suicide machine to kill patients suffering from both physical and mental disorders since the early 1990s.
● In 1994, Oregon voters passed Proposition 16, which legalized physician-assisted suicide (PAS) under certain conditions. Appeals slowed the implementation of the law, but voters again affirmed the concept in 1997.
● In 1995, the SUPPORT study, published in the *Journal of the American Medical Association*, showed that advance directives were often not used or honored and that many patients con-

tinued to die painful, isolated, and technologically oriented deaths.

● The U.S. Supreme Court ruled in 1997 that there is no constitutional right to assistance in committing suicide and thus opened the door for states to make laws prohibiting *or* allowing assisted suicide. In 1998, Michigan (in response to Michigan resident Jack Kevorkian's activities) passed a law prohibiting assisted suicide. In late 1998 Dr. Kevorkian was charged with murder after videotaping himself euthanizing a patient.

Requests made or actions considered or taken to control the character of care or to end the life of the patient may include the following (AMA, 1992):

● Withholding or withdrawing life-sustaining treatment: This may include the often difficult-to-define extraordinary measures (resuscitation) or more usual measures, such as intravenous fluids or oxygen. There is no ethical or legal difference between withholding or withdrawing life-sustaining treatments or measures (ANA, 1994).
● Providing palliative treatment that may have fatal side effects: This is termed double-effect treatment or reasoning (Cavanaugh, 1996). The principle of double effect is most often encountered in situations of intractable symptoms, such as pain. The ANA's position is clear on this matter: "The increasing titration of medication to achieve adequate symptom control, even at the expense of maintaining life or hastening death secondarily is ethically justified" (ANA, 1995, p. 2).
● Euthanasia, that is, action taken to end a life for merciful purposes, which includes the following:
 1. Involuntary euthanasia performed on a competent person without that person's consent
 2. Nonvoluntary euthanasia performed on an incompetent person
 3. Voluntary euthanasia performed on a competent person at that person's request

(now often termed physician-assisted death [PAD])
● Assisted suicide: The difference between assisted suicide and assisted death or euthanasia is the degree of health professional participation. In the former, the professional facilitates the death, and in the latter, he or she directly causes death. PAS or PAD are the means by which patients may legally in some cases (currently only in Oregon) and sanctioned by tradition in other cases (see the previous discussion about specific events) bring life to an intentional end. The most common means of PAS are writing prescriptions or furnishing medications in sufficient amounts to cause death and with the knowledge that they will be used to commit suicide. Instructions on using the medications to cause death may be included. PAD goes a step farther and includes the physician helping administer the medication(s).

A key issue in the previous discussion is whether the action causes death in a person who would not otherwise die at the time of the action. The position of the American Society of Clinical Oncology (ASCO) on assisted suicide is to "neither condone nor condemn" (ASCO, 1998, p. 1987). Nursing, however, is more directive about the issue: "The nurse does not act deliberately to terminate the life of any person" (ANA, 1985, p. 3), a position sustained in the ANA's Position Statement on Assisted Suicide (1994).

While a full appraisal of the debate on euthanasia and assisted suicide or death is beyond the scope of this work, it may be helpful to explore a few of the key issues that exist within the fundamental question of assisted death. These are posed in the following list as questions.

● Does assisted suicide or death incontrovertibly violate the principle of nonmaleficence? If it does not, how well founded is the fear expressed by some that sanctioning assisted death could put its practitioners and society on a potentially destructive "slippery slope" that could end with violation of the most fundamental ethical principles? Of particular concern here is the possibility of sanctioned euthanasia among nonconsenting aged or incompetent people.

● Does the availability of sanctioned assisted suicide or death result in the termination of suffering among the terminally ill who choose this option?

● Is assisted suicide or death, radical though it may be, nevertheless almost a moral imperative in some cases of extraordinary circumstances and suffering? Most health care providers in this work have been witness to terrible suffering. Nevertheless, while struggling to develop competency in caring for people who are dying, some would question whether the number of unmanageable patients is great enough to warrant a change in centuries-old moral traditions (Brescia, 1991).

● Can guidelines on sanctioned assisted suicide or death be consistently interpreted and implemented? It is known that in the Netherlands for example, guidelines are interpreted and implemented in various ways and at times, ignored (AMA Council on Scientific Affairs, 1996).

● Does the availability of sanctioned assisted suicide or death increase individual autonomy? Some argue that the power of the physician is increased, while others assert that patient autonomy is increased.

● Assisted suicide or death can decrease the often crippling financial costs of advanced disease; might this mean that the commitment to care diminishes? Some find that there is little evidence for concern (Brock, 1992), while others posit a realistic danger that euthanasia, like other aspects of the health care system, would be used unequally in the poor and others without adequate medical coverage (Scofield, 1991).

● Would sanctioned euthanasia affect efforts for improvement in the competent care of the terminally ill? Unquestionably, suicidal ideation often stems from uncontrolled symptoms and other suffering, and beneficence— manifested as absolute dedication to relieving pain and suffering—is a moral imperative in terminal care.

Summary

Hospice and palliative care are fraught with nonacademic ethical issues and dilemmas. The nurse is confronted with decisions that profoundly affect the lives of patients, their families, themselves, and their colleagues. The ANA Nurses' Code addresses the fundamental ethical principles, but these issues are not easily addressed, nor are the dilemmas easily resolved. The struggle with these life and death questions is, however, one of the most fundamental and significant struggles, and nurses' efforts to act and react intelligently, responsibly, and morally within that struggle are imbued with an undeniable nobility.

REFERENCES

American Academy of Hospice and Palliative Medicine. (1997). *Comprehensive end-of-life care and physician-assisted suicide*[On-line]. Author.

American Medical Association, Council on Ethical and Judicial Affairs. (1992). Decisions near the end of life. *Journal of the American Medical Association, 267*(16), 2229–2233.

American Medical Association, Council on Scientific Affairs. (1996). Good care of the dying patient. *Journal of the American Medical Association, 275*(6), 474–478.

American Nurses Association. (1985). *Code for nurses with interpretive statements.* Kansas City, MO: Author.

American Nurses Association. (1994). *Position statement on assisted suicide.* Washington, DC: Author.

American Nurses Association. (1995). *Position statement on promotion of comfort and relief of pain in dying patients.* Washington, DC: Author.

American Society of Clinical Oncology. (1998). Cancer care during the last phase of life. *Journal of Clinical Oncology, 16*(5), 1986–1996.

Beauchamp, T. L., & Childress, J. F. (1994). *Principles of biomedical ethics* (4th ed.). New

York: Oxford University Press.

Bernal, E. W. (1992). The nurse as patient advocate. *Hastings Center Report, 22*(4), 18–23.

Brescia, F. J. (1991). Killing the known dying: Notes of a death watcher. *Journal of Pain and Symptom Management, 6*(5), 337–339.

Brock, D. W. (1992). Voluntary active euthanasia. *Hastings Center Report, 22*(2), 10–22.

Butow, P. N., Maclean, M., Dunn, S. M., Tattersall, M. H. N., & Boyer, M. J. (1997). The dynamics of change: Cancer patients' preferences for information, involvement, and support. *Annals of Oncology, 8,* 857–863.

Callahan, D. (1992). When self-determination runs amok. *Hastings Center Report, 22*(2), 52–55.

Caruso-Herman, D. (1989). Concerns for the dying patient and family. *Seminars in Oncology Nursing, 5*(2), 120–123.

Cavanaugh, T. A. (1996). The ethics of death-hastening or death-causing palliative analgesic administration to the terminally ill. *Journal of Pain and Symptom Management, 12*(4), 248–254.

Collins, J. (1998). Commentary: Symptom management in children at the end of life. *Journal of Pain and Symptom Management, 15*(4), 259–260.

Davison, B. J., & Degner, L. F. (1998). Promoting patient decision making in life-and-death situations. *Seminars in Oncology Nursing, 14*(2), 129–136.

Feinberg, A. W. (1997). Coming to terms with the end of life. *Hospital Practice,* December, 13–15.

Humphry, D. (1991). *Final exit.* Eugene, OR: The Hemlock Society.

Kleinman, A. (1997). Intimations of solidarity? The popular culture responds to assisted suicide. *Hastings Center Reports, 27*(5), 34–36.

Latimer, E. J. (1991). Ethical decision-making in the care of the dying and its application to clinical practice. *Journal of Pain and Symptom Management, 6*(5), 329–336.

Ramsey, P. (1970). *The patient as person.* New Haven: Yale University Press.

Roy, D. J., & MacDonald, N. (1998). Ethical issues in palliative care. In D. Doyle, G. W. C. Hanks, & N. MacDonald (Eds.), *Oxford textbook of palliative medicine* (2nd ed.) (pp. 97–138) Oxford: Oxford University Press.

Saunders, C. M. (1978a). Appropriate treatment, appropriate death. In C. M. Saunders (Ed.), *The management of terminal disease* (pp. 1–9). London: Edward Arnold.

Saunders, C. M. (1978b). The philosophy of terminal care. In C. M. Saunders (Ed.), *The management of terminal disease* (pp. 193–202). London: Edward Arnold.

Scanlon, C. (1998). Unraveling ethical issues in palliative care. *Seminars in Oncology Nursing, 14*(2), 137–144.

Scofield, G. R. (1991). Privacy (or liberty) and assisted suicide. *Journal of Pain and Symptom Management, 6*(5), 280–288.

SUPPORT Principal Investigators. (1995). A controlled trial to improve care for seriously ill hospitalized patients. *Journal of the American Medical Association, 274*(20), 1591–1598.

Thomasina, D. C. (1997). Ethical issues in cancer nursing practice. In S. I. Groenwald, M. H. Frogge, M. Goodman, & C. H. Yarbro (Eds.), *Cancer nursing: Principles and practice* (4th ed.) (pp. 1608–1624). Boston: Jones and Bartlett.

Van Eyes, J. (1991). The ethics of palliative care. *Journal of Palliative Care, 7*(3), 27–32.

CHAPTER 9

Stress and Health Care Providers

KEY POINTS

● Working with people who are dying is inherently stressful.

● In hospice, palliative care, and related settings, there are sources of stress other than being in the presence of dying and death.

● A variety of strategies exist to deal with stress. Recognition of manifestations of stress is an important and often difficult first step.

● To everything there is a season, and sometimes there is a season to pull back from the presence of suffering, dying, and death.

It is no surprise that it is stressful to work with people who are dying. Numerous books, studies, articles, and countless dissertations document sources of and responses to stress among health care providers. Sometimes it seems that so much data are generated in such detail that the object (health care providers) of the study becomes only an object to be compared with another object or group of objects.

This chapter looks at stress and burnout in hospice and palliative care. In working in hospice, palliative care, or other end-of-life environments, health care providers should maintain awareness that this work directly addresses the ultimate questions and issues of life. Of course it is hard work, and of course it is stressful.

Manifestations and Sources of Stress

Manifestations (signs and symptoms, sometimes overlapping) of stress reaction or burnout among health care providers (Olson, 1997; Vachon, 1997; Vachon, 1998) include the following:

● *Psychological*: Anxiety, depression, unhappiness, boredom, frustration, (groundless) guilt, low self-esteem or sense of inadequacy, or alcohol or other drug (including prescription) abuse are obvious indications of a problem.
● *Physical*: Fatigue, headache, sleep pattern disturbances, appetite changes with weight loss or gain, abdominal pain, diarrhea, consti-

pation, and physical symptoms of anxiety (eg, tight chest, heart palpitations, shortness of breath, dizziness) or depression (eg, psychomotor retardation, fatigue, constipation, decreased libido) can all be indications of difficulty managing stress.

● *Social:* Family conflict or lack of "a life" is common among staff working long hours or in demanding environments or who are frequently on-call.

● *Spiritual:* All the basic spiritual needs or issues may be impacted by work-related stress. The work or life outside the work may begin to feel meaningless and hopeless, and a sense of isolation from patients, others, and God may occur.

● *Professional:* Any of the above may carry over into professional life. Development of a *pattern* of conflict with patients, colleagues, or others is a common manifestation, as is a pattern of low morale or overattachment or underattachment to clients. Increased absenteeism or changing jobs out of frustration may also occur.

Sources of Stress

To understand stress and burnout, it is helpful to identify some of the potential sources of stress that exist when caring for people who are terminally ill (Holland, Rei, Kufe, & Bast, 1997; Olson, 1997; Vachon, 1998):

● *The specific nature or characteristics of the work itself:* A major source of stress in working with people who are dying is the regular contact with the most fundamental human fear—fear of death—and with suffering, hopelessness, meaninglessness, and uncertainty. Related to this is the psychological and social isolation that may attend this unique work (others' everyday concerns may seem trivial).

● *The general nature or characteristics of the work itself:* Work in any area of health care is often characterized by too much work, too

much responsibility, role ambiguity, disrespect, and too little pay.

● *Patients and families:* Working in terminal care often means working with people who are anxious, angry, or depressed. Some patients and families are people with whom one otherwise might not associate. Others are people with whom one becomes close. In either case, confrontation with death and suffering cannot help but be internalized to some extent.

● *Personality or individual variables:* Each staff member brings a unique grouping of strengths and liabilities to the health care setting, and these influence the perception of and response to stress.

Regardless of the specific sources of stress for a particular person or group, the undeniable fact is that stress exists, and it will not go away. What can be done about stress—what *must* be done—is to modify the response to stressors. There are organizational measures for dealing with stress, but in the final analysis, it is the responsibility of each individual to deal with her or his stress.

Strategies for Dealing with Stress

The following are suggestions for strategies in dealing with stress. It is unlikely that anyone will use all the following. However, most should be operational:

● *Recognition of stress:* The first step in a healthy response to stress is to recognize and accept that stress exists and that everyone who works with the dying is at risk for negative effects of stress. Whether one is feeling the effects of stress or not, measures should be taken to prevent its negative effects. People do not always feel stress as such. Rather than recognize feelings for what they are, some may experience them instead as the desire to have a few more drinks (and a little more often), to enter into an impulsive relationship, to get angry more often (justifiably, of course), or as a host of other behaviors that seem, if not perfectly correct, then at least as viable as any other kind of truthful response.

● *Education and experience*: Education and experience are correlated with decreased burnout (Driedger & Cox, 1991). In other words, expertise, or competence, is an effective means of decreasing anxiety and stress. Competent practitioners do better work and tend to feel better about themselves and their work and so do their patients. The first and most important competence is clinical competence.

● *Communication skills*: Among the other important competencies is the ability to communicate and understand other people's communications, particularly in stressful situations. The ability to deal with other people's (and one's own) anger is especially important. Sociocultural competencies, such as learning about cultures other than one's own, are also essential in this multicultural society.

● *Social support*: The support of others is a vital, positive factor for working effectively with people who are dying (Holland et al., 1997). Basically, this work is almost impossible to do alone. While other sources exist, it is not uncommon, though this seems surprising, to find situations where support from colleagues is lacking or inadequate. Staff meetings or support groups are a common means of generating social or organizational support among peers.

● The freedom to express feelings—a component of some social support systems, but not of others—is important. Formal case conferences, for example, are not usually appropriate forums for expressing strong feelings. Team meetings may be more appropriate, and team support groups are often the most appropriate. A consistent need to express grief, anger, and so forth probably indicates a high level of stress and unmet needs. Whatever the setting, it is important that every practitioner have a person or people in whom she or he can confide any of their feelings about the work.

As noted at the beginning of this chapter, social support on a higher level may come from the awareness that this work directly addresses the ultimate questions and issues of life. Health care providers should look at the work they do (not at others' opinions of it) and recognize its importance.

● *Spiritual support*: Spiritual support is another logical and often neglected aspect of dealing with the stress inherent in working with people who are suffering and dying. Whether or not one is aware of them, spiritual values are intrinsic to human life (Jung, 1953). While it is inappropriate to urge personal spiritual values on patients or other staff, it is equally inappropriate to exclude those values from our own needs and practices in a workplace where dying and death are the order of every day.

● The search for spiritual support has become increasingly more complicated in western society. Inspirational or self-help books, programs, and organizations abound, but the seeker—especially when the need is greatest, as is the case in working with the dying—can ultimately remain more perplexed than nourished. Regardless of one's experience and outlook, throughout human history, people have come together in places of worship to find meaning, hope, relatedness, or simply common cause with one another. The spiritual healing power of tradition and ritual alone, particularly when it touches chords in early memory and experience, is sometimes overlooked.

● *Reasonable goals*: Setting reasonable goals is another factor essential to minimizing or managing stress. If a practitioner works toward unreasonable patient goals, such as keeping all symptoms well managed and all family relationships reconciled, and simultaneously toward unreasonable practitioner goals, such as remaining understanding in all circumstances and always meeting all needs, then failure, frustration, and high stress are the inevitable outcome. If, on the other hand, goals are individualized and reasonable, in terms of each patient and of self, then failure, frustration, and stress are decreased. Prioritizing goals also helps. Sometimes even reasonable goals cannot be achieved, hence the question, which goals should come first and which last?

● *Collaborative relationships with patients and families*: A constructive, cooperative relationship with patients and families is helpful in dealing with grief and stress. This sort of relationship is characterized by balance between overinvolvement and underinvolvement with patients and families. Overinvolvement is characterized by a pattern of nurse–patient relationships consistently based on emotion. Such relationships actually reflect nurses relating to their own responses to patients, rather than to the patients themselves (Travelbee, 1971). Underinvolvement is characterized by a pattern of interacting with patients and families as though they were problems or situations in need of diagnoses or burdens. Paradoxically, a pattern of deep involvement with individual patients and families is advocated by some as a means of humanizing practice (Martin & Julian, 1987).

● *Achieving a sense of closure*: Another aspect of nurse–patient relationships that reduces grief and stress is achieving a sense of closure when the patient dies (Eakes, 1990). Whether through spending time with a family after the death, attending the funeral, or by other means, it is generally helpful to find some way of achieving a sense of closure in some nurse–patient relationships.

● *Lifestyle management*: Taking measures to live in a healthier manner is a key aspect of modifying the response to stress. Taking time completely away from work; making time for physical exercise, improved diet, adequate sleep, and conscious pacing of life in general (and of practice in particular); separating work from home; and using drugs and alcohol judiciously are the basic measures to improve lifestyle. Time for reflection is also important. Vachon (1997) suggests using the 10-year rule in making decisions related to lifestyle management: "Ten years from now, which will matter more, that this (task) was a few days or weeks late or that I consistently sacrificed myself or members of my personal network for career goals, many of which may have been imposed by others?"

● *Counseling*: Sometimes the healer is wounded and needs outside help. Individual or group counseling outside the work environment is indicated when regularly used measures are not helpful or when the stress becomes overwhelming.

● *Organizational measures*: While individuals need to take primary responsibility for coping with their own stress, it is important that organizations also address the issue. A vital organizational or "environmental" coping mechanism is for staff members to feel that they belong to a team (Holland et al., 1997). Building a team usually requires mindful effort on the part of formal or informal leaders. Efforts to incorporate group dynamics, motivational techniques, and other aspects of team building are well spent. Other organizational measures to reduce or help staff better cope with stress include responding to and acting on staff problems as much as possible, working to create a milieu that is conducive to coping with stress, taking care in staff selection, and ensuring that administrative policies are congruent with human needs (Vachon, 1987).

A Final Thought

Sometimes it is just too much. Why on earth did anyone ever think that working with skill and grace in hospice, palliative care, oncology, critical care, and so forth was something that could be done indefinitely? Some people should have left this field a long time ago. It is okay to be tired, to be ready for a change, to do something else. To have done this work at all is a blessing and an honor.

REFERENCES

Driedger, S. M., & Cox, D. (1991). Burnout in nurses who care for PWAs. *AIDS Patient Care, 5*(4), 197–203.

Eakes, G. G. (1990). Grief resolution in hospice nurses. *Nursing and Health Care, 11*(5), 243–248.

Holland, J. F., Rei, E., Kufe, D. W., & Bast, R. C. (1997). Principles of medical oncology. In J. F. Holland, R. C. Bast, D. L. Morton, E. Frei, D. W. Kufe, & R. C. Weichselbaum (Eds.), *Cancer medicine* (4th ed.) (pp. 755–765). Baltimore: Williams & Wilkins.

Jung, C. G. (1953). Psychology and alchemy. In J. Jacobi & R. F. C. Hull (Eds.), *C.G. Jung: Psychological reflections* (pp. 338–339). Princeton, NJ: Princeton University Press.

Martin, C. A., & Julian, R. A. (1987). Causes of stress and burnout in physicians caring for the chronically and terminally ill. In L. F. Paradis (Ed.), *Stress and burnout among providers caring for the terminally ill and their families*. New York: The Haworth Press.

Olson, M. (1997). *Healing the dying*. Albany: Delmar Publishers.

Travelbee, J. (1971). *Interpersonal aspects of nursing* (2nd ed.). Philadelphia: F. A. Davis.

Vachon, M. L. S. (1997). Staff burnout: Sources, diagnosis, management, and prevention. In E. Bruera & R. K. Portenoy (Eds.), *Topics in palliative care* (Vol. 2) (pp. 247–293). New York: Oxford University press.

Vachon, M. L. S. (1998). Caring for the caregiver in oncology and palliative care. *Seminars in Oncology Nursing, 14*(2), 152–157.

Vachon, M. L. S. (1987). *Occupational stress in the care of the critically ill, the dying, and the bereaved*. Washington, D.C.: Hemisphere Publishing.

Pain and Symptom Management

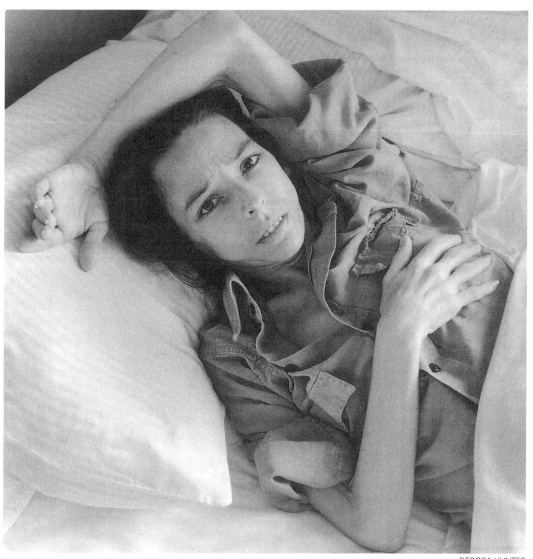

DEBORA HUNTER

Managing symptoms is the *sine qua non* of palliative care. Pain is often the most problematic and feared symptom, but other symptoms such as dyspnea, nausea and vomiting, cachexia, fatigue, and confusion can be souces of immense suffering.

The prevalence of pain in patients with advanced cancer ranges from 50%–80% depending on tumor type, research model, and other intrinsic or extrinsic factors (Foley, 1997). In most patients with cancer, the problem of unmanaged pain is unnecessary and due to errors in or lack of assessment or proper treatment (American Pain Society [APS], 1992). Despite significant advances in knowledge of pain treatment modalities, results are too often poor, even in some hospices (Abraham, 1998; APS, 1992).

The first section of Pain and Symptom Management (Chapters 10-12) offers clinical responses to the problem of pain, including basic principles of pain management; an overview of types of pain, pain syndromes, and assessment techniques; and techniques of pain management. While pain at the the end of life has been the focus of much research, other symptoms have received less attention. Priorities for research on other symptoms include cachexia, fatigue, nausea and vomiting, and especially, dyspnea (American Society of Clinical Oncology, 1998). The second section of Pain and Symptom Management is divided into chapters about symptoms and/or body systems: neurologic, respiratory, skin, oral, gastrointestinal, genitourinary, dehydration/fatigue/ sleep, oncologic emergencies and paraneoplastic syndromes, and imminent death.

There is more to pain and symptom management than clinical issues. Some of the social, cultural, and political issues that influence pain and other symptoms are discussed in Chapter 10. Underlying any change in negative influences within the nurse's control is the issue of attitude toward pain and symptom management. If the attitude is one of acceptance of health care system traditions of patients living in unnecessary pain, then patients will continue to live in unnecessary pain. If the attitude is one of searching for answers to end-of-life problems and not accepting the status quo, then fewer patients will live in unnecessary pain.

Change—even for the better—does not come easily. However, "pain initiatives" across the western world are beginning to show across-the-board improvements in pain status when institutional and individual resources are dedicated to improving pain management. These efforts should also be brought to bear on the other sources of suffering at the end-of-life.

REFERENCES

Abraham, J.L. (1998). Promoting symptom control in palliative care. *Seminars in Oncology Nursing, 14*(2), 95–109.

American Pain Society. (1992). *Principles of analgesic use in the treatment of acute pain and cancer pain* (3rd ed.). Skokie, IL: Author.

American Society of Clinical Oncology. (1998) Cancer care at the end of life Journal of Clinical Oncology, 16(5), 1986–1996.

Foley, K.M. (1997). Management of cancer pain. In V.T. DeVita, S. Hellman, & S.A. Rosenburg (Eds.), *Cancer: Principles and practice of oncology* (5th ed.) (pp. 2807–2841). Philadelphia: Lippincott-Raven.

Pain: Principles of Management

In years past, pain was considered only as a physiologic phenomenon. Unfortunately, this view of pain is still held by some nurses and physicians. Pain, however, is a highly individual and multidimensional phenomenon, with numerous influences on its magnitude and quality (Dalton & Lamb, 1995; Kjaer, 1997). Pain is the most frequently observed symptom of advanced cancer and is virtually universal among patients dying from AIDS (Donnelly & Walsh, 1995; Kaplan et al., 1996). The relief of pain and other symptoms is usually the first step in addressing the problem of suffering.

Pain and Suffering

Pain is defined as "an unpleasant sensory and emotional experience associated with actual or potential tissue damage, or described in terms of such damage" (American Pain Society [APS], 1992, p. 2). Suffering, on the other hand, is personal distress or affliction and to "some extent is universal among people who are dying, even those who have no physical discomfort" (Byock, 1997, p. 82). A person in pain may suffer, and a person not in pain also may suffer. In some cases, a person in pain may not suffer, such as in a person who experiences the "Anzio effect," in which pain is part of some good news, such as a war wound sufficiently serious to result in leaving combat.

Suffering is a unique and lived experience related to loss and may involve all dimensions of being. Although it is a fundamental personal and human experience, it should not be assumed to be present or absent in a particular person or group. To intervene in suffering, it is necessary to reach some understanding of the experience of the person who is suffering. Because the expression of suffering is more accessible to practitioners than the experience, it is necessary in most cases to take a holistic and team approach to the problem (Kahn & Steeves, 1995; Waller & Caroline, 1996).

Previously it was noted that the purpose of hospice and palliative care is to relieve suffering and promote healing. The effort to reduce suffering is the practice of mercy—the heart of hospice and palliative care. People who work with people who are dying do not often use words such as mercy, compassion, and kindness. They are more comfortable with terms that fit better with goals, objectives, and outcomes; however, their higher role and purpose are practicing mercy and succoring the suffering.

Influences on Pain

Many physiologic, psychological, sociocultural, spiritual, and institutional factors can positively or negatively influence the experience of pain (Cleland & Gebhart, 1997; McGuire, 1996; Waller & Caroline, 1996). Although practitioners and researchers tend to focus on factors that exacerbate pain, the absence or presence of some factors can positively influence the pain experience. Factors that may positively or negatively influence pain and suffering include the following:

● The nature or type of the pain (eg, neuropathic versus somatic; rapidly accelerating versus stable)
● Presence or absence of other symptoms, such as nausea or dyspnea
● Fear or lack of fear of pain
● Presence or absence of other fears or anxieties, especially those surrounding death
● Previous success or failure in coping with pain
● Depression or emotional well-being
● Spiritual distress or well-being
● Family or other interpersonal conflict or support
● Hopelessness (despair) or hope

● The meaning of the pain to the patient, family, and staff
● Preconceived notions on the part of practitioners (eg, that there should be less pain than the patient is experiencing or that pain should or should not be experienced)

One of the worst situations is that in which pain is combined with other factors, and the other factors and the pain begin to reinforce and amplify one another. For example, pain leads to anxiety, anxiety to conflict, conflict to anxiety, anxiety to physical tension and increased pain, increased pain to depression, and so on, in a vicious downward cycle (Fig. 10-1).

Physiology of Pain

Though an age-old problem, the pathophysiology of pain is not yet fully understood. A complete discussion of the pathophysiology of pain is beyond the scope of this book, but a summary of salient points (Foley, 1997; Paice, 1996) may shed some light on how pain occurs.

Nociceptive pain occurs when there is insult to superficial or deep structures, with tissue damage causing the release of stimulatory substances, such as prostaglandins, serotonin, and histamine. These excite sensory nerve endings, which depolarize and transmit the nociceptive impulse (painful message) through the peripheral nervous system by way of the highly myelinated, rapidly conducting A delta fibers and unmyelinated, slower conducting C-fibers (both of which are nociceptors). These lead to the dorsal horn of the spinal cord where sensory input is largely modulated through release of neurotransmitters, excitatory amino acids, and other substances. The neurotransmitters cause excitation within ascending nervous tracts leading to the brain stem and medulla and then to the thalamus where cognitive and emotional perceptions of the impulses occur. Visceral and somatic pain are examples of nociceptive pain. Non-nociceptive

Pain begins
↘
Anxiety
↙
Interpersonal difficulties
↘
Increased anxiety
↙
Physical tension
↘
Increased pain
↙
Depression
↘
Increased pain and despair

FIGURE 10–1. Pain Cycle: A Downward Spiral

pain (ie, neuropathic pain) occurs when there is pathologic or functional change in the peripheral or central nervous systems (Martin & Hagen, 1997).

Descending pathways (from the brain to the spinal cord) also modulate or inhibit the pain transmission through actions such as the release of substances, such as serotonin and norepinephrine. Opiate receptors are found on ascending and descending pain pathways and elsewhere in the central nervous system.

Factors Leading to Problems in Pain Management

Despite significant advances in pain management, pain remains a serious and unnecessary problem for many patients with advanced disease (Ahmedzai & Brooks, 1997; Levin, Berry, & Leiter, 1998). Pain is a serious problem because it results in vast suffering, and the suffering is unnecessary. Simple means exist to manage pain in approximately 90% of patients with pain from cancer (Schug, Zech, & Dörr, 1990), and alternative means exist to treat the pain in the other 10% (Foley, Bonica, &

Ventafridda, 1990), but pain treatment in cancer and AIDS continues to be inadequate and inconsistent. The problem is readily addressed, but sadly, it could have been handled by now: The "most common reason for unrelieved pain . . . is the failure of staff to routinely assess pain and pain relief" (APS, 1992, p. 2). Other reasons for unrelieved pain are as follows:

● Some nurses and physicians lack knowledge about currently accepted concepts of pain management.
● Staff or patients have social or cultural fears or myths concerning cancer pain and using opioids to manage the pain. The two most pernicious of these are that pain is inevitable and that using opioids is bad and will result in loss of control and addiction. Staff also fear patient respiratory depression.
● Some patients, and unfortunately, staff believe that pain is a given in cancer.
● There are social or legal impediments to using opioids (ie, administrative [nonmedical] systems monitor narcotic prescriptions).
● There may be problems in communication among staff and between staff and patients. Such problems can be disease related, interpersonal, cultural, or linguistic.
● Certain disease characteristics are more likely to result in poor pain control. These include neuropathic pain, bone pain, rapid disease progression, metastatic disease, and pain of rapid onset and brief duration (Ahmedzai & Brooks, 1997; Foley, 1997).
● Certain patient characteristics are associated with poor pain control: eg, expressing suffering and psychological difficulties through pain and difficulty expressing feelings in general.

Principles of Effective Pain Management

The World Health Organization (WHO, 1986) provides an uncomplicated, three-step oral drug therapy to manage pain in patients with pain from cancer (see the section Managing

Specific Pain Situations in Chapter 12). WHO guidelines for managing pain are essentially the same as those promoted since the mid-1960s by Saunders and others in the hospice movement. For the approximately 10% of patients whose pain is not manageable through the WHO therapy, other effective techniques exist (Foley et al., 1990; APS, 1992), and these are discussed later in the chapter. The following is a list of basic principles for effective pain management (Kjaer, 1997; Waller & Caroline, 1996):

● Whenever possible, treat the cause of the pain, especially if the pathology may further impact the quality of the patient's life.
● Use medications or techniques appropriate to the severity and specific type of pain (see Chapter 12).
● Give medications in amounts sufficient to control the pain and at intervals appropriate to the medication's duration of action. Understand that frequent dose changes may be required, especially early in treatment. When changing medications, use equianalgesic conversions (see Chapter 12).
● Use noninvasive or oral medications when possible. Controlled release morphine is the first drug of choice for patients with chronic cancer pain.
● Give medications around the clock at regular intervals (prophylactically) based on knowledge of phamacokinetics and duration of action so that a relatively constant titer is maintained, and the patient does not reexperience pain. Awaken the patient to receive medications on schedule.
● Use adjuvant medications, such as non-steroidal anti-inflammatory drugs, cortico-steroids, anticonvulsants, antidepressants, and phenothiazines, as indicated by the type of pain, but avoid polypharmacy.
● Assess for and treat side effects or complications, and anticipate problems when a side effect is likely (eg, constipation from narcotics or nausea in a client with a history of nausea). All patients and families should have instructions and means *on hand* to manage breakthrough pain.
● Assess for tolerance: As noted previously, some patients are reluctant to complain. Regular assessment is thus necessary.
● Assess for and intervene in psychosocial and spiritual issues related to the pain.
● Do not look only to pharmacology or to any other single means of controlling pain. A variety of effective psychological interventions exist, and there are situations in which radiation, neurosurgery, or other interventions are the treatment of choice.
● Approach each patient as an individual who brings unique beliefs, strengths, and weaknesses to the immense experience of cancer pain.
● Teach these principles of pain management to the patient, family, and others involved with care.

Goals, Objectives, and Responsibilities in Pain Management

The goal of pain management in patients with chronic cancer pain is to "achieve continuous suppression of pain" (Babul, Darke, Anslow, & Krishnamurthy, 1992, p. 400). Complete eradication of pain without some sedation is difficult to achieve. The effort is nevertheless directed toward the golden mean of a completely pain free and completely alert patient. Pain is approached in two ways: as a problem in itself and as a means of preventing or minimizing other problems. This second approach is sometimes neglected, especially in palliative care.

Nursing care is the cornerstone of pain management (Swenson, 1997), and the nurse's responsibility in pain management is clear: Nurses are responsible and accountable for implementation and coordination of the plan for management of cancer pain (Spross, McGuire, & Schmitt, 1991). The nursing scope of practice in managing pain, established by the Oncology Nursing Society (Spross et al., 1991), is as follows:

- Describing the phenomenon
- Identifying aggravating and relieving factors
- Determining the meaning of the pain to the individual
- Determining etiology
- Determining definitions of optimal relief
- Deriving nursing diagnoses
- Assisting in determining interventions
- Evaluating efficacy of interventions

Another key responsibility is to "titrate prescribed analgesics and adjuvant drugs" (Wilkie, 1990, p. 339). Clearly, nurses' roles in managing pain and other symptoms are expanding.

REFERENCES

Ahmedzai, S., & Brooks, D. (1997). Transdermal Fentanyl versus sustained relief morphine in cancer pain: Preference, efficacy, and quality of life. *Journal of Pain and Symptom Management, 13*(5), 254–261.

American Pain Society. (1992). *Principles of analgesic use in the treatment of acute pain and cancer pain* (3rd ed.). Skokie, IL: Author.

Babul, N., Darke, A. C., Anslow, J. A., & Krishnamurthy, T. N. (1992). Pharmacokinetics of two novel rectal controlled-release morphine formulations. *Journal of Pain and Symptom Management, 7*(7), 400–405.

Byock, I. (1997). *Dying well.* New York: Riverhead Books.

Cleland, C. L., & Gebhart, G. F. (1997) Principles of nocioception and pain. In *Springhouse Guide to Expert Pain Management.* Springhouse, PA: Springhouse.

Dalton, J. A., & Lamb, C. (1995). Tailoring treatment approaches to the individualized needs of cancer patients with pain. *Cancer Nursing, 18*(3), 180–188.

Donnelly, S., & Walsh, T. D. (1995). The symptoms of advanced cancer. *Seminars in Oncology, 22*(2, Suppl. 3), 67–72.

Foley, K. M. (1997). Management of cancer pain. In V. T. DeVita, S. Hellman, & S. A. Rosenburg (Eds.), *Cancer: Principles and practice of oncology* (5th ed.) (pp. 2807–2841). Philadelphia: Lippincott-Raven.

Foley, K. M., Bonica, J. J., & Ventafridda, V. (Eds.). (1990). *Proceedings of the Second International Congress on Cancer Pain.* New York: Raven Press.

Kahn, D. L., & Steeves, R. H. (1995). The significance of suffering in cancer care. *Seminars in Oncology Nursing, 11*(1), 9–16.

Kaplan, R., Conant, M., Cundiff, D., Maciewicz, R., Ries, K., Slagle, S., Slywka, J., & Buckley, B. (1996). Sustained release morphine sulfate in the management of pain associated with acquired immune deficiency syndrome. *Journal of Pain and Symptom Management, 12*(3), 150–160.

Kjaer, M. (1997). The therapy of cancer pain and its integration into a comprehensive supportive care strategy. *Annals of Oncology, 8*(Suppl. 3), s15–s19.

Levin, M. L., Berry, J. I., & Leiter, J. (1998). Management of pain in terminally ill patients: Physician reports of knowledge, attitudes, and behavior. *Journal of Pain and Symptom Management, 15*(1), 27–40.

Martin, L. A., & Hagen, N. A. (1997). Neuropathic pain in cancer patients: Mechanisms, syndromes, and clinical controversies. *Journal of Pain and Symptom Management, 14*(2), 99–117.

McGuire, D. B. (1996). The multiple dimensions of cancer pain: A framework for assessment and management. In D. B. McGuire, C. H. Yarbro, & B. R. Ferrell (Eds.), *Cancer pain management* (2nd ed.) (pp. 1–17), Boston: Jones and Bartlett.

Paice, J. A. (1996). Pain. In S. L. Groenwald, M. H. Frogge, M. Goodman, & C. H. Yarbro (Eds.), *Cancer symptom management* (pp. 100–125), Boston: Jones and Bartlett.

Schug, S. A., Zech, D., & Dörr, U. (1990). Cancer pain management according to WHO analgesic guidelines. *Journal of Pain and Symptom Management, 5*(1), 27–32.

Spross, J. A., McGuire, D. B., & Schmitt, R. M. (1990). Oncology Nursing Society position paper on cancer pain. Part III: Nursing administration, nursing administration, pediatric cancer pain, and appendices. *Oncology Nursing Forum, 17*(6), 943.

Spross, J. A., McGuire, D. B., & Schmitt, R. M. (1991). *Oncology Nursing Society position paper on cancer pain.* Pittsburgh: Oncology Nursing Press.

Swenson, C. J. (1997). Pain management. In S. E.

Otto (Ed.), *Oncology nursing* (3rd ed.) (pp. 746–787), St. Louis: C.V. Mosby.

Taylor, E. J., & Ersek, M. (1996). Ethical and spiritual dimensions of cancer pain management. In D. B. McGuire, C. H. Yarbro, & B. R. Ferrell (Eds.), *Cancer pain management* (2nd ed.) (pp. 41–60), Boston: Jones and Bartlett.

Waller, A., & Caroline, N. L. (1996). *Palliative care in cancer.* Boston: Butterworth-Heineman.

Wilkie, D. J. (1990). Cancer pain management: State of the art nursing care. *Nursing Clinics of North America, 25*(2), 331–343.

World Health Organization. (1986). *Cancer pain relief and palliative care.* Geneva: Author.

Zhukovsky, D. S., Gorowski, E., Hausdorff, J., Napolitano, B., & Lesser, M. (1995). Unmet analgesic needs in cancer patients. *Journal of Pain and Symptom Management, 10*(2), 113–119.

CHAPTER 11

Pain: Assessment

KEY POINTS

- Pain from cancer, human immunodeficiency virus (HIV) infection, and other disorders can be classified as acute, chronic, intermittent, or mixed.

- Pain can be further classified as visceral, somatic, neuropathic, or mixed.

- An awareness of the many specific pain syndromes provides further understanding of pain in advanced disease.

- All staff who assess pain should use the same tool, and the assessment of pain should cover specific parameters.

- Several effective tools exist for the assessment of pain; these tools should be used, as should the research on which they are based.

Classification of Pain

Cancer pain syndromes, first elucidated by Kathleen Foley in 1975, provide a means by which pain can be classified and clinically understood. Understanding pain syndromes and other characteristics of pain helps determine (1) etiologies and thus treatment and (2) the potential for complications of advancing disease.

Understanding the classifications and characteristics of the different types of pain is important in the early clinical identification of disease progression and identification of development of complications. Moreover, there are differences in the treatment of different types of pain and different syndromes.

The two general types of pain are acute and chronic, and these may be understood both in terms of temporal aspects and their meaning(s) to and effects on the patient.

Acute pain results from tissue damage, has a beginning and end, and usually resolves when the damage is resolved. Acute pain is generally associated with physical signs, such as tachycardia, hypertension, diaphoresis, mydriasis, and pallor (American Pain Society [APS], 1992).

Chronic pain is "the persistence of pain for more than three months, with a less well-defined temporal onset" than acute pain (Foley, 1997, p. 2810). Bonica (1990) notes that chronic pain persists "beyond the usual course of an acute disease or a reasonable time for an injury to heal or . . . is associated with a chronic pathologic process that causes continuous pain or the pain recurs at intervals for months or years" (p. 19). Although at least the initial mechanisms are the same in the etiology of chronic and acute pain, chronic pain is more complex than acute, both in terms of pathophysiology (of the pain itself and in its effects on other symptoms) and global effects on the patient's life (Foley, 1997). Chronic pain is not necessarily accompanied by the physical signs characteristic of acute pain.

Cancer pain can be acute, chronic, intermittent, or mixed (APS, 1992) and because of the global nature of the disease, can also be a combination of these, as can pain in HIV infection. Cancer pain is further classified physiologically as somatic, visceral, or neuropathic:

● Somatic pain is described as constant, localized, aching, gnawing, or sharp, such as pain from bony metastases or following surgery (Foley, 1997), with bone pain being a common cause of severe somatic pain in patients with cancer. Bone pain is often worse at night and may not be relieved by lying down (Coleman, 1997).

● Visceral pain is described as constant, poorly localized, deep, or squeezing and is sometimes referred to cutaneous sites. Abdominal or thoracic viscera are the origin of visceral pain, and examples include shoulder pain from diaphragmatic paralysis or liver or lung metastases, pancreatic pain, and pain from bowel obstruction. Acute visceral pain may be accompanied by autonomic symptoms, such as nausea and vomiting (Foley, 1997).

● Neuropathic pain is described as burning, stabbing, shocklike, or viselike and may occur "on a background of burning, constricting sensation" (Payne, 1990, p. 22). There are three types of dysesthesias, or "unpleasant abnormal sensation, whether spontaneous or evoked" (Lindbloom et al., 1986): (1) Allodynia is pain that results from a stimulus that does not normally cause pain but rather typically would cause a feeling of pressure or temperature. (2) Hyperalgesia is exaggerated pain from a stimulus that normally would cause less pain. (3) Hyperpathia is an exaggerated response to a stimulus, especially a repeated stimulus (Martin & Hagen, 1997). While not referred,

neurologic pain can be projected to the a dermatome (Walsh, 1989). Brachial plexopathy due to Pancoast's tumor or breast cancer, sacral plexopathy, postherpetic neuralgia, and phantom limb pain are examples of neuropathic etiologies. There are three major categories of neuropathic pain: (1) deafferentation pain from damage, such as from incision or trauma to an ascending afferent pathway; (2) sympathetically maintained pain from trauma; and (3) peripheral neuropathic pain from nerve injury, such as that from chemotherapy (Martin & Hagen, 1997).

These classes of pain may occur alone or in combination, with most patients with cancer having both somatic and visceral and 15% to 20% of patients with cancer having a more difficult to manage neuropathic pain (Foley, 1997). Somatic and visceral pain may also be combined with neuropathic pain, such as in tumor infiltration of nerve and spine. Somatic and visceral pain may also "be complicated by sympathetically maintained pain," which is described as "severe, burning . . . with dysesthesias and hyperpathia, as well as skin and bone changes" (Payne, 1989, p. 2267).

Somatic and visceral pain respond well to treatment by reduction of the tumor, opioids plus adjuvant medications, and sometimes neurosurgical or anesthetic treatment. Neuropathic pain does not respond as well to these treatments and is thus more challenging to treat. Adjuvant analgesics, including tricyclic antidepressants, anticonvulsants, local anesthetics, neuroleptics, and other measures assume a greater importance in neuropathic pain (Martin & Hagen, 1997). The management of pain is described in greater detail in Chapter 12.

Pain Syndromes

This section is an introduction to common pain syndromes. Readers are referred to Foley (1997), Martin & Hagen (1997), and other experts for more detailed information on specific cancer pain syndromes. Direct tumor involvement accounts for most pain in most patients with cancer, with invasion of bone being "probably the most common" cause of pain in patients with cancer (Springhouse, 1997, p. 116). Back pain may be a sign of spinal cord compression and hence should be carefully evaluated.

Pain from Bony Metastases

This pain is somatic but may involve parts of the nervous system:

● Generalized or multifocal involvement of bone, including multiple bony metastases and expansion of marrow are the most frequent causes of bone pain. Besides vertebrae, early metastases are commonly found in ribs and pelvis. Later metastases are found in the skull, femora, humeri, scapulae, and sternum (Enck, 1991).
● Metastasis to the base of skull usually results in regional pain as the first symptom; cranial nerve involvement, other neurologic signs, and changes in the range of motion of the neck are common.
● Metastasis to vertebral bodies results in regional pain, which is the first and sometimes only symptom. Central back pain (90%) with or without radicular pain is the most common. Neurologic signs and symptoms may follow (eg, motor followed by sensory impairment). The outcome of untreated vertebral body metastases may be spinal cord compression, an oncologic emergency that is discussed more completely under neurologic problems. Quick action is required when vertebral involvement is suspected. Signs and symptoms are related to the (spinal) level of involvement, except that pain is sometimes referred (eg, from L_1 or T_{12} to the ipsilateral iliac crest or sacroiliac joint).

Pain From Invasion of Viscera

This pain is visceral but may involve parts of the nervous system:

● Pain from invasion, compression, distension, or stretching of viscera (eg, pancreas, stomach, intestine) may be dull, boring, lancinating, or colicky, depending on site and other factors. Pain from hepatic metastases is of two types: most patients have right upper quadrant body wall pain; some have poorly localized abdominal pain radiating to flanks and back (Waldman, Feldstein, Donohoe, & Waldman, 1988). Related syndromes include peritoneal carcinomatosis and malignant perineal pain.
● Obstruction of a hollow viscus (any large internal organ) may result in cramping or colicky pain and loss of organ function. Intestinal and ureteral obstruction are examples.

Neuropathic Pain Syndromes

● Pain secondary to pathology in cranial nerves results in cranial neuralgias and may include bone destruction and somatic pain and neurologic abnormalities, such as palsies, numbness, weakness, Horner's syndrome (unilateral ptosis, miosis, sinking eyeball, and anhidrosis and flushing of the affected side), and others.
● Postherpatic neuralgia may persist for 2 or more months after the infection.
● Tumor-related mononeuropathy, such as rib metastases, may cause intercostal nerve injury (or neuropathies elsewhere according to lesions, eg, extremities).
● Other neuralgias may occur from cancer involvement of any sensory nerves or other disease-related pain.
● Radiculopathies (dermatomal pain) may be unilateral or bilateral and are exacerbated by coughing, sneezing, reclining, and other activity. Headache and neurologic deficits may occur, depending on the etiology of the pain. Because the origin of the pain in patients with cancer may be epidural or leptomeningeal mass, the possibility of spinal cord compression should always be considered. Radiculopathies may also be encountered in patients with AIDS.
● There are three types of nerve plexi syndromes:
　1. Cervical plexopathy is most commonly found in patients with head and neck tumors or cervical node metastases. Pain

may occur in several areas of the head or neck according to the site(s) of tumor involvement.

2. Brachial plexopathy is most common in patients with lymphoma or lung or breast cancer. Severe regional pain (shoulder, arm, scapula, sometimes extending to fingers) usually is the first symptom. Pain may be aching, with burning dysesthesias of the hand. Motor and sensory changes occur in the affected arm. Progressive pain or Horner's syndrome indicates probable extension into epidural space. Patients with brachial plexopathy are at risk for cord compression.

3. Lumbosacral plexopathy is most common in patients with regional tumors or metastasis (eg, gynecologic, genitourinary, colorectal). Aching pain in the lumbosacral area, groin, or leg (usually ipsilateral) is the most common first symptom. Continuous or paroxysmal dysesthesias may also occur. Lower extremity weakness and sensory loss are common. Cord compression may occur.

● Paraneoplastic peripheral neuropathies in patients with cancer may include dysesthesias, parasthesias, and other neurologic deficits. Peripheral neuropathies are common in patients at any stage of HIV or AIDS. The most common are distal axonal neuropathy and sensory polyneuropathy (Price & Brew, 1997).

● Headache from central pain syndromes is more often due to bone destruction than to neurologic damage. The headache from increased intracranial pressure may be severe, experienced before getting out of bed, and may improve about an hour after arising. Accompanying symptoms are changes in mentation, nausea, and vomiting (Glick & Glover, 1995). A more complete discussion of increased intracranial pressure can be found in Chapter 13. Headache is common in patients with HIV infection and may be due to a variety of infections or other etiologies (see Chapter 27 on HIV infection).

Pain Associated with Therapy

Postoperative pain in this section is considered pain that may continue or recur well past surgery.

● Postmastectomy pain usually occurs in the arm, axilla, or chest wall and may occur as late as several months after surgery. It is described as tight and burning, exacerbated with movement. Late occurrence of pain may also signal presence of disease.

● Post-thoracotomy pain is at the surgical site and is often associated with tumor.

● Postradical neck dissection pain may be constant and burning only or accompanied by dysesthesia and intermittent shocklike pain secondary to brachial plexus damage. This pain may occur weeks to months after surgery. Radical neck surgery may damage motor nerves and result in aching neck or shoulder pain. Recurrent cancer may also cause pain at or near the dissection site.

● Postamputation or phantom limb pain that recurs after initial resolution may or may not signal disease recurrence. Pain is usually burning and cramping. Phantom pain also occurs at the site of a (removed) shoulder, breast, anus, bladder, or other site, especially if there was pain in the missing part prior to removal.

Postchemotherapy Pain

● Peripheral neuropathies may result from vinca alkaloids and hexamethamelamine. The pain usually resolves 4 to 6 weeks after therapy. Antiretrovirals, such as dideoxycyttidine and dideoxythimidine, can cause peripheral neuropathy.

● Steroid pseudorheumatism (ie, myalgia and arthralgia with no objective signs of inflammation) may result from withdrawal of steroids. Withdrawal of steroids significantly exacerbates bone pain.

● Aseptic bone necrosis (usually) of the femoral or humeral head may follow chronic steroid therapy and other cancer therapy. The

problem presents with pain, followed by progressive loss of function in the affected limb.
● Mucositis may result from methotrexate, 5-fluorouracil, or other chemotherapeutic agents.

Postradiation Pain

The incidence of postradiation damage is decreasing because of improved radiotherapy techniques.

● Radiation fibrosis of nerve plexi (brachial or lumbosacral) can cause numbness or paresthesia occurring from 6 months to 20 years after treatment.
● Radiation myelopathy usually presents with neurologic deficits (paresis of one side and motor loss on the other), but some patients have pain as an early symptom.
● Radiation-induced peripheral nerve tumors may occur in the irradiated area as many as 20 years after radiation therapy.
● Radiation-induced bone necrosis: See previous discussion of aseptic bone necrosis.
● Mucositis: See previous discussion of mucositis.
● Other: Pain from cardiac tamponade, hypercalcemia, muscle spasms, myofascia, peptic ulcer, cystitis, osteoporosis, constipation, immobility, inflammation secondary to infection, decubitus ulcers, and postherpetic neuralgia may be directly, indirectly, or not at all related to the cancer or cancer therapy.

Staging Pain

Though not yet in wide use, the Edmonton Staging System for Cancer Pain provides an organized means of gaining insight into the status and prognosis of patients experiencing pain (Bruera et al., 1995). This system incorporates critical dimensions of pain previously discussed in this chapter:

● Mechanism of pain: Visceral, bone or soft tissue, neuropathic, mixed, or unknown

● Pain characteristics: The absence or presence of incidental pain (ie, pain brought on by movement, including swallowing, urination, or activity)
● Previous opioid exposure: Low, moderate, or high doses
● Cognitive function: Normal or impaired
● Psychological distress: Major distress absent or present
● Tolerance (to opioids): Lesser or greater escalation of dose
● History (of substance-related disorder): absent or present

Staging is I to III, with the greater number of dimensions present yielding the higher stage and poorer prognosis (with respect to response to analgesic treatment). Neuropathic pain is associated with poorer prognosis.

Assessment of Pain

Knowledge of pain syndromes, symptoms other than pain, and psychosocial and spiritual issues in terminal illness are interfaced with assessment parameters to develop an understanding of the nature and meaning of the patient's pain. Because cancer pain is largely a subjective and multidimensional experience, communication among patient, nurse, physician, and others is of the utmost importance: More difficulty in communicating means more problems in management.

While nurses and physicians often underestimate and undertreat patient pain, there seems to be a trend toward more accurate assessment and treatment of pain, at least in oncology settings (Levin, Berry, & Leiter, 1998). Patient estimations of pain, the "gold standard" (Bruera, Fainsinger, Miller, & Kuehn, 1992), are the best source of information. "Believe the patient's complaint of pain" (Foley, 1997, p. 2817).

The first assessment question should generally be something like, "Tell me about the pain." This general, unspecific question gives the patient the opportunity to say what is on his or her mind and perhaps to give critical insight into the situation. Initially directing the patient's thoughts to specific questions may result in submerging key information, which the patient needs to communicate, in a sea of assessment questions and the struggles of a sick, hurting person to comprehend and answer. The final assessment question should be to ask the patient if he or she has any further thoughts about the pain or the pain control.

Comprehensive assessment parameters follow. Many patients have difficulty being specific. The practitioner must be patient and persistent in such cases. It is essential that pain be *systematically* assessed by all staff and that assessments be *systematically* communicated among staff. This measure alone has a salutary effect on pain. Pain in cancer and HIV infection is dynamic and changes with disease progression and other factors and hence must be assessed regularly throughout care.

The assessment parameters given below are based on WHO (1986) guidelines, the short-form McGill Pain Questionnaire, the Memorial Pain Assessment Card, and the Wisconsin Brief Pain Questionnaire. WHO guidelines are known to be effective, and the other three are multidimensional and have good reliability and validity (Foley, 1997; McGuire, 1992). Pain assessment tools are included at the end of this chapter. These incorporate most of the parameters given in the following list.

Pain Assessment Parameters

● Severity: There are several types of scales to help assess the severity of pain. A verbal rating scale, also termed a categoric scale, offers words such as "none," "mild," "moderate," "severe," and "overwhelming" for patients to choose in describing the intensity of pain. A visual analogue scale uses a straight 10-cm line with one end representing no pain and the other the worst possible pain (see Figs. 11-1 and 11-2). Adding numeric integers to the

scale, such as on the Brief Pain Inventory (BPI) produces a graphic rating scale (GRS). The client marks the line at the place he or she most feels the pain. A cogent call has been made for standardizing the clinical rating of pain intensity using a 0 to 10 rating scale, not only within institutions, but also *among* institutions (Dalton & McNaull, 1998). Imagine how much time has been spent at thousands of institutions discussing 1 to 5 or 1 to 10 or the excruciatingly large number of words to describe pain. Enough of this indulgence!

● Location(s) and radiation: It is important to help the patient be as specific as possible. Most pain assessment tools include line drawings of a human figure. Patients shade in the areas on these drawings where they feel pain and thus document information that is helpful in determining etiology. The practitioner can use a different color marker, or clear overlays, to mark surgery, radiation, known metastases, or other significant sites of pain indicated.

● Quality: The patient's own words should be used in documentation. Terms like dull, aching, sharp, shooting, burning, etc. point to the classification or origins of the pain. Unpleasant sensations other than pain should be documented.

● Duration: When did it start? Is it constant or intermittent?

● Influencing factors (other than medications) and patterns: What makes the pain better or worse? When is pain most severe and least severe? Is it constant, does it comes and go gradually, or is it paroxysmal? Is it worse at a particular time of day or night? Are there any emotional, spiritual, or other factors that affect the pain?

● Other physical symptoms, especially those that are new or increasing: Motor, sensory, and range of motion changes may indicate neurologic involvement. Nausea and vomiting may be associated with significant processes, such as increased intracranial pressure and hypercalcemia.

● Functional status or impact of pain on (1) activity, (2) mood, (3) enjoyment of life, (4)

No pain_____Worst possible pain

FIGURE 11–1. VAS-Type Scale (Standard Length of Scale is 10 cm)

sleep, (5) sociability, and (6) any other relevant aspect of life. Pain impact or pain-related disability is one of the primary components in chronic pain classification attempts (Vallerand, 1998).

● Patient psychological and spiritual state: Anxiety, depression, hopelessness, and other states of mind can have profound effects on pain and the ability to communicate with others about pain or other symptoms.

● Meaning of the pain to the patient (and at times, the family).

● Pain history: Data should be gathered on whether pain occurred suddenly or developed gradually and whether it developed after a particular event (eg, changes in medications—especially analgesics and steroids—coughing

spells, falls). What medications or treatments succeeded in controlling the pain, and what failed?

● Effects of current medication(s): Assessing the effects of medication(s) is a complex issue, sometimes complicated by polypharmacy. Baseline data include the following:
1. Name of medication(s)
2. Effects
3. Length of effects
4. Problems patient and family think result from the medication(s)
5. Patient and family feelings about the medication(s)
6. History of medication(s) taken for pain
7. Any over-the-counter, alternative, homeopathic, or herbal remedies used

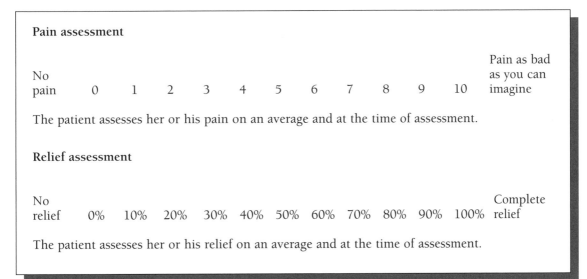

Pain assessment

| No pain | 0 | 1 | 2 | 3 | 4 | 5 | 6 | 7 | 8 | 9 | 10 | Pain as bad as you can imagine |

The patient assesses her or his pain on an average and at the time of assessment.

Relief assessment

| No relief | 0% | 10% | 20% | 30% | 40% | 50% | 60% | 70% | 80% | 90% | 100% | Complete relief |

The patient assesses her or his relief on an average and at the time of assessment.

FIGURE 11–2. Brief Pain Inventory or Graphic Rating Scale. The Brief Pain Inventory (BPI) makes the VAS easier for patients to understand by using a 10-cm line numbered 0–10 as shown above.

● Client understanding of treatment and treatment goals and patient goals for treatment

Of course, not all of these parameters are assessed in every patient encounter. They should all, however, be included in every initial assessment. A short form or tool, such as GRS, and specific questions based on the patient's current and potential pain status should be used for more frequent assessment. Among hospitalized patients with stable pain, a brief assessment should be conducted once every 8 hours. Among patients whose pain is not stable or well managed, assessment should be more frequent.

Examples of forms that can be used as functional tools are shown in Figure 11-3, Initial Pain Assessment Tool and Figure 11-4, Flow Sheet—Pain (for monitoring pain on an hourly or other periodic basis).

It is not enough to ask the patient, "How are you feeling today?"

Patient's Name _____ Age _____ Date _____
Room _____

Diagnosis _____ Physician _____

Nurse _____

I. LOCATION: Patient or nurse mark drawing.

II. Intensity: Patient rates the pain. Scale used _____
   Present:
   Worst pain gets:
   Best pain gets:
   Acceptable level of pain:

III. QUALITY: (Use patient's own words, e.g., prick, ache, burn, throb, pull, sharp) _____
_____

IV. ONSET, DURATION, VARIATIONS, RHYTHMS: _____
_____

V. MANNER OF EXPRESSING PAIN: _____
_____

VI. WHAT RELIEVES THE PAIN? _____
_____

VII. WHAT CAUSES OR INCREASES THE PAIN? _____
_____

VIII. EFFECTS OF PAIN: (Note decreased function, decreased quality of life.)
   Accompanying symptoms (e.g., nausea) _____
   Sleep _____
   Appetite _____
   Physical activity _____
   Relationship with others (e.g., irritability) _____
   Emotions (e.g., anger, suicidal, crying) _____
   Concentration _____
   Other _____

IX. OTHER COMMENTS: _____
_____

X. PLAN: _____
_____

Note: Reproduced with permission from *Pain: Clinical Manual for Nursing Practice* by M. McCaffery and A. Beebe, 1989, St. Louis: The C.V. Mosby Company.

FIGURE 11–3. Initial Pain Assessment Tool

Patient _____ Date _____

*Pain rating scale used _____

Pain rating acceptable to patient: _____

Analgesic(s) prescribed: _____

Time	Pain rating	Analgesic	R	P	BP	Level of arousal	Other†	Plan & comments

*Pain rating: A number of different scales may be used. Indicate which scale is used and use the same one each time. For example, 0–10 (0 = no pain, 10 = worst pain).

†Possibilities for other columns: bowel function, activities, nausea and vomiting, other pain relief measures. Identify the side effects of greatest concern to patient, family, physician, nurses.

Note. Reproduced with permission from *Pain: Clinical Manual for Nursing Practice* by M. McCaffery and A. Beebe, 1989, St. Louis: The C.V. Mosby Company.

FIGURE 11–4. Flow Sheet—Pain

REFERENCES

American Pain Society. (1992). *Principles of analgesic use in the treatment of acute pain and cancer pain* (3rd ed.). Skokie, IL: Author.

Bonica, J. J. (1990). Definitions and taxonomy of pain. In J. J. Bonica (Ed.), *The Management of pain* (2nd ed.) (pp. 18–27). Philadelphia: Lea & Febiger.

Bruera, E., Fainsinger, R. L., Miller, M. J., & Kuehn, N. (1992). The assessment of pain intensity in patients with cognitive failure: A preliminary report. *Journal of Pain and Symptom Management, 7*(5), 267–270.

Bruera, E., Schoeller, T., Wenk, R., MacEachern, T., Marcelino, S., Hanson, J., & Suarez-Almazor, M. (1995). A prospective multicenter assessment of the Edmonton staging system for cancer pain. *Journal of Pain and Symptom Management, 10*(5), 348–355.

Coleman, R. E. (1997). Skeletal complications of malignancy. *Cancer Supplement, 80*(8), 1588–1594.

Dalton, J. A., & McNaull, F. (1998). A call for standardizing the clinical rating of pain intensity using a 0 to 10 rating scale. *Cancer Nursing, 21*(1), 46–49.

Enck, R.E. (1991). Understanding and managing bone metastases. *American Journal of Hospice & Palliative Care, 8*(3), 3–4.

Foley, K. M. (1997). Management of cancer pain. In V. T. Ventifridda, S. Hellman, & S. A. Rosenberg (Eds.), *Cancer: Principles and practice of oncology* (5th ed.) (pp. 2807–2841). Philadelphia: Lippincott-Raven.

Glick, J. H., & Glover, D. (1995). Oncologic emergencies. In G. P. Murphy, W. Lawrence, & R. E. Lenhard (Eds.), *Textbook of clinical oncology* (2nd ed.) (pp. 597–618). Atlanta: The American Cancer Society.

Kjaer, M. (1997). The therapy of cancer pain and its integration into a comprehensive supportive care strategy. *Annals of Oncology, 8*(Suppl. 3), s15–s19.

Levin, M. L., Berry, J. I., & Leiter, J. (1998). Management of pain in terminally ill patients: Physician reports of knowledge, attitudes, and behavior. *Journal of Pain and Symptom Management, 15*(1), 27–40.

Martin, L. A., & Hagen, N. A. (1997). Neuropathic pain in cancer patients: Mechanisms, syndromes, and clinical controversies. *Journal of Pain and Symptom Management, 14*(2), 99–117.

McGuire, D. B. (1992). Comprehensive and multidimensional assessment and measurement of pain. *Journal of Pain and Symptom Management, 7*(5), 312–319.

Payne, R. (1989). Cancer pain: Anatomy, physiology, and pharmacology. *Cancer, 63*(11), 2266–2274.

Payne, R. (1990). Pathophysiology of cancer pain. In K. M. Foley, J. J. Bonica, & V. Ventafridda (Eds.). *Proceedings of the Second International Congress on Cancer Pain* (pp. 1–5). New York: Raven Press.

Price, R.W. & Brew, B.J. (1997). Central and peripheral nervous system complications. In V.T. DeVita, S. Hellman, & S.A. Rosenberg (Eds.) *AIDS: Etiology, diagnosis, treatment and prevention* (4th ed) (pp. 331–353). Philadelphia: Lippincott– Raven.

Springhouse. (1997). *Expert pain management.* Springhouse, PA: Author.

Vallerand, A. P. (1998). Development and testing of the Inventory of Functional Satus-Chronic Pain. *Journal of Pain and Symptom Management, 15*(2), 125–133.

Waldman, S. D., Feldstein, G. S., Donohoe, C. D., & Waldman, K. A. (1988). The relief of body wall pain secondary to malignant hepatic metastases by intercostal nerve block with bipivicaine and methylprednisolone. *Journal of Pain and Symptom Management, 3*(1), 39–43.

World Health Organization. (1986). *Cancer pain relief and palliative care.* Geneva: Author.

Zhukovsky, D. S., Gorowski, E., Hausdorff, J., Napolitano, B., & Lesser, M. (1995). Unmet analgesic needs in cancer patients. *Journal of Pain and Symptom Management, 10*(2), 113–119.

CHAPTER 12

Management of Pain

- The World Health Organization's three-step analgesic ladder remains the standard model for pain management in advanced disease.

- Opioids (especially morphine) are the mainstay in pain management in terminal illness.

- Opioids have a number of side effects, all of which are manageable under nearly all circumstances.

- Understanding types of pain and pain syndromes is important to effective treatment of pain.

- Combining opioids with adjuvant medications usually produces more effective analgesia.

- Oral is the preferred route of administration for the ongoing management of chronic pain. However, other routes and methods are also used for ongoing management, especially rectal and continuous subcutaneous infusion.

- Other widely accepted measures to treat pain are used in specific circumstances (eg, radiation for pain due to spinal metastases).

- Psychological, spiritual, and alternative or complementary methods of pain control may in some cases be helpful in pain management, but seldom as primary means of management.

- Special considerations are involved in treating pain in patients who are very young or very old. Patients with substance-related disorders require special consideration and expertise.

Effective pain management in advanced cancer is based on knowledge of pain syndromes, thorough and ongoing assessments, knowledge of treatment modalities, and commitment of staff to using all three of the above. Developing this fourth dimension of effective pain management—a strong commitment—is as much a matter of changing attitudes as it is of increasing knowledge. The commitment must be individual and institutional if progress is to be made. The essential attitude should be that pain *can* be managed, and opioids *are* safe to use.

Opioids, principally morphine, are the mainstay in managing cancer pain. Indeed, oral (PO) medications (with morphine being the primary medication), used according to World Health Organization (WHO) guidelines (Fig. 12-1), effectively manage pain in approximately 90% of patients (Portenoy, 1998; Schug, Zech, & Dörr, 1990).

Pharmacologic Management of Pain: Medications

Mild Analgesics: Nonopioids

Nonopioid analgesics include acetaminophen and nonsteroidal anti-inflammatory drugs (NSAIDs), such as aspirin, indomethacin, ibuprofen, fenoprofen, and naproxyn. With analgesic, antipyretic, and anti-inflammatory properties, the NSAIDs are the analgesics of first choice for mild pain. It has long been accepted that bone pain, even when severe, responds best when NSAIDs are added to opioids—the opioid-sparing effect (Mercadante et al., 1997). However, there also are now questions about whether NSAIDs add to the effectiveness of opioids in managing bone pain (Foley, 1997). Acetaminophen has analgesic and antipyretic, but not anti-inflammatory, properties and hence is of less value to treating chronic cancer pain.

FREEDOM FROM CANCER PAIN

STEP 3
Opioid for moderate to severe pain
± nonopioid
± adjuvant

When pain persists or increases, proceed to Step 3

STEP 2
Opioid for mild to moderate pain
± non opioid ±
adjuvant

When pain persists or increases, proceed to Step 2

STEP 1
Nonopioid
± adjuvant

Note. From World Health Organization (p. 9), 1990: Author.

FIGURE 12–1. World Health Organization Three-Step Analgesic Ladder

Gastrointestinal (GI) side or toxic effects are a limiting factor in the use of most NSAIDs. GI effects are exacerbated or occur more frequently in older patients, patients who are taking corticosteroids, and patients with a history of ulcers. Aspirin and the other NSAIDs have adverse effects on the GI, hematopoietic, hepatic, and renal systems, especially with chronic use. Acetaminophen has fewer adverse effects than aspirin, except in patients with liver disease (a significant liability for patients with lung, breast, GI, and genitourinary tumors: see Unit III, Advanced Cancer: Metastatic Spread, Common Symptoms, and Assessment) or alcoholism. NSAIDs carry increased risk of hepatic toxicity in clients who regularly take alcohol, phenobarbital, carbamazepine, phenytoin, and sulfinpyrazone. All the mild analgesics share the liability of ceiling effect (ie, analgesia does not increase and toxic-ity occurs at higher doses).

Mild Analgesics: Opioids

Mild opioids include codeine, hydrocodone, and propoxyphene. In the past, oxycodone was often classified as a mild opioid but is now considered by many to be a strong opioid (Benziger et al., 1997). However, oxycodone is recommended by some experts for mild to moderate pain (Foley, 1997). Mild opioids are useful primarily when added to an NSAID that is not completely effective in controlling mild to moderate pain. Mild opioids are often manufactured in combination with NSAIDs (eg, acetaminophen with codeine). These formulations give practitioners less flexibility in adjusting dosages that when using the opioid and NSAID in stand-alone formulations so that one can be adjusted without changing the other.

Codeine alone or used routinely is best avoided for pain management in advanced disease because side effects are significant (Walsh, 1990a) and because the analgesia of a typical dose does not exceed that of the NSAIDs. Propoxyphene has the liabilities of minimal analgesic effects in many clients, long half-life, tendency to accumulate with chronic use, and

overdose complicated by convulsions (Waller & Caroline, 1996).

The side effects of the mild opioids are essentially the same in nature as those of the strong opioids, which are discussed later in this chapter.

Mixed Agonist/Antagonist and Partial Agonist Opioids

Opioid agonist/antagonists include pentazocine (Talwin), butorphanol (Stadol), and nalbuphine (Nubain). Buprenorphine (Buprenex) is a partial agonist. These are best avoided for clients with chronic cancer pain because they do not produce greater analgesia than other opioids and they are associated with greater psychomimetic side effects than are other (agonist) opioids. They also precipitate withdrawal in opioid-dependent patients or when combined with opioids.

Strong Opioid Analgesics

Morphine is the "gold standard in cancer pain treatment" (Ahmedzai, 1997). Other strong opioid analgesics effective for moderate to severe pain are hydromorphone (Dilaudid), levorphanol (Levo-Dromoran), and transdermal fentanyl (Duragesic patches) (American Pain Society [APS], 1992; Foley, 1997; Ahmedzai, 1997).

● *Hydromorphone* has long been used for patients with cancer. Before the development of high-potency morphine, hydromorphone was the best means of parenteral pain relief in cachectic patients. Hydromorphone has a short half-life and hence is especially useful in elderly patients.
● *Levorphanol* is a synthetic opioid with a plasma half-life of 12 to 16 hours; therefore, patients who are elderly or have renal or hepatic disorders should be carefully monitored if levorphanol is used.
● *Transdermal fentanyl* is especially useful for patients whose pain is relatively stable or for those who cannot take medications by mouth. Transdermal fentanyl takes 12 to 16 hours to

produce a significant therapeutic effect and 48 hours to produce steady-state blood concentrations (APS, 1992). Other medications are therefore required until analgesia is achieved. Fentanyl has a short half-life and is available in parenteral and oral transmucosal forms, both of which are effective for breakthrough pain.

● *Oxycodone* is increasingly recognized as effective even for patients with severe pain and is now available in sustained release form (OxyContin). In clinical practice, many see oxycodone as more appropriate for moderate pain. Oxymorphone, the active metabolite of oxycodone, may cause less itching than other opioids. Oxymorphone is currently available in intravenous and rectal forms.

● *Methadone* is a second-line analgesic with liabilities including very long half-life (17 to 24 or more hours) and a 4- to 8-hour duration of action. Therefore, methadone should be avoided in patients who are elderly or have renal or hepatic disorders.

● *Heroin* is illegal in the United States. Taken orally, its effects are essentially the same as morphine. Intravenous heroin is, of course, the drug of choice for intravenous (IV) drug users. There is nothing clinically wrong about using heroin in managing cancer pain, but it is not superior to legal opioids and has a greater attraction for IV drug users.

● *Meperidine* (Demerol) is a poor choice for managing chronic cancer pain because regular use can result in central nervous system (CNS) excitability, leading to seizures, especially in patients with renal dysfunction (Foley, 1997). However, intramuscular (IM) meperidine is effective for painful procedures or for other occasional "pain emergencies."

OPIOID SIDE EFFECTS

The side effects of opioids are well known and in some cases may limit their use. However, use is more often limited by unrealistic concerns about adverse effects, such as respiratory depression and addiction (Paice, 1991). Consideration should be given to rotating opioids (with equianalgesic conversion from one

to another) in patients with troublesome side effects or difficult-to-manage pain (Ahmedzai, 1997). The principal side or adverse effects of opioids (APS, 1992; Foley, 1997; Swenson, 1997) include the following:

● *Respiratory depression* is potentially the most dangerous side effect. Because respiratory depression seldom occurs in patients who regularly take opioids, its importance in patients with terminal cancer is sometimes exaggerated (Walsh, 1990a). Tolerance to respiratory depression from opioids develops quickly with regular use (Foley, 1997), and respiratory depression occurs most frequently in patients with severe pain who receive large first-time doses (APS, 1992) and in patients with rapidly changing respiratory status (Walsh, 1990a). Patients whose pain is newly relieved often fall asleep, which adds to depressant effects and creates the possibility of airway obstruction by the tongue. Such patients should be closely observed 3 to 4 hours past the peak plasma level of the drug (APS, 1992). If naloxone is indicated by respiratory depression to the extent that there is threat to life, it should be carefully titrated to prevent pain breakthrough and the patient monitored for aspiration (endotracheal tube is recommended by Foley for comatose patients) and seizures.

● *Sedation* is usually an early (initiating) side effect of opioid use, decreasing 2 to 5 days after a consistent dose is established. Sedation may, however, increase several days after analgesia is achieved with medications that have a long half-life. Sedation results from medication effects on the CNS but may also be related to exhaustion from chronic pain. If sedation is due to exhaustion, the patient should be arousable and oriented when awake. Interventions for sedation include (1) accepting sedation for several days; (2) gradual decrease in dose of opioids; (3) caffeine beverages or other stimulants, such as amphetamine or methylphenidate (Ritalin), given until early afternoon; or (4) decreasing or eliminating all sedating medications, except those that are essential (Haviley et al., 1992). Sedation or a decrease in consciousness emerging as a new development when a medication regimen is established may be a sign of changes in disease processes. Also see the discussion of respiratory depression on the previous page.

● *Nausea and vomiting.* Like sedation, this is most often an initiating side effect of opioids and usually lasts no more than 7 days. If nausea and vomiting do occur, antiemetics, usually beginning with a phenothiazine, such as prochlorperazine or haloperidol, are given on schedule and gradually withdrawn after 5 to 7 days (increased time intervals between taking the medicine) (Rousseau, 1995). Nausea and vomiting due to gastric stasis (side effect of the opioid) last beyond the initiating period and usually respond to metoclopramide. Some patients respond to a change in opioid, and others benefit from a change in regimen (eg, from immediate release oral to controlled release) or route (eg, from oral to rectal or continuous subcutaneous infusion) (APS, 1992). Correct equianalgesic conversions are important—and a common source of error—when changing routes or medications (see the section on equianalgesic conversions later in this chapter). Practitioners must be alert to the possibility of nausea and vomiting originating in etiologies other than opioids (eg, bowel obstruction, hypercalcemia, increased intracranial pressure).

● *Constipation* is part of chronic opioid use, especially when the patient is also taking NSAIDs, is immobile, is ingesting inadequate fluids and fiber, or is depressed. A bowel regimen consisting of adequate fluids, the avoidance of constipating foods, and a stool softener and cathartic should be initiated *at the same time* opioids are started. Doses "far above" those required for routine bowel management may be needed (Foley, 1997, p. 2828). Increasing fiber is not sufficient to prevent constipation in a person who is using opioids. Preventing constipation is discussed more fully in Chapter 17, Gastrointestinal Problems.

● *Confusion* may be an initiating effect of opioid therapy (especially with older patients) or may result from excessive dosing or in some cases inadequately controlled pain (Duggleby & Lander, 1994; Waller & Caroline, 1996). A change in the amount of opioid given resolves confusion from the latter two causes. Hallucinations, accompanied by sudden mood changes without confusion or thought disorder, develop in small numbers of patients. Symptoms respond to haloperidol or a change in opioid (Bruera, Schoeller, & Montejo, 1992). Confusion may also result from brain metastases, hypercalcemia, medications other than opioids, and other causes (see Chapter 13).

● *Multifocal myoclonus and CNS hyperirritability* may occur with high doses of any opioid but are most common in patients receiving repeated doses of meperidine. Along with discontinuing the meperidine (and substituting morphine), a benzodiazepine may be required for several days as the meperidine is cleared or if myoclonus is due to opioids other than meperidine (Twycross & Lichter, 1998). See Chapter 13, on Neurological Problems for information on treating myoclonus recalcitrant to treatment with diazepam. Muscle spasm can be treated with diazepam 10 mg PO hs or baclofen 10 mg PO tid (Waller & Caroline, 1996).

● *Urinary retention* is a transient side effect and is due to increased tone of the detrussor muscle and contraction of the vessicle sphincter. Retention occurs most often in older patients. Belladonna and opium suppositories decrease muscle tone, but catheterization may be required.

● *Dry mouth* may be due as much to the anticholinergic properties of antidepressants as to opioids. Mouth swabs, hard candy, and other such measures may be used.

● *Pruritus* is a common but not necessarily distressing side effect of opioids, especially intraspinal. Fentanyl and oxymorphone (Numorphan) cause less itching than do other strong opioids (APS, 1992). Diphenhydramine (Benadryl) or hydroxyzine (Vistaril) are used to decrease pruritus (Waller & Caroline,

1996). Most patients develop tolerance to pruritus (see Chapter 15, Skin Problems).

● *Allergic reaction* is a concern of some patients. Exploration of patient claims of allergy to codeine or other opioids often reveals that sometime in the past the patient became nauseated or suffered other side effects after taking the medication. See previous discussion of nausea, confusion, pruritus, and other side effects.

● *Addiction or dependence* is feared by patients and professionals. The risk of addiction in medical-surgical patients of any kind is insignificant: In one study of 11,882 clients given opioids, four developed problems of addiction (Porter & Jick, 1980). Research at St. Christopher's Hospice showed that patients who regularly used heroin for pain control and who discontinued the medication because the etiology of the pain was resolved did not experience problems of addiction or dependence following discontinuation (Twycross, 1978). Several fears or issues are subsumed under that of "addiction":

1. Addiction, or more accurately, substance dependence, is "a cluster of cognitive, behavioral, and physiological symptoms indicating (continued use) of the substance despite significant substance-related problems (with) repeated self-administration that usually results in tolerance, withdrawal, and compulsive drug-taking behavior" (American Psychological Association [APA], 1994).

2. Physical dependence is the use of a substance to the extent that cessation of use results in a withdrawal syndrome. Physical dependence is distinguished from substance dependence or addiction by the absence of repeated self-administration and compulsive drug-seeking and taking (Kemp, 1996). Contrary to dramatic portrayals of drug addicts writhing in an agony of withdrawal, discontinuing oral opioids for patients with cancer pain results in marked discomfort, increased pain, insomnia, tremors, mild to moderate anxiety, and diaphoresis (Walsh, 1990a).

Gradual discontinuation of opioids decreases distress. "Clock-watchers" and other patients who are labeled as "a problem" with respect to analgesics are almost invariably patients whose pain is poorly managed, often with injections of inadequate amounts of medication given at intervals exceeding the duration of action of the medication. These patients are iatrogenically dependent and iatrogenically suffering.

3. Tolerance is a state in which ever-larger doses of medication are required to achieve the same effect, and there is an underlying fear that it does not take long to reach a point at which no dose is effective. ("They're saving the strong stuff for when the pain gets really bad.") Tolerance develops (or does not develop) at different rates among different patients. It is first manifested by a decrease in duration of analgesia (APS, 1992). Practitioners should take care that the need for increased medication is not a sign of disease progression rather than tolerance. Tolerance is addressed by shortening the interval at which medications are given, increasing the dose (sometimes doubling the dose, according to Foley, 1997), adding adjuvant medications, or switching to another opioid. Cross-tolerance between opioids is not complete, and the APS (1992) recommends that when switching opioids, the patient should be started on one-half the equianalgesic dose, then titrated upward according to relief of pain. Failure to control pain with strong opioids initially is not a problem of tolerance but an indication that more analgesic or adjuvant medication or different techniques are needed. Switching medications under these circumstances is an exercise in futility, and using one-half the equianalgesic dose is an exercise in cruelty.

While a matter of concern, opioid side effects are nearly always manageable, and fears that they might be a problem or that they might be difficult to manage are not legitimate reasons for not aggressively treating pain.

Adjuvant Medications

Adjuvant medications are used to treat pain that responds incompletely to opioids, to enhance the effects of opioids, to decrease side effects of opioids, and to treat associated symptoms. Adjuvant medications include tricyclic antidepressants (TCAs), anxiolytics, corticosteroids, anticonvulsants, and phenothiazines.

TREATING PAIN THAT RESPONDS INCOMPLETELY TO OPIOIDS: NEUROPATHIC PAIN

Two types of pain, neuropathic and bone, commonly do not respond completely to opioids alone. Medications for neuropathic pain include the following:

● The TCAs, such as amitriptyline (Elavil), doxepin (Sinequan), imipramine (Tofranil), desipramine (Norpramin), and nortriptyline (Pamelor), are commonly used for neuropathic pain, especially superficial dysesthesias in advanced cancer and HIV infection. The serotonin selective reuptake inhibitor paroxetine (Paxil) is also used for neuropathic pain. TCAs have analgesic effects that are apparently independent of their antidepressant effects. TCAs also affect the depression and anxiety that both accompany and influence the pain of advanced disease. The sedative properties of TCAs (except for desipramine and nortriptyline) mean that they can be used for insomnia and for improving mood and pain. Doses are lower in patients with advanced cancer than for those whose primary diagnosis is depression. Effects are usually experienced in 24 to 48 hours versus the 2 to 3 weeks required in patients with a psychiatric diagnosis of depression. The starting dose for amytriptyline is 25 mg and for elderly patients, 10 mg, both in a single bedtime dose. This may be titrated up to 75 mg (Foley, 1991). Side effects, such as dry mouth, palpitations, blurred vision, constipation, and edema, are often transitory (Monks, 1990). TCAs are also used for pain in multiple sclerosis.

● Anticonvulsants used for neuropathic pain, especially lancinating dysesthesias, include carbamazepine (Tegretol), phenytoin (Dilantin), clonazepam (Klonopin), valproate (Depakote), and gabapentin (Neurontin) (Portenoy, 1993; Rosenberg, Harrell, Ristic, Werner, & de Rosayro, 1997). Anticonvulsants should be started at low doses and gradually increased to the same therapeutic ranges as for seizure disorders. Serum levels of anticonvulsants and complete blood counts should be monitored. Neutropenia is a potential untoward effect of carbamazepine. Patients should thus be carefully monitored for infection, especially if blood work is not regularly done. Increased doses of cortico-steroids may be required for patients taking phenytoin.

● Corticosteroids, including dexamethasone (Decadron), prednisolone (Cortolone, Delta-Cortef), and prednisone are examples of the corticosteroids commonly used for symptom control, including neuropathic pain, especially that from nerve compression (Waller & Caroline, 1996). Corticosteroids reduce pain through reducing inflammation and produce at least transitory improvement of appetite, increased strength, and improved sense of well-being. Specific indications for corticosteroids include pain from bone metastases, brachial or lumbosacral plexopathy, and metastatic arthralgia. Corticosteroids are also used to ameliorate increased intracranial pressure, spinal cord compression, and superior vena cava syndrome (Walsh, 1990b). The side effects of chronic use should not be an issue in patients with advanced terminal cancer. Several side effects, however, should be noted: (1) Because it may cause sleep disturbances, prednisone should not be taken at night, and (2) rapid withdrawal exacerbates pain, hence withdrawal should be gradual (APS, 1992).

● Oral and other anesthetics (eg, mexiletine or lidocaine) are second-line options for treating neuropathic pain refractory to previously discussed treatments. Toxicity is a concern, and patients should be closely monitored with electrocardiograms and blood levels drawn.

● Cutaneous local anesthetics, including lidocaine and eutectic mixture of local anesthetics (EMLA, containing lidocaine and prilocaine), are effective for such skin pain as postherpatic neuralgia.

● Capsaicin cream applied topically helps relieve superficial neuropathic and musculoskeletal pain. Skin discomfort from the cream may be experienced, and contact with eyes and mucous membranes must be avoided.

● Other medications for neuropathic pain include the following:

1. Clonidine (Catapres) can be given orally or transdermally. Clonidine is an antihypertensive drug with high potential for side effects, including sedation, dizziness, and fatigue.

2. Clonazepam is a benzodiazepine with a half-life of 20 to 80 hours and may cause somnolence and cognitive impairment, especially with the repeated dosing necessary for neuropathic pain.

3. Methotrimeprazine (Levoprome) is the only phenothiazine with significant analgesic, anxiolytic, sedative, and antiemetic properties. Methotrimeprazine is recommended for intermittent use and in patients with bowel obstruction when other measures have failed.

4. N-methyl-D-aspartate antagonists (ketamine and dextromethorphan) and calcitonin have been effective in some cases, but their safety and efficacy in long-term management are not yet known.

5. Levodopa (with benserazide) has been tested with promising results.

TREATING PAIN THAT RESPONDS INCOMPLETELY TO OPIOIDS: BONE PAIN

Bone pain is common in metastatic disease. Among the cancers that most frequently spread to bone are multiple myeloma, breast, prostate, lung, thyroid, renal, and melanoma (Coleman, 1997). Bone pain is often worse at night, so it may be necessary to increase evening doses of analgesics. Adjuvant medications effective in treating bone pain include the following:

● The NSAIDs are discussed in the section on mild analgesics: nonopioids. At this point in the development of palliative care, their use in bone pain is standard in most settings.

● Corticosteroids are also discussed in the previous section treating neuropathic pain.

● Biphosphonates, such as pamidronate (Aredia), are given intravenously to treat hypercalcemia and are known to be effective for bone pain through reduction of osteoclast activity. Etidronate (Didronel) is available for oral and intravenous use. Clodronate is considered less effective for treatment of hypercalcemia (Warrell, 1997) but has been shown to be efficacious in the treatment of bone pain (Ernst et al., 1997).

● Calcitonin, a standard medication for hypercalcemia, is thought by some to relieve bone pain.

● Gallium nitrate has sometimes been used to treat bone pain.

● Strontium 89 is slow to yield results and suppresses bone marrow. It has been used for patients with otherwise low risk for bone marrow suppression and life expectancy greater than 3 months.

● Bony metastases may cause pathologic fractures, which, coupled with increasing life expectancy in cancer, means that orthopedic measures are commonly used (Payne, 1997).

Radiotherapy is also effective in the treatment of painful bony metastases (Janjan, 1996). See discussion of this and other measures later in this chapter.

OTHER ADJUVANT MEDICATIONS

Antianxiety medications are commonly used in terminal illness, but they are not indicated in managing chronic pain nor are they as useful as antidepressants in addressing issues associated with chronic pain. Anxiety is common to patients with terminal illness and depression or pain. In some cases, the primary issue may be depression rather than the anxiety. If the depression is resolved, the anxiety also is likely to be resolved; if the anxiety is resolved, the depression remains.

Managing Specific Pain Situations

Adjuvant medications are not specified in most of the following cases because of variation in circumstances. However, consideration should be given to adjuvant medications in all patients. Anxiety and depression exacerbate pain and hence should always be addressed. Rescue medications should be available in all cases. As with other situations, troublesome side effects of opioids and other medications are treated prophylactically whenever possible. Radiation, chemotherapy, and other measures to correct the etiology are the first choice, but for a variety of reasons, they are not always possible (Payne, 1997).

● Mild to moderate somatic or visceral pain is treated with a nonopioid, such as acetaminophen or an NSAID, plus an adjuvant medication, if indicated, or an opioid, such as oxycodone, plus an NSAID or an adjuvant medication.
● Moderate to severe somatic or visceral pain is treated with opioids combined with adjuvant medications or NSAID as described previously.
● Neuropathic pain usually requires an adjuvant medication as described previously (also see the following discussion of postherpatic neuralgia).

Difficult-to-Manage Pain

Several specific pain problems and measures for relief are summarized in the following discussion. Challenging or intractable pain situations usually require involvement of an oncology pain specialist. As noted previously, addressing the etiology of the pain is the treatment of choice when possible and reasonable, given side effects of treatment, expected outcome(s), and the patient's life expectancy.

● Breakthrough pain may occur despite relatively well-managed pain status. All patients, including those whose pain is stable, should have means available to manage breakthrough pain. The parenteral route is generally the fastest means of relieving breakthrough pain, but immediate-release oral opioids are also used. Several days of two to three episodes of breakthrough pain indicate a need to increase the regular dose of SR opioid (Casciato, 1995).
● Severe bilateral or midline lower body pain (eg, of pelvis) not relieved by opioids and not eligible for radiation therapy (radiation is a first choice if possible) is responsive to epidural opioids or local anesthetics.
● Neuropathic pain not responsive to pharmacologic measures described previously may require local anesthetic by one of several routes, nerve block, or other neurosurgical measures. Readers are referred to Foley, 1997.
● Postherpatic neuralgia is significantly reduced by giving amitriptyline preemptively (along with acyclovir) before it is a problem (Bowsher, 1997).
● Patients with cachexia or dysphagia can sometimes take suppositories. If not or if analgesia is unsatisfactory, continuous subcutaneous infusion of an opioid with bolus capability is an option, or if bolus is not possible, hydromorphone (Dilaudid HP, 10 mg/mL) or morphine HP can be given for pain flare-ups.
● Steroid pseudorheumatism is the appearance of myalgias, arthralgias, and other symptoms after steroids are reduced.
● Myofascial or focal muscle pain is characterized by local aching and the resulting muscle stress or splinting from adjacent pathology. If opioids are not effective, measures such as trigger point injections (of saline or local anesthetic) may be effective. Massage and heat may also help, and muscle relaxants may be useful.
● Pathologic fractures are treated (when possible) by means already discussed and by internal stabilization, usually with good results (Harrington, 1997).
● Headache from increased intracranial pressure tends to be deep, dull (not throbbing), and may be worse on arising in the morning. Palliative treatment options include corticosteroids, radiation, shunt placement, and other neurosurgical measures.
● Lymphedema, or soft-tissue swelling with

pain, can be treated pharmacologically with corticosteroids and occasionally with diuretics. Other measures include massage, containment hose, and pneumatic pumps (Farncombe, Daniels, & Cross, 1994).

● Infection may cause or contribute to pain, and in the complexities of advanced disease care (especially home), this may sometimes be missed. Immunosuppression is, of course, a huge problem in cancer and AIDS.

● Intestinal colic occurs in approximately 75% of patients with inoperable obstruction. Colicky pain is treated by discontinuing stimulant laxatives (senna, biscodyl) and gastrokinetic agents (metoclopramide, cisapride) and using antispasmodic agents, such as loperamide 2 mg PO qid, or if the patient is unable to tolerate oral medications, transdermal scopolamine or hyoscine. Opioids may also be necessary (Baines, 1998; Ripamonti, 1994). See the discussion of intestinal obstruction in Chapter 17, Gastrointestinal Problems.

● Rectal or bladder spasm pain or tenesmus is partially or completely relieved with belladonna and opium suppositories or chlorpromazine (Waller & Caroline, 1996). Intractable urogenital pain may be relieved with lumbar sympathetic block.

● Body wall pain secondary to chest wall tumor infiltration is effectively treated with intracostal nerve block. Peripheral nerve blocks are also used for craniofacial and radicular pain but not neuropathic pain (Foley, 1997).

● Malignant ulcers are treated with metronidazole (Flagyl) or clindamycin (Cleocin) and kept clean (Waller & Caroline, 1996) (see Chapter 15, Skin Problems).

● Dysuria (from urinary tract infection) is treated with phenazopyridine (Pyridium) and antibiotic therapy according to etiologic agent (Waller & Caroline, 1996).

● Intractable pain may require sedation with opioids and intravenous barbiturates. Terminal sedation may be achieved with midazolam 60 to 100 mg/24 h continuous SQ (subcutaneous) infusion (or diazepam 10–20 mg PR tid–qid) and haloperidol 20 to 40 mg/24 h (Twycross & Lichter, 1998).

Routes and Administration

Oral medications given in sufficient amounts at regular and appropriate intervals and with diligent attention to preventing side effects are remarkably effective in controlling pain. Patients unable to swallow tablets can often take morphine or other suspensions. While intervals between medication doses are based on duration of action, the peak drug effect for most opioids (morphine, hydromorphone, oxycodone) occurs in 1.5 to 2 hours (except for controlled-release opioids). Therefore, if analgesia is not achieved in that time and if side effects of non–controlled-release opioids are mild, the patient can safely take a second dose (APS, 1992).

Controlled-release morphine (eg, MS Contin, Oramorph SR, Kadian) provide longer duration of action than do immediate-release morphine sulfate, hydromorphone, and other opioids. The duration of action for MS Contin and Oramorph is 12 hours, but 8-hour intervals are required for some patients. Kadian has a 24-hour duration of action and may be given every 12 hours (same daily amount of morphine as with 24-hour dosing) (Broomhead et al., 1997). Controlled-release oxycodone is also available. For home care patients in particular, this means greater convenience and fewer mistakes. Hospitalized patients also prefer the less frequently given controlled-release morphine over immediate release. Controlled-release morphine is also available in suspension and has efficacy, duration of action, and adverse effects similar to the better known tablets. Rescue medications should be available for all patients. Converting from immediate-release opioids to controlled release is covered in the section on equianalgesic conversions.

The oral route is significantly less expensive than others; for example, patient-controlled analgesia (Ferrell & McCaffery, 1991).

There are, however, other effective routes and situations in which they are indicated:

● Transdermal (TTS) fentanyl (Duragesic) is especially useful for patients whose pain is relatively stable. Patient satisfaction tends to be good, and there is less constipation than with morphine (Ahmedzai & Brooks, 1997). Adverse side effects include, but are not limited to, sleep disturbances, cardiovascular depression and stimulation, respiratory depression, and muscle rigidity (Stanley, 1992). TTS Fentanyl takes 12 to 16 hours to produce a significant therapeutic effect and 48 hours to produce steady-state blood concentrations, and effects last approximately 16 hours after removal (APS, 1992; Swenson, 1997).

● Rectal medications are effective and less expensive than the high-tech routes discussed in the following section. Patients with dysphagia or those who are unable to tolerate oral medications are good candidates for the rectal route. Some degree of variation in analgesia is common, but correct placement (approximately one finger length or at least 1.5 in deep) helps achieve more consistent analgesia. Opioids may be given rectally in suppositories or the medications in tablet or capsule form inserted directly into the rectum. "Homemade" opioid microenemas are an easily prepared and inexpensive means of administering opioids rectally. These microenemas provide faster onset and longer duration of action than the same medications given orally (Ripamonti & De Conno, 1997). The latter means also allows patients to take much higher doses than available in commercially available suppositories. Analgesia from rectal opioids, including sustained-release morphine, is equal or slightly greater than from oral medications, but peak effects are usually reached 2 to 3 hours later than with oral sustained-release morphine (Warren, 1996). If the patient is dehydrated or the rectum dry for other reasons, 10 mL warm water should be instilled in the rectum to aid dissolution of tablets. Multiple tablets should be enclosed in a gelatin capsule to avoid multi-

ple insertions. Parenteral solutions and enteric-coated tablets should be avoided. See Warren (1996) for a complete discussion of rectal medications. Medications given rectally include the following:

● Opioids: morphine, hydromorphone, levorphanol, oxycodone, and methadone
● NSAIDs: ibuprofen, aspirin, and naproxen
● Adjuvants: carbamazepine and valproic acid
● Anxiolytics: diazepam, lorazepam, midazolam, and clonazepam
● Antiemetics: metoclopramide and prochlorperazine; others available in suppository form

● IM injections are most appropriate for acute pain (eg, for postsurgical, myocardial infarction). Appropriate uses of IM injections in chronic cancer pain are occasionally (1) prior to painful procedures and (2) for severe breakthrough pain. IM injections are not appropriate for managing chronic cancer pain. Liabilities of IM injections include the pain of administration, difficulty in reaching a steady-state of analgesia, and potential for muscle or soft tissue fibrosis or sterile abscesses.

● Intravenous infusion is most appropriate for newly admitted patients with out-of-control pain or for patients whose pain or side effects are not managed by oral or other means (eg, clients with cachexia, dysphagia, and bowel obstruction). The IV bolus gives the most rapid onset of effect of any routes and is thus used to bring pain under control. The peak effect of IV morphine is reached in 15 to 30 minutes; therefore, if analgesia is not experienced by the time of peak effect and if side effects are not problematic, another bolus may be given (APS, 1992). Continuous IV infusion (CIVI) gives effective ongoing analgesia with minimal side effects in most patients with cancer but presents more problems in client care management than oral methods. IV infusions (usually pumps) are used successfully by some for home care patients. Again, client care management is more challenging and IV complications can often be more of a problem at home than in the hospital.

● Subcutaneous injection (eg, of high-potency hydromorphone) is appropriate for cachectic patients under the circumstances given previously.

● Continuous subcutaneous infusion (CSCI) of opioids using a pump is used most appropriately for cachectic and dysphagic patients for whom IVs are difficult to start or maintain. Patient-controlled analgesia (PCA) may also be delivered subcutaneously. A combination of CSCI with provisions for extra or rescue doses is best. Unless an IV line is already established, CSCI is superior to CIVI for home care (Bruera, 1990). Common medications are morphine HP and hydromorphone HP. The infusion site should be changed weekly unless local signs (redness and swelling) appear sooner (Swenson, 1997). Dose escalation occurs for most home care patients about every 7 days, once analgesia reaches a steady state (Bruera, 1990).

● Epidural or intrathecal intraspinal infusion uses less opioid (usually fentanyl or morphine) than systemic administration. Intraspinal infusion is used most appropriately for patients who are unable to tolerate opioids; achieve relief, especially of regional pain below T_1, by other routes (APS, 1992; Mercadante, 1994); or have pain due to epidural metastases (Applegren et al., 1997). Medications are delivered epidurally in a single dose, intermittently by schedule or demand, by continuous infusion, or intrathecally in a single dose. While complications are not a major liability, cost and ensuring that staff have necessary expertise are significant issues (Manfredi, Chandler, Patt, & Payne, 1997).

● PCA pumps can deliver medications intravenously, subcutaneously, or epidurally. They are used successfully in surgical, oncology, and other settings, including the home, and new systems are rapidly being developed. While the effectiveness of PCA versus expert oral management of pain remains an issue of debate, it is clear that in at least the 10% of patients with cancer whose pain is not controlled with oral medications, PCAs are an option. However, the problems in this 10% category are often found in the neuropathic nature of the pain, so opioids are less effective regardless of the route. PCAs do have two qualities that make them more attractive to some: (1) Some patients have a significantly greater sense of control over the pain and other aspects of their situation and (2) the high-tech nature of PCA is comforting to some. For these patients, PCAs can be symbolic of the power of technology and proof that caregivers have not surrendered. (Others may experience the high-tech nature of PCAs as intrusive.) Problems of PCAs include cost, which can be more than $4,000/mo (Ferrell & Griffith, 1994); need for staff expertise; and potential for complications, most of which occur in PCAs that incorporate predetermined interval demand doses and continuous background infusion, which are the features needed to manage pain adequately. Another problem is the question of what happens with patients who develop cognitive failure.

● Buccal/sublingual delivery systems (eg, fentanyl "suckers") are in limited use.

● Exploration of less common means of administering opioids continues, including intracerebroventricular, buccal/sublingual, topical/transcutaneous, and intranasal routes.

Equianalgesic Conversions

Opioids have equivalent analgesic (equianalgesic) properties among routes and medications, but these vary according to medication and route. Converting from one medication or route to another carries significant potential for error. For chronic cancer pain, 30 mg of oral morphine is approximately equivalent to 10 mg IM morphine. Giving 10 mg of oral morphine in place of 10 mg IM morphine guarantees pain.

To make conversions, use equianalgesic charts (Tables 12-1 through 12-4) to determine the appropriate initial dose, then titrate to effect. Examples follow:

● 10 mg morphine IM every 4 hours is equivalent to 30 mg morphine PO every 4 hours; 20 mg morphine IM every 4 hours is equivalent to 60 mg morphine PO every 4 hours.

● 60 mg morphine PO or 20 mg IM is equivalent to 15 mg hydromorphone PO or 3 mg IM.

To change from continuous IV opioids (eg, morphine) to oral, the amount of morphine taken in 24 hours is determined. Using the IM equivalency, that amount is converted to the oral equivalent for 24 hours, and the 24-hour dose is divided by six (for immediate-release morphine) to determine how much oral morphine to give every 4 hours. To determine the amount to give for single IV boluses (when pain is not controlled), half of the IM dose is used (APS, 1992).

Equianalgesic data on rectal opioids are not well established, and there is variation in response to opioids. The early work of McCaffery and Beebe (1989) has held true: Rectal and oral doses are similar in effect, but some patients experience somewhat greater analgesia and sedation with rectal opioids (Warren, 1996). Insertion depth influences the analgesic effects of any suppository, and bowel movement after insertion may eliminate the suppository.

Analgesic Tables

To convert from other routes or medications to controlled-release morphine, the first conversion is to oral immediate-release morphine, which is administered until pain is relieved. After pain relief is achieved, the 24-hour dose of immediate-release oral morphine is determined and divided by two for every-12-hour dosing.

For example, the patient's pain is acceptably managed with morphine 20 mg IM every 4 hours. This equals 120 mg IM every 24 hours, and 360 mg PO every 24 hours. The every-12-hour (Oramorph and MS Contin) dose is 180 mg, and the 24-hour (Kadian) dose is 360 mg (capsule doses = 100 mg, 50 mg, and 20 mg; hence, exact dosing is not possible in this example).

Tables 12-1 to 12-4 summarize a few salient points—in connection with the previous discussion on conversions and dosages—concerning the medications listed there. Readers should also refer to current texts, journals, and other sources for complete information on administering, adjusting, or prescribing these medications.

Only commonly used analgesics are included in these tables. Mixed agonist-antagonists and partial agonists are not included because their use in chronic cancer pain is seldom appropriate. It must also be borne in mind that a variety of factors influence drug effects and side effects. These include patient size, disease status, pain intensity, other medications taken, and so forth. Discriminative clinical judgment is thus always necessary to administer, adjust, and prescribe these medications effectively.

Other Pain Relief Measures

A number of other techniques exist to reduce pain and to alleviate the symptoms causing pain:

● *Acupuncture and related techniques:* Acupuncture, cold laser therapy, and acupressure use stimulation of specific peripheral nerves (acupoints) to achieve analgesia.

● *Topical medications:* Menthol salves are used worldwide for pain. Tiger Balm, Monkey Holding a Peach, and various "sports balms" can all give surprising results for superficial pain, especially for patients with a tradition of using such medications (eg, Asians). Capsaicin cream is discussed previously in this chapter.

● *Cold or heat therapy:* Cold or heat therapy affects some pain by reducing inflammation (cold) or increasing blood flow (heat). Heat therapy also helps relaxation.

● *Radiation Therapy:* Radiation therapy reduces tumor size and is useful in several dif-

| TABLE 12-1 | Analgesics for Mild to Moderate Pain (Nonopioid Analgesics) |

Analgesic	Oral Dose Range	Dosing Schedule (Hours)	Maximum Dose (mg/24 h)*	Comments
Acetylsalicylic acid (eg, aspirin)	500–1000	4–6	6000	Give with caution to patients with renal dysfunction, hematologic disorders, or in combination with steroids. Gastrointestinal (GI) upset may occur. Half-life increases with dose. Do not give to children younger than 12 y. Rectal suppositories are available for children and adults.
Acetaminophen (eg, Tylenol)	500–1000	4–6	6000	Give with caution to patients with renal dysfunction or anemia. Minimal GI side effects. Rectal suppositories are available.
Ibuprofen (eg, Motrin, Nuprin, Advil)	400–800	4–8	4200	200 mg gives greater analgesia than aspirin 650 mg. Fewer GI and hematologic side effects than aspirin.
Naproxen (Naprosyn)	250–500	12	1000	Side effects are similar to aspirin but with a slower onset and longer duration of action. Sometimes given in doses as high as 1500 mg/d. Available in suspension.
Choline magnesium trisalicylate (Trilisate)	1500 × 1, then 1000 q12h	12	4000	Side effects are fewer than for aspirin. Platelets are unaffected.
Diflunisal (Dolobid)	1000 × 1, then 500 q12h	12	1500	Precautions are similar to those for aspirin. Initial loading dose shortens onset time.
Fenoprofen	800	6–8	3200	See ibuprofen.
Indomethacin	75	8–12	200	GI and central nervous system side effects are greater than propionic acids (eg, ibuprofen, naproxen, fenoprofen). Available in sustained release and rectal formulations.

*At high doses, stool should be checked for blood, and regular liver function tests, blood urea nitrogen and creatinine assessments, and urinalysis performed (Portenoy, 1998).
   Table references: American Pain Society, 1992; Foley, 1997; Portenoy, 1998.

ferent pain syndromes or situations (Foley, 1997): (1) Pressure on nerves from tumor growth responds well to radiation therapy; (2) tumor infiltration of nerves is less responsive; (3) bone pain from isolated metastases responds well to radiation (spinal metastases are commonly treated with radiation, chemotherapy, and corticosteroids [Janjan, 1996]); and (4) obstructive syndromes, such as superior vena cava syndrome, respond to radiation. Depending on several factors, the effects of radiation may be rapid or slow and in some cases include edema and hence temporarily increased symptoms.

● *Chemotherapy:* Chemotherapy can produce analgesia by reducing tumor size (of certain

TABLE 12-2	Opioid Analgesics for Mild to Moderate Pain*			
Analgesic	Oral Dose (mg)	IM Dose (mg)	Duration of Action (Hours)	Comments
Codeine	200	130	2–4	Side and adverse effects are similar to stronger opioids; 32 mg is approximately equianalgesic to 650 mg aspirin. Give with caution to patients with impaired ventilation, asthma, increased intracranial pressure, or liver failure. Often combined with nonsteroidal anti-inflammatory drugs.
Oxycodone	30	15	2–4	Available as a single agent or in combination with aspirin or acetaminophen. Also available as sustained release.
Hydrocodone	—	—	3–4	Available combined with acetaminophen.
Propoxyphene (Darvon)	—	—		May accumulate because of lengthy half-life (12 h), especially with regular use; 65 mg is approximately equivalent to 650 mg aspirin. Usefulness is limited in terminal illness.

*Doses given are similar in effect to 10 mg morphine sulfate IM or 30 mg PO (repeated dose).
  Table references: American Pain Society, 1992; Foley, 1997; Portenoy, 1998.

tumors) and possibly by affecting the tumor milieu, which includes tumor secretions and reactive host cells. Most patients with recurrent breast cancer develop bone metastases accompanied by pain and potential pathologic fractures. Some chemotherapeutic agents inhibit the bone metabolism that accompanies bone metastases. Others help prevent hypercalcemia and decrease pain and pathologic fractures, and still others inhibit bone formation. Chemotherapy can thus prevent pain, as in the first two situations, or can cause pain, as in the last (MacDonald, 1990).

● *Anesthetic measures:* Anesthetic measures include trigger point injections and nerve blocks. Blocks may be temporary or permanent. If temporary blocks effectively control pain, then permanent blocks may be used (Foley, 1997).

● *Surgery:* Neurosurgical approaches are most effective for well-defined localized pain (Foley, 1997) and are used when other approaches are unsuccessful.

Psychological and Related Interventions

While many nurses are aware of nonpharmacologic measures to manage pain, few use them regularly in practice. The following interventions are not a primary means of managing pain or other symptoms, and they are certainly not meant to be used as a kind of "smorgasbord" of suggestions for patients. Serious effort on the part of nurses to develop expertise in one or more of these interventions is an impor-

TABLE 12-3   Opioid Analgesics for Moderate to Severe Pain*

Analgesic	Oral Dose (mg)	IM Dose (mg†)	Duration of Action (Hours)	Comments
Morphine	30 (repeated dose) 60 (single dose)	10	3–4	Available in sustained release (12 and 24 h [12 h may have effective duration of 8 h]) tablets and immediate release (3–4 h) tablets, suspension, and suppositories. Can be given PO, PR, IM, IV, SQ. Sustained-release tablets are sometimes put in a capsule and given PR with good results.
Hydromorphone (Dilaudid)	7.5	1.5	3–4	Can be given PO, PR, IM, IV, SQ. Not currently available in sustained release.
Meperidine (Demerol)	300	75	2–4	Use in terminal illness is limited. Not recommended for long-term use.
Methadone	20	10	4–8	Tendency to accumulate in tissue and may result in oversedation. Use with care in older patients.
Levorphanol	4	2	4–8	Risk of accumulation exists.
Oxymorphone	No oral form	1 (10 mg PR)	3–4	Oral form not available.
Oxycodone	30	15	2–4	Available in sustained release. Used by some for moderate pain and by some for moderate to severe pain.
Fentanyl (see fentanyl table)	—	—	24–72	Transdermal fentanyl is a noninvasive means of managing stable pain.

*Doses for medications other than morphine are similar in effect to 10 mg morphine sulfate IM or 30 mg PO (repeated dose). All opioids should be given with caution to patients with respiratory deficit, increased intracranial pressure, and liver or renal dysfunction.
†For single IV bolus, use ½ the IM dose.
References: American Pain Society, 1992; Foley, 1997; Portenoy, 1998; Warren, 1996.

tant goal. Effort, expertise, and confidence in using nonpharmacologic methods are necessary before they can be effective, and their implementation is often hampered by the very pain nurses are trying to help clients control. To some degree, all of these techniques allow clients to develop an ability to control themselves and their situation.

● *Social support* has a definite but difficult-to-define relationship with morbidity and mortality. Many patients with cancer tend to withdraw socially, so their suffering increases. Support comes from the patient's significant others and from staff. Increasing the support of others is discussed in Chapter 3. The traditional nursing intervention—giving support or lending comfort—is made up of an important series of actions that develops in the process of building the nurse–patient relationship.

● *Counseling,* that is, intervention to help the patient integrate the health-illness experience with other life experiences, is clearly indicated in the multidimensional pain experience. Counseling based on the short-term crisis intervention model is appropriate for patients with cancer pain. A key aspect of the crisis intervention model is to apply past coping

TABLE 12-4	Fentanyl (Transdermal Duragesic Patch) Dose Prescription Based Daily 24-Hour Morphine Dose		
Oral 24-Hour Morphine (mg/d)	IM 24-Hour Morphine (mg/d)	Duragesic Dose μg/h	
45–134	8–22	25	
135–224	23–37	50	
225–314	38–52	75	
315–404	53–67	100	
405–494	68–82	125	
495–584	83–97	150	
585–674	98–112	175	
675–764	113–127	200	
765–854	128–142	225	
855–944	143–157	250	
945–1034	158–172	275	
1035–1124	173–187	300	

Reprinted with permission from Janssen Pharmaceutica (Manufacturer of Duragesic).

skills to the current situation, even though the current situation may be perceived as more of a crisis than past events. Goals are limited and applied to the treatment plan (compliance, for example) and to dealing with the pain itself.

● *Distraction* is considered a cognitive coping technique that encompasses several other techniques, including controlled attention, music therapy, singing, conversation, rhythmic breathing, and so forth. Children sometimes use play as a distraction to deal with pain, and as previously noted, this sometimes results in their pain being underestimated by others (Hester, Jacox, Miaskowski, & Ferrell, 1992). Visualization is a related technique, as is focusing on pictures, such as those of saints or deities.

● *Focusing* includes learned or acquired mental exercise techniques, such as (1) transforming pain into the image of something else that can be controlled by turning it off and then exercising the control; (2) transforming the context or situation, for example, transforming the self

who is sick into the self participating in combat; and (3) dissociating the pain from the body (Fishman, 1990).

● *Relaxation* strategies include guided imagery and progressive muscle relaxation, both of which are helpful in managing pain. This technique is most effective when strategies are combined; it is also similar to the focusing described previously.

● *Hypnosis* has long been used in managing pain, especially for chronic pain. Hypnosis modifies the patient's perception of pain through increasing the ability to concentrate. As is true of all the other interventions in this section, not all patients respond well to any one technique, hypnosis included.

● *Biofeedback* enables some patients, to some extent, to alter specific body functions, including muscle tension, which helps overcome the pain-bracing syndrome.

Spiritual Interventions

● *Prayer,* whether repetitive, such as in some meditative prayers, or intercessory, is effective for some people. Others may be dismayed and further disheartened that prayer may have no effect on the experience of pain.

● *Meditation* is a term meaning to contemplate or to keep the mind focused, either on itself or on something outside of self. It covers a variety of disciplines and has been most consistently taught and practiced in eastern religions, like Buddhism. There are also other conceptions of contemplation, for example, in Catholicism (Merton, 1953), where meditation may be understood as a form of private devotion or spiritual exercise consisting of deep, continued reflection on some religious theme. The idea of practicing meditation is that, through the discipline, the pain may decrease in importance or be better understood and thus be less distressing (Ram Dass & Gorman, 1985).

Alternative or Unconventional Therapies

The term alternative therapies is used here to designate measures for which little accepted (in the scientific world) research exists. While some advocates of alternative therapy refuse or dismiss modern medicine, others see a role for alternative therapy and modern medicine working together as complementary therapy (Cattau, 1997). The dangers of unconventional therapies are that (1) they are sometimes substituted for proven therapies, (2) some are very expensive and may result in discontinuing other beneficial medications or activities, and (3) some are toxic (eg, iscador [mistletoe], pennyroyal, lily of the valley).

Less than 20% of patients with HIV infection or cancer use alternative therapies (Carwein & Sabo, 1997; Jacob, 1997), and the number may decrease late in advanced disease. Most of the following measures are taken from Cattau (1997) and Jacob (1997). Some of the measures noted previously might also be classified as alternative:

● *Acupressure* operates on the same principles as acupuncture, except that finger and hand pressure are used along the meridians through which life energy is thought to be conducted.
● *Aromatherapy* uses botanical oils, such as rose, lavender, and others, that are added to bath water, massaged into the skin, added to tea, or used to scent a room.
● *Ayurveda* is the "knowledge of life" that is drawn from ancient Hindu texts.
● *Diet* measures include a vast array of diet supplements and total diet plans.
● *Herbal therapy and flower or "essence" therapy:* Herbs and various plant substances have long been used to heal illness and are the basis of many modern medications.
● *Homeopathy* uses a variety of herbs, minerals, and other materials to promote natural defenses against disease.
● *Juice therapy* incorporates (often large quantities of) fruit or vegetable juices to treat or prevent illness.
● *Marijuana* is used by some patients to treat nausea, anxiety, anorexia, or pain. Smoking marijuana rather than taking dronabinol (Marinol) or other commercial oral medica-

tions yields better control over effects for some and greater pleasure for others.
● *Reflexology* is based on the belief that specific areas of the foot are linked to other areas of the body; hence, massaging a particular area is thought to heal the connected part.
● *Sound therapy* uses music to calm a person or even treat illness.
● *Vitamin and mineral therapy* is sometimes called megavitamin therapy because it requires ingesting large quantities of several or sometimes one vitamin to treat or prevent illness.

Regardless of practitioner beliefs about efficacy or ethical issues related to these and other measures, it is important to understand that people do use such measures, and it is better to know than not to know about their use.

Special Populations

Children and Older Adults

Pain in infants and children has traditionally been undertreated (Berde, 1991). Children and babies older than 6 months experience approximately the same clinical effects from opioids as do young adults, while infants younger than 6 months are at higher risk of apnea from opioids than others, so they must be more closely monitored (APS, 1992). Oral opioids are effective for most children. After oral administration, continuous IV infusion and continuous subcutaneous infusion are the preferred routes of administration of medications. PCA appears to be effective for children able to understand how to use it effectively. IM injections should be avoided whenever possible because of children's fears (McGrath, 1998; Sellman, 1996).

Assessment is a major challenge in treating children with pain, especially those younger than 4 years. Parents are often used to obtain a pain history and give information on words or terms their children use for pain. However, depending on parents to assess pain is as unsatisfactory as depending on anyone else other than the patient: Accuracy is unlikely.

Behavioral clues in children with chronic pain are as unreliable as in adults. Children may even use a game or other types of play as a means of distraction to cope with pain. *Some children deny pain rather than take IM or even subcutaneous injections.* A number of self-report tools and scales are in use. Among them are the following, which appear to produce effective results (McGrath, 1998): the Faces Scale, Poker Chip Tool, visual analogue scales, and "pain thermometers." Most children older than 4 use self-report tools satisfactorily, and children older than 8 are able to use numerical scales (Hester et al., 1992). Readers should consult the pediatric literature for specifics on children and pain.

Pain is incorrectly considered by some as not as great a problem among older adults as it is among younger adults (Brescia et al., 1990). Older adults have greater sensitivity to opioids (and their side effects) than do younger adults and are at greater risk from accumulation and toxicity from medications with a lengthy plasma half-life, such as methadone and levorphanol. The primary difference between older and other adults is that older adults *complain* less of pain.

Patients with Substance-Related Disorders

The prevalence of addiction or substance-related disorders among patients with acute or cancer pain is unknown, but it is likely to be in the 19% to 25% range found among hospitalized patients (Savage, 1993). The prevalence of substance-related disorders among patients with AIDS is high: 25% of male patients in the United States contracted the disease through IV drug use, and nearly one half of infected women contracted the disease through IV drug use (Centers for Disease Control and Prevention, 1995). The prevalence of alcoholism among patients with AIDS is likely to be at least as great as in the general population.

Addiction is widely used synonymously with substance dependence in both popular and professional literature. Substance dependence is defined in the fourth edition of the *Diagnostic and Statistical Manual of Mental Disorders* as "a cluster of cognitive, behavioral, and physiological symptoms indicating (continued use) of the substance despite significant substance-related problems . . . (with) repeated self-administration that usually results in tolerance, withdrawal, and compulsive drug-taking behavior" (APA, 1994). Physical dependence is the use of a substance to the extent that cessation of use results in a withdrawal syndrome. Physical dependence is chiefly distinguished from substance dependence or addiction by the absence of problems, compulsive drug-taking, and repeated self-administration. Tolerance is the need to increase doses to achieve the same effect (of analgesia). Disease progression may also result in the need to increase doses to achieve the same analgesia.

PROBLEMS OF PAIN MANAGEMENT FOR PATIENTS WITH SUBSTANCE-RELATED DISORDERS

Problems of pain management for patients with substance-related disorders—whether active or in remission—center around the tension between (1) using psychoactive medications with a distinct potential for abuse or dependence and (2) effectively managing pain. It is thus difficult for some patients with substance disorders to find *and* maintain a balance between therapeutic effective use and misuse. Some patients underuse opioids in an attempt to avoid activation of dependence. Others may overuse medications to alleviate psychological distress to the detriment of activities of daily living and pain management. Others may go on binges of opioid consumption, sometimes mixed with tranquilizers, hypnotics, and other medications or alcohol and thus experience toxic side effects and subsequent poor pain status (McCorquodale, DeFaye, & Bruera, 1993). Still others may have overwhelming psychological distress that negates the salutary effects of opioids to the extent that escalating doses result in toxic effects (Lawlor, Walker, Bruera, & Mitchell, 1997).

Physicians and nurses contribute to or cause problems in pain management by underprescribing or underadministering because of not understanding pain management or misunderstanding or even being hostile toward people with substance disorders, especially when the pain is directly linked to the substance disorder (Cross & Urbanski, 1994). Health care providers with expertise in substance disorders may complicate the picture by viewing opioid use for pain management as addictive behavior (Savage, 1993).

Pain management is complicated by patients with substance-related disorders typically having a lower pain tolerance than other patients (Savage, 1993) and often requiring either higher doses or more frequent administration of analgesic medications (Selwyn, 1992). Psychopathology may exist as a precipitating factor in clients developing a substance-related disorder or may exist as a sequela of drug use (separate from the use itself) or as both a precipitating factor and sequela. Because of the complex interrelated physical, psychosocial, and spiritual problems involved in drug use, it is generally very difficult to manage pain adequately in patients with an active substance-related disorder (Kemp, 1996).

IDENTIFICATION OF SUBSTANCE-RELATED DISORDERS IN PATIENTS WITH PAIN

Substance-related disorders are underidentified in most health care settings. Detecting a substance-related disorder may be a process that occurs over time as the health care team comes to know the patient. The presence or absence of many of the following factors may not directly indicate a drug problem. Assessment of a patient's potential for or actual abuse of opioids or other medications includes the following:

● Is there a history of a substance-related disorder? When obtaining a history, the nurse should be alert to patient resentment of questions about substance use, rationalization of misuse, and history of weekend binges. The "CAGE questions" provide a quick, simple assessment format for alcoholism and other substance abuse (Ewing, 1984). Two to three affirmative answers to the following questions indicate a distinct possibility of dependence; four affirmative answers indicate a high likelihood of dependence. The questions are worded exactly as in the original CAGE research:

● C: Have you ever felt you ought to cut down on your drinking?
● A: Have people annoyed you by criticizing your drinking?
● G: Have you ever felt bad or guilty about your drinking?
● E: Have you ever had a drink first thing in the morning to steady your nerves or get rid of a hangover (eyeopener)?

● Finding the patient in an intoxicated state points clearly to at least a potential problem.
● Are there physical or other problems possibly related to substance-related disorders?
● Are medications taken reliably, and is the patient in control of use? Claims that medications were lost should be viewed with suspicion, especially if occurring more than once.
● Does the patient seek drugs? Obtaining prescriptions from more than one source, traveling long distances to obtain medications, having a history of multiple unsatisfactory interactions with health providers, and reporting drug "allergies" that limit treatment to opioids alone may indicate a problem.
● Are there other indications that a problem might exist or might develop? A patient in recovery from substance dependence should be carefully monitored for precipitating circumstances, such as psychosocial setbacks, death of a loved one, development of increased depression or anxiety, sudden changes in behavior, or disease exacerbation.

MANAGING PAIN

Care is challenging when a patient has chronic pain and is in recovery from a substance-related disorder. The patient may resist using a medication with the potential for abuse and if willing to use the medication, is at significant risk of abusing that medication or other substances. The more recent the history of dependence, the greater the potential for again becoming dependent. Indeed, some patients with a clear understanding of their own potential for abuse may make a conscious and fully informed decision for pain over opioid use.

GUIDELINES FOR CHRONIC PAIN MANAGEMENT IN ADVANCED DISEASE FOR PATIENTS WITH SUBSTANCE-RELATED DISORDERS

The health care provider should use the following guidelines when managing pain in patients with substance-related disorders:

● Use accepted and current means of effective pain assessment and management as described elsewhere in this chapter.
● Understand (and impart to other team members) the dynamics of substance-related disorders, especially the power of the compulsion to use substances and manipulative behaviors associated with these disorders. When possible, involve a specialist in substance-related disorders in patient care and with assisting the team to work effectively with the involved patient and family.
● Use frank, open communication with the patient and family about the substance-related problem. Involve the patient and family in planning care, and use a written care plan.
● Even for patients in recovery, promote regular and increased involvement with the recovery program.
● When using opioid medications, (1) use medications with lower abuse potential (especially sustained-release morphine tablets) and (2) avoid medications with the highest abuse potential (especially hydromorphone and morphine). Patients with substance-related disorders may require larger amounts of analgesics than other patients. Patients on methadone maintenance should receive analgesics in addition to their regular dose of methadone.
● Limit pain assessment to one nurse and one physician, and limit prescription writing to one physician only.

● Involvement of a substance disorders specialist is necessary for a simultaneous attempt at withdrawal from substances (including alcohol) and pain management (Kemp, 1996).

Pain management may still be a challenge even with all these measures activated, and relapse may occur. Nevertheless, the health team should strive for the highest possible level of pain management in patients with substance-related disorders.

REFERENCES

Ahmedzai, S. (1997). Current strategies for pain control. *Annals of Oncology, 8*(Suppl. 3), s21–s24.

Ahmedzai, S., & Brooks, D. (1997). Transdermal fentanyl versus sustained release morphine in cancer pain: Preference, efficacy, and quality of life. *Journal of Pain and Symptom Management, 13*(5), 254–261.

American Pain Society. (1992). *Principles of analgesic use in the treatment of acute pain and cancer pain* (3rd ed.). Skokie, IL: Author.

American Psychological Association. (1994). *Diagnostic and statistical manual of mental disorders* (4th ed.). Washington, DC: Author.

Applegren, L., Nordborg, C., Sjoberg, M., Karlsson, P-A., Nitescu, P., & Curelaru, I. (1997). Spinal epidural metastasis: Implications fpr spinal analgesia to treat "refractory" cancer pain. *Journal of Pain and Symptom Management, 13*(1), 25–42.

Baines, M. J. (1998). The pathophysiology and management of malignant intestinal obstruction. In D. Doyle, G. W. C. Hanks, & N. MacDonald (Eds.), *Oxford textbook of palliative medicine* (2nd ed.) (pp. 526–534). New York: Oxford University Press.

Benziger, D. P., Miotto, J., Grandy, R. P., Thomas, G. B., Swanton, R. E., & Fitzmartin, R. D. (1997). A pharmacokinetic/pharmacodynamic study of controlled-release oxycodone. *Journal of Pain and Symptom Management, 13*(2), 75–82.

Berde, C. B. (1991). The treatment of pain in children. In M. R. Bond, J. E. Charlton, & C. J. Woolf (Eds.), *Proceedings of the VIth World Congress on Pain* (pp. 435–440). Amsterdam: Elsevier.

Bowsher, D. (1997). The effects of pre-emptive treatment of postherpatic neuralgia with amitriptyline: A randomized, double-blind, placebo-controlled trial. *Journal of Pain and Symptom Management, 13*(6), 327–331.

Brescia, F. J., Adler, D., Gray, G., Ryan, M. A., Cimino, J., & Mamtini, R. (1990). Hospitalized advanced cancer patients: A profile. *Journal of Pain and Symptom Management, 5*(4), 221–227.

Broomhead, A., Kerr, R., Tester, W., O'Meara, P., Maccarrone, C., Bowles, R., & Hodsman, P. (1997). Comparison of once-a-day sustained-release morphine formulation with standard oral morphine treatment for cancer pain. *Journal of Pain and Symptom Management, 14*(2), 63–73.

Bruera, E. (1990). Subcutaneous administration of opioids in the management of cancer pain. In K. M. Foley, J. J. Bonica, & V. Ventafridda (Eds.), *Proceedings of the Second International Congress on Cancer Pain* (pp. 210–218). New York: Raven Press.

Bruera, E. (1991). Update on adjuvant drugs for cancer pain treatment. In M. R. Bond, J. E. Charlton, & C. J. Woolf (Eds.), *Proceedings of the VIth World Congress on Pain* (pp. 459–465). Amsterdam: Elsevier.

Bruera, E., Schoeller, T., & Montejo, G. (1992). Organic hallucinosis in patients receiving high doses of opiates for cancer pain. *Pain, 48*(3), 397–399.

Casciato, D. A. (1995). Symptom care. In D. A. Casciato & B. B. Lowitz (Eds.), *Manual of clinical oncology* (3rd ed.) (pp. 76–97). Boston: Little, Brown and Company.

Carwein V. L., & Sabo, C. E. (1997). The use of alternative therapies for HIV infection: Implications for patient care. *AIDS Patient Care and STDs, 11*(1), 79–85.

Cattau, D. (1997). All you really need is chi. *The Park Ridge Center Bulletin, 2,* 6–11.

Centers for Disease Control and Prevention. (1995). *HIV/AIDS surveillance report (mid year edition).* Atlanta: Author.

Coleman, R. E. (1997). Skeletal complications of malignancy. *Cancer Supplement, 80*(8), 1588–1594.

Cross, R. L., & Urbanski, B. A. (1994). Providing pain control for the critically ill substance abuse patient. *Dimensions in Critical Care Nursing, 13,* 282–283.

Duggleby, W., & Lander, J. (1994). Cognitive status and postoperative pain: Older adults. *Journal of Pain and Symptom Management, 9*(1), 19–27.

Ernst, D. S., Brasher, P., Hagen, N., Paterson, A. H.

G., MacDonald, R. N., & Bruera, E. (1997). A randomized controlled trial of intravenous clodronate in patients with metastatic bone disease and pain. *Journal of Pain and Symptom Management, 13*(6), 319–326.

Ewing, J. A. (1984) Detecting alcoholism: The CAGE questionnaire. *Journal of the American Medical Association, 252,* 1905–1907

Farncombe, M., Daniels, G., & Cross, L. (1994). Lymphedema: The seemingly forgotten complication. *Journal of Pain and Symptom Management, 9*(4), 269–276.

Ferrell, B. R., & Griffith, H. (1994). Cost issues related to pain management: Report from the Cancer Pain Panel of the Agency for Health Care Policy and Research. *Journal of Pain and Symptom Management, 9*(4), 221–234.

Fishman, B. (1990). The treatment of suffering in patients with cancer pain: Cognitive-behavioral approaches. In K. M. Foley, J. J. Bonica, & V. Ventafridda (Eds.), *Proceedings of the Second International Congress on Cancer Pain* (pp. 301–316). New York: Raven Press.

Foley, K. M. (1997). Management of cancer pain. In V. T. DeVita, S. Hellman, & S. A. Rosenburg (Eds.), *Cancer: Principles and practice of oncology* (5th ed.) (pp. 2807–2841). Philadelphia: Lippincott-Raven.

Foley, K. M. (1989). Controversies in cancer pain. *Cancer, 63*(11), 2257–2265.

Harrington, K. D. (1997). Orthopedic surgical management of skeletal complications of malignancy. *Cancer Supplement, 80*(8), 1614–16227.

Hester, N. O., Jacox, A., Miaskowski, C. & Ferrell, B. (1992). Excerpts from guidelines for the management of pain in infants, children, and adolescents. *Maternal-Child Nursing, 17,* 146–152.

Inturrisi, C. E. (1990). Opioid analgesic therapy in cancer pain. In K. M. Foley, J. J. Bonica, & V. Ventafridda (Eds.), *Proceedings of the Second International Congress on Cancer Pain* (pp. 133–154). New York: Raven Press.

Jacob, J. J. (1997). Unproven alternative methods of cancer treatment. In V. T. DeVita, S. Hellman, & S. A. Rosenburg (Eds.), *Cancer: Principles and practice of oncology* (5th ed.) (pp. 2993–3001). Philadelphia: Lippincott-Raven.

Janjan, N. A. (1996). Radiotherapeutic management of spinal metastases. *Journal of Pain and Symptom Management, 11*(1), 47–56.

Kemp, C. E. (1996). Managing chronic pain in patients with advanced disease and substance related disorders. *Home Healthcare Nurse, 14*(4), 255–263.

Lawlor, P., Walker, P., Bruera, E., & Mitchell, S. (1997). Severe opioid toxicity and somatization of psychosocial distress in a cancer patient with a background of chemical dependence. *Journal of Pain and Symptom Management, 13*(6), 356–361.

MacDonald, N. (1990). The role of medical and surgical oncology in the management of cancer pain. In K. M. Foley, J. J. Bonica, & V. Ventafridda (Eds.), *Proceedings of the Second International Congress on Cancer Pain* (pp. 27–39). New York: Raven Press.

Manfredi, P. L., Chandler, S. W., Patt, R., & Payne, R. (1997). High-dose epidural infusion of opioids for cancer pain: Cost issues. *Journal of Pain and Symptom Management, 13*(2), 118–121.

McCaffery, M., & Beebe, A. (1989). *Pain: Clinical manual for nursing practice.* St. Louis: C.V. Mosby.

McGrath, P. A. (1998). Pain contol (pediatric). In D. Doyle, G. W. C. Hanks, & N. MacDonald (Eds.), *Oxford textbook of palliative medicine* (2nd ed.) (pp. 1013–1031). New York: Oxford University Press.

McCorquodale, S., De Faye, B., & Bruera, E. (1993). Pain control in an alcoholic cancer patient. *Journal of Pain and Symptom Management, 8*(2), 177–180.

Mercadante, S., Sapio, M., Caligara, M., Serratta, R., Dardanoni, G., & Barresi, L. (1997). Opioid-sparing effect of diclofenac in cancer pain. *Journal of Pain and Symptom Management, 14*(1), 15–20.

Mercadante, S. (1994). Intrathecal morphine and bupivacaine in advanced cancer pain patients implanted at home. *Journal of Pain and Symptom Management, 9*(3), 201–207.

Merton, T. (1953). *Bread in the wilderness.* New York: New Directions Books.

Monks, R. (1990). Psychotropic drugs. In J. J. Bonica (Ed.), *The management of pain* (pp. 1676–1689). Philadelphia: Lea & Febiger.

Paice, J. A. (1991). Unraveling the mystery of pain. *Oncology Nursing Forum, 18*(5), 843–849.

Payne, R. (1997). Mechanisms and management of bone pain. *Cancer Supplement, 80*(8), 1608–1613.

Portenoy, R. K. (1993). Management of neuropathic pain. In C. R. Chapman & K. M. Foley (Eds.), *Current and emerging issues in cancer pain: Research and practice* (pp. 351–369). New York: Raven Press.

Portenoy, R. K. (1998). Three step analgesic ladder for management of cancer pain. *Oncology Special Edition, 1*(1), 71–74.

Portenoy, R. K. (1989). Cancer pain: Epidemiology and syndromes. *Cancer, 63*(11), 2298–2307.

Porter, J., & Jick, H. (1980). Addiction rare in patients treated with narcotics. *New England Journal of Medicine, 302*(2), 123.

Ram Dass, & Gorman, P. (1985). *How can I help?* New York: Alfred A. Knopf.

Ripamonti, C. (1994). Management of bowel obstruction in advanced cancer patients. *Journal of Pain and Symptom Management, 9*(3), 193–200.

Ripamonti, C., & De Conno, F. (1997). Rectal opioid medications: Our experience. *Journal of Pain and Symptom Management, 13*(5), 250–251.

Rosenberg, J. M., Harrell, C., Ristic, H., Werner, R. A., & de Rosayro, A. M. (1997). The effect of gabentin on neuropathic pain. *The Clinical Journal of Pain, 13*(3), 251–255.

Rousseau, P. (1995). Antiemetic therapy in adults with terminal disease: A brief review. *American Journal of Hospice and Palliative Care, 12*(6), 13–18.

Savage, S. R. (1993). Addiction in the treatment of pain: Significance, recognition, and management. *Journal of Pain and Symptom Management, 8*(5), 265–278.

Sellman, G. L. (1996). Pain management. In W. E. Nelson, R. E. Behrman, R. M. Kliegman, & A. M. Arvin (Eds.), *Nelson textbook of pediatrics* (15th ed.) (pp. 287–290). Philadelphia: W.B. Saunders.

Selwyn, P. A. (1992). Medical aspects of human immunodeficiency virus infection and its treatment in injecting drug users. In J. H. Lowinson, P. Ruiz, & R. B. Millman (Eds.), *Substance abuse: A comprehensive textbook* (2nd ed.) (pp. 744–774). Baltimore: Williams & Wilkins.

Schug, S. A., Zech, D., & Dörr, U. (1990). Cancer pain management according to WHO analgesic guidelines. *Journal of Pain and Symptom Management, 5*(1), 27–32.

Stanley, T. H. (1992). The history and development of the fentanyl series. *Journal of Pain and Symptom Management, 7*(3), Supplement, S3–S7.

Swenson, C. J. (1997). Pain management. In S. E.

Otto (Ed.), *Oncology nursing* (3rd ed.) (pp. 746–791). St Louis: C.V. Mosby.

Twycross, R. G. (1978). Relief of pain. In C. M. Saunders (Ed.), *The management of terminal disease* (pp. 65–98). London: Edward Arnold.

Twycross, R., & Lichter, I. (1998).The terminal phase. In D. Doyle, G. W. C. Hanks, & N. MacDonald (Eds.), *Oxford textbook of palliative medicine* (2nd ed.) (pp. 977–992). New York: Oxford University Press.

Waller, A., & Caroline, N. L. (1996). *Handbook of palliative care in cancer.* Boston: Butterworth-Heinemann.

Walsh, T. D. (1990a). Prevention of opioid side effects. *Journal of Pain and Symptom Management, 5*(6), 362–367.

Walsh, T. D. (1990b). Adjuvant analgesic therapy in cancer pain. In K. M. Foley, J. J. Bonica, & V. Ventafridda (Eds.), *Proceedings of the Second International Congress on Cancer Pain* (pp. 155–169). New York: Raven Press.

Warrell, R. P. (1997). Metabolic emergencies. In V. T. DeVita, S. Hellman, & S. A. Rosenburg (Eds.), *Cancer: Principles and practice of oncology* (5th ed.) (pp. 2486–2511). Philadelphia: Lippincott-Raven.

Warren, D. E. (1996). Practical use of rectal medications in palliative care. *Journal of Pain and Symptom Management, 11*(6), 378–387

Neurologic Symptoms

Neurologic problems, such as delirium, occur to some extent in most patients with terminal illness, especially as death nears (Roth-Roemer, Fann, & Syrjala, 1997). Common neurologic problems in terminal illness include confusion (delirium, dementia), terminal restlessness (with or without confusion), seizures, motor or sensory deficits, coma (discussed in Chapter 21), increased ICP, SCC, and other problems, such as plexopathies, brain metastases, and paraneoplastic syndromes (PNSs). These problems are due to central nervous system (CNS) metastases (to brain, meninges, spinal cord) or primary tumors of the CNS; to nonmetastatic processes, such as side effects of treatment, infections, metabolic disorders, nutritional disorders, neurologic PNSs, and primary neurologic disease (Holland, 1997); and in patients with AIDS, commonly to AIDS dementia complex, cytomegalovirus infection,

cryptococcal meningitis, toxoplasmic encephalitis, or direct HIV-1 infection (Price & Brew, 1997). Please see Chapter 21 for a discussion of coma, Chapter 27 for a discussion of the neurologic problems of AIDS, and Chapter 29 for a discussion of Alzheimer's disease.

Confusion: Delirium and Dementia

Symptoms

In general, delirium is an acute cognitive disorder of varying severity that includes disorientation (most often to time and seldom to person), attention deficits, either agitation or lethargy, and illusions or hallucinations (Walsh, 1989). There are often changes in mental status from hour to hour, and symptoms may worsen at night ("sundowning"). Hallucinations or other troubling psychologi-

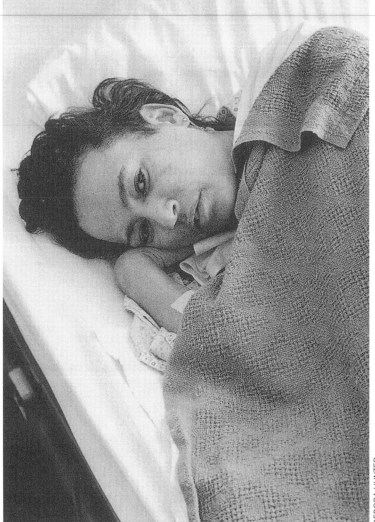

DEBORA HUNTER

cal events may be manifested only by change in mood and may not be voluntarily reported (Bruera, Schoeller, & Montejo, 1992). At least in early stages, delirium is often unrecognized by nurses and physicians and hence is untreated (Roth-Roemer et al., 1997).

Dementia is a chronic gradual decrease in cognition that may begin with slight memory losses or other deficits that are either unrecognized or excused by the client and others. In its early stages, dementia may be mistaken for depression. Dementia predisposes patients to episodes of delirium, except in the last stages of a chronic illness such as Alzheimer's disease or AIDS dementia complex.

In both delirium and dementia, there may be a decreased control over expression of personality tendencies, with suppressed memories or urges and unconscious material surfacing—to the distress of the patient and family.

TABLE 13-1	Common Causes of Confusion in Patients With Cancer
Treatment side effects	Opioids, steroids, phenothiazines, sedatives, antiemetics, anticholinergics, radiation (to brain)
	Withdrawal of treatment: benzodiazepines, corticosteroids, opioids
	Other drug withdrawal: alcohol, nicotine, barbiturate
Primary disease	Brain or other CNS metastases, primary tumor, increased ICP
Distant effects of primary disease or other condition	Electrolyte imbalance (eg, hypercalcemia, hyponatremia, hypoglycemia, acidosis, alkalosis)
	CNS paraneoplastic syndromes (especially with lung, breast, and ovarian cancer)
	Pain
	Other symptoms/problems, including anemia, dehydration, dyspnea, fecal impaction, hypovolemia, urine retention
	Nutritional deficiencies (eg, cachexia, vitamin B_{12} deficiency)
Other causes	Organ failure, including liver, kidney, lung, thyroid, adrenals
	Infection (and sometimes antibiotics)
	Nonmalignant disease (Alzheimer's disease, atherosclerosis, AIDS dementia)
	Psychiatric disorder

Etiologies

Acute confusion (delirium) may be due to a variety of etiologies, including medications, metabolic disorders, nonmalignant CNS disease, pain, infections, fecal impaction or urine retention, sleep deprivation, heart disease, or endocrine disorders. Among the causes of chronic confusion (dementia) are Alzheimer's disease, AIDS dementia, atherosclerosis, intracranial tumors (see following discussion of increased ICP), drugs, anemia, vitamin B_{12} deficiency, PNS, and chronic social isolation (Bruera et al., 1992; Holland, 1997). Because patients with advanced cancer are at risk for almost all of the above, changes in mentation, such as confusion, must be carefully assessed rather than automatically attributed to the disease (see Table 13-1). There are also numerous potential etiologies for confusion in clients with HIV infection.

Assessment of a confused patient includes (1) physical assessment, especially medication review and review of metabolic disorders, including hypercalcemia, hyponatremia, and hypoglycemia, and (2) a standardized mental status examination (eg, the Mini-Mental State Examination, shown in Figure 13-1, or the Memorial Delirium Assessment Scale) (Breitbart et al., 1997).

Interventions

The best option in treating confusion is to modify the etiology (eg, resolve pain, fecal impaction, urinary retention, insomnia, or hypercalcemia; reduce tumor edema; or change medications). In many cases, the etiology cannot be changed, either because the CNS changes are irreversible (eg, Alzheimer's disease) or because the confusion is part of the dying process (eg, hypercalcemia in a moribund patient). Symptomatic treatment includes the following:

● Antipsychotic medications, especially haloperidol (Haldol) 0.5 to 1.0 mg orally (PO) is given two to four times daily to decrease confusion and is sometimes combined with lorazepam (Ativan) to treat both confusion and agitation (Holland, 1997). For mild confusion, Waller and Caroline (1996) recommend haloperidol 1 mg PO tid and for severe confusion, parenteral (intramuscular [IM] or intravenous [IV]) haloperidol 1 to 2 mg repeated every 30 to 60 minutes twice as needed until acute confusion or agitation is controlled, then switching to the oral route. Diphenhydramine 25 to 50 mg PO tid to qid may also be started to prevent extrapyramidal reactions. Waller

FIGURE 13-1. *Mini-Mental State Examination*

Maximum score 30. Score <20 suggests significant cognitive impairment.

I. Orientation (Maximum score 10)	Date (e.g., January 21)	1_____
	Year	2_____
Ask "What is today's date?" Then ask specifically for parts omitted; e.g., "Can you also tell what season it is?"	Month	3_____
	Day (e.g., Monday)	4_____
Ask "Can you tell me the name of this hospital?"	Season	5_____
"What floor are we on?"	Hospital	6_____
"What town (or city) are we in?"	Floor	7_____
"What county are we in?"	Town/City	8_____
What state are we in"	County	9_____
	State	10_____

II. Registration (Maximum score 3)

Ask the subject if you may test his/her memory. Then say "Ball," "Flag," "Tree," clearly and slowly, about one second for each. After you have said all 3 words, ask subject to repeat them. This first repetition determines the score (0–3) but keep saying them (up to 6 trials) until the subject can repeat all 3 words. If he/she does not eventually learn all three, recall cannot be meaningfully tested

"Ball"	11_____
"Flag"	12_____
"Tree"	13_____

Record number of trials_____

III. Attention and calculation (Maximum score 5)

Ask the subject to begin at 100 and count backward by 7. Stop after 5 subtractions (93, 86, 79, 72, 65). Score one point for each correct number.

If the subject cannot or will not perform this task, ask him/her to spell the word "world" backward (D, L, R, O, W). The score is one point for each correctly placed letter, e.g., DLROW = 5, DLORW = 3. Record how the subject spelled "world" backward:

"93"	14_____
"86"	15_____
"79"	16_____
"72"	17_____
"65"	18_____
OR	
Number of correctly placed letters	19_____

IV. Recall (Maximum score 3)

Ask the subject to recall the three words you previously asked him/her to remember (learned in Registration).

"Ball"	20_____
"Flag"	21_____
"Tree"	22_____

V. Language (Maximum score 9)

Naming: Show the subject a wrist watch and ask "What is this?" Repeat for pencil. Score one point for each item named correctly.

Repetition: Ask the subject to repeat, "No ifs, ands, or buts." Score one point for correct repetition.

Watch	23_____
Pencil	24_____
Repetition	25_____

3-Stage Command: Give the subject a piece of blank paper and say, "Take the paper in your right hand, fold it in half and put it on the floor." Score one point for each action performed correctly.

Takes in right hand	26_____
Folds in half	27_____
Puts on floor	28_____
Closes eyes	29_____

Reading: On a blank piece of paper, print the sentence, "Close your eyes" in letters large enough for the subject to see clearly. Ask subject to read it and do what it says. Score correctly only if he/she actually closes his/her eyes.

Writing: Give the subject a blank piece of paper and ask him/her to write a sentence. It is to be written spontaneously. It must contain a subject and verb and make sense. Correct grammar and punctuation are not necessary.

Writes sentence   30_____

Copying: On a clean piece of paper, draw intersecting pentagons, each side about an inch, and ask subject to copy it exactly as it is. All 10 angles must be present and two must intersect to score one point. Tremor and rotation are ignored

Draws pentagons   31_____

For example:

Score: Add number of correct responses. In section III include items 14–18 or item 19, not both. (Maximum total score 30)

Rate subject's level of consciousness: (a) coma, (b) stupor, (c) drowsy, (d) alert

Total score _____

Reprinted with permission from Folstein, M.F., Folstein, F.E., and McHugh, P.R. (1975) Mini-mental state: a practical method for grading the cognitive state of patients for the clinician. *Journal of Psychiatric Research.* 12. 189–198.

and Caroline also recommend a trial of dexamethasone if brain metastases are or might be the cause of confusion, and blood chemistries are normal. Terminal agitation with delirium can be treated first with nembutal suppository 60 to 120 mg rectally q4h. If nembutal is not effective, droperidol 1.25 to 2.5 mg IV or IM is given, and if droperidol is not effective (or if neuromuscular activity is predominant), the other medications are discontinued and midazolam 1 to 2 mg/h subcutaneously (SQ) or IV is given until symptoms are managed. For severe agitation with delirium, midazolam can be given 1 mg q10 minutes until symptoms are under control. The hourly maintenance dose is 25% to 33% of required induction dose and diphenhydramine 25 to 50 mg PO tid to qid is used for extrapyramidal side effects (Hospice and Palliative Nurses Association [HPNA], 1997). Note that lorazepam (80% bioavailability) and clonazepam (bioavailability unknown) are effective when given rectally for terminal restlessness (Warren, 1996). Chlorpromazine 12.5 mg IV q4 to 12h or 25 mg PR q4 to 12h is a much less expensive alternative to midazolam and helps relieve dyspnea (Waller & Caroline, 1996).

● The patient's environment should be as familiar as possible and be well lighted (including a night light). Sensory overload should be avoided, especially at night, and brief, clear, and often repeated explanations given of procedures and other stimulating events. Because confusion is frightening to the patient, frequent reassurance should be given. Frequent reminders of person, place, and time may be helpful, including having a clock and a calendar present. Some patients are calmed by television, and some are not. Changes in staff should be avoided. Regular visits by family and friends should be encouraged and the effects of visits assessed. The patient should be dressed and groomed daily as long as possible. Environmental safety should be assessed. Unsupervised smoking should be discouraged. The value (to patient and family) of a structured schedule cannot be overemphasized. Structure can be promoted by writing out a schedule or a routine for the patient and others.

● Support to the family is essential. General psychosocial support, teaching, and frequent reassurance are helpful. Counseling or psychotherapy is especially helpful in dealing with anger or "wrong" thoughts, such as wishing the patient would die because he or she is a burden. See Chapter 29 for a further discussion of family issues related to degenerative neurologic disorders.

Terminal Restlessness

Terminal restlessness occurs in significant numbers (widely varying reports) of people in the last days or hours of life (Twycross & Lichter, 1998). Terminal restlessness is characterized by the following:

● Frequent, nonpurposeful motor activity
● Inability to concentrate or relax
● Distressed vocalizing
● Disturbances in sleep and rest patterns
● Fluctuating levels of consciousness, cognitive failure, or anxiety
● Potential progression to agitation (HPNA, 1997; Woodruff, 1997)

There are many potential etiologies of terminal restlessness, which in advanced stages of illness are extremely difficult to discern and in many cases are overlapping (see Table 13-1). Etiologies that may respond to intervention (eg, pain, change in medication or ability to metabolize medications, urinary retention, fecal impaction) are identified and treated. Terminal restlessness should be differentiated from akathisia, a syndrome of subjective feelings of restlessness and objective signs of pacing, rocking, and related agitated behaviors classified as extrapyramidal symptoms resulting from the use of antipsychotic medications (Brietbart, Chochinov, & Passik, 1998). In the absence of an identifiable etiology, terminal restlessness is treated as discussed previously under delirium, except that midazolam is the drug of choice in the absence of delirium (Twycross & Lichter, 1998). Chlorpromazine may also be used for terminal restlessness (Waller & Caroline, 1996).

Seizures

Any patient with intracranial tumor(s) or advanced AIDS is at risk for seizures. Almost 50% of clients with lung cancer and up to 75% of patients with melanoma will develop metastases to the brain, and of these, as many as 40% may have seizures at some point in the disease (Loeffler, Patchell, & Sawaya, 1997). Factors that may precipitate seizures in a patient with epilepsy or intracranial tumors include noncompliance with anticonvulsants, metabolic changes (uremia, hypoglcemia, hyponatremia), sleep deprivation, excess alcohol or withdrawal from alcohol or drugs, stress or anxiety, sepsis, and medications, including tricyclic antidepressants. Isolated grand mal seizures are managed or prevented with phenytoin and focal seizures (no loss of consciousness with motor, sensory, or psychic manifestations) are managed with carbamazepine (Waller & Caroline, 1996). Phenytoin accelerates the metabolism of corticosteroids (and other drugs), so dosages of corticosteroids should be increased. Occasionally corticosteroids will mask allergic reactions to phenytoin (usually manifested by skin rash) long enough for complications to develop.

If a patient does have a seizure, it is likely that additional seizures will occur. Teaching the family what to do when a seizure occurs then becomes important. Teaching points include the following:

● Medication administration, side effects, and what to do if a dose is missed (make up if omission remembered inside of 24 hours)
● Warning signs of seizure (prodromal phase), which are not always present
● Safety measures, including easing the patient to the floor or bed when a seizure begins, not restraining the patient, and not trying to force anything into the patient's mouth
● Ensuring that there is no airway obstruction or vomitus
● When to call for assistance (prolonged seizure, second seizure soon after first, injury)

Myoclonus

Myoclonus, a sudden involuntary contraction or twitching of muscles, is often multifocal and occurs most frequently with large doses of opioids; dopamine antagonists, such metoclopramide; neuroleptics, such as haloperidol; withdrawal of benzodiazepines, anticonvulsants, and other medications; or as a combination of organ failure and medications. Myoclonus is associated with CNS disease and renal or hepatic failure, especially in the final days or hours of life.

Treatment of myoclonus includes first addressing the etiology, if possible, such as decreasing dosages. Decreasing dosages may be possible if renal or hepatic failure is occurring. The following are medications for myoclonus (Twycross & Lichter, 1998):

● Diazepam 5 to 10 mg/h PR until settled and 10 mg PR once or twice daily thereafter
● Midazolam 5 to 10 mg SQ qh until settled and 10 to 30 mg/24 h SQ infusion thereafter
● Clonazepam 0.5 mg/h SQ until settled and 1 to 2 mg/24 h SQ infusion thereafter

Motor Sensory Deficits

Motor and sensory deficits in terminal illness are due to a variety of etiologies, including tumor growth, PNSs, metabolic disorders, treatment, and infections. Motor and sensory complications of AIDS include peripheral neuropathies, autonomic neuropathies, and myopathies. Peripheral neuropathies are common at all stages of HIV infection and AIDS. Some motor or sensory deficits are cardinal signs of disease progression and constitute serious complications in cancer and AIDS. Motor and sensory PNSs include the following:

● Polymyositis or dermatomyositis causes symmetric and proximal muscle weakness. Dermatomyositis includes a violaceous rash and periorbital edema and erythema. The syndrome progresses to include dark plaques on knuckles, elbows, and similar areas.
● Lambert-Eaton myasthenic syndrome, unlike many other PNSs, often occurs late in the course of illness and may resolve spontaneously. Problems include loss of motor function, but sensory function is not lost.
● Neuropathies include symmetric distal sensorimotor polyneuropathy associated with hematologic disorders.
● Myopathy is associated with carcinoid syndrome.

Also see the section on PNSs at the end of this chapter.

Increased Intracranial Pressure

Brain metastases are a common symptomatic complication of metastatic cancer, and increased ICP often results. The incidence of brain metastases is increasing because of increased survival of patients with tumors likely to metastasize to the brain.

Headache from increased ICP varies in site and associated symptoms, according to the site of the lesion(s). Typically, the pain is progressive and is usually accompanied by progressive neurologic deficits. Signs and symptoms depend on the nature of the lesion(s) and in addition to or in the absence of pain may include decreased level of or changes in consciousness, seizures, weakness, nausea and vomiting, bowel and bladder dysfunction, reflex changes, and evidence of cranial nerve involvement (Loeffler et al., 1997). Papillede-

ma (often with visual changes), vomiting, and headache are the classic triad of increased ICP. Headache may be most severe in early morning and may awaken the patient, but this occurs in less than half of patients with increased ICP (Loeffler et al., 1997). Bradycardia simultaneous with increased systolic blood pressure is an "early significant finding" in increased ICP (Chernecky & Krech, 1991). Personality changes and cognitive deficit may occur gradually or suddenly. Memory and judgment are affected, and agitation or depressed consciousness may be severe.

Signs and Symptoms of Brain Metastases

Brain metastases result in a variety of neurologic and other manifestations. The most common (Loeffler et al., 1997) follow:

● Headache, altered mental status
● Hemiparesis, focal weakness, gait ataxia
● Hemisensory loss, speech changes
● Seizure and papilledema

Treatment, if feasible given the patients stage of illness, includes radiation therapy, surgery, chemotherapy, and other measures described previously, especially under increased ICP.

Etiologies

Increased ICP is most often due to tumor (metastatic) and associated edema, causing pressure, displacement, or obstruction in the brain itself (especially the cortex) but also at the skull and dura or meninges. Untreated brain metastases result in a median survival of about 1 month (Mack, 1995).

Interventions

Treatment of increased ICP focuses on reducing pressure and managing associated symptoms (eg, pain, vomiting, agitation, confusion, and other neurologic deficits). Treatment must include explanations and psychosocial support. The idea of cancer in the brain and associated actual or potential symptoms is frightening. Seizures, personality changes, and loss of control are especially feared.

● Radiation is the standard treatment for brain metastases, and surgery is a common measure for reducing ICP due to single metastasis in the absence of disseminated disease.
● Dexamethasone is used to palliate symptoms of increased ICP, either alone or in conjunction with surgery or radiation (16–36 mg IV, then 4 mg IV or PO qid) (Waller & Caroline, 1996). Chemotherapy and other measures, including shunting for hydrocephalus, are used in some cases.
● Nausea and vomiting are prevented with antiemetics.
● Activities that increase ICP include suctioning, turning, straining, Valsalva maneuver, hip flexion, and lying prone. Activities that are unavoidable should be spaced over time. Valsalva maneuvers can be reduced by preventing constipation. Passive turning for alert patients may help. The patient's head should be elevated at least 20 degrees. Patient safety is a significant consideration. Hypertension and fever should be kept under control.
● The treatment of confusional states or deficits is directed to reducing ICP and failing that, to managing symptoms. The care of patients with confusion is discussed previously in this chapter.
● Associated symptoms may include sensory deficits, visual deficits, aphasia, dysarthria, aprosodia (inability to comprehend or express variations in pitch and other speech patterns), and dysphagia. Adaptive measures (eg, braces) are sometimes indicated, but when the disease is rapidly progressive are futile. Range of motion should be maintained up until death. Speech or occupational therapy consultation is indicated in some cases.
● Pain is best managed with steroids and treatments discussed previously. An opioid plus a phenothiazine can be used if these measures are ineffective (Woodruff, 1997).

Spinal Cord Compression (SCC)

Injury to the spinal cord (usually epidural) or cauda equina results in markedly increased suffering for the patient and significant challenges for all concerned in providing care. Paraplegia, incontinence, constipation, pain, and potential for skin breakdown are the direct sequelae of SCC.

Symptoms

Pain is the most common first symptom of SCC. The pain is generally constant, dull, aching, progressive back pain, usually at or near the lesion. The pain is exacerbated by recumbency, movement, coughing, sneezing, neck flexion, or Valsalva maneuver. Pain may also be radicular from back to front and improved by sitting or standing up (Janjan, 1996; Waller & Caroline, 1996). Neurologic deficits, the second major manifestation of SCC, usually occur after the onset of pain and usually begin with weakness or motor disabilities, most often in the lower extremities (Fuller, Heiss, & Oldfield, 1997). In the early stages, neurologic deficits are not necessarily apparent. A significant number of patients with weakness (30%) become paraplegic within 1 week of onset of the weakness (Janjan, 1996). Evaluation of equilibrium, lower extremity strength, reflexes, and gait, including heel-toe walking, should thus be part of the ongoing physical assessment. Neurologic deficits often become permanent.

Autonomic dysfunction is the third category of symptoms and, because it tends to occur late, is associated with a poor prognosis (Fuller et al., 1997). Autonomic symptoms include bladder dysfunction, consisting of retention manifested by frequent, small voiding. Bowel dysfunction, numbness, paresthesias, and sexual impotence may also occur. Impaired genitourinary sensation, saddle anesthesia, and diminished sensation in the lumbosacral dermatomes is indicative of cauda equina metastases (Glick & Glover, 1995).

Once lost, autonomic function often is not regained.

Etiologies

The most common sites of SCC are the thoracic area (70%), lumbosacral area (20%), and cervical area (10%) (Fuller et al., 1997). SCC is usually due to bone metastasis resulting in bone destruction or pressure or traction on, or stretching of, nerve structures. The prognosis is good when diagnosis is early and treatment is appropriate, but delayed diagnosis frequently plays a key role in the development of disabilities, as does rapid onset of symptoms (Belford, 1997). Tumors most commonly associated with cord compression include (but are not limited to) lung, breast, and prostate (Janjan, 1996). Any metastasis to the spine presents the potential for SCC.

Interventions

The importance of early identification of SCC cannot be overstressed in relation to the success of treatment and prevention of devastating complications. Patient and family involvement in detection is important and should be a standard of care for patients at risk.

● Dexamethasone is the initial treatment for suspicion of SCC (based on history and physical examination), followed by either radiation therapy or surgery, or in some cases, chemotherapy (Waller & Caroline, 1996).
● Radiotherapy is indicated for patients without neurologic deficits or for radioresponsive tumors and is standard treatment after surgery unless contraindicated (Fuller et al., 1997).
● Surgery (laminectomy) is sometimes the treatment of choice (eg, when there is bone deformity, inability to receive further radiation, high cervical compression, or radioresistant tumor) (Ratanatharathorn & Powers, 1991). When possible, surgery is followed by radiotherapy (Janjan, 1996).
● Chemotherapy may be used in a few cases of especially sensitive tumors or when there is recurrence, and radiation or surgery are not possible (Ratanatharathorn & Powers, 1991).

Disabilities are seldom reversible, so once they occur, adaptive measures begin. When there is extensive damage to the spine, the patient is maintained as immobile as possible.

Other Neurologic Problems

Plexopathies

Brachial plexopathy (including Horner's syndrome), lumbosacral plexopathy, and peripheral neuropathies are discussed briefly in the section on neuropathic pain. Adverse effects of radiation and chemotherapy are usually found and treated earlier in the course of disease. Vascular complications of the CNS (eg, ischemic or hemorrhagic lesions) are found at autopsy in almost 15% of deceased patients (Obbens, 1993), but their treatment is not generally considered a part of palliative or hospice care except as they result in troublesome symptoms or are part of manifestations of other problems (eg, disseminated intravascular coagulation).

Neurologic Paraneoplastic Syndromes

Neurologic PNSs, while rare (less than 1% of patients with cancer), can result in a variety of cognitive, sensory, and motor deficits. PNSs frequently present before cancer is diagnosed and are most commonly associated with small cell carcinoma of the lung and ovarian, renal, and stomach cancers (Mack, 1995). CNS PNSs occurring in adults include the following:

● Paraneoplastic cerebellar degeneration results in ataxia, nystagmus, inability to communicate, and global loss of function.
● Paraneoplastic sensory neuropathy/encephalomyelitis results in loss of proprioception, pain, sensory ataxia, urinary retention, and other disabilities, with many patients becoming bedridden, even though the motor system is spared.

● Lambert-Eaton myasthenic syndrome includes loss of motor but not sensory function.

● Cancer-associated retinopathy or optic neuritis progresses from obscurations and night blindness to total blindness.

● Limbic encephalitis begins with personality changes, and progresses to profound short-term memory loss and seizures, hallucinations, and hypersomnia.

● Brain stem encephalitis results in vertigo, nystagmus, facial numbness, oculomotor changes, dysphagia, dysarthria, and deafness.

The PNSs are poorly understood, except that many are known to have an autoimmune pathogenesis. Treatment is generally ineffective, and palliative treatment may also be challenging.

REFERENCES

Belford, K. (1997). Central nervous system cancers. In S. L. Groenwald, M. H. Frogge, M. Goodman, & C. H. Yarbro (Eds.), *Cancer nursing: Principles and practice* (4th ed.) (pp. 980–1035). Boston: Jones and Bartlett.

Breitbart, W., Rosenfield, B., Roth, A., Smith, M. J., Cohen, K., & Passik, S. (1997) The Memorial Delirium Assessment Scale. *Journal of Pain and Symptom Management, 13*(3), 128–137.

Brietbart, W., Chochinov, H. M., & Passik, S. (1998). Psychiatric aspects of palliative care. In D. Doyle, G. W. C. Hanks, & N. MacDonald (Eds.), *Oxford textbook of palliative medicine* (2nd ed.) (pp. 933–954). New York: Oxford University Press.

Bruera, E., Schoeller, T., & Montejo, G. (1992). Organic hallucinosis in patients receiving high doses of opiates for cancer pain. *Pain, 48*(3), 397–399.

Chernecky, C., & Krech, R. L. (1991). Complications of advanced disease. In S. B. Baird, R. McCorkle, & M. Grant (Eds.), *Cancer nursing* (pp. 864–874). Philadelphia: W.B. Saunders.

Folstein, M. F., Folstein, S. E., & McHugh, P. R. (1975). Mini-mental state: A practical method for grading the cognitive state of patients for the clinician. *Journal of Psychiatric Research, 12,* 189–198.

Fuller, B. G., Heiss, J., & Oldfield, E. H. (1997). Spinal cord compression. In V. T. DeVita, S. Hellman, & S. A. Rosenberg (Eds.), *Cancer: Principles and practice of oncology* (5th ed.) (pp. 2476–2485). Philadelphia: Lippincott-Raven.

Glick, J. H., & Glover, D. (1995). Oncologic emergencies. In G. P. Murphy, W. Lawrence, & R. E. Lenhard (Eds.), *Clinical oncology* (2nd ed.) (pp. 597–618). Altanta: American Cancer Society.

Holland, J. C. (1997). Principles of psycho-oncology. In J. F. Holland, E. Frei, R. C. Bast, D. W. Kufe, D. L. Morton, & R. W. Weischselbaum (Eds.), *Cancer medicine* (4th ed.) (pp. 1327–1346). Baltimore: Williams & Wilkins.

Hospice and Palliative Nurses Association. (1997). *Terminal restlessness.* Pittsburgh: Author.

Janjan, N. A. (1996). Radiotherapeutic management of spinal metastases. *Journal of Pain and Symptom Management, 11*(1), 47–56.

John, W. J., Patchell, R. A., & Foon, K. A. (1997). Paraneoplastic syndromes. In V. T. DeVita, S. Hellman, & S. A. Rosenberg (Eds.), *Cancer: Principles and practice of oncology* (5th ed.) (pp. 2397–2422). Philadelphia: Lippincott-Raven.

Loeffler, J. S., Patchell, R. A., & Sawaya, R. (1997). Metastic brain cancer. In V. T. DeVita, S. Hellman, & S. A. Rosenburg (Eds.), *Cancer: Principles and practice of oncology* (5th ed.) (pp. 2523–2536). Philadelphia: Lippincott-Raven.

Mack, E. E. (1995) Neuromuscular complications. In D. A. Casciato & B. B. Lowitz (Eds.) *Manual of clinical oncology* (3rd ed.) (pp. 513–526). Boston: Little, Brown and company.

March, P. A. (1998). Terminal restlessness. *American Journal of Hospice and Palliative Care, 15*(1), 51–53.

Obbens, E. A. M. T. (1993). Neurological problems in palliative medicine. In D. Doyle, G. W. C. Hanks, & N. MacDonald (Eds.), *Oxford textbook of palliative medicine* (pp. 460–472). New York: Oxford University Press.

Prados, M. D., & Wilson, C. B. (1993). Neoplasms of the central nervous system. In J. F. Holland, E. Frei, R. C. Bast, D. W. Kufe, D. L. Morton, & R. W. Weischselbaum (Eds.), *Cancer medicine* (3rd ed.) (pp. 1080–1119). Philadelphia: Lea & Febiger.

Price, R. W., & Brew, B. J. (1997). Central and peripheral nervous system complications. In V. T. DeVita, S. Hellman, & S. A. Rosenberg (Eds.), *AIDS: Etiology, diagnosis, treatment and preven-*

tion (4th ed.) (pp. 331–353). Philadelphia: Lippincott-Raven.

Ratanatharathorn, V., & Powers, W. E. (1991). Epidural spinal cord compression from metastatic tumor: Diagnosis and guidelines for management. *Cancer Treatment Reviews, 18*(1), 55–71.

Roth-Roemer, S., Fann, J., & Syrjala, K. (1997). The importance of recognizing and measuring delirium. *Journal of Pain and Symptom Management, 13*(3), 125–127.

Twycross, R., & Lichter, I. (1998). The terminal phase. In D. Doyle, G. W. C. Hanks, & N. MacDonald (Eds.), *Oxford textbook of palliative medicine* (2nd ed.) (pp. 977–992). New York: Oxford University Press.

Waller, A., & Caroline, N. L. (1996). *Handbook of palliative care in cancer*. Boston: Butterworth-Heinemann.

Walsh, T. D. (1989). Confusion. In T. D. Walsh (Ed.), *Symptom control* (pp. 57–68). Oxford: Blackwell Scientific Publications.

Warren, D. E. (1996). Practical use of rectal medications in palliative care. *Journal of Pain and Symptom Management, 11*(6), 378–387.

Woodruff, R. (1997). *Symptom control*. Melbourne: Asperula.

CHAPTER 14

Respiratory and Cardiovascular Problems

KEY POINTS

● Respiratory problems, especially dyspnea, are among the most distressing problems of advanced disease.

● Some palliative measures for respiratory symptoms are based on symptom etiology. Identification of the etiology of respiratory symptoms is often possible based on clinical signs and symptoms.

● Palliation of respiratory symptoms usually requires both nursing and medical measures.

● Cardiovascular problems are common sequelae of cancer treatment and other processes, but the primary cardiovascular problem of terminal illness directly related to cancer is pericardial effusion and cardiac tamponade.*

Respiratory problems are common in patients with advanced cancer, especially those with lung cancer and metastasis to the lungs, but they may also occur in other patients with advanced cancer, even without evidence of lung involvement (Ahmedzai, 1998). Respiratory problems are common in AIDS and are most frequently related to *Pneumocystis carinii* pneumonia, mycobacterial infections, histo-

*Also see Chapter 30, End-Stage Cardiovascular and Pulmonary Disease.

This chapter is adapted from an article published in *The American Journal of Hospice and Palliative Care*, 14(1), 26–30 and is used with permission.

plasmosis, and coccidiomycosis (Janson & Carrieri-Kohlman, 1998). In clients with advanced disease, dyspnea is often multicausal and may be associated with one or several of three pathophysiologic abnormalities: (1) increased respiratory effort to compensate for increased load, such as pleural effusion or obstruction; (2) increased proportion of respiratory muscle required to maintain respiration, such as in respiratory muscle weakness, and (3) increased ventilatory requirements, such as in hypoxemia, hypercapnia, or anemia (Kuebler, 1996; Ripamonti & Bruera, 1997).

The high incidence of respiratory problems in terminal illness is due to several factors, including the following:

- Lung cancer is by far the number one cause of cancer deaths.
- Almost all lethal cancers tend to metastasize to the lungs.
- Patients may be immunosuppressed as a result of disease or treatment.
- Pulmonary function may be compromised as a result of radiation or chemotherapy.
- Interrelated risk or causative factors, such as cachexia, debility, immobility, and dehydration, are often present.
- Previous disease, such as chronic asthma, bronchitis, emphysema, and other respiratory disorders, may be present.
- Among older patients, there is a normal decrease in pulmonary function.

Dyspnea, cough, and hemoptysis are the most common symptomatic respiratory problems of terminal illness.

Dyspnea

Dyspnea is the most common and troublesome respiratory problem of patients with advanced cancer and is also common in AIDS and degenerative neurologic diseases. Dyspnea may be defined as breathlessness, shortness of breath, or "difficult or labored breathing" (Harwood, 1996, p. 31). Dyspnea is not necessarily the same as tachypnea, hyperpnea, or hyperventilation, though these tend to exacerbate dyspnea. Anxiety and dyspnea may exacerbate one another in a cycle of anxiety → dyspnea → anxiety → dyspnea so that treatment of dyspnea usually includes treatment of anxiety. Dyspnea may occur on exertion or at rest and is influenced by factors such as exercise, posture, cough, and environmental conditions.

There are a number of specific causes of dyspnea. The more common causes and identifying characteristics of dyspnea in patients with cancer are shown in Table 14-1. Although this information is specific to cancer, several of the causes, especially pneumonia, are also common in patients with other diagnoses.

Many causes of dyspnea are treatable, and when possible, it is important for the practitioner to determine the specific etiology of dyspnea in the patient so that the cause rather than only the symptom is addressed.

Although advanced disease is an indication for withdrawal of *some* diagnostic and treatment measures, there are no clear-cut criteria for what is appropriate at various stages of disease. At least in early stage, and in some cases, late stage disease, definitive diagnosis results in decreased morbidity but not necessarily change in survival (Stover & Kaner, 1996). Invasive diagnostic procedures are associated with varying complication rates, ranging from around 8% for bronchoscopy and video-assisted thorascopic surgery to 30% for needle aspiration (Stover & Kaner, 1996).

The severity of dyspnea is based on the patient's self-report and may be measured on an ongoing basis with a visual analogue scale consisting of a 10-centimeter scale with five markers indicating dyspnea ranging from "no dyspnea (or) shortness of breath" to "dyspnea (or) shortness of breath as bad as it can be" (Harwood, 1996). Dyspnea is also commonly measured with a verbal categoric scale using words such as "none-mild-moderate-severe" (Kuebler, 1996). A variety of other tools are in use, including the Chronic Respiratory Questionnaire, Borg Category Scale, Oxygen Cost Diagram, and others. Pulmonary function tests are of limited value in understanding the severity of dyspnea among patients with advanced cancer (Ripamonti & Bruera, 1997). Progression of dyspnea—especially rapid—is highly significant.

Managing Dyspnea

Treatment of dyspnea is directed first to the cause and symptom(s) and if efforts to address the cause are unsuccessful, then to palliation of the symptom. Most of the causes listed previously are amenable to treatment, at least in early stages or when the patient is relatively strong. Palliative treatment of dyspnea (Ahmedzai, 1998; DeCamp, Mentzer, & Sugarbaker, 1997) includes supportive measures:

TABLE 14-1   Characteristics and Causes of Dyspnea in Patients with Cancer

Characteristic of Dyspnea	Potential Cause
Progressive or rapidly increasing dyspnea, blood in sputum, noisy breathing, chronic cough, choking, or pneumonia.	*Obstruction* from primary or secondary tumor (eg, in bronchus or upper airways) or enlarged lymph nodes.
Dyspnea with cough and chest pain (trachea displacement toward unaffected side with large effusion). Breath sounds usually decreased but may vary according to area of lung. Pleural effusions are usually unilateral, except when due to heart failure or lymphangitis carcinomatosis.	*Pleural effusion* (most common with lung, breast cancer, and lymphoma but may occur with any malignancy).
Dyspnea with elevated temperature, chills, purulent or rusty sputum (but not always present), decreased breath sounds. There may also be pleural effusion present. Bone marrow and other transplantations are a major risk factor for fungal pulmonary infections.	*Pneumonia* is common. Risk factors include immunologic compromise, debility, immobility, and ineffective breathing or cough. Bacterial pneumonia is common (especially *Streptococcus pneumoniae*), but other pathogens are also found. Fungal infections, such as invasive pulmonary aspergillosis and zygomycosis, are found in immunocompromised patients with cancer, and cryptococcosis and histoplasmosis are found in patients with AIDS. Fungal infections are particularly a problem in transplant patients.
Sudden onset of dyspnea with rapid breathing, rapid heart rate, cough, chest pain, and blood in sputum.	*Pulmonary emboli* are often related to debility and immobility. Among the tumors most often associated with emboli are leukemia, prostate, breast, and colon.
Dyspnea with cough, chest pain relieved by leaning forward. There may be syncope, weakness, pleural effusion, edema, distension of neck veins, tachypnea, and the clinical triad of tachycardia, muffled heart tones, and hypotension.	*Pericardial effusion* (fluid around the heart) may precede the cardiac emergency of *cardiac tamponade* (fluid compression of the heart). Pericardial effusions are often associated with primary lung tumors or breast cancer, lymphoma, leukemia, and metastatic melanoma.
Dyspnea with abdominal distension (from fluid) and tenderness, general discomfort, need to keep head elevated to breathe, rapid breathing rate, and pleural effusion. There may be gastrointestinal (GI) symptoms, such as early satiation, indigestion, and other GI symptoms.	*Ascites* is often related to tumors in ovaries, endometrium, breast, stomach, pancreas, and colon. Hepatomegaly may also cause dyspnea.
Dyspnea on exertion with general fatigue, weakness, rapid heart rate, and headache.	*Anemia* is often related to tumors in the liver and colon, leukemia, multiple myeloma and is secondary to chemotherapy.
Dyspnea with engorged neck veins, facial or arm swelling, changes in consciousness, cough, hoarseness, and noisy breathing.	*Superior vena cava syndrome* is an oncologic emergency most often associated with mediastinal (chest) tumors, including lymphomas.
Dyspnea with general weakness, anorexia, severe weight loss (cachexia), or the presence of a paraneoplastic syndrome.	*Respiratory muscle weakness* is often associated with paraneoplastic syndromes, anorexia, or cachexia.
Dyspnea with tachypnea, decreased chest wall movement unilaterally, deviated apical impulse and trachea, varying breath sounds but decreased on affected side.	*Atelectasis* may result from tumor or exudate compression or may follow surgery or other treatment.
Symptoms similar to emphysema. Dyspnea unexplained by other causes.	*Lymphangitis carcinomatosis* (infiltration of pulmonary lymph) is a potential cause.

(continued)

TABLE 14-1	Characteristics and Causes of Dyspnea in Patients with Cancer *(Continued)*
Characteristic of Dyspnea	**Potential Cause**
Dyspnea from far advanced disease and complications, including pleural or cardiac effusion, pulmonary edema from cardiac failure, lymphangitis carcinomatosis, carcinomatous infiltration of chest wall, paralysis, or pneumonia	*Loss of function* can result from any of these causes.
Dyspnea unexplained by other causes; history of bone marrow transplant.	*Bronchiolitis obliterans* (may occur 6 wk to 2 y after treatment).
Dyspnea associated with chronic bronchitis, emphysema, asthma, tuberculosis, neuromuscular disorder, congestive heart failure, or other heart disease.	*Preexisting conditions.*
Dyspnea associated with radiation or chemotherapy.	*Treatment sequelae,* such as radiation pneumonitis or fibrosis or damage to pulmonary capillary bed from chemotherapeutic agents, such as bleomycin or mitomycin. Radiation pneumonitis occurs 1–2 mo after treatment, while fibrosis may appear 6–12 mo after radiation.
Dyspnea not related to other etiologies/symptoms.	Dyspnea may also be associated with fatigue or other debilitating effects of advanced disease.
"Death rattle" or noisy respirations when death is imminent.	*Inability to manage secretions:* This is not dyspnea but is included here because of the distress it causes family members.
In all cases, the role of anxiety should be considered in exacerbating dyspnea; hence, treatment of anxiety usually should accompany treatment of dyspnea, especially when dyspnea is refractory to treatment.	

Ahmedzai, 1993; DeCamp, Mentzer, & Sugarbaker, 1997; Harwood, 1996, Ripamonti & Bruera, 1997; Stover & Kaner, 1996.

● Keeping the patient's head or torso elevated helps, or when one lung is obstructed, lying on the obstructed side may help.

● Limit activity to what is necessary and prioritize and space the activity (eg, eat first, then rest, then bathe). However, decreased activity increases the risk of pneumonia.

● The patient's room should be cool, and humidity should be low. Irritants, such as smoke, should be eliminated. Increasing ventilation helps, in particular, a *slight* cool breeze past the patient's face helps reduce dyspnea.

● Anxiety is nearly always a problem with dyspnea, and emotional upsets should be minimized. Reassurance may help, and some patients may be able to use relaxation techniques. Morphine, the most effective medication to reduce dyspnea in most cases, also reduces anxiety (see the following discussion).

● If dyspnea is due to ascites, diet and fluid may be restricted.

● Regular and frequent oral care helps decrease discomfort related to dry mouth and infection.

● If life expectancy and patient functional status allow, respiratory or pulmonary rehabilitation is appropriate.

Medical Interventions

Morphine is effective in improving the quality of breathing and decreasing both dyspnea and anxiety. Nebulized morphine in doses in addition to those given for pain is more effective for dyspnea than morphine by other routes. Waller and Caroline (1996) recommend starting with morphine 2.5 mg plus dexamethasone 2.0 mg in 2.5 mL of normal saline every 4 hours and as needed and titrating the morphine to effect. More recently, Zeppetella (1997) achieved good results within 24 hours starting with nebulized morphine 20 mg every 4 hours (two 10 mg/mL ampules mixed with 2 mL normal saline).

Oxygen is helpful but not indefinitely. Antianxiety or low-dose antipsychotic medications are sometimes used for restlessness, but morphine may be more appropriate. Inhaled corticosteroids or bronchodilators are useful when the cause of dyspnea is related to chronic bronchitis, emphysema, asthma, or other related disease or for wheezing (Ahmedzai, 1998).

Respiratory panic is treated with midazolam, chlorpromazine, or morphine. The patient should not be left alone at such times. For severe dyspnea in advanced disease, "substantial obtundation" may be the only available palliative treatment strategy (American Medical Association, 1996).

There are a variety of treatment options for the specific causes of dyspnea (Ahmedzai, 1998; DeCamp et al., 1997; Feldman & Klugman, 1997; Harwood, 1996; Kappe, 1997; Ripamonti & Bruera, 1997; Stover & Kaner, 1996; Waller & Caroline, 1996). Some treatments, however, are limited to early stages and stronger patients.

● Obstruction is treated palliatively with opioids, steroids, or in some cases, surgery. Chemotherapy or radiation may be used when there is a lengthy life expectancy.
● The fluid of pleural effusion can be aspirated and the area of effusion treated with talc powder or a talc slurry.
● Pneumonia is treated according to the pathogenic organism and risk factors reduced if possible. Resistant bacterial pathogens are increasing, and the treatment of fungal respiratory infections is difficult. Immunocompromised patients (transplant and AIDS) are especially difficult to diagnose and treat.
● Pulmonary embolus is a life-threatening condition requiring immediate treatment, including oxygen and anticoagulation therapy, except when death is imminent.
● Pericardial effusion also demands quick medical treatment, usually in the hospital, or tamponade may occur.
● Lymphangitis carcinomatosis, a condition of advanced disease, is treated with steroids, usually with slight success.
● Ascites may be treated with drawing off the fluid, diuretics, chemotherapy, or surgery (shunt).
● Anemia is usually treated with transfusion for significant, but often temporary, improvement.
● Superior vena cava syndrome may require emergency treatment, radiation and corticosteroids, or in some cases, chemotherapy.
● Bronchiolitis obliterans is treated with steroids.
● Loss of function or respiratory muscle weakness is difficult to treat other than supportively.
● Preexisting or other conditions are treated as they are in any circumstances unless the patient is severely weakened, in which case some options are not available.
● Radiation pneumonitis is treated with corticosteroids, while pulmonary fibrosis is a permanent condition.
● Fatigue or debilitation is addressed as discussed previously in the section Managing Dyspnea.

"Death rattle" is managed by elevating the head and when the rattle is due to inability to manage salivary secretions, an anticholinergic medication such as scopolamine (Hyoscine) in a single injection of 0.4 to 0.6 mg hydrobromide or 20 mg butylbromide is used (Bennett, 1996). Scopolamine is less effective when the secretions are bronchial in origin and accumulate over several days. Larger infusions of scopolamine or atropine early in the process may help. Other measures (Bennett, 1996; Waller & Caroline, 1996) include furosemide (Lasix) plus atropine; nebulized atropine, morphine, and dexamethasone; and scopolamine patch. Gentle suctioning may also be used but to little lasting effect.

Cough

Cough is most commonly a problem in bronchogenic cancer. Cough is also a complication of terminal illness and chronic illness, such as bronchitis, and of respiratory or cardiac problems, such as obstruction, loss of function, pneumonia, thromboembolus, pericardial effusion, superior vena cava syndrome, and congestive heart failure. Pathologic or severe cough may cause or contribute to loss of sleep, muscle strain, increased blood pressure, headache, ruptured blood vessels, and bone fracture (Hagen, 1991). Causes of cough are summarized in Table 14-2.

Managing Cough

Helping when cough is a problem includes at least some of the measures discussed in the section about dyspnea; some measures, however, are different (eg, increasing humidity). Measures to alleviate cough (Ahmedzai, 1998; Cowcher & Hanks, 1990; Waller & Caroline, 1996) include the following:

● Keeping the patient's head elevated helps, or when one lung is obstructed, lying on the obstructed side may help.
● Air should be warmed and humidified and irritants (eg, smoke) removed.
● Deep breathing and effective (deep) coughing may help.

Medical Management

If the causative factor cannot be resolved, the cough is treated according to its characteristics as follows:

● For dry, hacking cough, a demulcent antitussive (with dextromethorphan) may help decrease cough and soothe the patient's pharynx. Morphine or other opioids are used to suppress the cough reflex and may be given in combination with antihistamines to reduce opioid-stimulated histamine. Waller and Caroline (1996) also recommend adding dexamethasone. For severe cough, 2 mL of 2% lidocaine in 1 mL normal saline can be given through a nebulizer.
● For productive cough, steam inhaler or nebulizer may be used to increase humidification and provide a mucolytic effect. Albuterol may also be used if indicated by the underlying disorder.
● For wet cough when the patient is too weak to manage sputum, morphine is indicated as discussed for a dry hacking cough, either alone or with atropine through a nebulizer. Dexamethasone may also be added to these nebulized medications (Waller & Caroline, 1996). Anxiolytic medications may also be needed, especially in the terminal phase.

Most of the treatment options for the specific causes of cough can be found in the previous discussion of dyspnea.

● Gastroesophageal reflux is treated by elevating the head, through dietary measures, and with H_2 receptor antagonists, such as famotidine and cimetidine.
● Bronchodilators and inhaled corticosteroids are used when they can affect airway narrowing (eg, in chronic obstructive pulmonary disease).
● Sinusitis due to bacterial infection is treated with antibiotics, antihistamines, and nasal corticosteroids.
● Except for heroic measures (including some medications, eg, some vasopressors), heart disease should generally continue to be treated as it was prior to the terminal disease.

Hemoptysis

A small amount of blood in the sputum is not necessarily a seriously unfavorable sign and may come from a site other than the respiratory system (eg, nose). However, hemoptysis, especially that which is progressive, may be a

TABLE 14-2	Common Causes of Cough
Characteristic of Cough	**Potential Cause**
Cough with dyspnea (see dyspnea factors in preceding section).	*Cough and dyspnea are often associated.*
Cough with choking.	*Aspiration* (inhalation of sputum, other material) is associated with a variety of conditions, including obstruction and fistula.
Dry hacking cough.	*Endobronchial cancer spread, pleural effusion, asthma.* *Side effect of ACE inhibitors* (eg, benazepril, captopril).
Cough with choking; patient weak, weight loss significant, has respiratory infection.	*Sputum retention.*
Cough (bovine) and hoarseness.	*Vocal cord paralysis* is common in primary or secondary tumors of neck or chest.
Cough with history or symptoms of cardiac disease, especially congestive heart failure (CHF), especially with anemia. CHF is characterized by fatigue, dyspnea, tachycardia, edema (legs and lungs), nocturia, chest pain, and cough.	*Congestive heart failure.* Cough that is worse at night may indicate *left failure;* while cough with frothy pink sputum may indicate *right failure.*
Cough precipitated by lying recumbant or that increases at night without retrosternal burning.	*Gastroesophageal reflux disease (GERD).*
Cough with hemoptysis (frothy, bright red blood usually distinguishes hemoptysis from hematemesis).	*Malignant pleural effusion* (see dyspnea above). *Pulmonary tumor* causing alveolar or pleural bleeding.
Cough with fever, upper airway congestion.	*"Cold" or upper airway infection.*
Cough with history of COPD or other respiratory disease. Associated with environmental factors, such as dry air, cigarette smoke.	*Preexisting* or other conditions.

Cowcher & Hanks, 1990; Waller & Caroline, 1996.

prelude to massive hemoptysis—a rare terminal occurrence. Causes of hemoptysis include infection or pathologic condition (eg, pneumonia, aspergillosis, bronchitis, tuberculosis or tumor erosion of a bronchus, especially in bronchogenic cancer). Note that pulmonary hemorrhage often does *not* result in hemoptysis (Stover & Kaner, 1996). Tumors in the esophagus may also produce hemoptysis. Among the infections that can cause hemoptysis are pneumonia, candidiasis, aspergillosis, and tuberculosis. Pulmonary embolus and sometimes other cardiac problems may also cause hemoptysis.

Managing Hemoptysis

Supportive measures (Cowcher & Hanks, 1990; Waller & Caroline, 1996) for hemoptysis are limited and include the following:

● Cough suppressant can be used if hemoptysis is associated with cough.
● If the specific source of bleeding is known, that side (right or left lung) can be kept lower than the other to minimize aspiration and choking.
● Reassurance is often appropriate because slight hemoptysis is not necessarily an ominous sign.

Medical Management

Medications or treatments specific to a treatable problem are used (eg, for pneumonia). Lesions can sometimes be irradiated or surgery performed. Massive hemoptysis in terminal illness is virtually always a terminal event, and the patient should be given intravenous opioid and anxiolytic medications.

Cardiovascular Problems in Cancer

Cardiovascular problems in cancer are limited primarily to pericardial effusions and cardiac tamponade; metastases to the heart; problems related to secondary problems of cancer (eg, anemia, hyperthyroidism, syndrome of inappropriate antidiuretic hormone secretion [SIADH], aldosteronism, amyloidosis); part of multiple systems organ failure; preexisting problems; effects of treatment; primary pericardial tumors, such as sarcoma or mesothelioma (and principally in the context of AIDS); or primary cardiac lymphoma. Except for pericardial effusion and cardiac tamponade, most of the previous problems that are due to cancer are difficult or futile to treat other than palliatively in the context of *terminal* cancer. Cardiac problems that develop as a result of anemia, SIADH, and so forth are sometimes treatable in terminal illness. Except in moribund patients, preexisting or other cardiac problems, such as dysrhythmias, are treated as they would be in any other patient. See Chapter 21 for a discussion of cardiac states as death approaches. Cardiovascular problems other than those related to cancer are discussed in Chapter 30.

Pericardial Effusions and Cardiac Tamponade

Cardiac tamponade (pathologic compression) is an oncologic emergency resulting from cardiac compression by a large pericardial effusion. The rate of effusion is significant, with rapid effusions resulting in more severe tamponade (Glick & Glover, 1995). Small or slow-growing effusions may be nonsymptomatic or, if the heart is encased by tumor or radiation fibrosis, significantly symptomatic (Glick & Glover, 1995; Ewer & Benjamin, 1993). Tumors most likely to metastasize to the heart are lung, breast, melanoma, acute leukemia, lymphoma, and gastrointestinal tumors (Chernecky & Krech, 1991).

The symptoms of pericardial effusion are dyspnea, cough, retrosternal chest discomfort, orthopnea, palpitations, weakness, fatigue, and dizziness. Progression to cardiac tamponade results in more severe manifestations, including chest pain, increased dyspnea (partially relieved by bending forward), cough, and ashen or plethoric face (Pass, 1997). Other manifestations of cardiac tamponade include tachycardia, tachypnea, decreased systolic and pulse pressures, changes in consciousness, peripheral cyanosis, neck vein distension, edema, and occasionally nausea, vomiting, and abdominal pain (Glick & Glover, 1995).

If the pericardium cannot be drained (pericardiocentesis) immediately, treatment may include administrating oxygen (but positive pressure breathing is contraindicated) and medications (isoproterenol) to improve cardiac contractions and filling. This may result in relief, but symptoms often return within 48 hours (Glick & Glover, 1995). For all but moribund patients, treatment (other than of the tumor) consists of drainage and pericardial sclerosis (Pass, 1997). Several effective means exist to achieve both, including pericardial catheter drainage and sclerosis using antibiotic, chemotherapy, systemic hormonal therapy, radiation therapy, and pericardiotomy (Glick & Glover, 1995; Pass, 1997).

REFERENCES

Ahmedzai, S. (1998). Palliation of respiratory symptoms. In D. Doyle, G. W. C. Hanks, & N. Mac-Donald (Eds.), *Oxford textbook of palliative medicine* (2nd ed.) (pp. 583–616). New York: Oxford University Press.

AMA Council on Scientific Affairs. (1996). Good care of the dying patient. *Journal of the American Medical Association, 275*(6), 474–478.

Bennett, M. I. (1996). Death rattle: An audit of hyoscine (scopolamine) use and review of management. *Journal of Pain and Symptom Management, 12*(4), 229–233.

Chernecky, R. E. & Krench, R. L. (1991). Complications of advanced disease. In S. B. Baird, R. McCorkle, & M. Grant (Eds.). *Cancer nursing: Principles and practice* (pp. 990–998). Boston: Jones and Bartlett.

Cowcher, K., & Hanks, G. W. (1990). Long term management of respiratory symptoms in advanced cancer. *Journal of Pain and Symptom Management,* 5(5), 320–330.

DeCamp, M. M., Mentzer, S. J., & Sugarbaker, D. J. (1997). Malignant effusive disease of the pleura and pericardium. *Chest,* 112(4 Suppl.), 291s–295s.

Ewer, M. S., & Benjamin, R. S. (1993). Cardiac complications. In J. F. Holland, E. Frei, R. C. Bast, D. W. Kufe, D. L. Morton, & R. W. Weischselbaum (Eds.), *Cancer medicine* (3rd ed.) (pp. 2332–2348). Philadelphia: Lea & Febiger.

Feldman, C., & Klugman, K. (1997). Pneumococcal infections. *Current Opinion in Infectious Diseases,* 10, 109–115.

Glick, J. H., & Glover, D. (1995). Oncologic emergencies. In G. P. Murphy, W. Lawrence, & R. E. Lenhard (Eds.), *Clinical oncology* (2nd ed.) (pp. 597–618). Altanta: American Cancer Society.

Hagen, N. A. (1991). An approach to cough in cancer patients. *Journal of Pain and Symptom Management,* 6(4), 257–262.

Harwood, K. V. (1996). Dyspnea. In S. L. Groenwald, M. H. Frogge, M. Goodman, & C. H. Yarbro (Eds.), *Cancer symptom management* (pp. 31–41). Boston: Jones and Bartlett.

Janson, S., & Carrieri-Kohlman, V. (1998). Respiratory changes. In M. E. Ropka & A. B. Williams (Eds.), *HIV Nursing and symptom management* (pp. 59–109). Boston: Jones and Bartlett.

Kappe, R. (1997). Fungal pulmonary infections. *Current Opinion in Infectious Diseases,* 10, 123–127.

Kuebler, K. K. (1996). *Hospice and palliative care clinical practice protocol: Dyspnea.* Pittsburgh: Hospice Nurses Association.

Pass, H. I. (1997). Malignant pleural and pericardial effusions. In V. T. DeVita, S. Hellman, & S. A. Rosenberg (Eds.), *Cancer: Principles and practice of oncology* (5th ed.) (pp. 1502–1539). Philadelphia: Lippincott-Raven.

Ripamonti, C., & Bruera, E. (1997). Dyspnea: Pathophysiology and assessment. *Journal of Pain and Symptom Management,* 13(4), 220–232.

Stover, D. E., & Kaner, R. J. (1996). Pulmonary complications in cancer patients. *CA-Cancer Journal for Clinicians,* 46, 303–320.

Waller, A., & Caroline, N. L. (1996). *Palliative care in cancer.* Boston: Butterworth-Heineman.

Zeppetella, G. (1997). Nebulized morphine in the palliation of dsypnoea. *Palliative Medicine,* 11, 267–272.

Skin Complications

● Virtually all patients with advanced chronic illness are at risk for skin complications for a variety of reasons.

● Pressure ulcers continue as a significant problem in chronic illness, especially among older patients.

● Skin complications affect physical and psychosocial dimensions.

● Some skin complications, such as fistulas and malignant lesions, may require creative effort on the part of the entire health care team.

● Infections affecting the skin present a variety of symptoms and problems in patients with cancer and especially AIDS.

Skin complications of patients with advanced cancer include pressure (decubitus) ulcers, malignant lesions, fistulas, paraneoplastic syndromes, pruritus, infections, and dermatologic sequelae of treatment (Gallagher, 1995; Mortimer, 1998). Skin problems are common in people with HIV infection and are discussed in this chapter under infections and in the chapter on HIV. Paraneoplastic syndromes are listed and discussed in the chapter on paraneoplastic syndromes. Compromises of the skin in advanced illness may encompass thinning, loss of elasticity, dehydration, deepening of sores and wrinkles, various pigmentation disorders, and problems related to immunosuppression, nutrition, and loss of mobility.

Pressure Ulcers

Pressure (or decubitus) ulcers are always a potential problem of advanced or chronic illness, especially among older patients. The results of pressure ulcers may include pain, infection, protein loss, multiplication of lesions, and increased demands on caregiver effort.

Etiologies and Assessment

Pressure ulcers result from pressure, sometimes exacerbated by trauma (eg, friction, bruises, or multiple, same-site injections), especially at or near bony prominences. The pressure results in occlusion of blood vessels and a lack of oxygen and other nutrients at that site. The development of pressure ulcers is influenced by multiple factors, including immobility and incontinence; and hydration, nutritional, circulatory, and mental status. Patients who are terminally ill are at significant risk of skin breakdown, especially as the disease reaches far advanced stages, and measures to prevent skin breakdown may conflict with comfort measures.

Assessment is mediated by the degree of risk for skin breakdown for a particular patient, the discomfort involved, and life expectancy. During bathing (or while massaging) is a good time to inspect the skin carefully. Special attention should be given to the sacrum, ischia, heels, ankles, and trochanters.

Different organizations have different means of pressure ulcer classification and description. It is important that everyone providing care to a particular patient use the same means of classification and description. A recognized and widely used classification of pressure ulcers (Miller, 1998) follows:

Grade I: Skin is intact with erythema that blanches under pressure.
Grade II: Erythema remains and skin does not blanch with pressure. There may be excoriation, vesiculation, or superficial break in the skin (epidermis).
Grade III: Lesion encompasses full thickness of skin loss but does not include subcutaneous tissue. Serosanguinous drainage is present, but not infection.
Grade IV: Lesion (cavity) extends into subcutaneous fat and deep fascia with destruction of muscle tissue. Eschar formation and infection are common.

Regardless of the classification system, describing and recording the patient's condition includes at a minimum the following: The diameter and depth should be measured (not estimated) and the lesion described (eg, presence of erythema, vesicles, drainage, eschar, or bony involvement). The patient's mobility, mental status, and other relevant factors should be noted. The odor, appearance of the dressing, other skin areas, bed linens, and so forth should be described. When appropriate, the family caregiver's mental, socioeconomic, and physical status should also be noted.

Independent Interventions

Because of associated morbidity and negative influence on quality of life, pressure ulcers are best prevented. Preventive measures include attention to frequent assessment; frequent turning; correct positioning; good hygiene; attention to mechanical factors, hydration and nutrition, pain status and immobility, the patient's other physical problems or factors of the patient's disease or treatment, the bed, and preventive devices; and using the knowledge and abilities of the caregiver(s) to the greatest extent possible. Prevention (Casciato, 1995; De Conno, Ventafridda, & Saita, 1991; Miller, 1998) includes the following:

● Turning the patient every 2 hours is the standard. Turning must be done with care to prevent external trauma from shearing force, bruising, and friction.
● Patients should be placed at oblique (30-degree) alternating angles on the bed rather than always straight up and down.
● Skin should be kept clean, dry, and as free as possible from urine, stool, drainage, or perspiration. Frequently cleansed skin is often excessively dry, so moisturizing lotions can be used judiciously. Powders should be avoided. Soaps used for skin and linens should be nonirritating.
● Mechanical and other factors should be avoided or modified. These include wrinkled or rough sheets, crumbs, tape, jewelry, patient fingernails, vigorous drying with towels, excessive heat, and other external factors that can contribute to decubitus ulcers.
● Protein deficiency is strongly linked with decubitus development. Hydration and nutrition should be maintained as long as possi-

ble, given the patient's desires and capabilities.

● Immobility is frequently implicated in decubitus ulcers and pain is a frequent cause of immobility. Overmedication with analgesics may result in immobility and not feeling the pain of developing problems. Depending on when death is expected, immobility from weakness or paralysis can be addressed with passive range of motion exercises. However, care should be taken that exercises are not discontinued weeks before death: Immobile patients can stiffen quickly and develop subsequent problems. It is essential that pain be controlled before range-of-motion exercises begin. Ideally, exercise also is a means of positive human contact.

● Other physical problems or factors that affect tissue perfusion and contribute to skin breakdown include dehydration, peripheral vascular disease, ascites, edema, infection, and anemia.

● Soft beds are better than hard, and special surfaces (eg, sheepskin or egg crate foam) are better than sheet over mattress alone. Sheepskin should be brushed daily and kept clean. An alternating pressure mattress is best, especially for high-risk patients or for those with skin breakdown. A waterbed is appropriate for some. Preventive devices, including sheepskin pads shaped to fit over heels and sheepskin or blankets between the knees, are helpful for debilitated patients.

● Family caregivers should understand procedures and prevention. Their ability to understand and provide good care should be assessed on an ongoing basis.

● If pressure ulcers develop, they should be treated using the previous principles of prevention and the following additional principles or techniques.

Interventions for Existing Pressure Ulcer

● *Relief of pressure and other contributing factors:* All treatments for existing ulcer are accompanied by the measures described previously. Key issues are relief of pressure, removal of other causative factors (urine, drainage), and prevention of infection.

● *Treatment of open ulcers:* Generally accepted measures (Miller, 1998; De Conno et al., 1991; Gallagher, 1995) include the following, with painful treatment preceded by analgesic administration:

● Grades I and II: Clean lesion with normal saline. Place polyurethane film over lesion, and change every 3 to 4 days and as needed.

● Grade III: Clean lesion with normal saline. (1) Use a hydrocolloid dressing and leave in place until water is transparent over lesion or there is leakage, *or* (2) apply calcium alginate and cover with a semiocclusive dressing. Change the dressing when there is leakage.

● Grade IV: Clean lesion with normal saline. Débridement is necessary and may include surgical intervention. Débridement is also achieved as follows: (1) Use a hydrocolloid dressing and leave in place until water is transparent over lesion or there is leakage; *or* (2) clean eschar with normal saline and apply hydrogel to eschar and cover with a film dressing; *or* (3) apply an enzymatic substance, such as collagenase (Miller writes that the eschar can be scored or the enzymatic injected under the eschar), and apply occlusive dressing; *or* (4) when the lesion is draining or infected—not dry—it can be cleaned with normal saline and a hydrophilic substance (polysaccharide dextranomer, such as Debrisan) put into cavity and covered with a semiocclusive dressing.

Infection is treated with oral antibiotics according to the probable or established microorganism.

Malignant Lesions: Fungating Tumors, Malignant Ulcers

Malignant skin lesions are visible (and often olfactory) manifestations of advanced disease, especially in breast cancer, but also in cancers of the lung, gastrointestinal (GI) tract, and urinary tract and in melanoma (Wagner & Lowitz, 1995).

Etiologies and Assessment

Malignant skin lesions may begin as nodular and progress to changes in skin color (red to purplish or in melanoma, black) and thence to skin breakdown as fungating (ulcerated and proliferating) tumors. Skin metastases also present as inflammation, as in Paget's disease of the nipple or vulva, or carcinoma erysipelatoides, which is also most common in breast cancer. Ulcerated skin lesions are susceptible to infection and thus to becoming malodorous and more painful.

Interventions

Care is directed to problems of pain, drainage, bleeding, odor, and risk or presence of infection. Interventions (Gallagher, 1995; Waller & Caroline, 1996) include the following:

● If the cleaning or débriding procedure is painful, an additional short-acting analgesic may be given before starting.
● Normal saline is used to cleanse and irrigate malignant lesions. It is possible for some patients to shower and use a gentle stream of water and mild soap.
● If débridement is indicated by purulence, apply an enzymatic substance, such as collagenase, and cover with an occlusive dressing *or* for black, necrotic tissue, a hydrophilic substance (polysaccharide dextranomer, such as Debrisan) is applied and covered with a semi-occlusive dressing.
● Minor bleeding is sometimes manageable with pressure or if that is not effective, gauze soaked in 1:1000 epinephrine over the bleeding area. A silver nitrate stick or Gelfoam is also used. Waller and Caroline suggest crushing a 1-g sucralfate tablet and mixing powder in 2 to 3 mL water-soluble gel and applying to the area.
● More extensive bleeding resulting from tumor extension is managed by radiation, cryosurgery, or embolization. Major, irreversible hemorrhage calls for sedation (De Conno et al., 1991). Dark towels can be used to minimize visual effects of bleeding.
● Foul odor is due to anaerobic microorganisms. Frequent cleaning is essential, and contrary to the usual use of normal saline, it may be necessary to use a disinfectant, such as povidone-iodine, hydrogen peroxide, or chlorhexidine. Infection should be treated topically with metronidazole 0.8% gel and often systemically as well with metronidazole 200 to 400 mg PO tid. The ideal dressing is a sterile, nonadherent permeable surface next to skin, absorbent middle layer, and outer layer with charcoal packing. Alternatives to metronidazole gel include magnesium hydroxide, yogurt, yogurt and buttermilk, or honey applied to the area. Good air circulation is helpful to some extent, as are ionizers.
● Drainage to adjacent areas should be prevented with dressings and other measures as described previously.
● Psychosocial issues are at the forefront in the management of these problems. Support and diversion are essential.

Fistulas

Fistulas occur as abnormal channels between internal structures or between an internal structure and the skin.

Etiologies and Assessment

Fistulas are most common in patients with GI cancers (enterocutaneous fistulas), those who have undergone radiation to pelvic organs (rectovaginal or rectovesical [bladder]), or those with head and neck cancer (pharyngocutaneous or tracheoesophageal) (Miller, 1998). Their presence is manifested by discharge or related symptoms in the case of enterocutaneous, rectovaginal, rectovesical, or pharyngocutaneous fistulas; or choking, coughing, and related symptoms in the case of tracheoesophageal fistulas.

Interventions

For patients with high-volume enterocutaneous fistula(s), surgery (proximal bowel diversion with colostomy) is performed to control sepsis and for palliation if the patient is able to tolerate surgery and has a reasonable life expectancy (Schwartzentruber, 1997). Palliative measure (Miller, 1998; Waller & Caroline, 1996; Woodruff, 1997) are directed to preventing or minimizing complications:

● Discharge is often copious, malodorous, and caustic. If possible, involvement of an enterostomal specialist should be sought as soon as a fistula develops. Ostomy bags may be used for patients with enterocutaneous fistulas depending on the volume of discharge. Location and (small) size of the fistula opening may warrant the use of pediatric ostomy bags. Fillers and carmellose paste help create a flat surface and complete seal. Stomahesive helps prevent excoriation and should be used from the beginning. Barrier creams are used on surrounding skin. In some cases, such as a fistula in a large wound, use of an ostomy bag may not be possible, and a low pressure suction tube may be required. Leakage is inevitable, and care must be taken to minimize its effects.
● High-volume discharge can be reduced with the use of octreotide 0.1 mg subcutaneously (SQ) tid, 0.2 to 0.3 mg/24 h SQ infusion, loperamide 2 to 4 mg PO qid, scopolamine 0.4 mg SQ qid, or 0.6 to 1.2 mg/24 h SQ infusion.
● Odor is managed by (1) frequent changing (or draining) of the appliance—always in a well-ventilated room, (2) use of charcoal dressings if an appliance is not used, and (3) control of infection with metronidazole PO as discussed previously under malignant ulcers.
● Rectovaginal or rectoperineal fistulas are very distressing to patients. Creative management, using tampons, sanitary pads, and other measures, tax the skills of the practitioner. Unflagging persistence in good treatment and effective management of the condition has a positive effect on the patient's physical and psychological well-being.

Paraneoplastic Syndromes

Paraneoplastic syndromes (PNSs) are problems that occur at a distance from the primary, or metastatic, tumors. They may affect any body system. Some occur as a first sign of cancer, some late in the disease. The only treatment for PNSs is treatment of the underlying malignancy and palliation of symptoms when possible, such as noted elsewhere in this chapter.

Etiologies and Assessment

Mechanisms of action may occur as ectopic hormone production, as autoimmune or immune responses, or as other, unknown responses. Cutaneous PNSs are rare and include the following (Haapoja, 1997; John, Patchell, & Foon, 1997):

Pigmented Paraneoplastic Syndromes

● Acanthosis nigricans is dark, thickened, "thorny" skin, especially in axillae and similar areas. Acanthosis nigricans is most commonly found in gastric and other adenocarcinomas.
● Tripe palms (often associated with acanthosis nigricans) is a hyperpigmented, soft thickening of tissue of palms; it is associated with gastric and lung cancer.
● Paget's disease includes a keratotic and erythematous patch over the areola or breast (sometimes vulva); it is associated with breast cancer.
● Sign of Leser-Trélat manifests as multiple keratotic and seborrheic (wartlike) lesions; it is associated with gastric adenocarcinoma, lymphoma, breast cancer.
● Sweet's syndrome appears suddenly as painful erythematous plaques or nodules, usually on upper extremities, head, and neck; it is associated with hematologic, genitourinary, breast, and GI cancers.
● Bazex's syndrome manifests as psoriasislike hyperkeratosis with pruritic scales on the face

and extremities; it is associated with gastric and respiratory cancers.

Erythematous Paraneoplastic Syndromes

● Erythema gyratum repens is progressive scaling erythema in concentric bands and pruritus over entire body; it is associated with lung, GI, uterine, and breast cancers.
● Dermatomyositis is muscle weakness and a rash that progresses from periorbital changes to purplish plaquelike lesions on knuckles, elbows, and similar areas; it is associated with breast and other cancers.
● Circinate erythema manifests as circular erythematous and pruritic lesions; it is associated primarily with lymphoma.
● Necrolytic migratory erythema includes circular patches of blistering and erosion with stomatitis; it is associated with pancreatic cancer.
● Flushing is intermittent episodes of facial and neck flushing; it is associated with carcinoids and thyroid tumors.

Endocrine and Metabolic Paraneoplastic Syndromes

● Porphyria cutanea tarda manifests as blisters on skin exposed to sunlight; it is associated with hepatocellular carcinoma.
● Systemic nodular panniculitis (Weber-Christian disease) is recurrent tender erythematous subcutaneous nodules, abdominal pain, and fat necrosis in bone marrow, lungs, and elsewhere; it is associated with pancreatic cancer.
● Cushing's syndrome and Addison's syndrome sometimes appear as PNSs.

There are other cutaneous PNSs, including pruritus not attributable to other causes.

Pruritus

Pruritus (itching) is usually a relatively insignificant problem but may become trouble-some to some patients and has the potential to lead to secondary problems of infection or skin breakdown.

Etiologies and Assessment

The most common primary skin problem resulting in pruritus in terminal cancer and advanced AIDS is dry skin (xerosis), resulting from age, debility, dry air, and related factors. In patients with AIDS, hyperkeratosis (thickening and plaque formation) or infection may also be a cause of pruritus. Also see the following discussion of skin infections and Chapter 27 on HIV infection.

Xerosis tends to worsen or occur more frequently in the winter months. Contact dermatitis also causes pruritus and is due to reaction to ointments, soap, and other substances with which skin comes into contact. Wet, macerated skin (eg, in contact with urine, sweat) also itches. In a few cases, pruritus is due to infestation with scabies, pediculosis, fleas, or mites.

Disease conditions resulting in pruritus include primary polycythemia, Hodgkin's disease, lymphoma, leukemia, and other tumor types and paraneoplastic syndromes (De Conno et al., 1991). Pruritus also develops secondarily to systemic processes, such as uremia and cholestasis, especially when there is obstructive jaundice. Itching may also be due to a psychological disorder and other problems indirectly related to terminal illness (eg, candidiasis, eczema).

Drugs that may cause pruritus due to histamine release include opioids (especially with initial use), aspirin, and vancomycin. Drugs that may cause pruritus due to allergic reaction include carbamazepine, penicillin, sulfonamides, streptomycin, and allopurinol. Drugs that may cause pruritus due to hepatic cholestasis are phenothiazines, captopril, and trimethoprim-sulfamethoxazole (Bactrim). In the absence of an apparent reason for pruritus, all medications should be reviewed. The perception of pruritus is increased by anxiety, dehydration, heat, and boredom (Cosby, 1998; Waller & Caroline, 1996).

Independent Interventions

Treating the cause is the best course. When this is not possible, the following measures (Cosby, 1998; Waller & Caroline, 1996) may reduce pruritus:

● Discontinue drugs causing allergic reaction.
● Local comfort measures include a cool (not hot) bath to which sodium bicarbonate may be added. The patient should not bathe more than once a day. After bathing, apply an emollient to damp skin, and apply the emollient three to five additional times each day for dry skin. Emollients such as Eucerin are significantly more effective than the more commonly used moisturizing and "intensive care" lotions. If scaling is present, use a keratolytic gel.
● Other nonpharmacologic measures include elimination of harsh perfumed soaps and detergents for bathing and linens, avoiding wool and other irritants, avoiding topical alcohol and other drying agents, keeping the patient's nails trimmed, treating insomnia (pruritus may be worse at night), reducing coffee and alcohol use, and providing distraction. It may be helpful for some patients to wear gloves at night. Cool compresses or even ice packs may help specific areas.
● Lotions to reduce itching include calamine or medicated lotions (2% phenol, menthol).
● Wet skin can be protected with zinc oxide paste, which is more effective than petroleum jelly.

Interdependent Interventions

Treating the cause is the best course. Palliative interventions (Casciato, 1995; De Conno et al., 1991; Waller & Caroline, 1996) include the following:

● Discontinue drugs causing allergic reaction.
● Nonspecific palliative measures include a sedating antihistamine at bedtime or bid, such as diphenhydramine 50 mg PO or hydroxyzine 10 to 25 mg PO, both of which also have anxiolytic properties. Promethazine 20 to 50 mg PO bid is also used. The antihistamines are more effective for pruritus due to allergy than other etiologies and are ineffective for pruritus due to cholestasis.
● Systemic and topical therapies should be combined for severe pruritus, including the medications noted previously and topical agents, such as calamine, medicated lotions (2% phenol, menthol), crotamiton 10% (Eurax), anesthetic gel (0.5%–2.0% lidocaine)—the latter applied every 2 hours for severe pruritus. Because of potential development of sensitization phenomenon, antihistamine ointments are discouraged by De Conno et al., but Amlot (1989) reports that in severe cases, potential benefits outweigh risks.
● Systemic corticosteroids are usually ineffective in systemic disease but for severe pruritus are worthy of a trial.
● Cholestasis, uremia, Hodgkin's disease, polycythemia, and so forth are treated to the extent possible in relation to the degree of debilitation. Aspirin is helpful only to patients with Hodgkin's disease and polycythemia vera. Cimetidine is effective in some patients with polycythemia vera. Odansetron 8 mg IV, then 8 mg PO bid is given for pruritus due to cholestasis. Infection is treated as discussed in the following section.

Infections

Skin infections in patients with terminal cancer are most commonly bacteriologic (eg, wound infection) but also may be viral, fungal, or mixed. As the use of immunosuppressive cancer therapy increases, an increase in variety of infections is to be expected. In patients with HIV infection, skin infections are frequently fungal but are also due to other pathogens and may be manifestations of more serious or disseminated infection. Infections are often complicated by some combination of immunosuppression, neutropenia, debility, and other factors. Some infections are preventable through effective hygiene, wound care, and to a lesser extent, maintenance of other aspects of health status. Skin infections should be treated on the basis of the microorganism involved. Pain and odor, if any, from the infection should be addressed as discussed under malignant lesions. Skin infections most commonly found in advanced illness (Cosby, 1998; Mortimer, 1998; Wagner & Lowitz, 1995) follow:

● Candidiasis is a fungal infection, usually of the mouth, vagina, or related areas, including the esophagus. *Candida* may also infect any warm, moist area of the body (eg, groin, armpit); may be found beneath finger or toenails; or when immunosuppression is severe may be disseminated. Candidiasis may occur along with other infections, such as herpes, and may result in secondary infections. Symptoms include discomfort or pain in the infected area. In the mouth, candidiasis appears as red patches, often with white or yellowish "cottage cheese" plaques or hardened areas that usually can be wiped off. There may also be fissures or cracks in mucosal tissue. Esophageal candidiasis causes painful and difficult swallowing. Vaginal and related candidiasis causes pain and itching.
● Herpes simplex virus or HSV type 1 (HSV-1) causes cold sores and eye infections, and HSV type 2 (HSV-2), causes genital herpes. Both are manifested by painful vesicular lesions and erosion on the lips or genitalia that usually resolve in 7 to 10 days. Herpes simplex lesions are often larger and tend to last longer and be more widespread in patients with HIV than in other patients. Fever, adenopathy, and malaise accompany more severe HSV infections.
● Herpes zoster or varicella zoster virus (VZV or "shingles") results from reactivation of varicella (chickenpox) infection. Lesions most commonly occur on the posterior thoracic area or flank along one to three dermatomes and include painful and pruritic macules, papules, plaques, and clusters of vesicles. Pain from VZV is neuropathic and characterized as burning. Pain (postherpatic neuralgia) may last for several months after lesions are no longer evident. It is wise to treat patients with VZV pre-emptively for postherpatic neuralgia before pain begins.

Less common infections include the following:

● Anogenital warts are caused by the human papillomavirus and are spread primarily by sexual contact. They may appear in and around the anus or genitalia as warts, bumps, or protrusions. They tend to spread and when profuse, cause discomfort and problems with elimination.
● Aspergillosis is a fungal (*Aspergillus*) infection occurring in the respiratory system and also in sinuses, central nervous system, liver, kidney, heart, and skin, especially in patients who are neutropenic or receiving chronic steroid therapy.
● Folliculitis is inflammation or infection of the hair follicles (sack from which each hair develops) from one of several causes, including bacterial, fungal, and "allergic" (related to eosinophil cells in the blood). Manifestations include inflammation and itching of the scalp or other areas of the body, with drainage, crusting, and loosened hair.
● Kaposi's sarcoma lesions may become ulcerated and infected (bacterial).
● Molluscum contagiosum is a viral infection characterized by small, painless, white, wartlike lesions that tend to spread. Molluscum contagiosum occurs anywhere on the body but most frequently on the face. The infection is not life threatening and is difficult to treat, except by freezing.
● Psoriasis is a chronic skin disease that may resemble seborrheic dermatitis. Symptoms include raised areas or plaques (scales) that are reddish or brown with pruritus and slight bleeding. Infection commonly occurs on the knees, elbows, and back. Treatment is with steroid creams. Antifungal medications are sometimes used.
● Seborrheic dermatitis causes patches of red, itching skin, especially on the face, chest, armpits, groin, eyebrows, and scalp. Dandruff

shampoo helps with seborrheic dermatitis of the scalp. Steroid and antifungal ointments are used, as are oral medications, such as keto-conazole.

Interventions

Interventions for skin infections (Cosby, 1998; Mortimer, 1998; Wagner & Lowitz, 1995) include the following:

● Treatment of oral candidiasis usually begins with topical nystatin or clotrimazole in suspension (swish and swallow) or troches. Topical creams or vaginal suppositories are used for vaginal candidiasis. Systemic therapy (fluconazole 150 mg PO once daily for 5 days or keto-conazole 200 mg PO once daily for 5 days) is used when infections are severe or frequently recurrent. Prophylactic or suppressive treatment (ongoing topical therapy plus weekly fluconazole PO) is not recommended but may be necessary when there is esophageal candidiasis or infections are frequent or severe. Regular and thorough oral care is important in prevention and early detection of candidiasis. The earlier treatment is initiated in the disease process, the easier the treatment and the better the prognosis will be.

● Herpes simplex virus or HSV-1 (primary infection) is treated with topical anesthetics, such as viscous lidocaine or benzalkonium chloride mouthwash. Recurrent infections are treated with topical ethyl ether soaked gauze placed on the lesion for 5 minutes, repeated in 12 to 24 hours, and again at 48 hours. As lesions heal, antibiotic ointment (bacitracin) can be applied to prevent secondary infection.

● Herpes zoster is treated with antiviral therapy (begin immediately), either acyclovir 800 mg PO five times daily for 7 days or famciclovir 250 mg PO tid for 7 days. For pain, opioids are increased and medications for neuropathic component are added, either amitriptyline 25 to 75 mg PO at bedtime for continuous pain *or* carbamazepine 200 to 800 mg PO at bedtime for shooting pain. Lesions can be treated with

cool saline compresses, Burow's solution (aluminum acetate), or calamine lotion. Preemptive treatment of postherpatic neuralgia with amitriptyline and antiviral (acyclovir) is recommended to reduce postherpatic neuralgia (Bowsher, 1997).

● Anogenital warts are treated by freezing, cauterizing, or chemically "burning off" the warts. There is no systemic therapy for anogenital warts.

● Aspergillosis is treated with amphotericin B. Patients who recover from aspergillosis are at risk for pulmonary hemorrhage.

● Folliculitis is treated according to causative agent: antibiotics for bacterial infection, antifungals for fungal infections, and ultraviolet light for eosinophilic folliculitis. Corticosteroids may also be used for inflammation.

● Infected Kaposi's sarcoma lesions are treated according to the causative pathogen.

● Molluscum contagiosum is difficult to treat, except by freezing.

● Psoriasis is treated with steroid creams. Antifungal medications are sometimes used.

● Seborrheic dermatitis is treated with steroid and antifungal ointments. Ketoconazole is used for resistant cases. Dandruff shampoo helps with seborrheic dermatitis of the scalp.

Dermatologic Sequelae of Treatment

Both radiation and chemotherapy can have ill effects on the skin.

Etiologies and Assessment

The effects of radiation are mediated by dose, skin condition, and other factors and are most severe in skin folds. Radiation injuries are less common with current treatment modalities than previously. Late reactions to radiation may be irreversible and include malfunction of dermal glands.

Patients with advanced cancer may receive radiation for palliation of symptoms, especially for bone pain. Early alterations in skin integrity include erythema, followed sometimes by blisters and desquamation. Other reactions include dryness, pruritus, edema, vesiculation, ulceration, weeping, pain, and alopecia. Secondary infection may also result.

Skin problems resulting from chemotherapy include necrosis from drug extravasation, alopecia, and allergic or hypersensitivity reactions. Other reactions include changes in pigmentation, photosensitivity, nail problems, folliculitis, and radiation recall reactions. In advanced disease, palliative chemotherapy is seldom given in amounts sufficient to cause skin reactions.

Interventions

Treatment includes measures to minimize problems, such as avoiding irritants (eg, harsh soaps, restrictive clothing, trauma). Skin should be cleansed gently with warm water and mild soap. Mild lotions may also be used. Treatment of ulcers and infections is the same as discussed elsewhere.

Treatment for extravasation includes ice packs for 24 hours after occurrence (except for vinca alkaloids) and wound care, if necessary.

REFERENCES

Amlot, P. (1989). Itch. In T. D. Walsh (Ed.), *Symptom control* (pp. 285–294). London: Blackwell Scientific Publications.

Bowsher, D. (1997). The effects of pre-emptive treatment of postherpatic neuralgia with amitriptyline: A randomized, double-blind, placebo-controlled trial. *Journal of Pain and Symptom Management, 13*(6), 327–331.

Casciato, D. A. (1995). Symptom care. In D. A. Casciato & B. B. Lowitz (Eds.), *Manual of clinical oncology* (3rd ed.) (pp. 76–97). Boston: Little, Brown and Company.

Cosby, C. (1998). Skin problems. In M. E. Ropka & A. B. Williams (Eds.), *HIV nursing and symptom management*. Boston: Jones and Bartlett.

De Conno, F., Ventafridda, V., & Saita, L. (1991). Skin problems in advanced and terminal cancer patients. *Journal of Pain and Symptom Management, 6*(4), 247–256.

Gallagher, J. (1995). Management of cutaneous symptoms. *Seminars in Oncology Nursing, 11*(4), 239–247.

Haapoja, I. S. (1997). Paraneoplastic syndromes. In S. I. Groenwald, M. H. Frogge, M. Goodman, & C. H. Yarbro (Eds.), *Cancer nursing: Principles and practice* (4th ed.) (pp. 702–720). Boston: Jones and Bartlett.

John, W. J., Patchell, R. A., & Foon, K. A. (1997). Paraneoplastic syndromes. In V. T. DeVita, S. Hellman, & S. A. Rosenberg (Eds.), *Cancer: Principles and practice of oncology* (5th ed.) (pp. 2397–2422). Philadelphia: Lippincott-Raven.

Miller, C. (1998). Nursing aspects of skin problems. In D. Doyle, G. W. C. Hanks, & N. MacDonald (Eds.), *Oxford textbook of palliative medicine* (2nd ed.) (pp. 642–656). New York: Oxford University Press.

Mortimer, P. S. (1998). Management of skin problems. In D. Doyle, G. W. C. Hanks, & N. MacDonald (Eds.), *Oxford textbook of palliative medicine* (2nd ed.) (pp. 617–627). New York: Oxford University Press.

Schwartzentruber, D. J. (1997). Surgical emergencies. In V. T. DeVita, S. Hellman, & S. A. Rosenberg (Eds.), *Cancer: Principles and practice of oncology* (5th ed.) (pp. 2500–2511). Philadelphia: Lippincott-Raven.

Wagner, R. F., & Lowitz, D. A. (1995). Cutaneous complications. In D. A. Casciato & B. B. Lowitz (Eds.), *Manual of clinical oncology* (3rd ed.) (pp. 473–480). Boston: Little, Brown and Company.

Waller, A., & Caroline, N. L. (1996). *Handbook of palliative care in cancer*. Boston: Butterworth-Heinemann.

Woodruff, R. (1997). *Symptom control in advanced cancer*. Melbourne: Asperula.

CHAPTER 16

Oral Problems

KEY POINTS

- Oral problems of advanced disease are related to primary disease processes, secondary infections or deterioration, or hygiene.

- Prevention of oral problems is a primary goal but becomes more difficult as patients deteriorate and immunosuppression increases.

- Assessment and treatment of oral problems are complicated by the relative frequency of mixed problems (eg, mucositis and infection).

- Infections may be fungal, viral, bacterial, or mixed.

Oral problems, ranging from pathologic processes to poor hygiene, contribute significantly to decreased quality of life in many patients with advanced cancer, especially those with hematologic malignancies and patients treated for head and neck cancer. The primary oral complications of cancer are mucositis (or stomatitis), oral ulcers, xerostomia (dry mouth), taste alteration (hypogeusia, ageusia, dysgeusia), and infections (fungal, viral, and bacterial). In some cases, anorexia, malnutrition, and cachexia result directly from oral complications. Patients with acquired immunodeficiency syndrome (AIDS) have an extremely high (> 70%) incidence of oral infections and other problems, including candidiasis, oral hairy leukoplakia, herpes simplex, recurrent aphthous ulcers, periodontal disease, and lesions due to opportunistic infections and cancer. Lesions from opportunistic infections (cytomegalovirus [CMV] and disseminated histoplasmosis) and cancer associated with AIDS are also common. Oral problems of AIDS are also discussed in Chapter 27.

General Interventions and Prevention

Oral care should be frequent and systematic and should take into consideration the fragility of the oral cavity of patients with advanced disease. Thus, the toothbrush should be soft, toothpaste mild, mouthwash mild and without alcohol, and water-pick device operated at a low (power of water jet) setting. Dental flossing should be done with great care, lest the floss cut into the patient's gums. Areas where lesions or pockets of infection exist should be the last areas flossed. Dentures should fit well and be carefully cleaned after every meal and should be removed at night and soaked in hydrogen peroxide for 10 minutes or overnight in a nystatin solution. Oral care for patients who are weak and cachectic may consist primarily of rinsing with salt water. Oral care should be given before sleep. Regular and systematic oral care can help reduce the likelihood of infections, especially bacterial.

General comfort measures begin with oral care every 4 hours. Discomfort may be relieved with warm salt water rinses, chewing sugar-free gum for dry mouth, and eating softer foods without strong flavors. Mouthwashes with alcohol should be avoided, as should alcoholic drinks, carbohydrates, sugars, and foods that are hot, acidic, or strong flavored. Note that some elixers have alcohol; hence, the patient may need to switch to tablets. Regular use of 1:1 hydrogen peroxide and water or chlorhexidine mouthwash (not to be swallowed) helps prevent or minimize mucositis, and chlorhexidine reduces the incidence of oropharyngeal candidiasis. If hydrogen peroxide rinses are used for ulcerated areas, they should be followed with normal saline rinse to prevent interference with healing (Beck, 1996; Freifeld, Walsh, & Pizzo, 1997; Ungvarski & Schmidt, 1995; Waller & Caroline, 1996).

Medications specific for oral pain due to mucositis and other painful oral conditions (unless contraindicated by other treatment) include the following (Berger & Kilroy, 1997):

● Diphenhydramine 30 mL 12.5 mg/5 mL plus 30 mL viscous lidocaine 2% plus 30 mL Maalox mixed: The patient should rinse with 15 mL four to six times daily.
● Diphenhydramine 30 mL 12.5 mg/5 mL plus 30 mL viscous lidocaine 2% plus tetracycline or penicillin 125 mg/5 mL suspension plus 45 mL nystatin oral suspension 100,000 U/mL plus hydrocortisone suspension 10 mg/5 mL plus 45 mL sterile water mixed: The patient should rinse with 15 mL four to six times daily. As is apparent, this formulation is designed to prevent infection and treat pain.
● Viscous lidocaine 2% solution or dyclonine hydrochloride 0.5% or 1% solution 10 to 15 mL every 2 to 3 hours.

● Proprietary anesthetic agents (Hurricaine, Dyclone, Oratect) and dressings (Zilactin and Orahesive) are recommended by Madeya (1996) because they do not have the systemic effects of lidocaine and some other agents.

Oral pain may also be partially relieved with popsicles, ice chips, or frozen yogurt. Topical agents (eg, lidocaine) can be applied before meals if pain interferes with eating, and if necessary, a short-acting analgesic can be given at an appropriate interval prior to eating.

Mucositis

Oral mucositis, sometimes referred to as stomatitis, is most commonly found in patients undergoing cancer treatment, especially patients with leukemia.

Etiologies and Assessment

Oral mucositis is an inflammation and ulceration of the oral cavity. Infection often develops and may be fungal, viral, or mixed. See descriptions of the various types of infections below. Mucositis is usually due to cancer treatment but also to a combination of the cancer itself and its treatment (Beck, 1996). The risk of mucositis is increased by poor oral hygiene, alcohol and tobacco use, preexisting oral infection, denture problems, vitamin deficiency, radiation therapy, or blood dyscrasias. In terminal stages, mucositis, if present, is usually complicated by infection.

Interventions

Interventions take into consideration the fact that oral complications are reduced, prevented, or identified early in their development through frequent, systematic oral care. Treatment includes regular oral care before and after meals and before bedtime. Oral care for a patient with mucositis (mediated by the degree of debilitation) typically consists of the following (Beck, 1996; Woodruff, 1997):

● Comfort measures should be instituted as described previously.

● Changes in mucosa or other symptoms indicating infection should be carefully monitored.

● Early culture should be taken of sites that appear infected.

● Xerostomia should be prevented with adequate fluid intake, use of lip lubricants, and additional measures, such as stimulation of saliva, synthetic saliva, and caries prophylaxis.

● If bleeding occurs, the patient should rinse with ice water and apply pressure. A wet tea bag that has been frozen may be used as a compress.

● Waller & Caroline (1996) suggest *Candida* infection prevention with clotrimazole troches 10 mg five times daily. For moderate to severe candidiasis, fluconazole 200 to 400 mg/d or a short course of amphotericin may be required (Freifeld et al., 1997).

● Bacterial infection may be treated with topical tetracycline suspension 250 mg mouthwash (2 minute swish, then swallow) qid.

● A topical corticosteroid (eg, triamcinolone 1% in orabase) may be applied topically qid.

Ulcers (or Aphthous Stomatitis)

Recurrent aphthous ulcers are the most common oral ulceration in people with AIDS. They are less common in patients with cancer.

Etiologies and Assessment
Aphthous ulcers are discrete and painful, shallow and usually surrounded by a ring of erythema, found in and out of the mouth, and are most common in the soft mucosa. Ulcers are a result of (1) the neutropenia found most often in patients with hematologic malignancies or human immunodeficiency virus infection; (2) local factors, such as trauma, infection, drug toxicity; or (3) unknown causes.

Interventions
Interventions for aphthous ulcers are the same as for mucositis (also see the section on infections).

Xerostomia (Dry Mouth)

Xerostomia is common during cancer treatment and in later stages of disease, especially when the patient is dehydrated.

Etiologies and Assessment
Xerostomia is characterized by thirst and discomfort. Secondary complications include development of oral lesions and infection and increased dental caries. These may be followed by decreased food intake and malnourishment. Xerostomia is very common in advanced disease and is due to a variety and often a combination of factors. Among these are a decrease in saliva caused by radiation, medications, infection, and other factors; erosion of buccal mucosa caused by disease, treatment, infection, and other factors; and dehydration caused by anorexia, vomiting, diarrhea, mouth breathing, oxygen therapy, difficulty swallowing, and other factors. Medications that may cause or contribute to xerostomia include anticholinergics, antidepressants, phenothiazines, antihistamines, morphine, anticonvulsants, and others.

Interventions
Interventions call for treatment that includes addressing specific etiologies when possible (eg, changing medications, reducing the dosage, treating the infection, or increasing fluids by mouth). Palliation of xerostomia (Madeya, 1996; Ventafridda, Ripamonte, Sbanotto, & De Conno, 1998; Woodruff, 1997) includes the following:

● Regular oral care should increase in frequency (every 2 hours), as should monitoring for infections or complications as described previously.

● Sodium bicarbonate reduces saliva viscosity and neutralizes the acidic oral environment associated with xerostomia.

● Specific infections are treated as described later in this chapter.

● Saliva can be stimulated or dryness offset by frequent fluids, citrus drinks, pineapple, crushed ice, sugar-free candies or gum, or pilocarpine 5 to 7.5 mg tid.

● Commercial artificial saliva products (carboxymethylcellulose or mucin based) help maintain oral hydration and are especially useful before meals and at bedtime.

● Glycerine, methylcellulose (Cologel), and normal saline (1:1:8) provide a saliva substitute.

● Pilocarpine and antholetrithione are effective in improving salivary flow during cancer treatment.

Xerostomia may sometimes be associated with dehydration and imminent death.

Taste Changes (Hypogeusia, Ageusia, Dysgeusia)

Common basic taste changes are hypogeusia (decreased ability to taste), ageusia (no ability to taste), and dysgeusia (distortions in taste).

Etiologies and Assessment

Common taste changes are decreased tolerance of bitter and increased tolerance of sweet tastes. There may also be an increased threshold of detection (ie, aversion) for all four basic tastes (sweet, sour, salty, bitter) in some patients. A common food aversion is for red meat and other urea-containing foods. Taste disorders may be caused by the illness itself, cancer treatment, medications, or protein, vitamin, or zinc deficiencies.

Interventions

Maximum nutrition with minimum intake is the general goal when taste disorders influence dietary intake. Interventions call for offering only foods that do not taste or smell unpleasant to the patient. If the problem is increased threshold to tastes, then hot, strong-smelling foods may be helpful. Acidic or tart foods may increase appetite or in the case of ageusia, stimulate the ability to taste. High-protein supplements in place of meat are often used. Alterna-

tive intake, such as nasogastric feeding or hyperalimentation, are seldom appropriate in terminal illness.

Infections

A variety of oral infections may occur in advanced illness. Infections may be due to a single pathogen but often are mixed. Poor oral hygiene is a common etiology or complicating factor. References for interventions are Beck, 1996; Freifeld et al., 1997; Waller & Caroline, 1996; and Woodruff, 1997.

Fungal Infections
CANDIDIASIS

Candidiasis is by far the most common fungal infection of cancer and AIDS, and by the terminal stage, it occurs in the majority of patients with either diagnosis. Oral candidiasis results in oral pain, odynophagia, and dysphagia and hence leads to decreased intake and malnutrition. In an otherwise healthy person, candidiasis is an uncomfortable annoyance. In a severely immunosuppressed person, the infection can progress from oral to esophageal to systemic infection and to death.

Candidiasis is characterized by oral discomfort, removable white ("cottage cheese") plaques, or flat red lesions of the mucosa without removable plaques. There may be cracks and fissures in oral mucosa and tongue. *Candida* esophagitis (with or without oral candidiases) causes dysphagia and often retrosternal pain, nausea, and vomiting. Candidiasis is often associated with steroids, antibiotics, and other immunosuppressive treatment. In cancer, patients with leukemia are at greatest risk, followed by those with lymphoma. Patients with AIDS are at the greatest risk.

An oral care protocol helps, if not in prevention, then certainly in early identification. Treatment of oral candidiasis usually begins with topical nystatin or clotrimazole in suspension (swish and swallow) or troches. Topical creams or vaginal suppositories are used for vaginal candidiasis. Systemic therapy (fluconazole 150 mg PO once daily for 5 days or ketoconazole 200 mg PO once daily for 5 days) is used when infections are severe or frequently recurrent. Prophylactic or suppressive treatment (ongoing topical therapy plus weekly oral fluconazole) is not recommended but may be necessary when there is esophageal candidiasis or infections are frequent or severe. Comfort measures are described previously. For patients with candidiasis, mouth washes should be avoided.

ASPERGILLOSIS

Aspergillosis, primarily pulmonary but also oral or esophageal, is increasingly found in patients who are neutropenic or receiving chronic steroid therapy. Systemic symptoms may be nonspecific, and oral symptoms include pain and erythema. Treatment is with amphotericin B. Patients who recover from (pulmonary) aspergillosis are at risk for pulmonary hemorrhage.

CRYPTOCOCCOSIS

Cryptococcosis infections affect the central nervous or pulmonary systems and may present as painless lesions similar to those of Kaposi's sarcoma or molluscum contagiosum. Treatment is with amphotericin B alone or with 5-fluorocytosine.

HISTOPLASMOSIS

Histoplasmosis is a fungal infection with manifestations similar to coccidioidomycosis. Symptoms of histoplasmosis include fever, weight loss, cough, abdominal pain, diarrhea, fatigue, oral ulcers, and skin lesions. Other organ systems may also be affected with related symptoms, and histoplasmosis may be disseminated. Treatment of histoplasmosis is with amphotericin B. Itraconazole and fluconazole are being tested in the treatment of histoplasmosis. After the first episode, lifelong suppressive treatment with itraconazole is instituted.

Viral Infections

HERPES SIMPLEX

Herpes simplex is a common viral infection of AIDS and cancer. Herpes simplex virus type 1 causes cold sores and eye infections, manifested by painful vesicular lesions and erosion, inflamed gingiva, or inflamed and crusted lips. The infection usually resolves in 7 to 10 days unless immunosuppression exists. Herpes simplex lesions are often larger and tend to last longer in patients with AIDS than in other patients. Treatment includes comfort measures as described previously and acyclovir 200 mg five times daily for 5 days.

ORAL HAIRY LEUKOPLAKIA

Oral hairy leukoplakia is a viral infection of the mouth. Symptoms include white nonremovable plaques (versus the removable plaques of *Candida*) especially on the sides of the tongue. Oral hairy leukoplakia is sometimes mixed with *Candida albicans*, so it may seem to respond to some extent to topical antifungals. Antifungals are ineffective in the treatment of oral hairy leukoplakia. Cryosurgery is sometimes used to control severe cases.

CYTOMEGALOVIRUS

Cytomegalovirus (CMV) is a ubiquitous virus related to the herpes simplex virus. Immunosuppression can result in the CMV affecting almost any or all body systems. Oral CMV infection is manifested by large, shallow ulcers. Treatment is with ganciclovir or foscarnet, but these do do not cure the infection, so ongoing suppressive treatment is used.

Bacterial Infections

ETIOLOGIES AND ASSESSMENT

Bacterial infections are characterized by small oral hemorrhages, periodontal pain, fever, signs of periapical abscess, and signs of secondary infection in adjacent structures; other signs of inflammation may be missing. The presence of marginal or necrotic gingivitis with erythema indicates infection with mouth anaerobes.

Bacterial infections result from a variety of pathogens and are common during and after chemotherapy; they may also occur as secondary infections in patients with mucositis, candidiasis, and other problems.

INTERVENTIONS

Interventions call for treatment including antibiotic therapy and dental care. Mouthwashes that help include (1) hydrogen peroxide 2% followed by normal saline rinse and (2) povidone-iodine and chlorhexidine 0.2%. Bacterial infections of the oral cavity are often due to mouth anaerobes (*Bacteroides, Clostridia*) or gram-positive cocci (*Staphylococcus aureus,* streptococci). Clindamycin or metronidazole are commonly used for the former and penicillin or a penicillinase-resistant penicillin for the latter. The tetracycline swish described in the discussion of aphthous ulcers may be appropriate (Freifeld et al., 1997; Ventafridda et al., 1998).

Halitosis

Halitosis in terminal illness is sometimes a sign of an underlying problem, always a source of discomfort to the patient, and sometimes a social barrier between the patient and others.

Etiologies and Assessment

Halitosis may simply be evidence of the poor oral hygiene or periodontal disease common in many people regardless of their health status otherwise. Halitosis may also indicate pathology as follows (Ventafridda et al., 1998; Waller & Caroline, 1996):

● Fetid or "sewer" breath may be evidence of infection from anaerobic organisms in the respiratory or gastrointestinal tracts.
● Sweet and sickly breath may indicate *Pseudomonas* infection.
● Ammonia breath is associated with uremia.
● Musty ammoniac breath may indicate hepatic failure.

● Any other preceding primary, secondary, or combined infections of the oral cavity lead to halitosis, especially when old blood or poor hygiene is present.

Interventions include treating the cause (eg, anaerobic infection with metronidazole, candidiasis with clotrimazole) and instituting oral hygiene measures, such as those described in the discussion of bacterial infections or elsewhere in this chapter.

REFERENCES

Beck, S. L. (1996). Mucositis. In S. L. Groenwald, M. H. Frogge, M. Goodman, & C. H. Yarbro (Eds.), *Cancer symptom management* (pp. 308–323). Boston: Jones and Bartlett.

Berger, A. M., & Kilroy, T. J. (1997). Oral complications. In V. T. DeVita, S. Hellman, & S. A. Rosenberg (Eds.), *Cancer: Principles and practice of oncology* (5th ed.) (pp. 2714–2725). Philadelphia: Lippincott-Raven.

De Conno, F., Ripamonti, C., Sbanotto, A., & Ventafridda, V. (1989). Oral complications in patients with advanced cancer. *Journal of Pain and Symptom Management, 4*(1), 20–29.

Freifeld, A. G., Walsh, T. J., & Pizzo, P. A. (1997). Infections in the cancer patient. In V. T. DeVita, S. Hellman, & S. A. Rosenberg (Eds.), *Cancer: Principles and practice of oncology* (5th ed.) (pp. 2659–2704). Philadelphia: Lippincott-Raven.

Madeya, M. L. (1996). Oral complications from cancer therapy: Part 2-nursing implications for assessment and treatment. *Oncology Nursing Forum, 23*(5), 808–821.

Ungvarski, P. J., & Schmidt, J. (1995). Nursing management of the adult client. In J. H. Flaskerud & P. J. Ungvarski (Eds.), *HIV/AIDS: A guide to nursing care* (3rd ed.) (pp. 134–184). Philadelphia: W.B. Saunders.

Ventafridda, V., Ripamonte, C., Sbanotto, A, & De Conno, F. (1998). Mouth care. In D. Doyle, G. W. C. Hanks, & N. MacDonald (Eds.), *Oxford textbook of palliative medicine* (2nd ed.) (pp. 691–707). New York: Oxford University Press.

Waller, A., & Caroline, N. L. (1996). *Handbook of palliative care in cancer.* Boston: Butterworth-Heinemann.

Woodruff, R. (1997). *Symptom control.* Melbourne: Asperula.

Gastrointestinal Problems

Common gastrointestinal (GI) problems include dysphagia, nausea and vomiting (N&V), hiccups, anorexia, cachexia, constipation, diarrhea, incontinence, and bowel obstruction. Xerostomia, stomatitis, and alterations in taste are sometimes addressed as GI problems, but in this work, they are addressed in the chapter on oral problems. Although there is conflicting information on the prevalence of specific GI problems in end-stage disease, the most common and troublesome are N&V, constipation, and anorexia (Seligman, Fink, & Massey-Seligman, 1998).

Most GI symptoms have at least the potential to affect several domains of life with overall adverse effects on quality of life. Cachexia, N&V, diarrhea, and others, for example, may contribute to other physical symptoms or problems, including discomfort and a quicker demise; serve as unmistakable reminders of disease progression and loss of function; and have a negative impact on social life, including being reminders that the family unit will soon undergo irrevocable change.

Dysphagia

Dysphagia may be manifested by drooling, tendency to hold food in the mouth, difficulty swallowing, choking, coughing, nasal regurgitation, or pain (odynophagia).

Etiologies and Assessment
The following are causes of dysphagia:

1. Mechanical obstruction or compression, such as tumor, lymph node(s), or stricture, especially in esophageal cancer
2. Neuromuscular dysfunction, such as invasion of cranial nerves, or neuromuscular disease, such as amyotrophic lateral sclerosis
3. Odynophagia or pain when swallowing caused by infection, such as candidiasis; treatment sequelae, such as stomatitis or mucositis; and irritation from a mechanical disorder, such as gastroesophageal reflux disease, or esophagitis from infection, treatment, or other causes
4. Asthenia or severe debilitation

Dysphagia may be due to dysfunction in one or all of the three phases of swallowing (Table 17-1): buccal, pharyngeal, or esophageal (Waller & Caroline, 1996; Woodruff, 1997).

Dysphagia may include difficulty swallowing solids only or solids and liquids and may progress to inability to manage saliva. Difficulty swallowing solids usually precedes difficulty swallowing liquids, except in neuromuscular disorders. When present with cognitive failure and weight loss of 10 kg or more, dysphagia with solids or liquids is an accurate indicator that death is likely to occur in less than 4 weeks (Bruera, Miller, Kuehn, MacEachern, & Hanson, 1992). In patients with AIDS, dysphagia is most commonly due to esophageal candidiasis or cytomegalovirus infection (Ungvarski & Schmidt, 1995).

Independent Interventions
It is critical to distinguish dysphagia caused by infection from dysphagia due to mechanical or neuromuscular defects. Interventions in dysphagia (Grant & Rivera, 1995; Ungvarski & Schmidt, 1995) include the following:

● Only soft, semisolid, or finely chopped foods should be eaten, and all food taken in small amounts at intervals through the day. It is often necessary to experiment with different foods and consistencies of foods, and these may change as the disease progresses.
● Dry or abrasive foods should be avoided unless softened by soaking in sauce, tea, bouillon, or milk (unless the latter causes problems with mucus). Most raw fruits and vegetables should be avoided, as should sticky foods, such as peanut butter or soft bread.

TABLE 17-1	Phases of Swallowing and Dysphagia	
Phase	**Characteristic**	**Potential Cause**
Buccal	Drooling, holding food in mouth	Stomatitis, mucositis, xerostomia, tumor involvement of cranial nerves (7, 9, 10, 12), asthenia
Pharyngeal	Choking, coughing, nasal regurgitation, food sticking high in throat	Tumor or lymph node obstruction or compression, central nervous system metastasis, pharyngitis from infection or irritation
Esophageal	Retrosternal pain, food sticking lower in throat	Tumor or lymph node obstruction or compression, esophagitis from infection, treatment, or irritation

● Attention should be paid to adequate caloric and protein intake.

● The patient should sit upright or even lean forward to eat. Fluids should be taken during and after meals. Using a straw to drink may help. The patient should avoid tilting her or his head back when swallowing. The patient's head and torso, if possible, should be kept elevated for 30 to 45 minutes after meals.

● When dysphagia is due to infection, spicy, acidic, salty, sticky, and excessively hot or cold foods should be avoided. Popsicles, however, may help with pain.

● Alcohol and tobacco exacerbate dysphagia.

● Having a suction machine available may help if choking is a problem. If choking is a problem, the patient should be monitored for airway obstruction and pneumonia.

● Oral hygiene should be maintained.

Interdependent Interventions

When dysphagia is due to infection, interventions are directed to resolving the infection. As dysphagia worsens or the patient deteriorates, palliative care may include esophagectomy (but this measure has a morbidity rate of more than 20% and a 1- to 2-month recovery period), radiation therapy, esophageal dilatation, photodynamic therapy, or endoprosthesis or esophageal stent (Coleman, 1997; Martins & Lynch, 1997). Total obstruction results in problems with drooling, which may be treated with scopolamine patch. A trial of dexamethasone is sometimes recommended for mechanical obstruction or tumor infiltration (Waller & Caroline, 1996).

The care of patients with esophageal stent is focused on preventing complications. The most troublesome complication is reflux of gastric contents leading to pneumonia. Measures to prevent complications (Coleman, 1997; Waller & Caroline, 1996) include the following:

● The head of the bed is kept elevated at all times and meals taken with the patient in an upright position.

● The patient should chew carefully and take small swallows of solids followed by a sip of fluid.

● Foods to avoid include soft breads, fish, hard-boiled eggs, stringy or pithy fruits and vegetables, and tough or stringy meats.

● To clear the tube, drink at least half of a glass of water or carbonated beverage at the end of each meal. Gastrostomy and jejunostomy allow nutritional support but do not relieve symptoms.

The clinician should explore with the patient and family the positive meanings of giving and receiving food in relation to the liabilities of attempting to eat in some situations in advanced disease.

Nausea and Vomiting

N&V are common in cancer and AIDS and have a marked negative impact on the overall quality of life in many patients, N&V lead to more specific problems of nutritional deficits, dehydration, electrolyte imbalance, and difficulty managing other disease processes, such as diabetes, congestive heart failure, and renal dysfunction. Nausea may range from vague abdominal discomfort to severe nausea with accompanying salivation, swallowing, cold sweat, tachycardia, and gastric relaxation. Vomiting may range from occasional retching ("dry heaves") to frequent profuse vomiting. Hereafter, this section refers only to N&V, but interventions apply to nausea, retching, or vomiting.

Etiologies and Assessment

When possible, the treatment of N&V is based on the mechanism(s) by which they are triggered. N&V occur when the vomiting center of the medulla is stimulated by afferent impulses from one or more of the following anatomic areas (Fessele, 1996; Mannix, 1998):

● Chemoreceptor trigger zone (CTZ), which is stimulated by metabolic products produced by uremia, ketoacidosis, hypercalcemia; tumor-generated toxins and chemotherapeutic agents; radiation; and opioids. Note that N&V resulting from opioid use is usually a side effect of opioid therapy initiation and will resolve in most patients in less than 1 week.

● Cerebral cortex, which is stimulated by anxiety and thoughts (eg, anticipatory nausea); sights, smells, and tastes; and increased intracranial pressure (ICP) which causes vomiting without nausea

● Vestibular system (the source of motion or position nausea) through the labyrinth of inner ear, the sensitivity of which can be increased by opioids

● Upper GI tract stimulated by pressure, distension, obstruction, or irritation with impulses from vagus and splanchnic nerves as is common in GI cancers, GI metastases, and other disease processes. GI tract stasis may also be affected by opioids and mechanical processes, such as ascites.

N&V may be due to one or more of the above (eg, opioid use can result in chemical stimulation of the CTZ, increased sensitivity of the vestibular system, and gastric stasis and decreased peristalsis). Specific etiologies of N&V in cancer or AIDS (Fessele, 1996; Mannix, 1998; Mercadante, 1997; Rousseau, 1995; Waller & Caroline, 1996) may include one or more of those given in Table 17-2. Because medical treatment is based on the most potent antagonist to the receptor and site, the most effective medications or other treatments are briefly noted in the table.

Independent Interventions

While etiologies are sometimes difficult to determine, one characteristic of N&V is that the problem, regardless of etiology, is often self-perpetuating or self-exacerbating. Independent interventions (Fessele, 1996; Rhodes, Johnson, & McDaniel, 1995; Ungvarski & Schmidt, 1995) include the following

● Determine and act on (ie, by providing information and encouragement through teaching) any misconceptions on the part of the patient and the family, for example, that nausea from opioids will be a long-lasting problem.

● Assist the patient or family to maintain a self-care journal to track symptoms, self-care responses, and outcomes.

● Modify diet (in the absence of a prescribed diet or diet that the patient has successfully used to combat N&V in the past, for example, during chemotherapy) according to the following guidelines:

1. Increase soft drinks, soda crackers, salty foods, fresh fruits, nonacidic juices, chicken soup or broth, Jello, bland or soft foods, colorless foods (eg, cottage cheese and vanilla ice cream), non–gas-forming foods, cold foods, and foods that the patient thinks will be tolerated.
2. Decrease fatty, fried, strong-smelling, or very sweet foods.
3. Avoid smells and sights of cooking; bathroom smells may also contribute to the problem and should be minimized.
4. Institute smaller, more frequent meals.
5. Track any patterns in time of nausea, and take larger meals when N&V are least problematic. Fasting may be necessary.
6. Ensure adequate hydration, except that it may help to minimize liquids before, during, and immediately after meals.
7. Rest after meals, but keep head elevated.

● Instruct the patient and family to keep the patient's head elevated and the room cool.

● Teach and support the patient and family in using imagery, music therapy, or distraction techniques (see Psychological Interventions in Chapter 11). Also, provide psychological support to patient and family.

Interdependent Interventions

As noted previously, N&V are best treated by resolving the underlying cause and by palliation based on the most potent antagonist to the receptor and site. The key is to prevent the problem or intervene as quickly as possible. When N&V are known to exist, medications are given on a regular schedule so that the

TABLE 17-2	Nausea and Vomiting: Etiologies and Interventions	
Site	**Syndromes/Etiologies**	**Medication(s)/Treatment(s)**
Chemoreceptor trigger zone (CTZ)	*Metabolic disorder,* such as hypercalcemia, ketoacidosis, uremia *Medications,* including opioids, steroids, digoxin, anticonvulsants, antibiotics *Toxins,* such as those from infection, gastritis, tumor products (cytokines)	Treat or prevent underlying cause (eg, hypercalcemia). Decrease or discontinue medication if not essential to treatment. Palliate with haloperidol, phenothiazine, metoclopramide; Corticosteroid can be used for N&V from hypercalcemia. N&V from chemotherapy may require multidrug combinations.
Cerebral cortex	*Anxiety* and thoughts (eg, anticipatory nausea), sights, smells, and tastes *Increased intracranial pressure (ICP)* from brain, meningeal metastases	Benzodiazepine, haloperidol, or cannabinoid can be used for anxiety and corticosteroids for increased ICP.
Vestibular system	*Sensitivity to stimulation* possibly increased by opioids	Antihistamine can be used, such as hydroxyzine or diphenhydramine.
Upper gastrointestinal tract	*Stasis* from opioids, anticholinergics; mechanical processes, such as ascites, hepatomegaly, gastritis *Distension, distortion* of viscera, such as with constipation, obstruction *Irritation* from gastric secretions, gastric carcinoma *Pancreatic disease* *In AIDS,* infection primary cause of N&V	Treat or prevent underlying cause (eg, infection, constipation, ascites). Metoclopramide is used for stasis (but not with obstruction). Reduce gastric secretions with H_2 blocker or $5\text{-}HT_3$ antagonists: omeprazole, odansetron, tropisetron. See discussion of obstruction later in this chapter.
Other	Pain, high fever, oral candidiasis, urinary tract infection, and N&V of unknown etiology	Treat cause and palliate.

patient does not reexperience the problem. For patients who have not had a problem with N&V, medications are given at the first sign of nausea. To be most effective (Bruera et al., 1996; Mannix, 1998; Waller & Caroline, 1996), medications are given in the following manner:

● According to the etiology of the N&V
● In therapeutic dosages so that nausea is eliminated
● Often in combination if single drug is ineffective (see regimen below)
● At proper (preventive, scheduled) intervals so that the client does not reexperience nausea
● By an effective route so that the patient does not lose medication through vomiting or inef-

fective absorption. Oral is the preferred route. If necessary, maintenance antiemetics may be given rectally. Initially, in cases of severe vomiting, medications may be given parenterally.

Antiemetics commonly used, singly or in combination, for patients with advanced disease (Bruera et al., 1996; Fessele, 1996; Mannix, 1998; Rhodes et al., 1995; Ungvarski & Schmidt, 1995; Waller & Caroline, 1996; Woodruff, 1997) include the following:

MECHANISM OF ACTION UNCLEAR

● Corticosteroid, such as dexamethasone 4 to 24 mg PO every morning (used for N&V from increased ICP, hypercalcemia, and in combination with other medications for difficult-to-treat N&V). Side effects include euphoria, other mood changes, fluid retention, and GI irritation.

ACTS ON CHEMORECEPTOR TRIGGER ZONE

Any of the drugs that act on the CTZ may result in extrapyramidal side effects, for which diphenhydramine or lorazepam should be given with every dose beginning with the first:

- Phenothiazine, such as prochlorperazine 5 to 10 mg PO tid or 25 mg PR bid (can also be given IM or IV). Side effects include sedation, dystonic reactions (trismus, torticollis, facial spasm, oculogyric crisis, anxiety), and orthostatic blood pressure changes.
- Orthopromide, such as metoclopramide 10 to 20 mg PO qid or tid (can be given IV), is also effective in gastric stasis. Side effects include sedation, dystonic reactions, akathisia, and tardive dyskinesia (involuntary chewing, vermicular tongue movements).
- Butyrophenone, such as haloperidol 0.5 to 3.0 mg PO tid (can be given 1–3 mg IM q2–4h for two to three doses to bring N&V under control). Side effects include sedation, dystonic reactions, other extrapyramidal side effects.

ACTS ON CEREBRAL CORTEX

- Benzodiazepine, such as diazepam 5 mg PO (can be given IV) or lorazepam 1 to 2 mg PO (also given IV). Side effects include sedation and amnesiac effect.
- Cannabinoid, such as dronabinol 2.5 to 5 mg PO q3–6 h. Some patients prefer to smoke marijuana rather than take oral medications as a source of cannabinoid. Side effects include sedation, euphoria, increased appetite.

ACTS ON VESTIBULAR SYSTEM

- Antihistamine, such as diphenhydramine 50 to 75 mg PO qid (also used to treat extrapyramidal effects from phenothiazines, butyphe-

nones, metoclopramide). Side effects include sedation and dry mouth.
- Anticholinergic, such as scopolamine 0.5 mg transdermal q3d. Side effects include anticholinergic effects, such as dry mouth, blurred vision, urinary retention, and constipation.

ACTS ON GASTROINTESTINAL TRACT

- Orthopromide, such as metoclopramide 10 to 20 mg PO qid or tid (can be given parenterally), which also acts on CTZ.
- Corticosteroid, such as dexamethasone 4 to 24 mg PO qam (can be given IV).
- H_2 blocker, such as hydroxyzine 6.25 mg tid. Side effects include anticholinergic effects.
- Serotonin antagonists, specifically 5-hydroxytryptamine (5-HT_3) antagonists, such as ondansetron 8 mg bid (can be given IV). Side effects include headache and constipation.

A protocol for N&V in patients with terminal illness (Bruera et al., 1996; Waller & Caroline, 1996) includes the following:

1. Treat cause (eg, hypercalcemia, increased ICP, infection) if possible, and palliate symptoms concurrently. If etiology is not apparent or not amenable to intervention, proceed as below.
2. Begin with metoclopramide.
3. If metoclopramide is not effective, add a second medication according to the suspected etiology of N&V: haloperidol if CTZ or dexamethasone if increased ICP or etiology is unclear.
4. If the two-drug regimen is ineffective, add an antihistamine (if not already used with the metoclopramide).
5. If the three-drug regimen is ineffective, add dexamethasone 4 mg if not already in use.
6. If the four-drug regimen is ineffective, add 5-HT_3 antagonist, such as ondansetron (other authors, such as Mystakidou, Befon, Liossi, & Vlachos, 1998, recommend using a 5-HT_3 antagonist as the initial drug).

Phenergan is commonly used in the acute hospital setting but seldom in hospice or palliative care.

Hiccups

When lasting a few minutes in a healthy person, hiccups are an annoyance. When hiccups occur as chronic problem in a person with advanced illness, hiccups are a troublesome symptom indicating the presence of underlying pathology.

Etiologies and Assessment

Hiccups are commonly caused by diaphragmatic irritation, gastric distension, esophagitis, phrenic nerve irritation, uremia, brain tumor, infection, or in a few cases, psychogenic origin (Woodruff, 1997).

Independent Interventions

"Home cures" are sometimes helpful in stopping hiccups (Twycross & Regnard, 1998; Woodruff, 1997):

● Swallowing two teaspoons of granulated sugar
● Rapidly drinking two glasses of liquid
● Swallowing dry bread
● Swallowing finely crushed ice
● Drinking from the wrong (far) side of a cup
● Tongue traction sufficient to result in a gag reflex
● Nasogastric suction
● Rebreathing into a paper bag
● Breath holding or hyperventilation

Some of these interventions may be limited by debilitation.

Interdependent Interventions

Medical and even surgical measures may be used when chronic hiccups have a significant negative effect on quality of life (eg, result in dehydration, insomnia, pain). The following are among the measures used to treat hiccups that are not responsive to the previous interventions (Twycross & Regnard, 1998; Waller & Caroline, 1996):

● Etiology should be resolved.
● Simethicone before or after meals and at bedtime may be sufficient when hiccups are due to gastric distension.
● If the above is not effective, metoclopramide 10 to 20 mg PO qid, either alone or with simethicone, has shown good results (see previous discussion of side effects). Waller & Caroline note that metoclopramide initially may be given IV or IM for faster results.
● Peppermint water is used when esophageal disorders are the etiology but not concurrently with metoclopramide.
● Chlorpromazine (25–50 mg PO tid) and haloperidol (1–4 mg PO tid) are effective in the treatment of hiccups. Either may be given parenterally. Side effects were noted previously.
● Anticonvulsants, including carbamazepine, phenytoin, and valproic acid are sometimes effective.
● Phrenic nerve interruption with bupivacaine or surgery is occasionally used.

Anorexia and Cachexia

Anorexia and accompanying weight loss are "the most common symptoms in terminal cancer patients" and occur, to some extent, in all cancers (Wachtel, Allen-Masterson, Reuben, Goldberg, & Mor, 1988, p. 73). Anorexia and weight loss are universal in patients with advanced AIDS.

If weight loss is due to poor appetite alone, nutritional support or other measures may stabilize or even increase the patient's weight in earlier stages of disease. In later stages, anorexia tends to progress to or be caused by cancer cachexia or in the case of AIDS, wasting syndrome. Though they are not exactly the same process, both cancer cachexia and wasting syndrome are complex syndromes that include anorexia, nausea, tissue wasting, skeletal muscle atrophy, asthenia, immune dysfunction, and metabolic changes (Bruera & Fainsinger, 1998; Casey, 1997a; Rivadeneira, Evoy, Fahey, Lieberman, & Daly, 1998). Cachexia is seldom, if ever, stabilized or reversed in far advanced illness (Fainsinger, 1997).

Etiologies and Assessment

With anorexia and weight loss common, and in most cases inevitable, among patients with terminal illness, identifying specific causes is an extremely challenging and ultimately futile task. Nevertheless, anorexia and weight loss from some etiologies are treatable, so assessment of anorexia and weight loss is an integral part of quality palliative care. The fundamental cause of weight loss is decreased intake. A general assessment includes determining intake patterns, food likes and dislikes, and the meaning of food or eating to the patient and family. Early in the disease, comprehensive and frequent assessments are appropriate (Casey, 1997a), but later assessments—even as basic as weight—are not helpful to the patient (Casciato, 1995). Common causes of anorexia and cachexia (Casey, 1997a; Grant & Rivera, 1995; Rivadeneira et al., 1998) include the following:

● A host of physical symptoms often contribute to or cause anorexia, such as pain, alterations in taste, stomatitis, dysphagia, odynophagia, dyspnea, nausea, vomiting, diarrhea, constipation, fatigue, various infections, and early satiety. In general, most people who are seriously ill or suffering distressing symptoms have poor appetites. Cancer and AIDS treatments are well known to often have deleterious effects on appetite or result in side effects leading to poor appetite or weight loss. Patients with HIV disease may develop primary muscle disease leading to weight loss.
● Metabolic alterations are common in cancer, and some may result in cachexia, including glucose intolerance, glucose turnover, insulin resistance, increased lipolysis, increased whole body turnover, increased skeletal muscle catabolism, negative nitrogen balance, and in at least some patients increased basal energy expenditure. The presence of cytokines (interleukins and tumor necrosis factor) produced by tumor or as an immune response to tumor are thought to mediate these metabolic abnormalities. In AIDS, metabolic alterations leading to wasting include hypermetabolism, endocrine dysfunction, and the presence of cytokines.
● Paraneoplastic syndromes, including hypercalcemia, may also cause anorexia or symptoms such as fatigue that lead to anorexia. Anorexia and cachexia are considered by some to be a paraneoplastic syndrome caused probably by cytokines as noted previously.
● Other problems of the GI tract leading to anorexia include hepatomegaly, splenomegaly, gastric compression, delayed emptying, malabsorption, and obstruction.
● Side effects of medications may directly result in anorexia (acyclovir, foscarnet, zidovudine, and others) or have side effects, such as nausea, taste changes, and diarrhea, that lead to anorexia.
● Psychological or spiritual distress may be another cause of anorexia and may include anxiety, depression, or feelings of hopelessness, all of which may result in little enthusiasm or energy for preparing or eating food.
● Poorly fitting dentures and other causes of dental or oral pain play a role in anorexia.

Independent Interventions

Interventions for treating the problems noted previously include the following (Bruera & Fainsinger, 1998; Casey, 1997b; Grant & Rivera, 1995; Ungvarski & Schmidt, 1995):

● If anorexia is due to a problem, such as particular symptoms, infection, early satiety, taste disorders, poorly fitting dentures, etc., then the problem is managed. Taste disorders are discussed in the chapter on oral problems.
● Altering diet may be helpful—at least to some extent. Small meals given on the patient's schedule and according to the taste and whims of the patient are the most helpful measure. Giving and taking food often have profound (and sometimes unrecognized) meaning to

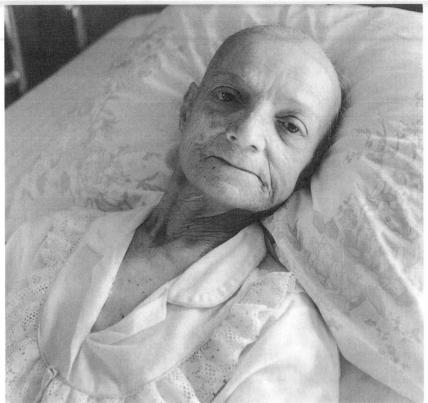

DEBORA HUNTER

patients and their families. Helping the family become proficient in preparing food appropriate to the terminal situation can have a positive effect on patient and family. Homemade milkshakes or Carnation Instant Breakfast are better tolerated by some patients than are dietary supplements and hence may have greater value (Miller & Albright, 1989). General guidelines for altering diet include the following:

1. The meaning to the patient and family of giving and taking food should be determined. It is possible, with some families, to encourage and instruct them in trying to redirect their food-related personal values from symbolic nurturing to symbolic sharing. Partaking of half a bite of food by sharing it in "sacred meals" eaten with loved ones constitutes a kind of victory over the disease (R. Bowie, personal communication, April, 1992). More often, however, strong and perhaps unconscious beliefs about food cannot be modified. Families may require frequent support in their helplessness and frustration related to diminished intake.

2. Small, frequent meals served on smaller plates and presented attractively may help. Dressing for meals and sitting at the table are helpful unless fatigue decreases appetite.

3. The patient should be offered foods with different tastes, textures, temperatures, seasonings, degrees of spiciness, degrees of moisture, colors, and so forth.

4. The patient should be offered different liquids. In general, liquids, except for nutritional supplements, should not be taken with meals. Cold, clear liquids are usually

well tolerated and enjoyed. Soft drinks, nonacidic fruit juices or seltzers, flavored Jello (liquid or congealed), popsicles, tea (warm or iced), and any other drinks that sound good to the patient should be offered.

5. The nutritional quality of intake should be evaluated and, if possible, modified to improve the quality. Patients who are not moribund may benefit from supplementary sources of protein and calories.

6. Early satiety, the feeling of fullness shortly after beginning to eat, is addressed by increasing the nutritional value of the first part of the meal and by following the measures discussed later under interdependent measures.

7. Procedures, treatments, psychological upsets, or other stressors or activities prior to meals should be limited.

8. Depression as the primary etiology of anorexia requires comprehensive interventions, as discussed in the section on depression in Chapter 2.

9. For patients living at home, making food as easy as possible to prepare or eat may increase consumption. Frozen foods, meals prepared ahead of time and then frozen, meals on wheels, and similar measures may thus help.

Interdependent Interventions

Options to address the problem of anorexia are limited and in the final stages of terminal illness are futile. Bruera and Fainsinger (1998), Fainsinger (1997), and Waller and Caroline (1996) offer the following interventions in anorexia:

● When possible, the underlying cause should be addressed, along with palliation of the symptom.

● Palliative treatment of anorexia/cachexia includes the following:

1. Megestrol acetate 160 to 800 mg PO daily (qid) in liquid suspension improves appetite and reduces N&V and alterations in taste. It is most useful for patients expected to live for weeks or months. Side effects may include fluid retention, menstrual irregularities, and tumor flare in patients with breast cancer. Megestrol is contraindicated in patients with thrombophlebitis.

2. Metoclopramide 10 mg PO tid is most helpful for patients with delayed gastric emptying or gastric paresis (leading to early satiety).

3. Corticosteroids (eg, dexamethasone 4–8 mg every morning) are most useful in patients with limited life expectancy or when a rapid effect is needed. Side effects include euphoria, other mood changes, fluid retention, and GI irritation.

4. Cannabinoids (eg, dronabinol 2.5–5 mg PO q3–6h) improve appetite and decrease nausea. Older patients may have unpleasant feelings from cannabinoids.

5. Antidepressants are used when depression is an etiology in anorexia.

● Enteral and parenteral nutrition are useful only in a small subset of patients with anorexia and advanced terminal illness—specifically, those with bowel obstruction and lengthy life expectancy (Fainsinger, 1997).

Constipation

Constipation is one of the most common and distressing problems of advanced cancer (Seligman et al., 1998) and may be defined as stools that are too small, too hard, too difficult to expel, and too infrequent in relation to what is usual for the patient. Feeling of incomplete evacuation may also be considered constipation (Wright & Thomas, 1995).

Etiologies and Assessment

About 50% of patients with terminal cancer are constipated (Wachtel et al., 1988). In addition to the decreased frequency of bowel movements, problems of constipation include the accompanying discomfort, fecal impaction with diarrhea and incontinence, anorexia, N&V, urinary retention and incontinence, and confusion. Severe constipation influences the absorption of oral medications, sometimes markedly increasing pain. Undiagnosed fecal impaction is a key factor in significant numbers of patients whose pain becomes unmanageable (Glare & Lickiss, 1992).

The patient's bowel history is significant. Constipation may be a lifelong pattern or may have a more recent etiology. However, in patients with far-advanced cancer, constipation may be an unalterable consequence of diminished intake and thus not necessarily a problem. Half of a patient's normal food intake may produce a bowel movement every other day, and a third the normal intake may produce a bowel movement every third day (Bisanz, 1997). Specific etiologies—often combined—in constipation (Agra et al., 1998; Waller & Caroline, 1996; Wright & Thomas, 1995) include the following:

● Medications are a common cause of constipation. In terminal illness, opioids are probably the most common cause. Other medications that may cause or contribute to constipation include anticholinergic agents; antacids; anticonvulsants; phenothiazines; nonsteroidal anti-inflammatory drugs; antiemetics, such as ondansetron; and certain chemotherapeutic agents.
● Conditions or problems associated with advanced disease contribute to constipation, including advanced age, weakness, immobility or decreased activity, depression, confusion, or sedation.
● Inadequate fluids and fiber are a common cause or contributing factor. An abundance of fiber and inadequate fluids may result in hard stools and tendency to impaction. A general decreased intake also contributes to decreased bowel movements.
● Changes in bowel habits may be indirectly related to illness (eg, decreased privacy or unfamiliar toilet facilities).
● Hypercalcemia or hypokalemia may result in constipation.

● Tumor invasion or growth (bowel, pelvic, other abdominal) may result in neurologic dysfunction or bowel compression, which is addressed separately below.

Independent Interventions

Independent interventions for treating constipation include the following (Bisanz, 1997; Wright & Thomas, 1995):

● When possible, intake should be modified to increase fiber and fluids and avoid constipating foods (eg, dairy products and fried foods). Large meals are more likely to stimulate bowel movements than small. However, "dietary modifications and bulk laxatives alone are seldom tolerable or adequate" (Levy, 1985, p. 403) for clients with advanced cancer who are taking opioids. As death nears, all intake inevitably decreases.
● When possible, activity should be increased (good pain management and other symptom management are necessary to do so).
● Patients and family should be assisted to resolve the anger or hopelessness that may lie behind depression.
● Privacy and bathroom assistive devices should be available.

Interdependent Interventions

Interdependent interventions for treating constipation are noted in the following list (Agra et al., 1998; Sykes, 1996; Waller & Caroline, 1996). When possible, laxatives should be given orally, although significant numbers of patients are accustomed to rectal laxatives or enemas.

● Bowel obstruction should be ruled out.
● When the patient is at risk for constipation (ie, taking opioids, with a decreased activity level, or with a decreased fluid intake), fluids and fiber should be increased, and the patient should be given a prophylactic stool softener (eg, diocytyl sodium sulfosuccinate) and a stimulant laxative (eg, senna [Senokot-S] 1–2 tabs PO). Ambulatory patients without risk

factors do not necessarily need laxative prophylaxis.

● When the patient is constipated (no bowel movement in 48 hours), fecal impaction should be ruled out (either fecal mass in rectal vault or higher and presenting as a nontender, movable, and indentable abdominal mass). If impaction by a large fecal mass exists, it may require physical (digital) disimpaction preceded by morphine and diazepam or in the case of hard stool, an olive oil (120 mL) retention enema 12 hours before disimpaction, then disimpaction followed by a high milk and molasses (see below) or saline enema. After impaction is resolved, a bowel regimen is instituted, beginning with independent measures as described above plus stool softener plus stimulant laxative. Digital removal of an impaction is contraindicated in people with neutropenia or thrombocytopenia (Donoghue, 1988).

● If stool is hard, constipation continues, and impaction is not present, fluids should be increased and the patient given an osmotic cathartic, such as lactulose or sorbitol, or if stronger action is required, magnesium sulfate (the latter is contraindicated with renal insufficiency).

● If constipation continues, a glycerin or bisacodyl suppository or sodium biphosphate enema may be added to the regimen.

● Some patients prefer enemas as a primary means of treating constipation. Sodium biphosphate (Fleets) enemas are convenient and effective. A milk and molasses enema is recommended because it is nonirritating. The formula for milk and molasses enema is 8 oz warm water and 3 oz powdered milk shaken together and then 4.5 oz molasses added and shaken until completely mixed. The enema can be given every 6 hours (three times) until results are achieved (Bisanz, 1997).

● Specific measures for patients with constipation (Waller & Caroline, 1996) include the following:

1. Soft fecal mass palpated in abdomen may be treated with a stimulant laxative, such as bisacodyl, or osmotic cathartic, such as magnesium salts (eg, Milk of Magnesia) except as contraindicated. If not resolved, an oil retention enema may be followed by a phosphate or milk and molasses enema.
2. Soft feces in the rectum may be treated with a stimulant laxative, such as senna or biscodyl.
3. Empty distended rectum and a history of constipation is treated with high enemas.
4. Painful hemorrhoids or anal fissures require a combination of bulk-forming agents (psyllium or cellulose) plus stool softener or surfactant laxative (docusate) plus analgesic anal suppositories (Anusol).

Diarrhea

Diarrhea occurs most often in patients with stomach or esophageal cancers (50%), followed by those with pancreatic, cervical, or uterine cancers. Patients with primary brain tumors are least likely to experience diarrhea (Wachtel et al., 1988). Patients with AIDS have a very high incidence of diarrhea—often refractory to treatment (Wilcox, 1997).

Etiologies and Assessment

A practical definition of diarrhea is an increase in one or more of the following parameters: daily stool weight, water content, or frequency (Mercadante, 1995). Diarrhea may be profuse, or there may be a pattern of expelling small amounts of watery stool. Incontinence of stool is a common confounding factor.

Diarrhea may be classified as large volume (increased water or intestinal secretion) or small volume (increased motility) The primary mechanisms of diarrhea are osmotic (water drawn into the colon), secretory (intestinal mucosa secretes fluid, often in response to infection), and motile (inflammatory response) (Wright & Thomas, 1995). A number of potential etiologies follow. General assessment of diarrhea includes usual patterns of elimination and, with respect to the diarrhea, determination of the onset, amount, appearance, associated symptoms, dietary patterns, and perirectal or stomal skin condition. Specific etiologies (Bisanz, 1997; Mercadante, 1995; Sykes, 1996; Ungvarski & Schmidt, 1995; Wright & Thomas, 1995) include the following:

● Gastrointestinal infection is the most common cause of diarrhea in AIDS and is a common cause of sudden-onset diarrhea in patients with cancer and immunosuppression. Infective agents include overgrowth of *Candida,* as well as bacteria, viruses, or fungi. Antibiotic therapy may also cause diarrhea. GI infections in AIDS are commonly caused by bacteria (*Salmonella, Shigella, Mycobacterium avium-intracellulare, Campylobacter*), fungi (*Candida*), protozoa (*Cryptosporidium, Isopora belli, Microsporidium, Entamoeba histolytica, Giardia*), and viruses (HIV enteropathy, cytomegalovirus, herpes simplex, adenovirus, astrovirus, picornavirus).

● Overuse of or too strong laxative therapy is a common cause of diarrhea in advanced cancer. Other medications that cause or contribute to diarrhea include antacids, diuretics, theophylline, and antibiotics.

● Cancer treatment, especially chemotherapy but also radiation, may result in increased peristalsis, inflammation, and overproduction of mucus with resulting diarrhea. Chronic treatment-related entercolitis may develop as long as 6 to 12 months after radiation therapy. Surgery (gastrectomy, ileal resection, colectomy) may sometimes result in diarrhea.

● Fecal impaction may cause small amounts of watery stool to be expelled around the impaction. See previous discussion of constipation.

● Diarrhea may be a sign of partial intestinal obstruction. Please see the section on obstruction at the end of this chapter.

● Nasogastric feeding—especially continuous—or enteric supplements of high osmolarity may cause diarrhea.

● Short bowel syndrome secondary to intestinal resection, other GI surgery, or other pathologic GI processes, including various malabsorption processes, may result in diarrhea.

● Cachexia may result in malabsorption and diarrhea.

● Pancreatic insufficiency is characterized by steatorrhea (ie, pale, bulky, greasy stools and gas).

● Some tumors tend to cause diarrhea, including neuroendocrine, small cell lung carcinoma, carcinoid tumors, ganglioneuroma, pheochromocytoma, pancreatic islet cell, and medullary thyroid carcinoma. In AIDS, Kaposi's sarcoma in the GI tract can cause diarrhea.

● Chronic diarrhea may also be due to diverticulitis, ulcerative colitis, colon tumor, hyperthyroidism, or diabetes.

● Stress can be a precipitating or contributing factor.

Independent Interventions

Independent interventions for treating diarrhea include the following (Bisanz, 1997; Mercadante, 1995; Ungvarski & Schmidt, 1995):

● Increase fluids, especially with commercial mixtures, such as Pedialyte. Homemade oral rehydration therapy mixture is 2 g salt, 50 g sugar, 1 L clean water, and small amount lemon or lime juice to flavor. Tap water may not be clean enough for patients with immunosuppression. Clients should take a minimum of 2 qt of noncarbonated fluids per day.

● The bowel should be rested with clear liquids and a light carbohydrate diet (eg, toast, rice, crackers).

● Diet can be modified, for example, by increasing low-residue foods high in protein and calories; small and frequent meals; eliminating high-lactose foods; avoiding spicy, greasy, or (GI) irritating foods, such as caffeine; and avoiding extremely cold or hot foods.

● Comfort measures include protective ointments or anesthetics applied to perirectal area (eg, A&D Ointment, hydrocortisone, or Tucks). Because skin problems almost invariably accompany chronic diarrhea, these comfort measures should begin before skin problems develop. After several days of diarrhea, even the softest toilet paper is painful. Squeeze bottles, one with warm soapy water to cleanse and the other with clear water to rinse are far superior to toilet paper. Commercial spray cleansers are also superior to toilet paper. After cleansing, a petroleum-based protective ointment should be applied to intact skin and a protective powder (eg, Stomahesive) applied to denuded areas followed by petroleum-based ointment. When the diarrhea pattern is one of small amounts of stool, adult diapers can be worn.

● Water supply, food storage, caregiver or patient hygiene, or other habits related to infection may need to be modified.

Interdependent Interventions

Interdependent interventions for treating diarrhea include the following (Mercadante, 1995; Sykes, 1998; Waller & Caroline, 1996):

● Laxatives should be discontinued.

● The primary antidiarrheal medications in terminal illness are (1) opioids, if the patient is not already taking them (eg, codeine, tincture of opium), or (2) loperamide 4 mg initially, then 2 mg after each loose stool (maximum 16 mg/24 h). Absorbent or bulk-forming agents (methyl cellulose) and adsorbents (kaolin) are slow to act and produce modest results, so they have little application in patients with advanced disease (Wilcox, 1997).

● If diarrhea is due to pancreatic insufficiency, pancreatic replacements are given, along with antidiarrheal medications (loperamide as above plus famotidine 20 mg PO bid to increase fat absorption). Diet modification includes high protein, high carbohydrates, and vitamin replacement.

● Radiation or chemotherapy enteritis, postgastrectomy dumping syndrome, and carcinoid syndrome can be treated with octreotide 100 to 300 µg SQ bid or over 24 hours in a continuous SQ infusion.

● Gastrointestinal infections are diagnosed and treated medically. The opportunistic infections of AIDS are extremely difficult to manage. Octreotide has been used (as above) with some success for the secretory diarrhea common in patients with AIDS.

● Fecal impactions are removed and preventive measures instituted. Digital removal of an impaction is contraindicated in neutropenia or thrombocytopenia (Donoghue, 1988).

● Interventions for obstructions are addressed below.

● Diverticulitis, colitis, hyperthyroidism, and tumors are treated medically and supportively. Not all treatment options may be open (eg, withholding fluids).

● Drug toxicity (especially laxatives, antacids, or antibiotics) is treated by changing the medication, if possible.

● The temporary use of antianxiety medications for patients with diarrhea may also be indicated.

Fecal Incontinence

Etiologies and Assessment

Fecal incontinence is most often due to diarrhea, whether from impaction, infection, or other causes. Temporary fecal incontinence is common. Combined incontinence of urine and feces is more resistant to treatment, especially when it occurs with slow onset (Hamdy, 1989).

For etiologies and assessment, see also preceding section on diarrhea. Note also the following points:

● Anxiety may play a role in some cases.

● Fecal incontinence is commonly associated with dementia, especially when incontinence is manifested with formed stools (Hamdy, 1989).

● Incontinence is occasionally related to the nature of the toilet the patient is using (for example, is the patient able to get to a sitting position?), its location, or the patient's inability to remove clothing.

Interventions

● Diarrhea and anxiety are treated according to the methods described previously. Other interventions are described on the next page.

● Dementia presents a major management problem. When death is not imminent, developing a bowel routine should be considered. If possible, placing the patient on the toilet shortly after breakfast and coffee is probably the easiest routine. Glycerine suppositories after breakfast also help but may not always work for patients with dementia. Constipation can be induced with (for example, codeine given every 4 hours with laxative suppositories or Fleets enemas every 2 or 3 days to force evacuation) (Hamdy, 1989). Codeine or other opioids may also help with agitation.

● Rearranging furniture and modifying clothing may also help.

Bowel Obstruction

Bowel obstruction is common in patients with abdominal tumors, especially ovarian (15%–42%) and colorectal (10%–28%), but also gastric, uterine, and to a lesser extent, other cancers (Mercadante, 1997; Ripamonti, 1995). Bowel obstruction presents difficult decisions. Practitioners skilled in palliative care may be comfortable with treating the problem palliatively, while those used to acute care tend to treat obstruction aggressively.

Etiologies and Assessment
Bowel obstruction results from tumor mass occluding the bowel lumen; tumor mass or organomegaly compressing the bowel; dysfunction of the neural plexus of the intestine, resulting in adynamic ileus or "narcotic bowel" and pseudo-obstruction; intussuception; treatment injury, such as adhesions, radiation injury, or neurotoxicity; and nonmalignant lesions, such as those in diverticulitis (Waller & Caroline, 1996). Some patients, especially those with ovarian cancer, may have more than one etiology. In the early stages of obstruction, there is usually intermittent colicky abdominal pain, increased bowel sounds, abdominal distension, and diarrhea. If the obstruction is

high, there may be little distension but profuse vomiting with vomitus containing bile and mucus. If the obstruction is due to adynamic ileus, there may not be colic. Few patients complain of constipation early in the process. In later stages, the pain becomes continuous with colicky components, abdominal distension increases, and the patient experiences N&V and constipation. Visible peristalsis, intermittent borborygmi, and anorexia are common. The most prevalent symptoms are N&V, intestinal colic, and other abdominal pain (Baines, 1998; Ripamonti, 1994).

Interventions
In the early or partial stages, patients with mechanical bowel obstruction can be treated with liquid or soft diet, stool softeners, analgesics, and antiemetics as follows (Baines, 1998; Mercadante, 1997; Waller & Caroline, 1996):

● Nausea and vomiting from a high obstruction are treated with haloperidol 1.5 mg qd, ± hydroxyzine 25 mg, ± octreotide 0.3 to 0.6 mg by continuous SQ infusion over 24 hours. N&V from a low obstruction may be treated with haloperidol 1.5 mg qd *or* metoclopramide 60 mg *if* the obstruction is incomplete, ± hydroxyzine 25 mg, or ± octreotide 0.3 mg by continuous SQ infusion over 24 hours. Dexamethasone 4 to 100 mg qd has also been effective in treating N&V and has sometimes restored bowel function. In bowel obstruction, some N&V is likely to occur no matter what interventions are used. Waller and Caroline state a goal of vomiting no more than once or twice daily. There is some indication that metoclopramide may help prevent complete obstruction.

● Colicky pain is treated by discontinuing stimulant laxatives (senna, biscodyl) and gastrokinetic agents (metoclopramide, cisapride) and using antispasmodic agents, such as loperamide 2 mg PO qid, or if the patient is unable to tolerate oral medications, transdermal scopolamine or hyoscine. Hyoscine also reduces the frequency and volume of vomiting and hence is a first-line treatment, which in some cases results in no further need for a nasogastric tube.

● Continuous abdominal pain is treated with morphine PO or continuous SQ infusion.

● Constipation and diarrhea are treated as discussed previously.

● Gastrointestinal intubation is used to remove gases and secretions as a means of resolving obstruction (25% success rate), palliate symptoms, instill medications, or prepare for surgery. Nasogastric suction is not usually considered a viable option in the ongoing management of obstruction in terminal illness.

● Surgery (resection, colostomy or ileostomy, or bypass) to resolve bowel obstruction in terminal illness is not automatically undertaken. Candidates for surgery should have a life expectancy of more than 2 months, good general performance status (ECOG = 2 or better; or Karnofsky Performance Status of D 50), no previous obstruction or abdominal surgery in the past year, no malignant ascites or liver failure, no lung metastases or pleural effusion, and no carcinomatosis or palpable abdominal mass. Even with careful patient selection, morbidity and mortality from the surgery are high, with mortality ranging from 18% to 35%.

● An alternative to the surgeries is the simpler percutaneous gastrostomy, which allows venting as needed.

Patients with "narcotic bowel syndrome" or adynamic ileus and advanced terminal illness can be treated by adding metoclopramide 60 mg/24 hours through continuous SQ infusion.

REFERENCES

Agra, Y., Sacristán, A., González, M., Ferrari, M., Portugués, A. & Calvo, M. J. (1998). Efficacy of senna versus lactulose in terminal cancer patients treated with opioids. *Journal of Pain and Symptom Management* 15(1), 1–7.

Baines, M. J. (1998). The pathophysiology and management of malignant intestinal obstruction. In D. Doyle, G. W. C. Hanks, & N. MacDonald (Eds.), *Oxford textbook of palliative medicine* (2nd ed.) (pp. 526–534). New York: Oxford University Press.

Bisanz, A. (1997). Managing bowel elimination problems in patients with cancer. *Oncology Nursing Forum*, 24(4), 679–686.

Bruera, E., & Fainsinger, R. L. (1998). Clinical management of cachexia and anorexia. In D. Doyle, G. W. C. Hanks, & N. MacDonald (Eds.), *Oxford textbook of palliative medicine* (2nd ed.) (pp. 548–557). New York: Oxford University Press.

Bruera, E., Miller, M. J., Kuehn, N., MacEachern, T., & Hanson, J. (1992). Estimate of survival of patients admitted to a palliative care unit: A prospective study. *Journal of Pain and Symptom Management*, 7(2), 82–86.

Bruera, E., Seifert, L., Watanabe, S., Babul, N., Darke, A., Harsanyi, Z., & Suarez-Almazor, M. (1996). Chronic nausea in advanced cancer patients: A retrospective assessment of a metoclopramide-based antiemetic regimen. *Journal of Pain and Symptom Management*, 11(3), 147–153.

Casciato, D. A. (1995). Symptom care. In D. A. Casciato & B. B. Lowitz (Eds.), *Manual of clinical oncology* (3rd ed.) (pp. 76–97). Boston: Little, Brown and Company.

Casey, K. M. (1997a). Malnutrition associated with HIV/AIDS: Definition and scope, epidemiology, and pathophysiology. *Journal of the Association of Nurses in AIDS Care*, 8(3), 24–32.

Casey, K. M. (1997b). Malnutrition associated with HIV/AIDS: Assessment and interventions. *Journal of the Association of Nurses in AIDS Care*, 8(3), 39–48.

Coleman, J. (1997). Esophageal, stomach, liver, gallbladder, and pancreatic cancers. In S. I. Groenwald, M. H. Frogge, M. Goodman, & C. H. Yarbro (Eds.), *Cancer nursing: Principles and practice* (4th ed.) (pp. 1082–1144). Boston: Jones and Bartlett.

Fainsinger, R. (1997). The modern management of cancer related cachexia in palliative care. *Progress in Palliative Care*, 5(5), 191–195.

Fessele, K. S. (1996). Managing the multiple causes of nausea and vomiting in the patient with cancer. *Oncology Nursing Forum*, 23(9), 1409–1415.

Glare, P., & Lickiss, J. N. (1992). Unrecognized constipation in patients with advanced cancer: A recipe for disaster. *Journal of Pain and Symptom Management*, 7(6), 369–371.

Grant, M. M., & Rivera, L. M. (1995). Anorexia, cachexia, and dysphagia: The symptom experience. *Seminars in Oncology Nursing*, *11*(4), 266–271.

Haapoja, I. S. (1997). Paraneoplastic syndromes. In S. I. Groenwald, M. H. Frogge, M. Goodman, & C. H. Yarbro (Eds.), *Cancer nursing: Principles and practice* (4th ed.) (pp. 702–720). Boston: Jones and Bartlett.

Hamdy, R. (1989). Fecal incontinence. In T. D. Walsh (Ed.), *Symptom control* (pp. 259–263). Oxford: Blackwell Scientific Publications.

Levy, M. H. (1985). Pain management in advanced cancer. *Seminars in Oncology*, *12*(4), 394–410.

Mannix, K. A. (1998). Palliation of nausea and vomiting. In D. Doyle, G. W. C. Hanks, & N. MacDonald (Eds.), *Oxford textbook of palliative medicine* (2nd ed.) (pp. 489–499). New York: Oxford University Press.

Martins, R. G., & Lynch, T. J. (1997). Esophageal cancer: Are you up to date? *Internal Medicine*, *18*(8), 18–36.

Mercadante, S. (1997). Assessment and management of mechanical bowel obstruction. In R. K. Portenoy & E. Bruera (Eds.), *Topics in palliative care* (Vol. 1) (pp. 113–130). New York: Oxford University Press.

Mercadante, S. (1995). Diarrhea in terminally ill patients: Pathophysiology and treatment, *Journal of Pain and Symptom Management*, *10*(4), 298–309.

Miller, R. J., & Albright, P. G. (1989). What is the role of nutritional support and hydration in terminal cancer patients. *American Journal of Hospice Care*, *6*(6), 33–38.

Mystakidou, K, Befon, S., Liossi, C., & Vlachos, L. (1998). Comparison of troisetron and chlorpromazine combinations in the control of nausea and vomiting in patients with advanced cancer. *Journal of Pain and Symptom Management*, *15*(3), 176–184.

Rhodes, V. A., Johnson, M. H., & McDaniel, R. W. (1995). Nausea, vomiting, and retching: The management of the symptom experience. *Seminars in Oncology Nursing*, *11*(4), 256–265.

Ripamonti, C. (1994). Management of bowel obstruction in advanced cancer patients. *Journal of Pain and Symptom Management*, *9*(3), 193–200.

Rivadeneira, D. E., Evoy, D., Fahey, T. J., Lieberman, M. D., & Daly, J. M. (1998). Nutritional support of the cancer patient. *CA—A Cancer Journal for Clinicians*, *48*(2), 69–80.

Rousseau, P. (1995). Antiemetic therapy in adults with terminal disease: A brief review. *American Journal of Hospice & Palliative Care*, *12*(1), 13–18.

Seligman, P. A., Fink, R., & Massey-Seligman, E. J. (1998). Approach to the seriously ill or terminal cancer patient who has a poor appetite. *Seminars in Oncology*, *25*(2) (Suppl. 6), 33–34.

Sykes, N. P. (1996). A volunteer model for the comparison of laxatives in opioid-related constipation. *Journal of Pain and Symptom Management*, *11*(6), 363–369.

Twycross, R. & Regnard, C. (1998). Dysphagia, dyspepsia, and hiccup. In D. Doyle, G. W. C. Hanks, & N. MacDonald (Eds.), *Oxford textbook of palliative medicine* (2nd ed.) (pp. 499–512). New York: Oxford University Press.

Ungvarski, P. J., & Schmidt, J. (1995). Nursing management of the adult client. In J. H. Flaskerud & P. J. Ungvarski (Eds.), *HIV/AIDS: A guide to nursing care* (3rd ed.) (pp. 134–184). Philadelphia: W.B. Saunders.

Wachtel, T., Allen-Masterson, S., Reuben, D., Goldberg, R., & Mor, V. (1988). The end stage cancer patient: Terminal common pathway. *The Hospice Journal*, *4*(4), 43–80.

Waller, A., & Caroline, N. L. (1996). *Handbook of palliative care in cancer*. Boston: Butterworth-Heinemann.

Walsh, T. D. (1990). Symptom control in patients with advanced cancer. *American Journal of Hospice and Palliative Care*, *7*(60), 20–29.

Wilcox, C. M. (1997). Chronic unexplained diarrhea in AIDS: Approach to diagnosis and management. *AIDS Patient Care and STDs*, *11*(1), 13–17.

Woodruff, R. (1997). *Symptom control in advanced cancer*. Melbourne: Asperula.

Wright, P. S., & Thomas, S. L. (1995). Constipation and diarrhea: The neglected symptoms. *Seminars in Oncology Nursing*, *11*(4), 289–297.

Genitourinary Problems

- Genitourinary problems of cancer are often associated with regional tumors or metastases.

- The most common genitourinary problems of advanced illness are urinary tract infection and incontinence.

- Early signs of obstructive uropathy, an oncologic emergency except in people who are imminently terminal, are sometimes attributed to expected deterioration from disease.

- Sexual problems among people who are terminally ill (and their partners) are seldom assessed by health professionals. Sex is not a major issue for most patients with far-advanced disease but is an issue for some in earlier stages of terminal illness.

The primary genitourinary (GU) problems are urinary frequency and urgency, incontinence, obstruction, and sexual dysfunction. GU dysfunction also occurs as a sign of spinal cord compression (see Chapter 13). Problems often affecting the GU system, such as candidiasis, fistulas, malignant ulcers, and pruritus, are discussed in Chapter 15.

Urinary Frequency and Urgency

Etiologies and Assessment
Urinary frequency and urgency are most commonly due to cystitis or inflammation of the urinary bladder resulting from a urinary tract infection (UTI) or prostatitis. UTI symptoms include dysuria (pain and burning on urination), frequency, and suprapubic pain. A history of UTIs, lower back pain, pyuria, hematuria, and bacturia is common in UTIs. See notes on catheter care later in this chapter. Other causes of frequency and urgency are increased volume from diabetes, hypercalcemia, diuretic treatment, or increased fluid intake; decreased bladder capacity from treatment or fecal impaction; or other causes, most of which are discussed under incontinence (Woodruff, 1997).

Interventions
When possible, the etiology is treated. A probable UTI is cultured, and while results are pending, treatment is started with trimethoprim-sulfamethoxazole 160 to 800 mg PO bid

to qid. Phenazopyridine 100 to 200 mg PO qid is given to decrease discomfort (Waller & Caroline, 1996).

Urinary Incontinence

Urinary incontinence is a troublesome problem for patients and caregivers. It is embarrassing and shameful to many people and is often taken fearfully as a sign of deterioration. For significant numbers of patients, incontinence is the deciding factor in submitting to extended care placement.

Etiologies and Assessment

The symptoms of urinary incontinence vary according to etiology. Specific etiologies and related symptoms include the following situations (Norman, 1998; Woodruff, 1997):

● Incontinence only at night may be the result of oversedation or related to polyuria from heart failure or diabetes. Incontinence primarily in the morning may be associated with diuretics given in the morning.
● Incontinence characterized by urge to void and polyuria but inability to control urine long enough to reach the toilet is termed *urge incontinence* and is commonly due to irritation, for example, from infection (see symptoms in previous discussion of urgency); tumor infiltration of bladder; or effects of cancer treatment. Spinal cord or central nervous system (CNS) lesions or anxiety may also cause urge incontinence.
● Incontinence characterized by suprapubic discomfort from distended bladder, inability to void completely, and small volume of urine is *overflow incontinence* and may be due to bladder outlet obstruction or dysfunction from tumor, calculi, or other internal or external mass or to malfunction of the detrusor muscle (eg, from anticholinergic medications, CNS lesions, or debility and confusion). The outcome is urine retention with some overflow and the likelihood of UTI.

● Incontinence that results from movement, lifting, coughing, laughing, etc. is considered *stress incontinence*. The etiology may be benign and related to postmenopausal changes or may be due to tumor infiltration of GU system or CNS or cord lesions.
● *Functional incontinence* is characterized by a lack of awareness that voiding has occurred coupled with cognitive impairment. Functional incontinence may occur in the final stages of illness.
● Incontinence in which there is no awareness of full bladder or urgency may result from retention or *atonic (neurogenic) bladder*. Causes include diabetic neuropathy, spinal cord injury, and other neurologic dysfunction. This form of incontinence is common with pelvic lesions.
● Incontinence as the result of urgency coupled with inability to reach the toilet in time is the most common form and may be due to problems of access, complicated by a variety of physical limitations. This form of incontinence may be benign with respect to mortality, or it may be due to primary brain tumors or metastasis. Some patients are simply unable to manage zippers, buttons, reaching a sitting position, or other mechanical impediments.
● The possibility of polyuria from hypercalcemia should be considered.
● Continuous incontinence may result from mechanical problems, such as vesicorectal, vesicocutaneous, or vesicovaginal fistula.
● The effects of pelvic radiation or surgery may include incontinence.

Independent Interventions

Caregiver and patient attitudes are of primary importance when incontinence exists. Some people are able to operate with the attitude that incontinence is just another problem to manage; more often, incontinence is viewed as a major problem and may become a major problem. The practitioner who approaches the problem with a positive, matter-of-fact attitude can help promote more functional attitudes in caregivers and patients. However, behavioral programs, such as those used for bladder training, are seldom appropriate for patients who are terminally ill. Independent interventions for treatment by caregivers include the following:

● Any specific etiologies noted previously should be identified and acted on if possible.
● Some aspect of the situation should be modified:
  1. Rearranging the environment, including (perhaps) obtaining portable commode
  2. Modifying the patient's clothing
  3. Establishing a voiding schedule (eg, q2h)
  4. Teaching patient to void as soon as the urge is felt
  5. Limiting fluids in the evening and decreasing sedatives to limit night incontinence
● The effects of incontinence can be minimized with the following measures:
  1. Urinals and towels should be used to catch and soak up the urine. Although such measures are thought by some to be unsuitable for long-term use, some caregivers use these measures for years with a family member who is chronically ill. Frequent changes are necessary, but in some cases, this situation is not as difficult to manage as is an indwelling catheter, and it does not have as many inherent liabilities as a catheter.
  2. Frequent skin care is also necessary. Vaseline or other barrier ointments or creams are helpful in protecting the skin.
  3. Attends or other products can be used to allow patients to go out for limited periods of time.

Interdependent Interventions

Independent interventions, especially skin care and teaching, remain vitally important. Interdependent interventions for treatment by caregivers include the following (Norman, 1998; Sahai, 1995; Woodruff, 1997).

● Incontinence due to drugs or disease is managed (if possible) by managing the etiology.
● Urge incontinence (bladder irritation) is commonly due to UTI, and if infection is present or likely (symptoms of frequency and dysuria are present but Gram's stain is negative), it is treated with an antibiotic (see discussion of UTI in the section on frequency and urgency). Phenazopyridine 100 to 200 mg PO tid is given for pain relief. An anticholinergic and antispasmodic medication, such as oxybutynin 2.5 to 5 mg PO bid to tid (depending on age, debility) reduces bladder or outlet spasms.
● Overflow incontinence due to anticholinergic medications may be relieved by discontinuing one or more of the medications with anticholinergic properties. If there is an obstruction from tumor or calculi, a urologist may be required. Obstruction from fecal impaction is managed as discussed in Chapter 17 on gastrointestinal symptoms. An indwelling catheter may be necessary if there is continued retention or continued obstruction. See notes on catheters below.
● Stress incontinence is traditionally treated with a bladder training program of pelvic exercises, scheduled voiding, and sometimes pessary or clamp. Usually, only an attempt at a voiding schedule is appropriate in terminal illness. Imipramine 25 to 50 mg PO at bedtime provides some anticholinergic effect and decreases incontinence.
● Functional incontinence often requires catheterization. However, if retention or discomfort is not present in a patient who is imminently terminal, catheterization should be avoided if possible, especially if urine volume is low.
● Incontinence due to atonic or neurogenic bladder can be treated with an anticholinergic drug, such as propantheline bromide 15 to 30 mg PO tid. Other anticholinergic drugs may also be helpful. Catheterization may be necessary.
● Hypercalcemia is prevented or treated as noted in Chapter 20 on paraneoplastic syndromes and oncologic emergencies.

● The problem of incontinence due to a fistula is sometimes partly relieved (depending on the site of the bladder end of the fistula) by regular and frequent voiding to keep the urine volume in the bladder relatively low. Catheterization may be necessary to reduce the flow from the fistula. Skin care at the fistula outlet or stoma is important. Urinary diversion is used when a patient has a long life expectancy.

● Incontinence due to pelvic radiation or surgery is treated according to the effects of treatment on the urinary tract (eg, fibrosis, scarring).

Notes on Catheter Use

The primary complication of urinary catheters is (sometimes asymptomatic) bacteriuria, which markedly increases in prevalence over time, until almost all patients catheterized for a month or more have bacteria in their urine. Encrustation and bladder spasms may also occur (Fainsinger et al., 1992). Gram-negative bacteria are the most common pathogens in UTIs, and patients receiving systemic antibiotics have an increased likelihood of infection from unusual urinary tract pathogens, such as *Pseudomonas* or *Candida*. Complications of UTI include ascending infection leading to pyelonephritis, prostatitis, abscesses, and sepsis (Russo, 1997). Measures to reduce complications (Berry, 1996; Fainsinger et al., 1992; Russo, 1997; Waller & Caroline, 1996) include the following:

● The patient and family must be taught to wash their hands before and after handling the catheter and related equipment. Thorough perineal care should occur twice daily, and the catheter should cleaned daily starting at the insertion point.

● Fluid intake should be increased to (preferably) 2 L/d.

● Because bladder capacity is often reduced, especially with pelvic disease, a 30-mL balloon should not be filled to capacity; 5 to 10 mL is adequate. The smaller balloon size causes less discomfort. A small diameter silicone catheter (12–16 French) with a 5-mL balloon is preferred over larger sizes.

● Leakage of urine around the catheter may be due to stimulation of the detrusor muscle, so relief may result from an antispasmodic medication, such as oxybutynin 2.5 to 5 mg PO bid to tid (depending on age, debility).

● Systemic antibiotics should be avoided if possible (unless the patient is septic). If antibiotic therapy is necessary, the patient should be monitored for secondary infection from *Pseudomonas*, *Candida*, or other resistant pathogen.

● The catheter should be irrigated with normal saline only when blocked or blockage is developing.

● The catheter should be removed as soon as possible (often not possible in terminal illness), and after removal, the patient should be started on a short course of antibiotic therapy.

Obstructive Uropathy

Obstructive uropathy is considered an oncologic emergency and leads ultimately to renal failure and death.

Etiologies and Assessment

The possibility of gradual—usually bladder neck—obstruction is indicated by changes in urinary habits, especially retention (manifested by hesitancy, urgency, nocturia, frequency, and decreased force of stream), flank pain, hematuria, intractable UTIs, and fatigue. Rapid obstruction of the ureter often results in severe pain. Alternating polyuria and oliguria suggest the possibility of partial kidney obstruction. Infection, calculi, and decreased renal function may occur. Regional mass (or masses) will sometimes be found on examination.

Obstructive uropathy is usually due to intra-abdominal, retroperitoneal, and pelvic cancers. Bladder outlet obstruction is most frequently associated with prostate, cervical, or bladder cancer (or benign prostatic hypertrophy), and ureteral obstruction is most frequently associated with para-aortic malignancies, such as lymphoma or sarcoma, and with regional nodal metastases. Other causes include renal calculi from chronic hypercalcemia, hyperuricemia, and UTI; cystitis; urethral strictures; and neurologic involvement (Glick & Glover, 1995; Norman, 1998).

Interventions

While a lower urinary tract obstruction can sometimes be relieved with an indwelling catheter, surgery is often necessary (Glick & Glover, 1995). The presence of tumor or other obstructive processes in or at the urethra or bladder results in difficulties and complications in catheter insertion; therefore, catheterization should be undertaken with care, and involvement of a urologist is advisable. Ureteral obstruction in nonmoribund patients usually requires surgery. Obstruction from a pelvic mass pressing on ureters can sometimes be relieved medically (eg, with dexamethasone).

Sexual Dysfunction

This section is concerned only with physical etiologies of sexual dysfunction. A more complete discussion of the subject can be found in Chapter 2.

Etiologies and Assessment

Sexual dysfunction in patients with advanced cancer often encompasses all phases of the sexual response cycle—desire, excitement, orgasm, and resolution (Anderson & Schmuch, 1991).

Pain (general or related to sexual functioning), stress, depression, and fatigue play significant roles in decreasing sexual activity, even when desire might otherwise exist. In general, tumors and treatments most associated with sexual functioning, especially physically but also psychologically, are also most associated with sexual dysfunction. Thus, primary and metastatic GU and regional (colon, rectum, lumbosacral) tumors and breast tumors produce significant dysfunction. CNS tumors,

especially those resulting in spinal cord compression, can cause sexual dysfunction. Many cancer treatments, including chemotherapy, hormone therapy, regional radiation, or surgery, can affect one or more sexual response(s). Other common factors influencing sexual response(s) in patients with advanced disease include opioids, alcohol, and a variety of other medications and substances and preexisting conditions, such as diabetes, hypertension, and arthritis (Mott-Smith & Stolberg, 1995).

Interventions

By the time the disease has progressed to terminal, little can be done to improve physiologic sexual functioning. However, with a life expectancy of months, effort to address problems may be rewarded with the patient and partner experiencing some degree of sexual intimacy. Pain, stress, depression, and other extrinsic factors may be relieved to some extent, but their "cure" (eg, opioids, tranquilizers, antidepressants) may also diminish sexual function. The reader is referred to Chapter 2 for a discussion of loss of sexual intimacy.

The presence of a colostomy or catheter inhibits many people. Counseling on positions or practices (see illustrations in Bruner & Iwamoto, 1996) may help couples understand alternatives to familiar positions. Specific physical problems and interventions in sexual dysfunction in women (Farias-Eisner, Walker, & Berek, 1995; Mott-Smith & Stolberg, 1995) include the following:

● Dyspareunia (difficult or painful intercourse) due to vaginal atrophy, shortened vaginal cuff, or loss of lubrication can be addressed with estrogen replacement therapy or creams, water-based vaginal lubricants, and counseling (eg, slow, shallow insertion and gentle thrusting; changing the angle of penetration; one of the partners using her or his lubricated hand at the base of the penis to give the sensation of deeper penetration).
● Vaginal stenosis may preclude sexual intercourse. People who are intent on intercourse may

achieve some satisfaction from tightly closed and lubricated thighs. Oral and anal sex may be satisfying to some. Vaginal dilation is seldom an appropriate intervention in terminal illness.

● Loss of libido due to hormonal changes may be treated with hormone replacement therapy. However, decreased libido may be a multifactorial problem not responsive to any one intervention.

Sexual problems (and interventions) specific to men include:

● Erectile impotence may be due to cancer, cancer treatment, diabetes, cardiovascular disease, and other processes. Oral sildenafil is a generally safe means of restoring erectile function (Morales, Gingell, Collins, Wicker, & Osterloh, 1998), though it may not be safe for debilitated terminally ill patients. A suction erection device or penile prosthesis may also be used.

● Retrograde ejaculation as a result of testicular cancer may be reversed with imipramine 25 to 50 mg PO qd.

● Dry orgasm resulting from chemotherapy or radiation may still be pleasurable. There is no treatment for dry orgasm, though the problem may resolve with time.

In all cases of sexual dysfunction, counseling and exploration of intimacy and sexual needs of both partners are essential.

REFERENCES

Anderson, B. L., & Schmuch, G. (1991). Sexuality and cancer. In A. I. Holleb, D. J. Fink, & G. P. Murphy (Eds.), *Clinical oncology* (pp. 606–616). Atlanta: American Cancer Society.

Berry, D. L. (1996). Bladder disturbances. In S. L. Groenwald, M. H. Frogge, M. Goodman, & C. H. Yarbro (Eds.). *Cancer symptom management* (pp. 467–483). Boston: Jones and Bartlett.

Bruner, D. W., & Iwamoto, R. R. (1996). Altered sexual health. In S. L. Groenwald, M. H. Frogge, M. Goodman, & C. H. Yarbro (Eds.), *Cancer symptom management* (pp. 523–551). Boston: Jones and Bartlett.

Fainsinger, R., MacEachern, T., Hanson, J., &

Bruera, E. (1992). The use of urinary catheters in terminally ill cancer patients. *Journal of Pain and Symptom Management, 7*(6), 333–338.

Farias-Eisner, R. P., Walker, D. L., & Berek, J. S. (1995). Gynecologic cancers. In D. A. Casciato & B. B. Lowitz (Eds.), *Manual of clinical oncology* (3rd ed.) (pp. 200–227). Boston: Little, Brown and Company.

Garnick, M. B. (1993). Urologic complications. In J. F. Holland, E. Frei, R. C. Bast, D. W. Kufe, D. L. Morton, & R.W. Weischselbaum (Eds.), *Cancer medicine* (3rd ed.) (pp. 2323–2331). Philadelphia: Lea & Febiger.

Glick, J. H., & Glover, D. (1995). Oncologic emergencies. In A. I. Holleb, D. J. Fink, & G. P. Murphy (Eds.), *Clinical oncology* (2nd ed.) (pp. 597–618). Atlanta: American Cancer Society.

Morales, A., Gingell, C., Collins, M., Wicker, P. A., & Osterloh, I. H. (1998). Clinical safety of oral sildenafil citrate (VIAGRA™) in the treatment of erectile dysfunction. *International Journal of Impotence Research, 10*(2), 69–74.

Mott-Smith, M., & Stolberg, L. (1995). Sexual function and pregnancy. In D. A. Casciato & B. B. Lowitz (Eds.), *Manual of clinical oncology* (3rd ed.) (pp. 200–227). Boston: Little, Brown and Company.

Norman, R. W. (1998). Genitourinary disorders. In D. Doyle, G. W. C. Hanks, & N. MacDonald (Eds.), *Oxford textbook of palliative medicine* (2nd ed.) (pp. 489, 667–676). New York: Oxford University Press.

Russo, P. (1997). Urologic emergecies. In V. T. DeVita, S. Hellman, & S. A. Rosenberg (Eds.), *Cancer: Principles and practice of oncology* (5th ed.) (pp. 2512–2522). Philadelphia: Lippincott-Raven.

Sahai, J. (1995). Urinary tract infections. In L. E. Young & M. A. Koda-Kimble (Eds.), *Applied therapeutics: The clinical use of drugs* (6th ed.) (pp. 63-1–63-17). Vancouver, WA: Applied Therapeutics.

Smith, P., & Bruera, E. (1995). Management of malignant ureteral obstruction in the palliative care setting. *Journal of Pain and Symptom Management, 10*(6), 481–486.

Waller, A., & Caroline, N. L. (1996). *Handbook of palliative care in cancer.* Boston: Butterworth-Heinemann.

Woodruff, R. (1997). *Symptom control.* Melbourne: Asperula.

Dehydration, Fatigue, and Sleep

Prior to the inception of hospice care and the development of expertise in palliative care for terminally ill patients, it was generally assumed that decreased fluid intake indicated a need for fluid replacement using intravenous infusion or nasogastric tube. With greater attention paid to the patient's quality of life, however, realization grew that in the latter stages of dying, changes in nutrition, fluid balance, and elimination are inevitable, and attempts to reverse or stabilize them (1) are often futile or even harmful and (2) do not have a significant effect on comfort levels (Burge, 1993; Twycross & Lichter, 1998; Vullo-Navich, Smith, Andrews, Tischler, & Veglia, 1998). However, there is some conflicting evidence that adequate hydration in patients with advanced terminal illness increases comfort and decreases confusion and metabolite accumulation (MacDonald, 1998). As in all other aspects of terminal care, the central issue of dehydration is the well-being of the patient: If death is imminent and there is not a specific attainable goal for rehydration, nothing is gained by attempting rehydration; if time or quality of life can be extended, rehydration is indicated.

Problems of Dehydration

The following are primary problems of dehydration in people who are terminally ill:

● Dehydration can result in renal failure with subsequent accumulation of opioid metabolites, leading to confusion, myoclonus, and seizures (Fainsinger, 1995).

● Electrolyte imbalances often occur in dehydrated patients (Fainsinger & deMoissac, 1998).

● Dehydration may be associated with increased incidence of confusion and restlessness in patients with advanced disease (MacDonald, 1998).

● Discomfort, especially problems from xerostomia and thirst, may result from dehydration (Twycross & Lichter, 1998).

Emotional issues are also often involved in the question of hydration. Although there may be no gain for the patient in taking in fluids, for the family and other caregivers, there may be a very strong desire to give fluids by mouth or even parenterally. Even though patients close to death often lose the desire for fluids, the issue for family and others sometimes remains a potent one.

Other Effects of Dehydration

Several authors (Twycross & Lichter, 1998; Waller & Caroline, 1996) note effects of dehydration that should be considered in decisions about means of hydration. Among these are the following:

● Decrease in urine output: Incontinence and its attendant psychological, cosmetic, care, and physical issues become less problematic. Decreased urine may obviate the need for catheterization or the effort associated with frequent cleaning and changing sheets and bedpans.

● Decrease in gastric secretions: A decrease in vomiting may be noted, especially when there is an intestinal obstruction.

● Decrease in pulmonary secretions and edema: In this respect, hydration may actually decrease quantity and quality of life. The futile trauma of suctioning pharyngeal secretions may also be avoided.

● Decrease in other fluid accumulations, such as ascites and peripheral edema: Decreased edema at any site, or in general, promotes comfort. Decreased edema at tumors may decrease pain from nerve compression.

● Hydration may result in increased awareness and thus increased pain perception.

Interventions in Dehydration

A definitive statement cannot yet be made that dehydration in patients who are in advanced stages of terminal disease should or should not be allowed to progress without treatment. If there are days or weeks of life left, rehydration by subcutaneous infusion of fluids (hypodermoclysis) or by rectal infusion (proctolysis) are better (simpler and less prone to complications) choices than intravenous fluids. Proctolysis, in particular, is essentially risk free and costs almost nothing (Bruera et al., 1998). If dehydration is significant (degree or time), it may be necessary to reduce medications, such as opioids, gradually to prevent metabolite accumulation and toxic effects (Fainsinger & deMoissac, 1998; MacDonald, 1998).

If neither quantity nor quality of life can be increased through rehydration, the issue in treatment is comfort related primarily to xerostomia and thirst. For patients with sufficient strength and who are able to swallow, oral fluids are helpful for both these problems and for the emotional well-being of caregivers. Giving and receiving drink is more than a physiologic issue. When a patient is unable to swallow, just a few drops of water or other fluid on the patient's lips lovingly and gently offered from a favorite cup or glass can be significant and even, in some respects, healing for all concerned. Intravenous or subcutaneous hydration do not necessarily relieve xerostomia or thirst.

Xerostomia and thirst are further treated by regular oral care (eg, every 2 hours) regardless of mental status. Depending on the patient's ability to swallow, oral care consists of the following:

● Small, frequent sips of fluids, including ice chips or chips of popsicle

● Gentle cleansing of the mouth with a soft, moist brush, and a trace of toothpaste

● Swabbing with glycerin, cologel, normal saline (1:1:8), methylcellulose, or lemon essence and water

● Very fine spray from an (eg, perfume) atomizer—available at minimal cost from drug or variety stores

Readers may also want to read the Chapters 16 and 21 on oral care and imminent death.

Fatigue (or Asthenia)

Fatigue (also known as asthenia) is a lack of vitality common in virtually all patients with advanced disease. Fatigue has physical and psychosocial components, often including weakness, tiredness, lethargy, dys-pnea on exertion, lack of motivation, difficulty concentrating, and anhedonia. In the chronic fatigue of advanced illness, rest and sleep do not appreciably restore vitality. Common etiologies of fatigue include the disease itself (including cytokine production), secondary infections, effects of treatment, insomnia, anemia, malnutrition, prolonged immobility, depression, paraneoplastic syndromes, and emotional exhaustion (Piper, 1998; Yellen, Cella, Webster, Blendowski, & Kaplan, 1997). Extreme fatigue often results in, or contributes to, sadness or depression; this, in turn, exacerbates the fatigue.

Fatigue is distinguished from weakness by the global nature of fatigue as opposed to the specific muscle weakness implied by complaints of weakness (Nail & Winningham, 1995). However, clarification of a patient's complaint of weakness (eg, "I feel weak all over") may result in a more accurate determination of fatigue.

Interventions in Fatigue

While fatigue may be a given in advanced disease, there are interventions to help patients live as fully as possible within the constraints of fatigue. The primary intervention is, if possible, to resolve the problem that causes the fatigue. Some of the etiologies discussed previously (eg, anemia, insomnia, depression, some drug side effects, and some cases of anorexia) are subject to resolution or modification. Supplemental steroid therapy may give transient relief but carries its own fatigue-related liability on withdrawal of treatment and returns diminish even during treatment (Cleary, 1998). Adequate fluids and nutrition help in some situations, as does exercise. In some other situations (eg, "multiple sclerosis fatigue" or far-advanced cancer or AIDS), fatigue is a given, and little, if anything, will change it. Change must then occur in the patient and environment.

Planned and paced activities help minimize the effects of fatigue (Ungvarski & Schmidt, 1995). There seems to be a universal tendency among patients of all sorts to overextend themselves when they are feeling better than usual. This is followed inevitably by hours, or even days, of recovery time. In helping plan activities, the nurse should assist the patient to identify activities that are essential *and* pleasant or uplifting. These are then prioritized, with the top priorities including some essentials and some pleasant or uplifting activities. This means that some activities that are important may have to be assigned to someone else. While giving up activities is difficult for many people, reassurances about who will accomplish the needed tasks and when they will be accomplished often ease the reluctance.

Many people find it difficult to reorder any aspect of their lives, especially in the context of illness. Nevertheless, reordering is necessary. In general, strength is usually greatest and fatigue least early in the day. For example, eating breakfast, resting, and then bathing—rather than the reverse order—may help some patients accomplish the top priority (nutritional intake) more often, despite their tendency to stick to old habits and bathe first.

Most people have difficulty resting when they feel well or at least well enough to continue an activity. Therefore, every planned activity should be either of short duration or divided into several stages, each one accompanied by *planned* rest. Finally, other modifications may be possible in the manner in which activities are conducted. For ambulatory patients, activities that can be accomplished while sitting rather than while standing might include showering, shaving, brushing teeth, putting on makeup, and preparing food. Furniture might need rearranging to increase sitting time. These measures may seem, on the face of it, simple and easy to accomplish. However, few people are able to initiate such changes themselves.

Modifying the environment helps in many cases. Ease of access with respect to placement of telephone, medications, drinking water, toilet chair, and other essentials decreases energy expenditure. Attention should be paid to the presence, for instance, of low-slung chairs, beds, and other furniture in which getting in and out require excessive effort. As a patient's energy decreases, the environment available to her or him should also decrease in size. Because the situation in terminal illness means that everyone is eventually limited to using only several rooms and finally to one room only, the room(s) chosen might as well be the best ones available. The quality of life for those who are dying seems to depend to a great extent on the ability to adapt well to the circumstances. A classic manifestation of adaptability in dying is having the patient's bed in the living room or den. Assistive devices can be installed to help the patient get in and out of the bath, go to the toilet, and so forth.

Fatigue and weakness or further disability can be mutually reinforcing: The greater the fatigue, the less exercise the patient can get, and the more weakness will result. Therefore, some kind of exercise is necessary for most patients, whether it be to accomplish a task or simply for its own sake (Piper, 1998). This may entail as little (or as much) as getting out of bed daily or passive range-of-motion exercises. Patients who do not require any exercise include those with end-stage heart disease and those who are moribund.

Heat plays a role in increasing fatigue. Baths or showers should be warm, not hot, and the patient's room temperature should be cool (Hubsky & Sears, 1992).

Finally, the patient's (and often also the family's) psychological or spiritual state may play a role in fatigue. Depression plays a role in many cases. Fatigue can even function as a sort of defense mechanism, which facilitates avoidance of unpleasant interactions. Addressing fatigue always includes a psychosocial component, especially dealing with ever-diminishing capabilities and resulting grief.

Sleep

Sleep disorders are common among the population in general and among people with terminal illness in particular. There are many kinds of sleep disorders, but this discussion is limited to insomnia. Insomnia is generally classified as difficulty falling asleep, frequent awakenings, early morning awakening, persistent sleepiness despite sleep of adequate duration, or any combination of these. Sleep disorders contribute to or result from physical or psychological symptoms of advanced illness.

Insomnia in terminal illness may have one or more of several etiologies (Czeisler & Richardson, 1998):

● Drug side effects (eg, theophylline, corticosteroids) or withdrawal from drugs or alcohol
● Effects of illness (eg, restless legs syndrome in anemia or renal failure, pruritus, pain, dyspnea, nausea)
● Symptom of illness (eg, delirium, depression)
● Psychophysiologic phenomenon (stress → insomnia → poor sleep habits → hyperarousal with efforts to fall asleep → cycle repeating)
● Fear and anxiety concerning dying, death, unfinished business, and related issues (related to the preceding)
● Poor sleep hygiene (eg, frequent or lengthy daytime napping)

Interventions for Insomnia

Managing sleep disorders begins with attempting to restore the normal sleep–wake cycle by (if possible) decreasing time spent in bed during the day. Intervention should be instituted for any apparent etiology (eg, pain, dyspnea). Addressing issues of anxiety, fear, and depression are part of restoring a normal cycle and may require medication as discussed in Chapter 2, counseling, and reassurance. Afternoon or evening coffee, other stimulants, evening diuretics, and other contributing factors should be eliminated or decreased.

Nonpharmacologic remedies for improving sleep include mild exercise, socializing during the day, decreasing environmental stimulants (eg, noise, light), using background noise (eg, a fan or soft music), warm bath before bedtime, light warm carbohydrate snack before bed, meditation at bedtime, prayer at bedtime, or reading from the Bible, Koran, or other holy book or devotional before bedtime.

Pharmacologic treatment of insomnia in terminal illness is usually with an intermediate-acting benzodiazepine (eg, temazepam 15 mg PO at bedtime, lorazepam 1 mg PO at bedtime, or oxazepam 10 mg PO at bedtime) (Sateia & Silberfarb, 1998). Short-term intermittent use of these or other medications should be attempted. Patients with advanced illness should be carefully monitored for oversedation or evidence of accumulation. Pharmacologic interventions should, in all cases, be accompanied by nonpharmacologic measures.

REFERENCES

Brescia, F. J. (1991). Killing the known dying: Notes for a death watcher. *Journal of Pain and Symptom Management, 6*(5), 337–339.

Bruera, E., Pruvost, M., Schoeller, T., Montejo, G., & Watanabe, S. (1998). Proctolysis for hydration of terminally ill cancer patients. *Journal of Pain and Symptom Management, 15*(4), 216–219.

Burge, F. I. (1993). Dehydration symptoms of palliative care cancer patients. *Journal of Pain and Symptom Management, 8*(7), 454–464.

Cleary, J. F. (1998). The reversible causes of asthenia. In E. Bruera & R. K. Portenoy (Eds.), *Topics in palliative care* (Vol. 2) (pp. 183–202). New York: Oxford University Press.

Collaud, T., & Rapin, C-R. (1991). Dehydration in dying patients: Study with physicians in French-speaking Switzerland. *Journal of Pain and Symptom Management, 6*(4), 230–240.

Czeisler, C. A., & Richardson, G. S. (1998). Disorders of sleep and circadian rhythms. In A. S. Fauci, E. Braunwald, K. J. Isselbacher, J. D. Wilson, J. B. Martin, D. L. Kasper, S. L. Hauser, & D. L. Longo (Eds.), *Harrison's principles of internal medicine* (14th ed.) (pp. 150–159). New York: McGraw-Hill.

De Conno, F., Ripamonti, C., Sbanotto, A., & Ventafridda, V. (1989). Oral complications in patients with advanced cancer. *Journal of Pain and Symptom Management, 4*(1), 20–29.

Fainsinger, R. (1995). Dehydration and palliative care. *Palliative Care Letter, 7*(1), insert 1.

Fainsinger, R., & deMoissac, D. (1998). Letter on hydration in terminal illness. *Journal of Intravenous Nursing, 21*(3), 138–139.

Hubsky, E. P., & Sears, J. H. (1992). Fatigue in multiple sclerosis: Guidelines for nursing care. *Rehabilitation Nursing, 17*(4), 176–180.

Irvine, D. M., Vincent, L., Bubela, N., Thompson, L., & Graydon, J., (1991). A critical appraisal of the research literature investigating fatigue in the individual with cancer. *Cancer Nursing, 14*(4), 188–199.

MacDonald, N. (1998). Ethical issues in hydration and nutrition. In E. Bruera & R. K. Portenoy (Eds.), *Topics in palliative care* (Vol. 2) (pp. 153–169). New York: Oxford University Press.

Musgrave, C. F. (1990). Terminal dehydration: To give or not to give intravenous fluids. *Cancer Nursing, 13*(1), 62–66.

Nail, L. M., & Winningham, M. L. (1995). Fatigue and weakness in cancer patients: The symptom experience. *Seminars in Oncology Nursing, 11*(4), 272–278.

Pickard-Holley, S. (1991). Fatigue in cancer patients. *Cancer Nursing, 14*(1), 13–19.

Piper, B. F. (1998). Fatigue. In M. E. Ropka & A. B. Williams (Eds.), *HIV nursing and symptom management* (pp. 449–470). Boston: Jones and Bartlett.

Sateia, M. J., & Silberfarb, P. M. (1998). Sleep. In D. Doyle, G. W. C. Hanks, & N. MacDonald (Eds.), *Oxford textbook of palliative medicine* (2nd ed.)

(pp. 751–767). New York: Oxford University Press.

Twycross, R., & Lichter, I. (1998).The terminal phase. In D. Doyle, G. W. C. Hanks, & N. MacDonald (Eds.), *Oxford textbook of palliative medicine* (2nd ed.) (pp. 977–992). New York: Oxford University Press.

Ungvarski, P. J., & Schmidt, J. A. (1995). Nursing management of the adult client. In J. H. Flaskerud & P. J. Ungvarski (Eds.), *HIV/AIDS: A guide to nursing care* (3rd ed.) (pp. 134–184). Philadelphia: W.B. Saunders.

Vullo-Navich, K., Smith, S., Andrews, M., Tischler, J. F., & Veglia, J. M. (1998). Comfort and incidence of abnormal serum sodium, BUN, creatinine and osmolality in dehydration of terminal illness. *American Journal of Hospice and Palliative Care, 15*(2), 77–84.

Yellen, S. B., Cella, D. F., Webster, K., Blendowski, C., & Kaplan, E. (1997). Measuring fatigue and other anemia-related symptoms with the Functional Assessment of Cancer Therapy (FACT) measurement system. *Journal of Pain and Symptom Management, 13*(2), 63–74.

Waller, A., & Caroline, N. L. (1996). *Handbook of palliative care in cancer.* Boston: Butterworth-Heinemann.

CHAPTER 20

Oncologic Emergencies and Paraneoplastic Syndromes

Most of the oncologic emergencies of terminal illness are covered in other chapters of this book as follows: increased intracranial pressure and spinal cord compression are discussed in Chapter 13; superior vena cava syndrome, airway obstruction, and cardiac tamponade are discussed in Chapter 14; and obstructive uropathy is discussed in Chapter 18.

Paraneoplastic syndromes (PNSs) are problems that occur at a distance from the primary or metastatic tumors. Mechanisms of action may occur as ectopic hormone production, autoimmune or immune responses, or other, unknown responses. Syndromes usually considered oncologic emergencies are discussed in the following section and include hypercalcemia and syndrome of inappropriate antidiuretic hormone (SIADH). Other PNSs are also discussed here and include endocrine,

neurologic, cutaneous, and those associated with lung, renal, and stomach cancers.

Any of these oncologic emergencies or PNSs may occur as part of the final stage of disease. In some cases, there is ultimately no reasonable treatment. In other cases, however, treatment may result in palliation or even reversal of symptoms.

Hypercalcemia

Hypercalcemia is the most common metabolic oncologic emergency of cancer. The tumors most commonly associated with hypercalcemia are multiple myeloma and breast (approximately 40%). Hypercalcemia is also relatively common in non-small cell lung cancer and renal cancers (Odell, 1997; Warrell, 1997).

Despite the association of hypercalcemia with bony metastases and hyperparathyroidism, two tumors that frequently involve bone—prostate cancer and small cell carcinoma of the lung (SCLC)—rarely result in hypercalcemia. It is now understood that hypercalcemia results from one of several processes that vary according to tumor, disease, and in breast cancer, hormonal therapy (Odell, 1997). Hypercalcemia is also associated with HIV infection and two related infections: coccidioidomycosis and tuberculosis (Warrell, 1997).

Two key factors that increase the risk of hypercalcemia are immobility and dehydration. Anorexia, nausea, vomiting, and pain contribute directly or indirectly to these. The use of thiazide diuretics, vitamin A and D, and some hormones also increases the risk of hypercalcemia (Waller & Caroline, 1996).

Clinical characteristics of hypercalcemia are similar in many respects to those of cancer and other advanced illnesses. The most common initial complaints are fatigue, lethargy, constipation, nausea, and polyuria (Warrell, 1997). Other clinical manifestations of hypercalcemia include the following:

● Neuromuscular: malaise, apathy, muscle weakness, fatigue, and hyporeflexia, possibly progressing to mental changes, seizures, and coma
● Gastrointestinal (GI): nausea, vomiting, anorexia, constipation, and abdominal pain
● Renal: polyuria and polydipsia and, ultimately, renal failure
● Cardiac: bradycardia and arrhythmias
● General: dehydration, weight loss, anorexia, and pruritus

A sudden increase in serum calcium levels (to 12–13 mg/mL) may result in cardiac arrhythmias and death, while a gradual increase, even though the level may be higher (14 mg/mL) may be better tolerated (Glick & Glover, 1995; Warren, 1997).

Clearly, prevention is important in the consideration of hypercalcemia. The patient whose physical, psychological, and spiritual pain are well managed is more likely to be mobile and take adequate fluids and is thus less likely to develop hypercalcemia (or other problems).

Treatment of moderate to severe or rapidly developing hypercalcemia begins with intravenous rehydration to promote urinary calcium excretion followed by intravenous pamidronate disodium 90 mg over 24 hours to decrease bone reabsorption. A lower dose of pamidronate (60 mg over 4 hours) provides 7 or more days of normal calcium levels (Odell, 1997; Waller & Caroline, 1996). Calcium supplements and vitamin A and D should be discontinued. Dietary calcium intake, except perhaps with lymphomas, can be continued.

Waller and Caroline (1996) suggest the following regimen for treating chronic hypercalcemia: (1) increasing fluids and activity; (2) giving etidronate (oral biphosphonate) 200 mg PO bid and prednisone 20 to 40 mg/d PO for lymphoma or multiple myeloma; and (3) avoiding thiazide diuretics, cimetidine, ranitidine, and calcium-containing preparations (though milk and related foods can be taken).

Syndrome of Inappropriate Antidiuretic Hormone

Syndrome of inappropriate antidiuretic hormone occurs most frequently in patients with SCLC and is common in patients with non-small cell carcinoma of the lung. SIADH is found less frequently in patients with head and neck cancer, and there are reports of SIADH in patients with lymphoma, leukemia, and cancers of the prostate, bladder, and GI system (John, Patchell, & Foon, 1997).

The primary manifestations of SIADH are water intoxication and hyponatremia. Characteristics of mild hyponatremia include anorexia, nausea, myalgias, and slight neurologic changes, such as irritability, lethargy, or headache. These can progress to hyporeflexia, increasing weakness, confusion, somnolence, and coma. Nausea and vomiting, anorexia, thirst, decreased urine output, and weight gain may also occur.

Treatment for SIADH ideally is treatment of the underlying cause—the tumor. For patients with a sodium level less than 130, fluids are restricted to 500 mL/24 h, and demeclocycline 600 mg/24 h is given (John et al., 1997). Patients with decreased fluid intake schedule should rinse their mouth hourly to compensate for decreased fluids. See measures for xerostomia in Chapter 16 on oral care.

Paraneoplastic Syndromes Not Usually Considered Emergencies

Endocrine Syndromes
ECTOPIC ADRENOCORTICOTROPIC HORMONE SYNDROME (ACTH)

Ectopic ACTH is most commonly found in patients with SCLC, pancreatic cancer, bronchial carcinoid tumors, and neural tumors. Because of rapid onset of the disorder and characteristics of advanced disease, patients with ectopic ACTH related to advanced cancer lack the typical moon facies, obesity of the trunk, purple straie, buffalo hump, hirsutism, and other stigmata of Cushing's syndrome. Characteristics include generalized weakness, weight loss, hypertension, and hypokalemia. If treatment of the underlying etiology is not possible, the current treatment of choice is ketoconazole 400 to 1200 mg/d (John et al., 1997).

HYPOGLYCEMIA

In terminally ill patients, hypoglycemia is found most often in patients with mesenchymal tumors and hepatic, adrenal, GI, and hematologic carcinomas (Odell, 1997). Symptoms include extreme fatigue, weakness, dizziness, tremors, and, if untreated, seizures. Treatment is ideally frequent food intake with no periods of fasting—obviously impossible in advanced terminal illness. Intravenous dextrose then becomes the only possibility (Glick & Glover, 1995).

HYPOCALCEMIA

Hypocalcemia is relatively uncommon and occurs most often in patients with advanced liver or breast cancer, especially with widespread bony metastases in the latter case, and in patients with visceral or mesenchymal tumors. Tetany is the primary characteristic of hypocalcemia. Related symptoms include paresthesias and muscle cramps. Neurologic symptoms include laryngospasm, lethargy, and changes in mentation. Seizures may also occur. Treatment is usually with intravenous calcium and magnesium if magnesium levels are decreased (Carlson & Casciato, 1995).

CARCINOID SYNDROME

Carcinoid syndrome results most frequently from neoplasm of the GI tract, usually accompanied by liver metastases, and from bronchogenic carcinomas and intracranial neoplasm. Carcinoid syndrome is characterized by flushing of the skin, especially facial, and diarrhea, bronchoconstriction, and cardiac anomalies. Wheezing and abdominal pain often accompany the flushing attacks. Flushing may be transient and mild or in the case of tumors arising in the foregut (bronchus, stomach, first portion of the duodenum, and pancreas), severe and ultimately disfiguring. Treatment is directed to the tumor. Failing that, flushing and diarrhea respond well to octreotide 6 to 20 µg/kg/d (Vinik & Perry, 1997).

Central Nervous System Paraneoplastic Syndromes

A number of (fortunately rare) central nervous system (CNS) PNSs exist. Many are associated with lung, breast, and ovarian cancers and other tumors. PNSs are challenging, if not impossible, to treat other than palliatively. The most common (John et al., 1997; Mack, 1995) follow:

● Polymyositis and dermatomyositis cause symmetrical and proximal muscle weakness. Dermatomyositis includes a violaceous rash and periorbital edema and erythema. The syndrome progresses to include dark plaques on knuckles, elbows, and similar areas.

● Lambert-Eaton myasthenic syndrome often occurs late in the course of illness and may resolve spontaneously.

● Neuropathies include symmetric distal sensorimotor polyneuropathy associated with hematologic disorders.

● Myopathy is associated with carcinoid syndrome.

● Paraneoplastic cerebellar degeneration results in ataxia, nystagmus, inability to communicate, and global loss of function.

● Paraneoplastic sensory neuropathy/encephalomyelitis results in loss of proprioception, pain, sensory ataxia, urinary retention, and other disabilities with many patients becoming bedridden, even though the motor system is spared.

● Cancer-associated retinopathy or optic neuritis progresses from obscurations and night blindness to total blindness.

● Limbic encephalitis begins with personality changes and progresses to profound short-term memory loss and seizures, hallucinations, and hypersomnia.

● Brain stem encephalitis results in vertigo, nystagmus, facial numbness, oculomotor changes, dysphagia, dysarthria, and deafness.

Cutaneous Paraneoplastic Syndromes
PIGMENTED CUTANEOUS PARANEOPLASTIC SYNDROMES

● Acanthosis nigricans is dark, thickened "thorny" skin, especially in axillae and similar areas. Acanthosis nigricans is most often found in gastric and other adenocarcinomas.

● Tripe palms (often associated with acanthosis nigricans) is a hyperpigmented, soft thickening of tissue of palms; it is associated with gastric and lung cancer.

● Paget's disease includes a keratotic and erythematous patch over areola or breast (sometimes vulva); it is associated with breast cancer.

● Sign of Leser-Trélat manifests as multiple keratotic and seborrheic (wartlike) lesions; it is associated with gastric adenocarcinoma, lymphoma, and breast cancer.

● Sweet's syndrome appears suddenly as painful erythematous plaques or nodules; it is associated with hematologic, GU, breast, and GI cancers.

● Bazex's syndrome manifests as psoriasislike hyperkeratosis with pruritic scales on the face and extremities; it is associated with gastric and respiratory cancers.

ERYTHEMATOUS CUTANEOUS PARANEOPLASTIC SYNDROMES

● Erythema gyratum repens is progressive scaling erythema in concentric bands and pruritus over entire body; it is associated with lung, GI, uterine, and breast cancer.

● Dermatomyositis is muscle weakness and a rash that progresses from periorbital changes to purplish plaquelike lesions on knuckles, elbows, and similar areas; it is associated with breast and other cancers.

● Circinate erythemas manifest as circular erythematous and pruritic lesions; they are associated primarily with lymphoma.

● Necrolytic migratory erythema includes circular patches of blistering and erosion with stomatitis; it is associated with pancreatic cancer.

● Flushing is intermittent episodes of facial and neck flushing; it is associated with carcinoid and thyroid tumors.

ENDOCRINE AND METABOLIC CUTANEOUS PARANEOPLASTIC SYNDROMES

● Porphyria cutanea tarda manifests as blisters on skin exposed to sunlight; it is associated with hepatocellular carcinoma.

● Systemic nodular panniculitis (Weber-Christian disease) is recurrent tender erythematous subcutaneous nodules, abdominal pain, and fat necrosis in bone marrow, lungs, and elsewhere; it is associated with pancreatic cancer.

● Cushing's syndrome and Addison's syndrome sometimes appear as PNS.

There are other cutaneous PNSs, including pruritus not attributable to other causes.

Other

Paraneoplastic syndromes associated with lung, stomach, and hepatic cell carcinomas are discussed in Unit III of this book. Syndromes associated with lung cancer include the following:

Paraneoplastic Syndromes Associated with Lung, Renal, and Stomach Cancers

Lung, renal, and stomach cancers are the most likely cancers to produce PNSs. These cancers and associated PNSs are discussed in greater detail in Unit III of this book.

Lung cancer is associated with PNSs including hypercalcemia, Eaton-Lambert syndrome (pseudomyasthenia), and other neurologic disorders, including encephalopathy, cerebellar degeneration, peripheral neuropathy, and others; hypertrophic osteoarthropathy, digital clubbing, polyarthritis; hematologic disorders, including thrombocytosis, hypercoagulation, thrombocytopenia, and anemia; and paraneoplastic ACTH (Cushing's) syndrome and SIADH. See Chapter 22 .

Among the PNSs associated with renal cancer are hypercalcemia and other metabolic disorders, including hyponatremia and hyperkalemia, increased erythrocyte sedimentation rate, anemia, hypertension, cachexia, neuromuscular disorders, and secondary amyloidosis. Nephrotic syndrome is usually a PNS rather than a result of tumor invasion or metastases. See Chapter 25 on renal cancer.

The types of PNSs associated with stomach cancer include acanthosis nigricans, dermatomyositis, polymyositis, circinate erythemas, dementia, cerebellar ataxia, thrombophlebitis, Cushing's syndrome, paraneoplastic chorionic gonadotropin secretion, and cachexia.

REFERENCES

Carlson, H. E., & Casciato, D. A. (1995). Metabolic complications. In D. A. Casciato & B. B. Lowitz (Eds.), *Manual of clinical oncology* (3rd ed.) (pp. 456–472). Boston: Little, Brown and Company.

Glick, J. H., & Glover, D. (1995). Oncologic emergencies. In G. P. Murphy, W. Lawrence, & R. E. Lenhard (Eds.), *Clinical oncology* (2nd ed.) (pp. 597–618). Altanta: American Cancer Society.

John, W. J., Patchell, R. A., & Foon, K. A. (1997). Paraneoplastic syndromes. In V. T. DeVita, S. Hellman, & S. A. Rosenberg (Eds.), *Cancer: Principles and practice of oncology* (5th ed.) (pp. 2397–2422). Philadelphia: Lippincott-Raven.

Mack, E. E. (1995) Neuromuscular complications. In D. A. Casciato & B. B. Lowitz (Eds.), *Manual of clinical oncology* (3rd ed.) (pp. 513–526). Boston: Little, Brown and Company.

Odell, W. D. (1997). Paraneoplastic syndromes. In J. F. Holland, R. C. Bast, D. L. Morton, E. Frei, D. W. Kufe, & R. W. Weischselbaum (Eds.), *Cancer medicine* (4th ed.) (pp. 1149–1165). Baltimore: Williams & Wilkins.

Vinik, A. I., & Perry, R. R. (1997). Neoplasms of the gastroenteropancreatic endocrine system. In J. F. Holland, R. C. Bast, D. L. Morton, E. Frei, D. W. Kufe, & R. W. Weischselbaum (Eds.), *Cancer medicine* (4th ed.) (pp. 1605–1639). Baltimore: Williams & Wilkins.

Waller, A., & Caroline, N. L. (1996). *Palliative care in cancer*. Boston: Butterworth-Heineman.

Warrell, R. P. (1997). Metabolic emergencies. In V. T. DeVita, S. Hellman, & S. A. Rosenberg (Eds.), *Cancer: Principles and practice of oncology* (5th ed.) (pp. 2486–2499). Philadelphia: Lippincott-Raven.

Imminent Death: The Last 48 Hours

The last days and hours of life are supremely challenging for everyone involved—the patient, family, care team, and others. Physical, psychosocial, and spiritual issues are often magnified, and the intensity of all aspects of care increases. There sometimes is an air of unreality mixed with the dawning realization that the end is near. Of course, there are endless variations in how patients and families enter this last phase. Some are joyous and some fearful; some are calm and some agitated; some are conscious and some comatose; some go willingly and some resist. However death occurs, care continues through the process of dying.

The abnormalities that *together* are most predictive of impending death (survival of less than 4 weeks) in patients with cancer are cognitive failure, dysphagia, and significant weight loss (Bruera et al, 1992). Advanced cancer, the above symptoms, and a major infection (pneumonia or septicemia) are predictive of imminent death (survival of less than 1 week). Additional indications of impending death are profound weakness, extended periods of drowsiness, and disinterest in foods or fluids (Twycross & Lichter, 1998). Biologic indices predictive of a poor prognosis include high white blood count, high neutrophil percentage, low lymphocyte percentage, low serum albumin level, low pseudocholinesterase level, and high proteinuria (Maltoni et al., 1997).

In patients with acquired immunodeficiency syndrome, the greatest risk of death occurs with (1) a decreased CD4 cell count and increased viral load and (2) the presence of the following opportunistic diseases or conditions (in decreasing order of magnitude of risk):

lymphoma, progressive multifocal leukoencephalopathy, disseminated *Mycobacterium avium* complex infection, and cytomegalovirus disease. Other conditions indicating reduced survival time include *Pneumocystis carinii* pneumonia, Kaposi's sarcoma, toxoplasmosis, cryptosporidiosis, dementia, wasting syndrome, and esophageal candidiasis (Chaisson, Gallant, Keruly, & Moore, 1998).

Symptoms that have been a problem previously often continue to cause difficulties and may increase in severity in the last weeks of life. Although there is seldom a "crescendo of pain" in the final days, there often is an increase in pain or other symptoms (especially dyspnea) (Twycross & Lichter, 1998). Changes in consciousness are common and include in the final week or weeks confusion or agitation. Social withdrawal is also common and does not necessarily mean distress or deterioration: There usually is little to say in the face of eternity. Drowsiness, unresponsiveness, and/or coma frequently occur in the final days.

Providing Care to Moribund Patients

The first intervention in caring for moribund (dying) patients is to teach the family what to do and what to expect. Family members and others involved with the patient often imagine that death is a catastrophic event, filled with terrible physical agony. Understanding that

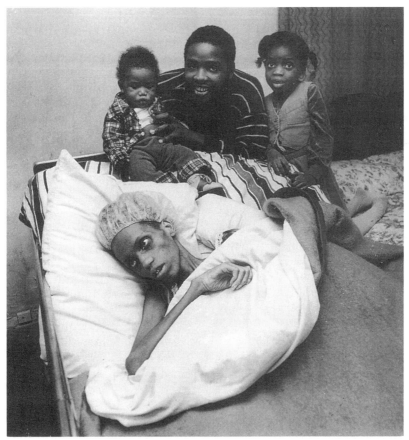

DEBORA HUNTER

this is seldom the case is immensely comforting. Now, more than ever, the family benefits from involvement in giving care. Providing care keeps people busy with giving love versus sitting or pacing and feeling helpless.

This is truly the last chance to say what needs saying and to do what needs doing. The nurse may need to be directive with a patient or family member, to help one or the other—or both—say healing words of forgiveness or acceptance. This is also the last chance to say goodbye. Some words can be a lovely, final gift; some people need help saying them.

Dying at home presents challenging decisions and often a need for great support to the family. Family members often have questions: "Is there anything more that would be done if she or he were in the hospital?" The presence or availability of the nurse when death occurs at home is extremely helpful.

Different political areas (eg, cities, counties) have different procedures for death at home. Knowing what will happen when authorities are informed of the death can prevent crises. Resuscitation, for example, is attempted by many emergency services, regardless of cause of death or of what the family says and sometimes in the presence of advance directives. It is necessary to learn about local procedures and make alternative plans if necessary. When death is due to advanced incurable disease and resuscitation is not desired by the patient, waiting for an hour or more after death to contact authorities is probably the simplest measure to prevent inappropriate resuscitation attempts. A physician, or in some areas, the hospice nurse can come to the home and pronounce death. With enough lead time, some medical examiner offices issue "do not resuscitate" bracelets or documents prior to death.

While it is not possible to predict the exact course of a person's death, certain events are common in the final few days or hours of life. These are given in the following section, along with a discussion of care. It is important to understand that not all of these occur in every person who is dying.

Dreams and Visions

Dreams and visions tend to increase in frequency in terminal patients during their final weeks and days. These are usually comforting to the person who is dying. Family members sometimes reject or devalue such occurrences. Powerful themes and symbols appear in these dreams and visions. Among these are a bridge or a river to cross, a door through which lies the "other side," a tunnel leading to the light, traveling, angels, religious figures, and deceased loved ones. Early on in the dying process, it is very helpful (to patient, family, and nurse) for the person who is dying to describe these experiences and to talk about what they mean. Later, when the person is able perhaps only to mumble, one simply listens to whatever is intelligible.

Withdrawal

Many patients withdraw, not in despair, but in acceptance of death (or life). These people speak very little, even to loved ones or to favorite caregivers. This is a natural part of the process, and it is very helpful to family members to understand that it is not depression or rejection of others in a negative sense. The person who withdraws in this way is probably looking toward eternity rather than to finite life. Once family members understand the process, it is usually well accepted.

Pain

Pain (like other symptoms) is treated with the same vigor as at any point in the illness. Assessment is more difficult in the final stages of life, and in many cases, the patient will not be able to communicate with words. In the absence of increased distress indicating increased pain or the presence of symptoms directly attributable to opioid overdose, pain medications should be continued as before, whether the patient is conscious or unconscious. The oral route for medications becomes less available, and rectal and subcutaneous routes assume more importance. See Warren (1996) for a complete discussion of the rectal route. If dehydration is significant, a downward titration of medications such as opioids may be necessary to prevent metabolite accumulation and toxic side effects (Fainsinger & deMoissac, 1998).

Terminal Anguish

As death approaches, some people are unable any longer to suppress (conscious process) or repress (unconscious process) painful, unresolved psychological material. This may lead to terminal anguish, characterized by restlessness, moaning, and similar behavior. Terminal anguish may be distinguished from agitated delirium by the absence of cognitive failure, hallucinations, or delusions (Hospice and Palliative Nurses Association [HPNA], 1997). If the patient is able to communicate and wants to do so, this may be a last opportunity to deal with whatever is the basis of the anguish. If the patient is unable to communicate verbally, the family or other loved ones should be helped to stay close to the patient and otherwise provide support with words, song, prayer, or whatever means suit the people and situation. See the discussion of neurologic symptoms for pharmacologic interventions in Chapter 13.

Neurologic Symptoms

Changes in consciousness include drowsiness, unresponsiveness, or coma; and in some patients, confusion or agitation. The latter is treated according to etiology (eg, with opioids for pain, and oxygen or opioids for dyspnea as described elsewhere in this text). There may be periods of lucidity interspersed with confusion or somnolence.

Terminal restlessness (agitation) with delir-ium can be treated first with nembutal suppository 60 to 120 mg PR q4h. If nembutal is not effective, droperidol 1.25 to 2.5 mg is given intravenously (IV) or intramuscularly, and if droperidol is not effective (or if neuromuscular activity is predominant), the other medications are discontinued, and midazolam 1 to 2 mg/h subcutaneously is given until symptoms are managed. For severe agitation with delirium, midazolam can be given 1 mg every 10 minutes until symptoms are under control. The hourly maintenance dose is 25% to 33% of required induction dose (HPNA, 1997).

Lorazepam (80% bioavailability) and clonazepam (bioavailability unknown) are effective when given rectally for terminal restlessness (Warren, 1996). Chlorpromazine 12.5 mg IV q4–12h or 25 mg PR q4–12h is a much less expensive alternative to midazolam and helps relieve dyspnea (Waller & Caroline, 1996).

Myoclonus (usually multifocal) may occur in the last hours or days of life. Treatment is with diazepam 5 to 10 mg PR every hour until settled and 10 mg PR once or twice daily thereafter (Twycross & Lichter, 1998). See Chapter 13 on neurologic problems for information on treating myoclonus recalcitrant to treatment with diazepam.

When agitation, anguish, and delirium are overwhelming, it is sometimes necessary to keep a patient sedated until death occurs. Terminal sedation may be achieved with midazolam 60 to 100 mg/24 h continuous subcutaneous infusion (or diazepam 10–20 mg PR tid–qid) and haloperidol 20 to 40 mg/24 h (Twycross & Lichter, 1998). Treatment of other symptoms continues and assessment is made to ensure that the agitation is not due to unmanaged pain, urine retention, or other treatable problems.

Patients who become unresponsive or comatose receive basic and nonintrusive care as follows: Artificial tears are used when the patient does not blink. Very gentle mouth care is provided as described in Chapter 16 on oral problems (xerostomia should be assumed). Even small amounts of water can cause choking. Minimal skin care is provided, primarily to keep the skin clean and dry (bowel movements are unusual and urine output is generally minimal). If the patient is incontinent, pads or heavy towels may be enough to avoid catheterization. Vital signs are seldom necessary. If the patient is not incontinent, retention should be monitored. The question of how much of what medications to give is difficult to answer definitively. Pain and antiemetic medications should generally be continued as before.

Anorexia

Anorexia occurs in most patients in the last weeks of life (Brescia, 1997). Some family members have an intense desire to give food to even the most cachectic moribund patients. This may be an unconscious means of nurturing and showing love (Zerwekh, 1991). However, insofar as feeding a loved one can be considered a sign of love and nurturing, it is a secondary and indirect sign; both patient and family will benefit from primary or more direct expressions of love. Forcing food on patients who are clearly dying may also be a form of denial or a manifestation of helplessness. Whatever the cause of the desire to give food, it is, at best, a burden for the patient. When dysphagia is the cause of anorexia, forcing food can result in choking. The nurse can (1) help family members clarify their feelings and goals in wanting the patient to eat and (2) teach them alternative means of expressing their love and care.

Dehydration

Some patients also refuse fluids in their final days or hours. This is discussed more fully in Chapter 19. Forcing fluids or initiating IV infusions for hydration is nearly always contraindicated in people who are imminently terminal. However, for patients who are not imminent, hypodermoclysis or rectal hydra-

tion (proctolysis) may help prevent (1) renal failure with subsequent accumulation of opioid metabolites, leading to confusion, myoclonus, and seizures; (2) electrolyte imbalances; and (3) confusion and restlessness in patients with advanced disease (Bruera et al., 1998). Depending on degree of debilitation and existing problems, aggressive IV hydration can actually increase pulmonary edema, peripheral edema, urine output, secretions, vomiting, and ascites. Xerostomia and thirst are the primary problems resulting from decreased fluids in patients who are close to death, neither of which is necessarily relieved by rehydration. Treatment consists of oral care at least every 2 hours; occasional sips, even of one to two drops, of fluid; and if the client cannot swallow, small amounts of fine spray from an atomizer. There is significant controversy about hydration in terminally ill patients, and readers are encouraged to reread Chapter 19.

Respiratory Symptoms

Respiratory symptoms are often a significant problem in imminently terminal patients. The character of agonal respirations (near the end of life) is generally increasingly shallow or labored as death nears. Periods of apnea increase in frequency, or respirations slow, then increase in rate, and then again slow. Cheyne-Stokes respirations (rhythmic waxing and waning of respiratory depth with regular periods of apnea) may also occur.

Problems include pulmonary secretions increasing and the patient having difficulty managing them (ie, difficulty coughing, clearing, and swallowing effectively). Dyspnea often increases as death nears, even when there is no lung or pleural involvement (Twycross & Lichter, 1998). The specific cause(s) of dyspnea should be sought, and the interventions chosen should be based on etiology, if possible. In general, interventions for dyspnea (Kemp, 1997) include oxygen, opioids (including by nebulizer), tranquilizers, steroids, hyoscine to decrease secretions, and independent comfort measures (eg, fan, elevated head, turning on side) as described in Chapter 14. Increased dyspnea and secretions, sometimes referred to as "death rattle," leads to anxiety in the family. There is sometimes what is or seems to be a final struggle for breath. Although suctioning may not extend either the length or quality of life, it may be comforting to the family. Hyoscine to treat the rattle is most effective if used early in the process of developing rattling respirations and least effective when secretions are bronchial in origin and accumulate over several days. Other measures (Bennett, 1996; Waller & Caroline, 1996) include furosemide (Lasix) and atropine; nebulized atropine, morphine, and dexamethasone; and scopolamine patch.

Cardiovascular

The pulse rate increases, and there is a corresponding decrease in cardiac efficiency; that is, the pulse (usually) is weak and irregular. Blood pressure decreases. Cyanosis, beginning distally and progressing, results from cardiac and respiratory deficiencies. The skin is usually cool and mottled. The patient may perspire, and edema may develop. Hyperthermia occurs occasionally from infection or tumor activity. Except for oxygen in some cases and comfort measures (eg, light blanket or sheet, physical presence, reassurance) in all cases, there is usually no intervention for these events in advanced terminal illness.

Nausea and Vomiting

Nausea and vomiting may occur in the last days and of course must be treated aggressively. Oral medications may not be possible, so rectal and subcutaneous routes should be used.

Elimination

Urine output decreases, usually as a result of decreased intake and decreased renal function, sometimes coupled with anticholinergic effects, impaction, and other processes. Incontinence or retention may also occur, and the patient should be regularly assessed for a distended bladder. Retention requires catheterization, while incontinence of relatively small volume may be manageable with towels and pads changed frequently, especially if the patient is not in pain.

Constipation may continue as a problem until death. Part of the process of dying is the gradual shutdown of all body functions, including bowel. The tendency to constipation may be counterbalanced by decreased food intake, hence less stool. In the final days, a stool every 3 or even 4 days may not be abnormal. Discomfort and the presence of indentable abdominal mass show the need for intervention. Fecal incontinence is usually a result of diarrhea (see Chapter 17).

Other

The eyes become sunken and glazed and are often half open. The senses are generally dulled, except that hearing may not be lost and sensitivity to light may remain. The ability to move decreases, beginning in the legs and progressing to the arms. The patient's body may become stiff and joints painful when moved.

Only essential medications are given in the final few days and hours. The essential medications under most circumstances in the last hours of life are morphine, antiemetics, furosemide, and hyoscine. Sedative-hypnotics, corticosteroids, or some other medications for problems, such as reflux esophagitis or bronchospasm, might also need to be continued (Waller & Caroline, 1996).

The most frequent causes of death in patients with cancer (Inagaki, Rodriguez, & Bodey, 1974) are as follows:

● Infection (47%) comes primarily from pneumonia and septicemia. Patients with tumors of the lung, head, and neck and with melanoma are most likely to die from pneumonia; patients with gastrointestinal and genitourinary tumors are more likely to develop septicemia but may also die from pneumonia. Obstructive tumors and neutropenia are often associated with death from infection.

● Organ failure (25%) is most frequently (in decreasing order) respiratory, cardiac, hepatic, central nervous system (CNS), and renal. Respiratory and CNS failure are caused by tumor; hepatic and renal failure are usually caused by tumor; and cardiac failure is caused in approximately equal numbers by heart disease or tumor.

● Infarction (11%) is most often of the lungs or heart. Lung infarction is a result of either tumor in the lung or distal thrombosis, causing embolization. Arteriosclerosis is the primary cause of myocardial infarction.

● Carcinomatosis or carcinosis (10%) is widespread metastatic disease and occurs most often in patients with melanoma or breast cancer. Cachexia or electrolyte imbalances are commonly associated with carcinomatosis.

● Hemorrhage (7%) occurs most frequently in the gastrointestinal tract and brain and is usually caused by gastrointestinal tumor or melanoma.

Ultimately, death from any of these or other causes is a result of a lack of oxygen to the brain (Nuland, 1994).

Teaching the Family and Final Points

Depending on room temperature, a light blanket or sheet should be used. Lighting should be whatever the patient has been using. Other than loved ones who heretofore have been unable to come, visitors should generally be only those (usually) few that have been with the patient in his or her final weeks. Conversation should not be hushed, and children should not be kept out. The brief presence of an infant grandchild is very appropriate.

The nurse should reassure the family (and other loved ones) about the normalcy of events and help them continue to provide as much care as possible. Knowing that the patient is likely to be able to hear is very helpful to family members and motivates them to talk to the patient. Family members should be encouraged to sit close to and touch the patient if this is not painful to the patient. They should be instructed to give gentle oral and skin care, limited perhaps to occasional moistening of the lips, wiping the brow, and so on. If at all possible, someone from the family should be with the patient at all times.

The importance of family involvement in care at this point cannot be too highly stressed. This time is a bridge from life to death and from caring to grief. Everything that happens in the last hours will be remembered by the family, and if family members were there and care was given, there will be an affirmation of the family and its caring for the one who died. There will still be grief, but there will also be the knowledge that the person who died was not alone in the final hours.

Finally, the duty to those who are dying comes down to this: "Watch with me." This is what we do and what we teach others to do in this time of truth.

After Death

Whether at home or in the hospital, there is a tendency to hurry through whatever happens after a person dies. In hospitals, for example, nurses often ask the family to leave a few minutes after the death while they "wrap" or otherwise prepare the body for transport to (of course) the basement. At home, the ambulance service may be called to transport the body a few minutes after the death. This rush is probably related to the family's pain and the staff's discomfort. There also may be *no* particular reason; this is just the way it is done.

It should be understood by all, after some consideration of the facts, that there is no reason to hurry. There usually is reason not to hurry. Slowing the after-death events means that the family has more time to begin understanding the reality of what has happened and to begin the process of saying goodbye. Spending time with the body before it is made up (as if going to a party) by the funeral home helps the family see that the person is truly gone physically. Some families want to wash the face or otherwise tend to the body. Some want to sit with the body, and some want to stay awhile, then go away, and then come back. Some want to keep the body at home until the next day. Whatever the case, the only reason not to encourage families to take as much time as they like has to do with public health rules, and these rules apply only to a few patients; even then, they are usually relevant only after the patient has been dead for at least 24 hours.

REFERENCES

Bennet, M. I. (1996). Death rattle: An audit of hyoscine (scopolamine) use and review of management. *Journal of Pain and Symptom Management, 12*(4), 229–233.

Brescia, F. J. (1997). Specialized care of the terminally ill. In V. T. DeVita, S. Hellman, & S. A. Rosenberg (Eds.), *Cancer: Principles and practice of oncology* (5th ed.) (pp. 2905–2912). Philadelphia: Lippincott-Raven.

Bruera, E., Pruvost, M., Schoeller, T., Montejo, G., & Watanabe, S. (1998). Proctolysis for hydration of terminally ill cancer patients. *Journal of Pain and Symptom Mangement, 15*(4), 216–219.

Bruera, E., Miller, M. J., Kuehn, N., MacEachern, T., & Hanson, J. (1992). Estimate of survival of patients admitted to a palliative care unit: A prospective study. *Journal of Pain and Symptom Management, 7*(2), 82–86.

Chaisson, R. E., Gallant, J. E., Keruly, J. C., & Moore, R. D. (1998). Impact of opportunistic disease on survival in patients with HIV infection. *AIDS 1998, 12*(1), 29–33.

Fainsinger, R., & deMoissac, D. (1998). Letter on hydration in terminal illness. *Journal of Intravenous Nursing, 21*(3), 138–139.

Hospice and Palliative Nurses Association. (1997). *Terminal restlessness.* Pittsburgh: Author.

Inagaki, J., Rodriguez, V., & Bodey, G. P. (1974). Causes of death in cancer patients. *Cancer, 33*(2), 568–573.

Kemp, C. E. (1997). Palliative care for respiratory problems in terminal illness. *American Journal of Hospice and Palliative Care, 14*(1), 26–30.

Maltoni, M., Pirovano, M., Nanni, O., Marinari, M., Indelli, M., Gramazio, A., Terzoli, E., Luzzani, M., De Marinis, F., Caracini, A., & Labianca, R. (1997). Biological indices predictive of survival in 519 Italian terminally ill cancer patients. *Journal of Pain and Symptom Management, 13*(1), 1–9.

Nuland, S. B. (1994). *How we die.* New York: Alfred A. Knopf.

Twycross, R., & Lichter, I. (1998).The terminal phase. In D. Doyle, G. W. C. Hanks, & N. MacDonald (Eds.), *Oxford textbook of palliative medicine* (2nd ed.) (pp. 977–992). New York: Oxford University Press.

Waller, A., & Caroline, N. L. (1996). *Handbook of palliative care in cancer.* Boston: Butterworth-Heinemann.

Warren, D. E. (1996). Practical use of rectal medications in palliative care. *Journal of Pain and Symptom Management, 11*(6), 378–387.

Zerwekh, J. (1991). Supportive care of the dying patient. In S. B. Baird, R. McCorkle, & M. Grant (Eds.), *Cancer nursing: A comprehensive textbook* (pp. 875–884). Philadelphia: W.B Saunders.

Advanced Cancer: Metastatic Spread, Common Symptoms, and Assessment

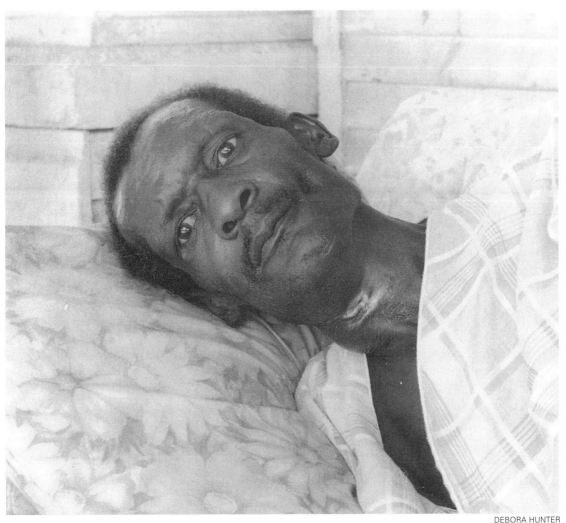

DEBORA HUNTER

ONE of the classic clinical issues in hospice and palliative care is the early identification of disease or problem progression. Early identification of progression often means that treatment of problems can be more effective and less aggressive. Heart failure and diabetes; and cancer and skin breakdown, dehydration, and constipation are examples of diseases and problems in which early identification of problems is essential.

The hospice and palliative care literature (eg, Doyle, Hanks, & MacDonald, 1998; Groenwald, Frogge, Goodman, & Yarbro, 1996; Waller & Caroline, 1996; Woodruff, 1997; and others) has typically focused on what to do when problems occur. Anticipation and prevention or early identification should be added to the hospice and palliative care armamentarium. These chapters examine the natural history and typical progression of the 18 primary tumor sites (listed below) that each cause more than 5,000 deaths per year in the United States

It is essential to remember that the listing of metastatic sites is not inclusive of all patients with a particular primary tumor site. Some patients have fewer metastatic sites and problems; some have other sites and problems; and in others, there may be little evidence of metastatic disease. Moreover, there is great variation in the intrinsic aggressiveness of tumors, even when similar in size and histology, hence speed and other factors in progression vary (Liotta & Kohn, 1997). Nevertheless, there is at least some predictability in the spread and behavior of tumors, and this predictability provides a vital tool in caring for patients with cancer (Lowitz & Casciato, 1995).

Metastasis is the most challenging aspect of cancer treatment and is the primary cause of mortality in patients with cancer (Woodhouse, Chuaqui, & Liotta, 1997). Metastasis is a complex process involving the following steps (LeMarbre & Groenwald, 1997; Liotta & Kohn, 1997):

1. Growth of the primary tumor and neovascularization (angiogenesis)
2. Invasion of tumor cells from primary tumor through adjacent structures, such as basement membrane
3. Spread of tumor cells into blood (intravasation) or lymphatic system (and tumor cells must survive immune surveillance in circulation)
4. Arrest in the capillary bed of an organ (often the first capillary bed encountered)
5. Movement from the capillary bed into the organ (extravasation)
6. Growth within the organ and establishment of a new tumor locus (colony formation)

Cancer also spreads by direct extension of the primary (or secondary) tumor from one structure or area to another.

This section is divided according to major organs and systems as follows:

● **Chapter 22**. Major organs: lung cancer, pancreatic cancer, liver cancer, brain cancer
● **Chapter 23**. Female reproductive: breast cancer, ovarian cancer, uterine cancer

Table Section III-1. Deaths from Cancer by Tumor Site			
Rank	Site	Deaths 1993	Estimated Deaths 1998
1	Lung	148,727	160,100
2	Colon and rectum	57,405	56,500
3	Breast	43,910	43,900
4	Prostate	34,865	39,200
5	Pancreas	26,445	28,900
6	Non-Hodgkin's lymphoma	20,576	24,900
7	Leukemia	20,772	21,600
8	Stomach	13,850	13,700
9	Ovary	12,870	14,500
10	Brain, central nervous system	11,993	13,300
11	Bladder	10,962	12,500
12	Esophagus	10,450	11,900
13	Kidney	10,322	11,600
14	Liver	10,063	13,000
15	Multiple myeloma	9,841	11,300
16	Oral cavity	8,241	8,000
17	Melanoma	6,712	7,300
18	Uterine	6,098	6,300

American Cancer Society, 1997; Landis, Murray, Bolden, & Wingo, 1998.

● **Chapter 24**. Gastrointestinal: colorectal cancer, stomach cancer, esophageal cancer, oral cancer
● **Chapter 25**. Urinary tract: renal, other urinary cancer (except bladder), bladder cancer, prostate cancer
● **Chapter 26**. Blood/lymph and skin: non-Hodgkin's lymphoma, leukemia, multiple myeloma, melanoma

For each primary site, there is a brief discussion of metastatic sites, symptoms, and oncologic emergencies common to that tumor. Oncology emergencies are always in **bold**. Metastatic sites are listed along with problems (assessment parameters) typical of those sites.

Tumors examined are shown in Table 1 above.

REFERENCES

American Cancer Society. (1997). *Cancer facts and figures*. Atlanta: Author.
Doyle, D., Hanks, G. W. C., & MacDonald, N. (1998). *Oxford textbook of palliative medicine* (2nd ed.). Oxford: Oxford University Press.
Groenwald, S. I., Frogge, M. H., Goodman, M., & Yarbro, C. H. (Eds.) (1996). *Cancer symptom management*. Boston: Jones and Bartlett.
Landis, S. H., Murray, T., Bolden, S., & Wingo, P. A. (1998). Cancer statistics, 1998. *CA—A Cancer Journal for Clinicians*, 48(1), 6–29.

LeMarbre, P. J., & Groenwald, S. L. (1997). Biology of cancer. In S. I. Groenwald, M. H. Frogge, M. Goodman, & C. H. Yarbro (Eds.), *Cancer nursing: Principles and practice* (4th ed.) (pp. 17–37). Boston: Jones and Bartlett.

Liotta, L. A., & Kohn, E. C. (1997). Invasion and metastasis. In J. F. Holland, R. C. Bast, D. L. Morton, E. Frei, D. W. Kufe, & R. C. Weichselbaum (Eds.), *Cancer medicine* (4th ed.) (pp. 165–180). Baltimore: Williams & Wilkins.

Lowitz, B. B., & Casciato, D. A. (1995). Principles of cancer biology and management. In D. A. Casciato & B. B. Lowitz (Eds.), *Manual of clinical oncology* (pp. 3–13). Boston: Little, Brown and Company.

Waller, A., & Caroline, N. L. (1996). *Handbook of palliative care in cancer.* Boston: Butterworth-Heinemann.

Woodhouse, E. C., Chuaqui, R. F., & Liotta, L. A. (1997). General mechanisms of metastasis. *Cancer, 80*(8), 1529–1537.

Woodruff, R. (1997). *Symptom control in advanced cancer.* Melbourne: Asperula.

CHAPTER 22

Major Organs (Lung, Pancreas, Liver, Brain): Metastatic Spread, Symptoms, and Assessment

Lung Cancer

Lung cancer is the leading cause of cancer death for both women and men, with 148,727 total deaths in 1993 and an estimated 160,100 deaths in 1998. In 1993, 56,234 women died from lung cancer—12,679 more than from breast cancer (American Cancer Society, 1997; Landis, Murray, Bolden, & Wingo, 1998).

The most common lung cancers according to World Health Organization classification are squamous cell (epidermoid), small cell (SCLC), adenocarcinoma, and large cell (Harwood, 1996). Lung cancers other than SCLC are increasingly referred to as non-small cell lung cancer (NSCLC). Characteristics of the different tumor types include the following:

● Squamous cell carcinomas usually arise in the bronchi, are slow growing, and tend to spread by local invasion, so have fewer distant sites of metastases. The very painful superior sulcus or Pancoast's tumors most often result from squamous cell carcinomas (Arcasoy & Jett, 1997). Common sites of metastases are contralateral thorax, lymph, bone, and liver (Ingle, 1997). Local progression is the usual cause of death (Hilderley, 1996).

● SCLC is the fastest growing and most aggressive of the lung cancers and is most likely to result in distant metastases (Martin & Comis, 1996). SCLC may also be combined with other types. Widespread metastasis is often found at diagnosis with the most common sites being bone, bone marrow, liver, lymph, central nervous system (CNS), and lung (Ingle, 1997; Tabbarah, Lowitz, & Livingston, 1995). SCLC tends to be endocrinologically active, so paraneoplastic syndromes (PNS) are more common in this tumor type.

● Adenocarcinoma, the most frequently occurring lung tumor, is associated with multiple pulmonary nodules, metastases to pleura and scalene (chest) nodes, and metastases to contralateral thorax, bones, liver, and brain (Tabbarah et al., 1995). Superior sulcus or Pancoast's tumors also are associated with adenocarcinomas (Arcasoy & Jett, 1997).

● Large cell carcinomas are the least common of the four major types. Metastatic patterns are similar to adenocarcinomas.

Pleural effusions are common in lung cancer (especially SCLC). Lung cancer may also metastasize to the heart (Chernecky & Krech-Fritskey, 1996). Metastases to adrenals are relatively common but usually asymptomatic (Ginsberg, Vokes, & Raben, 1997).

The tendency for widespread metastases and the intrinsic pulmonary symptoms in lung cancer present a complicated clinical challenge. Common selected symptoms of lung cancer include dyspnea and a combination of other pulmonary symptoms, persistent and often severe pain, fever (sometimes of unknown origin), nausea or vomiting, constipation, diarrhea, anorexia and weight loss, lymphadenopathy, and neurologic sequelae of brain metastases (Ginsberg et al., 1997; Tabbarah et al., 1995).

Lung cancer is associated with a number of PNSs (Ginsberg, et al., 1997; Haapoja, 1997; Humphrey, Ward, & Perri, 1995):

- Hypercalcemia is most common in NSCLC.
- Eaton-Lambert syndrome (pseudomyasthenia) most often occurs in SCLC and is characterized by severe muscle weakness and fatigue.
- Other neurologic disorders are rare, but a variety may occur, including encephalopathy, cerebellar degeneration, peripheral neuropathy, and others.
- Hypertrophic osteoarthropathy is common in NSCLC and is characterized by inflammation of the joints of the fingers and toes and sometimes also of the distal ends of long bones.
- Digital clubbing may accompany hypertrophic osteoarthropathy or may occur independently. Polyarthritis, similar to rheumatoid arthritis, may also occur.
- Hematologic disorders include thrombocytosis, hypercoagulation, thrombocytopenia, and anemia.
- Paraneoplastic adrenocorticotropic hormone (Cushing's) syndrome occurs most frequently in SCLC.
- Syndrome of inappropriate antidiuretic hormone secretion (SIADH) is common in SCLC.
- Nephrotic syndrome is usually a PNS rather than a result of tumor invasion or metastases.

The oncologic emergencies most often associated with lung cancer are **pericardial effusion** leading to cardiac tamponade, **superior vena cava syndrome**, **tracheal obstruction**, **spinal cord compression**, **increased intracranial pressure** (ICP, from metastasis to the brain or carcinomatosis meningitis), **hypercalcemia**, and **SIADH** (hyponatremia) (Ginsberg et al., 1997; Glick & Glover, 1995; Hilderly, 1996). See Table 22-1.

Pancreatic Cancer

Cancer of the pancreas is the fifth leading cause of cancer death for women and men and occurs about equally in both populations. There were 26,445 deaths from pancreatic cancer in 1993 and the estimation of deaths in 1998 is 28,900 (American Cancer Society, 1997; Landis et al., 1998).

Almost all tumors of the pancreas, 95% of which arise from the exocrine portion, are adenocarcinomas. Pancreatic cancer is usually diagnosed at an advanced stage so that survival time is often limited. The most common sites of metastases are liver, lungs, bone, bowel, and regional and distal lymph nodes (Evans, Abbruzzese, & Rich, 1997; Weiss, 1992).

Common symptoms include pain, especially abdominal or middle to upper back, anorexia, early satiety, xerostomia, sleep disturbances, weight loss, fatigue, weakness, nausea, constipation, and dyspepsia (Evans et al., 1997; Krech & Walsh, 1991). Abdominal pain is often vague and sometimes intermittent; it may be dull, boring, and worse at night. Mid to upper back pain is frequently a result of tumor invasion of the celiac and mesenteric plexus and may be relieved by sitting up, bending forward, or lying in a curled up position (Ottery & McLaughlin-Hagan, 1996).

A variety of other problems, primarily gastrointestinal, are also common. Obstruction of the pancreatic duct may cause pancreatic insufficiency with resulting malabsorption and steatorrhea. Ascites may develop late in the course of the disease, and jaundice is common. Diarrhea is especially troublesome in later stages (Wachtel et al., 1988). Cachexia and fatigue, often accompanied by dyspnea, are common at presentation and universal in later stages.

Paraneoplastic syndromes found in patients with pancreatic cancer are Cushing's syndrome and SIADH (Haapoja, 1997).

The oncologic emergency most often associated with pancreatic cancer is **SIADH** (Haapoja, 1997). See Table 22-2.

TABLE 22-1	Lung Cancer: Spread, Problems, and Assessment	
Metastatic Spread	**Problems**	**Assessment Parameters**
Thorax, bilaterally, including lymph be	Dyspnea	Pleural effusion: Dyspnea with cough and chest pain (trachea displacement toward unaffected side with large effusion). Breath sounds are usually decreased but may vary according to area of lung. Pleural effusions are usually unilateral, except when due to heart failure or lymphangitis carcinomatosis. Pneumonia: Dyspnea with elevated temperature, chills, purulent or rusty sputum (but not always present), decreased breath sounds. Pleural effusion may also present. Bone marrow and other transplantations are a risk factor for fungal pulmonary infections. **Obstruction** (from tumor, lymphadenopathy): Progressive or rapidly increasing dyspnea, blood in sputum, noisy breathing, chronic cough, choking, and/or pneumonia. **Pulmonary embolus:** Sudden onset of dyspnea with rapid breathing, rapid heart rate, cough, chest pain, and blood in sputum. **Pericardial effusion → Cardiac tamponade:** Dyspnea with cough and chest pain relieved by leaning forward. There may be syncope, weakness, pleural effusion, edema, distension of neck veins, tachypnea, and the clinical triad of tachycardia, muffled heart tones, and hypotension. **Superior vena cava syndrome:** Dyspnea with engorged neck veins, facial or arm swelling, changes in consciousness, cough, hoarseness, and noisy breathing. Respiratory muscle weakness: Dyspnea with general weakness, anorexia, severe weight loss (cachexia), or the presence of a paraneoplastic syndrome. Atelectasis: Dyspnea with tachypnea, decreased chest wall movement unilaterally, deviation of apical impulse and trachea, varying breath sounds but decreased on affected side. Lymphangitis carcinomatosis: Symptoms similar to emphysema; dyspnea unexplained by other causes. Loss of function: Dyspnea from far advanced disease and complications, including pleural or cardiac effusion, pulmonary edema from cardiac failure, lymphangitis carcinomatosis, carcinomatous infiltration of chest wall, paralysis, or pneumonia. Bronchiolitis obliterans: Dyspnea unexplained by other causes; history of bone marrow transplant. Treatment sequelae: Potential causes include radiation pneumonitis or fibrosis or damage to pulmonary capillary bed from chemotherapeutic agents, such as bleomycin or mitomycin. Radiation pneumonitis occurs 1–2 mo after treatment, while fibrosis may appear 6–12 mo after radiation. Dyspnea may also result from other processes and preexisting conditions.
	Pain	Pain may be mixed somatic and neuropathic, with chest wall and pleural involvement. Superior sulcus tumor or Pancoast's syndrome includes (1) very severe neuropathic pain in the shoulder, sometimes radiating to the head, neck, scapula, axilla, chest, or arm and (2) Horner's syndrome—weakness and atrophy of hand muscles with ipsilateral ptosis, miosis, and anhidrosis.
	Cough	Cough may be associated with **obstruction,** pleural effusion, pulmonary edema from lymphangitis carcinomatosis, pneumonia, **pulmonary embolus,** pericardial effusion or **tamponade,** vocal cord paralysis, respiratory muscle weakness, congestive heart failure, or other preexisting conditions.

TABLE 22-1	Lung Cancer: Spread, Problems, and Assessment *(Continued)*	

Metastatic Spread	Problems	Assessment Parameters
	Hemoptysis	Bronchogenic tumor is a common cause. Other causes include pneumonia, **pulmonary embolus,** nonmalignant disease, and extra-pulmonary source. Irreversible hemorrhage is possible with end-stage cancer.
	Lymphadenopathy	The primary problem of lymphadenopathy in lung cancer is pressure from lymph nodes on internal structure (eg, superior vena cava). Lymphedema may also occur: enlarged lymph, edema (area or lower extremities); pain; cellulitis, lymphangitis.
Liver	Pain	Liver pain may be upper right abdominal or nonspecific, characteristic of visceral pain. It may radiate to right scapula and worsen at night.
	Ascites	Abdominal distension, bulging flanks, fluid wave, weight gain, and discomfort; anorexia, early satiety, indigestion, decreased bowel mobility; dyspnea, orthopnea, tachypnea; weakness, fatigue.
Bone	Pain	Bone pain is usually localized, constant, dull, aching, or sharp and is worse at night.
		Spinal cord compression (from pathologic fracture or compression of cord without fracture): back pain is the first symptom and may be local (somatic: constant, dull, aching), radicular, or both. It is exacerbated by movement, neck flexion, and straight leg raising and is decreased by sitting up. It is tender to percussion. Neurologic deficits usually follow pain. They may begin subtly and include extremity weakness, ataxia, stumbling; urine retention, bowel dysfunction, numbness.
Marrow	Bleeding disorder	Thrombocytopenia: bleeding occurs in skin, mucous membranes, and gastrointestinal or genitourinary tracts. Disseminated intravascular coagulation may also occur.
Brain, central nervous system (CNS)	CNS symptoms	**Increased intracranial pressure** (ICP): Progressive pain is usually present and may be more severe in the morning. Classic triad of increased ICP = papilledema (often with visual changes), vomiting, and headache. Confusion, seizures, or other CNS problems may also result from brain metastases (see Chapter 13).
Paraneoplastic syndromes changes (PNS)	Metabolic and related changes	**Hypercalcemia:** (Often nonspecific) symptoms include fatigue, weakness, anorexia, nausea, polyuria, polydipsia, and constipation; progressing to in mentation, seizures, and coma.
		Syndrome of inappropriate antidiuretic hormone secretion (SIADH, hyponatremia): Anorexia, nausea, myalgia (including abdominal wall), slight neurologic changes; progression to increased neurologic changes: confusion, lethargy, seizures.
		Other PNS: Eaton-Lambert syndrome (pseudomyasthenia) with severe muscle weakness and fatigue. Other neurologic PNS include encephalopathy, cerebellar degeneration, peripheral neuropathy, and others. Hypertrophic osteoarthropathy is characterized by inflammation of the joints of the fingers and toes and sometimes of the distal ends of long bones. Digital clubbing may accompany hypertrophic osteoarthropathy or may occur independently. Polyarthritis, similar to rheumatoid arthritis, may also occur. Hematologic disorders include thrombocytosis, hypercoagulation, thrombocytopenia, and anemia. Paraneoplastic ACTH (Cushing's) syndrome occurs most frequently in small cell lung cancer (SCLC).

(continued)

TABLE 22-1	Lung Cancer: Spread, Problems, and Assessment *(Continued)*	
Metastatic Spread	**Problems**	**Assessment Parameters**
Kidney		Hematuria, flank pain, flank mass. Nephrotic syndrome is usually a paraneoplastic syndrome rather than a result of tumor invasion or metastases.
Other	Various problems	Anemia: Dyspnea, weakness, fatigue, tachycardia, headache. Anemia also may be considered a paraneoplastic syndrome.
		Problems of therapy (eg, opioids, corticosteroids, tricyclic antidepressants, radiation, chemotherapy).
		Fatigue, dysphagia, or other debilitating effects of advanced disease.
		Fever of unknown origin (common with liver involvement).
		Cardiac disorders.
		Preexisting problems.

Liver Cancer

Primary liver (hepatic) and biliary passages cancer is the 14th leading cause of cancer death overall with 10,063 deaths in 1993 and an estimated 13,300 deaths in 1998 (American Cancer Society, 1997; Landis et al., 1998). Liver cancer is especially common in persons from sub-Saharan Africa and parts of Asia and is associated with cirrhosis, hepatitis, and other factors (Carr, Flickinger, & Lotze, 1997).

The liver is a common site of metastases from many cancers at other sites. Liver involvement is usually a grim sign, and the extent of hepatic tissue replacement by tumor is the primary prognostic indicator. Signs and symptoms of advanced liver metastases include jaundice, ascites, increased abdominal girth, hepatomegaly, fever, pain, anorexia, fatigue, weight loss, and abdominal fullness (Daly & Kemeny, 1997).

Most primary hepatic tumors are fast-growing hepatocellular carcinomas with a high mortality rate. Most tumor growth is within the liver, and metastases do not always occur. Metastases are usually to lung(s), portal vein, and lymph (Coleman, 1997).

Common symptoms of liver cancer include abdominal pain, epigastric pressure, fullness, and discomfort. Anorexia, weight loss, and fatigue are common, as is hepatosplenomegaly, ascites, jaundice, and fever (Carr et al., 1997; Coleman, 1997).

The PNSs are common in hepatic cell carcinoma. The most important and common are hypoglycemia, erythrocytosis, and hypercholesterolemia (Engstrom, McGlynn, & Hoffman, 1997), Other PNSs include hypercalcemia, dysfibrinogenenemia, carcinoid syndrome, sexual changes, and porphyria cutanea tarda (Carr et al., 1997).

Death from a primary hepatic neoplasm is usually from liver failure (Tabbarah et al., 1995) or related to the wasting and weakness of the disease (Frogge, 1990). In the latter case, patients may develop rapidly progressive pulmonary congestion and pneumonia.

Oncologic emergencies associated with hepatic cancer include **hypercalcemia** and **hypoglycemia** (Carr et al., 1997; Tabbarah et al., 1995) (Table 22-3).

Brain Cancer

Primary brain and CNS cancer is the 10th leading cause of cancer death overall with 11,993 deaths in 1993 and an estimated

TABLE 22-2	Pancreatic Cancer: Spread, Problems, and Assessment	

Metastatic Spread	Problems	Assessment Parameters
Regional extension (see liver and bowel below)	Pain	Abdominal pain is often vague and sometimes intermittent. It may be dull, boring, and worse at night.
		Mid to upper back pain is a result of tumor invasion of the celiac and mesenteric plexus. It may be relieved by sitting up, bending forward, or lying in a curled up position.
	Gastrointestinal symptoms	Early satiety, dyspepsia, xerostomia, jaundice (and pruritus, especially at night), constipation, anorexia, weight loss, cachexia, diarrhea.
		Malabsorption (of fat): Steatorrhea, which includes malodorous fatty stools, bloating, or diarrhea.
Liver	Pain	Pain may be upper right abdominal or nonspecific and is characteristic of visceral pain. Pain may radiate to the right scapula and worsen at night.
	Ascites	Abdominal distension, bulging flanks, fluid wave, weight gain, and discomfort; early satiety, indigestion, decreased bowel mobility (potential for obstruction); dyspnea, orthopnea, and tachypnea; weakness and fatigue; anorexia.
Lung	Dyspnea (see Chapter 14)	Pleural effusion: Dyspnea with cough and chest pain (trachea displacement toward unaffected side with large effusion). Breath sounds are usually decreased but may vary according to area of lung. Pleural effusions are usually unilateral, except when due to heart failure or lymphangitis carcinomatosis.
		Pneumonia: Dyspnea with elevated temperature, chills, purulent or rusty sputum (but not always present), decreased breath sounds. Pleural effusion may also be present. Bone marrow and other transplantations are a risk factors for fungal pulmonary infections.
		Respiratory muscle weakness: Dyspnea with general weakness, anorexia, severe weight loss (cachexia), or the presence of a paraneoplastic syndrome.
Bone	Pain	Pain is usually localized to site(s) of lesion to at least some extent. **Cord compression** is not common in pancreatic cancer.
Lymph	Lymphadenopathy	Lymphedema: Lower extremities, pain; cellulitis, lymphangitis; or enlarged internal nodes may result in pressure or internal structures (vessels or organs).
Other	Paraneoplastic syndromes	Cushing's syndrome and **syndrome of inappropriate antidiuretic hormone secretion:** Personality changes, weight gain, weakness, anorexia, nausea, vomiting, lethargy, seizures, coma.
		Fatigue cachexia, dysphagia, or other debilitating effects of advanced disease.
		Problems of therapy (eg, opioids, corticosteroids, tricyclic antidepressants, radiation, chemotherapy). Fever of unknown origin (common with liver involvement).

TABLE 22-3 Liver Cancer: Spread, Problems, and Assessment

Metastatic Spread	Problems	Assessment Parameters
Liver, regional	Pain	Liver pain may be upper right abdominal or nonspecific, characteristic of visceral pain. It may radiate to right scapula and worsen at night.
	Ascites	Abdominal distension, bulging flanks, fluid wave, weight gain, and discomfort; anorexia, early satiety, indigestion, decreased bowel mobility, dyspnea, orthopnea, tachypnea; weakness, fatigue. Jaundice is common in later stages.
	Bleeding	Bleeding into the peritoneal cavity from vessels of or associated with the liver may occur and be extensive.
	General abdominal symptoms	Epigastric fullness, pressure, discomfort; early satiety, constipation, diarrhea; anorexia, cachexia.
Lung(s)	Dyspnea (see Chapter 14)	Pleural effusion: Dyspnea with cough and chest pain (trachea displacement toward unaffected side with large effusion). Breath sounds are usually decreased but may vary according to area of lung. Pleural effusions are usually unilateral.
		Pneumonia: Dyspnea with elevated temperature, chills, purulent or rusty sputum, decreased breath sounds. Pleural effusion may also be present.
		Respiratory muscle weakness: Dyspnea with general weakness, anorexia, severe weight loss (cachexia), or the presence of a paraneoplastic syndrome.
Lymph	Lymphadenopathy	Regional lymphadenopathy resulting in pressure on viscera or vessels if extensive.
Paraneoplastic syndromes (PNSs)	Hypoglycemia	Sudden onset → sweating, tremors, hunger. Chronic → weakness, fatigue, dizziness, confusion, somnolence, seizures, coma.
	Erythrocytosis (polycythemia)	Elevated hematocrit, hemoglobin, and red blood cell count → hyperviscosity with resulting changes in mentation, headache, fatigue, and dizziness and increased cardiac workload.
	Hypercholesterolemia	Potential for vascular deterioration; risk for heart and other end-organ damage.
		Other PNSs include **hypercalcemia,** carcinoid syndrome, dysfibrinogenaenemia, sexual changes, and porphyria cutanea tarda. Cachexia may be considered a PNS.
Other	Various problems	Weakness, fatigue, cachexia, and muscle wasting are common in liver cancer.
		Fever of unknown origin is sometimes considered a PNS.
		Problems of therapy (eg, opioids, corticosteroids, tricyclic antidepressants, nonsteroidal anti-inflammatory drugs, other cancer treatment).
		Problems related to debilitation.

13,300 deaths in 1998. Brain cancer deaths are about equally divided between women and men (American Cancer Society, 1997, Landis et al, 1998). After leukemia, CNS tumors are the second leading cause of death from childhood cancer. CNS metastases are common with several systemic cancers, notably lung and breast, but also colon, kidney, testis, melanoma, and others. The number of people dying from CNS metastases is more than 10 times the number dying from primary brain tumors (Prados & Wilson, 1997).

Most (malignant) primary brain tumors are astrocytomas and glioblastomas, with the latter being the most malignant stage of astrocytomas (Louis & Cavenee, 1997). These tumors are characterized by local invasiveness and rarely metastasize beyond the CNS (Prados & Wilson, 1997).

While differences in growth rate and other factors exist among the various brain tumors, depending on the location of tumor, problems are generally similar (Table 22-4). Problems of brain cancer (and metastases) are due to one or more of the following (Thapar & Laws, 1995):

● Increased ICP resulting from tumor mass, obstruction of cerebrospinal fluid, or edema
● Destruction or distortion of brain mass
● Compression or distortion of cranial nerves
● Electrochemical changes leading to seizures

General problems of brain cancer include headache, nausea, vomiting, seizures, or

TABLE 22-4	Brain Cancer: Spread, Problems, and Assessment	
Metastatic Spread	**Problems**	**Assessment Parameters**
Local extension	General central nervous system (CNS) symptoms	**Increased intracranial pressure** (ICP): Headache is usually present and may be more severe in the morning. Classic triad of increased ICP = papilledema (often with visual changes), vomiting, and headache. In adults, projectile vomiting indicates a rapid increase in ICP. Disequilibrium may also occur.
		Seizures are most often focal (partial) or partial complex versus grand mal or tonic-clonic generalized seizures.
	Site-specific CNS symptoms	Frontal lobes: Changes in mental status, aphasia, hemiparesis.
		Temporal lobe: Changes in speech, memory, and perception (hearing , vision, taste, and hallucinations in some cases); seizures.
		Parietal lobe: Changes (sometimes dramatic) in sensation.
		Occipital lobe: Sensory changes, including hallucinations, inability to recognize familiar people or objects, visual changes, seizures.
		Thalamus: Increased ICP, hemiparesis, pain syndromes.
		Hypothalamus: Endocrine changes (eg, diabetes, acromegaly, Cushing's syndrome, syndrome of inappropriate antidiuretic hormone secretion).
		Cerebellum: Coordination and motor changes.
		Brain stem: Cranial nerve deficits and extremity weakness.
		Spinal cord: Neurologic deficits, including extremity weakness, ataxia, urine retention, bowel dysfunction, numbness.
		Meninges (usually metastases): Neurologic dysfunction, including seizures and mental changes.
Other	Various problems	Fatigue, cachexia, dysphagia, or other debilitating effects of advanced disease.
		Problems of therapy, especially corticosteroids and long-term effects of other treatment.

changes in consciousness or personality. Headaches are usually associated with increased ICP, so they may be more severe in the morning, aggravated by actions that increase ICP (eg, straining, coughing), and accompanied by papilledema (often with visual changes), nausea, and vomiting. Projectile vomiting is associated with rapid increase in ICP. Only about 30% of patients with brain tumors develop seizures, sometimes late in the course of illness (Prados & Wilson, 1997). Specific problems of brain cancer depend largely on the site of the tumor (Belford, 1997).

Early identification of developing problems in advanced brain cancer may not lend itself as satisfactorily to early intervention as with some other tumors. Treatment options may be limited, especially in patients who have already received multimodality treatment. Nevertheless, early clinical identification of disease progression should be attempted and will in some cases result in symptom relief.

Oncologic emergencies associated with brain tumors are **increased ICP** and **spinal cord compression**.

REFERENCES

American Cancer Society. (1997). *Cancer facts and figures*. Atlanta: Author.

Arcasoy, S. M., & Jett, J. R. (1997). Superior pulmonary sulcus tumors and Pancoast's syndrome. *New England Journal of Medicine, 337*(19), 1370–1376.

Belford, K. (1997). Central nervous system cancers. In S. I. Groenwald, M. H. Frogge, M. Goodman, & C. H. Yarbro (Eds.), *Cancer nursing: Principles and practice* (4th ed.) (pp. 980–1035). Boston: Jones and Bartlett.

Carr, B. I., Flickinger, J. C., & Lotze, M. T. (1997). Hepatobiliary cancers. In V. T. DeVita, S. Hellman, & S. A. Rosenberg (Eds.), *Cancer: Principles and practice of oncology* (5th ed.) (pp. 1087–1114). Philadelphia: Lippincott-Raven.

Chernecky, C. C., & Krech-Fritskey, R. (1996). Complications of advanced disease. In R. McCorckle, M. Grant, M. Frank-Stromberg, & S. B. Baird (Eds.), *Cancer nursing* (2nd ed.) (pp. 1145–1156). Philadelphia: W.B. Saunders.

Coleman, J. (1997). Esophageal, stomach, liver, gallbladder, and pancreatic cancers. In S. I. Groenwald, M. H. Frogge, M. Goodman, & C. H. Yarbro (Eds.), *Cancer nursing: Principles and practice* (4th ed.) (pp. 1082–1144). Boston: Jones and Bartlett.

Daly, J. M., & Kemeny, N. E. (1997). Metastatic cancer to the liver. In V. T. DeVita, S. Hellman, & S. A. Rosenberg (Eds.), *Cancer: Principles and practice of oncology* (5th ed.) (pp. 2551–2570). Philadelphia: Lippincott-Raven.

Engstrom, P. F., McGlynn, K., & Hoffman, J. P. (1997). Primary neoplasms of the liver. In J. F. Holland, R. C. Bast, D. L. Morton, E. Frei, D. W. Kufe, & R. C. Weichselbaum (Eds.), *Cancer medicine* (4th ed.) (pp. 1923–1938). Baltimore: Williams & Wilkins.

Evans, D. B., Abbruzzese, J. L., & Rich, T. A. (1997). Cancer of the pancreas. In V. T. DeVita, S. Hellman, & S. A. Rosenberg (Eds.), *Cancer: Principles and practice of oncology* (5th ed.) (pp. 1054–1087). Philadelphia: Lippincott-Raven.

Frogge, M. H. (1990). Gastrointestinal cancer: Esophagus, stomach, liver, and pancreas. In S. L. Groenwald, M. H. Frogge, M. Goodman, & C. H. Yarbro (Eds.), *Cancer nursing: Principles and practice* (3rd ed.) (pp. 806–844). Boston: Jones and Bartlett.

Ginsberg, R. J., Vokes, E. E., & Raben, A. (1997). Non-small cell lung cancer. In V. T. DeVita, S. Hellman, & S. A. Rosenberg (Eds.), *Cancer: Principles and practice of oncology* (5th ed.) (pp. 858–911). Philadelphia: Lippincott-Raven.

Glick, J. H., & Glover, D. (1995). Oncologic emergencies. In G. P. Murphy, W. Lawrence, & R. E. Lenhard (Eds.), *Clinical oncology* (2nd ed.) (pp. 597–618). Altanta: American Cancer Society.

Haapoja, I. S. (1997). Paraneoplastic syndromes. In S. I. Groenwald, M. H. Frogge, M. Goodman, & C. H. Yarbro (Eds.), *Cancer nursing: Principles and practice* (4th ed.) (pp. 702–720). Boston: Jones and Bartlett.

Harwood, K. (1996). Non-small cell lung cancer: An overview of diagnosis, staging, and treatment. *Seminars in Oncology Nursing, 12*(4), 285–294.

Hilderley, L. J. (1996). Radiation therapy for lung cancer. *Seminars in Oncology Nursing, 12*(4), 304–311.

Humphrey, E. W., Ward, H. B., & Perri, R. T. (1995). Lung cancer. In G. P. Murphy, W. Lawrence, & R.

E. Lenhard (Eds.), *Clinical oncology* (2nd ed.) (pp. 220–235). Altanta: American Cancer Society.

Ingle, R. J. (1997). Lung cancers. In S. I. Groenwald, M. H. Frogge, M. Goodman, & C. H. Yarbro (Eds.), *Cancer nursing: Principles and practice* (4th ed.) (pp. 1260–1290). Boston: Jones and Bartlett.

Krech, R. L., & Walsh, T. D. (1991). Symptoms of pancreatic cancer. *Journal of Pain and Symptom Management, 6*(6), 360–367.

Landis, S. H., Murray, T., Bolden, S., & Wingo, P. A. (1998). Cancer statistics, 1998. *CA—A Cancer Journal for Clinicians, 48*(1), 6–29.

Louis, D. N., & Cavenee, W. K. (1997). Molecular biology of central nervous systems neoplasms. In V. T. DeVita, S. Hellman, & S. A. Rosenberg (Eds.), *Cancer: Principles and practice of oncology* (5th ed.) (pp. 2013–2022). Philadelphia: Lippincott-Raven.

Martin, V. R., & Comis, R. L. (1996). Small cell carcinoma of the lung: An updated overview. *Seminars in Oncology Nursing, 12*(4), 295–303.

Ottery, F. D., & McLaughlin-Hagan, M. (1996). Gastric and related cancers. In R. McCorckle, M. Grant, M. Frank-Stromberg, & S. B. Baird (Eds.), *Cancer nursing* (2nd ed.) (pp. 634–651). Philadelphia: W.B. Saunders.

Prados, M. D., & Wilson, C. B. (1997). Neoplasms of the central nervous system. In J. F. Holland, R. C. Bast, D. L. Morton, E. Frei, D. W. Kufe, & R. C. Weichselbaum (Eds.), *Cancer Medicine* (4th ed.) (pp. 1471–1514). Baltimore: Williams & Wilkins.

Tabbarah, H. J., Lowitz, B. B., & Livingston, R. B. (1995). Lung cancer. In D. A. Casciato & B. B. Lowitz (Eds.), *Manual of clinical oncology* (pp. 133–144). Boston: Little, Brown and Company.

Thapar, K., & Laws, E. R. (1995). Tumors of the central nervous system. In G. P. Murphy, W. Lawrence, & R. E. Lenhard (Eds.), *Clinical oncology* (2nd ed.) (pp. 198–219). Altanta: American Cancer Society.

Wachtel, T., Allen-Masterson, S., Reuben, D., Goldberg, R., & Mor, V. (1988). The end stage cancer patient: Terminal common pathway. *The Hospice Journal, 4*(4), 4380.

Weiss, L. (1992). Comments on hematogenous metastatic patterns in humans as revealed by autopsy. *Clinical and Experimental Metastasis, 10*(3), 191–199.

CHAPTER 23

Female Reproductive Cancer (Breast, Ovarian, Uterine): Metastatic Spread, Common Symptoms, and Assessment

Breast Cancer

Breast cancer is the second leading cause of cancer death among women, with 43,555 deaths among women and 355 deaths among men in 1993. It is estimated that there will be 43,900 deaths from breast cancer in 1998 (American Cancer Society, 1997; Landis, Murray, Bolden, & Wingo, 1998). The mean time from diagnosis to death from breast cancer is 6.7 years, and most fatal breast cancers are unilateral invasive ductal carcinomas (Haskell & Casciato, 1995).

Metastatic spread is often detected first in regional (especially sentinel) lymph, but distal metastases may already have occurred or may occur without evidence of lymph involvement (Dowlatshahi, Fan, Snider, & Habib, 1997). There is great variation in tumor growth rate (doubling time) and clinical course in breast cancer. Breast cancer does not metastasize to a single focus (Henderson, 1995), so the norm in advanced disease is multiple sites of metastases and multiple problems. The most common significant sites of distal metastases (on autopsy) are liver, lung, and bone (>60%) and thyroid and brain (>20%). The most common sites of bone metastases are the red marrow of the axial skeleton, proximal ends of long bones, ribs, and vertebral column (Mundy, 1997). Other sites of metastases include (but are not limited to) in descending order of frequency skin, kid-

ney, skeletal muscle, and heart. Of the cancers with highest morbidity and mortality, breast cancer is the most likely to metastasize to skin (19.5%) and after primary bone cancer, second most likely to metastasize to skeletal muscle (Weiss, 1992).

Pain is more common among patients with breast cancer than most other primary sites, perhaps because of its high incidence (second only to prostate cancer) of bone metastasis (Wachtel, Allen-Masterson, Reuben, Goldberg, & Mor, 1988). Pain, pathologic fractures, lymphedema, skin lesions and sequelae of liver, lung, and other metastasis present difficult clinical challenges. Pathologic fractures, central nervous system symptoms, malignant pleural effusions, and uremia are common clinical problems. Paraneoplastic problems associated with advanced breast cancer include acanthosis nigricans, neuromuscular disorders, and hypercalcemia (Haskell & Casciato, 1995).

Exact figures are not available, but it is known that patients with breast cancer often die from infection and after patients with melanoma, are more likely to die from carcinomatosis (Inagaki, Rodriguez, & Bodey, 1974). Haskell, Giuliano, Thompson, and Zarem (1990, p. 129) report that about 50% of clients with breast cancer die from "the malignant process itself."

The oncologic emergencies most common in patients with breast cancer are **pericardial**

DEBORA HUNTER

effusion leading to cardiac tamponade, **increased intracranial pressure** (including from carcinomatosis meningitis), **spinal cord compression, airway obstruction, disseminated intravascular coagulation,** and **hypercalcemia** (Glick & Glover, 1995; Waller & Caroline, 1996). **Hypercalcemia** and **spinal cord compression** are the most common oncologic emergencies in breast cancer (Waller & Caroline, 1996) (Table 23-1).

Ovarian Cancer

Ovarian cancer is the ninth leading cause of cancer death overall and fifth leading cause of cancer death in women. There were 12,870 deaths from ovarian cancer in 1993, and the estimation of deaths in 1998 is 14,500. Ovarian cancer results in the greatest number of cancer deaths from gynecologic cancer but after uterine (endometrial) cancer is the second most common gynecologic cancer (American Cancer Society, 1997; Landis et al., 1998).

About 85% of ovarian tumors are one of several epithelial cell types. Metastasis is primarily through intraperitoneal seeding to the liver, diaphragm, bladder, small bowel, and large bowel. Other common sites of metastasis include bone and lung. Involvement of pelvic and abdominal lymph is common and can result in the accumulation of malignant ascitic fluid (Clark, 1997; Weiss, 1992).

Metastatic Spread	Problems	Assessment Parameters
Bone	Pain without pathologic fracture	Bone pain is usually localized to some extent and may be described as constant, aching, gnawing, sharp. It is often worse at night and may not be relieved by lying down. Pain may also be from other processes.
	Pathologic fracture	Severe, sharp, localized pain. Spinal cord compression from pathologic fracture is possible.
		Spinal cord compression (from pathologic fracture or compression of cord without fracture): Back pain is the first symptom and may be local (somatic: constant, dull, aching), radicular, or both. It is exacerbated by movement, neck flexion, straight leg raising and is decreased by sitting up. It is tender to percussion. Neurologic deficits usually follow pain. They may begin subtly and include extremity weakness, ataxia, stumbling; urine retention, bowel dysfunction, numbness.
	Metabolic changes	**Hypercalcemia** (often nonspecific): Symptoms include fatigue, weakness, anorexia, nausea, polyuria, polydipsia, and constipation, progressing to changes in mentation, seizures, coma.
Regional lymph and structures	Lymphadenopathy	Involvement of lymph nodes may result in lymphadema (subcutaneous) with edema, pain, cellulitis, or lymphangitis. Enlarged internal nodes may result in pressure on internal structures, such as vessels (eg, superior vena cava).
	Cardiac changes (also see metastases to heart below)	**Superior vena cava syndrome:** Dilated neck or thoracic veins; facial edema, plethora; tachypnea; cyanosis; edema upper extremities; cough, hoarseness.
		Pericardial effusion → Cardiac tamponade: Retrosternal chest pain relieved by sitting forward; orthopnea; cough; tachypnea; tachycardia; decreased cardiac output (decreased cerebral blood, peripheral cyanosis, decreased systolic and pulse pressures, pulsus paradoxus); occasional nausea and vomiting and abdominal pain.
Liver	Pain	Pain may be upper right abdominal or nonspecific and characteristic of visceral pain. It may radiate to right scapula and worsen at night
	Ascites	Abdominal distension, bulging flanks, fluid wave, weight gain, and discomfort; anorexia, early satiety, indigestion, decreased bowel mobility; dyspnea, orthopnea, tachypnea; weakness, fatigue.
Lung(s)	Dyspnea, cough, hemoptysis (multiple etiologies) (see Chapter 14)	Pleural effusion: Dyspnea with cough and chest pain (trachea displacement toward unaffected side with large effusion). Breath sounds are usually decreased but may vary according to area of lung. Pleural effusions are usually unilateral.
		Pneumonia: Dyspnea with elevated temperature, chills, purulent or rusty sputum, decreased breath sounds. Pleural effusion may also be present.
		Embolus: Sudden onset of dyspnea with rapid breathing, rapid heart rate, cough, chest pain, and blood in sputum.
		Obstruction: Progressive or rapidly increasing dyspnea, blood in sputum, noisy breathing, chronic cough, choking, or pneumonia.
		Preexisting conditions, such as chronic obstructure pulmonary disease or ascites may also cause dyspnea.
Brain, meninges	Central nervous system (CNS) symptoms	**Increased intracranial pressure** (ICP): Progressive pain is usually present and may be more severe in the morning. Classic triad of increased ICP = papilledema (often with visual changes), vomiting, and headache.
		Confusion, seizures, or other CNS problems may also result from brain metastases (see Chapter 13).

TABLE 23-1	Breast Cancer: Spread, Problems, and Assessment *(Continued)*

Metastatic Spread	Problems	Assessment Parameters
Skin	Lesions	Metastatic lesions are often painful and have an unpleasant odor. Skin lesions may also be due to inflammatory carcinoma, Paget's disease, or ulceration from underlying disease.
Heart	Cardiac changes	Arrhythmias, congestive heart failure; see pericardial effusion and cardiac tamponade.
Kidney	Genitourinary symptoms	Hematuria, flank pain, flank mass. Nephrotic syndrome is usually a paraneoplastic syndrome rather than a result of tumor invasion or metastases.
	Uremia	Decreased urine, changes in blood pressure, congestive heart failure, stomatitis, nausea and vomiting, gastrointestinal bleeding, bowel changes, lethargy, changes in mentation.
Thyroid	Regional changes	Thyroid nodules, hoarseness, dysphagia; stridor; lymphadenopathy.
Other	Various problems	Anemia from several potential etiologies: Weakness, anorexia, headache, tachycardia.
		Paraneoplastic syndromes, including acanthosis nigricans, neuromuscular disorders, and hypercalcemia.
		Fatigue cachexia, dysphagia, or other debilitating effects of advanced disease.
		Problems of therapy (eg, opioids, corticosteroids, antidepressants, radiation, chemotherapy).
		Disseminated intravascular coagulation.
		Fever of unknown origin (common with liver involvement).
		Infection is a frequent cause of death. Carcinomatosis is more common in breast cancer than with any other tumor except for melanoma.

Frequently encountered problems of advanced ovarian cancer include problems of the respiratory, gastrointestinal, and genitourinary (GU) systems. Ascites and pleural effusion are very common. Cachexia, nausea and vomiting, and constipation are common and may be due to the extensive abdominal involvement or more specific problems, such as intestinal obstruction. Changes in peristalsis and absorption may develop from adhesions among the bowel loops or from metastases to the mesentery causing dysfunction of autonomic innervation (Berek, Dembo, & Ozols, 1993). In a study of patients with intestinal obstruction at St. Christopher's Hospice, patients with primary ovarian cancer exceeded all other patients combined (>50%) in a diagnosis of obstruction (Baines, 1990).

The pelvis is often filled with tumor or peritoneal carcinomatosis; therefore, pelvic or perineal pain (mix of neuropathic, visceral, and somatic pain) is common as are GU tract problems, including ureteral obstruction with uremia and vagina bleeding. Lymphatic and venous obstruction lead to pedal and genital edema and contribute to other obstructive processes and pain. Invasion of rectum or bladder results in bleeding, sloughing of tumor into bowel or urine, and bowel or bladder outlet obstruction (Farias-Eisner, Walker, & Berek, 1995; Ozols, Schwartz, & Eifel, 1997).

Paraneoplastic syndromes are commonly associated with ovarian cancer (Farias-Eisner et al., 1995) and may include neurologic syndromes (most frequently peripheral neuropathies, dementia, amyotrophic lateral sclerosislike syndrome, and cerebellar ataxia),

TABLE 23-2	Ovarian Cancer: Spread, Problems, and Assessment	
Metastatic Spread	**Problems**	**Assessment Parameters**
Intraperitoneal seeding to large and small bowel, mesentery	Obstruction	Intestinal obstruction: Nausea and vomiting, intestinal colic, other abdominal pain, diarrhea.
	Other gastrointestinal (GI) symptoms	Nausea and vomiting, anorexia, cachexia; changes in peristalsis, absorption, or innervation of the GI system. Constipation or less frequently, diarrhea. Abdominal distension is common.
Regional lymph, other structures	Lymphadenopathy	Lymphedema (area of lower extremities): Pain, cellulitis, lymphangitis, occasionally genital edema; pressure on internal structures.
	Obstruction	**Obstructive uropathy** (ureteral from tumor or lymphadenopathy): Hesitancy, urgency, nocturia, frequency, decreased force of stream, polyuria alternating with oliguria.
	Uremia	Oliguria or anuria, fatigue, headache, anorexia, nausea and vomiting, fetid breath, changes in mentation.
	Perineal pain	Severe pain; most often neuropathic but also mixed neuropathic with visceral or somatic.
		Other genitourinary symptoms, including vaginal bleeding; blood or tumor sloughing into urine or bowel.
Liver	Pain	Pain may be upper right abdominal or nonspecific and characteristic of visceral pain. Pain may radiate to the right scapula and worsen at night.
	Ascites	Abdominal distension, bulging flanks, fluid wave, weight gain, and discomfort; anorexia, early satiety, indigestion, decreased bowel mobility (potential for obstruction); dyspnea, orthopnea, and tachypnea; weakness and fatigue, pruritus.
Lung or diaphragm	Dyspnea, other pulmonary symptoms (see Chapter 14)	Pleural effusion: Dyspnea with cough and chest pain (trachea displacement toward unaffected side with large effusion). Breath sounds are usually decreased but may vary according to area of lung. Pleural effusions are usually unilateral, except when due to heart failure or lymphangitis carcinomatosis.
		Pneumonia: Dyspnea with elevated temperature, chills, purulent or rusty sputum (but not always present), decreased breath sounds. Pleural effusion may also be present. Bone marrow and other transplantations are a risk factors for fungal pulmonary infections.
		Obstruction (from tumor, lymphadenopathy): Progressive or rapidly increasing dyspnea, blood in sputum, noisy breathing, chronic cough, choking, or pneumonia.
		Pulmonary embolus: Sudden onset of dyspnea with rapid breathing, rapid heart rate, cough, chest pain, and blood in sputum.
		Respiratory muscle weakness: Dyspnea with general weakness, anorexia, severe weight loss (cachexia), or the presence of a paraneoplastic syndrome.
		Atelectasis: Dyspnea with tachypnea, decreased chest wall movement unilaterally, deviation of apical impulse and trachea, varying breath sounds but decreased on affected side.
		Preexisting or concurrent conditions, such as chronic obstructive pulmonary disease or ascites, may contribute to dyspnea.

(continued)

TABLE 23-2	Ovarian Cancer: Spread, Problems, and Assessment *(Continued)*	
Metastatic Spread	**Problems**	**Assessment Parameters**
Bone	Pain	Bone pain is usually localized, constant, dull, aching, or sharp and is worse at night.
		Spinal cord compression from pathologic fracture is possible but not common in ovarian cancer.
Paraneoplastic syndromes (PNSs)	Neurologic PNSs	Peripheral neuropathies, dementia, amyotrophic lateral sclerosislike syndrome, and cerebellar ataxia.
	Other PNSs	Cushing's syndrome, **hypercalcemia,** and thrombophlebitis.
Other	Various problems	Fatigue cachexia, dysphagia, or other debilitating effects of advanced disease.
		Problems of therapy (eg, opioids, corticosteroids, tricyclic antidepressants, radiation, chemotherapy). Fever of unknown origin (common with liver involvement).

Cushing's syndrome, hypercalcemia, and thrombophlebitis.

Death is often from infection (septicemia or pneumonia), electrolyte imbalance, or cardiovascular collapse (Inagaki et al., 1974; Walczak, Klemm, & Guarnieri, 1997).

The oncologic emergencies most often associated with ovarian cancer are **obstructive uropathy** (ureteral obstruction) and **bronchial obstruction** (Glick & Glover, 1995) (Table 23-2).

Uterine Cancer

Uterine or endometrial cancer is the 18th leading cause of cancer death overall and sixth leading cause of cancer death in women. There were 6098 deaths in 1993 and the estimated number of deaths in 1998 is 6300. While uterine cancer is the most common gynecologic cancer, it results in fewer fatalities than ovarian, the second most common gynecologic cancer (American Cancer Society, 1997; Landis et al., 1998).

The most common endometrial cancer (of the corpus uteri or uterine body) is endometroid adenocarcinoma. Other adenocarcinoma cell types and other endometrial cancers (eg, sarcomas) tend to have a less favorable prognosis. Endometrial cancer spreads by invasion of the myometrium (the smooth muscle coat of the uterus) to the bladder, cervix, vagina, and elsewhere and by metastases to the peritoneum, lymph, and adnexa (ovaries and uterine tubes). Kidneys, brain, bone, and lungs may also be involved (Cohen & Thomas, 1997; Weiss, 1992).

TABLE 23-3	Uterine Cancer: Spread, Problems, and Assessment	
Metastatic Spread	**Problems**	**Assessment Parameters**
Primary tumor growth and regional spread by way of extension or seeding	Pelvic/perineal pain	Severe pain; most often neuropathic but also mixed neuropathic with visceral or somatic.
	Pelvic structure involvement (also see kidney, below)	Fistulas: Perirectal, rectovaginal, and others.
		Bladder, urinary dysfunction.
		Vaginal tumors: Fungating, ulcerative, or invasive; vaginal bleeding (sometimes heavy).

(continued)

TABLE 23-3 Uterine Cancer: Spread, Problems, and Assessment *(Continued)*

Metastatic Spread	Problems	Assessment Parameters
	Abdominal pain	Visceral, deep squeezing pain.
	Obstruction, other abdominal symptoms	Intestinal obstruction: Nausea and vomiting, intestinal colic, other abdominal pain, diarrhea; constipation.
		Obstruction or dysfunction of other structures is possible (eg, kidney, bladder). Peritoneal effusion may occur.
		Jaundice, pruritius.
Lymph	Lymphadenopathy	Lymphedema of lower extremities. Pain; cellulitis, lymphangitis; obstruction of or pressure on internal structures.
Liver	Pain	Pain may be upper right abdominal or nonspecific and is characteristic of visceral pain. Pain may radiate to the right scapula and worsen at night.
	Ascites	Abdominal distension, bulging flanks, fluid wave, weight gain, and discomfort; anorexia, early satiety, indigestion, decreased bowel mobility (potential for obstruction); dyspnea, orthopnea, and tachypnea; weakness and fatigue.
Lungs	Dyspnea, other respiratory symptoms (see Chapter 14)	Pleural effusion: Dyspnea with cough and chest pain (trachea displacement toward unaffected side with large effusion). Breath sounds are usually decreased but may vary according to area of lung. Pleural effusions are usually unilateral.
		Pneumonia: Dyspnea with elevated temperature, chills, purulent or rusty sputum, decreased breath sounds. Pleural effusion may also be present.
		Embolus: Sudden onset of dyspnea with rapid breathing, rapid heart rate, cough, chest pain, and blood in sputum.
		Preexisting conditions, such as chronic obstructive pulmonary disease or ascites may also cause dyspnea.
Brain	Central nervous system (CNS) symptoms	**Increased intracranial pressure** (ICP): Progressive pain is usually present and may be more severe in the morning. Classic triad of increased ICP = papilledema (often with visual changes), vomiting, and headache.
		Confusion, seizures, or other CNS problems may also result from brain metastases (see Chapter 13).
Kidney	Genitourinary symptoms	Hematuria, flank pain, flank mass. Nephrotic syndrome is usually a paraneoplastic syndrome rather than a result of tumor invasion or metastases.
	Uremia	Decreased urine, changes blood pressure, CHF, stomatitis, nausea and vomiting, gastrointestinal bleeding, bowel changes, lethargy, changes in mentation.
Bone	Pain	Pain is usually localized at least to some extent. Spinal cord compression from pathologic fractures of the spine is possible. Pain may be associated with other processes.
	Various problems	Fatigue cachexia, dysphagia, anemia, or other debilitating effects of advanced disease.
		Problems of therapy (eg, opioids, corticosteroids, tricyclic antidepressants, radiation, chemotherapy).

The presence of widespread pelvic disease often presents challenges in management. Pelvic or perineal pain from invasion of structures and nerve plexi may be a mix of neuropathic, visceral, and somatic pains. Fistulas, vaginal tumors, and skin breakdown may develop and be very difficult to manage. Bowel obstruction, ascites, jaundice, and respiratory distress may develop (Averette & Nguyen, 1995; Cohen & Thomas, 1997).

There are no oncologic emergencies typically associated with uterine cancer (Glick & Glover, 1995) (Table 23-3).

REFERENCES

American Cancer Society. (1997). *Cancer facts and figures*. Atlanta: Author.

Averette, H. E., & Nguyen, H. (1995). Gynecologic cancer. In G. P. Murphy, W. Lawrence, & R. E. Lenhard (Eds.), *Clinical oncology* (2nd ed.) (pp. 552–579). Atlanta: American Cancer Society.

Baines, M. J. (1990). Management of malignant intestinal obstruction in patients with advanced cancer. In K. M. Foley, J. J. Bonica, & V. Ventafridda (Eds.), *Advances in pain research and therapy, Volume 16: Proceedings of the Second International Congress on Cancer Pain* (pp. 327–335). New York: Raven Press.

Berek, J. S., Dembo, A., & Ozols, R. F. (1993). Ovarian cancer. In J. F. Holland, E. Frei, R. C. Bast, D. W. Kufe, D. L. Morton, & R. W. Weischselbaum (Eds.), *Cancer medicine* (3rd ed.) (pp. 1659–1690). Philadelphia: Lea & Febiger.

Clark, J. C. (1997). Gynecologic cancers. In S. E. Otto (Ed.), *Oncology nursing* (3rd ed.) (pp. 196–226). St. Louis: C.V. Mosby.

Cohen, C. J., & Thomas, G. M. (1997) Endometrial cancer. . In J. F. Holland, R. C. Bast, D. L. Morton, E. Frei, D. W. Kufe, & R. C. Weichselbaum (Eds.), *Cancer medicine* (4th ed.) (pp. 2263–2280). Baltimore: Williams & Wilkins.

Dowlatshahi, K., Fan, M., Snider, H. C., & Habib, F. A. (1997). Lymph node micrometastases from breast carcinoma. *Cancer, 80*(8), 1188–1197.

Farias-Eisner, R. P., Walker, D. L., & Berek, J. S. (1995). Gynecologic cancers. In D. A. Casciato & B. B. Lowitz (Eds.), *Manual of clinical oncology* (pp. 200–227). Boston: Little, Brown and Company.

Glick, J. H., & Glover, D. (1995). Oncologic emergencies. In G. P. Murphy, W. Lawrence, & R. E. Lenhard (Eds.), *Clinical oncology* (2nd ed.) (pp. 597–618). Atlanta: American Cancer Society.

Haskell, C. M., & Casciato, D. A. (1995). Breast cancer. In D. A. Casciato & B. B. Lowitz (Eds.), *Manual of clinical oncology* (pp. 183–199). Boston: Little, Brown and Company.

Haskell, C. M., Giuliano, A. E., Thompson, R. W., & Zarem, H. A. (1990). Breast cancer. In C. M. Haskell (Ed.), *Cancer treatment* (3rd ed.) (pp. 123–164). Philadelphia: W.B. Saunders.

Henderson, I. C. (1995). Breast cancer. In G. P. Murphy, W. Lawrence, & R. E. Lenhard (Eds.), *Clinical oncology* (pp. 198–219). Atlanta: American Cancer Society.

Inagaki, J., Rodriguez, V., & Bodey, G. P. (1974). Causes of death in cancer patients. *Cancer, 33*(2), 568–573.

Landis, S. H., Murray, T., Bolden, S., & Wingo, P. A. (1998). Cancer statistics, 1998. *CA—A Cancer Journal for Clinicians, 48*(1), 6–29.

Mundy, G. R. (1997). Mechanisms of bone metastasis. *Cancer, 80*(8), 1546–1556.

Ozols, R. F., Schwartz, P. E., & Eifel, P. J. (1997). Ovarian cancer, fallopian tube carcinoma, and peritoneal carcinoma. In V. T. DeVita, S. Hellman, & S. A. Rosenberg (Eds.), *Cancer: Principles and practice of oncology* (5th ed.) (pp. 1502–1539). Philadelphia: Lippincott-Raven.

Wachtel, T., Allen-Masterson, S. Reuben, D. Goldberg, R, & Mor, V. (1988). The end stage cancer patient: Terminal common pathway. *The Hospice Journal, 4*(4), 4380.

Walczak, J. R., Klemm, P. R., & Guarnieri, C. (1997). Gynecologic cancers. In S. I. Groenwald, M. H. Frogge, M. Goodman, & C. H. Yarbro (Eds.), *Cancer nursing: Principles and practice* (4th ed.) (pp. 1145–1198). Boston: Jones and Bartlett.

Waller, A., & Caroline, N. L. (1996). *Handbook of palliative care in cancer*. Boston: Butterworth-Heinemann.

Weiss, L. (1992). Comments on hematogenous metastatic patterns in humans as revealed by autopsy. *Clinical and Experimental Metastasis, 10*(3), 191–199.

CHAPTER 24

Gastrointestinal Cancer (Colorectal, Stomach, Esophageal, and Oral): Metastatic Spread, Common Symptoms, and Assessment

Colorectal Cancer

Colorectal cancer is the second leading cause of cancer death overall, with 57,405 deaths in 1993 and an estimated 54,900 deaths in 1997 (46,600 colon and 8,300 rectum). Estimated deaths for 1998 are expected to total 56,500. Colorectal cancer deaths are about equally divided between women and men (American Cancer Society [ACS], 1997; Landis et al., 1998).

Almost 60% of primary colorectal tumors are in the left or descending colon, sigmoid colon, or rectosigmoid. The most common tumor type found in the colon is adenocarcinoma, and in the appendix, rectum, and small bowel, carcinoid tumors are common. Tumors of the anus are commonly epidermoid or cloagenic tumors (Steele, 1995). Metastatic spread (except for carcinoid tumors) is to regional lymph (perineal, inguinal, retroperineal). Distal sites are primarily liver, lung, and bone, with liver metastases nearly always preceding lung metastases (Weiss, 1992). Adjacent structures may also be invaded, causing such problems as rectovaginal fistulas or pelvic pain or tenesmus (Jessup, Menck, Fremgen, & Winchester, 1997).

Many patients with colorectal cancer have a colostomy, and the combination of colostomy, cachexia, and other processes of advanced cancer result in significant challenges in care. With or without a colostomy, bowel problems are common. Bowel obstruction occurs most frequently with tumors of the descending and sigmoid colon (Steele, 1995). A significant number of patients with colorectal cancer develop widespread metastases to pelvic organs and nerve plexi, with an attendant difficult-to-manage mix of neuropathic, visceral, and somatic perineal pain.

Steele (1995) has developed a helpful guide showing expected variations in symptoms in colon and rectal cancer:

- Ascending (right) colon cancer is characterized by ill-defined pain, brick-red bleeding, weakness, and infrequent obstruction.
- Descending (left) colon cancer is characterized by colicky pain (worsened by eating), red blood mixed with stool, infrequent weakness, and frequent obstruction.
- Rectal cancer is characterized by steady, gnawing pain, bright red blood coating stool, infrequent weakness, and infrequent obstruction.

Perforation (usually through the tumor) also occurs and carries a significantly increased risk of death (Jessup et al., 1997).

The systemic effects of carcinoid tumors usually occur only when there is liver metastasis. Symptoms, which vary according to tumor site, include flushing, diarrhea, bronchoconstrictions, enlarged and painful liver, and cardiac lesions. Bowel obstruction from fibrosis of the mesentery cannot be treated surgically (Carlson, Lowitz, & Casciato, 1995).

Most patients with colorectal cancer die (listed in descending order) from infection, septicemia, pneumonia, and peritonitis, and patients with colorectal cancer are more likely to die from hemorrhage than any other cause (Inagaki, Rodriguez, & Bodey, 1974).

The oncologic emergency most often associated with colorectal tumors is **obstructive uropathy** (Glick & Glover, 1995) (Table 24-1).

Stomach Cancer

Stomach or gastric cancer is the eighth leading cause of cancer death in women and men. It occurs more often in men than women (8:5). There were 13,850 deaths in 1993, and the estimation of deaths in 1998 is 13,700 (ACS, 1997; Landis et al, 1998).

Most stomach cancers are adenocarcinomas. Metastasis is primarily through the lymphatic system, but also directly through the stomach wall to adjacent organs (liver, pancreas, intestine) or mesentery, through blood, and direct seeding of the peritoneum. Lung, bone, and brain metastases may also occur (Coleman, 1997; Weiss, 1992).

The major problems of stomach cancer are usually directly related to the primary tumor and include constant abdominal pain, pain after eating, nausea and vomiting, belching, early satiety, distaste for meat, regurgitation, dysphagia, and dyspepsia. Anemia, jaundice, weakness, and fatigue are common. Anorexia and weight loss are sometimes related to decreased gastric function, pain, and other problems of advanced disease. Cachexia is common in advanced disease. Other problems of advanced gastric cancer include peritoneal and pleural effusions, high obstruction (stomach to small bowel), and bleeding. Hematemesis, melanemesis, or melena may occur (Coleman, 1997; Tabbarah, 1995).

The types of paraneoplastic syndromes associated with stomach cancer include acanthosis nigricans, dermatomyositis, polymyositis, circinate erythemas, dementia, cerebellar ataxia, thrombophlebitis, Cushing's syndrome, paraneoplastic chorionic gonadotropin secretion, and cachexia (Huapoja, 1997; Tabbarah, 1995).

The oncologic emergencies most often associated with stomach cancer are **increased intracranial pressure** and **cardiac tamponade** (Glick & Glover, 1995) (Table 24-2).

Esophageal Cancer

Carcinoma of the esophagus is the 12th leading cause of cancer death overall, with a male-to-female ratio of approximately 3:1. In 1993, there were 10,450 deaths from carcinoma of the esophagus, and the estimated number of deaths in 1998 is 11,900 (ACS, 1997; Landis et al., 1998).

The most common tumor type in esophageal cancer is squamous cell in the upper and middle sections of the esophagus and increasingly adenocarcinoma in the thoracic esophagus (ie, below the clavicles), where most esophageal cancers occur (Ellis, Huberman, & Busse, 1995). Both squamous cell carcinomas and adenocarcinomas may take different forms, including malignant ulcer (site of hemorrhage), circumferential stricture, or mass within the esophageal lumen (Skinner, Altorki, Minsky, & Kelsen, 1997). Carcinoma of the upper (cervical) esophagus tends to spread by invasion of adjacent structures, including carotid arteries, pleura, recurrent laryngeal nerves, trachea, and larynx. Tumors of the middle (thoracic) esophagus tend to spread to the left main stem bronchus, pleura, and related structures. Tumors of the lower (lower thoracic and cardiac) esophagus tend to invade the pericardium, aorta, diaphragm, and phrenic nerve (Coleman, 1997). Lymphatic spread follows patterns similar to direct spread, with about 75% of patients presenting at diagnosis with mediastinal node or distant metastasis (Tabbarah, 1995). Hematogenous spread is commonly to liver, lung, bone, and kidney. Brain

TABLE 24-1 |

Metastatic Spread	Problems	Assessment Parameters
Colon	Bowel obstruction	Colon obstruction: Intermittent (colicky) or continuous pain, nausea and vomiting, diarrhea, or constipation. In colon obstruction, the abdomen is distended, and bowel sounds are hyperactive.
	Constipation	May or may not be related to obstruction.
	Nausea and vomiting Anorexia	May or may not be related to obstruction.
	Bleeding/anemia	Persistent bleeding, especially with rectal cancer. Anemia: Weakness, fatigue, anorexia, headache, tachycardia, dyspnea.
Regional lymph and structures	Lymphadenopathy	Lymphedema (area lower extremities): Pain, cellulitis, lymphangitis; pressure on internal structures.
	Obstructive uropathy	**Obstructive uropathy:** Hesitancy, urgency, nocturia, frequency, decreased force of stream, urinary tract infection.
		Partial kidney obstruction: Polyuria alternating with oliguria.
	Fistula	Pain, odor, discharge depending on site.
	Perineal pain	Severe pain, most often neuropathic, but also mixed neuropathic with visceral or somatic.
Liver	Pain	Liver pain may be upper right abdominal or nonspecific, characteristic of visceral pain. It may radiate to right scapula and worsen at night.
	Ascites	Abdominal distension, bulging flanks, fluid wave, weight gain, and discomfort; anorexia, early satiety, indigestion, decreased bowel mobility; dyspnea, orthopnea, tachypnea; weakness, fatigue.
Lung(s)	Dyspnea, other pulmonary (see Chapter 14)	Pleural effusion: Dyspnea with cough and chest pain (trachea displacement toward unaffected side with large effusion). Breath sounds are usually decreased but may vary according to area of lung. Pleural effusions are usually unilateral.
		Pneumonia: Dyspnea with elevated temperature, chills, purulent or rusty sputum, decreased breath sounds. Pleural effusion may also be present.
		Embolus: Sudden onset of dyspnea with rapid breathing, rapid heart rate, cough, chest pain, and blood in sputum.
		Obstruction: Progressive or rapidly increasing dyspnea, blood in sputum, noisy breathing, chronic cough, choking, or pneumonia.
		Preexisting conditions, such as chronic obstructive pulmonary disease or ascites, may also cause dyspnea.
Bone	Pain	Bone pain is usually localized, constant, dull, aching, or sharp and is worse at night.
		Spinal cord compression from pathologic fractures of the spine or compression of cord without fracture is possible. Pain may be associated with other processes.
Other	Various problems	Carcinoid syndrome: This usually occurs only when there is liver metastasis. Symptoms may include flushing, diarrhea, bronchoconstrictions, enlarged and painful liver, cardiac lesions, bowel obstruction.
		Fatigue, cachexia, dysphagia, anemia, other problems of advanced debilitating disease.
		Problems of therapy (eg, opioids, corticosteroids, antidepressants, radiation, chemotherapy).
		Skin integrity may become a major challenge if rectal discharge develops or if colostomy is present.

TABLE 24-2	Stomach Cancer: Spread, Problems, and Assessment	
Metastatic Spread	**Problems**	**Assessment Parameters**
Primary tumor growth and regional spread	Gastrointestinal (GI) disturbances	Abdominal pain (gnawing, constant, or pain after eating), dyspepsia; nausea and vomiting; belching, regurgitation; early satiety; dysphagia; diarrhea; peritoneal effusions. Hematemesis, melanemesis, melena.
	Obstruction	Stomach/small bowel obstruction: Severe, colicky epigastric pain; vomiting (bile, mucus); abdomen not distended (though distension from peritoneal effusion may be present). Jaundice, pruritus.
Liver	Pain	Pain typically upper right abdominal or nonspecific, characteristic of visceral pain. Pain may radiate to right scapula and worsen at night.
	Ascites	Abdominal distension, bulging flanks, fluid wave, weight gain, and discomfort; anorexia, early satiety, indigestion, decreased bowel mobility; dyspnea, orthopnea, tachypnea; weakness, fatigue.
Regional lymph, other structures	Lymphadenopathy	Lymphedema, obstruction of adjacent organs (see obstructive uropathy) or structures, pain; cellulitis, lymphangitis.
Lung(s)	Dyspnea, other respiratory symptoms (see Chapter 14)	Pleural effusion is common: Dyspnea with cough and chest pain (trachea displacement toward unaffected side with large effusion). Breath sounds are usually decreased but may vary according to area of lung. Pleural effusions are usually unilateral, except when due to heart failure or lymphangitis carcinomatosis. Pneumonia: Dyspnea with elevated temperature, chills, purulent or rusty sputum (but not always present), decreased breath sounds. Pleural effusion may also be present. Bone marrow and other transplantations are risk factors for fungal pulmonary infections. **Obstruction** (from tumor, lymphadenopathy): Progressive or rapidly increasing dyspnea, blood in sputum, noisy breathing, chronic cough, choking, or pneumonia. **Pulmonary embolus:** Sudden onset of dyspnea with rapid breathing, rapid heart rate, cough, chest pain, and blood in sputum.
Bone	Pain	Pain is usually localized, constant, dull, aching, or sharp. It may be worse at night.
Brain	Central nervous system (CNS) symptoms	**Increased intracranial pressure** (ICP): Pain is usually present and may be more severe in the morning. Progressive neurologic deficits (motor, sensory, cognitive). Classic triad of increased ICP = papilledema (often with visual changes), vomiting, and headache. Confusion, seizures, other CNS symptoms.
Other	Cardiac problems	**Pericardial effusion → Tamponade:** Retrosternal chest pain relieved by sitting forward; orthopnea; cough; tachypnea; tachycardia; decreased cardiac output (decreased cerebral blood, peripheral cyanosis, decreased systolic and pulse pressures, and pulsus paradoxus [weaker during inspiration]); occasional nausea and vomiting and abdominal pain.
	Paraneoplastic syndromes	Acanthosis nigricans: Dark, thickened "thorny" skin, especially in axillae and similar areas.

(continued)

TABLE 24-2	Stomach Cancer: Spread, Problems, and Assessment *(Continued)*	
Metastatic Spread	**Problems**	**Assessment Parameters**
		Dermatomyositis: Muscle weakness and a rash that progresses to plaquelike lesions. Polymyositis is the muscle weakness without skin changes.
		Circinate erythemas: Circular erythematis lesions.
		Dementia, cerebellar ataxia.
		Venous thrombosis, thrombophlebitis.
		Cushing's syndrome.
		Chorionic gonadotropin secretion.
		Cachexia.
	Anemia	Weakness, fatigue, headache, tachypnea.
	Other	Fatigue cachexia, dysphagia, or other debilitating effects of advanced disease.
		Problems of therapy (eg, opioids, corticosteroids, tricyclic antidepressants, radiation, chemotherapy).

metastasis occurs in almost 20% of patients (Skinner et al., 1997; Weiss, 1992).

The most common problem of carcinoma of the esophagus is dysphagia, which usually does not occur until there is about 90% tumor involvement or narrowing of the lumen (Skinner et al., 1997). Dysphagia generally begins with solids, progresses to liquids, and even to saliva. Odynophagia (painful swallowing) is present in about 50% of patients. Dysphagia leads to at least three major problems: (1) malnutrition, weight loss, and eventually cachexia; (2) dehydration; and (3) aspiration pneumonia from food spilling over into the lungs or from regurgitation. A chronic cough may point to aspiration or a tracheoesophageal fistula. Hoarseness indicates laryngeal nerve involvement, and chronic hiccups and paralysis of the arm or diaphragm indicate phrenic nerve involvement. Hemoptysis may be from an ulcerative tumor or, if massive, may indicate aortic or carotid involvement. Pain can arise from the primary tumor, especially if ulcerative, or from invasive or metastatic extension (Coleman, 1997; Skinner et al., 1997; Tabbarah, 1995). Pain in the ear indicates pharyngeal metastases (Calcaterra & Juillard, 1990).

Palliative care may include esophagectomy (but this measure has a morbidity rate of more than 20% and a 1- to 2-month recovery period), radiation therapy, esophageal dilatation, photodynamic therapy, or endoprosthesis (Coleman, 1997; Martins & Lynch, 1997).

Death commonly occurs from inanition or pneumonia (Tabbarah, 1995).

The oncologic emergencies typically associated with carcinoma of the esophagus include **hypercalcemia, tracheal obstruction,** and **increased intracranial pressure** (Coleman, 1997; Glick & Glover, 1995). Invasion of the aorta or carotid arteries may result in massive hemorrhage (Table 24-3).

Oral Cancer

Oral cancer is the 16th leading cause of cancer death in women and men. About twice as many men as women die from oral cancer, but the percentage of women is increasing. There were 8241 deaths from oral cancer in 1993, and the estimation of deaths in 1998 is 8000 (ACS, 1997; Landis et al., 1998).

TABLE 24-3	Esophageal Cancer: Spread, Problems, Assessment	
Metastatic Spread	**Problems**	**Assessment Parameters**
Primary tumor growth, regional extension	Decreased esophageal lumen	Dysphagia: Inability to swallow solids, liquids, and eventually in some cases, saliva. (Dysphagia may also be due to involvement of esophageal nerve plexus.) Odynophagia: Painful swallowing. Cachexia, weight loss from inability to eat or drink, dehydration. Aspiration pneumonia from food spill-over (see pneumonia below). **Tracheal obstruction:** Hemoptysis, wheezing, cough, dyspnea.
	Fistula	Chronic cough after swallowing liquids may be due to cough-swallow sequence from tracheoesophageal fistula.
	Regional nerve involvement	Hoarseness from laryngeal nerve involvement. Chronic hiccups, paralyzed arm or diaphragm from phrenic nerve involvement. Dysphagia for solids and liquids from esophageal nerve plexus damage.
	Pain	Pain: Related to the above. Pain from esophageal obstruction tends to be retrosternal, throat, or intrascapular.
	Bleeding	Hemorrhage (massive) from carotid artery or aorta involvement. Hemoptysis from ulcerative primary tumor.
Lung(s)	Dyspnea (see Chapter 14)	Pleural effusion: Dyspnea with cough and chest pain (trachea displacement toward unaffected side with large effusion). Breath sounds are usually decreased but may vary according to area of lung. Pleural effusions are usually unilateral. Pneumonia: Dyspnea with elevated temperature, chills, purulent or rusty sputum, decreased breath sounds. Pleural effusion may also be present. **Embolus:** Sudden onset of dyspnea with rapid breathing, rapid heart rate, cough, chest pain, and blood in sputum. **Obstruction:** Progressive or rapidly increasing dyspnea, blood in sputum, noisy breathing, chronic cough, choking, or pneumonia. Preexisting conditions, such as chronic obstructive pulmonary disease or ascites, may also cause dyspnea.
Liver	Pain	Pain may be upper right abdominal or nonspecific and characteristic of visceral pain. It may radiate to right scapula and worsen at night.
	Ascites	Abdominal distension, bulging flanks, fluid wave, weight gain, and discomfort; anorexia, early satiety, indigestion, decreased bowel mobility; dyspnea, orthopnea, tachypnea; weakness, fatigue.
Bone	Pain	Bone pain is usually localized to some extent and may be described as constant, aching, gnawing, sharp. It is often worse at night and may not be relieved by lying down. Pain may be from other processes. Spinal cord compression is possible but is not common in esophageal cancer.
	Metabolic changes	**Hypercalcemia:** Symptoms include fatigue, weakness, anorexia, nausea, polyuria, polydipsia, and constipation, progressing to changes in mentation, seizures, and coma.

(continued)

TABLE 24-3	Esophageal Cancer: Spread, Problems, Assessment *(Continued)*	
Metastatic Spread	**Problems**	**Assessment Parameters**
Brain	Central nervous system (CNS) symptoms	**Increased ICP**: Progressive pain is usually present and may be more severe in the morning. Classic triad of increased ICP = papilledema (often with visual changes), vomiting, and headache. Confusion, seizures, headache, or other CNS problems may also result from brain metastases.
Other	Various problems	Problems of therapy (eg, opioids, corticosteroids, tricyclic antidepressants, radiation, chemotherapy). Fatigue, cachexia, other debilitating problems of advanced disease.

Most fatal oral cavity tumors are in the mouth, followed by the pharynx, other oral cavity, tongue, and a very few on the lip (ACS, 1997). The lip, however, is the most common site of oral cancer. The most common tumor type is squamous cell carcinoma. Tumor spread is primarily by regional submucosal extension and, when the tumor is deeper into the oropharynx, also by regional (especially cervical) nodes. Local invasion can include bone, nerves, muscle, submucosa, and area structures, such as the tongue or soft tissue of the neck where malignant ulceration may occur. When metastasis does occur, it usually is late and to lung, liver, or bone (Clayman, Lippman, Laramore, & Hong, 1997; Jacobs & Pinto, 1995).

The problems of advanced oral cancer are both general and according to the areas or structures involved (Clayman et al., 1997; Parker, Rice, & Casciato, 1995; Talmi et al., 1997):

● General problems of oral cancer: pain (usually locoregional and often facial), dysphagia, odynophagia, communication deficits, odor (from tumor necrosis), problems secondary to treatment, and lymphadenopathy
● Oral cavity (floor of mouth, tongue, buccal mucosa, gingiva, hard palate): local pain, difficulty chewing, dysphagia, tumor necrosis, and lymphadenopathy
● Oropharynx: odynophagia, otalgia (ear-ache), dysphagia, trismus (trigeminal nerve dysfunction causing spasms of the masticatory muscles resulting in "lockjaw"), and lymphadenopathy
● Nasopharynx: headache, epistaxis, nasal obstruction, sore throat, hearing loss, neck pain, lymphadenopathy, and cranial nerve involvement (2nd–6th and 9th–12th), resulting in neurologic deficits, such as ptosis, trigeminal neuralgia, regional weakness, dysphagia, Horner's syndrome, and related problems. Destruction of bony structures can cause severe pain and neurologic deficits, such as shoulder weakness.
● Hypopharynx: odynophagia, dysphagia, otalgia, cough, hoarseness, aspiration pneumonia, and lymphadenopathy
● Larynx (and glottic areas): hoarseness, dysphagia, odynophagia, otalgia, airway obstruction, tumor erosion, lymphadenopathy
● Nasal cavity and paranasal sinuses: chronic nasal regurgitation, pain, bleeding, visual disturbances, trismus, ulcerating masses, and lymphadenopathy

The results of many of the problems of oral cancer are malnutrition and at least the potential for ineffective breathing. Pain is a challenging problem because there is often a mix of neuropathic and somatic pain.

Hypercalcemia is the only oncologic emergency typically associated with oral cancer. Hemorrhage occurs in some cases (Table 24-4).

TABLE 24-4	Oral Cancer: Spread, Problems, and Assessment	
Metastatic Spread	**Problems**	**Assessment Parameters**
Regional extension and associated damage	General problems of oral cancer	Pain may be neuropathic or mixed and may result from the cancer or treatment.
		Dysphagia, odynophagia, and related problems and complications are common. Dysphagia may be complicated by paralysis of the tongue or other neurologic complications involving swallowing, the lips, and area sensory function and chronic aspiration or nasal regurgitation.
		Lymphadenopathy with resultant pressure on cranial nerves and other structures.
		Odor and pain from tumor necrosis.
		Chronic aspiration results in frequent choking and may result in pneumonia. Reluctance to take fluids results in dehydration.
		Tumor necrosis, especially deep tumors, results in foul odor and taste; malignant ulceration occurs.
		External (fungating) tumors present problems of pain, odor, and appearance.
		Hemorrhage may occur from extension of tumor to blood vessels (and nerves) found in the oropharynx and neck.
		Communication difficulties may include hearing, vision, and speaking changes.
Specific areas of involvement	Oral cavity	Local pain, difficulty chewing, dysphagia, tumor necrosis, and lymphadenopathy.
	Oropharynx	Odynophagia, otalgia, dysphagia, trismus (trigeminal nerve dysfunction causing spasms of the masticatory muscles resulting in "lockjaw"), and lymphadenopathy.
	Nasopharynx	Headache, epistaxis, nasal obstruction, sore throat, hearing loss, neck pain, lymphadenopathy, and cranial nerve involvement (2–6 and 9–12), resulting in neurologic deficits, such as ptosis, trigeminal neuralgia, regional weakness, dysphagia, Horner's syndrome, and related problems. Destruction of bony structures can cause severe pain and neurologic deficits, such as shoulder weakness.
	Hypopharynx	Odynophagia, dysphagia, otalgia, cough, hoarseness, aspiration pneumonia, and lymphadenopathy.
	Nasal cavity and paranasal sinuses	Chronic nasal regurgitation, pain, bleeding, visual disturbances, trismus, ulcerating masses, and lymphadenopathy.
Lung	Dyspnea (see Chapter 14)	Pleural effusion: Dyspnea with cough and chest pain (trachea displacement toward unaffected side with large effusion). Breath sounds are usually decreased but may vary according to area of lung. Pleural effusions are usually unilateral.
		Pneumonia: Dyspnea with elevated temperature, chills, purulent or rusty sputum, decreased breath sounds. Pleural effusion may also be present.
		Obstruction: Progressive or rapidly increasing dyspnea, blood in sputum, noisy breathing, chronic cough, choking, or pneumonia.
		Preexisting conditions, such as chronic obstructive pulmonary disease or ascites, may also cause dyspnea.

(continued)

TABLE 24-4	Oral Cancer: Spread, Problems, and Assessment *(Continued)*

Metastatic Spread	Problems	Assessment Parameters
Liver	Pain	Pain may be upper right abdominal or nonspecific and characteristic of visceral pain. Pain may radiate to the right scapula and worsen at night.
	Ascites	Abdominal distension, bulging flanks, fluid wave, weight gain, and discomfort; anorexia, indigestion, decreased bowel mobility; dyspnea, orthopnea, and tachypnea; weakness, fatigue.
Bone	Pain	Bone pain is usually localized, constant, dull, aching, or sharp and is worse at night. Local (head and neck) involvement may result in complex pain syndromes with neuropathic and somatic pain with neurologic deficits from cranial nerve involvement.
		Spinal cord compression (from pathologic fracture) is not common in oral cancer.
Other	Various problems	**Hypercalcemia** (often nonspecific): Symptoms include fatigue, weakness, anorexia, nausea, polyuria, polydipsia, and constipation, progressing to changes in mentation, seizures, and coma.
		Fatigue cachexia, dysphagia, anemia, or other debilitating effects of advanced disease.
		Problems of therapy (eg, opioids, corticosteroids, tricyclic antidepressants, radiation, chemotherapy).

REFERENCES

American Cancer Society. (1997). *Cancer facts and figures*. Atlanta: Author.

Calcaterra, T. C., & Juillard, G. J. F. (1990). Head and neck neoplasms: Larynx and hypopharynx. In C. M. Haskell (Ed.), *Cancer treatment* (3rd ed.) (pp. 389–395). Philadelphia: W.B. Saunders.

Carlson, H. E., Lowitz, B. B., & Casciato, D. A. (1995). Endocrine neoplasms. In D. A. Casciato & B. B. Lowitz (Eds.), *Manual of clinical oncology* (3rd ed.) (pp. 268–287). Boston: Little, Brown and Company.

Coleman, J. (1997). Esophageal, stomach, liver, gallbladder, and pancreatic cancers. In S. I. Groenwald, M. H. Frogge, M. Goodman, & C. H. Yarbro (Eds.), *Cancer nursing: Principles and practice* (4th ed.) (pp. 1082–1144). Boston: Jones and Bartlett.

Clayman, G. L., Lippman, S. M., Laramore, G. E., & Hong, W. K. (1997). Head and neck cancer. In J. F. Holland, R. C. Bast, D. L. Morton, E. Frei, D. W. Kufe, & R. C. Weichselbaum (Eds.), *Cancer medicine* (4th ed.) (pp. 1645–1710). Baltimore: Williams & Wilkins.

Ellis, F. H., Huberman, M., & Busse, P. (1995). Cancer of the esophagus. In G. P. Murphy, W. Lawrence, & R. E. Lenhard (Eds.), *Clinical oncology* (2nd ed.) (pp. 293–303). Atlanta: American Cancer Society.

Glick, J. H., & Glover, D. (1995). Oncologic emergencies. In G. P. Murphy, W. Lawrence, & R. E. Lenhard (Eds.), *Clinical oncology* (2nd ed.) (pp. 597–618). Atlanta: American Cancer Society.

Huapoja, I. S. (1997). Paraneoplastic syndromes. In S. I. Groenwald, M. H. Frogge, M. Goodman & C. H. Yarbro (Eds.). *Cancer nursing: Principles and practice* (4th ed.) (pp. 702–720). Boston: Jones and Bartlett.

Inagaki, J., Rodriguez, V., & Bodey, G. P. (1974). Causes of death in cancer patients. *Cancer, 33*(2), 568–573.

Jacobs, C. D., & Pinto, H. (1995). Head and neck cancers. In J. S. MacDonald, D. G. Haller, & R. J. Mayer (Eds.), *Manual of oncologic therapeutics* (3rd ed.) (pp. 162–169). Philadelphia: J.B. Lippincott.

Jessup, J. M., Menck, H. R., Fremgen, A., & Winchester, D. P. (1997). Diagnosing colorectal carcinoma: Clinical and molecular approaches.

CA—A Cancer Journal for Clinicians, 47(2), 70–92.

Landis, S. H., Murray, T., Bolden, S., & Wingo, P. A. (1998). Cancer statistics, 1998. *CA—A Cancer Journal for Clinicians,* 48(1), 6–29.

Martins, R. G., & Lynch, T. J. (1997). Esophageal cancer: Are you up to date? *Internal Medicine,* 18(8), 18–36.

Parker, R. G., Rice, D. H., & Casciato, D. A. (1995). Head and neck cancers. In D. A. Casciato & B. B. Lowitz (Eds.), *Manual of clinical oncology* (pp. 113–132). Boston: Little, Brown and Company.

Skinner, D. B., Altorki, N. K., Minsky, B. D., & D. P. Kelsen. (1997). Neoplasms of the esophagus. In J. F. Holland, R. C. Bast, D. L. Morton, E. Frei, D. W. Kufe, & R. C. Weichselbaum (Eds.), *Cancer medicine* (4th ed.) (pp. 1861–1878). Balti-more: Williams & Wilkins.

Steele, G. (1995). Colorectal cancer. In G. P. Murphy, W. Lawrence, & R. E. Lenhard (Eds.), *Clinical oncology* (2nd ed.) (pp. 236–250). Altanta: American Cancer Society.

Tabbarah, H. J. (1995). Gastrointestinal tract cancers. In D. A. Casciato & B. B. Lowitz (Eds.), *Manual of clinical oncology* (3rd ed.) (pp. 145–182). Boston: Little, Brown and Company.

Talmi, Y. P., Waller, A., Bercovici, M., Horowitz, Z., Pfeffer, M. R., Adunski, A., & Kronenberg, J. (1997). Pain experienced by patients with terminal head and neck carcinoma. *Cancer,* 80(6), 1117–1123.

Weiss, L. (1992). Comments on hematogenous metastatic patterns in humans as revealed by autopsy. *Clinical and Experimental Metastasis,* 10(3), 191–199.

CHAPTER 25

Urinary Tract Cancer (Kidney, Bladder, and Prostate): Metastatic Spread, Common Symptoms, and Assessment

Kidney Cancer

Kidney (renal) cancer is the 13th leading cause of cancer death overall, with 10,322 deaths in 1993 and 11,600 deaths estimated in 1998. Kidney cancer affects about twice as many men as women (American Cancer Society, 1997; Landis, Murray, Bolden & Wingo, 1998).

Renal cell carcinomas, usually adenocarcinomas, are the most common tumor type (Richie, Kantoff, & Shapiro, 1997). Spread is through blood to liver, lungs, and bones; through lymph; and by direct extension to adjacent structures, including the renal vein, vena cava, and viscera (Lind & Hagan, 1997). The contralateral kidney may also be affected, and uremia is common. Metastases to the skin may also occur (Waller & Caroline, 1996).

Problems of kidney cancer include those common to metastatic disease in liver, lungs, bones, and nodes. Flank pain, palpable renal mass, and hematuria are the "classic triad" of renal carcinoma symptoms (Kassabian & Graham, 1995). Anemia, weight loss, night sweats, fever, and (in men) sudden onset of varicocele are common (Sokoloff, deKernion, Figlin, & Belldegrun, 1996). Liver dysfunction in the absence of hepatic involvement also occurs, and hyponatremia and hyperkalemia are common (Waller & Caroline, 1996). Paraneoplastic syndromes and "unusual problems" (Young, 1998, p. 1306; Richie et al., 1997; Waller & Caroline, 1996) are common and include the following:

- Hypercalcemia
- Other metabolic disorders, including hyponatremia and hyperkalemia
- Increased erythrocyte sedimentation rate
- Anemia
- Hypertension
- Cachexia
- Neuromuscular disorders
- Secondary amyloidosis
- Fever of unknown origin

Oncologic emergencies associated with renal cancers include **increased intracranial pressure, spinal cord compression, bronchial obstruction, ureteral obstruction,** and **hypercalcemia** (Glick & Glover, 1995; Richie et al., 1997; Waller & Caroline, 1996) (Table 25-1).

Bladder Cancer

Bladder cancer is the 11th leading cause of cancer death overall, with 10,962 deaths in 1993 and an estimated 12,500 deaths in 1998. Bladder cancer kills about twice as many men as women (American Cancer Society, 1997; Landis et al., 1998).

TABLE 25-1	Kidney Cancer: Spread, Problems, and Assessment	
Metastatic Spread	**Problems**	**Assessment Parameters**
Kidney	Classic symptoms	Classic triad of renal cancer symptoms: Flank pain, abdominal mass, hematuria. Weakness, anemia, anorexia.
	Uremia	Note that renal failure is rarely a result of primary renal cancer. Symptoms include oliguria or anuria, fatigue, headache, anorexia, nausea and vomiting, fetid breath, changes in mentation.
	Obstruction	**Obstructive uropathy:** Hesitancy, urgency, nocturia, frequency, decreased force of stream, urinary tract infection. Partial kidney obstruction: Polyuria alternating with oliguria.
Lymph	Lymphedema	Lymphedema: Enlarged lymph, edema (especially leg), pain; cellulitis, lymphangitis; pressure on internal structures.
Liver	Pain	Liver pain may be upper right abdominal or nonspecific, characteristic of visceral pain. It may radiate to right scapula and worsen at night.
	Ascites	Abdominal distension, bulging flanks, fluid wave, weight gain, and discomfort; anorexia, early satiety, indigestion, decreased bowel mobility; dyspnea, orthopnea, tachypnea; weakness, fatigue.
Lung(s)	Dyspnea, other respiratory symptoms (see Chapter 14)	Pleural effusion: Dyspnea with cough and chest pain (trachea displacement toward unaffected side with large effusion). Breath sounds are usually decreased but may vary according to area of lung. Pleural effusions are usually unilateral.
		Pneumonia: Dyspnea with elevated temperature, chills, purulent or rusty sputum, decreased breath sounds. Pleural effusion may also be present.
		Embolus: Sudden onset of dyspnea with rapid breathing, rapid heart rate, cough, chest pain, and blood in sputum.
		Obstruction: Progressive or rapidly increasing dyspnea, blood in sputum, noisy breathing, chronic cough, choking, or pneumonia.
		Preexisting conditions, such as chronic obstructive pulmonary disease or ascites, may also cause dyspnea.
Brain	Central nervous system (CNS) symptoms	**Increased ICP:** Progressive pain is usually present and may be more severe in the morning. Classic triad of increased ICP = papilledema (often with visual changes), vomiting, and headache.
		Confusion, seizures, or other CNS problems may also result from brain metastases or paraneoplastic syndromes (see Chapter 13).
Bone	Pain	Bone pain is usually localized, constant, dull, aching, or sharp. It is worse at night.
	Cord compression	**Spinal cord compression** (from pathologic fracture or compression of cord without fracture): Back pain is the first symptom and may be local (somatic: constant, dull, aching), radicular, or both. It is exacerbated by movement, neck flexion, straight leg raising and decreased by sitting up. It is tender to percussion. Neurologic deficits usually follow pain and may begin subtly and include extremity weakness, ataxia, stumbling; urine retention, bowel dysfunction, numbness.
Skin	Lesions	They are usually found on lower abdominal wall, genitalia, scalp and also on nose, eyelids, or fingertips.

(continued)

TABLE 25-1   Kidney Cancer: Spread, Problems, and Assessment *(Continued)*

Metastatic Spread	Problems	Assessment Parameters
Distant effects	Paraneoplastic syndromes, other distant effects	**Hypercalcemia** (often nonspecific): Symptoms include fatigue, weakness, anorexia, nausea, polyuria, polydipsia, and constipation, progressing to changes in mentation, seizures, and coma. Other metabolic disorders, including hyponatremia and hyperkalemia, increased erythrocyte sedimentation rate, anemia, hypertension, cachexia, neuromuscular disorders, secondary amyloidosis, fever of unknown origin.
Other	Various problems	Fatigue cachexia, dysphagia, anemia, or other debilitating effects of advanced disease. Problems of therapy (eg, opioids, corticosteroids, tricyclic antidepressants, radiation, chemotherapy).

About 90% of bladder cancers are transitional cell carcinoma (from the epithelium), and the remainder are adenocarcinoma, squamous cell, or small cell carcinoma (Kantoff, Zietman, & Wishnow, 1997). Invasion of the bladder muscle is universal in patients with advanced bladder cancer. Local sites of invasion may include adjacent structures, such as the prostate, uterus, vagina, pelvic bone, or abdominal wall (Kelly & Miaskowski, 1996). Metastases are most frequently found in regional and other lymph nodes followed by liver, lung, bone, and kidney (Kantoff et al., 1997; Lamm & Torti, 1996, Weiss, 1992).

Elimination problems are prominent and include "irritable bladder" (dysuria, frequency, urgency), stranguria (pain with straining to urinate), ureteral or bladder neck obstruction, or hematuria (which may be life threatening). Uremia may also occur. There is often a risk for urinary tract or related infection (and sepsis). Patients who have been extensively treated may have one of a variety of elimination aids, such as urinary diversion surgery (Kantoff et al., 1997).

Extension to pelvic nerve plexi, lymph, bone, or viscera can result in mixed somatic, visceral, and neuropathic perineal pain + elimination problems and perhaps significant lower extremity edema—a "formidable challenge" of management (Stillman, 1990, p. 364). Spread to adjacent structures, such as sigmoid colon, rectum, prostate, or vagina, can create major problems (eg, fistula) in hygiene and care.

The oncologic emergency most commonly associated with bladder cancers is **obstructive uropathy** (Kantoff et al., 1997) (Table 25-2).

Prostate Cancer

Cancer of the prostate is the second leading cause of cancer among men and the fourth leading cause of cancer death overall. There were 34,865 deaths from prostate cancer in 1993, and the estimation of deaths in 1998 is 39,200. The incidence of prostate cancer surpasses that of lung cancer in men and is expected to continue to increase as the population ages (American Cancer Society, 1997; Landis et al., 1998).

More than 99% of prostate cancers are adenocarcinomas. The most common site (almost 70% on autopsy) of metastases is bone (mostly osteoblastic lesions). The most common sites of bony metastases (in descending order of frequency) are pelvis and sacrum, spine, femur, ribs, and scapulae. Local extension is common, and lymph (pelvic, abdominal, and thoracic), adjacent structures, lungs, and liver may be involved (Elmajian, Agha, & Culkin, 1997; Weiss, 1992). The course of prostate cancer is generally (but not always) indolent but progressive (Herr, 1997).

TABLE 25-2 Bladder Cancer: Spread, Problems, and Assessment

Metastatic Spread	Problems	Assessment Parameters
Primary tumor growth and regional spread	Perineal pain	Severe pain, most often neuropathic, but also mixed neuropathic with visceral or somatic.
	Pelvic structure involvement	Fistulas: Perirectal, rectovaginal, and others. Vaginal tumors: Fungating, ulcerative, or invasive. Abdominal pain.
	Obstruction	**Obstructive uropathy:** Hesitancy, urgency, nocturia, frequency, decreased force of stream, urinary tract infection (UTI). Renal calculi may develop secondary to UTIs. Partial kidney obstruction: Polyuria alternating with oliguria.
	Other elimination problems	Irritable bladder: Dysuria, frequency, urgency; incontinence; retention; hematuria. Impaired bladder emptying secondary to nerve involvement. Extensive pelvic disease can result in neurologic impairment or urinary dysfunction. Intestinal obstruction: Nausea and vomiting, intestinal colic, other abdominal pain, diarrhea, constipation.
	Lymphadenopathy	Lymphedema (area or lower extremities): Pain, cellulitis, lymphangitis; pressure on viscera, nerve plexi resulting in pain, obstruction.
Liver	Pain	Liver pain may be upper right abdominal or nonspecific, characteristic of visceral pain. It may radiate to right scapula and worsen at night.
	Ascites	Abdominal distension, bulging flanks, fluid wave, weight gain, and discomfort; anorexia, early satiety, indigestion, decreased bowel mobility; dyspnea, orthopnea, tachypnea; weakness, fatigue; changes in color of urine and stool; pruritus.
Lung(s)	Dyspnea, other pulmonary symptoms (see Chapter 14)	Pleural effusion: Dyspnea with cough and chest pain (trachea displacement toward unaffected side with large effusion). Breath sounds usually decreased but may vary according to area of lung. Pleural effusions are usually unilateral. Pneumonia: Dyspnea with elevated temperature, chills, purulent or rusty sputum, decreased breath sounds. Pleural effusion may also be present. **Embolus:** Sudden onset of dyspnea with rapid breathing, rapid heart rate, cough, chest pain, and blood in sputum. **Obstruction:** Progressive or rapidly increasing dyspnea, blood in sputum, noisy breathing, chronic cough, choking, or pneumonia. Preexisting conditions, such as chronic obstructive pulmonary disease or ascites, may also cause dyspnea.
Bone	Pain	Bone pain is usually localized at least to some extent and is constant, dull, aching, or sharp. It is worse at night. **Spinal cord compression** from pathologic fractures of the spine or compression of cord without fracture is possible. Pain may be associated with other processes.
Kidneys	Uremia	Oliguria or anuria, fatigue, headache, anorexia, nausea and vomiting, fetid breath, changes in mentation. Also see obstruction.
Other	Anemia	Anemia from several potential etiologies: Weakness, fatigue, anorexia, headache, tachycardia, dyspnea.
	Various problems	Fatigue cachexia, dysphagia, or other debilitating effects of advanced disease. Problems of therapy (eg, opioids, corticosteroids, tricyclic antidepressants, radiation, chemotherapy).

There is a higher incidence of pain often related to bone metastases and lumbosacral invasion. Pelvic and related complications are common and may include lower extremity edema from lymphadenopathy, urinary dysfunction (retention, dribbling, urgency, frequency, hematuria), and neurologic impairment (Herr, 1997; Kassabian & Graham, 1995; Oesterling, Fuks, Lee, & Scher, 1997).

Sexuality is an issue for many patients with prostate cancer (and their spouses). Treatment impacting sexuality may include prostatecto-my, surgical or medical castration, and frequent invasive procedures to alleviate genitourinary problems, such as obstruction and bleeding. The presence of pelvic disease also has an impact on sexuality (Herr, 1997).

The oncologic emergencies most common in patients with prostate cancer are **spinal cord compression** (rare), **obstructive uropathy, and SIADH, and disseminated intravascular coagulation** (Elmajian et al., 1997; Glick & Glover, 1995). Note that despite a very high incidence of bone metastases, hypercalcemia is not common (Table 25-3).

TABLE 25-3	Prostate Cancer: Spread, Problems, and Assessment	
Metastatic Spread	**Problems**	**Assessment Parameters**
Bone: Most common sites are pelvis and sacrum, spine, femur, ribs, scapulae.	Pain	Pain is usually localized to some extent. Pathologic fractures are possible. Pain may be from other processes.
		Spinal cord compression: Back pain may be local (somatic: constant, dull, aching), radicular, or both. It is exacerbated by movement, neck flexion, straight leg raising and decreased by sitting up. It is tender to percussion. Neurologic deficits begin subtly and are not necessarily apparent to the patient: weakness, ataxia, stumbling; urine retention, bowel dysfunction, impotence, numbness.
Regional lymph and other structures	Lymphadenopathy	Lymphedema (especially lower extremities): Pain, cellulitis, lymphangitis.
		Extensive pelvic disease can result in neurologic impairment or urinary dysfunction.
	Obstruction, other genitourinary (GU) problems	**Obstructive uropathy** (ureteral): Hesitancy, urgency, nocturia, frequency, decreased force of stream alternating with oliguria.
		Uremia: Nausea, vomiting, lethargy, oliguria. Other GU problems, including retention (monitor for urinary tract infection), dribbling, urgency, hematuria.
	Pain	Severe pelvic/perineal pain, most often neuropathic with visceral and/or somatic aspects.
Lungs	Dyspnea, other respiratory symptoms (see Chapter 14)	Pleural effusion: Dyspnea with cough and chest pain (trachea displacement toward unaffected side with large effusion). Breath sounds are usually decreased but may vary according to area of lung. Pleural effusions are usually unilateral, except when due to heart failure or lymphangitis carcinomatosis.
		Pneumonia: Dyspnea with elevated temperature, chills, purulent or rusty sputum (but not always present), decreased breath sounds. Pleural effusion may also be present. Bone marrow and other transplantations are risk factors for fungal pulmonary infections.

(continued)

TABLE 25-3	Prostate Cancer: Spread, Problems, and Assessment *(Continued)*	
Metastatic Spread	**Problems**	**Assessment Parameters**
		Respiratory muscle weakness: Dyspnea with general weakness, anorexia, severe weight loss (cachexia), or the presence of a paraneoplastic syndrome.
Liver	Pain	Pain may be upper right abdominal or nonspecific, characteristic of visceral pain. It may radiate to right scapula and worsen at night.
	Ascites	Abdominal distension, bulging flanks, fluid wave, weight gain, and discomfort; anorexia, early satiety, indigestion, decreased bowel mobility; dyspnea, orthopnea, tachypnea; weakness, fatigue.
Other	Various problems	Fatigue cachexia, dysphagia, anemia, or other debilitating effects of advanced disease.
		Problems of therapy (eg, opioids, corticosteroids, tricyclic antidepressants, radiation, chemotherapy).
		Sexuality problems and issues.

REFERENCES

American Cancer Society. (1997). *Cancer facts and figures.* Atlanta: Author.

Elmajian, D. A., Agha, A. A., & Culkin, D. J. (1997). Metastatic prostate cancer: An update. *Hospital Medicine, August,* 48–52.

Herr, H. W. (1997). Quality of life in prostate cancer patients. *CA—A Cancer Journal for Clinicians,* 47(4), 207–217.

Kantoff, P. W., Zietman, A. L., & Wishnow, K. (1997). Bladder cancer. In J. F. Holland, R. C. Bast, D. L. Morton, E. Frei, D. W. Kufe, & R. C. Weichselbaum (Eds.), *Cancer medicine* (4th ed.) (pp. 2105–2123). Baltimore: Williams & Wilkins.

Kassabian, V. S., & Graham, S. D. (1995). Urologic and male genital cancers. In G. P. Murphy, W. Lawrence, & R. E. Lenhard (Eds.), *Clinical oncology* (2nd ed.) (pp. 293–303). Atlanta: American Cancer Society.

Kelly, L. P., & Miaskowski, C. (1996). An overview of bladder cancer: Treatment and nursing implications. *Oncology Nursing Forum,* 23(3), 459–468.

Lamm, D. L., & Torti, F. M. (1996). Bladder cancer, 1996. *CA—A Cancer Journal for Clinicians,* 46(2), 93–112.

Landis, S. H., Murray, T., Bolden, S., & Wingo, P. A. (1998). Cancer statistics, 1998. *CA—A Cancer Journal for Clinicians,* 48(1), 6–29.

Lind, J., & Hagan, L. (1997). Bladder and kidney cancer. In S. I. Groenwald, M. H. Frogge, M. Goodman, & C. H. Yarbro (Eds.), *Cancer nursing: Principles and practice* (4th ed.) (pp. 889–915). Boston: Jones and Bartlett.

Oesterling, J., Fuks, Z., Lee, C. T., & Scher, H. I. (1997). Cancer of the prostate. In V. T. DeVita, S. Hellman, & S. A. Rosenberg (Eds.), *Cancer: Principles and practice of oncology* (5th ed.) (pp. 1322–1386). Philadelphia: Lippincott-Raven.

Richie, J. P., Kantoff, P. W., & Shapiro, C. L. (1997). Renal cell carcinoma. In J. F. Holland, R. C. Bast, D. L. Morton, E. Frei, D. W. Kufe, & R. C. Weichselbaum (Eds.), *Cancer medicine* (4th ed.) (pp. 2085–2096). Baltimore: Williams & Wilkins.

Sokoloff, M. H., deKernion, J. B., Figlin, R. A., & Belldegrun, A. (1996). Current management of renal cell carcinoma. *CA—A Cancer Journal for Clinicians,* 46(5), 284–302.

Stillman, M. J. (1990). Perineal pain. In K. M. Foley, J. J. Bonica, & V. Ventafridda (Eds.), *Advances in pain research and therapy, volume 16: Proceedings of the Second International Congress on Cancer Pain* (pp. 359–377). New York: Raven Press.

Waller, A., & Caroline, N. L. (1996). *Handbook of palliative care in cancer.* Boston: Butterworth-Heinemann.

Weiss, L. (1992). Comments on hematogenous metastatic patterns in humans as revealed by autopsy. *Clinical and Experimental Metastasis,* 10(3), 191–199.

Young, R. C. (1998). Metastatic renal-cell carcinoma: What causes occasional dramatic regressions? *New England Journal of Medicine,* 338(18), 1305.

CHAPTER 26

Blood/Lymph and Skin Cancer (Non-Hodgkin's Lymphoma, Leukemia, Multiple Myeloma, Melanoma): Metastatic Spread, Common Symptoms, and Assessment

Non-Hodgkin's Lymphoma

Non-Hodgkin's lymphoma (NHL) is the sixth leading cause of cancer death and affects men and women about equally. There were 20,576 deaths from NHL in 1993, and an estimated 24,900 deaths are expected in 1998 (American Cancer Society, 1997; Landis, Murray, Bolden, & Wingo, 1998). There is an increase in the number of patients with NHL secondary to acquired immunodeficiency syndrome (AIDS) and other factors (Skarin & Dorfman, 1997).

A cancer of the lymphoid system, NHL results from the uncontrolled growth of lymphocytes. There are a number of different types of NHL, and several classification systems are used. The different types of NHL grow at different rates, often in unpredictable patterns, and the slow-growing (low-grade or indolent) NHLs may transform to a more aggressive type. In some cases (10%–15%), the aggressive (intermediate/high-grade) types may develop into a leukemic phase. NHLs are sometimes referred to as "bulky" or "nonbulky," with the former being more problematic (Rosenthal & Eyre, 1995; Skarin & Dorfman, 1997).

In terminal stages, NHL is disseminated and includes extranodal sites and widespread lymph involvement. Common nodal sites include (in descending order of frequency) multiple sites, head and neck, intra-abdominal, inguinal/leg, axilla/arm, intrathoracic, and Waldeyer's ring (nasopharynx). The most common extranodal sites are (in descending order of frequency) stomach, brain, skin, bone marrow, small intestine, lung, and skull/orbit. Note however, that spread to other sites is not uncommon, including (but not limited to) thyroid, breast, ovaries, testes, parotid gland, and colon (Glass, Karnell, & Menck, 1997). Many patients with NHL, especially those with AIDS and bone marrow involvement, are immunosuppressed and hence susceptible to common and uncommon infections, including herpes zoster, candidiasis, aspergillosis, pneumococcal sepsis, *Pneumocystis carinii* pneumonia, and other infections (Yarbro & McFadden, 1997).

A variety of treatment complications (late) may result from high-dose multiagent chemotherapy, radiation, and other treatment modalities. These include lung injury, cardiac complications, immunosuppression, sterility, and radiation myelopathy (Yarbro & McFadden, 1997).

The oncologic emergencies most common in patients with lymphoma are **superior vena cava syndrome** (NHL is the second most likely cancer to cause this), **spinal cord compression**, **ureteral obstruction**, **increased intracranial pressure** (from carcinomatous meningitis), and **hyperuricemia** (Glick & Glover, 1995; Yarbro & McFadden, 1997) (Table 26-1).

TABLE 26-1	Non-Hodgkin's Lymphoma: Spread, Problems, and Assessment	
Metastatic Spread	**Problems**	**Assessment Parameters**
Lymph, often widespread	Lymphadenopathy	Nodes usually are not painful. Lymphadenopathy may be generalized. Associated problems include the following: Lymphedema: Enlarged lymph, edema (area, upper or lower extremities), pain, cellulitis, lymphangitis.
	Genitourinary problems	**Obstructive uropathy** (ureteral): Hesitancy, urgency, nocturia, frequency, decreased force of stream, polyuria alternating with oliguria. **Hyperuricemia,** uric acid nephropathy leading to acute renal failure: nausea, vomiting, lethargy, oliguria.
	Gastrointestinal (GI) problems	Dysphagia; pain from pressure on viscera, especially abdominal.
	Pulmonary	Dyspnea from lung infiltration, lymphangitis carcinomatosis, pulmonary edema. See pleural effusion below.
	Cardiovascular	**Superior vena cava syndrome:** Dilated neck or thoracic veins; facial edema, plethora; tachypnea; cyanosis; edema upper extremities; cough, hoarseness.
Extranodal: GI tract, including small intestine	GI disturbances	Abdominal pain, often from bulky tumor. Also diarrhea, constipation, intestinal obstruction.
	Liver pain	Pain may be upper right abdominal or nonspecific and characteristic of visceral pain. Pain may radiate to the right scapula and worsen at night.
	Ascites	Abdominal distension, bulging flanks, fluid wave, weight gain, and discomfort; anorexia, indigestion, decreased bowel mobility; dyspnea, orthopnea, and tachypnea; weakness, fatigue.
Brain	Central nervous system (CNS) symptoms	**Increased intracranial pressure** (ICP): Progressive pain is usually present and may be more severe in the morning. Classic triad of increased ICP = papilledema (often with visual changes), vomiting, and headache. Confusion, seizures, or other CNS problems may also result from brain or meningeal metastases (see Chapter 13).
Skin	Lesions	Skin lesions found in patients with non-Hodgkin's lymphoma include indurated and erythematous diffuse lesions (T-cell lymphomas); dermatomyositis, which begins with edema, erythema, and bluish-red discoloration, progresses to purplish plaques, and may include muscle weakness; circinate erythemas, which may be pruritic; acquired ichthyosis, which has the appearance of fish scales; and Sweet's syndrome, which appears suddenly and includes painful erythematous plaques or nodules.
Bone marrow	Decreased bone marrow function	Immunosupression: Increased infection rate, including herpes zoster, candidiasis, aspergillosis, pneumococcal sepsis, *Pneumocystis carinii* pneumonia, and others. Bleeding disorders.

(continued)

TABLE 26-1	Non-Hodgkin's Lymphoma: Spread, Problems, and Assessment *(Continued)*	
Metastatic Spread	**Problems**	**Assessment Parameters**
Lung (also see lymph)	Dyspnea (see Chapter 14)	Pleural effusion: Dyspnea with cough and chest pain (trachea displacement toward unaffected side with large effusion). Breath sounds are usually decreased but may vary according to area of lung. Pleural effusions are usually unilateral, except when due to heart failure or lymphangitis carcinomatosis.
		Other respiratory problems may develop, including **embolus,** pneumonia, respiratory muscle weakness. Also see late effects of treatment below. Preexisting and other conditions may lead to respiratory problems (eg, chronic obstructive pulmonary disease, ascites).
Late effects of treatment	Various problems	Lung injury, cardiac complications, immunosuppression, sterility, and radiation myelopathy.
Other	Various problems	**Spinal cord compression:** Back pain may be local (somatic: constant, dull, aching), radicular, or both and is exacerbated by movement, neck flexion, straight leg raising. It is decreased by sitting up and is tender to percussion. Neurologic deficits begin subtly and may not be apparent to the patient: weakness, ataxia, stumbling; urine retention (frequent, small voiding); bowel dysfunction, impotence; numbness. Systemic symptoms, such as fever, night sweats, weight loss, fatigue, weakness, immune disorders.
		Problems of current therapy (eg, opioids, corticosteroids, tricyclic antidepressants).
		Debilitating problems of advanced disease (eg, fatigue, cachexia, dysphagia, anemia).

Leukemia

Leukemia is the seventh leading cause of cancer death in the United States with 19,707 deaths in 1993 and 21,600 deaths estimated in 1998. Leukemia affects slightly more men than women and is the leading cause of cancer death in children (American Cancer Society, 1997; Landis et al., 1998).

The most common types of leukemias causing death in western counties (in descending order) are as follows:

1. Acute myeloid (or myelogenous) leukemia (AML), which affects mostly adults
2. Chronic lymphocytic leukemia (CLL), which affects mostly older people and is the most common type of leukemia

3. Chronic myeloid (or myelogenous) leukemia, which affects all ages
4. Acute lymphocytic leukemia (ALL), which affects mostly children (Foon & Casciato, 1995a; 1995b; Krause, 1998).

All leukemias are similar in many respects, but differences do exist, especially with respect to patients being more or less prone to the various common problems of leukemia. For the purposes of hospice or palliative care, the leukemias may be considered together, except, of course, in a specialized setting (eg, hematology palliative unit).

Infection, bleeding, anemia, fatigue, and pain are among the most serious and common problems of advanced disease. Infections or related complications are the most common cause of death in CLL and may include pneumonia, septicemia, urinary tract infection, and perirectal abscess or cellulitis; infections may be viral or bacterial, and some may be opportunistic (Krause, 1998; Ososki, 1997). Because early manifestations of infection may be subtle, slight changes indicating infection must be methodically sought. Anemia is almost universal, and bleeding (related to thrombocytopenia or less frequently, disseminated intravascular coagulation) may be found in the skin, mucous membranes, and gastrointestinal (GI) or genitourinary tracts (Foon & Casciato, 1995A; Ososki, 1997). Fatigue, weakness, and dyspnea may be related to anemia or other processes. Weight loss is common throughout the course of illness and is universal in later stages. The course of leukemia is most often slow with much treatment, so patients may be physically and emotionally exhausted by the end stages. Bone or joint pain from leukemic infiltration is common, especially in children.

The central nervous system (CNS), eyes, and testis are known as "sanctuary sites" for localized relapse, especially in ALL (Scheinberg, Maslak, & Weiss, 1997). Of these, the CNS is the most commonly affected. Headache or other neurologic changes, such as nausea, vomiting, vision blurring, or cranial nerve changes, may herald CNS involvement, including increased intracranial pressure. Changes in mentation, especially when accompanied by shortness of breath, may signal leukostasis—white cell clotting (sludging) in microvasculature—which is most common in AML (Foon & Casciato, 1995A). Leukemic infiltration of eyes causes visual changes, and infiltration of testes causes testicular swelling.

Other problems found frequently in patients with leukemia are lymphadenopathy, fever (related to infection or increased metabolic rate), night sweats, abdominal pain and organomegaly, and weight loss (Ososki, 1997). Patients with advanced disease may also be liable to late effects of therapy, including cardiomyopathy (with congestive failure and pericarditis) and neuropsychiatric symptoms

(Maguire-Eisen & Edmonds, 1992). Pleural effusions or pleural leukemic infiltrates may occur late in the disease, with the latter associated with pulmonary infection, such as *Pneumocystis carinii* pneumonia.

The later stages of chronic myeloid leukemia may be marked by the occurrence of "blast crisis," characterized by fever of unknown origin, increased anemia and thrombocytopenia, and decreased response to any therapy. A good response to therapy in a blast crisis often results in meningeal leukemia (Silver, 1993).

Death is usually from infection, bleeding, or other complications (Foon & Casciato, 1995b).

The oncologic emergencies most common in patients with leukemia are **increased intracranial pressure** (including from cerebral hemorrhage and carcinomatosis meningitis), **obstructive uropathy**, and **cardiac tamponade**. Tumor lysis syndrome is usually a complication of treatment and includes hyperuricemia, hyperkalemia, hyperphosphatemia, and hypocalcemia, with the outcome of cardiac arrhythmias, acute renal failure, and tetany (Glick & Glover, 1995; Foon & Casciato, 1995a; Scheinberg et al., 1997) (Table 26-2).

Multiple Myeloma

Multiple myeloma (MM) is the 15th leading cause of cancer death for women and men and is about equally divided between the two groups. There were 9841 deaths from MM in 1993, and there will be an estimated 11,300 deaths from MM in 1998 (American Cancer Society, 1997; Landis et al., 1998).

Along with Waldenström's macroglobulinemia and heavy chain disease, MM is a plasma cell neoplasm and in some sources is referred to as plasma cell myeloma. Proliferation of plasma cells (immunoglobulin) occurs most commonly in bones, bone marrow, and extraosseous sites, such as kidneys and heart (Anderson, 1997).

TABLE 26-2	Leukemia: Spread, Problems, and Assessment	
Metastatic Spread	**Problems**	**Assessment Parameters**
Bone marrow dysfunction	Bleeding	Thrombocytopenia: Bleeding occurs in skin, mucous membranes, and gastrointestinal (GI) or genitourinary (GU) tracts. Disseminated intravascular coagulation may also occur.
	Infection	Granulocytopenia, neutropenia. Signs and symptoms of infection in early stages may be absent. Infections may bacterial or viral and may include pneumonia, septicemia, skin infections (eg, herpes), perirectal abscess, GI or GU tract, cellulitis. Fever of unknown origin may or may not be related to infection.
	Fatigue	Thrombocytopenia, erythrocytopenia, other processes result in anemia: weakness, fatigue, tachycardia, headache, dyspnea.
Brain, central nervous system (CNS)	CNS symptoms (see Chapter 13)	**Increased intracranial pressure** (ICP) (from cerebral infiltration or meningeal leukemia): Progressive pain may be more severe in the morning. Classic triad of increased ICP = papilledema (often with visual changes), vomiting, and headache. Confusion, seizures, or other CNS problems may also result from brain involvement. Cranial nerve involvement → findings related to specific cranial nerve affected. Changes in mentation with shortness of breath may indicate leukostasis.
Lymph	Lymphadenopathy	Lymphedema: Enlarged lymph, edema, obstruction of adjacent organs (see obstructive uropathy) or structures, pain.
Liver, GI tract	Pain, hepatomegaly	Liver pain may be upper right abdominal or nonspecific, characteristic of visceral pain. It may radiate to right scapula and worsen at night.
	Ascites	Abdominal distension, bulging flanks, fluid wave, weight gain, and discomfort; anorexia, early satiety, indigestion, decreased bowel mobility; dyspnea, orthopnea, tachypnea; weakness, fatigue.
	GI disturbances	Hemorrhage, bleeding, abdominal pain.
Lung(s)	Dyspnea, cough, hemoptysis (see Chapter 14)	Pleural effusion: Dyspnea with cough and chest pain (trachea displacement toward unaffected side with large effusion). Breath sounds are usually decreased but may vary according to area of lung. Pleural effusions are usually unilateral. Pneumonia: Dyspnea with elevated temperature, chills, purulent or rusty sputum, decreased breath sounds. Pleural effusion may also be present. Preexisting conditions, such as chronic obstructive pulmonary disease or ascites, may contribute to dyspnea.
Kidney	Obstruction	**Obstructive uropathy** (ureteral): Hesitancy, urgency, nocturia, frequency, decreased force of stream, polyuria alternating with oliguria.
	GU symptoms	Hematuria, flank pain, flank mass. Nephrotic syndrome is usually a paraneoplastic syndrome rather than a result of tumor invasion or metastases.
Bones, joints	Pain	Bone pain and joint swelling are common (somatic pain).
Skin	Skin lesions	Leukemia cutis (infiltration), purpura, ecchymosis, petechiae, infection (eg, herpes), pain.
Oral cavity	Various problems	Oral lesions and gingival problems are common.

(continued)

TABLE 26-2	Leukemia: Spread, Problems, and Assessment *(Continued)*	
Metastatic Spread	Problems	Assessment Parameters
Sanctuary sites	Brain	Involvement of CNS (see above).
	Eyes	Visual changes, especially blurring.
	Testes	Testicular swelling.
Other	Various problems	Problems of therapy (eg, opioids, corticosteroids, tricyclic antidepressants, radiation, chemotherapy). Late effects of therapy include cardiomyopathy with congestive failure and pericarditis.
		Pericardial effusion → **Cardiac tamponade.**
		Dyspnea with cough, chest pain relieved by leaning forward. There may be syncope, weakness, pleural effusion, edema, distension of neck veins, tachypnea, and the clinical triad of tachycardia, muffled heart tones, and hypotension.
		Fatigue cachexia, dysphagia, or other debilitating effects of advanced disease.

Bone pain, often extreme, is the most common problem of MM. Osteolytic lesions are the primary cause of the bone pain. Pathologic fractures are common and may occur in the spine, ribs, skull, pelvis, and proximal long bones (Bataille & Harousseau, 1997). Hypercalcemia develops in about 25% of patients with MM. Hypercalcemia and bone pain may become synergistic with pain or pathologic fractures, leading to immobility, hypercalcemia, and increased likelihood of pathologic fractures. These processes also contribute to the development of pneumonia and other problems of immobility.

Bone marrow involvement leads to anemia, manifested by fatigue and weakness; to thrombocytopenia and attendant bleeding; and to neutropenia, which (along with other processes) predisposes patients to recurrent and refractory infections, especially urinary and respiratory. Acute leukemia develops in a few patients with MM (Salmon & Cassady, 1997; Sheridan, 1996).

Renal involvement occurs in 20% to 50% of patients, and acute renal failure may be precipitated most commonly by dehydration and by infection, hyperuricemia, pyelonephritis, hypercalcemia, "myeloma kidney," and deposits of calcium and amyloid in the heart, blood vessels, and GI tract. Hydration must therefore be aggressive and hypercalcemia prevented as much as possible (Salmon & Cassady, 1997; Sheridan, 1996).

Neurologic dysfunction includes peripheral neuropathies, nerve root compression, and spinal cord compression from collapse of vertebral bodies (Berenson & Casciato, 1995).

Hyperviscosity syndrome occurs in about 5% of patients with MM, leading to symptoms of fatigue, headache, changes in mentation, and visual disturbances. Vascular effects of sludging may include myocardial ischemia and circulatory insufficiency (Anderson, 1997).

Cardiac failure is relatively common and is due primarily to infiltration of myocardium with amyloids, hyperviscosity syndrome, or anemia (Anderson, 1997).

Death is usually from infection or renal failure (Bataille & Harousseau, 1997).

The oncologic emergencies most common in patients with MM are **hypercalcemia**, **spinal cord compression**, and **hyperuricemia** (Bataille & Harousseau, 1997; Glick & Glover, 1995; Morris & Holland, 1997) (Table 26-3).

TABLE 26-3	Multiple Myeloma: Spread, Problems, and Assessment	
Metastatic Spread	**Problems**	**Assessment Parameters**
Proliferation of plasma cells in bones	Pain	From pressure, pathologic fractures are common. Primary sites are spine, ribs, skull, pelvis, proximal long bones. **Spinal cord compression:** Back pain may be local (somatic: constant, dull, aching), radicular, or both. It is exacerbated by movement, neck flexion, straight leg raising and is decreased by sitting up. It is tender to percussion. Neurologic deficits begin subtly and may not be apparent to the patient: weakness, ataxia, stumbling; urine retention (frequent, small voiding); bowel dysfunction, impotence; numbness lower extremities.
	Metabolic changes	**Hypercalcemia** (often nonspecific): Symptoms include fatigue, weakness, anorexia, nausea, polyuria, polydipsia, and constipation; progressing to changes in mentation, seizures, and coma.
	Immobility	Related to or influenced by pain, pathologic fractures, hypercalcemia. Evaluate for pneumonia.
Marrow involvement	Bleeding	Thrombocytopenia: Bleeding in skin, mucous membranes, GI, or GU tract. Anemia: Fatigue, weakness, headache, tachypnea, dyspnea.
	Infection(s)	Neutropenia: Frequent infections, especially pneumonia, urinary tract.
Kidney	Renal failure	Acute renal failure, **hyperuricemia** related to dehydration, infection, pyelonephritis, hypercalcemia, "myeloma kidney," and systemic amyloid deposits. Symptoms include oliguria, fluid retention, engorged neck veins, bounding pulse, first a decrease then an increase in blood pressure, electrolyte abnormalities, GI symptoms. Renal failure may be irreversible.
Heart, circulatory	Cardiac failure	Due to amyloid infiltration of myocardium, hyperviscosity syndrome, or anemia. Hyperviscosity syndrome: Decreased circulation, fatigue, headache, visual disturbances, changes in mentation.
Other	Neurologic problems	Peripheral neuropathies, nerve root compression, or **spinal cord compression** (usually from vertebral collapse): Back pain is the first symptom and may be local (somatic: constant, dull, aching), radicular, or both. It is exacerbated by movement, neck flexion, straight leg raising and is decreased by sitting up. It is tender to percussion. Neurologic deficits usually follow pain, may begin subtly, and include extremity weakness, ataxia, stumbling; urine retention, bowel dysfunction, numbness. Fatigue cachexia, dysphagia, or other debilitating effects of advanced disease. Problems of therapy (eg, opioids, corticosteroids, tricyclic antidepressants, radiation, chemotherapy).

Melanoma

Cutaneous Melanoma (CM) is the 17th leading cause of cancer death with 6712 deaths in 1993 and an estimated 7300 deaths in 1998. CM affects about twice as many men as women. Incidence is increasing worldwide and in the United States has more than doubled in the past 10 years (American Cancer Society, 1997; Landis et al., 1998).

Primary sites of metastases of melanoma are regional lymph, then skin, subcutaneous tissue, and lung. Other major sites of metastases include liver, bone, and brain. GI metastases occur and may lead to small bowel obstruction, intussusception, or chronic bleeding (Urist, Miller, & Maddox, 1995). Melanoma is significantly more likely than any other tumor to spread to almost all vital organs, resulting in carcinomatosis (Inagaki, Rodriguez, & Bodey, 1974) and thus a vast array of problems. Distant sites of metastases may include (in addition to the above) heart, adrenal gland, spleen, pancreas, thyroid, bone marrow, pleura, diaphragm, ovaries, prostate, genitourinary tract, breast, and even placenta and fetus (Morton, Essner, Kirkwood, & Parker, 1997; Wagner & Casciato, 1995). Ulceration of the primary tumor may occur, resulting in odor and other challenges in care. The course of CM is variable, and in some cases patients with distant metastases may remain stable for long periods of time.

The oncologic emergencies commonly associated with melanoma include **pericardial effusion** leading to tamponade, **increased intracranial pressure** from brain metastases or carcinomatosis meningitis, **airway obstruction**, and **hemorrhage** from GI involvement (Glick & Glover, 1995; Waller & Caroline, 1996) (Table 26-4).

TABLE 26-4	Melanoma: Spread, Problems, and Assessment	
Metastatic Spread	**Problems**	**Assessment Parameters**
Primary tumor growth; skin, subcutaneous tissue	Skin	The primary tumor may ulcerate. Multiple skin metastases cause pain, odor, pruritus, bleeding. Lesions are sometimes inflammatory. Subcutaneous deposits are common.
Lymph: regional, distant	Lymphadenopathy	Lymphedema: Enlarged lymph, edema (area or lower extremities), pain, cellulitis, lymphangitis. Extensive pelvic disease can result in neurologic impairment or urinary dysfunction (the vulva is a common primary site).
Lung(s)	Dyspnea, other pulmonary symptoms (see Chapter 14)	Pleural effusion: Dyspnea with cough and chest pain (trachea displacement toward unaffected side with large effusion). Breath sounds are usually decreased but may vary according to area of lung. Pleural effusions are usually unilateral. Pneumonia: Dyspnea with elevated temperature, chills, purulent or rusty sputum, decreased breath sounds. Pleural effusion may also be present. **Embolus:** Sudden onset of dyspnea with rapid breathing, rapid heart rate, cough, chest pain, and blood in sputum. **Obstruction:** Progressive or rapidly increasing dyspnea, blood in sputum, noisy breathing, chronic cough, choking, or pneumonia. Preexisting conditions, such as chronic obstructive pulmonary disease or ascites, may also cause dyspnea.

(continued)

TABLE 26-4 Melanoma: Spread, Problems, and Assessment *(Continued)*

Metastatic Spread	Problems	Assessment Parameters
Liver	Pain	Liver pain may be upper right abdominal or nonspecific, characteristic of visceral pain. It may radiate to right scapula and worsen at night.
	Ascites	Abdominal distension, bulging flanks, fluid wave, weight gain, and discomfort; anorexia, early satiety, indigestion, decreased bowel mobility; dyspnea, orthopnea, tachypnea; weakness, fatigue.
Bone	Pain	Bone pain is usually localized, constant, dull, aching, or sharp and is worse at night.
		Spinal cord compression (from pathologic fracture or compression of cord without fracture): Back pain is the first symptom and may be local (somatic: constant, dull, aching), radicular, or both. It is exacerbated by movement, neck flexion, straight leg raising and is decreased by sitting up. It is tender to percussion. Neurologic deficits usually follow pain, may begin subtly, and include extremity weakness, ataxia, stumbling; urine retention, bowel dysfunction, numbness.
Brain	Central nervous system (CNS) symptoms	**Increased intracranial pressure** (ICP): Progressive pain is usually present and may be more severe in the morning. Classic triad of increased ICP = papilledema (often with visual changes), vomiting, and headache.
		Confusion, seizures, or other CNS problems may also result from brain metastases (see Chapter 13).
Gastrointestinal (GI) system	Bleeding	Occult bleeding. Sometimes massive hemorrhage from stomach.
	Pain, obstruction	Obstruction, intussusception, often from multiple sites. Small bowel may be involved: Severe epigastric colicky pain; vomiting bile and mucus; abdomen not distended.
Heart	Cardiac dysfunction	Arrhythmias, congestive heart failure.
		Pericardial effusion → **Cardiac tamponade:** Dyspnea with cough and chest pain relieved by leaning forward. There may be syncope, weakness, pleural effusion, edema, distension of neck veins, tachypnea, and the clinical triad of tachycardia, muffled heart tones, and hypotension.
Kidney	Genitourinary problems	Hematuria, flank pain, flank mass.
		Uremia: Decreased urine, changes in blood pressure, congestive heart failure, stomatitis, nausea and vomiting, GI bleeding, bowel changes, lethargy, changes in mentation.
Other	Various problems	Anemia: Dyspnea, weakness, fatigue, tachycardia, headache. Anemia also may be considered a PNS.
		Fatigue cachexia, dysphagia, or other debilitating effects of advanced disease.
		Fever of unknown origin (common with liver involvement).
		Preexisting problems.
		Problems of therapy (eg, opioids, corticosteroids, tricyclic antidepressants, radiation, chemotherapy).

REFERENCES

American Cancer Society. (1997). *Cancer facts and figures*. Atlanta: Author.

Anderson, K. C. (1997). Plasma cell tumors. In J. F. Holland, R. C. Bast, D. L. Morton, E. Frei, D. W. Kufe, & R. C. Weichselbaum (Eds.). *Cancer medicine* (4th ed.) (pp. 2809–2828). Baltimore: Williams & Wilkins.

Bataille, R., & Harousseau, J-L. (1997). Multiple myeloma. *New England Journal of Medicine*, 336(23), 1657–1664.

Berenson, J. R., & Casciato, D. A. (1995). Plasma cell disorders. In D. A. Casciato & B. B. Lowitz (Eds.), *Manual of clinical oncology* (pp. 386–401). Boston: Little, Brown and Company.

Foon, K. A., & Casciato, D. A. (1995a). Chronic leukemias. In D. A. Casciato & B. B. Lowitz (Eds.), *Manual of clinical oncology* (pp. 402–417). Boston: Little, Brown and Company.

Foon, K. A., & Casciato, D. A. (1995b). Acute leukemia. In D. A. Casciato & B. B. Lowitz (Eds.), *Manual of clinical oncology* (pp. 431–445). Boston: Little, Brown and Company

Glass, A. G., Karnell, L. H., & Menck, H. R. (1997). The national cancer data base report on non-Hodgkin's lymphoma. *Cancer*, 80(12), 2311–2320.

Glick, J. H., & Glover, D. (1995). Oncologic emergencies. In G. P. Murphy, W. Lawrence, & R. E. Lenhard (Eds.), *Clinical oncology* (2nd ed.) (pp. 597–618). Atlanta: American Cancer Society.

Inagaki, T., Rodriguez, V., & Bodey, G. P. (1974). Causes of death in cancer patients. *Cancer*, 33(2), 568–573.

Krause, J. C. (1998). Chronic lymphocytic leukemia: A brief review. *Cleveland Clinic Journal of Medicine*, 65(1), 42–48.

Landis, S. H., Murray, T., Bolden, S., & Wingo, P. A. (1998). Cancer statistics, 1998. *CA—A Cancer Journal for Clinicians*, 48(1), 6–29.

Maguire-Eisen, M., & Edmonds, K. S. (1992). Leukemias. In J. C. Clark & R. F. McGee (Eds.), *Core curriculum for oncology nursing* (pp. 480–487), Philadelphia: W.B. Saunders.

Morris, J. C., & Holland, J. F. (1997). Oncologic emergencies. In J. F. Holland, R. C. Bast, D. L. Morton, E. Frei, D. W. Kufe, & R. C. Weichselbaum (Eds.), *Cancer medicine* (4th ed.) (pp. 3337–3367). Baltimore: Williams & Wilkins.

Morton, D. l., Essner, R., Kirkwood, J. M., & Parker, R. G. (1997). Malignant melanoma. In J. F. Holland, R. C. Bast, D. L. Morton, E. Frei, D. W. Kufe, & R. C. Weichselbaum (Eds.). *Cancer medicine* (4th ed.) (pp. 1923–1938). Baltimore: Williams & Wilkins.

Ososki, R. L. (1997). Leukemia. In S. Otto (Ed.), *Oncology nursing* (3rd ed.) (pp. 284–311). St. Louis: C.V. Mosby.

Rosenthal. D. S., & Eyre, H. J. (1995). Hodgkin's disease and non-Hodgkin's lymphoma. In G. P. Murphy, W. Lawrence, & R. E. Lenhard (Eds.), *Clinical oncology* (2nd ed.) (pp. 451–469). Altanta: American Cancer Society.

Salmon, S. E., & Cassady, J. R. (1997). Plasma cell neoplasms. In V. T. DeVita, S. Hellman, & S. A. Rosenberg (Eds.), *Cancer: Principles and practice of oncology* (5th ed.) (pp. 2344–2387). Philadelphia: Lippincott-Raven.

Scheinberg, D. A., Maslak, P., & Weiss, M. (1997). Acute leukemias. In V. T. DeVita, S. Hellman, & S. A. Rosenberg (Eds.), *Cancer: Principles and practice of oncology* (5th ed.) (pp. 2293–2321). Philadelphia: Lippincott-Raven.

Sheridan, C. A. (1996). Multiple myeloma. *Seminars in Oncology Nursing*, 12(1), 59–69.

Silver, R. T. (1993). Chronic myeloid leukemia. In J. F. Holland, E. Frei, R. C. Bast, D. W. Kufe, D. L. Morton, & R. W. Weischselbaum (Eds.), *Cancer medicine* (3rd ed.) (pp. 1934–1946). Philadelphia: Lea & Febiger.

Skarin, A. T., & Dorfman, D. M. (1997). Non-Hodgkin's lymphomas: Current classification and management. *CA—A Cancer Journal for Clinicians*, 47(6), 351–372.

Urist, M. M., Miller, D. M., & Maddox, W. A. (1995). Malignant melanoma. In G. P. Murphy, W. Lawrence, & R. E. Lenhard (Eds.), *Clinical oncology* (2nd ed.) (pp. 305–310). Atlanta: American Cancer Society.

Wagner, R. F., & Casciato, D. A. (1995). Skin cancers. In D. A. Casciato & B. B. Lowitz (Eds.), *Manual of clinical oncology* (pp. 288–299). Boston: Little, Brown and Company.

Waller, A., & Caroline, N. L. (1996). *Handbook of palliative care in cancer*. Boston: Butterworth-Heinemann.

Yarbro, C. H., & McFadden, M. E. (1997). Malignant lymphomas. In S. I. Groenwald, M. H. Frogge, M. Goodman, & C. H. Yarbro (Eds.), *Cancer nursing: Principles and practice* (4th ed.) (pp. 1291–1318). Boston: Jones and Bartlett.

Management of Other Terminal Illnesses

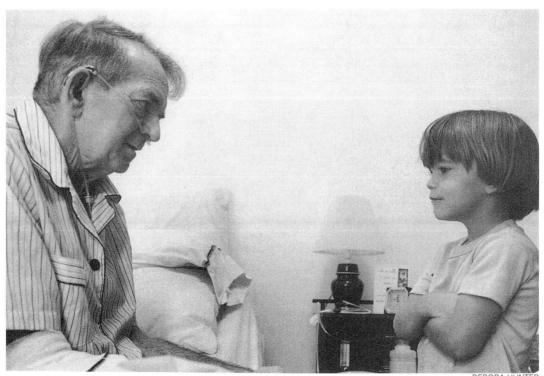

DEBORA HUNTER

INTRODUCTION

Although cancer is the most commonly seen disease in hospice and palliative care settings, other illnesses are responsible for the great majority of deaths overall. Cancer, however, presents a complex and somehow more appropriate (for hospice and palliative care) clinical picture than most other illnesses. In particular, at some point in the progression of cancer, it is apparent to those who understand cancer that the patient will die from the disease. This section of the book is concerned with terminal care for patients with diseases other than cancer:

● Human immunodeficiency virus (HIV) infection (AIDS)
● Degenerative neurologic disorders (multiple sclerosis, Parkinson's disease, amyotrophic lateral sclerosis, myasthenia gravis)
● Alzheimer's disease
● Cardiovascular and chronic obstructive pulmonary disease

Care for patients who are dying from these diseases is often complicated by one or both of two factors:

● Several (eg, AIDS and heart disease) have an uncertain trajectory. In many cases, it is difficult to determine with certainty that curative treatment should be withdrawn and palliative treatment instituted.
● In other diseases (eg, Alzheimer's, multiple sclerosis [MS]), the disease process is extremely slow, and satisfactory systems of care do not exist to any significant extent.

In this section of the book, beginning approaches to the problems of these diseases are explored.

The concepts of palliative care for patients with cancer are generally applicable to other patients as well. For example, although pain syndromes in HIV infection or MS differ in some respects from those in cancer, the general approach to assessment and treatment is quite similar. Approaches to gastrointestinal, urinary tract, and other problems are also similar. Moreover, *it is not always necessary to draw a line between curative and palliative care. Competent curative treatment of an illness should never preclude competent management of symptoms.*

Although similar in many respects to the psychosocial issues common in cancer, psychosocial issues for the diseases in this section are different in other respects. AIDS, for example, carries at least the potential for several unique psychosocial problems, including the potential for transmission and negative implications in how the patient may have contracted the disease (eg, intravenous drug use or homosexual activity). The slow neurodegenerative disorders often mean unimaginable physical, psychological, and spiritual stress on caregivers. Still, many of the basic principles of care remain similar.

CHAPTER 27

Acquired Immunodeficiency Syndrome

The worldwide spread of acquired immunodeficiency syndrome (AIDS) and its causative agent, human immunodeficiency virus type 1 (HIV-1), is the most dramatic health problem of the modern world. As of 1997, in the United States alone, more than 386,000 people have died from AIDS since the pandemic began in 1981 (Centers for Disease Control and Prevention [CDC], 1998a).

Epidemiology and Characteristics of the Disease

Worldwide, approximately 23 million people (40% female) are infected with HIV-1, and currently approximately 500,000 infants are infected each year (CDC, 1997; CDC, 1998b). Barring an unforeseen breakthrough in treatment, all of these infected individuals will develop AIDS.

In the United States, the epidemiology of AIDS is shifting from a population composed mainly of homosexual and bisexual men and intravenous drug users to a more diverse grouping. Although men who have sex with men remain the most affected group, HIV-infected individuals now include steadily increasing numbers of children and heterosexual women and men. African Americans and Hispanic Americans account for a disproportionate share of cases of HIV infection (CDC, 1998a).

The virus is transmitted through sexual intercourse, blood and blood products, and perinatally or through breast milk from an infected mother to her infant. The onset of clinical symptoms varies from 2 weeks after exposure to as long as 12 years (Flemmig & Visscher, 1997). About 50% of infected individuals experience symptoms of acute retroviral or seroconversion syndrome (primary HIV-1 infection), and about 50% are asymptomatic. Disease progression is marked by progressively decreased CD4+ lymphocytes, increased viral load, and the presence of opportunistic infections (Saag, 1997).

Opportunistic infections are the major clinical manifestation of HIV disease and are the primary cause of morbidity and mortality in HIV disease (Chaisson & Moore, 1997; Piemme, 1998). The incidence of opportunistic infections increases with immunosuppression marked by decreased CD4+ counts and increased viral load (Temesgen & Wright, 1997). In general, the more frequent, varied, and severe the infections, the poorer the prognosis. The greatest risk of death occurs with decreased CD4 cell count and increased viral load and presence of the following opportunistic diseases or conditions (in decreasing order of magnitude of risk): lymphoma, progressive multifocal leukoencephalopathy (PML), disseminated *Mycobacterium avium* complex infection (MAC), and cytomegalovirus (CMV) disease. Other conditions indicating reduced survival time include *Pneumocystis carinii* pneumonia (PCP), Kaposi's sarcoma (KS), toxoplasmosis, cryptosporidiosis, dementia, wasting syndrome, and esophageal candidiasis (Chaisson, Gallant, Keruly, & Moore, 1998).

The disease may be categorized based on CD4 counts and a combination of clinical features (Saag, 1997) as follows:

1. Initial or primary HIV infection (acute retroviral or seroconversion syndrome) is often characterized as similar to the flu or mononucleosis. Primary HIV infection is described in the section Physical Problems of AIDS.
2. Early HIV-1 is defined by a CD4+ count greater than 500 cells mm^3. Clinical manifestations commonly include lymphadenopathy, dermatologic abnormalities, and, to a lesser extent, oral lesions.
3. Intermediate stage HIV disease is defined by a CD4+ count between 200 and 500 cells mm^3. Clinical manifestations include increased frequency, severity, and variety of skin and oral lesions; intermittent constitutional symptoms, such as headache, fatigue, arthralgias, and myalgias; and increased frequency of common infections.
4. Late stage HIV disease is defined by a CD4+ count between 50 and 200 cells mm^3. CDC guidelines published in 1993 defined AIDS as a CD4+ count of less than 200 cells mm^3 or presence of AIDS-defining clinical conditions, such as PCP, KS, toxoplasmosis, cryptococcosis, cryptosporidiosis, esophageal candidiasis, and others. In late stage HIV disease, constitutional symptoms increase, as do neurologic disorders, HIV-associated cancers, hematologic disorders, and hormonal disorders.
5. Advanced HIV disease is defined by a CD4+ count of less than 50 cells mm^3. Opportunistic infections associated with advanced stage disease include MAC disease, cryptococcal meningitis, CMV retinitis, invasive aspergillosis, PML, disseminated histoplasmosis, coccidioidomycosis, and bartonellosis. Opportunistic infections may occur concurrently or relapse. Central nervous system (CNS) disorders are more common, severe, and progressive. Anorexia and gastrointestinal (GI) malabsorption are common and contribute to HIV wasting syndrome.
6. Terminal HIV results from the inability to control symptoms of the disease or available treatments becoming ineffective.

Patients with AIDS present several major challenges to practitioners involved with terminal, palliative, or hospice care (Kemp & Stepp, 1995). Some of these challenges are described in the following list.

● The severity, complexity, and unpredictable trajectory of AIDS makes caring for patients with advanced disease a challenge for nonspecialists in AIDS.
● There is sometimes difficulty discerning which treatments are palliative and which are curative. Intravenous infusions, blood transfusions, and expensive suppressive therapy are uncommon in most hospice settings. Moreover, some patients treat themselves with alternative therapies. Even in the terminal stage of AIDS, many patients, especially young adults, cling to the hope for a cure and thus are not willing to accept hospice care.
● Challenging psychosocial problems often attend AIDS, including lifestyle-related family or intrapersonal conflict, caregiver fears of infection, uncertainty regarding the course of illness, and the problems attending any advanced and fatal disease. Care is complicated in some cases by intravenous or other drug use (remote or current).
● Funding for services is often inadequate.

Nevertheless, hospice care and hospice principles (especially related to quality of life and symptom management) are vitally important in the continuum of services for patients with AIDS. At some point, patients with AIDS are terminally ill, and further aggressive treatment and resuscitation are futile.

Transmission Precautions

Regardless of the specifics of infection transmission, in all cases, it is essential to practice universal precautions and to instruct and aid others, especially those who are immunosuppressed, in avoiding infection. See Box 27-1 for a description of universal precautions against infection transmission.

Treatment of AIDS

Holistic treatment of HIV is organized according to five axes of care:

1. The psychosocial and spiritual health of the patient and of his or her significant others is addressed throughout the course of illness.
2. Nutrition and exercise are especially important early on in the process of HIV and AIDS. In the terminal stage, the ability to exercise or take in nutrition is greatly diminished.
3. Prevention or early identification of deterioration is emphasized throughout the disease. Avoidance of complications is increasingly difficult as CD4+ counts decrease.
4. The patient and family are educated about the illness in general and especially about changes in symptoms that require urgent attention.
5. Medical therapy and nursing measures related to it are generally directed to anti-HIV measures, prophylaxis of opportunistic infections, treatment of specific conditions, and management of symptoms.

Beginning in 1995, new, more active antiretroviral therapies led to sharply decreased morbidity and mortality rates. Triple combination antiretroviral therapy or highly active antiretroviral therapy (HAART) consists of two nucleosides (to compete with the synthesis of proviral deoxyribonucleic acid [DNA]) and a protease inhibitor (to inhibit the protease enzyme that is necessary for the final stage of the HIV life cycle). HAART is the current standard of care and results in the greatest reduction in morbidity and mortality (Palella et al., 1998; Sherer, 1998). Nucleoside reverse transcriptase inhibitors currently include zidovudine, didanosine, zalcitabine, lamivudine, and stavudine. Protease inhibitors include ritonavir, indinavir, nelfinavir, and saquinavir. Nonnucleoside reverse transcriptase block DNA activity and include nevirapine and delavirdine. Drugs in advanced stages of investigation are abacavir, efavirenz, amprenavir, and adefovir (Carpenter et al., 1998). However, despite gains made through routine prophylaxis and improved retroviral therapy, opportunistic infections and diseases continue to occur, sometimes with changes in presentation so that they are not always as readily identified as before (Jacobson & French, 1998; Sepkowitz, 1998). From 10% to 20% of patients fail to respond to HAART (Sherer, 1998).

Medical treatment for HIV infection is based on the following principles of therapy (CDC, 1998c):

1. Ongoing HIV replication leads to immune system damage and progression to AIDS.
2. Plasma HIV ribonucleic acid (RNA) levels (viral load) indicate the magnitude of HIV replication and associated rate of CD4+ cell destruction, and CD4+ cell counts indicate immune damage already suffered. Regular measurement of both parameters is necessary to determine when to initiate or modify antiretroviral treatment.
3. Disease progression rates vary among individuals, and treatment decisions should be individualized according to CD4+ cell counts and plasma HIV RNA levels.
4. Maximum achievable suppression of HIV replication is the goal of therapy. Combination antiretroviral therapy lowers HIV RNA levels below what can currently be measured, hence selection of the most effective antiretroviral variants is limited.
5. The most effective means to accomplish lasting suppression of HIV replication is the simultaneous initiation of combinations of effective anti-HIV drugs with which the patient has not already been treated and that are not cross-resistant with anti-HIV drugs with which the patient has already been treated.

Box 27-1. Universal Precautions

From 1981 to 1997, 22 cases of occupationally acquired HIV infection of nurses have been documented (Centers for Disease Control, 1998a). Percutaneous injury is by far the most common means of exposure (Marcus & Bell, 1997). Risk for HIV infection from percutaneous injury (Cardo et al, 1997) is increased by the following:

1. Deep injury
2. Injury with a device visibly contaminated with blood
3. Injury with a needle placed in the source patient's artery or vein
4. Exposure to a source patient who died of AIDS within 2 months of the exposure

While the risk of HIV infection to health care workers (HCW) is very small, practitioners must always protect themselves *and* others from disease transmission. The following is a summary of blood and other body fluid precautions that does not substitute for the current policies and procedures that every health care organization should have. Policies and procedures should be based on Centers for Disease Control and Prevention (CDC) guidelines. Note that the best means of protecting oneself from the most common means of HIV transmission—needle-stick—is to pay careful attention to what one is doing. Note also that patients with advanced AIDS have other infections, some of which are transmitted in the same manner as HIV and some of which are not. Tuberculosis, for example, is most often contracted by inhalation of airborne droplets and is a distinct risk for HCW (see below).

Fluids to which universal precautions apply (including materials contaminated by these fluids): Blood, semen, vaginal fluid, amniotic fluid, cerebrospinal fluid, pericardial fluid, peritoneal fluid, pleural fluid, synovial fluid, breast milk, saliva (if contaminated with blood). Universal precautions do not apply to the following unless blood is present: feces, nasal secretions, sputum, sweat, tears, urine, vomitus (Bolyard & Bell, 1997).

Handwashing: Hands should be washed between each patient contact and after contact with blood, bloody fluids, secretions, excretions, and contaminated items, regardless of whether gloves are worn.

Hands should be washed after gloves are removed. Hands should be washed between tasks and different sites on the same patient's body. Plain nonantimicrobial soap should be used for handwashing unless there are special circumstances as defined by infection control policies and procedures.

Gloves: Gloves are worn when contact is possible with a patient's blood, bloody fluids, secretions, excretions, and contaminated items. Gloves should be changed between patients; between tasks on the same patient, when contaminated; and as soon as possible after they are torn or punctured. Clean gloves should be put on before touching mucous membranes and nonintact skin. Hands should be washed after removing gloves. Disposable latex or vinyl gloves should not be reused. Utility gloves can be decontaminated and reused but should be discarded if deterioration or break occurs.

Gowns: Gowns or aprons are not routinely necessary. They are best used when there is the possibility of contact with body fluids that might get on the practitioner's skin or clothing (eg, when changing dressings with heavy drainage or during procedures involving splashes or sprays). Gowns should be changed (and hands washed afterward) when soiled and between patients.

Masks, protective eyewear: Masks and protective eyewear or face shields are used when splashes or sprays of body fluids are anticipated (eg, suctioning, bronchoscopy, surgery, and débridement).

Needles and sharp instruments: Careful handling of syringes and sharp instruments is necessary, especially if contaminated with blood or other body secretions. Percutaneous injury is the greatest threat, but contamination of skin, mucous membranes, clothing, or other surfaces may carry some degree of risk, especially to other patients. Used needles should never be recapped before disposal in a sharps container, and care should be taken that needles or other sharp instruments are not pointed toward the body or others. Sharps disposal containers should be rigid, puncture-proof, and not be completely filled, nor should any item be forced into a sharps container. Care should be taken to account for all sharps to ensure that none is mixed in with linens, paper items, trash, or other such materials.

(continued)

Box 27-1. Universal Precautions *(Continued)*

Linens: Linens and related items contaminated with blood, bloody fluids, secretions, or excretions should be disposed of according to agency policies and in such a way that prevents contamination of skin, mucous membranes, and clothing or transfer of microorganisms to other patients. In the home, linens and other soiled fabrics should be washed in hot water with detergent in a 25-minute washing cycle.

Environmental control: Agency policies and procedures should include means of disinfecting surfaces, such as beds, bedrails, bedside tables, and other contaminated items or instruments.

Other: Mouthpieces, resuscitation bags, and other ventilation equipment should be used in place of mouth-to-mouth resuscitation.

Tuberculosis and other airborne infections: CDC guidelines should be followed and, depending on circumstances, may include engineering controls for ventilation, personal respirators, masks, and other such equipment and precautions.

References: Bolyard & Bell, 1997; Cardo et al., 1997; CDC, 1998a; Ropka & Grant, 1998.

6. Antiretroviral drugs used in combination therapy should always be used according to optimum schedules and dosages.
7. Effective antiretroviral drugs are limited in number and mechanism of action, and cross-resistance exists among some drugs; therefore, any change in therapy increases future therapeutic limitations.
8. Women should receive optimal antiretroviral therapy regardless of pregnancy status.
9. The same principles of antiretroviral therapy apply to HIV-infected children, adolescents, and adults, although there are unique considerations with children.
10. People with acute primary HIV infection should be treated with combination antiretroviral therapy.
11. People infected with HIV, including those with undetectable viral loads, should be considered infectious and should thus not expose others or themselves to infection.

Other treatment may be a combination of curative and palliative care or may be designed only to slow wasting. Many medications used to treat AIDS and its associated infections are likely to produce toxic effects. The balance between desired and untoward effects is often difficult to establish. (See Table 27-1 for a listing of commonly used drugs for patients with AIDS, the indications for their use, common side effects and toxicities, and interactions and contraindications.)

Practitioners should be aware that alternative healing practices are used by some patients with HIV infection. Many such practices are benign and may have some positive effect at least on attitude (eg, relaxation therapy, massage, acupressure, and yoga). There is not, however, any significant body of research demonstrating efficacy of any alternative therapy with respect to CD4+ counts, viral loads, or opportunistic infections. Buyer's clubs are found in most large cities, and some medications and herbal preparations specifically developed for alternative AIDS treatment are available through the mail. Some are benign and possibly helpful. Others involve powerful chemical-biologic agents, such as compound Q, that may have difficult-to-predict, adverse effects. In addition, some medications available by prescription (eg, itraconazole, ddc) are also obtainable through buyer's clubs. It is essential for the practitioner to determine what medications, agents, or herbs clients are taking. However, to make this determination, it is important to approach patients free of judgments and prejudices.

Text continues on page 288

TABLE 27.1	Commonly Used Drugs for Patients Infected with Human Immunodeficiency Virus (HIV)		
Drug Name	**Primary Indications**	**Common Side Effects, Toxicities**	**Interactions and Contraindications (consult insert, other materials)**
Acyclovir (Zovirax)	Herpes zoster/simplex	Oral: Headache, nausea, vomiting, diarrhea, vertigo, hematuria Parenteral: Lethargy, potential for renal dysfunction, confusion, coma	Zidovudine, opioids (meperidine), probenicid
Amphotericin B	Fungal infections	Fever, chills, hypokalemia, anemia, visual changes, renal failure, parasthesias, tinnitus, hearing loss, shortness of breath, seizures, pruritus, hematologic disorders	Corticosteroids, dapsone, digoxin flucytosine, mechlorethamine, TMP/SMX, zidovudine
Delavirdine (Rescriptor)	HIV infection	Rash, changes in liver function	Antacids, astemizole, carbamazepine, clarithromycin, didanosine, diltiazem, erythromycin, indinavir, itraconazole, midazolam, nifedipine, phenytoin, prednisone, quinidine, rifabutin, rifampin, ritonavir, saquinovir, terfenadine, testosterone, triazolam, warfarin
Didanosine [ddI] (Videx)	Advanced HIV infection and intolerance to, or deterioration during, zidovudine (AZT) therapy	Seizures, headache, peripheral neuropathy, cardiomyopathy, chills, fever, diarrhea, abdominal pain, pancreatitis Signs of pancreatitis should be reported promptly. Patients at risk for pancreatitis (independently of ddI use) should be closely monitored	Alpha interferon, antacids, cimetidine, ciprofloxacin (and other quinolone antibiotics), dapsone, ganciclovir, itraconazole, ketoconazole, pentamidine, quinolone antibiotics, ranitidine, ribavarine, tetracyclines, TMP/SMX, vincristine, zalcitabine, zidovudine
Ethambutol	Mycobacterium infection (tuberculosis, *Mycobacterium arium* complex [MAC])	Arthralgias, fever, rash, parasthesias, visual changes, abdominal pain, nausea and vomiting, anorexia, headache, confusion	Aluminum hydroxide
Fluconazole (Diflucan)	Fungal infections: cryptococcal meningitis, candidiasis	Abnormal liver function, nausea, abdominal pain, dizziness, headache, skin rash	Anticoagulants, astemizole, cyclosporin, methylpred- nisone, phenytoin, rifampin, sulfonylurea oral hypo- glycemics (eg, tolbutamide), terfenadine, zidovudine

TABLE 27.1	Commonly Used Drugs for Patients Infected with Human Immunodeficiency Virus (HIV) *(Continued)*		
Drug Name	**Primary Indications**	**Common Side Effects, Toxicities**	**Interactions and Contraindications (consult insert, other materials)**
Foscarnet sodium (Foscavir)	Cytomegalovirus (CMV) retinitis	Renal failure, seizures, polydipsia, nausea, anorexia, electrolyte imbalances (Ca, phosphatemia), fatigue, irritability	Pentamidine
Ganciclovir (Cytovene)	CMV retinitis; disseminated CMV	Cytopenic changes, abnormal liver function, phlebitis, nausea, abdominal pain, anorexia, headache, changes in mentation, skin rash	Amphotericin B, antineoplastic drugs, corticosteroids, dapsone, didanosine, flucytosine, foscarnet, pentamidine, pyrimethamine
Indinavir (Crixivan)	HIV infection	Nephrolithiasis, gastrointestinal (GI) intolerance, nausea, headache, asthenia, blurred vision, rash, metallic taste, thrombocytopenia, hyperglycemia	Astemizole, cisapride, delavirdine, didanosine, ergot alkaloids, ketoconazole, midazolam, nevirapine, rifabutin, rifampin, terfenadine, triazolam
Interferon alfa-2a recombinant (Intron-A, Roferon-A)	Kaposi's sarcoma	Leukopenia, congestive cardiomyopathy, liver enzyme changes, weight loss, flulike symptoms, alopecia, fatigue	Zidovudine
Isoniazid (INH)	TB, MAC	Decreased appetite, sore throat, nausea and vomiting, diarrhea, asthenia, parasthesias, changes in liver function, bleeding/bruising, seizures, depression	Alcohol, aluminum hydroxide, rifampin
Itraconazole (Sporanox)	Histoplasmosis, blastomycosis	Nausea, fatigue, rash, K depletion, edema	Astemizole, cisapride, terfenadine
Ketoconazole (Nizoral)	Candidiasis, other fungal infections	Hepatitis, nausea, diarrhea, headache, dizziness, drowsiness, skin rash, photophobia	Alcohol, antacids, anticoagulants, astemizole, cimetidine, cisapride, corticosteroids, cyclosporin, H_2 blockers, isoniazid, paclitaxel, pheny-toin, ranitidine, rifampin, sucralfate, terfenadine, theophylline, triazolam, hepatotoxic drugs
Lamivudine (3TC, Epivir)	HIV infection	Neutropenia, rash, insomnia, fever, headache, asthenia, diarrhea, parasthesias	TMP/SMX, zidovudine, drugs toxic to pancreas or peripherally neurotoxic
Nelfinavir (Viracept)	HIV infection	Diarrhea, hyperglycemia	Astemizole, cisapride, delavirdine, ergot alkaloids, ethinyl estradiol, indinavir, midazolam, norethindrone, rifabutin, rifampin, saquinavir, terfenadine, triazolam

TABLE 27.1   **Commonly Used Drugs for Patients Infected with Human Immunodeficiency Virus (HIV) *(Continued)***

Drug Name	Primary Indications	Common Side Effects, Toxicities	Interactions and Contraindications (consult insert, other materials)
Nevirapine (Viramune)	HIV infection	Rash, thrombocytopenia, fever	Amoxicillin, astemizole, cimetadine, cisapride, clarithromycin, clavulonic acid, corticosteroids, dapsone, delavirdine, didanosine, ethinyl estradiol, itraconazole, indinavir, ketoconazole, midazolam, norethindrone, oral contraceptives, phenytoin, rifabutin, rifampin, ritonavir, saquinavir, terfenadine, ticarcillin, TMP/SMX, tolbutamide, triazolam, trimetrexate, warfarin, zidovudine
Pentamidine isethionate - aerosol (Nebupent)	*Pneumocystis carincii* pneumonia (PCP) Prophylaxis	Chest pain, coughing, congestion, dyspnea, pharyngitis, skin rash, pneumothorax	Zidovudine
Pentamidine isethionate - IV and IM (Pentam)	PCP treatment	Blood dyscrasias, hyperglycemia or hypoglycemia, hypotension, changes in heart rate and rhythm, skin rash	Ganciclovir, zidovudine
Pyrimethamine (Daraprim)	Toxoplasmosis treatment, PCP	Folic acid deficiency (including bleeding, diarrhea, stomatitis, dysphagia), seizures, nausea, fever, anorexia, fatigue, skin rash, motor dysfunction Leucovorin is sometimes given in conjunction with pyrimethamine to prevent bone marrow suppression	Ganciclovir, zidovudine
Rifabutin (Mycobutin)	MAC disease (treatment and prophylaxis)	Decreased liver enzymes and creatinine, rash, fever, leukopenia, GI distress, hemolysis, arthralgias	Dapsone, fluconazole, ketoconazole, methadone, nelfinavir, zidovudine, myelosuppressive agents (chemotherapy)
Rifampin (Rifadin)	TB, MAC	Chills, dyspnea, fever, headache, myalgia, rash, pruritis, changes liver function, bleeding, nausea and vomiting, urinary changes, diarrhea, asthenia	Aminosalicylic acid, anticoagulants, antacids, atovaquone, chloramphenicol, oral contraceptives, dapsone, fluconazole, methadone, nelfinavir, saquinavir,

TABLE 27.1	Commonly Used Drugs for Patients Infected with Human Immunodeficiency Virus (HIV) *(Continued)*		
Drug Name	**Primary Indications**	**Common Side Effects, Toxicities**	**Interactions and Contraindications (consult insert, other materials)**
Ritonavir (Norvir)	HIV infection	GI intolerance, nausea and vomiting, diarrhea, paresthesias, hepatitis, asthenia, taste changes, hyperglycemia, elevated triglycerides, transaminase, CPK, and uric acid	Clarithromycin, desipramine, didanosine, ethinyl estradiol, TMP/SMX, theophylline, zidovudine
Saquinavir (Invirase, Fortovase)	HIV infection	GI intolerance, nausea and vomiting, headache, abdominal pain, dyspepsia, increased transaminase enzymes, hyperglycemia	Astemizole, carbamazepine, cimetidine, cisapride, delavirdine, dexamethasone, ergot alkaloids, ketoconazole, midazolam, nelfinavir, nevirapine, phenobarbitol, phenytoin, rifabutin, rifampin, ritonavir, terfenadine, triazo-lam
Stavudine (Zerit)	HIV infection	Peripheral neuropathy, hepatotoxicity, anemia, headache, nausea	Didanosine, zidovudine, drugs toxic to liver or pancreas, or causing peripheral neuropathy
Trimethoprim and sulfamethoxazole (Bactrim, Septra)	PCP treatment, salmonella, other infections	Leukopenia, thrombocytopenia, hepatitis, fever, skin rash, changes in urine, muscle and joint pain, dysphagia, diarrhea, nausea, dizziness, headache	Phenytoin
Zalcitabine (HIVID, ddC)	Used in combination with AZT to treat adults with decreased CD4+ count and significant deterioration	Peripheral neuropathy, pancreatitis	Antacids, cimetidine, interferon alpha, metoclopramide, ribavarin, zidovudine
Zidovudine (AZT, Retrovir)	HIV infection	Leukopenia, anemia, neutropenia, changes in platelet count, diarrhea, nausea, fever, dizziness, skin rash, headache, insomnia, myopathy	Acetaminophen, acyclovir, adriamycin, amphotericin B, dapsone, didanosone, fluconazole, foscarnet, ganciclovir, interferon alpha, indomethacin, methadone, myelosuppressive drugs (doxorubicin, vinblastine), pentamidine, phenytoin, probenecid, pyrimethamine, ribavarin, stavudine, TB drugs, drugs toxic to kidneys

(CDC, 1998b; Flaskcrud & Ungvarski, 1995; Pharmaceutical Manufacturers Association, 1992; Temesgen & Wright, 1997; Wilkes & Williams, 1998)

Physical Problems of AIDS

Disease-related problems of HIV infection may be classified according to opportunistic infection or disease, by body system(s) affected, or by other means. This chapter uses a clinical manifestations categorization similar to that used by DeVita, Hellman, and Rosenberg (1997) in which material is organized (for the most part) according to both infections and body systems as follows:

● Acute retroviral syndrome
● Generalized lymphadenopathy
● Protozoal infections (PCP, toxoplasmosis, cryptosporidiosis, microsporidiosis, isoporiasis, cyclosporiasis)
● Fungal infections (candidiasis, cryptococcosis, histoplasmosis, coccidioidomycosis, aspergillosis)
● Bacterial infections (tuberculosis [TB], MAC disease, *Mycobacterium genovense*, bacterial pneumonia, sinusitis, salmonella)
● Viral infections (herpesvirus [herpes simplex virus, HSV, varicella zoster virus, VZV], CMV, PML, Epstein-Barr virus [EBV], oral hairy leukoplakia, genital warts, molluscum contagiosum, hepatitis)
● HIV-related cancers (KS and non-Hodgkin's lymphoma)
● Neurologic complications (including AIDS dementia complex and neuromuscular disorders)
● Hematologic complications (anemia, neutropenia, thrombocytopenia)
● Oral complications (opportunistic infections, aphthous ulcers, peridontal disease, xerostomia)
● Skin complications (opportunistic infections, seborrheic dermatitis, acute exanthum, syphilis, folliculitis, impetigo, drug reactions)
● Respiratory complications (opportunistic infections and cancers)
● Gastrointestinal complications (opportunistic infections, wasting syndrome, esophagitis, nausea and vomiting, diarrhea)
● Renal complications
● Children with HIV infection

Each of these problems is discussed in this chapter. However, only the most common problems and infections are covered. Many others occur in AIDS (eg, pneumonitis, heart disease, other sexually transmitted diseases). Readers should also make use of the chapters with information on specific symptoms and their management found throughout this book.

Acute Retroviral Syndrome

Acute retroviral (or seroconversion) syndrome, or primary HIV-1 infection, is nonspecific and similar to viremia or mononucleosis, with common manifestations of fever, night sweats, malaise, myalgia, sore throat, anorexia, nausea, diarrhea, large liver and spleen, lymphadenopathy, rash, and in some cases meningitis. Before the advent of improved antiretroviral therapy in the late 1990s, treatment was symptomatic and supportive, and the syndrome could be expected to resolve in weeks to months. Currently, patients with acute primary HIV infection should be treated with HAART to suppress virus replication (CDC, 1998).

Generalized Lymphadenopathy

Lymphadenopathy may begin with the primary HIV infection and persist throughout the course of the disease as lymphadenopathy syndrome. In the context of AIDS, lymphadenopathy is not a major problem, except that significant enlargement of thoracic or abdominal nodes may be a sign of other complications, such as TB, MAC disease, histoplasmosis, or lymphoma. Contrary to early impressions, the loss of lymphadenopathy is a sign of disease progession (Saag, 1997).

Protozoal Infections
PNEUMOCYSTIS CARINII PNEUMONIA

Mortality rates from PCP began to decline with the advent of anti-*Pneumocystis* therapy in the late 1980s and declined further after HAART came into wide use. Nevertheless, PCP remains associated with death among HIV-infected patients (Jacobson & French, 1998).

While PCP may progress rapidly, the onset is often insidious, with unexplained fever, weight loss, and fatigue gradually developing for as long as several months. Common presenting manifestations are exertional dyspnea, interstitial infiltrates, oral candidiasis, dry rales, chest tightness, and clear sputum (Decker & Masur, 1997; Selwyn et al, 1998). Sputum examination using saline mist inhalation ("induced sputum") is currently the best non-invasive means of diagnosis (Decker & Masur, 1997).

Primary therapy for PCP is currently either trimethoprim/sulfamethoxazole (TMP/SMX) given orally or intravenously, or pentamidine given intravenously, with the latter having more toxic effects. Other effective treatments include TMP in combination with dapsone; clindamycin and primaquine; atovaquone (alone or in combination with pentamidine); and trimetrexate. Adjunctive corticosteroids are recommended to improve respiratory status. TMP/SMX is also taken for primary prophylaxis (CD4+ count of <200 cells mm^3) or secondary prophylaxis (long-term preventive therapy for patients with a history of PCP). TMP/SMX is also prophylactic against toxoplasmosis. Pentamidine may be taken in an aerosol, but the resultant metallic taste is disliked by most patients, and the aerosol produces coughing in many patients and some danger of infecting others with coexisting pulmonary TB. Supportive care is similar to that described under specific problems in earlier chapters, except that practitioners should understand that significant relief occurs through treatment of the PCP rather than symptom control. Supplemental oxygen and sometimes ventilation may be necessary as temporary measures (Decker & Masur, 1997).

TOXOPLASMOSIS (TOXOPLASMIC ENCEPHALITIS)

Toxoplasma gondii is a protozoan found in a variety of foods, especially undercooked meat. Soil and feces (especially cat) are other common sources. Infection usually occurs in people with CD4+ counts of less than 100 cells mm^3. The most common site of symptomatic infection is the CNS, but GI, pulmonary, and other toxoplasmosis infections occur.

Symptoms may at first be vague, developing over several days from dull, constant headache and slight mental changes to neurologic deficits. Symptoms of progression include fever, fatigue, headache, motor weakness, altered mental status (including confusion, lethargy, delusions, cognitive impairment, coma), seizures, and other neurologic deficits.

Treatment is usually with a combination of pyrimethamine and sulfadiazine or pyrimethamine and clindamycin orally. Medication toxicity is not uncommon, especially bone marrow suppression, hence folinic acid (leucovorin calcium) is given orally or parenterally to prevent or treat marrow toxicity. Clarithromycin, azithromycin, and atovaquone may also be effective. People who are *Toxoplasma* positive and whose CD4+ count is less than 100 should receive prophylactic treatment, and those who have had toxoplasmosis require lifelong suppressive therapy, in both cases on antitoxoplasmosis agents, such as TMP/SMX or pyrimethamine plus sulfadiazine and leucovorin. TMP/SMX is also prophylactic against PCP (Decker & Masur, 1997; Sepkowitz, 1998).

CRYPTOSPORIDIOSIS

Cryptosporidiosis is a protozoan (*Cryptosporidium*) infection of the GI tract and is associated with contact with human and animal feces, including contact with diaper-age children, soil, contaminated drinking or swimming water, young farm animals, and pets. It is also associated with anal sex.

Cryptosporidiosis manifests with secretory diarrhea (sometimes more than 20 stools per day), abdominal cramping, gas, and rapid weight loss. Nausea and vomiting may also occur. In some cases, there may be a brief bout of diarrhea followed by a symptom-free period. When HIV infection is advanced (eg, CD4+ count <50), diarrhea may result in electrolyte imbalances and dehydration.

At the time this is written, there are no treatments known to be effective in treating cryptosporidiosis other than combination antiretroviral therapy (Foudraine et al., 1998). Paromomycin has also shown some limited effectiveness, as has azithromycin (Bruzzese & Kaplowitz, 1998; Decker & Masur, 1997). Treatment focuses on palliation of symptoms, including fluid replacement, to prevent dehydration and electrolyte imbalances, nutritional supplements, treatment of pain, and symptomatic treatment of GI symptoms. Octreotide is sometimes helpful in reducing chronic diarrhea in AIDS (Wilcox, 1997) (see Chapter 17). There are no effective prophylactic or suppressive medications. Obviously, careful precautions to prevent spread of cryptosporidiosis are important. The usual decontaminants (eg, diluted household bleach, 5% formaldehyde, iodophor) are not effective in killing the *Cryptosporidium* pathogen. Full-strength bleach or 5% ammonia are effective disinfectants when applied for more than 15 minutes.

MICROSPORIDIOSIS

Microsporidia infection appears to be a significant cause of (often intermittent) diarrhea in patients with CD4+ counts less than 50 whose GI problems are not attributable to another cause (Wilcox, 1997). Microsporidiosis is characterized by nonbloody diarrhea with colicky abdominal pain and weight loss. Fever and anorexia are usually not present. Combination antiretroviral therapy is probably the most effective treatment for microsporidiosis. Albendazole may be helpful, as may metronidazole (Decker & Masur, 1997). Treatment focuses on palliation of symptoms as described previously and in Chapter 17.

ISOSPORIASIS

Isospora belli infection is usually of the small intestine. In the United States, isosporiasis is associated most frequently with people from Latin America. The symptoms of isosporiasis are similar to those cryptosporidiosis, except that steatorrhea and fever are more common.

Treatment and suppression of isosporiasis is usually with TMP/SMX. Other medications used to treat or suppress isosporiasis include pyrimethamine, metronidazole, and quinacrine (Decker & Masur, 1998).

CYCLOSPORIASIS

Cyclospora infection is similar to crytosporidiosis in presentation. TMP/SMX is effective in treatment and secondary prophylaxis.

Fungal Infections
ORAL AND OTHER CANDIDIASIS

Oropharyngeal candidiasis is the most common oral fungal infection in patients with HIV infection, occurring in about 90% of people who are HIV positive. Vaginal or perineal candidiasis is common in women with AIDS (Filler, 1997). Prevalence increases as CD4+ counts decrease. Esophageal candidiasis indicates AIDS, as does *Candida* infection of the trachea, bronchi, or lungs.

Oropharyngeal candidiasis appears in four major forms. These may be mixed with one another or with other lesions, such as HSV (Grbic & Lamster, 1997):

● Pseudomembranous: removable white ("cottage cheese") plaques on the tongue, palate, buccal mucosa, and labial mucosa, which, if removed, leave erythematous and possibly bleeding mucosa
● Erythematous: flat red lesions with no removable plaques
● Angular chelitis: fissures at the corners of the mouth
● Chronic hyperplastic: white plaques that are not removable

Most oropharyngeal candidiasis is accompanied by pain and sometimes dysphagia, which contribute to difficulty in eating and subsequent malnutrition. Perineal or vaginal candidiasis is characterized by pain, pruritus, discharge, and red lesions. Esophageal candidiasis symptoms include dysphagia, odynophagia, feeling of obstruction, or retrosternal, burning pain. Patients presenting with odynophagia are often presumed to have esophageal candidiasis (Sepkowitz, 1998).

Treatment for oropharyngeal candidiasis includes topical agents (nystatin or clotrimazole) for patients with relatively high CD4+ counts and systemic antifungal azoles, especially fluconazole, but also itraconazole or ketoconazole for patients with decreased CD4+ (Filler, 1997). Recurrence is common, but there is controversy about whether routine prophylaxis is indicated (Polis & Kovacs, 1997). Candidemia occasionally occurs, often due to central venous catheter (Launay et al., 1998)

CRYPTOCOCCOSIS

Cryptococcus neoformans infection commonly presents as a CNS disorder and as pulmonary or disseminated disease; it is the primary cause of meningitis in patients with AIDS (Polis & Kovacs, 1997). The infection begins in the lungs through inhalation of spores and spreads through the bloodstream to the meninges. Headache and fever are the most frequently reported initial symptoms. Other manifestations include nausea and vomiting, changes in mental status, and meningeal signs (eg, stiff neck). If unchecked, disseminated disease may occur, with problems occurring according to the affected system, and increased CNS manifestations, such as confusion or seizures. Respiratory symptoms include fever, cough, dyspnea, and pleuritic pain (Piemme, 1998). Therapy includes (1) amphotericin B alone or in combination with flucytosine or (2) fluconazole, with the latter used for mild, nonmeningeal disease. Relapse is common and maintenance therapy, usually with fluconazole, is recommended but is not always successful (Bruzzese & Kaplowitz, 1998; Sepkowitz, 1998).

HISTOPLASMOSIS

Histoplasma capsulatum infection manifests with fever, weight loss, and respiratory complications. Histoplasmosis may also present in disseminated form, including GI system (splenomegaly or hepatomegaly), CNS involvement (meningitis or increased intracranial pressure), hematologic abnormalities (thrombocytopenia, neutropenia, and anemia), and skin or oral lesions. Amphotericin B is used to treat histoplasmosis initially. Recurrence is common and itraconazole or fluconazole is used for maintenance therapy (Polis & Kovacs, 1997).

COCCIDIOIDOMYCOSIS

Coccidioides immitus infection is primarily a pulmonary infection similar in presentation to histoplasmosis, with fever, weight loss, cough, and malaise. Pulmonary infiltrates, effusions, and cavitation may occur. Extrapulmonary infection may affect the CNS, skin, lymphatics, or liver. Therapy includes amphotericin B or fluconazole or itraconazole. Maintenance therapy uses fluconazole, itraconazole, or (second line) amphotericin B (Bruzzese & Kaplowitz, 1998). Patients with HIV infections should avoid arid areas of the southwestern United States where *C. immitus* is endemic.

ASPERGILLOSIS

Aspergillus species infection causes invasive pulmonary and obstructing bronchial disease in immunocompromised patients. Onset may be insidious, with cough, dyspnea, and fever, but ultimately aspergillosis is a fulminating disease. Treatment attempts have included amphotericin B and itraconazole, both with limited success (Polis & Kovacs, 1997).

Bacterial Infections
TUBERCULOSIS

Tuberculosis is caused by *Mycobacterium tuberculosis*. The prevalence of TB in the United States is increasing, in part due to TB in patients with AIDS. TB infection is a distinct threat to health care workers and to others who come into contact with infected patients; guidelines for protection and regular testing are available from CDC. In patients with AIDS, skin tests may give false-negative results because of the anergy common in people with immunosuppression. In contradistinction to many other opportunistic infections, TB tends to occur in patients whose CD4+ counts are relatively high (>300 mm^3). Symptoms include cough, dyspnea, hemoptysis, lymphadenopathy, chest pain, and constitutional symptoms, such as fever, night sweats, weight loss, and fatigue. As CD4+ counts decline, extrapulmonary TB increases, manifested according to the affected organ system and commonly including lymphadenopathy, CNS symptoms, soft-tissue masses, bone marrow depression, liver dysfunction, and other GI symptoms (Piemme, 1998). Extrapulmonary disease or rapid course of pulmonary disease is associated with a higher risk of death.

Treatment is complicated by an increasing incidence of multidrug-resistant TB in clients with HIV infection and others. Current standard treatment (there are many variations) for active TB is isoniazid, vitamin B$_6$, rifampin for 6 months, pyrazinamide, and ethambutol for 2 months. Prophylaxis is achieved with isoniazid, vitamin B$_6$ for 12 months or rifampin, and pyrazinamide for 2 months (Bruzzese & Kaplowitz, 1998). Staff who work with patients who have or are suspected to have TB should be tested at regular intervals.

MYCOBACTERIUM AVIUM INTRACELLULARE COMPLEX (MAC)

Organisms of MAC are commonly found in food and water. In people who are not HIV positive, MAC poses little threat, but in HIV-infected people, MAC is the most common bacterial systemic opportunistic infection and is indicative of increased risk of death (Chaisson et al., 1998). Related mycobacteria cause TB and Hansen's disease (leprosy).

Infection with MAC may begin with fever, night sweats, anorexia, weight loss, malaise, and fatigue. The GI tract is a common site of infection, with symptoms of abdominal pain, hepatosplenomegaly, chronic diarrhea, nausea and vomiting, and other GI disturbances. MAC

may be disseminated to almost all body systems with symptoms related to the affected body systems. See the following discussion of neuromuscular and related disorders.

Treatment is usually with various multidrug regimens (eg, clarithromycin or azithromycin, rifabutin, and ethambutol). Prophylaxis is with one of the above medications (Bruzzese & Kaplowitz, 1998).

MYCOBACTERIUM GENOVENSE

Mycobacterium genovense causes symptoms similar to MAC and is treated similarly.

BACTERIAL PNEUMONIA

Streptococcus pneumonia, Haemophilus influenzae, Staphylococcus aureus, Moraxella catarrhalis, other *Streptococcus* and *Haemophilus* species, and *Pseudomonas aeruginosa* are all relatively common community-acquired pathogens causing pneumonia. Organisms involved in hospital-acquired pneumonia are most commonly *Enterobacter* spp., *Klebsiella pneumoniae, P. aeruginosa,* and *S. aureas* (Zurlo & Lane, 1997). Symptoms include dyspnea, elevated temperature, chills, purulent or rusty sputum (but not always present), decreased breath sounds, and sometimes sinusitis. Pleural effusion may also be present. TMP/SMX is effective in most cases except for nosocomial infection. Alternatives include clarithromycin or azithromycin. People with HIV infection should be immunized with pneumococcal vaccine and consideration given to vaccination for *H. influenzae* type B (Bruzzese & Kaplowitz, 1998).

SINUSITIS

Sinusitis is common among HIV-infected patients. Symptoms include nasal congestion (yellowish), fever, postnasal drip, headache, and facial pain. Sinusitis is sometimes the presenting problem of *P. aeruginosa* and other pneumonias (Piemme, 1998). Treatment is with TMP/SMX, amoxicillin-clavulanate, or cefuroxime axetil (Zurlo & Lane, 1997).

SALMONELLA

Salmonella species are commonly implicated in acute GI illnesses resulting from contaminated food or water or pet reptiles and other animals. Symptoms in people with immunocompromise include fever, chill, anorexia, diarrhea, and less commonly, abdominal cramping, headache, and myalgias (Piemme, 1998). Salmonella and other bacterial infections in patients with AIDS are characterized by recurrence and by a high incidence of bacteremia (Kotler, 1997). The small or large bowel may be affected, and diarrhea is usually profuse and accompanied by cramping, bloating, nausea, and weight loss. Treatment is with ampicillin for 1 to 4 weeks, then amoxicillin to complete a 2- to 4-week course (if sensitive). Alternatives include a fluoroquinolone for 2 to 4 weeks, or a third-generation cephalosporin, such as cefotaxime or ceftriaxone or TMP/SMX. Maintenance therapy is with TMP/SMX, amoxicillin, or ciprofloxacin (Bruzzese & Kaplowitz, 1998).

Viral Infections

HERPES

Herpesvirus infections are very common in HIV-infected people and include HSV and VZV, both of which are characterized by painful vesicular lesions and periods of latency after primary infection.

The HSV-1 is transmitted primarily mouth to mouth through oral mucous membranes and saliva, and HSV-2 is transmitted primarily by sexual contact. HSV usually presents as painful vesicles, pustules, and erosions on the lips, genitalia, or anus with fever, adenopathy, and malaise. With HIV infection, the lesions are sometimes more widespread (eg, to cheeks, perineum). HSV infection of the CNS, viscera (especially esophagus), retina, and elsewhere occur. HSV lesions may be mixed with *Candida* or other lesions.

Shingles or VZV results from childhood varicella (chickenpox) infection, which lies dormant unless immunosuppression occurs. VZV infection is manifested by neuropathic radicular pain along one to three dermatomes and includes painful and pruritic macules, papules, plaques, and clusters of vesicles. People with immunosuppression may have widespread and treatment-resistant lesions and neurologic, eye, and other involvement. Pain (postherpatic neuralgia) may last for several months after lesions are no longer evident.

Acute HSV and VZV reactivations are treated with acyclovir. Suppressive therapy when there is a history of frequent reactivations or neurologic sequelae is also with acyclovir. Other medications effective in the treatment of HSV are valacyclovir, famciclovir, and if acyclovir-resistant, foscarnet or cidovir (if being used to treat CMV disease) (Bruzzese & Kaplowitz, 1998; Grbic & Lamster, 1997; Mirowski et al., 1998).

CYTOMEGALOVIRUS (CMV)

Most HIV-infected people are seropositive for CMV, but clinically important infections do not usually occur until advanced stages of HIV infection (CD4+ <100 cells/mm^3) (Schacker & Corey, 1997). CMV disease is associated with increased risk for death (Chaisson et al., 1998). Although CMV infection may be disseminated, the most common specific sites of CMV infection are as follows:

● The GI tract CMV syndromes include esophagitis, gastritis, intestinal ulcers, ileitis, intestinal perforation, colitis, hepatitis, pancreatitis, cholangitis, and wasting. Lower GI tract infection is characterized by symptoms of diarrhea, fever, abdominal pain, rebound tenderness, and no other stool pathogens present. CMV colitis is associated with extreme wasting. Esophageal CMV is characterized by symptoms of odynophagia, dysphagia, and retrosternal chest pain.
● Infection with CMV in the eye includes symptoms of (usually) unilateral visual field loss, decreased acuity, and the presence of "floaters." Untreated, the infection results in blindness.

● Central nervous system CMV infection causes encephalitis, (ascending) polyradiculopathy, and myelitis. CMV encephalitis is characterized by dementia, decreased level of consciousness, cranial nerve abnormalities, and seizures.
● The respiratory system is a less common site of infection, but respiratory CMV is a common cause of pneumonitis.

Ganciclovir or foscarnet (or both combined) is the main treatment option for CMV. Cidofovir has also been shown to be effective. Secondary prophylaxis is with ganciclovir (Bruzzese & Kaplowitz, 1998; Parente & Bianchi-Porro, 1998; Schacker & Corey, 1997).

PROGRESSIVE MULTIFOCAL LEUKOENCEPHALOPATHY (PML)

Progressive multifocal leukoencephalopathy is caused by the human papovavirus (JC virus). Disability occurs as a result of selective demyelination, leading to focal neurologic deficits, such as hemiparesis, hemianopsia, aphasia, hemisensory deficit, and ataxia. Changes in consciousness are less common. While zidovudine, interferon, or cytosine arabinoside may sometimes be helpful, there is no proven curative, prophylactic, or suppressive treatment for PML. PML is associated with significantly increased risk of death (Chaisson et al., 1998). Also see chapters on neurologic problems, degenerative neurologic diseases, and Alzheimer's disease. Although the diseases are different, many principles of care are not.

EPSTEIN-BARR VIRUS (INFECTIOUS MONONUCLEOSIS)

The EBV is of the same family of viruses as herpes, CMV, and others. EBV causes infectious mononucleosis, is found in oral hairy leukoplakia, and may have a role in the development of HIV-associated non-Hodgkin's lymphoma (EBV has a definite role in other lymphomas). Mononucleosis causes fatigue, swollen lymph glands, fever, and sore throat. Treatment is primarily bedrest and supportive care.

ORAL HAIRY LEUKOPLAKIA

Oral hairy leukoplakia is a viral (EBV) infection of the mouth, characterized by white nonremovable plaques (versus the removable plaques of *Candida*) especially on the sides of the tongue. Oral hairy leukoplakia is sometimes mixed with *Candida albicans* so may seem to respond to some extent to topical antifungals. Effective treatment is through acyclovir at doses similar to those used for HSV. Foscarnet may also be effective, but in any case, the lesions usually return (Greenspan & Greenspan, 1997).

GENITAL WARTS

Genital warts are caused by the human papillomavirus (HPV) and are spread primarily by sexual contact. They may appear in and around the anus, genitalia, or mouth as warts, bumps, or protrusions. They tend to spread and when profuse, cause discomfort and problems with elimination. HPV-associated neoplasms include invasive cervical and anal cancers (Kiviat, 1997). Treatment of genital warts is through freezing, cauterizing, or chemically "burning off" the warts. There is no systemic therapy for genital warts.

MOLLUSCUM CONTAGIOSUM

Molluscum contagiosum is a viral infection characterized by small, painless, white, wart-like, rounded papules that tend to spread. Molluscum contagiosum occurs anywhere on the body but occurs most frequently on the face. The infection is not life threatening and is difficult to treat, except by freezing individual lesions.

HEPATITIS

Hepatitis is an inflammation of the liver, usually viral in origin. There are several types of viral hepatitis (HBV, HCV), which are spread by several means (eg, food, sex, intravenous drug use). Manifestations of hepatitis include abdominal pain, organomegaly, nausea and vomiting, anorexia, fever, weakness, fatigue, ascites, jaundice, and pruritus. Treatment is primarily supportive, bedrest and avoidance of further insult to the liver. Interferon and acyclovir are used under some circumstances. Vaccination against hepatitis B is usually recommended for patients with HIV infection.

HIV-Related Cancers

HIV-related cancers include most notably Kaposi's sarcoma (KS) and non-Hodgkin's lymphoma (NHL). There is also increased risk of developing cervical, anal, lung, and brain cancer and multiple myeloma or seminoma (Aboulafia & Mitsuyasu, 1997; Goedert et al., 1998; Johnson et al., 1997). Among patients with HIV-related cancers, there are reports of increased survival resulting from HAART (Lebbe et al., 1997; McGowan & Shah, 1998).

KAPOSI'S SARCOMA (KS)

KS is the most common cancer among people with HIV infection, especially homosexual and bisexual men with AIDS. HIV-related KS is more aggressive than other forms of KS.

Early manifestations of KS are painless slightly raised or nodular pigmented skin lesions (darker in dark-skinned patients) of varied size. There may also be "patch-stage" lesions that form plaques and become nodular. Common skin lesion sites are the nose, arms, legs, feet, and roof of mouth. Skin lesions are sometimes painful and, if ulcerated, may become sites for secondary infections. Lymphadema associated with lesions most often occurs in the face, genitals, and legs. KS may also spread to the respiratory system or GI tract. Symptoms from pulmonary KS include dyspnea, cough, hemoptysis, and fever. Symptoms from GI KS are less common and may include abdominal pain and GI bleeding.

Treatment of KS is based on the stage and rate of progression of the disease. In general, antiretroviral and anti-infective therapies should be optimized and chemotherapy started with one or a combination of agents. Local treatment of cutaneous lesions includes local radiotherapy, liquid nitrogen, and intralesional injection (Miles, Aboulafia, & Mitsuyasu, 1997).

NON-HODGKIN'S LYMPHOMA (NHL)

Although less common than KS in patients with AIDS, NHL is associated with a higher risk for death (Chaisson et al., 1998). Lymphoma is a disease of the immune system and involves lymph and bone marrow. AIDS-related associated NHL is characterized by lymphadenopathy and rapid spread to the CNS, bone marrow, GI tract, and liver, and it carries a poor prognosis (see Chapter 26).

Manifestations of AIDS-related NHL include systemic symptoms, such as unexplained fever, drenching night sweats, or weight loss of more than 10%. In as many as 25% of patients with AIDS-related NHL, the disease is found only in the CNS with a variety of neurologic problems resulting and a very poor prognosis. Other symptoms of NHL are according to the affected site(s).

The primary treatment for NHL is chemotherapy, usually multiagent. Depending on the stage and grade of the cancer, CD4+ cell count, and other factors, response to chemotherapy may range from good (more than 24 months survival) to poor (less than 4 months survival). Treatment is complicated by the compromised immune systems of the person with NHL and the toxicity of the more effective chemotherapeutic agents. Radiation is usually the treatment of choice for CNS lymphoma (Miles et al., 1997).

Neurologic Manifestations

Central nervous system manifestations of HIV infection include AIDS dementia complex (ADC), neurologic symptoms of primary HIV infection, cerebral toxoplasmosis, cryptococcal meningitis, PML, CMV infection, mycobacterial infections, HSV or VZV infection, syphilis, other infections, and CNS neoplasms (primary and metastatic NHL). Peripheral nervous system and muscle disorders include peripheral neuropathies and myopathies (Price & Brew, 1997). ADC and peripheral nervous system and muscle disorders are discussed in the following section. The other nervous system complications are discussed under specific infections and disorders.

AIDS DEMENTIA COMPLEX

Sometimes termed HIV-associated dementia, ADC is a complex of cognitive, motor, and behavioral dysfunction that develops slowly late in the course of HIV infection, often after several major opportunistic infections. To a lesser extent, ADC sometimes exists in the absence of other manifestations of AIDS. ADC is increasingly thought to be caused by HIV-1 rather than CMV or some other pathogen as was previously thought. Common clinical features include the following:

● Cognitively, patients gradually deteriorate from slightly slowed thinking, difficulty concentrating, and forgetfulness to confusion, amnesia, mutism, and global dementia.
● Motor dysfunction often begins with poor handwriting, tremors, unsteady gait, poor balance (especially with fast head turns), and lower extremity weakness. Eventually a cane is needed to walk, then a walker, and finally the client is bedfast and incontinent.
● Behavior varies, but it is common for patients to become withdrawn and apathetic. Some patients, however, have mania. Insight decreases late in the process, so patients are often aware of their mental deterioration.

The condition is complicated by all the psychosocial features common to AIDS: depression, anxiety, fear, isolation, and so forth (Ownby & Ownby, 1998; Price & Brew, 1997).

Treatment or prophylaxis of ADC is with zidovudine, and results are generally encouraging (Price & Brew, 1997). HAART may also slow or reverse ADC progression. Neuroleptic medications (eg, haloperidol) are indicated for agitation, delirium, and related problems (Ownby & Ownby, 1998). Susceptibility to side effects of antipsychotics (eg, extrapyramidal symptoms) is increased in patients with ADC and probably in other patients with HIV infection. Please see Chapter 13 on neurologic symptoms and neuromuscular diseases for further information on patients with neurologic problems.

Neuromuscular and Related Complications

Neuromuscular complications of HIV infection include peripheral neuropathies, autonomic neuropathies, and myopathies. Peripheral neuropathies are common at all stages of HIV infection and AIDS. They may be due to HIV infection or unknown causes, opportunistic infections (especially CMV or herpes), or medications (Galantino, 1991).

Peripheral neuropathies are a common cause of pain in patients with AIDS. (Please see the section on Neuropathic Pain in Chapter 12.) The most common neuropathy is distal symmetrical (painful sensory) polyneuropathy, which begins early in HIV infection (Price & Brew, 1997). This is characterized by progressive bilateral distal paresthesias, beginning in the feet. Pain, sensory loss, weakness, and muscle atrophy may occur.

An important neuropathy is the ascending polyradiculopathy caused by CMV. This progressive sensorimotor neuropathy is characterized by pain and early bowel and bladder dysfunction. Early treatment (with ganciclovir) is started on the basis of clinical suspicion. Other peripheral neuropathies exist but are less common than those described here.

Autonomic neuropathies may be manifested by impotence, bowel and bladder impairment, abnormal sweating, and presyncope (Simpson & Wolfe, 1991). Incontinence is common in ADC.

Myopathies include progressive muscle weakness and myalgia, especially of the thighs (Simpson & Wolfe, 1991). Long-term zidovudine use may result in wasting of buttock muscles and lower extremity weakness.

Hematologic Complications

Hematologic complications of AIDS commonly include anemia, neutropenia, or thrombocytopenia. Etiologies include infections (including HIV-1), immune destruction of platelets, possibly nutritional deficiencies, cancer, and medications.

ANEMIA

Anemia is common in patients with AIDS and worsens as the disease progresses and anemia-inducing factors accrue (antiretroviral and other medications, infections that affect the bone marrow, and malignancies). Symptoms include fatigue, weakness, headache, tachypnea, and dyspnea. Treatment includes transfusion of red blood cells. Improvement may also be seen with changes in medications, resolution of infections, and administration of erythropoietin (Viele, 1998).

NEUTROPENIA

Decreased neutrophils, lymphocytes, and other blood abnormalities are related primarily to myelosuppression, often exacerbated by medications. The risk for infection is increased, and if neutropenia is severe (absolute neutrophil count <500 cells/mm^3), prophylactic medications for infection suppression may be started (Viele, 1998).

THROMBOCYTOPENIA

Decreased platelets and anemia usually occur concurrently in HIV infection. Causes of thrombocytopenia include decreased bone marrow production and immune and nonimmune destruction sometimes associated with drug use. Manifestations include bleeding in skin, mucous membranes, and GI or GU tracts. Therapy includes zidovudine or dapsone. Corticosteroids may provide brief improvement. Interferons and globulins tend to provide brief improvement. Splenectomy or splenic irradiation may be necessary (Doweiko & Groopman, 1997). Patients with bleeding disorders should avoid medications that are associated with increasing bleeding, such as acetylsalicylic acid and other aspirin products, anticoagulants (eg, heparin), dipyridamole (Persantine), and alcohol. Patients should avoid trauma, tight or constrictive clothing, anal examinations or sex, and constipation. Nutrition and hydration should be maintained.

Oral Complications

Oral complications (Grbic & Lamster, 1997; Mirowski et al., 1998) include fungal (candidiasis and occasionally histoplasmosis and cryptococcosis), bacterial (especially periodontal disease and rarely mycobacterial infections), viral (HSV, VZV, CMV, oral hairy leukoplakia, and HPV), neoplastic (KS, non-Hodgkin's lymphoma), and nonneoplastic lesions (aphthous ulcers and salivary gland disease). Peridontal disease, aphthous ulcers, and xerostomia are discussed in the following section; the other disorders are discussed under the etiologic agents.

RECURRENT APHTHOUS ULCERS (OR STOMATITIS)

Aphthous ulcers are single or multiple painful oral ulcers surrounded by a red halo. Their cause is unknown, but they are associated with immunosuppression in both HIV infection and cancer treatment. Topical steroids (rinse and expectorate) are effective in most cases (Greenspan & Greenspan, 1997).

PERIODONTAL DISEASE

The three primary forms of periodontal disease found in people with HIV include (1) linear gingival erythema, a bright red band of gingival erythema; (2) rapidly progressive gingivitis with ulcers, bleeding, and pain; and (3) rapidly progressive periodontal disease, including bone lesions and necrosis. Treatment includes regular oral care (including irrigation with chlorhexidine for linear gingival erythema and with povidine-iodine for periodontal disease), oral surgery procedures (surgical débridement), and metronidazole or amoxicillin-clavulanate or clindamycin (Greenspan & Greenspan, 1997).

XEROSTOMIA

Dry mouth is commonly a result of anticholinergic effects of medications, such as antidepressants, antihistamines, anxiolytics, ddl, and others. HIV-salivary gland disease features enlarged salivary glands and benign cysts of the glands, thus causing xerostomia.

Skin Complications

Common skin disorders in patients with AIDS include herpesvirus infections (HSV, VZV); candidiasis; noninfectious problems, such as seborrheic dermatitis and drug reactions; and infectious disorders or manifestations of infectious disorders, such as acute exanthem of HIV infection, molluscum contagiosum infection, HPV infections, syphilis, and bacterial infections (eg, folliculitis, impetigo, furuncles, and conjunctivitis). Skin disorders, such as candidiasis, HSV, VZV, oral hairy leukoplakia, and skin disorders related to CMV, *P. carinii* infection, mycobacterial infections, KS, and NHL, are discussed under etiologic agents. Other, less serious skin disorders related to HIV are discussed in the following sections.

SEBORRHEIC DERMATITIS

Seborrheic dermatitis is the most common noninfectious skin disorder found in patients with AIDS. It is characterized by erythema, or fine white scaling without erythema, usually on the scalp, face, eyebrows, back, axillae, and groin. Blepharitis and otitis externa are common. Treatment is difficult because the condition worsens as the disease progresses and shows a poor response to topical agents (eg, glucocorticoids) and limited response to ketoconazole (Safai, 1997).

ACUTE EXANTHEM

Acute exanthum is an early manifestation of HIV infection and consists of small pink macules and papules on the trunk and extremities, fever, and pharyngitis.

SYPHILIS

Like other infections in patients with AIDS, syphilis may have more severe symptoms, including a number of atypical skin changes.

FOLLICULITIS

Usually due to staphylococcal infection, folliculitis is characterized by pruritic erythema, pustules, or papules on the face, trunk, or groin. Folliculitis may also be caused by a variety of other pathogens, or there may be no identifiable pathogen. Lesions may progress to abscesses, furuncles, or carbuncles. Treatment is according to pathogen or in some cases with UVB phototherapy (Lim, Vallurapalli, Meola, & Sater, 1997).

IMPETIGO

Impetigo is due to *Staphylococcus* or *Streptococcus* infection and in clients with AIDS is usually found in the inguinal or axillary regions. Typically, painful red macules progress to bullae, which eventually rupture. Treatment is with topical or systemic antibiotics (Cockerell, 1992).

DRUG REACTIONS

Drugs whose use commonly results in skin reactions are TMP/SMX (and other sulfonamides), fluconazole, zidovudine, delavirdine, efavirenz, and indinavir.

Respiratory Complications

The major respiratory symptoms (dyspnea, cough, hemoptysis) are all found in patients with HIV infection. Opportunistic infections most commonly associated with respiratory symptoms are PCP, mycobacterial infections, histoplasmosis, coccidioidomycosis, and bacterial pneumonia. Aspergillosis and other less common infections and disseminated infections also result in respiratory complications. KS and non-Hodgkin's lymphoma may involve the pulmonary system, especially in late stages. See the chapter on respiratory symptoms for palliative care options.

Gastrointestinal Complications

Gastrointestinal problems are common in patients with HIV infection and are often due to one or more infection(s). While many opportunistic infections affect the GI tract, CMV and MAC are especially important. GI problems of patients with AIDS include anorexia and weight loss (notably, HIV wasting syndrome), esophagitis, nausea and vomiting, and diarrhea. Problems of nutrition are extremely important in HIV infection. This section is divided broadly into discussions of the problems noted previously. GI problems resulting from infection and cancer are discussed in the sections on infections and AIDS-related cancers. Symptom control specific to patients with AIDS is discussed at appropriate points in this section; additional material on symptom control can be found in Chapter 17.

ANOREXIA AND WEIGHT LOSS

Progressive, involuntary weight loss occurs in almost all patients with AIDS. In the United States, wasting syndrome, characterized by unintentional weight loss of at least 10%, occurs in 25% of patients with AIDS in the last 6 months of life (Sattler, Briggs, Antonipillai, Allen, & Horton, 1998). Malnutrition and decreased immune response are mutually exacerbating, and weight loss increases the risk of dying (Casey, 1997). The loss of lean body mass is of particular importance in morbidity and mortality related to wasting (Strawford & Hellerstein, 1998).

Weight loss is due to factors such as complex alterations in metabolism, reduced intake, or malabsorption. Reduced intake or malabsorption may be due to odynophagia from infection, oral pain from gingivitis, depression, nausea and vomiting or diarrhea from GI infection or medications, and other such (sometimes) treatable problems (Casey, 1997). Multifactorial and complex alterations in metabolism may be precipitated by decreased intake and include hypometabolism or hypermetabolism; alterations in metabolism of carbohydrates, lipids, and protein; altered cytokine profiles; and endocrine dysfunction (Casey, 1997; Strawford & Hellerstein, 1998).

As with other forms of cachexia, wasting syndrome (due to alterations in metabolism) in patients with AIDS does not usually respond to nutritional therapy (Strawford & Hellerstein, 1998). Less severe wasting or wasting due to

decreased intake or treatable opportunistic infections, however, may respond to nutritional therapy. In general, supplements and diet should be high calorie and high protein and taken in small and more frequent amounts. Because of frequency of complications, especially infection, total parenteral nutrition is seldom indicated. Because there is enormous variation in content of nutritional supplements, it is wise to use the expertise of a registered dietitian in examining dietary alternatives, even in the terminal stage of AIDS.

Medical treatment of wasting syndrome is first with HAART and with some combination of other therapies, including exercise, androgen therapy, appetite stimulants (megestrol oral suspension, cannabinoids), human growth hormone, L-glutamine, and bovine immuno-globulin preparations (Sherer, 1998). There is, however, a 10% to 20% failure rate with HAART, and in some cases increased weight in response to therapy is due not to increased lean body mass, but increased fat, so is not to the patient's benefit (Strawford & Hellerstein, 1998).

ESOPHAGITIS

Esophageal pathology is characterized by dysphagia, odynophagia, retrosternal pain, nausea, anorexia, and weight loss. Esophagitis is most commonly secondary to candidiasis, HSV, or CMV infection. Other causes include reflux esophagitis, KS lesions, lymphoma, or peptic ulcer disease.

NAUSEA AND VOMITING

Nausea and vomiting in HIV-infected patients is commonly due to (1) GI infections, which may be bacterial, viral, fungal, or protozoal, and (2) medication side effects (especially amphotericin B, zidovudine, pentamidine, TMP/SMX, and other antibiotics). Other causes of nausea and vomiting not specific to HIV are discussed in Chapter 17.

DIARRHEA

Diarrhea is an overwhelming problem for many patients with AIDS. AIDS complicated by chronic diarrhea is almost twice as expensive to treat as AIDS not complicated by chronic diarrhea, and the patient's quality of life is significantly reduced (Lubeck, Bennett, Mazonson, Fifer, & Fries, 1993). The more common GI infections that cause diarrhea are cryptosporidia, microsporidia, CMV, disseminated MAC disease, and salmonella. Other less common GI infections that may feature diarrhea include giardiasis, amebiasis, shigella, and various systemic fungal infections. There are also significant numbers of patients with diarrhea in whom an etiologic agent cannot be found (Kotler, 1997; Wilcox, 1997).

The most effective treatment for diarrhea due to opportunistic infection may be HAART (Foudraine et al., 1998) and should be combined with palliative measures (often multimodal), such as those discussed in Chapter 17. In general, when there is weight loss and diarrhea, supplements or diet should be isotonic, lactose free, high calorie, high protein, low fat, and taken in small and more frequent amounts (Kotler, 1997). Oral rehydration therapy solutions are hypocaloric, and excessive use may lead to additional weight loss (Kotler, 1997). There is significant variation in response to diet and experimentation, and an individual patient's response is often necessary to gauge correctly treatment modality.

Renal Complications

Renal complications in HIV-infected people include the following:

1. Fluid and electrolyte disorders, especially hyponatremia, but also hypokalemia, hyperkalemia, hypernatremia, hypocalcemia, and hyperuricemia
2. Acute renal failure from a wide variety of causes, including antiviral, antibiotic, and other medications; infections and related symptoms; obstruction; and other causes
3. Urinary tract infections from common and uncommon pathogens
4. Glomerular disease, primarily nephrotic syndrome, and especially focal segmental glomerulosclerosis (FSGS) in patients of African descent

Zidovudine has been used with varied success to treat FSGS. For some patients, chronic dialysis is the only option (Kopp & Balow, 1997).

Children With HIV

As increasing numbers of women are infected with HIV, so too will increasing numbers of infants be infected by mother–infant transmission. Some children and adolescents also will be infected as a secondary effect of intravenous drug use, homosexual and heterosexual contacts, and sexual abuse. Transmission through transfusion, which devastated young hemophiliacs in the 1980s, is not currently a problem of large dimension as it was before universal testing was initiated in blood banks. From 1991 to 1996, 2860 children younger than 13 years died from AIDS (CDC, 1998a). (Each year approximately three times as many children die from cancer as from AIDS [Landis et al., 1998]). The suffering of children with AIDS is compounded by the frequency with which entire families are HIV infected (Butler & Pizzo, 1992).

While many aspects of HIV infection are similar in children and adults, there are some important age-specific characteristics. Infants who are symptomatic before 12 months tend to develop more opportunistic infections, contract HIV-related encephalopathy, and have a poorer prognosis. Infection may be manifested by failure to thrive, lymphadenopathy, organomegaly, and increased incidence of common childhood illness. Infections (eg, PCP) may be more severe in children than in adults. CNS involvement is also more common in children than in adults (Grubman, Conviser, & Oleske, 1992). The median survival age has increased to 9 years for most perinatally infected children (Butz & Joffe, 1998). As in other highly specialized situations, practitioners should seek current and specialized resources to help in understanding children with HIV infection.

REFERENCES

Aboulafia, D. M., & Mitsuyasu, R. T. (1997). Lymphomas and other cancers associated with acquired immunodeficiency syndrome. In V. T. DeVita, S. Hellman, & S. A. Rosenberg (Eds.), *AIDS: Etiology, diagnosis, treatment, and prevention* (4th ed.) (pp. 319–330). Philadelphia: Lippincott-Raven.

Berger, T. G. (1990). Dermatologic care in the AIDS patient: A 1990 update. In M. A. Sande & P. A. Volberding (Eds.), *The medical management of AIDS* (2nd ed.) (pp. 114–130). Philadelphia: W.B. Saunders.

Bolyard, E. A., & Bell, D. M. (1997). Universal precautions in the health care setting. In V. T. DeVita, S. Hellman, & S. A. Rosenberg (Eds.), *AIDS: Etiology, diagnosis, treatment, and prevention (4th ed.)* (pp. 655–664). Philadelphia: Lippincott-Raven.

Bruzzese, V. L., & Kaplowitz, L. G. (1998). Pharmacological treatment of opportunistic infections. In M. E. Ropka & A. B. Williams (Eds.), *HIV nursing and symptom management* (pp. 143–168). Boston: Jones and Bartlett.

Butler, K. M. & Pizzo, P. A. (1992). HIV infection in children. In V. T. DeVita, S. Hellman, & S. A. Rosenberg (Eds.), *AIDS: Etiology, diagnosis, treatment, and prevention* (3rd ed.) (pp 285–312). Philadelphia: J. B. Lippincott.

Butz, A. M., & Joffe, A. (1998). Infants, children, and adolescents. In M. E. Ropka & A. B. Williams (Eds.), *HIV nursing and symptom management* (pp. 632–676). Boston: Jones and Bartlett.

Cardo, D. M., Culver, D. H., Ciesielski, C. A., Srivastava, P. U., Marcus, R., Abiteboul, D., Heptonstall, J., Ippolito, G., Lot, F., McKibben, P. S., Bell, D. M., & the CDCP Needlestick Surveillance Group. (1997). A case-control study of HIV seroconversion in health care workers after percutaneous exposure. *New England Journal of Medicine, 337*(21), 1485–1490.

Carpenter, C. C. J., Fischl, M. A., Hammer, S. M., Hirsch, M. S., Jacobsen, D. M., Katzenstein, D. A., Montaner, J. S. G., Richman, D. D., Saag, M. S., Schooley, R. T., Thompson, M. A., Vella, S.,

Yeni, P. G., & Volberding, P. A. (1998). Antiretroviral therapy for HIV infection in 1998. *JAMA, 280*(1), 78–86.

Casey, K. M. (1997). Malnutrition associated with HIV/AIDS: Definition and scope, epidemiology, and pathophysiology. *Journal of the Association of Nurses in AIDS Care, 8*(3), 24–32.

Centers for Disease Control. (1998a). *HIV/AIDS Surveillance Report, 9*(2), 1–43.

Centers for Disease Control. (1998b). Administration of zidovudine during late pregnancy and delivery to prevent perinatal HIV transmission - Thailand 1996-1998. *Morbidity and Mortality Weekly Report, 47*(8), 751–754.

Centers for Disease Control. (1998c). Report of the NIH Panel to Define Principles of Therapy of HIV Infection. *Morbidity and Mortality Weekly Report, 47*(RR-5), 1–37.

Centers for Disease Control. (1997). World AIDS Day—December 1, 1997. *Morbidity and Mortality Weekly Report, 46*(46), 1085.

Chaisson, R. E., & Moore, R. D. (1997). Prevention of opportunistic infections in the era of improved antiretroviral therapy. *Journal of Acquired Immune Deficiency Syndrome, 16*(Suppl. 1), S14–S22.

Chaisson, R. E., Gallant, J. E., Keruly, J. C., & Moore, R. D. (1998). Impact of opportunistic disease on survival in patients with HIV infection. *AIDS 1998, 12*(1), 29–33.

Cockerell, C. J. (1992). Cutaneous and histologic signs of HIV infection other than Kaposi's sarcoma. In G. P. Wormser (Ed.), *AIDS and other manifestations of HIV infection* (2nd ed.) (pp. 463–476). New York: Raven Press.

Decker, C. F., & Masur, H. (1997). *Pneumocystis* and other protozoa. In V. T. DeVita, S. Hellman, & S. A. Rosenberg (Eds.), *AIDS: Etiology, diagnosis, treatment, and prevention* (4th ed.) (pp. 215–229). Philadelphia: Lippincott-Raven.

DeVita, V. T., Hellman, S., & Rosenberg, S. A. (Eds.) (1997). *AIDS: Etiology, diagnosis, treatment, and prevention*. Philadelphia: Lippincott-Raven.

Doweiko, J. P., & Groopman, J. E. (1997). Hematologic complications of human immunodeficiency virus infection. In V. T. DeVita, S. Hellman, & S. A. Rosenberg (Eds.), *AIDS: Etiology, diagnosis, treatment, and prevention* (4th ed.) (pp. 429–442). Philadelphia: Lippincott-Raven.

Dworkin, B. M. (1992). Gastrointestinal manifestations of AIDS. In G.P. Wormser (Ed.), *AIDS and other manifestations of HIV infection* (2nd ed.) (pp. 419–432). New York: Raven Press.

Ehrhardt, A. A. (1992). Trends in sexual behavior and the HIV pandemic. *American Journal of Public Health, 82*(11), 1459–1461.

Filler, S. G. (1997). The diagnosis and treatment of candidiasis: Current therapeutic options. *AIDS Patient Care and STDs, 11*(Suppl. 1), S10–S14.

Flaskerud, J. H., & Ungvarski, P. J. (Eds.) (1995). *HIV/AIDS: A guide to nursing care* (3rd ed.). Philadelphia: W.B. Saunders.

Flemming, D. S. & Visscher, B. R. (1997). Epidemiology and HIV transmission. In J. L. Fahey & D. S. Flemming (Eds.), *AIDS/HIV: Reference guide for medical professionals* (4th ed.) (pp. 1–56). Baltimore: Williams & Wilkins.

Foudraine, N. A., Weverling, G. J., van Gool, T., Roos, M. T. L., de Wolf, F., Koopmans, P. P., van den Broek, P. J., Meenhorst, P. L., van Leewen, R., Lange, J. M. A., & Reiss, P. (1998). Improvement of chronic diarrhea in patients with advanced HIV-1 infection during potent antiretroviral therapy. *AIDS 1998, 12*(1), 35–41.

Galantino, M. L. (1991). Pain management and neuromuscular reeducation for the HIV patient. *AIDS Patient Care, 5*(2), 81–85.

Goedert, J. J., Cote, T. R., Virgo, P., Scoppa, S. M., Kingma, D. W., Gail, M. H., Jaffe, E. S., & Biggar, R. J. (1998). Spectrum of AIDS-associated malignant disorders. *The Lancet, 351,* 1833–1839.

Gompels, M.M., Hill, A., Jenkins, P., Peters, B., Tomlinson, D., Harris, J.R.W., Stewart, S., & Pinching, A.J. (1992). Kaposi's sarcoma in HIV infection treated with vincristine and bleomycin. *AIDS, 6*(10), 1175–1180.

Grbic, J. T., & Lamster, I. B. (1997). Oral manifestations of HIV infection. *AIDS Patient Care and STDs, 11*(1), 18–24.

Greenspan, J. S., & Greenspan, D. (1997). Oral disease in human immunodeficiency infection. In V. T. DeVita, S. Hellman, & S. A. Rosenberg (Eds.), *AIDS: Etiology, diagnosis, treatment, and prevention* (4th ed.) (pp. 355–363). Philadelphia: Lippincott-Raven.

Grubman, S., Conviser, R., & Oleske, J. (1992). HIV infection in infants, children, and adolescents. In G. P. Wormser (Ed.), *AIDS and other manifestations of HIV infection* (2nd ed.) (pp. 201–216). New York: Raven Press.

Jacobson, M. A., & French, M. (1998). Altered natural history of AIDS-related opportunistic infections in the era of potent combination antiretroviral therapy. *AIDS 1998, 12*(Suppl. A), S157–S163.

Johnson, C. C., Wilcosky, T., Kvale, P., Rosen, M., Stansell, J., Glassroth, J., Reichman, L., Wallace, J., Markowitz, N., Thompson, J. E., & Hopewell, P. (1997). Cancer incidence among an HIV-infected cohort. *American Journal of Epidemiology, 146*(6), 470–475.

Jones, J. L., Hanson, D. L., Dworkin, M. S., Kaplan, J. E., & Ward, J. W. (1998). Trends in AIDS-related opportunistic infections among men who have sex with men and among injecting drug users, 1991-1996. *Journal of Infectious Diseases, 178*(1), 114–120.

Kemp, C. E., & Stepp, L. (1995). Palliative care for patients with acquired immunodeficiency syndrome. *American Journal of Hospice and Palliative Care, 12*(6), 14–27.

Kiviat, N. B. (1997). Human papillomavirus and hepatitis viral infections in human immunodeficiency virus-infected persons. In V. T. DeVita, S. Hellman, & S. A. Rosenberg (Eds.), *AIDS: Etiology, diagnosis, treatment, and prevention* (4th ed.) (pp. 281–294). Philadelphia: Lippincott-Raven.

Kopp, J. B., & Balow, J. E. (1998). Renal complications. In V. T. DeVita, S. Hellman, & S. A. Rosenberg (Eds.), *AIDS: Etiology, diagnosis, treatment, and prevention* (4th ed.) (pp. 423–428). Philadelphia: Lippincott-Raven.

Kotler, D. P. (1997). Gastrointestinal manifestations of human immunodeficiency virus infection. In V. T. DeVita, S. Hellman, & S. A. Rosenberg (Eds.), *AIDS: Etiology, diagnosis, treatment, and prevention* (4th ed.) (pp. 365–391). Philadelphia: Lippincott-Raven.

Landis, S. H., Murray, T., Bolden, S., & Wingo, P. A. (1998). Cancer statistics, 1998. *Ca—A Cancer Journal for Clinicians, 48*(1), 6–29.

Launay, O., Lortholary, O., Bouges-Michel, C., Jarrouse, B., Bentata, M., & Guillevin, L. (1998). Candidemia: A nosocomial complication in adults with late-stage AIDS. *Clinical Infectious Diseases, 26*(5), 1134–1141.

Lebbe, C., Blum, L., Pellet, C., Blanchard, G., Verola, O., Morel, P., Danne, O., & Calvo, F. (1998). Clinical and biological impact of antiretroviral therapy with protease inhibitors on HIV-related Kaposi's sarcoma. *AIDS 98, 12*(7), 45–49.

Lim, H. W., Vallurapalli, S., Meola, T., & Sater, N. A. (1997). *Journal of the American Academy of Dermatology, 37*(3 pt 1), 414–417.

Lubeck, D. P., Bennett, C. L., Mazonson, P. D., Fifer, S. K., & Fries, J. F. (1993). Quality of life and health service use among HIV-infected patients with chronic diarrhea. *Journal of Acquired Immune Deficiency Syndromes, 6*(5), 478–484.

McGowan, J. P., & Shah, S. (1998). Long-term remission of AIDS-related primary central nervous system lymphoma associated with highly active antiretroviral therapy. *AIDS 98, 12*(8), 952–954.

Miles, S. A., Aboulafia, D. M., & Mitsuyasu, R. I. (1997). AIDS-related malignancies. In V. T. DeVita, S. Hellman, & S. A. Rosenberg (Eds.), *Cancer: Principles and practice of oncology* (5th ed.) (pp. 2445–2467). Philadelphia: Lippincott-Raven.

Mirowski, G. W., Hilton, J. F., Greenspan, D., Canchola, A. J., MacPhail, L. A., Maurer, T., Berger, T. G., & Greenspan, J. S. (1998). Association of cutaneous and oral diseases in HIV-infected men. *Oral Diseases, 4*(1), 16–21.

Ownby, K., & Ownby, J. (1998). Neurological manifestations. In M. E. Ropka & A. B. Williams (Eds.), *HIV Nursing and symptom management* (pp. 233–290). Boston: Jones and Bartlett.

Palella, F. J., Delaney, K. M. Moorman, A. C., Loveless, M. O., Fuhrer, J., Satten, G. A., Aschman, D. J., Holmberg, S. D., & the HIV Outpatient Study Investigators (1998). Declining morbidity and mortality among patients with advanced human immunodeficiency virus infection. *New England Journal of Medicine, 338*(13), 853–860.

Parente, F., & Bianchi-Porro, G. (1998). Treatment of cytomegalovirus esophagitis in patients with acquired immune deficiency syndrome: A randomized controlled study of foscarnet versus ganciclovir. *American Journal of Gastroenterology, 93*(3), 317–322.

Pharmaceutical Manufacturers Association. (1992). *AIDS medicines.* Washington, D.C.: Author:

Piemme, J. A. (1998). Opportunistic infections. In M. E. Ropka & A. B. Williams (Eds.), *HIV nursing and symptom management* (pp. 110–142). Boston: Jones and Bartlett.

Polis, M. A., & Kovacs, J. A. (1997). Fungal infections in patients with acquired immunodeficiency. In V. T. DeVita, S. Hellman, & S. A. Rosenberg (Eds.), *AIDS: Etiology, diagnosis, treatment, and prevention* (4th ed.) (pp. 231–243). Philadelphia: Lippincott-Raven.

Price, R. W. & Brew, B. J. (1997). Central and peripheral nervous system complications. In V. T. DeVita, S. Hellman, & S. A. Rosenberg (Eds.), *AIDS: Etiology, diagnosis, treatment, and prevention* (4th ed.) (pp. 331–354). Philadelphia: Lippincott-Raven.

Ropka, M. E., & Williams, A. B. (Eds.) (1998). *HIV nursing and symptom management.* Boston: Jones and Bartlett.

Saag, M. S. (1997). Clinical spectrum of human immunodeficiency virus diseasea. In V. T. DeVita, S. Hellman, & S. A. Rosenberg (Eds.), *AIDS: Etiology, diagnosis, treatment, and prevention* (4th ed.) (pp. 203–214). Philadelphia: Lippincott-Raven.

Safai, B. (1997). Noninfectious organ-specific complications of HIV infection. In V. T. DeVita, S. Hellman, & S. A. Rosenberg (Eds.), *AIDS: Etiology, diagnosis, treatment, and prevention* (4th ed.) (pp. 393–403). Philadelphia: Lippincott-Raven.

Sattler, F., Briggs, W., Antonipillai, I., Allen, J., & Horton, R. (1998). Low dihydrotestosterone and weight loss in the AIDS wasting syndrome. *Journal of Acquired Immune Deficiency Syndromes and Human Retrovirology, 18*(2), 246–251.

Schacker, T., & Corey, L. (1997). Herpesvirus infections in human immunodeficiency virus-infected persons. In V. T. DeVita, S. Hellman, & S. A. Rosenberg (Eds.), *AIDS: Etiology, diagnosis, treatment, and prevention* (4th ed.) (pp. 267–280). Philadelphia: Lippincott-Raven.

Selwyn, P. A., Pumerantz, A. S., Durante, A., Alcabes, P. G., Gourevitch, M. N., Boiselle, P. M., & Elmore, J. G. (1998). Clinical predictors of pneumocystis carinii pneumonia, bacterial pneumonia and tuberculosis in HIV-infected patients. *AIDS 1998, 12*(8), 885–893.

Sepkowitz, K. A. (1998). Effect of prophylaxis on the clinical manifestations of AIDS-related opportunistic infections. *Clinical Infectious Diseases, 26*(4), 806–810.

Sherer, R. (1998). Current antiretroviral therapy and its impact on human immunodeficiency virus-related wasting. *Seminars in Oncology, 25*(2, Suppl 6), 92–97.

Simpson, D. M., & Wolfe, D. E. (1991). Neuromuscular complications of HIV infection and its treatment. *AIDS, 5*(8), 917–926.

Strawford, A., & Hellerstein, M. (1998). The etiology of wasting in the human immunodeficiency virus and acquired immunodeficiency syndrome. *Seminars in Oncology, 25*(2, Suppl. 6), 76–81.

Temesgen, Z., & Wright, A. J. (1997). Recent advances in the management of human immunodeficiency virus infection. *Mayo Clinic Proceedings, 72*(9), 854–859.

Viele, C. S. (1998). Hematologic abnormalities. In M. E. Ropka & A. B. Williams (Eds.) *HIV nursing and symptom management* (pp. 387–399). Boston: Jones and Bartlett.

Wilcox, C. M. (1997). Chronic unexplained diarrhea in AIDS: Approach to diagnosis and management. *AIDS Patient Care and STDs, 11*(1), 13–17.

Wilkes, G., & Williams, A. (1998). Pharmacological issues in HIV treatment. In M. E. Ropka & A. B. Williams (Eds.), *HIV Nursing and symptom management* (pp. 59–109). Boston: Jones and Bartlett.

Zurlo, J. J., & Lane, H. C. (1997). Other bacterial infections. In V. T. DeVita, S. Hellman, & S. A. Rosenberg (Eds.), *AIDS: Etiology, diagnosis, treatment, and prevention* (4th ed.) (pp. 355–363). Philadelphia: Lippincott-Raven.

CHAPTER 28

Degenerative Neurologic Disorders: Multiple Sclerosis, Parkinson's Disease, Amyotrophic Lateral Sclerosis, and Myasthenia Gravis

KEY POINTS

● Although none of the neurodegenerative diseases is among the leading causes of death in the United States, patients with neurodegenerative disorders comprise an important population that benefits from hospice and palliative care.

● Each neurodegenerative disease has unique characteristics that must be understood if quality hospice or palliative care is to be provided.

● All the neurodegenerative diseases have common characteristics and problems, such as lengthy trajectory, dysphagia, inability to perform independent activities of daily living, and respiratory compromise.

● All the neurodegenerative diseases present challenging ethical dilemmas in the end stages, such as whether to use assisted ventilation and if so when to discontinue ventilation.

● The basic principles of hospice and palliative care are readily applicable to care for patients with any of the neurodegenerative diseases.

While not listed among the 15 leading causes of death in the United States (Centers for Disease Control and Prevention [CDC], 1997), degenerative neurologic disorders are the primary diagnosis in some patients receiving palliative care. The physiologic decline of terminally ill patients with neurologic disorders is dissimilar in some respects to that of patients suffering from other major illness, but pneumonia, the sixth leading cause of death (CDC, 1997), is a common ending. Common also is the enormous physical, psychosocial, and spiritual stress placed on family caregivers as they work to care for a suffering family member.

This chapter examines the most widespread degenerative neurologic disorders: multiple sclerosis (MS), Parkinson's disease (PD), amy-otrophic lateral sclerosis (ALS), and myasthe-nia gravis (MG). (Alzheimer's disease is dis-cussed in Chapter 29.) Each disorder is discussed individually, and unique aspects are identified.

Multiple Sclerosis

Multiple sclerosis is a complex chronic degenerative neurologic disorder featuring inflammatory demyelination of the central nervous system (CNS) due probably to an autoimmune response (Ewing & Bernard, 1998). Several forms or patterns of MS exist (Hickey, 1997), and not all are fatal:

● Relapsing/remitting MS (65% of cases) is characterized by relapses with remission and return to baseline. Relapsing/remitting MS may convert to chronic progressive MS.
● Relapsing/progressive disease (15% of cases) is characterized by relapses and failure to return to baseline.
● Chronic progressive MS (20% of cases) is characterized by progressive deterioration with cerebellar and spinal cord dysfunction.

MS usually begins between the ages of 20 and 40 and has a trajectory lasting as long as 30 or more years (Adams & Victor, 1989). Disabilities from MS are varied, often involving multiple functions of the nervous system, and including the following (taken in large part from Hickey, 1997 and also Caracini & Martini, 1998):

Sensory Symptoms
Paraesthesias and numbness are common, especially in extremities. Dysesthetic central pain, low back pain, and painful leg spasms are usually the most disabling types of chronic pain experienced by patients with MS. Other types of pain include trigeminal neuralgias, painful tonic seizures, headache, and spasticity-related pain.

Motor Symptoms
Ataxia, paresis, and other neurologic deficits may manifest first in the lower extremities and eventually become global in nature. Intentional tremors of the extremities eventually affect the head. Spasticity is common and includes paroxysmal and painful spasms of extremities.

Cerebellar Symptoms
Cerebellar ataxia is characterized by slurred or scanning speech (ie, speech with regular pauses), nystagmus, loss of coordination, vertigo, vomiting, and sometimes very severe intentional tremors.

Cranial Nerve Involvement
Any or all the cranial nerves may be affected, especially the optic nerve, resulting in optic neuritis, a partial or total and often temporary or improving loss of vision in one or both eye(s). Diplopia is also common, as are tinnitus and unformed auditory hallucinations.

Other Symptoms
Brain stem involvement can be characterized by facial paralysis or myokymia (brief muscle contractions). Urinary dysfunction (hesitancy, urgency, frequency, and incontinence) and sexual dysfunction are common and related in many cases to autonomic changes, including detrusor muscle spasm or neurogenic bladder. Bowel dysfunction is common in late-stage disease. Seizures or tetanic spasms occur in some patients.

Fatigue
Fatigue is a common chronic symptom of MS and increases as the disease progresses. "MS fatigue" does not always have an apparent etiology other than the disease itself.

Psychological and Cognitive Changes
Mental changes in MS range from euphoria or unconcern about the disease to euthymia or depression. While the euphoria sometimes found in patients with MS has received much attention, depression is more common and

increases with disease progression (Mohr, Goodkin, Gatto, & Van der Wende, 1997). Depression has been inconclusively studied as a response, a sign or symptom, and a precipitating factor in MS. Bipolar disorder may also be disproportionately represented among patients with MS (Miller & Hens, 1993). Isolation, helplessness, hopelessness, and increased dependence are hallmarks of advanced MS, and with the lengthy trajectory of the disease, they fit well with the concept of chronic sorrow (Gulick & Bugg, 1992; Hainsworth, Burke, Lindgren, & Eakes, 1993).

Multiple sclerosis dementia occurs in later stages of the disease and is characterized by euphoria, emotional lability, and depression. Cognitive dysfunction is not necessarily profound but may include memory loss and inability to use new information (Pelosi, Geesken, Holly, Hayward, & Blumhardt, 1997). However, global dementia, or a confused psychosis, may also occur (Adams & Victor, 1989).

Palliative Care in Multiple Sclerosis

Treatment of MS is palliative and experimental. Steroids are commonly used during periods of exacerbation, and muscle relaxants or tranquilizers used for spasticity or related symptoms (Hickey, 1997). Beta interferon is used to slow progression, and other chemotherapeutic agents are used as well.

Several factors are known to exacerbate MS symptoms at any stage of disease. These include overexertion, heat (environmental, water, and other sources), infection, fever, anxiety, and emotional stress.

Pain is a common problem in patients with MS—especially in far advanced disease. The most common pain is neuropathic (central pain, dysesthesias, trigeminal neuralgia, and others). Because depression is common, the tricyclic antidepressants are important in treating neuropathic pain in MS. Headache and painful spasms of the extremities are also common, as is dull, aching lower back pain (Caracini & Martini, 1998). Please refer to

Unit II of this book, in particular to discussions of neuropathic and also somatic pain in Chapters 11 and 12.

The primary cause of death in patients with MS is, predictably, pneumonia. One study has shown a startling second leading cause of death: In this study, 28.6% of MS deaths were attributed to suicide by (in descending order) overdose, gunshot, and starvation (Sadovnick, Eisen, Ebers, & Paty, 1991). Results have not been replicated. Severe urinary tract infections are common in the later stages (Hickey, 1997).

Some problems, such as depression, neuropathic pain, pneumonia, urinary dysfunction (or infection if a catheter is inserted), and constipation, are almost universal in late-stage MS. Therefore, anticipatory assessment and, in some cases, prophylactic treatment should be instituted for these problems.

Parkinson's Disease

Parkinson's disease is a chronic, degenerative, slowly progressive disease of the basal ganglia with disease onset most frequently around age 60 years (Hickey, 1997). Pathologic CNS changes include the loss of pigmented neurons and the presence of Lewy bodies in the substantia nigra with no known cause (Lusis, 1997). The primary characteristics of PD are muscle rigidity, resting tremors, bradykinesia (slow movement), and stooped and unstable posture. Major manifestations (Adams & Victor, 1989; Hickey, 1997; Lusis, 1997) are discussed in the following sections.

Tremors

Resting tremors are common, especially of the hands ("pill-rolling"), feet, and face. Fine motor control gradually diminishes.

Muscle Rigidity

Bradykinesia is a result of muscle rigidity and is part of the akinetic phenomena of PD. Other akinetic phenomena are "cogwheeling" or difficulty reaching a target with one continuous movement, fatigue with rapid movement, and freezing or complete immobility, which is seen most often when the patient attempts movement. Small, shuffling steps are characteristic of PD.

Postural Changes
An increasingly stooped and unstable posture leads to injury and (along with other impairments) ultimately to the patient becoming bedridden.

Autonomic Changes
Autonomic deterioration includes drooling, oily skin, dysphagia, increased perspiration, constipation, orthostatic hypotension, and urinary frequency and hesitation.

Other Secondary Changes
Characteristic changes of PD include masklike facies, monotone voice, blurred vision, changes in olfaction, and cognitive changes.

Psychological Disturbances
Depression, with prevalence rates as high as 50%, is common in patients with PD. It is not known whether the depression is a reaction to PD or a part of the disease (Bunting & Fitzsimmons, 1991). Besides depression, delirium and dementia are the most common psychological problems of patients with PD. Hallucinations, usually nonthreatening and visual but also auditory, are relatively common among patients with PD, especially those with cognitive impairment (Inzelberg, Kipervasser, & Korczyn, 1998). Frustration, accompanied by irritation and anger, is almost universal among patients with PD (Marr, 1991).

Progression of Parkinson's Disease
As the disease progresses, all movement is slowed, including chewing, swallowing, and speaking; and the patient becomes increasingly immobile. Freezing or complete immobility is seen most often when the patient attempts movement. Vision may blur, and the ability to speak diminishes. About 10% to 30% of patients are likely to have moderate to severe dementia (Adams & Victor, 1989).

Palliative Care in Parkinson's Disease
Levodopa remains the most effective medication for all stages of PD (Chase, 1998). Levodopa is often given as Sinemet (combination of levodopa and carbidopa). There is a "wearing off" phenomenon of levodopa therapy that results in varied responses and progressive worsening of the disease. Changes in blood levels of levodopa result in the "on-off phenomenon," in which the patient suddenly becomes immobile. Involuntary movements, including dyskinesias, dystonia, choreoathetosis, and restlessness, sometimes result from long-term levodopa and related medication use. Bromocriptine (Parlodel) and pergolide (Permax) are dopamine agonists that decrease the fluctuation in motor response to levodopa. Anticholinergics (eg, benztropine) help decrease tremors and rigidity. Other medications, including amantadine and the monoamine oxidase inhibitor selegiline, are also used (Hickey, 1997). It is important that caregivers understand the limitations and implications of levodopa use and the measures necessary for safe administration. These include eliminating vitamin B_6 supplements, decreasing alcohol intake, decreasing protein intake, taking medications with meals, taking measures to relieve xerostomia (see Chapter 16), wearing elastic stockings, and monitoring for depression (Hickey, 1997).

Care of the bedridden patient takes into account the physical, psychological, and caregiver problems and issues noted at the end of this and the Chapter 29. Heat should be avoided, range of motion maintained, skin breakdown avoided (see Chapter 15), dysphagia addressed (Chapter 17), and problems of elimination managed (see Chapters 17 and 18). The degenerative nature of PD, physical and psychological demands of caregiving, decreased social interaction, and other stressors all play a role in the significant and stressful burden the disease places on caregivers. By the end stage, the primary caregiver is likely to be globally exhausted.

Amyotrophic Lateral Sclerosis (ALS)

ALS, or motor neuron disease (also known as Lou Gehrig's disease), is a progressive degenerative disease of the motor neurons of the spinal cord or brain stem. Onset is usually after age 50, the etiology is unknown, the time from onset to death is typically 2 to 5 years, and there is currently no cure (Jackson & Bryan, 1998).

Typically, ALS is manifested initially by difficulty using first one hand and then the other. Hand and forearm atrophy and weakness spread to the upper arms and shoulders. In later stages, ALS is characterized by lower extremity spasticity and hyperreflexia. Fasciculations (small muscle contractions) are common. The atrophy and weakness spread to the neck and tongue, with resultant dysarthria, dysphagia, drooling, and wasting and tremors of the tongue. Muscles of the trunk and lower extremities eventually deteriorate. Muscle cramps are frequent, and patients may feel aching pain or a sense of coldness in the affected areas. Involvement of chest and shoulder muscles contributes to dyspnea. Swallowing and managing secretions become increasingly difficult, and aspiration often results. Ultimately, the patient becomes quadriplegic and unable to speak, swallow, or breathe. ALS does not affect vision, hearing, intellectual ability, or bladder or bowel function (Borasio & Voltz, 1997; Jackson & Bryan, 1998; National Hospice Organization [NHO], 1996).

Psychologically, ALS is a devastating disease. The patient experiences, with intact intellect, an inexorable decline, including steadily increasing difficulty in breathing, which may, in the final analysis, be better than going through the process with dementia. Social isolation, anger, and depression are common. Many patients with ALS are emotionally labile, and outbursts of crying or laughing may occur. If problematic, these may be treated with amitriptyline, fluoxetine, or other medications. Amitriptyline also helps decrease drooling, so it may be the first choice (Borasio & Voltz, 1997). Stresses on the family are similar to those on families of patients with any fatal degenerative neurologic disease.

Palliative Care in Amyotrophic Lateral Sclerosis

Treatment of ALS is symptomatic and supportive. Medications for symptoms include baclofen, tizanidine, memantine, or tetrazepam for spasticity; quinine sulfate, carbamazepine, vitamin E, phenytoin, magnesium, or verapamil for cramps and fasciculations; and amitriptyline, trihexyphenidyl, clonidine, ipratropium bromide, or butylsopolamine for excess salivation and drooling (Borasio & Voltz, 1997; Hickey, 1997). Reducing salivation results in xerostomia (see Chapter 16). Intake of food, fluids, and medications becomes a major challenge. Some patients eventually resist food and fluid for fear of choking. Dysphagia progresses to the point that feeding by gastrostomy or jejunostomy is required to maintain nutritional status (Caracini & Martini, 1998), though some patients refuse such measures. Small amounts of morphine (eg, 2.5 mg PO every 4 hours) can be given for severe hunger pangs (Oliver, 1989). Because choking and aspiration are inevitable, suction equipment should be available. Pain from the effects of immobility and other (usually neuromuscular) causes is common, and opioids are often required for pain and dyspnea (Oliver, 1998).

Dyspnea in ALS progresses from slight breathlessness to chronic respiratory insufficiency with chronic nocturnal hypoventilation to hypercapnic coma. It is important to explain to clients that the hypercapnic coma results in "peaceful death during sleep" as opposed to the feared choking to death (Borasio & Voltz, 1997, p. S12). Noninvasive intermittent ventilation is an option to mechanical ventilation using tracheostomy.

Because of the patient's inability to hold his or her head or otherwise move, manage secretions, or breath adequately, the end stages of ALS require intensive patient care. Unless the patient gives specific directions to the contrary, mechanical ventilation is likely. Patients who have had full explanations of the course of ALS often do not choose assisted ventilation (NHO, 1996). Once mechanical ventilation is started, it cannot be discontinued without significant respiratory distress (ie, the patient usually dies). It is wise and humane to give an opioid before a patient is removed from a ventilator.

Myasthenia Gravis (MG)

MG is a chronic, progressive autoimmune neuromuscular disease characterized by chronic fatigue and muscle weakness, which partially improve with rest (Kernich & Kaminski, 1995). Onset in women is frequently between the ages of 20 and 30 years and for men, after age 50. The course of MG is variable. With stable ocular myasthenia, the disease may never generalize, and with mild generalized MG, the disease is responsive to medications. With moderate generalized MG, the response to medications is less satisfactory, and with acute fulminating MG, there is poor drug response and high mortality. The progression of MG also varies widely. Hyperplasia of the thymus gland is usually present in people with MG, and thymectomy results in a remission rate of approximately 40% if performed early in the disease (Hickey, 1997; Kernich & Kaminski, 1995).

Typically, repeated activity of a muscle group results in loss of contractile power and progressive paresis. MG usually begins with chronic fatigue, but in some cases, rapid onset occurs, often following an upper respiratory infection or emotional distress (Adams & Victor, 1989). While symptoms vary among different patients, a usual course of a more severe form of MG includes progressive weakness of voluntary muscles (extremities, facial, chewing, speaking, and swallowing), drooping eye-

lids, visual disturbances, and distortion of the face. The effects of weakened respiratory muscles and decreased tidal volume and vital capacity are complicated by difficulties swallowing and managing secretions. The result is often aspiration pneumonia (Hood, 1990; Litchfield & Noroian, 1989).

Two sorts of crises occur with some frequency in patients with MG. Myasthenic crisis is a sudden escalation of MG symptoms and even with increased medications, may result in respiratory paralysis. Intubation and respiratory support are necessary, and when the crisis is resolved, these are removed. Cholinergic crisis is characterized by slowly developing weakness, increased secretions, and decreased respiratory function, all often preceded by abdominal cramping and diarrhea. Cholinergic crisis is managed similarly to myasthenic crisis (Hickey, 1997).

Psychological responses to MG are similar to responses to other degenerative illnesses. Isolation, helplessness, anger, and depression are familiar to most patients with MG and to their families.

Palliative Care in Myasthenia Gravis
Treatment of advanced MG includes anticholinesterase drugs and corticosteroids. Plasmapheresis is used for severe disease and provides improvement for as long as 6 weeks. Patients with severe MG require the same intensive care as patients with other severe neuromuscular diseases, especially related to respiratory problems (dyspnea, aspiration, pneumonia), dysphagia, asthenia, pain (eg, from immobilty), and emotional responses to slow neurologic deterioration.

Problems of End-Stage Degenerative Neurologic Diseases

Common problems of end-stage degenerative neurologic diseases are also discussed in Chapter 29. Some problems, however, are discussed here:

● Dysphagia is common in all degenerative neurologic diseases. Intake of food, fluids, and medications becomes a major challenge. While there is variation among individuals, semisolid or soft foods and finally liquid supplements are required. It is essential that the patient be sitting up with head bowed slightly forward (likely requiring support) for all oral intake. Distractions during mealtimes should be minimized. Straws should not be used by clients whose lips do not function well. Fluids and solids should not be mixed, and meals should be finished with a small amount of water. The patient should force a cough after eating and should remain sitting for at least an hour if possible (Twycross & Regnard, 1998). Please see Chapter 17 for a more complete discussion of dysphagia.

● Pneumonia may result from aspiration or immobility. Maintaining mobility, or at least range of motion, in a long-term, bedridden patient is a major challenge, especially when, as in the case of some neuromuscular diseases, activity further exacerbates disease symptoms.

● Isolation is common in all chronic illnesses. The degenerative neurologic diseases are perhaps more isolating because of their lengthy trajectory, the inability of patients to communicate, and the sometimes off-putting symptoms, such as drooling, facial distortion, and frequent choking. Socially, end-stage disease is usually characterized by either long-term care or by caregiving provided by one family member, often a physically and emotionally exhausted spouse who provides both care and the patient's sole social contact (O'Brien, 1993). Because social support and hope are strongly related, the reality of patient and caregiver is often grim. Psychosocial care and support take on increased importance. Each family should receive case management services, including carefully planned, intentional psychosocial support, preferably in a coordinated team effort.

● Caregiver exhaustion is common and is compounded by caregivers frequently ignoring their own health (O'Brien, 1993). Regular monitoring of caregiver health is thus indicated. Respite services help, but as noted elsewhere, offers of intermittent services may not be received with the enthusiasm expected by some health providers. It is well to remember that these caregivers are nearly always in the midst of an unimaginably difficult and painful marathon that lasts for years. For those able or willing to leave the patient, disease-specific support groups are usually helpful

For more information, please see the section on providing care in Chapter 29.

REFERENCES

Adams, R. D., & Victor, M. (1989). *Principles of neurology*. New York: McGraw-Hill Information Services.

Borasio, G. D., & Voltz, R. (1997). Palliative care in amyotrophic lateral sclerosis. *Journal of Neurology*, 244(Suppl. 4), S11–S17.

Bunting, L. K. (1991). Depression in Parkinson's disease. *Journal of Neuroscience Nursing*, 21(5), 158–164.

Caracini, A., & Martini, C. (1998). Neurological problems. In D. Doyle, G. W. C. Hanks, & N. MacDonald (Eds.), *Oxford textbook of palliative medicine* (2nd ed.) (pp. 727–749). New York: Oxford University Press.

Centers for Disease Control and Prevention. (1997). Mortality patterns-Preliminary data, United States, 1996. *Morbidity and Mortality Weekly Report*, 46(40), 941–944.

Chase, T. N. (1998). The significance of continuous dopaminergic stimulation in the treatment of Parkinson's disease. *Drugs*, 55(Suppl. 1), 1–9.

Ewing, C., & Bernard, C. C. (1998). Insights into the etiology and pathogenesis of multiple sclerosis. *Immunological Cellular Biology*, 76(1), 47–54.

Gulick, E. E., & Bugg, A. (1992). Holistic health patterning in multiple sclerosis. *Research in Nursing and Health*, 15(3), 175–185.

Hainsworth, M. A., Burke, M. L., Lindgren, C. L., & Eakes, G. G. (1993). Chronic sorrow in multiple sclerosis. *Home Healthcare Nurse*, 11(2), 9–13.

Hickey, J. V. (1997). Selected degenerative diseases of the nervous system. In J. V. Hickey (Ed.), *The clinical practice of neurological and neurosurgical nursing*. Philadelphia: Lippincott-Raven.

Hood, L. J. (1990). Myasthenia gravis: Regimens and regimen-associated problems in adults. *Journal of Neuroscience Nursing, 22*(6), 358–354.

Inzelberg, R., Kipervasser, S., & Korczyn, A. D. (1998). Auditory hallucinations in Parkinson's disease. *Journal of Neurosurgical Psychiatry, 64*(4), 533–555.

Jackson, C. E., & Bryan, W. W. (1998). Amyotrophic lateral sclerosis. *Seminars in Neurology, 18*(1), 27–39.

Kernich, C. A., & Kaminski, H. J. (1995). Myasthenia gravis: Pathophysiology, diagnosis, and collaborative care. *Journal of Neuroscience Nursing, 27*(4), 207–215.

Litchfield, M., & Noroian, E. (1989). Changes in selected pulmonary functions in patients diagnosed with myasthenia gravis. *Journal of Neuroscience Nursing, 21*(6), 375–381.

Lusis, S. A. (1997). Pathophysiology and management of idiopathic Parkinson's disease. *Journal of Neuroscience Nursing, 29*(1), 24–31.

Marr, J. (1991). The experience of living with Parkinson's Disease. *Journal of Neuroscience Nursing, 23*(5), 325–330.

Miller, C. M., & Hens, M. (1993). Multiple sclerosis: A literature review. *Journal of Neuroscience Nursing, 25*(3), 174–179.

Mohr, D. C., Goodkin, D. E., Gatto, N., & Van der Wende, J. (1997). Depression, coping, and level of neurological impairment in multiple sclerosis. *Multiple Sclerosis, 3*(4), 254–258.

Morgante, L. A., Madonna, M. G., & Pokoluk, R. (1989). Research and treatment in multiple sclerosis: Implications for nursing practice. *Journal of Neuroscience Nursing, 21*(5), 285–289.

National Hospice Organization. (1996). *Medical guidelines for determining prognosis in selected non-cancer diseases.* Arlington, VA: Author.

O'Brien, M. T. (1993). Multiple sclerosis: Health-promoting behaviors of spousal caregivers. *Journal of Neuroscience Nursing, 25*(2), 105–112.

Oliver, D. (1998). Opioid medication in the palliative care of motor neuron disease. *Palliative Medicine, 12*(2), 113–115.

Pelosi, L., Geesken, J. M., Holly, M., Hayward, M., & Blumhardt, L. D. (1997). Working memory impairment in early multiple sclerosis. *Brain, 120*(pt. 11), 2039–2058.

Sadovnick, A. D., Eisen, K., Ebers, G. L., & Paty, D. W. (1991). Causes of death in patients attending multiple sclerosis clinics. *Neurology, 41*(8), 1193–1196.

Twycross, R., & Regnard, C. (1998). Dysphagia, dyspepsia, and hiccup. In D. Doyle, G. W. C. Hanks, & N. MacDonald (Eds.), *Oxford textbook of palliative medicine* (2nd ed.) (pp. 499–512). New York: Oxford University Press.

CHAPTER 29

Alzheimer's Disease

KEY POINTS

● Alzheimer's disease is a devastating physical, psychological, spiritual, and social disorder.

● Alzheimer's disease has profound effects of family and other such caregivers. The "36-hour day" is a reality for caregivers.

● In late stages, Alzheimer's disease affects almost all body systems.

● Caring for caregivers is a challenge and an honor for nurses and others.

Alzheimer's disease (AD) or dementia of the Alzheimer type and similar neurodegenerative or dementing diseases affect approximately 4 million Americans, and, with about 100,000 deaths annually, constitute the fourth leading cause of death among adults, according to the Alzheimer's Association. The incidence of AD in the population over 65 years of age is about 10%, and in the population over 85 years, it is more than 45% (Alzheimer's Association, 1998). While some specifics may differ slightly, the care discussed under AD applies also to other dementing illnesses, such as vascular dementia, dementia due to head trauma, Huntington's disease, and others.

Characteristics

Alzheimer's disease is characterized by progressive and insidious deterioration of memory and other cognitive, psychosocial, and physical functions. From the moderately impaired stage through the profoundly impaired stage, patients are likely to experience delirium, delusions, hallucinations, and depression. Distinguishing between AD, delirium, and depression is sometimes difficult (American Psychiatric Association [APA], 1997). The AD process averages about 7.5 years from onset to death but may last anywhere from 3 to 20 years (Alzheimer's Association, 1998).

Alzheimer's disease is manifested by such problems as memory loss, catastrophic reactions (exaggerated response to a situation), demanding behavior, night waking, hiding articles, and decreased ability to communicate. It is important to understand that while cognitive loss in general is predictable, each patient loses different abilities at different times (APA, 1997). Use of the brief Mini-Mental State Examination (Folstein, Folstein, & McHugh, 1975) is a recommended means of assessing cognitive function in clients with AD (Lerner, Hedera, Koss, Stuckey, & Friedland, 1997).

The brief Mini-Mental State Examination is included in Chapter 13 (Figure 13-1). To be most meaningful, the examination should be conducted at regular intervals, preferably by the same person.

There are treatment options that primarily function to slow the progression of AD in some patients (APA, 1997). By late or terminal stage, there are ethical questions about whether such measures are beneficial to the patient, and the answer, generally, is no (Post, 1997).

In most patients, the ability to communicate is profoundly affected to the extent that by the end stage, meaningful communication is completely lost. This and other deficits result in increased isolation for the patient and frustration in family and professionals, which tends to further increase isolation (Lee, 1991).

In general, AD progresses from forgetfulness to increasing confusion to "ambulatory dementia" and finally to a severe, increasingly vegetative state (APA, 1997). While these are not clearly defined stages, they are fairly typical. The stage characterized by ambulatory dementia (ie, Alzheimer's dementia) is very troublesome for all concerned, and in many cases this is the stage at which the family is no longer able to care for the patient at home (Foreman & Grabowski, 1992). Agitation and other restless behavior, such as wandering, cursing, threatening, and repetitive statements or questions, are common (Moore, 1997), especially late in the day ("sundowning").

Each stage brings its unique difficulties and contributes to a crescendo of deterioration in the patient and pain for the family. In the end stage, patients are unable, for the most part, to recognize others, familiar objects, and even body parts. Patients may be unable to eat, chew, or swallow. Rather than speak, patients may groan or scream. The terminal stage of AD is characterized by all the following deficits: inability to speak more than six words, walk, bathe properly, dress without assistance, stand, sit up, smile, hold the head up, or swallow food and the presence of urinary and fecal incontinence (National Hospice Organization [NHO],

1996). Comorbid conditions indicating decreased survival time include (within the past year) aspiration pneumonia, pyelonephritis or other upper urinary tract infection, septicemia, multiple stage three to four decubitus ulcers, fever recurrent after antibiotics, and coma (Jacob Perlow Hospice, 1991; NHO, 1996).

Effects of Alzheimer's Disease on Caregivers

A key characteristic of the disorder is the unrelenting nature of the deterioration and the concomitant, steadily increasing load on the patient's family. In a very real sense, AD becomes a global family disease that often affects the physical, psychosocial, and spiritual health of all concerned (Moore, 1997).

Physical problems for caregivers center around exhaustion and its consequences. Most are relatives, either a spouse or daughter, and most are elderly. The care is demanding and increases in difficulty as the disease progresses. Regardless of disease stage, there is always something to do. The physical work of cleaning and caring for the patient is compounded by the need for constant vigilance to prevent the consequences of demented decisions and behaviors. As the patient deteriorates, total patient care becomes necessary. Caregivers are thus at risk themselves for physical deterioration.

Psychosocial problems are legion. Finances and medical bills are often an unresolved problem operating in the background. Social isolation and ambivalence toward the object of loss, both key factors in grief and morbidity, are frequently operational in caregivers of patients with AD (Moore, 1997). Social isolation occurs, at least in part, because of the never-ending care demands. Ambivalence is related to caregiver role changes and to negative changes in the patient's personality and behavior. Ambivalent feelings, such as love for the person that was and anger, disgust, or death wishes for the person that is, may result in terrible guilt. Grief is profound and is complicated by the death of the personality before the body, by the lack of time (psychological space) in which to grieve, and by a lack of social sanction and support in grieving. In a caregiver with previously inadequate coping skills or other risk factors for complicated grief, there is significant risk of developing chronic sorrow (see Chapter 6). Caregiver health is compromised by fatigue, and this further complicates the psychological state. Family conflict is almost inevitable. Caregivers are also confronted with "negative choices" or dilemmas for which there is no good answer, only inevitable pain. Current and anticipated financial burdens complete the picture.

Applying the concept of spiritual needs to caring for a relative with AD shows the clear potential for encountering unmet needs. What is the *meaning* in this deterioration and loss of dignity? What *hope* is there? What *relatedness* does the patient have with God? How angry with God is the caregiver? How angry with the caregiver is God? Is anyone involved *transcending* anything? Answers to these questions do not come easily when a loved one has AD. Ultimately, through giving care as long and as well as possible, they are answered to at least some extent. (See later discussion of caregiver spiritual issues.)

Providing Care

Introduction

In the early stages, most patients are cared for at home, while in later stages, most are institutionalized. The key issue in where care is given is not, however, the level of cognitive and physical deterioration, but socioeconomic factors. Factors leading to staying in the community rather than being institutionalized include living with children, being male (ie, increased likelihood of having a caregiver), and having a higher income (Ford, Roy, Haug, Folmar, & Jones, 1991).

Regardless of where care is given, there is often a reluctance to ask for help or even to let others help with the care. Many caregivers approach the task with the realization that community support is inadequate and that there is nobody better able than themselves to give the care. While such an attitude might be attributed to guilt, "martyring," or other such processes, the reality is that in many instances, these caregivers are correct in their assessment of the situation. When one has been at the job for 5 years and is looking at possibly another 5 years, then the 2 to 4 months of 2 hours a day, 3 days a week services covered by Medicare may not seem that significant.

With some notable exceptions, home hospice programs have generally been reluctant to admit more than a few patients with AD. Reasons for this include the slow deterioration (uncertain prognosis) of patients with AD versus those with cancer, the inability of patients to communicate, and other factors. Professional inexperience and knowledge deficit with respect to end-stage AD also play a significant role. However, the NHO (1996) has clarified prognostic guidelines, and admissions of patients with AD to hospices may be increasing. Note should be taken of the severity of disabilities under hospice guidelines. Unfortunately, in most cases, patients who have reached this state will already be in long-term care, hence most home hospices will not admit significant numbers of patients with AD.

Physical Problems

Physical problems in the end-stage (see previous discussion) are due in large part to immobility and may include a general deterioration in functional ability, with neurologic deficits (dementia, communication difficulties, agitation, and other neurologic deficits), unknown pain status, compromised immune function, impaired respiratory function, impaired cardiovascular function, dysphagia, impaired gastrointestinal function, malnutrition, impaired urinary function, decreased range of motion and strength, and skin breakdown, along with any other preexisting problems (APA, 1997; NHO, 1996; Volicer & Hurley, 1997). Each of these is discussed in the following sections. Care for caregivers is also discussed.

GENERAL GUIDELINES

A guiding principle throughout the course of AD is consistency in caregivers and routine. While consistency does not by any means ensure a trouble-free situation, a lack of consistency does guarantee difficulties. The patient usually has to be repeatedly reminded of even the regular caregiver's identity.

NEUROLOGIC DEFICITS

DEMENTIA. The confusion of earlier stages usually gives way to an increasingly vegetative state. Measures used in earlier stages should be continued. Validation therapy (ie, attempting to understand the meaning of the patient's attempts at communication) should be continued as a way to make emotional contact—even if it is a one-way attempt. Communication is continued as discussed below.

COMMUNICATION DIFFICULTIES. When possible, sensory aides, such as hearing aides and eyeglasses, should be kept on and in working order. Other helpful suggestions include using simple instructions; speaking slowly and distinctly, repeating phrases, and speaking in short sentences; and demonstrating instructions or actions (eg, cleaning dentures). The patient with end-stage AD is seldom responsive to these measures.

A significant issue in communication is that the patient is unable to report pain or other problems to others. See the following discussion of pain.

AGITATION. Although agitation or its expression decreases in the final stage of AD, measures should be continued or instituted to reduce anxiety and other causes of agitation or delirium. A calm environment with minimal visual, audio, and other stimuli helps prevent or reduce anxiety. Some patients are calmed by television, and some are not. The patient's response should be determined and action

based on the response. Audiotapes of music appropriate for the patient are a better choice for some than television. If the patient has a history of sundowning, stimuli should be further decreased in the evening. A light should be left on, and the presence of the caregiver may help. Agitation may not necessarily be due to AD. Other potential causes include hyponatremia, hypoglycemia, hypercalcemia, medications, pain, sleep deprivation, and fecal impaction or urinary retention (Martin, 1990). Antipsychotics (eg, risperidone or clozapine) are indicated for treatment of psychosis or agitation (APA, 1997). The treatment of agitation is complicated by increased risk among elderly and demented patients (especially women) for side effects of antipsychotic medications, hence starting doses should be low. Benzodiazepines (eg, lorazepam or oxazepam) are used for occasional agitation or when anxiety is prominent (APA, 1997) (also see Chapter 13).

OTHER NEUROLOGIC PROBLEMS. Neurologic problems of AD are often complicated by other neurologic problems at a greater prevalence than among people without AD. These problems include parkinsonism, cerebrovascular accident, myoclonus, and seizures (Volicer & Hurley, 1997).

PAIN

Patients with advanced AD cannot complain of pain and thus it is not known to what extent they experience pain. It is known that patients with AD use fewer nonsteroidal anti-inflammatory drugs than elderly people without dementia, and it has been hypothesized that this may be due to an affective component of pain (Scherder & Bouma, 1997). The best way to approach pain is to assume that it is as likely as it was when the person was able to communicate. The presence of problems that ordinarily would cause pain (eg, urinary tract infection, exacerbations of arthritis, chronic cough, immobility) should be treated as if the patient was able to verbalize complaints. The rectal route becomes increasingly important as the patient deteriorates.

COMPROMISED IMMUNE FUNCTION

Patients with AD have expected age-related decreased immune function along with impaired cell-mediated immunity associated with dementia (Volicer & Hurley, 1997). Moreover, institutionalization exposes patients to nosocomial infections. Respiratory and urinary tract infections are major and common complications of AD.

IMPAIRED RESPIRATORY FUNCTION

Lung capacity decreases, secretions thicken and increase, expectoration decreases, and aspiration increases, resulting in increased risk for pneumonia—the cause of death in more than 50% of patients with AD (Volicer & Hurley, 1997). Use of sedatives and presence of feeding tubes also contribute to the risk.

IMPAIRED CARDIOVASCULAR FUNCTION

Lying immobile and recumbent significantly increases cardiac workload, especially in the presence of extant cardiac disease. Edema, often found in the sacral area, contributes to skin breakdown. Other problems include orthostatic hypotension and risk for thrombosis (Mobily & Kelley, 1991).

DYSPHAGIA

Difficulty swallowing manifested by drooling or retaining or spitting out food may be due to lip, tongue, or jaw impairment, while coughing or choking after or while swallowing indicates pharyngeal problems. Interventions for dysphagia include giving small meals and small bites of food, giving adequate time to chew and swallow, reminding the patient to swallow, and giving (in most instances) liquids with thicker consistencies. Care should be taken when giving oral medications. Large tablets, in particular, are difficult to swallow and the rectal route is often required in late stages. Dysphagia may also be due to problems other than progression of AD. Bacterial, fungal, or viral infection or esophageal cancer may cause dysphagia, odynophagia, or painful swallowing. Family members should be taught what measures to take in case of choking. Readers are encouraged to refer to Chapter 17.

IMPAIRED GASTROINTESTINAL FUNCTIONS

Incontinence and constipation are common, and there is a potential for impaction. A bowel routine is essential. See the sections on constipation and diarrhea in Chapter 17. As the patient deteriorates and consumes less food, bowel movements also decrease.

MALNUTRITION

Weight loss is common and may be related to hypermetabolic state, increased energy expenditure (in active stages of disease), decreased food intake (related to depression, confusion, dysphagia, and other factors), or changes in lean body mass (Volicer & Hurley, 1997). Sequelae of malnutrition include increased risk of skin breakdown, infection, and other physical deterioration. Negative nitrogen balance from immobility and decreased intake and hypercalcemia from calcium loss are both possible in advanced AD (Mobily & Kelley, 1991).

IMPAIRED URINARY FUNCTIONS

Problems of impaired urinary function include urinary tract infections, perineal infections, renal calculi, and increased likelihood of skin breakdown (Volicer & Hurley, 1997). Adequate fluids (except for diuresing fluids, like coffee or tea) help prevent the first three but contribute, perhaps, to the last problem. Use of urinary catheters virtually ensures urinary tract infections but is necessary in many cases. Ideal fluid intake (3000 mL of fluids during the day) is seldom realistic. Diuretics are best given in the morning, especially if there is no catheter. Toileting schedules should be designed around the patient's elimination schedule (see Chapter 18).

DECREASED RANGE OF MOTION AND STRENGTH

Passive range of motion sometimes seems futile to families who associate exercise with rehabilitation. In this case, however, the purpose is not rehabilitation, but prevention of contractures and their sequelae of further decreased range of motion, pain, and skin breakdown. Decreased range of motion also affects strength, as discussed below. In the end stage, there is little that can be done about decreased strength other than whatever small gain occurs through passive range of motion. Passive range of motion also limits cardiovascular deterioration. Immobility also decreases skeletal strength and increases the likelihood of stress or pathologic fracture (Mobily & Kelley, 1991) and thus may further decrease mobility.

SKIN BREAKDOWN

This problem is related to immobility, incontinence, and nutritional deficits. Preventive measures include regular assessment, frequent turning, meticulous hygiene, reduction of mechanical factors (wrinkles, crumbs, and so forth on the sheet), adequate hydration and nutrition, and use of egg crate mattress, special bed, sheepskin, and other protective devices (see Chapter 15).

Caring for the Caregiver

By the end stage, nearly all caregivers are physically and emotionally exhausted from countless "36-hour days" (Mace & Rabins, 1981). They have worked hard and, at times, been reviled for their work by the patient, seen their sense of security vanish, kept on through days and weeks and months of despair, lost friends and friendships of family members, seen services that they thought would be helpful come and go, grieved and grieved again for the patient and themselves, and looked to a grim future. Thus, when practitioners offer help to these caregivers, it should be with the understanding that help is being offered to heroes.

In the traditional sense of heroism—with fear and uncertainty as their only companions, standing "alone in the night" against an implacable enemy, wounded in body and spirit, true to their vows—*they are heroes*. Most are also experts in caregiving.

Practitioners working with end-stage Alzheimer's patients may profit from an approach that combines a sense of humility with respect and honor toward these heroic caregivers, rather than one in which the health care worker arrives on the scene as the "expert," controlling all the services that can make the big difference. The objective for practitioners should be to fit their care with the needs and situation of patient and family.

It should also be borne in mind that, for many caregivers, turning over their responsibilities to another is extremely difficult (Wilson, 1989). When their role is relinquished, partially or completely, the caregiver often hovers in the room or frets in the next room. Some health care providers have difficulty with this behavior. Rather than resist it, however, it is better for practitioners to enlist caregivers' help, to ask them for information about the needs and functioning of that particular patient. Once they are satisfied that care is adequate, caregivers are more likely to give up some part of their responsibility and to experience a subsequent sense of relief from anxiety.

Psychosocial care also often centers around finances or medical bills, stress, and grief. In fact, all of these are pressing issues for most patients and families, and they should be addressed in relation to their importance. Readers are referred to the information on this subject in Chapter 3, Psychosocial Needs, Problems, and Interventions: The Family (As noted previously, "family" is best thought of as whoever is doing the work. Certainly blood relatives and spouses are family, but in the fierce arena of caregiving, anyone who gives care on a consistent basis is family.)

Specific caregiver problems having to do with AD and with other long-term neurologic diseases include the following issues:

● The organization needed to pay medical bills is often neglected in favor of using the time for providing physical care to the patient, thus creating a sense of financial dread in the family that serves as a background to all their other problems.

● Caregivers' sense of social isolation is difficult, if not impossible, to resolve. For most people, the situation is inherently isolating, and time spent away from the client may seem even more stressful than their duties themselves.

● Ambivalence (eg, love and hate) toward the patient is common and natural but also difficult for the caregiver to accept or address. Guilty feelings often result from recognition of anger. At least two people are represented in the person with AD: the person who was and the demented, sometimes abusive, and even violent person who is. The latter person may be viewed as responsible for destroying the life and the feelings created by the former. The reality is that the exhaustion and despair of the caregiver would not exist if not for the person with AD.

● Grief is a major issue and includes grief for what is already lost in the patient, for the altered relationship that exists between patient and caregiver, and for oneself. There is also anticipatory grief for what the future will bring in relation to these situations. Grief in the context of AD is complicated by the nature of the disease: The personality dies but not the body. Chronic sorrow may exist.

● Exhaustion is probably inevitable, even when part or even all of the care is given over to others.

● Family conflict (excluding the patient) is common and often includes guilt and blaming. "Help-rejecting complaining" is common on the part of the caregiver. Communications are influenced by old, unresolved issues and complicated by the caregiver's physical and emotional exhaustion.

● Spiritual issues are sometimes incompletely addressed. Although Chapters 3 and 4 offer a more complete discussion of these needs, several questions are addressed here in the context, not of supplying universal answers to suit every situation, but rather of providing some frame of reference. What, for example, is the meaning in this deterioration and loss of dignity inherent in the situation of the AD patient? The meaning may not be found so much in what is happening to the patient, as in what the caregiver is doing. In other words, a better question may be, "What is the meaning of this level of love, devotion, or just plain hard-headedness?" Another question is, "What hope is there?" Again, if the focus is more on the caregiver, the question may be, "What hope is there in a person, family, or society that works this hard to do the right thing in the face of despair and of certain defeat of the flesh?" Finally, caregivers may question the patient's relationship with God, while their own relationships can be fairly predictable, generally falling into one of three phases, according to the situation of the moment: either they depend on God, they question the existence (or motives) of God who allows such suffering, or they are very angry with God.

In all cases, families should be linked with community resources, such as the Alzheimer's Association. Experience, however, teaches health care providers that some people can have negative experiences with organizations in general and are reluctant to use them. Health care providers may need to act as advocates or to otherwise assist families in finding and receiving services.

The Alzheimer's Association is currently located at 919 North Michigan Avenue, Suite 1000, Chicago, IL, 60611. The current phone number outside Illinois is 1-800-621-0379 and in Illinois, 1-800-572-6037. The Internet address is *www.alz.org*.

REFERENCES

Alzheimer's Association. (1998). *Statistics/prevalence*. Chicago: Author.

American Psychiatric Association. (1997). *Practice guidelines for the treatment of patients with Alzheimer's disease and other dementias of late life*. Washington, DC: Author.

Folstein, M. F., Folstein, S. E., & McHugh, P. R. (1975). Mini-mental state: A practical method for grading the cognitive state of patients for the clinician. *Journal of Psychiatric Research, 12,* 189–198.

Ford, A. B., Roy, A. W., Haug, M. R., Folmar, S. J., & Jones, P. K. (1991). Impaired and disabled elderly in the community. *American Journal of Public Health*, 81(9), 1207–1209.

Foreman, M. D., & Grabowski, R. (1992). Diagnostic dilemma: Cognitive impairment in the elderly. *Journal of Gerontological Nursing*, 18(9), 5–12.

Jacob Perlow Hospice. (1991). *Functional assessment staging (FAST) adapted for Alzheimer's disease*. New York: Author.

Lee, V. K. (1991). Language changes and Alzheimer's disease: A literature review. *Journal of Gerontological Nursing*, 17(1), 16–20.

Lerner, A. J., Hedera, P., Koss, E., Stuckey, J., & Friedland, R. P. (1997). Delirium in Alzheimer disease. *Alzheimer Disease and Associated Disorders*, 11(1), 16–20.

Mace, N. L., & Rabins, P. V. (1981). *The 36 hour day: A family guide to caring for persons with Alzheimer's disease, related dementing illnesses, and memory loss in later life*. Baltimore: Johns Hopkins University Press.

Martin, E. W. (1991). *Confusion in the terminally ill: Diagnosis and management*. Seattle: National Hospice Organization Annual Meeting.

Marzinski, L. R. (1991). The tragedy of dementia: Clinically assessing pain in the confused, nonverbal elderly. *Journal of Gerontological Nursing*, 17(6), 25–28.

Mobily, P. R., & Kelley, L. S. (1991). Iatrogenesis in the elderly. *Journal of Gerontological Nursing*, 17(9), 5–10.

Moore, I. (1997). Living with Alzheimer's: Understanding the family's and patient's perspective. *Geriatrics*, 52(Suppl. 2), S33–S36.

National Hospice Organization. (1996). *Medical guidelines for determining prognosis in selected non-cancer diseases*. Arlington, VA: Author.

Post, S. G. (1997). Slowing the progression of Alzheimer disease: Ethical issues. *Alzheimer Disease and Associated Disorders*, 11(Suppl. 5), S34–S36.

Scherder, E. J. A., & Bouma, A. (1997). Is decreased use of analgesics in Alzheimer disease due to a change in the affective component of pain? *Alzheimer Disease and Associated Disorders*, 11(3), 171–174.

Volicer, L., & Hurley, A. C. (1997). Physical status and complications in patients with Alzheimer disease: Implications for outcome studies. *Alzheimer Disease and Associated Disorders*, 11(Suppl. 6), 60–65.

Willoughby, J., & Keating, N. (1991). Being in control: The process of caring for a relative with Alzheimer's disease. *Qualitative Health Research*, 1(1), 27–50.

Wilson, H. S. (1989). Family caregiving for a relative with Alzheimer's dementia: Coping with negative choices. *Nursing Research*, 38(2), 94–98.

CHAPTER 30

End-Stage Cardiovascular and Pulmonary Disease

KEY POINTS

● Philosophically, providing hospice or palliative care for patients with cardiovascular disease is challenging because of difficulties defining which interventions are palliative and which are curative.

● The basic principles of hospice and palliative care may be applied to patients with end-stage cardiovascular or respiratory disease.

● Palliative care for patients with respiratory disease is a classic example of double-effect treatment.

Cardiovascular Disease

Cardiac problems in advanced cancer are discussed in Chapter 14.

Heart disease is the leading cause of death in the United States (Centers for Disease Control and Prevention [CDC], 1997). Patients who are terminally ill from cardiovascular disease are principally those with (1) advanced congestive heart failure (CHF) or (2) acute myocardial infarction (AMI), with extensive damage to the myocardium. The patient with CHF may be managed well at home during much of the course of illness, while the patient with AMI may live for several days in a cardiac unit. In either case, care is focused on palliation of cardiac symptoms, and resuscitation or other extraordinary measures are not used. It is therefore essential that all legal documents concerning the patient's wishes about resuscitation be completed and that all concerned parties clearly understand the patient's wishes.

Providing palliative care may be philosophically difficult for some staff in acute and critical care units, where the goal is preserving life at all costs (O'Brien, Walsh, & Dunn, 1998). Even when it is clear that the primary goals of care are to ensure comfort and dignity, it is sometimes difficult to determine what is palliative, what is aggressive, and what lies between. There is disagreement about whether, for example, antibiotic, vasoactive, or anticoagulant drugs should be withdrawn or given; whether or not—or how much—suctioning should occur; whether intravenous hydration should be given; and whether sedating doses of opioids for patients in acute respiratory distress are a form of euthanasia (Makielski & Broom, 1992; Solomon et al., 1993). In cardiology, palliative care may be focused on extending life to a greater extent than palliative care in cancer and may include defibrillator implantation, heart transplantation, and other such measures, though exclusion criteria for transplantation include poor prognosis and other such limitations (Fisher, Balke, & Freudenberger, 1997).

National Hospice Organization (1996) guidelines for determining decreased prognosis in cardiac disease include the following:

● The patient has symptoms of CHF and is functionally classified as New York Heart Association Class IV (inability to carry out any physical activity without discomfort, symptoms of heart failure or anginal syndrome present at rest, and increase in discomfort with any physical activity).
● The patient is being optimally treated with diuretics and vasodilators, preferably angiotensin-converting enzyme inhibitors but continues to have persistent symptoms of CHF. (Newer medications may be included in "optimal treatment" in the future.)
● In patients treated as described, survival is further decreased by (1) symptomatic supraventricular or ventricular arrhythmias resistant to antiarrhythmia therapy, (2) history of cardiac arrest and resuscitation, (3) history of unexplained syncope, (4) cardiogenic brain embolism, or (5) concomitant HIV disease.

Because of increasing numbers of older people and increasing numbers of patients surviving AMI, the incidence and prevalence of CHF are increasing (Fisher et al., 1997). Although CHF is commonly classified as left or right ventricular failure, patients with end-stage CHF are likely to have both left and right—or biventricular—failure (Braunwald, 1987). Important symptoms of advanced CHF include dyspnea on exertion and at rest, edema, chest pain, difficulty sleeping (including paroxysmal nocturnal dyspnea [PND]), nocturia, cognitive deficits, headache, weakness, and fatigue (Quaal, 1992). Pain, discomfort, or other problems stemming from other etiologies are also common, and in the context of heart disease, these may not be readily recognized or treated (Gu & Belgrade, 1993).

Palliative Care in Heart Disease

Dyspnea is usually associated with left ventricular failure and is related to pulmonary congestion and increased airway resistance. The slight congestion and breathlessness of early CHF can progress to pulmonary edema and feelings of smothering, tachycardia, agitation, and pink, frothy hemoptysis (Quaal, 1992). In addition to therapy intended to minimize deterioration of the patient's cardiac status (eg, diuretic, antiarrhythmic, vasodilator), the following measures (O'Brien et al., 1998; Quaal, 1992) can be taken:

● Nondrug measures should be implemented, including positioning (sitting in a high Fowler's position), use of a fan, reassurance, and other measures discussed in Chapter 14.
● Oxygen is given.
● An opioid, usually quick-release morphine, is given. Patients with advanced CHF living at home should have morphine on hand. (In cancer care, crises appear to occur more often at night; in CHF, respiratory crises really do occur more often at night.) Opioids improve the quality of respirations and relieve anxiety.
● Factors that increase dyspnea (eg, anxiety, heat) should be minimized.

Dyspnea is likely to increase when death is imminent, and it may be necessary to give sedating doses of opioids as the patient struggles to breathe and becomes agitated.

It may seem irrelevant to discuss diet with these patients. However, failure to maintain sodium restrictions (no more than 4 g/d) can have a distinct effect on the speed with which a patient develops pulmonary edema and thus experiences breathing difficulty. Sodium restrictions are therefore maintained. Fluid restrictions (no more than 2 L/d) should also be followed (McNamara, Alvarez, Rosenblum, Murali, & Feldman, 1997).

Systemic edema is associated with right ventricular failure, and while it does not necessarily lead to pulmonary edema, systemic edema adds significantly to the cardiac load. In patients with advanced CHF, who are bedridden most of the time, edema is found in the sacral, posterior thighs, or other dependent areas. Ascites also develops and in some cases is extensive enough that it forces the diaphragm up while the patient is recumbent and thus limits lung capacity. Ascites also increases intra-abdominal pressure, causing nausea and anorexia.

Dyspnea and cardiac function may be further exacerbated by respiratory infection, especially in a bedridden patient. Palliation in this case might include antibiotics and possibly increased diuretics but not necessarily hospitalization and use of powerful drugs with a high incidence of adverse effects. There is controversy about when antibiotics should and should not be given and about which antibiotics should be given in end-stage disease.

Another factor in dyspnea, fatigue, and even angina is anemia. Severe anemia may also cause tachypnea and intermittent claudication and may result in further deterioration of the patient's cardiovascular status.

Common etiologies of chest pain in advanced CHF include angina and AMI and to lesser extent, pulmonary embolism, stress, and other processes. The characteristics and treatment of these vary. Stable angina is a squeezing or heavy, painful sensation lasting more than 2 and less than 15 minutes, predictable with a certain degree of activity, and relieved with nitroglycerin. Unstable angina occurs even at rest and is unrelieved with nitroglycerin. AMI is similar in quality but greater in intensity than angina, lasts longer, and is not relieved with nitroglycerin or rest. Pain from pulmonary embolism is sharp, stabbing, and continuous (Haak & Huether, 1992). In general, pain is not as much a problem in advanced heart disease as cancer or HIV disease because (1) the disease itself tends to be inherently less

painful and (2) improvements in management of cardiac disease have lessened problems of pain (O'Brien et al., 1998).

Difficulty sleeping is a frequent complaint of patients with advanced heart disease. Patients with CHF are also likely to have PND, the frightening experience of suddenly waking up struggling to breathe. PND further complicates whatever prior difficulties the patient was having with sleep, anxiety, depression, and fear (eg, the relatively common fear of dying during sleep). Sitting up and taking oxygen provides relief from the dyspnea, if not from the fear. Because PND is related to fluid imbalance, careful attention to measures to maintain balance is important. Small doses of quick-release morphine (eg, 5 mg PO at bedtime) may be given for night breathlessness and a sedative (eg, temazepam 10–20 mg PO at bedtime or thioridazine 10 mg at bedtime) for sleep or sedation (O'Brien et al., 1998).

Nocturia, a nuisance for those with little disability, becomes a significant problem for patients with advanced disease and may in some cases manifest as incontinence (Graham, 1989). Indeed, nights in general are often a problem. Inability or difficulty ambulating and confusion from sleeping medications can make urinating a difficult procedure and result in further loss of sleep. Attention to the patient's fluid balance may help relieve nocturia. For example, taking diuretics in the morning and limiting fluids in the evening may significantly decrease nocturia.

Cognitive deficits and headache are most common in older patients (Haak & Huether, 1992). These may be due to a combination of cerebral atherosclerosis and to the complex of anxiety, depression, insomnia, dyspnea, and other processes active in advanced heart disease. Patients with atherosclerosis are also more likely to have Cheyne-Stokes respirations (Braunwald, 1987). Confusion may be due to dementia or delirium. In delirium, confusion may be reversible, so it is important to determine the etiology. (Please see the discussion of confusion in Chapter 13.)

Weakness and fatigue are intrinsic to advanced heart disease. At some point in the process of advanced disease, exercise, no matter how light, results in an increase in afterload and decrease in cardiac performance. Exercise thus becomes a liability and is in no way beneficial to the patient. Hyponatremia—characterized by lethargy, anorexia, weakness, and abdominal cramps—may develop, often as a consequence of excessive treatment with diuretics.

In the final stages, a regimen based on the same palliative principles as in terminal cancer may be the best approach. Pain and respiratory symptoms are managed aggressively with cardiac medications, opioids, oxygen, and other measures; constipation is prevented (straining can cause death); other symptoms are managed; patient and family support is optimized; and other hospice or palliative care measures are initiated (Stephany, 1996a).

Pulmonary Disease

The pulmonary diseases most commonly encountered in terminal care situations are the chronic obstructive pulmonary diseases (COPD) or chronic obstructive lung diseases (COLD)—emphysema and bronchitis. COPD is now the fourth leading cause of death in the United States (CDC, 1997). The general principles of care for these patients usually apply as well to patients with other diagnoses, such as pulmonary fibrosis, coal worker's pneumoconiosis, silicosis, and so forth. Clients with cystic fibrosis are almost always cared for by staff on units dedicated to that disease and are not discussed in this chapter.

Chronic Bronchitis

Chronic bronchitis is an airway or bronchial disease characterized by an increase in the size and number of submucous glands of the large bronchi, increase in the number of goblet cells of the mucosa, and thickening of the bronchial submucosa. Inflammatory changes and, later, fibrosis occur. Secretions pool and plug first small, then larger bronchioles. The net result is air moving through less space and more mucus. Chronic cough and expectoration are the cardinal symptoms, and as the disease progresses, dyspnea increases. Concurrently, retained mucus and other processes incline the patient to frequent respiratory infections, which, in turn, worsen the patient's pulmonary status during the infection and afterward. Right-sided heart failure is a frequent complication. To this complicated clinical picture, right ventricular failure adds edema, hepatomegaly, and ascites, thus creating further difficulty in breathing. Finally, small airway obstruction contributes to the patient developing emphysema. Chronic bronchitis is marked by a variable course, with debilitating infections followed by (ever-shorter) periods of recovery (Picella, 1997; Stephany, 1996b).

Emphysema

Emphysema is an alveolar disease, characterized by hyperinflation of the lungs and loss of the alveolar, or gas-exchanging, surfaces. The lungs lose elasticity and form bullae (nonfunctional spaces or vesicles), and air-trapping occurs. Cardinal manifestations are slowly progressive dyspnea with prolonged expiration phase and cough. Dyspnea or respiratory effort results in first voluntary inactivity as the patient prevents dyspnea and conserves strength and later involuntary inactivity. Patients with advanced emphysema are sometimes called "fighters" because of their unending struggle to breathe. Inadequate nutrition is related to the effort required to eat. Malnutrition and inactivity, coupled with dyspnea, result in a characteristically wasted appearance. Respiratory infections increase in frequency and severity. Right ventricular failure may occur as death nears. The course of emphysema is characterized by a steady decline, with periods of acute exacerbation from infections or bronchitis (Dettenmeier, 1992; Picella, 1997; Stephany, 1996b).

DEBORA HUNTER

Palliative Care in Pulmonary Disease

Caring for patients with advanced and terminal COPD means caring for bedridden, dyspneic, anxious patients with exhausted and sometimes resentful families. Because the illness is chronic and slowly progressive, by the time the client is terminal, the family usually (but not always) has experience in providing care and dealing with equipment. Family resentment is sometimes related to family dynamics unrelated to illness, sometimes to physical and psychological exhaustion (COPD is a noisy disease), and sometimes to the fact that some patients continue to smoke as long as they are able to lift the cigarette to their lips and despite the spectacular coughing that results from each inhalation.

The medical management of far-advanced COPD, which usually encompasses both bronchial and alveolar disease, may include bronchoactive drugs (eg, anticholinergics), methylxanthines (eg, theophylline, aminophylline), and sympathomimetics (albuterol, terbutaline, metaproterenol) (Honig & Ingram, 1998). Mucolytic agents intended to liquefy secretions are no more effective than adequate hydration, and anti-inflammatories, such as corticosteroids, are best used when there is decreased response to the previously noted measures (Honig & Ingram, 1998). The therapeutic and lethal doses of theophylline are close, and advanced disease increases the likelihood of adverse reactions (Johanssen, 1994). Antibiotics are used intermittently to treat, suppress, or prevent infection.

Dyspnea is, of course, an ongoing and progressive problem. Oxygen is necessary and frequently so is suctioning (Flenley, 1984). Oxygen must be carefully managed, because increasing oxygen decreases ventilatory drive.

Opioids, especially morphine, and increasingly through a nebulizer (but also oral, rectal, or sublingual), are used to decrease dyspnea and anxiety. In the absence of pain, doses of morphine are usually low (2.5–5 mg/2 mL normal saline delivered through nebulizer) (O'Brien et al., 1998; Picella, 1997).

Progressive coughing occurs and is exacerbated by increasing weakness, hence coughing accomplishes less clearing and makes increasing energy demands. Ultimately, dysphagia develops and the patient is unable to cough and protect the airway. Oral secretions, bronchial secretions, and cardiopulmonary congestion combine to increase respiratory distress. Opioids have antitussive properties and the ability to decrease dyspnea and anxiety. See cautionary note below regarding depressant medications. Also see Chapter 14.

Anxiety is almost universal in patients with far-advanced COPD (Johannsen, 1994). Short-acting benzodiazepines, such as lorazepam 0.5 mg PO tid or qid or alprazolam 0.25 to 0.5 PO tid or qid, are commonly used for anxiety in advanced cancer (Holland, 1997) and are also appropriate in COPD with care taken to avoid depressant effects (see caution below) (O'Brien et al., 1998). In the final stage of disease, agitation also commonly occurs. Terminal restlessness in COPD is managed as in other terminal illnesses: Antipsychotic medications, especially haloperidol (Haldol) 0.5 to 1.0 mg PO is given two to four times daily to decrease confusion and is sometimes combined with lorazepam (Ativan) to treat both confusion and agitation (Holland, 1997). For severe agitation with delirium, midazolam can be given 1 mg every 10 minutes until symptoms are under control. The hourly maintenance dose is 25% to 33% of required induction dose, and diphenhydramine 25 to 50 mg PO tid to qid is used for extrapyramidal side effects (Hospice and Palliative Nurses Association, 1997). Note that lorazepam (80% bioavailability) and clonazepam (bioavailability unknown) are effective when given rectally for terminal restlessness (Warren, 1996). Intravenous chlorpromazine 12.5 mg q4–12h or 25 mg PR q4–12h is a much less expensive alternative to midazolam and helps relieve dyspnea (Waller & Caroline, 1996). Note, however, agitation, insomnia, and increasing dyspnea may herald acute respiratory failure, and some pulmonary specialists state without equivocation that "depressant drugs that impair ventilatory drive should be avoided at all times in patients with severe COLD" (Honig & Ingram, 1998, p. 1458).

The patient's environment should contain a minimum of irritants. Tobacco or other smoke, dust, pollen, high ozone levels, and strong perfumes all have an adverse effect on patients with COPD. Air should not be completely dry as with some forms of indoor heating or air conditioning. Some patients require a humidifier. Days in which the humidity is high are difficult for patients with COPD.

Adequate fluids are important in keeping secretions liquefied. Postural drainage, percussion, and the like are not possible in patients with end-stage COPD. Suctioning may be necessary but in some patients creates great difficulties with coughing. Dyspnea is such that patients are unable to remain in any position other than semi-Fowler's. Oxygen is usually administered at 2 to 3 L/min (but up to 10 L/min) 18 to 24 hours a day through nasal cannula or mask (Stephany, 1996b).

Patients with advanced COPD are always at risk for respiratory infections. Infection initiates a vicious cycle of airway infection, inflammation, and loss of pulmonary function (Niederman, 1997). Patients at home should have their temperature taken at least daily, and lung sounds and sputum volume and appearance should be regularly evaluated for signs of infection (though not all sputum is purulent in the presence of infection).

Patients should rest before meals. Meals should be small and high in protein. Gas-forming, difficult to chew, and very hot or very cold foods should be avoided. Fluid intake must be maintained.

Most clients with COPD die in the hospital. The struggle to breathe as death approaches is more than most families are able to handle. Acute respiratory failure (likely precipitated by infection) is a common event in advanced disease. Manifestations include increased volume, viscosity, and purulence of secretions. Airways are increasingly obstructed and inflamed; secretions increase; hypoxia and CO_2 retention increase; and the patient commonly is agitated, dyspneic, and unable to sleep (Honig & Ingram, 1998). The need for sedation and relief of dyspnea versus the deleterious effects of depressant medications is a dramatic illustration of the ethical challenges of double-effect treatment.

REFERENCES

Braunwald, E. (1987). Heart failure. In E. Braunwald, K. J. Isselbacher, R. G. Petersdorf, J. D. Wilson, J. B. Martin, & A. S. Fauci (Eds.), Harrison's principles of internal medicine (11th ed.) (pp. 905–916). New York: McGraw-Hill.

Centers for Disease Control and Prevention. (1997). Mortality patterns—preliminary data, United States, 1996. Morbidity and Mortality Weekly Report, 46(40), 941–944.

Dettenmeier, P. A. (1992). Pulmonary nursing care. St. Louis: Mosey-Year Book.

Fisher, M. L., Balke, C. W., & Freudenberger, R. (1997). Therapeutic options in advanced heart failure. Hospital Practice, December 15, 97–106.

Flenley, D. (1984). Palliative care in respiratory diseases. In D. Dole (Ed.), Palliative care: The management of far-advanced illness. Philadelphia: The Charles Press.

Graham, I. (1989). Edema. In T. D. Walsh (Ed.), Symptom control. Oxford: Blackwell Scientific Publications.

Gu, X., & Belgrade, M. J. (1993). Pain in hospitalized patients with medical illnesses. Journal of Pain and Symptom Management, 8(1), 17–21.

Haak, S. W., & Huether, S. E. (1992). The person with angina pectoris. In C. E. Guzzetta & B. M. Dossey (Eds.), Cardiovascular nursing: Holistic practice (pp. 221–249). St. Louis: Mosby-Year Book.

Holland, J. C. (1997). Principles of psycho-oncology. In J. F. Holland, E. Frei, R. C. Bast, D. W. Kufe, D. L. Morton, & R. W. Weischselbaum (Eds.), Cancer medicine (4th ed.) (pp. 1327–1346). Baltimore: Williams & Wilkins.

Honig, E. G., & Ingram, R. H. (1998). Chronic bronchitis, emphysema, and airway obstruction. In A. S. Fauci, E. Braunwald, K. J. Isselbacher, J.

D. Wilson, J. B. Martin, D. L. Kasper, S. L. Hauser, & D. L. Longo (Eds.), Harrison's principles of internal medicine (14th ed.) (pp. 1451–1460). New York: McGraw-Hill.

Hospice and Palliative Nurses Association. (1997). Terminal restlessness. Pittsburgh: Author.

Johanssen, J. M. (1994) Chronic obstructive pulmonary disease: Current comprehensive care for emphysema and bronchitis. Nurse Practitioner, 19(1), 59–67.

Makielski, M., & Broom, C. (1992). Administering pain medications for a terminal patient. Dimensions of Critical Care Nursing, 11(3), 157–161.

McNamara, D., Alvarez, R. J., Rosenblum, W., Murali, S., & Feldman, A. (1997). Managing symptomatic heart failure in 1997. Internal Medicine, 18(6), 18–28.

National Hospice Organization. (1996). Medical guidelines for determining prognosis in selected non-cancer diseases. Arlington, VA: Author.

Niederman, M. S. (1997). COPD—The role of infection. Chest, 112(Suppl. 6), 301S–302S.

O'Brien, T., Walsh, J., & Dunn, F. G. (1998). ABC of palliative care: Non-malignant conditions. British Medical Journal, 316, 286–289.

Picella, D. V. (1997). Palliative care for the patient with end stage respiratory illness. Respiratory Nursing, 8(4), 1–10.

Quaal, S. J. (1992). The person with heart failure and cardiogenic shock. In C. E. Guzzetta & B. M. Dossey (Eds.), Cardiovascular nursing: Holistic practice (pp. 302–354). St. Louis: Mosby-Year Book.

Solomon, M. Z., O'Donnell, L., Jennings, B., Guilfoy, V., Wolf, S. M., Nolan, K., Jackson, R., Koch-Weser, D., & Donnelly, S. (1993). Decisions near the end of life: Professional views on life-sustaining treatments. American Journal of Public Health, 83(1), 14–23.

Stephany, T. (1996a). Low-tech hospice home care for end-stage heart disease. American Journal of Hospice and Palliative Care, 13(3), 35–36.

Stephany, T. (1996b). Palliative nursing care during end-stage COPD. American Journal of Hospice and Palliative Care, 13(5), 20–21.

Waller, A., & Caroline, N. L. (1996). Handbook of palliative care in cancer. Boston: Butterworth-Heinemann.

Warren, D. E. (1996). Practical use of rectal medications in palliative care. Journal of Pain and Symptom Management, 11(6), 378–387.

Epilogue

This epilogue is essentially the same as in the first edition. It was written then in a state of physical and emotional exhaustion and as truly as I can write. It is also dedicated to Cicely Saunders, who showed us most of what we know.

The purpose or mission of terminal care is to facilitate an internal and external physical, psychosocial, and spiritual environment in which there is the opportunity for reconciliation with God, others, and self. Terminal care thus provides the opportunity to realize the purpose of life, for these three reconciliations are nothing other than the purpose of life. As we know—all too well—not everyone experiences these reconciliations. Some never experience any reconciliation, yet the work goes on. Our charge in this work is to comfort "all the comfortless" (Saunders, 1978, p. 202).

An Exploration of the Purpose or Mission of Terminal Care

To "facilitate" means to make easier or help toward something. In caring for people who are dying, the nurse makes it easier for the patient to move toward reconciliation; the nurse does not make it happen. Expecting all patients and families to do well (however "well" might be defined) is to guarantee failure and ultimately disappointment and cynicism.

The "internal environment" means the patient's physical, psychosocial, and spiritual experiences in the process of dying. Pain and other symptoms should be managed; the patient should not be physically or psycholog-

ically alone; and there should be the opportunity for the patient and others to rediscover or further explore the life of the spirit.

The "external environment" refers to the patient's surroundings, especially other people, such as family and friends (and including the nurse). At least as important as the individual is the way in which the individuals interact and the psychosocial and spiritual atmosphere they bring. The physical, psychosocial, and spiritual well-being of these others must not be ignored.

"Reconciliation with God" presupposes that all beings were or are of God and that many have fallen or feel fallen away from that vital connection. To come back into harmony puts one back in his or her real place and beyond the fear, anxiety, and resignation that living brings to so many.

"Reconciliation with others" means to restore relationships. Terminal illness brings an immediacy that may result in healed relationships. At times, however, it is not possible to become peaceable with another because the other is dead or otherwise incapable of participating in reconciliation. In such instances, reconciliation is to accept that the relationship was and is broken.

"Reconciliation with self" refers to acceptance of those aspects of life that one wishes were not so. There is no sentient life without regrets. Some regrets are about mistakes and missed opportunities. Some are about things over which there was no control. In most cases, there is no way to change what was, so accepting self is the only avenue.

In the Preface to this book, I wrote that this work takes us to "an ancient and essential human function: the priestly function of accompanying another through suffering and to the awesome finality of death."

> *In all their affliction he was afflicted, and the angel of his presence saved them; in his love and in his pity he redeemed them; he lifted them up and carried them all the days of old. (Isaiah 63:9)*

Finally, caring for people who are dying is an expression of faith.

REFERENCE

Saunders, C. M. (1978). *The management of terminal disease.* London: Edward Arnold.

INDEX

Note: Page numbers in *italics* indicate illustrations; those followed by t indicate tables; and those followed by b indicate boxed material.

A

Abdominal pain. *See* Pain
Absent grief, 80
Acanthosis nigricans, 170, 214
  in stomach cancer, 251t
Acceptance
  of death, 31-32
  forgiveness and, 53
Acetaminophen, 123-124, 135t
Acetylsalicylic acid, 123-124, 135t
Acquired immunodeficiency syndrome (AIDS), 279-301. *See*
  HIV/AIDS
ACTH, ectopic, 213
Activity and exercise, 207-208
Acupressure, 139
Acute exanthem, in HIV/AIDS, 298
Acute leukemia, 267-268, 269t-270t
Acute pain, 111-112. *See also* Pain
Acute retroviral syndrome, 288
  in HIV/AIDS, 288
Acyclovir (Zovirax)
  for herpes simplex infection, 180, 293
  for herpes zoster, 174, 293
  for HIV/AIDS, 281-283, 284t
Addiction. *See also* Substance abuse
  definition of, 127, 140
  opioid, 127, 140-142
    pain management and, 140-142
Adolescents. *See also* Children
  as caregivers, 45
  response of to death, 44-46
Adrenocorticotropic hormone (ACTH), ectopic, 213
Advance directives, 13, 37-38
  death at home and, 218
  ethical aspects of, 91-92
Advocacy, for poor, 75
African Americans, 71-72
After death care, 222-223
  for Buddhists, 65
  for Hindus, 64
  for Jews, 58
  for Muslims, 62
Ageusia, 179
Agitation
  in Alzheimer's disease, 316
  in imminent death, 219
  terminal, 150-151
    in chronic obstructive pulmonary disease, 326
AIDS. *See* HIV/AIDS

Airway obstruction
  in bladder cancer, 262t
  in breast cancer, 242, 243t
  in colorectal cancer, 251t
  in esophageal cancer, 254t
  in lung cancer, 233t
  in malignant melanoma, 272, 272t
  in oral cancer, 256t
  in ovarian cancer, 245t, 246
  in renal cancer, 260t
Akathisia, 150
  diphenhydramine for, 148, 150
Akinesia, in Parkinson's disease, 307-308
Alcoholism. *See also* Substance abuse
  assessment for, 141
  in Native Americans, 69
  pain management in, 140-142
Allergic reactions
  to drugs, 171
    in HIV/AIDS, 298
  to opioids, 127
Allodynia, 112
Alprazolam
  for anxiety, 23
  for chronic obstructive pulmonary disease, 326
Al Qur'an, 61, 62
Alternative therapies, 139
  for HIV/AIDS, 283
Alzheimer's disease, 313-319
  cardiovascular problems in, 317
  caregiver needs and problems in, 314-315, 318-319
  clinical manifestations of, 313-314
  dysphagia in, 317
  gastrointestinal problems in, 317
  home vs. institutional care in, 315
  hospice care for, 7, 315
  interventions in, 315-318
  malnutrition in, 317
  motor deficits in, 317-318
  neurologic deficits in, 316
  pain in, 316-317
  physical problems in, 315-318
  progression of, 314
  respiratory problems in, 317
  terminal stage of, 314
  urinary elimination in, 317
Ambivalence, in caregivers, 314-315, 319
Ambulatory dementia, 314
American Indians, 68-69

331